DAVID BUSCH'S
NIKON® D7000

GUIDE TO DIGITAL SLR PHOTOGRAPHY

David D. Busch

Course Technology PTR
A part of Cengage Learning

D1088141

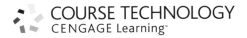

COURSE TECHNOLOGY
CENGAGE Learning™

Australia, Brazil, Japan, Korea, Mexico, Singapore, Spain, United Kingdom, United States

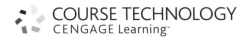

COURSE TECHNOLOGY
CENGAGE Learning™

David Busch's Nikon® D7000
Guide to Digital SLR Photography
David D. Busch

Publisher and General Manager, Course Technology PTR:
Stacy L. Hiquet

Associate Director of Marketing:
Sarah Panella

Manager of Editorial Services:
Heather Talbot

Marketing Manager:
Jordan Castellani

Executive Editor:
Kevin Harreld

Project Editor:
Jenny Davidson

Series Technical Editor:
Michael D. Sullivan

Interior Layout Tech:
Bill Hartman

Cover Designer:
Mike Tanamachi

Indexer:
Katherine Stimson

Proofreader:
Sara Gullion

For product information and technology assistance, contact us at **Cengage Learning Customer & Sales Support, 1-800-354-9706.**

For permission to use material from this text or product, submit all requests online at **cengage.com/permissions**. Further permissions questions can be e-mailed to **permissionrequest@cengage.com**.

Nikon is a registered trademark of Nikon Corporation in the United States and/or other countries.

All other trademarks are the property of their respective owners.

All images © David D. Busch unless otherwise noted.

Library of Congress Control Number: 2010941296

ISBN-13: 978-1-4354-5942-7

ISBN-10: 1-4354-5942-3

Course Technology, a part of Cengage Learning
20 Channel Center Street
Boston, MA 02210
USA

Cengage Learning is a leading provider of customized learning solutions with office locations around the globe, including Singapore, the United Kingdom, Australia, Mexico, Brazil, and Japan. Locate your local office at: **international.cengage.com/region**.

Cengage Learning products are represented in Canada by Nelson Education, Ltd.

For your lifelong learning solutions, visit **courseptr.com**.

Visit our corporate Web site at **cengage.com**.

Printed in China
3 4 5 6 7 15 14 13

For Cathy

Acknowledgments

Once again thanks to the folks at Course Technology PTR, who recognized that a camera as popular as the Nikon D7000 deserves in-depth full-color coverage at a price anyone can afford. Special thanks to executive editor Kevin Harreld, who always gives me the freedom to let my imagination run free with a topic, as well as my veteran production team including project editor Jenny Davidson and technical editor Mike Sullivan. Also thanks to Bill Hartman, layout; Katherine Stimson, indexing; Sara Gullion, proofreading; Mike Tanamachi, cover design; and my agent, Carole Jelen, who has the amazing ability to keep both publishers and authors happy.

About the Author

With more than a million books in print, **David D. Busch** is the world's #1 selling digital camera guide author, and the originator of popular digital photography series like *David Busch's Pro Secrets* and *David Busch's Quick Snap Guides.* He has written nearly two dozen hugely successful guidebooks and compact guides for Nikon digital SLR models, several dozen additional user guides for other camera models, as well as many popular books devoted to dSLRs, including *Mastering Digital SLR Photography, Third Edition* and *Digital SLR Pro Secrets.* As a roving photojournalist for more than 20 years, he illustrated his books, magazine articles, and newspaper reports with award-winning images. He's operated his own commercial studio, suffocated in formal dress while shooting weddings-for-hire, and shot sports for a daily newspaper and upstate New York college. His photos have been published in magazines as diverse as *Scientific American* and *Petersen's PhotoGraphic*, and his articles have appeared in *Popular Photography & Imaging, The Rangefinder, The Professional Photographer*, and hundreds of other publications. He's also reviewed dozens of digital cameras for CNet and *Computer Shopper*. His advice has been featured on National Public Radio's *All Tech Considered*.

When About.com named its top five books on Beginning Digital Photography, debuting at the #1 and #2 slots were Busch's *Digital Photography All-In-One Desk Reference for Dummies* and *Mastering Digital Photography.* During the past year, he's had as many as five of his books listed in the Top 20 of Amazon.com's Digital Photography Bestseller list—simultaneously! Busch's 100-plus other books published since 1983 include bestsellers like *David Busch's Quick Snap Guide to Using Digital SLR Lenses.*

Busch earned top category honors in the Computer Press Awards the first two years they were given (for *Sorry About The Explosion* and *Secrets of MacWrite, MacPaint and MacDraw*), and he later served as Master of Ceremonies for the awards. Visit his website at http://www.dslrguides.com/blog.

Contents

PART I: GETTING STARTED WITH YOUR NIKON D7000

Chapter 1
Nikon D7000: Thinking Outside of the Box   5

Chapter 2
Nikon D7000 Quick Start   25

Chapter 3
Nikon D7000 Roadmap   47

PART II: BEYOND THE BASICS

Chapter 4
Getting the Right Exposure   95

Chapter 5
Mastering Autofocus Options   133

Chapter 6
Live View and D-Movies   153

Chapter 7
Advanced Techniques   179

PART III: ADVANCED TOOLS

Chapter 8
Setup: Playback and Shooting Menus   213

Chapter 9
Setup: The Custom Settings Menu   275

Chapter 10
Setup: The Setup Menu, Retouch Menu, and My Menu   311

Chapter 11
Working with Lenses   345

Chapter 12
Making Light Work for You   395

PART IV: ENHANCING YOUR EXPERIENCE

Chapter 13
Useful Software for the Nikon D7000   443

Chapter 14
Nikon D7000: Troubleshooting
and Prevention   459

Glossary   489

Index   501

Preface

You don't want good pictures from your new Nikon D7000—you demand *outstanding photos*. After all, the D7000 is the most advanced mid-level camera that Nikon has ever introduced. It boasts 16.2 megapixels of resolution, and blazing-fast automatic focus. But your gateway to pixel proficiency is dragged down by the slim booklet included in the box as a manual.

You know everything you need to know is in there, somewhere, but you don't know where to start, and you probably don't like the idea of having to read your manual on a computer screen. In addition, the camera manual doesn't offer much information on photography or digital photography. Nor are you interested in spending hours or days studying a comprehensive book on digital SLR photography that doesn't necessarily apply directly to your D7000.

What you need is a guide that explains the purpose and function of the D7000's basic controls, how you should use them, and *why*. Ideally, there should be information about file formats, resolution, aperture/priority exposure, and special autofocus modes, but you'd prefer to read about those topics only after you've had the chance to go out and take a few hundred great pictures with your new camera. Why isn't there a book that summarizes the most important information in its first two or three chapters, with lots of illustrations showing what your results will look like when you use this setting or that? This is that book.

If you can't decide on what basic settings to use with your camera because you can't figure out how changing ISO or white balance or focus defaults will affect your pictures, you need this guide. I won't talk down to you, either; this book isn't padded with dozens of pages of checklists telling you how to take a travel picture, a sports photo, or how to take a snapshot of your kids in overly simplistic terms. There are no special sections devoted to "real world" recipes here. All of us do 100 percent of our shooting in the real world! So, I give you all the information you need to cook up great photos on your own!

Introduction

I've owned every Nikon digital SLR since the D70 (16 different models in all), and none of them made the first impression that the D7000 did. The first time I picked up this camera, the absolutely stunning image quality and feature set of the Nikon D7000 threw me for a loop, which is why I decided to spend an extra three months developing a comprehensive guidebook for this camera, rather than rushing to be the first one on the shelves with a cursory overview of its capabilities. If you waited for this book, I guarantee it will have been worth the wait.

David Busch's Nikon D7000 Guide to Digital SLR Photography deals with one of the best cameras Nikon has ever offered for such a low price. Although there have been some controversies (real or perceived) over its image quality, when it comes right down to it, the feature set of this camera, its resolution, and high ISO performance instantly made the much more expensive Nikon D300s obsolete. I dumped both my D700 and D300s, and *this* is the camera I use when I want a smaller bodied camera when I travel light (especially overseas).

But, despite its bulging feature list, the D7000 retains the ease of use that smoothes the transition for those new to digital photography. For those just dipping their toes into the digital pond, the experience is warm and inviting. The Nikon D7000 isn't a snapshot camera—it's a point-and-shoot (if you want to use it in that mode) for the thinking photographer.

Once you've confirmed that you made a wise purchase decision, the question comes up, *how do I use this thing?* All those cool features can be mind numbing to learn, if all you have as a guide is the manual furnished with the camera. Help is on the way. I sincerely believe that this book is your best bet for learning how to use your new camera, and for learning how to use it well.

If you're a Nikon D7000 owner who's looking to learn more about how to use this great camera, you've probably already explored your options. There are DVDs and online tutorials—but who can learn how to use a camera by sitting in front of a television or computer screen? Do you want to watch a movie or click on HTML links, or do you want to go out and take photos with your camera? Videos are fun, but not the best answer.

There's always the manual furnished with the D7000. It's compact and filled with information, but there's really very little about *why* you should use particular settings or features. Its organization may make it difficult to find what you need. Multiple cross-references may send you searching back and forth between two or three sections of the book to find what you want to know. The basic manual is also hobbled by black-and-white line drawings and tiny monochrome pictures that aren't very good examples of what you can do.

Also available are third-party guides to the D7000, like this one. I haven't been happy with some of these guidebooks, which is why I wrote this one. The existing books range from skimpy and illustrated by black-and-white photos to lushly illustrated in full color but too generic to do much good. Photography instruction is useful, but it needs to be related directly to the Nikon D7000 as much as possible.

I've tried to make *David Busch's Nikon D7000 Guide to Digital SLR Photography* different from your other D7000 learn-up options. The roadmap sections use larger, color pictures to show you where all the buttons and dials are, and the explanations of what they do are longer and more comprehensive. I've tried to avoid overly general advice, including the two-page checklists on how to take a "sports picture" or a "portrait picture" or a "travel picture." Instead, you'll find tips and techniques for using all the features of your Nikon D7000 to take *any kind of picture* you want. If you want to know where you should stand to take a picture of a quarterback dropping back to unleash a pass, there are plenty of books that will tell you that. This one concentrates on teaching you how to select the best autofocus mode, shutter speed, f/stop, or flash capability to take, say, a great sports picture under any conditions.

This book is not a lame rewriting of the manual that came with the camera. Some folks spend five minutes with a book like this one, spot some information that also appears in the original manual, and decide "Rehash!" without really understanding the differences. Yes, you'll find information here that is also in the owner's manual, such as the parameters you can enter when changing your D7000's operation in the various menus. Basic descriptions—before I dig in and start providing in-depth tips and information—may also be vaguely similar. There are only so many ways you can say, for example, "Hold the shutter release down halfway to lock in exposure." But not *everything* in the manual is included in this book. If you need advice on when and how to use the most important functions, you'll find the information here.

David Busch's Nikon D7000 Guide to Digital SLR Photography is aimed at both Nikon and dSLR veterans as well as newcomers to digital photography and digital SLRs. Both groups can be overwhelmed by the options the D7000 offers, while underwhelmed by the explanations they receive in their user's manual. The manuals are great if you already know what you don't know, and you can find an answer somewhere in a booklet arranged by menu listings and written by a camera vendor employee who last threw together instructions on how to operate a camcorder.

Once you've read this book and are ready to learn more, I hope you pick up one of my other guides to digital SLR photography. Five of them are offered by Course Technology PTR, each approaching the topic from a different perspective. They include:

David Busch's Compact Field Guide for the Nikon D7000

Readers have told me they love my 400-plus page guidebooks written specifically for their cameras, but asked me to condense the most essential information about settings, menus, and options into a pocket-sized format they can tuck in a camera bag. Well, you can throw away your cheat sheets and command cards. My *Compact Field Guide* for your D7000 is an on-the-go reference you can refer to as you shoot. It's a spiral-bound, lay-flat book with advice on using every setting and control your D7000 offers. While my "big books" contain everything you need to know, the compact versions make sure you'll have the must-have information, when you need it.

Quick Snap Guide to Digital SLR Photography

Consider this a prequel to the book you're holding in your hands. It might make a good gift for a spouse or friend who may be using your D7000, but who lacks even basic knowledge about digital photography, digital SLR photography, and Nikon photography. It serves as an introduction that summarizes the basic features of digital SLR cameras in general (not just the D7000), and what settings to use and when, such as continuous autofocus/single autofocus, aperture/shutter priority, EV settings, and so forth. The guide also includes recipes for shooting the most common kinds of pictures, with step-by-step instructions for capturing effective sports photos, portraits, landscapes, and other types of images.

David Busch's Quick Snap Guide to Using Digital SLR Lenses

A bit overwhelmed by the features and controls of digital SLR lenses, and not quite sure when to use each type? This book explains lenses, their use, and lens technology in easy-to-access two- and four-page spreads, each devoted to a different topic, such as depth-of-field, lens aberrations, or using zoom lenses.

David Busch's Quick Snap Guide to Photo Gear

Which three filters *must* you own—and which filters are obsolete in the era of digital photography? What's the best type of tripod or monopod for sports, landscape, or wildlife photography? Shoulder bags, sling bags, backpacks, and travel cases: which make the most sense to you? Of all the different gadgets for close-up photography, which are the best? Do I need a special memory card for my camera? What does a radio trigger do? You'll find the answers to all these questions in my guidebook for choosing and using the best photo gear and accessories.

Mastering Digital SLR Photography, Third Edition
This book, completely revamped with six brand new chapters for this latest edition, is an introduction to digital SLR photography, with nuts-and-bolts explanations of the technology, more in-depth coverage of settings, and whole chapters on the most common types of photography. While not specific to the D7000, this book can show you how to get more from its capabilities.

Digital SLR Pro Secrets
This is my more advanced guide to dSLR photography with greater depth and detail about the topics you're most interested in. If you've already mastered the basics in *Mastering Digital SLR Photography*, this book will take you to the next level.

Family Resemblance

If you've owned previous models in the Nikon digital camera line, and copies of my books for those cameras, you're bound to notice a certain family resemblance. Nikon has been very crafty in introducing upgraded cameras that share the best features of the models they replace, while adding new capabilities and options. You benefit in two ways. If you used a Nikon D90 prior to switching to the latest D7000 model, you'll find that the parts that haven't changed have a certain familiarity for you, making it easy to make the transition to the newest model. There are lots of features and menu choices of the D7000 that are exactly the same as those in the most recent models, or even "big siblings" like the D300s. This family resemblance will help level the learning curve for you.

Similarly, when writing books for each new model, I try to retain the easy-to-understand explanations that worked for previous books dedicated to earlier camera models, and concentrate on expanded descriptions of things readers have told me they want to know more about, a solid helping of fresh sample photos, and lots of details about the latest and greatest new features. Rest assured, this book was written expressly for you, and tailored especially for the D7000.

Who Are You?

When preparing a guidebook for a specific camera, it's always wise to consider exactly who will be reading the book. Indeed, thinking about the potential audience for *David Busch's Nikon D7000 Guide to Digital SLR Photography* is what led me to taking the approach and format I use for this book. I realized that the needs of readers like you had to be addressed both from a functional level (what you will use the D7000 for) as well as from a skill level (how much experience you may have with digital photography, dSLRs, or Nikon cameras specifically).

From a functional level, you probably fall into one of these categories:

- Professional photographers who understand photography and digital SLRs, and simply want to learn how to use the Nikon D7000 as a backup camera, or as a camera for their personal "off-duty" use.

- Individuals who want to get better pictures, or perhaps transform their growing interest in photography into a full-fledged hobby or artistic outlet with a Nikon D7000 and advanced techniques.

- Those who want to produce more professional-looking images for their personal or business website, and feel that the Nikon D7000 will give them more control and capabilities.

- Small business owners with more advanced graphics capabilities who want to use the Nikon D7000 to document or promote their business.

- Corporate workers who may or may not have photographic skills in their job descriptions, but who work regularly with graphics and need to learn how to use digital images taken with a Nikon D7000 for reports, presentations, or other applications.

- Professional webmasters with strong skills in programming (including Java, JavaScript, HTML, Perl, etc.) but little background in photography, but who realize that the D7000 can be used for sophisticated photography.

- Graphic artists and others who already may be adept in image editing with Photoshop or another program, and who may still be using a film SLR (Nikon or otherwise), but who need to learn more about digital photography and the special capabilities of the D7000 dSLR.

Addressing your needs from a skills level can be a little trickier, because the D7000 is such a great camera that a full spectrum of photographers will be buying it, from absolute beginners who have never owned a digital camera before up to the occasional professional with years of shooting experience who will be using the Nikon D7000 as a backup body. (I have to admit I tend to carry my D7000 with me everywhere, even if I intend to take most of my photos with another camera.)

Before tackling this book, it would be helpful for you to understand the following:

- **What a digital SLR is:** It's a camera that shows an optical (not LCD) view of the picture that's being taken through the (interchangeable) lens that actually takes the photo, thanks to a mirror that reflects an image to a viewfinder, but flips up out of the way to allow the sensor to be exposed. Today, such cameras also offer an optional Live View feature if you want to preview your images on the LCD, especially when prepping to shoot movies.

- **How digital photography differs from film:** The image is stored not on film (which I call the *first* write-once optical media), but on a memory card as pixels that can be transferred to your computer, and then edited, corrected, and printed without the need for chemical processing.

- **What the basic tools of correct exposure are:** Don't worry if you don't understand these; I'll explain them later in this book. But if you already know something about shutter speed, aperture, and ISO sensitivity, you'll be ahead of the game. If not, you'll soon learn that shutter speed determines the amount of time the sensor is exposed to incoming light; the f/stop or aperture is like a valve that governs the quantity of light that can flow through the lens; the sensor's sensitivity (ISO setting) controls how easily the sensor responds to light. All three factors can be varied individually and proportionately to produce a picture that is properly exposed (neither too light nor too dark).

It's tough to provide something for everybody, but I am going to try to address the needs of each of the following groups and skill levels:

- **Digital photography newbies:** If you've used only point-and-shoot digital cameras, or have worked only with non-SLR film cameras, you're to be congratulated for selecting one of the very best entry-level digital SLRs available as your first dSLR camera. This book can help you understand the controls and features of your D7000, and lead you down the path to better photography with your camera. I'll provide all the information you need, but if you want to do some additional reading for extra credit, you can also try one of the other books I mentioned earlier. They complement this book well.

- **Advanced point-and-shooters moving on up:** There are some quite sophisticated pocket-sized digital cameras available, including those with many user-definable options and settings, so it's possible you are already a knowledgeable photographer, even though you're new to the world of the digital SLR. You've recognized the limitations of the point-and-shoot camera: even the best of them have more noise at higher sensitivity (ISO) settings than a camera like the Nikon D7000; the speediest still have an unacceptable delay between the time you press the shutter and the photo is actually taken; even a non-interchangeable super-zoom camera with 12X to 20X magnification often won't focus close enough, include an aperture suitable for low-light photography, or take in the really wide view you must have. Interchangeable lenses and other accessories available for the Nikon D7000 are another one of the reasons you moved up. Because you're an avid photographer already, you should pick up the finer points of using the D7000 from this book with no trouble.

■ **Film SLR veterans new to the digital world:** You understand photography, you know about f/stops and shutter speeds, and thrive on interchangeable lenses. If you have used a newer film SLR, it probably has lots of electronic features already, including autofocus and sophisticated exposure metering. Perhaps you've even been using a Nikon film SLR and understand many of the available accessories that work with both film and digital cameras. All you need is information on using digital-specific features, working with the D7000 itself, and how to match—and exceed—the capabilities of your film camera with your new Nikon D7000.

■ **Experienced dSLR users broadening their experience to include the D7000:** Perhaps you started out with the Nikon D70 back in 2004, or a D100 before that. It's very likely that some of you used the 6-megapixel Nikon D40 before the bug to advance to more megapixels bit you. You may have used a digital SLR from Nikon or another vendor and are making the switch. You understand basic photography, and want to learn more. And, most of all, you want to transfer the skills you already have to the Nikon D7000, as quickly and seamlessly as possible.

■ **Pro photographers and other advanced shooters:** I expect my most discerning readers will be those who already have extensive experience with Nikon intermediate and pro-level cameras. I may not be able to teach you folks much about photography, but, even so, an amazing number of D7000 cameras have been purchased by those who feel it is a good complement to their favorite advanced dSLR. Others (like myself) own a camera like the Nikon D300s and find that the D7000 fills a specific niche incredibly well, and, is useful as a backup camera, because the D7000's 16-megapixel images are often just as good as those produced by more "advanced" models. You pros and semi-pros, despite your depth of knowledge, should find this book useful for learning about the features the D7000 has that your previous cameras lack or implement in a different way.

Who Am I?

After spending years as the world's most successful unknown author, I've become slightly less obscure in the past few years, thanks to a horde of camera guidebooks and other photographically oriented tomes. You may have seen my photography articles in *Popular Photography & Imaging* magazine. I've also written about 2,000 articles for magazines like *Petersen's PhotoGraphic* (which is now defunct through no fault of my own), plus *The Rangefinder, Professional Photographer,* and dozens of other photographic publications. But, first, and foremost, I'm a photojournalist and made my living in the field until I began devoting most of my time to writing books. Although I love writing, I'm happiest when I'm out taking pictures, which is why I took off 11 days just before I began writing this book to travel to Barcelona, Spain, and then, when the book was finished, immediately embark for Old San Juan in Puerto Rico. Last year, my travels also took me to "exotic" locations that included Florida, San Diego, and Ireland. You'll find photos of some of these visual treasures within the pages of this book.

Like all my digital photography books, this one was written by a Nikon devotee with an incurable photography bug. My first Nikon SLR was a venerable Nikon F back in the 1960s, and I've owned most of the newer digital models since then.

Over the years, I've worked as a sports photographer for an Ohio newspaper and for an upstate New York college. I've operated my own commercial studio and photo lab, cranking out product shots on demand and then printing a few hundred glossy 8 × 10s on a tight deadline for a press kit. I've served as a photo-posing instructor for a modeling agency. People have actually paid me to shoot their weddings and immortalize them with portraits. I even prepared press kits and articles on photography as a PR consultant for a large Rochester, N.Y., company, which shall remain nameless. My trials and travails with imaging and computer technology have made their way into print in book form an alarming number of times, including a few dozen on scanners and photography.

Like you, I love photography for its own merits, and I view technology as just another tool to help me get the images I see in my mind's eye. But, also like you, I had to master this technology before I could apply it to my work. This book is the result of what I've learned, and I hope it will help you master your Nikon D7000 digital SLR, too.

As I write this, I'm currently in the throes of upgrading my website, which you can find at www.nikonguides.com, adding tutorials and information about my other books. There's a lot of information about several Nikon models right now, but I'll be adding tips and recommendations about the Nikon D7000 (including a list of equipment and accessories that I can't live without) in the next few months. I hope you'll stop by for a visit. I've also set up a wish list of Nikon cameras, lenses, and accessories on Amazon.com for those who want to begin shopping now. I hope you'll stop by for a visit to my blog at http://www.dslrguides.com/blog, where you'll find a list of any typos sharp-eyed readers have reported. You'll find my equipment recommendations at http://astore.amazon.com/nikonphoto-20.

Part I

Getting Started with Your Nikon D7000

This first part of the book, consisting of just three short chapters, is designed to familiarize you with the basics of your Nikon D7000 as quickly as possible, even though I have no doubt that you've already been out shooting a few hundred (or thousand) photographs with your pride and joy.

After all, inserting a memory card, mounting a lens, stuffing a charged battery into the base, and removing the lens cap to fire off a shot or two isn't rocket science. Even the rawest neophyte can rotate the mode dial (located at top left on the camera body) to the P (Programmed auto) indicator or green Auto icon. Point the D7000 at something interesting and press the shutter release. Presto! A pretty good picture will pop up on the color LCD on the back of the camera. It's easy!

But in digital photography, there is such a thing as *too* easy. If you bought a D7000, you certainly had no intention of using the camera as a point-and-shoot snapshooter. After all, the D7000 is a tool suitable for the most advanced photographic pursuits, with an extensive array of customization possibilities. As such, you don't want the camera's operation to be brainless; you want *access* to the advanced features to be easy.

You get that easy access with the Nikon D7000. However, you'll still need to take the time to learn how to use these features, and I'm going to provide everything you need to know in these first three chapters to begin shooting:

- **Chapter 1:** This is a "Meet Your D7000" introduction, where you'll find information about what came in the box with your camera and, more importantly, what *didn't* come with the camera that you seriously should consider adding to your arsenal. I'll also cover some things you might not have known about charging the D7000's battery, choosing a memory card, setting the time and date, and a few other pre-flight tasks. This is basic stuff, and if you're a Nikon veteran, you can skim over it quickly. A lot of this first chapter is intended for newbies, and even if you personally don't find it essential, you'll probably agree that there was some point during your photographic development (so to speak) that you wished this information was spelled out for you. There's no extra charge!

- **Chapter 2:** Here, you'll find a Quick Start aimed at those who may not be old hands with Nikon cameras having this level of sophistication. The D7000 has some interesting new features, including one of the most advanced autofocus systems ever seen in a mid-level camera body (and which deserves an entire chapter of its own later in this book). But even with all the goodies to play with and learning curve still to climb, you'll find that Chapter 2 will get you shooting quickly with a minimum of fuss.

■ **Chapter 3:** This is a Streetsmart Roadmap to the Nikon D7000. Confused by the tiny little diagrams and multiple cross-references for each and every control that send you scurrying around looking for information you know is buried somewhere in the small and inadequate manual stuffed in the box? This chapter uses multiple large full-color pictures that show every dial, knob, and button, and explain the basics of using each in clear, easy-to-understand language. I'll give you the basics up front, and, even if I have to send you deeper into the book for a full discussion of a complex topic, you'll have what you need to use a control right away.

Once you've finished (or skimmed through) these three chapters, you'll be ready for Part II, which explains how to use the most important basic features, such as the D7000's exposure controls, nifty new autofocus system, and the related tools that put Live View and movie making tools at your fingertips. Then, you can visit Part III, the advanced tools section, which explains all the dozens of setup options that can be used to modify the capabilities you've learned to use so far, how to choose and use lenses, and introduces the Nikon D7000's built-in flash and external flash capabilities. I'll wind up this book with Part IV, which covers image software, printing, and transfer options and includes some troubleshooting that may help you when good cameras (or memory cards) go bad.

1

Nikon D7000: Thinking Outside of the Box

Whether you subscribe to the "my camera is just a tool" theory, or belong to the "an exquisite camera adds new capabilities to my shooting arsenal" camp, picking up a new Nikon D7000 is a special experience. Those who simply wield tools will find this camera as comforting as an old friend, a solid piece of fine machinery ready and able to do their bidding as part of the creative process.

Other photographers see the low-light capabilities (up to ISO 25600), the rapid-fire 6 frames-per-second continuous shooting, anvil-like ruggedness, and ultra-high 16.2-megapixel resolution of the D7000, and gain a sense of empowerment. *Here* is a camera with fewer limitations and more capabilities for exercising renewed creative vision. In either case, using less mawkish terms, the D7000 is one of the coolest cameras Nikon has ever offered. Whether you're upgrading from another brand, from another Nikon model (like the D90), or (O brave one!) your D7000 is your first digital camera and/or SLR, welcome to the club.

But, now that you've unwrapped and recharged the beast, mounted a lens, and fueled it with a memory card, what do you *do* with it? That's where this chapter—and the chapters that follow—should come in handy. Like many of you, I am a Nikon user of long standing. And, like other members of our club, I had to learn at least some aspects of my newest camera for the very first time at some point. Experienced pro, or Nikon newbie, you bought this book because you wanted to get the most from a very powerful tool, and I'm here to help.

Depending on your path to the camera, the Nikon D7000 is either the company's most ambitious amateur camera, or most affordable entry-level "pro" camera, which are both distinctions that I find almost meaningless in the greater scheme of things. I know consummate professionals who produce amazing images with a D90; experienced wedding photographers who evoke the most romantic photos from an old Nikon D200. The Nikon D7000 is a professional camera in most of the traditional senses: built like a tank with a magnesium body, reliable for hundreds of thousands of exposures, capable of lightning-fast autofocusing and superb image quality, whether you're shooting in a studio or drenched in driving rain. But whether your *images* are of professional quality, both technically and inspirationally, depends on what's between your ears, and how you apply it. The goal of this book is to provide you with the information you need to put your brain cells together with your Nikon's electro-mechanical components to work productively.

There's a lot to learn, but you don't have to master every detail all at once. Some of the other camera guides I've seen winnow this information down to about one-third as many pages. Indeed, I find it odd that those guidebooks use the same basic template for the advanced D7000 cameras as for a resolutely amateur-level model like the Nikon D3100. A camera like the D7000 has a lot more depth than that, and deserves the in-depth coverage you'll find here.

Whether you've already taken a dozen or twelve hundred photos with your new camera, now that you've got that initial creative burst out of your system, you'll want to take a more considered approach to operating the camera. This chapter and the next are designed to get your camera fired up and ready for shooting as quickly as possible. After all, the D7000 is not a point-and-shoot camera, even though it does boast easy-to-use Scene mode options.

So I'm going to provide a basic pre-flight checklist that you need to complete before you really spread your wings and take off. You won't find a lot of detail in these first two chapters. Indeed, I'm going to tell you just what you absolutely *must* understand, accompanied by some interesting tidbits that will help you become acclimated to your D7000. I'll go into more depth and even repeat some of what I explain here in later chapters, so you don't have to memorize everything you see. Just relax, follow a few easy steps, and then go out and begin taking your best shots—ever.

Even if you're a long-time Nikon shooter, I hope you won't be tempted to skip this chapter or the next one. I realize that you probably didn't purchase this book the same day you bought your camera and that, even if you did, the urge to go out and take a few hundred—or thousand—photos with your new camera is enticing. As valuable as a book like this one is, nobody can suppress their excitement long enough to read the instructions before initiating play with a new toy.

No matter how extensive your experience level is, you don't need to fret about wading through a manual to find out what you must know to take those first few tentative snaps. I'm going to help you hit the ground running with this chapter, which will help you set up your camera and begin shooting in minutes. You won't find a lot of detail in this chapter. Indeed, I'm going to give you the basics, accompanied by some interesting tidbits that will help you become acclimated. I'll go into more depth and even repeat some of what I explain here in later chapters, so you don't have to memorize everything you see. Because I realize that some of you may already have experience with Nikon cameras similar to the D7000, each of the major sections in this chapter will begin with a brief description of what is covered in that section, so you can easily jump ahead to the next if you are in a hurry to get started.

First Things First

This section helps get you oriented with all the things that come in the box with your Nikon D7000, including what they do. I'll also describe some optional equipment you might want to have. If you want to get started immediately, skim through this section and jump ahead to "Initial Setup" later in the chapter.

The Nikon D7000 comes in an impressive gold box filled with stuff, including connecting cords, booklets, a CD, and lots of paperwork. The most important components are the camera and lens (if you purchased your D7000 with a lens), battery, battery charger, and, if you're the nervous type, the neck strap. You'll also need a memory card as one is not included. If you purchased your D7000 from a camera shop, as I did, the store personnel probably attached the neck strap for you, ran through some basic operational advice that you've already forgotten, tried to sell you a memory card, and then, after they'd given you all the help you could absorb, sent you on your way with a handshake.

Perhaps you purchased your D7000 from one of those mass merchandisers that also sell washing machines and vacuum cleaners. In that case, you might have been sent on your way with only the handshake, or, maybe, not even that if you resisted the efforts to sell you an extended warranty. You save a few bucks at the big box stores, but you don't get the personal service a professional photo retailer provides. It's your choice. There's a third alternative, of course. You might have purchased your camera from a mail order or Internet source, and your D7000 arrived in a big brown (or purple/red) truck. Your only interaction when you took possession of your camera was to scrawl your signature on an electronic clipboard.

In all three cases, the first thing to do is to carefully unpack the camera and double-check the contents with the checklist on one end of the box, helpfully designated under a "This package includes" listing. While this level of setup detail may seem as superfluous as the instructions on a bottle of shampoo, checking the contents *first* is always a good idea. No matter who sells a camera, it's common to open boxes, use a particular camera for a demonstration, and then repack the box without replacing all the pieces and parts afterwards. Someone might actually have helpfully checked out your camera on your behalf—and then mispacked the box. It's better to know *now* that something is missing so you can seek redress immediately, rather than discover two months from now that the video cable you thought you'd never use (but now *must* have) was never in the box. I once purchased a brand-new Nikon dSLR kit that was supposed to include a second focusing screen; it wasn't in the box, but because I discovered the deficiency right away, the dealer ordered a replacement for me post haste.

At a minimum, the box should have the following:

- **Nikon D7000 digital camera.** It almost goes without saying that you should check out the camera immediately, making sure the back- and top-panel LCDs aren't scratched or cracked, the memory and battery doors open properly, and, when a charged battery is inserted and lens mounted, the camera powers up and reports for duty. Out-of-the-box defects like these are rare, but they can happen. It's probably more common that your dealer played with the camera or, perhaps, it was a customer return. That's why it's best to buy your D7000 from a retailer you trust to supply a factory-fresh camera.

- **Rechargeable Li-ion battery EN-EL15.** You'll need to charge this 7.0V, 1900mAh (milliampere hour) battery before use, and then navigate immediately to the Setup menu's Battery Info Entry to make sure the battery accepted the juice and is showing a 100% charge. (You'll find more on accessing this menu item in Chapter 10.) You'll want a second EN-EL15 battery as a spare (trust me), so buy one as soon as possible.

- **Quick charger MH-25.** This charger comes with both a power cable and a power adapter that can be used instead of the cable to plug the charger directly into a wall outlet.

- **EG-D2 audio/video cable.** Use this supplied cable to connect your D7000 to a standard definition (analog) television through the set's yellow RCA video jack when you want to view the camera's output on a larger screen. Although the D7000 can be connected to a high-definition television, you'll need to buy a high-definition multimedia interface (HDMI) cable to do that. No HDMI cable is included with the camera.

■ **USB cable UC-E4.** You can use this cable to transfer photos from the camera to your computer (I don't recommend that because direct transfer uses a lot of battery power), to upload and download settings between the camera and your computer (highly recommended), and to operate your camera remotely using Nikon Camera Control Pro software (not included in the box). This cable is a standard one that works with the majority of digital cameras—Nikon and otherwise—so if you already own one, you now have a spare.

■ **AN-DC1 neck strap.** Nikon provides you with a neck strap emblazoned with your camera model. It's not very adjustable, and, while useful for showing off to your friends exactly which nifty new camera you bought, the Nikon strap also can serve to alert observant unsavory types that you're sporting a higher-end model that's worthy of their attention. I never attach the Nikon strap to my cameras (although once I put a D3x strap on a Nikon D40 as a jest), and instead opt for a more serviceable strap from Op-Tech (www.optechusa.com) or, best of all, an UPstrap (www.upstrap-pro.com). An UPstrap is shown in Figure 1.1, with its patented non-slip pad that keeps your D7000 on your shoulder, and not crashing to the ground. If you order one of these, tell inventor-photographer Al Stegmeyer that I sent you.

■ **BF-1B body cap.** The body cap keeps dust from infiltrating your camera when a lens is not mounted. Always carry a body cap (and rear lens cap) in your camera bag for those times when you need to have the camera bare of optics for more than a minute or two. (That usually happens when repacking a bag efficiently for transport, or when you are carrying an extra body or two for backup.) The body cap/lens cap nest together for compact storage.

Figure 1.1
Third-party neck straps like this UPstrap model are often preferable to the Nikon-supplied strap.

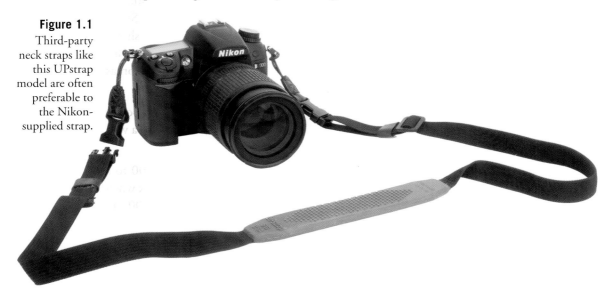

Note

If you happen to have one of the earlier BF-1 body caps for older film cameras, do not use it, as it may damage the lens mount's protruding autofocus screw, which focuses lenses that don't have an autofocus motor built in.

- **DK-21 eyecup.** This is the square rubber eyecup that comes installed on the D7000. It slides on and off the viewfinder. If you prefer, you can also use round, screw-in eyepiece accessories, such as the DK-3 circular rubber eyecup or DG-2 eyepiece 2x magnifier by substituting the Nikon No. 2370 eyepiece adapter for the DK-23 eyecup.

- **DK-5 eyepiece cap.** This small piece can be clipped over the viewfinder window to prevent strong light sources from entering the viewing system when your eye is not pressed up against it, potentially affecting exposure measurement. That can be a special problem when the camera is mounted on a tripod, because additional illumination from the rear can make its way to the 1005-segment CCD that interprets light reaching the focusing screen. I pack this widget away to keep from losing it. As a practical matter, you'll never find it when you really need it, and covering the viewfinder with your hand (hover *near* the viewfinder window rather than touch it, to avoid shaking a tripod-mounted camera) works almost as well.

- **BS-1 accessory shoe cover.** This little piece of plastic protects the electrical contacts of the "hot" shoe on top of the D7000. You can remove it when mounting an electronic flash, Nikon GP-1 GPS device, or other accessory, and then safely leave it off for the rest of your life. I've never had an accessory shoe receive damage in normal use, even when not protected. The paranoid among you who use accessories frequently can keep removing/mounting the shoe cover as required. Find a safe place to keep it between uses, or purchase replacements for this easily mislaid item. (Visit www.bocaphoto.com for many Nikon-related items.)

- **LCD monitor cover BM-11.** The glass covering the D7000's big 3-inch LCD is tough, but this plastic cover adds another layer of protection, and it can be replaced for a few dollars if scratched. If I were going to worry about shielding the LCD from damage, I'd use a less obtrusive acrylic cover from DaProducts (www.daproducts.com) at a cost of about $6. My big problem with Nikon's clip-on protector is that it easily fogs up when you breathe on it. I'll show you some alternatives in Chapter 14.

- **User's manuals.** Even if you have this book, you'll probably want to check the user's guide that Nikon provides, if only to check the actual nomenclature for some obscure accessory, or to double-check an error code. Google "Nikon D7000 manual PDF" to find a downloadable, non-printable version that you can store on your laptop, a CD-ROM, or other media in case you want to access this reference when the paper version isn't handy. If you have an old memory card that's too small to be usable on a modern dSLR (I still have some 128MB and 256MB cards), you can store the PDF on that. But an even better choice is to put the manual on a low-capacity USB "thumb" drive, which you can buy for less than $10. You'll then be able to access the reference anywhere you are, because you can always find someone with a computer that has a USB port and Adobe Acrobat Reader available. You might not be lucky enough to locate a computer with a memory reader.

- **Quick Start guide.** This little booklet tucked away in the camera's paperwork offers a reasonable summary of the Nikon D7000's basic commands and settings, and can be stowed in your camera bag.

- **Software CD-ROM.** Here you'll find the Nikon ViewNX2 software, a useful image management program. I'll cover a variety of other software offerings later in Chapter 13 of this book.

- **Warranty and registration card.** Don't lose these! You can register your Nikon D7000 by mail or online (in the USA, the URL is www.nikonusa.com/register), and you may need the information in this paperwork (plus the purchase receipt/invoice from your retailer) should you require Nikon service support.

Don't bother rooting around in the box for anything beyond what I've listed previously. There are a few things Nikon classifies as optional accessories, even though you (and I) might consider some of them essential. Here's a list of what you *don't* get in the box, but might want to think about as an impending purchase. I'll list them roughly in the order of importance:

- **Secure Digital card.** First-time digital camera buyers are sometimes shocked that their new tool doesn't come with a memory card. Why should it? The manufacturer doesn't have the slightest idea of what capacity or speed card you prefer, so why should they pack one in the box and charge you for it? That's especially true for the Nikon D7000, which is likely to be purchased by photographers who have quite definite ideas about their ideal memory card. Perhaps you want to use tiny 4GB cards—and lots of them. I've met many paranoid wedding photographers who like to work with a horde of smaller cards (and then watch over them *very* protectively), on the theory that they are reducing their chances of losing a significant chunk of the event or reception at one time (of course, that's why you hire a second shooter as backup). Others, especially sports photographers, instead prefer a 16GB or 32GB card with room to spare. If you are shooting fast action at high frame rates, or transfer lots of photos to your computer with a speedy card reader, you might opt for the speediest possible memory card. Buy one (or two, or three) of your own and have your flash memory ready when you unpack your D7000.

- **Extra EN-EL15 battery.** I mentioned the need for an extra battery earlier, and I'll mention it here, again. Even though you might get 1,000 or more shots from a single battery, it's easy to exceed that figure in a few hours of shooting sports at 6 fps. Batteries can unexpectedly fail, too, or simply lose their charge from sitting around unused for a week or two. Buy an extra (I own four, in total), keep it charged, and free your mind from worry.

- **Nikon Capture NX 2 software.** You can download a free try-out copy of this software from Nikon's website, but if you want to use it after the free period expires, you'll need to buy it.

- **Camera Control Pro 2 software.** This is the utility you'll use to operate your camera remotely from your computer. Nikon charges extra for this software, but you'll find it invaluable if you're hiding near a tethered, tripod-mounted camera while shooting, say, close-ups of hummingbirds. There are lots of applications for remote shooting, and you'll need Camera Control Pro to operate your camera. Buy a suitably longer USB cable, too, unless you plan to use the Nikon WT4a wireless transmitter (described below).

- **Add-on speedlight.** One of the best uses for your Nikon D7000's built-in electronic flash is as a remote trigger for an off-camera speedlight such as the Nikon SB-900. Your built-in flash can function as the main light, diffused and used for fill, or dialed down in power so it has virtually no effect on the finished photo at all (other than triggering your remote flash units). But, you'll have to own one or two (or more) external flash units to gain that flexibility. If you do much flash photography at all, consider an add-on speedlight as an important accessory.

- **Remote control cable MC-DC2.** You can plug this one-meter long accessory electronic release cable into the socket hidden behind a rubber cover on the side of the D7000, and then fire off the camera without the need to touch the camera itself. In a pinch, you can use the D7000's self-timer to minimize vibration when triggering the camera, or even take advantage of the mirror up (M-UP) and delayed release features to reduce camera shake. (These are all described later in this book.) But when you want to take a photo at the exact moment you desire (and not when the self-timer happens to trip), or need to eliminate all possibility of human-induced camera shake, you need this release cord.

- **ML-L3 infrared remote.** The D7000 has a pair of infrared sensors on the front and back panels that can receive signals from this optional remote control. They work best when used while facing the camera, or directly behind (rather than to either side), but, unlike the MC-DC2 remote, you can be positioned farther away than one meter.

- **Nikon GP-1 global positioning system (GPS) device.** This accessory attaches to the accessory shoe on top of the Nikon D90 and captures latitude, longitude, and altitude information, which is imprinted in a special data area of your image files. The "geotagging" data can be plotted on a map in Nikon ViewNX or other software programs. I'll explain more about this feature in Chapter 7.

- **AC adapter EH-5a.** There are several typical situations where this AC adapter for your D7000 can come in handy: when you're cleaning the sensor manually and want to totally eliminate the possibility that a lack of juice will cause the fragile shutter and mirror to spring to life during the process; when in the studio shooting product photos, portraits, class pictures, and so forth for hours on end; when using your D7000 for remote shooting as well as time-lapse photography; for extensive review of images on your standard-definition or high-definition television; or for file transfer to your computer. These all use prodigious amounts of power, which can be provided by this AC adapter. (Beware of power outages and blackouts when cleaning your sensor, however!)

- **Multi-power battery pack MB-D11.** Lots of photographers consider this battery pack/vertical grip to be an essential item (I'm going to cover it in detail later in this book), but you must buy it as an extra. The price is reasonable at less than $250. Unfortunately, it is delivered "bare," with no extra power sources at all. You'll need to purchase AA batteries (alkalines or rechargeables) for the supplied AA battery tray, or have an extra EN-EL15 battery to use this accessory. (I *told* you that you'd need that extra battery.)

- **DR-6 right-angle viewer.** Fastens in place of the standard square rubber eyecup and provides a 90-degree view for framing and composing your image at right angles to the original viewfinder, useful for low-level (or high-level) shooting. (Or, maybe, shooting around corners!)

- **DK-21M magnifying eyepiece.** Provides a 1.17X magnification factor of the entire viewing area (unlike the 2X DG-2 eyepiece, which enlarges the center of the image), making it easier to check focus. You might have to move your eye around a little to see all the indicators outside the image frame, but this magnifier is still suitable for everyday use.

- **SC-28 TTL flash cord.** Allows using Nikon speedlights off-camera, while retaining all the automated features.

- **SC-29 TTL flash cord.** Similar to the SC-28, this unit has its own AF-assist lamp, which can provide extra illumination for the D7000's autofocus system in dim light (which, not coincidentally, is when you'll probably be using an electronic flash).

Initial Setup

This section helps you familiarize yourself with the three important controls most used to make adjustments: the multi selector and the main and sub-command dials. You'll also find information on charging the battery, setting the clock, mounting a lens, and making diopter vision adjustments. If you're comfortable with all these things, skim through and skip ahead to "Changing Default Settings" in the next section.

Once you've unpacked and inspected your camera, the initial setup of your Nikon D7000 is fast and easy. Basically, you just need to charge the battery, attach a lens, and insert a memory card. I'll address each of these steps separately, but if you already are confident you can manage these setup tasks without further instructions, feel free to skip this section entirely. While most buyers of a D7000 tend to be experienced photographers, I realize that some readers are ambitious, if inexperienced, and should, at the minimum, skim the contents of the next section, because I'm going to list a few options that you might not be aware of.

Mastering the Multi Selector and Command Dials

I'll be saving descriptions of most of the controls used with the Nikon D7000 until Chapter 2, which provides a complete "roadmap" of the camera's buttons and dials and switches. However, you may need to perform a few tasks during this initial setup process, and most of them will require the MENU button and the multi selector pad. The MENU button is easy to find: it's located to the left of the LCD, the first button in the series of four located to the left of the LCD. It requires almost no explanation; when you want to access a menu, press it. To exit most menus, press it again.

The multi selector pad may remind you of the similar control found on many point-and-shoot cameras, and other digital SLRs. It consists of a thumbpad-sized button with projections at the North, South, East, and West positions, plus a button in the center. It can also be pushed in diagonal directions to give you Northeast, Southeast, Southwest, and Northwest orientations. (See Figure 1.2.)

The multi selector on the D7000 functions slightly differently than its counterpart on some other cameras. For example, some point-and-shoot models assign a function, such as white balance or ISO setting, to one of the directional buttons (usually in conjunction with a function key of some sort). The use of the multi selector varies, even within the Nikon dSLR line up. For example, many Nikon digital SLRs (such as the Nikon D50/D70/D80) have no center button in the multi selector at all. Other Nikon cameras (such as the D300/D300s and D3/D3x) allow assigning a function of your choice to the multi selector center button.

Figure 1.2
The multi selector pad has four directional positions for navigating up/down/left/ right, and a center button to confirm your selection.

OK button

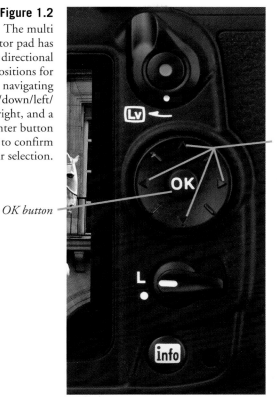

Directional buttons

With the D7000, the multi selector is used extensively for navigation, for example, to navigate among menus on the LCD or to choose one of the 39 focus points, to advance or reverse display of a series of images during picture review, or to change the kind of photo information displayed on the screen. The center button is used to select a high-lighted item from a menu.

So, from time to time in this chapter (and throughout this book) I'll be referring to the multi selector and its left/right/up/down buttons, and center button.

The main command dial and sub-command dial are located on the rear and front of the D7000, respectively. The main command dial is used to change settings such as shutter speed, while the sub-command dial adjusts an alternate or secondary setting. For example, in Manual exposure mode, you'd use the sub-command dial to change the aperture, while the main command dial is used to change the shutter speed. (In both cases, the dial is "active" for these adjustments only when the D7000's exposure meter is On.) The meter will automatically go to sleep after an interval (you'll learn how to specify the length of time in Chapter 9), and you must waken the camera (just tap the shutter release button) to switch the meter back on and activate the main and sub-command dials.

Setting the Clock

It's likely that your Nikon D7000's internal clock hasn't been set to your local time, so you may need to do that first. If so, the flashing CLOCK indicator on the top-panel LCD will be the giveaway. You'll find complete instructions for setting the four options for the date/time (time zone, actual date and time, the date format, and whether you want the D7000 to conform to Daylight Savings Time) in Chapter 10. However, if you think you can handle this step without instruction, press the MENU button, use the multi selector (that thumb-friendly button I just described, located to the immediate right of the back panel LCD) to scroll down to the Setup menu, press the multi selector button to the right, and scroll down to Time Zone and Date choice, and press right again. The options will appear on the screen that appears next. Keep in mind that you'll need to reset your camera's internal clock from time to time, as it is not 100-percent accurate.

Battery Included

Your Nikon D7000 is a sophisticated hunk of machinery and electronics, but it needs a charged battery to function, so rejuvenating the EN-EL15 lithium-ion battery pack furnished with the camera should be your first step. A fully charged power source should be good for approximately 1,050 shots, based on standard tests defined by the Camera & Imaging Products Association (CIPA) document DC-002. Nikon's own standards are quite a bit more optimistic (it predicts as many as 4,500 shots from a single charge). In the real world, of course, the life of the battery will depend on how much image review you do, how many shots you take with the built-in flash, and many other factors. You'll want to keep track of how many pictures *you* are able to take in your own typical circumstances, and use that figure as a guideline, instead.

A BATTERY AND A SPARE

I always recommend purchasing Nikon brand batteries (for about $50) over less-expensive third-party packs, even though the $30 substitute batteries may offer more capacity at a lower price (some may even top the 1,900 mAh offered by the Nikon battery). My reasoning is that it doesn't make sense to save $20 on a component for a $1,200 camera, especially since batteries have been known to fail in potentially harmful ways. You need only look as far as Nikon's own recall of its earlier EN-EL3 batteries, which forced the company to ship out thousands of free replacement cells. You're unlikely to get the same support from a third-party battery supplier that sells under a half-dozen or more different product labels and brands, and may not even have an easy way to get the word out that a recall has been issued.

If your pictures are important to you, always have at least one spare battery available, and make sure it is an authentic Nikon product.

All rechargeable batteries undergo some degree of self-discharge just sitting idle in the camera or in the original packaging. Lithium-ion power packs of this type typically lose a few percent of their charge every few days, even when the camera isn't turned on. The small amount of juice used to provide the "shots remaining" figure on the top-panel monochrome LCD when the D7000 is turned off isn't the culprit; Li-ion cells lose their power through a chemical reaction that continues when the camera is switched off. So, it's very likely that the battery purchased with your camera is at least partially pooped out, so you'll want to revive it before going out for some serious shooting.

Charging the Battery

When the battery is inserted into the MH-25 charger properly (it's impossible to insert it incorrectly), a Charge light begins flashing, and remains flashing until the status lamp glows steadily indicating that charging is finished, in about 2.5 hours. You can use the supplied connector cable (at left in Figure 1.3) or attach a handy plug adapter that allows connecting the charger directly to a wall outlet (as shown at right in Figure 1.3). When the battery is charged, flip the lever on the bottom of the camera and slide the battery in, as shown in Figure 1.4. Check the Setup menu's Battery Info entry as I recommended earlier to make sure the battery is fully charged. If not, try putting it in the charger again. One of three things may be the culprit: a.) the actual charging cycle sometimes takes longer than you (or the charger) expected; b.) the battery is new and needs to be "seasoned" for a few charging cycles, after which it will accept a full charge and deliver more shots; c.) you've got a defective battery. The last is fairly rare, but before you start counting on getting a particular number of exposures from a battery, it's best to make sure it's fully charged, seasoned, and ready to deliver.

Final Steps

Your Nikon D7000 is almost ready to fire up and shoot. You'll need to select and mount a lens, adjust the viewfinder for your vision, and insert a memory card. Each of these steps is easy, and if you've used any Nikon before, you already know exactly what to do.

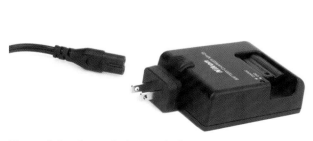

Figure 1.3 Charge the battery before use.

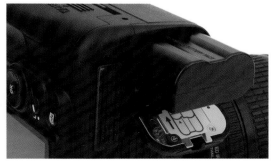

Figure 1.4 Insert the battery in the camera; it only fits one way.

I'm going to provide a little extra detail for those of you who are new to the Nikon or SLR worlds.

Mounting the Lens

As you'll see, my recommended lens mounting procedure emphasizes protecting your equipment from accidental damage and minimizing the intrusion of dust. If your D7000 has no lens attached, select the lens you want to use and loosen (but do not remove) the rear lens cap. I generally place the lens I am planning to mount vertically in a slot in my camera bag, where it's protected from mishaps, but ready to pick up quickly. By loosening the rear lens cap, you'll be able to lift it off the back of the lens at the last instant, so the rear element of the lens is covered until then.

After that, remove the body cap by rotating the cap towards the release button. You should always mount the body cap when there is no lens on the camera, because it helps keep dust out of the interior of the camera, where it can settle on the mirror, focusing screen, interior mirror box, and potentially find its way past the shutter onto the sensor. (While the D7000's sensor cleaning mechanism works fine, the less dust it has to contend with, the better.) The body cap also protects the vulnerable mirror from damage caused by intruding objects (including your fingers, if you're not cautious).

Once the body cap has been removed, remove the rear lens cap from the lens, set it aside, and then mount the lens on the camera by matching the alignment indicator on the lens barrel with the raised white bump on the camera's lens mount. (See Figure 1.5.) Rotate the lens toward the shutter release until it seats securely. Some lenses are trickier to mount than others, particularly telephotos and telephoto zooms with swiveling collars that allow the lens to be fastened to a tripod. You might need to rotate the collar so the tripod foot doesn't bump into the front overhang of the D7000's prism.

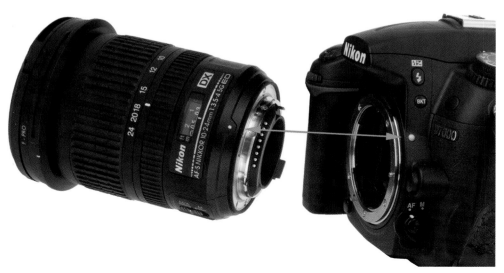

Figure 1.5
Match the indicator on the lens with the white dot on the camera mount to properly align the lens with the bayonet mount.

DEALING WITH ERRORS

After you've mounted your lens properly (or *think* you have), you might find various error codes appearing on the top-panel LCD, viewfinder, and back-panel color LCD. Here are the most common error codes, and what you should do next:

- **FE E.** This error code, with a smaller uppercase F followed by two Es indicates that you've mounted a lens that has an aperture ring, but haven't set the lens to its smallest f/stop (usually f/22 or f/32). Nikon autofocus lenses with an aperture ring have a lock lever that allows you to set the minimum aperture and lock it there so that this problem doesn't occur. However, you may have unlocked the aperture ring when you needed to set the aperture manually with the lens mounted on an older camera that didn't allow setting the aperture electronically. Or, you might have mounted the lens on a non-autoaperture extension tube, bellows, or other accessory.

- **E r r.** Some other error has taken place. Release the shutter, turn off the camera, remove the lens, and remount it. Try another lens. If the message persists, then there is a problem unrelated to your lens, and your D7000 may need service.

Set the focus mode switch on the lens to AF or M-AF (autofocus). If the lens hood is bayoneted on the lens in the reversed position (which makes the lens/hood combination more compact for transport), twist it off and remount with the "petals" (found on virtually all Nikon lens hoods) facing outward. (See Figure 1.6.) A lens hood protects the front of the lens from accidental bumps, and reduces flare caused by extraneous light arriving at the front element of the lens from outside the picture area.

Figure 1.6
A lens hood protects the lens from extraneous light and accidental bumps.

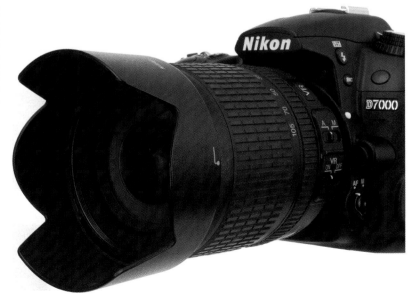

Adjusting Diopter Correction

Those of us with less than perfect eyesight can often benefit from a little optical correction in the viewfinder. Your contact lenses or glasses may provide all the correction you need, but if you are a glasses wearer and want to use the D7000 without your glasses, you can take advantage of the camera's built-in diopter adjustment, which can be varied from −3 to +1 correction. Press the shutter release halfway to illuminate the indicators in the viewfinder, then rotate the diopter adjustment dial next to the viewfinder (see Figure 1.7) while looking through the viewfinder until the indicators appear sharp.

Diopter correction wheel

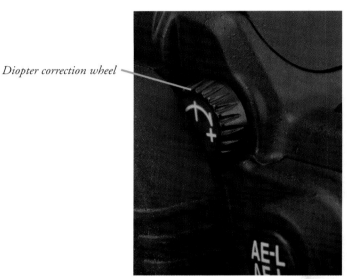

Figure 1.7
Viewfinder diopter correction from −3 to +1 can be dialed in.

If more than one person uses your D7000, and each requires a different diopter setting on the camera itself, you can save a little time by noting the number of clicks and direction (clockwise to increase the diopter power; counterclockwise to decrease the diopter value) required to change from one user to the other. Should the available correction be insufficient, Nikon offers nine different Diopter-Adjustment Viewfinder Correction lenses for the viewfinder window, ranging from −5 to +3, at a cost of $15-$20 each.

Inserting a Secure Digital Memory Card

You've probably set up your D7000 so you can't take photos without a memory card inserted. (There is a No Memory Card? entry, Custom Settings menu CSM #f8 that enables/disables shutter release functions when a memory card is absent—learn about that in Chapter 9.) So, your final step will be to insert a memory card. Slide the door on the back right edge of the body towards the back of the camera to release the cover, and then open it. (You should only remove a memory card when the camera is switched off, or, at the very least, the yellow-green memory access light that indicates the camera is writing to the card is not illuminated.)

MORE ABOUT CSM OPTIONS IN CHAPTER 9

The next section will suggest other "default" settings you might want to adjust before you get started. You'll find a complete list of Custom Settings menu options and parameters in Chapter 9.

Inside, you'll find two SD card slots. (See Figure 1.8.) You can use one card, or two. The slot closest to the top of the camera is Slot 1; the other is Slot 2. If you load only one card, it's customary to insert it in Slot 1, but the camera will operate even if the only SD card in use is placed in Slot 2.

Figure 1.8
The memory card in either slot is always inserted with the label facing the back of the camera.

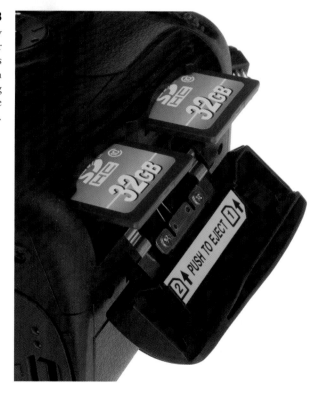

Insert the memory card with the label facing the back of the camera oriented so the edge with the contacts (metallic "fingers" with a Secure Digital card) goes into the slot first. Close the door, and, if necessary, format the card. A Secure Digital card can be removed just by pressing it inward; it will pop out far enough that you can extract it.

Formatting a Memory Card

There are four ways to create a blank memory card for your D7000, and two of them are wrong. Here are your options, both correct and incorrect:

- **Transfer (move) files to your computer.** When you transfer (rather than copy) all the image files to your computer from the memory card (either using a direct cable transfer or with a card reader, as described later in this chapter), the old image files are erased from the card, leaving the card blank. Theoretically. Unfortunately, this method does *not* remove files that you've labeled as Protected (by pressing the Protect button to the left of the LCD while viewing the image on the LCD), nor does it identify and lock out parts of your memory card that have become corrupted or unusable since the last time you formatted the card. Therefore, I recommend always formatting the card, rather than simply moving the image files, each time you want to make a blank card. The only exception is when you *want* to leave the protected/unerased images on the card for awhile longer, say, to share with friends, family, and colleagues.

- **(Don't) Format in your computer.** With the memory card inserted in a card reader or card slot in your computer, you can use Windows or Mac OS to reformat the memory card. Don't! The operating system won't necessarily install the correct file system. The only way to ensure that the card has been properly formatted for your camera is to perform the format in the camera itself. The only exception to this rule is when you have a seriously munged memory card that your camera refuses to format. Sometimes it is possible to revive such a corrupted card by allowing the operating system to reformat it first, then trying again in the camera.

- **Setup menu format.** To use one of the recommended methods to format a memory card, press the MENU button, use the up/down buttons of the multi selector (that thumb-pad-sized control to the right of the LCD) to choose the Setup menu (which is represented by a wrench icon), navigate to the Format Memory Card entry with the right button of the multi selector, choose which memory card to format (Slot 1 or Slot 2), and select Yes from the screen that appears. Press OK to begin the format process.

- **Two-button format.** The second recommended method requires no menus. Hold down the metering mode button (on top of the camera, just southwest of the shutter release button) and the trash can button (on the upper-left corner of the back) simultaneously for about two seconds. (A Format label [color-coded red], appears next to each button, as shown in the yellow boxes in Figure 1.9.) The characters For and the exposures remaining displays will blink in the viewfinder and top-panel LCD. If you have memory cards inserted in both the Secure Digital card slots, Slot 1 will be selected. If you'd rather format the other card, rotate the main command dial to select that slot. Then press the pair of buttons again, and the D7000 will format your card. To cancel the format, press any other button.

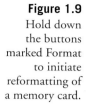

Figure 1.9
Hold down the buttons marked Format to initiate reformatting of a memory card.

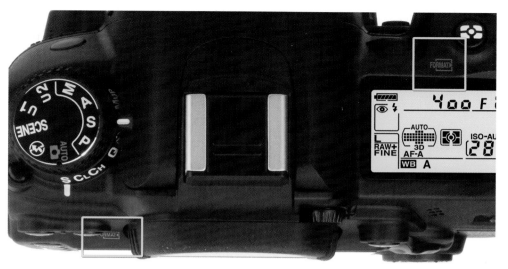

HOW MANY SHOTS?

The D7000 provides a fairly accurate estimate of the number of shots remaining on the top-panel LCD at all times (even when the camera is turned off), as well as at the lower-right edge of the viewfinder display when the display is active. (Tap the shutter release button to activate it.)

It is only an estimate, because the actual number will vary, depending on the capacity of your memory card, the file format(s) you've selected, and the content of the image itself. (Some photos may contain large areas that can be more efficiently compressed to a smaller size.)

For example, an 8GB card can hold about 813 JPEG Fine shots in full resolution (Large) format; 1,600 shots using Normal JPEG compression; or 3,100 shots with Basic JPEG compression. When numbers exceed 1,000, the D7000 displays a figure and decimal point, followed by a K superscript, so that 3,100 shots (or thereabouts) is represented by $[3.1]^K$ in the LCD and viewfinder. The D7000 offers three different resolution settings that provide different numbers of exposures: Large (4928 × 3264; 16.1 megapixels), Medium (3696 × 2448; 9.0 megapixels), and Small (2464 × 1632; 4 megapixels). For example, JPEG Basic using the Small resolution setting yields 11K exposures on a single 8GB memory card!

Using RAW/NEF format (more on that later) reduces the number of shots. An 8GB card has enough room for 300-400 RAW photos in Nikon's NEF format (depending on the type of compression you choose, as described later) or 191 pictures if you're shooting RAW+JPEG Fine pairs. Table 1.1 shows some typical capacities for an 8GB memory card. You should know that the D7000 has various compression options for JPEG and RAW files, as well as 12-bit and 14-bit dynamic range settings for the RAW format; we'll look into those options in more detail in Chapter 8.

Table 1.1 shows the typical number of shots you can expect using 12-bit color depth and an 8GB memory card. (Hold down the QUAL button [the bottom button in the column to the left of the back-panel LCD] and rotate the main command dial to change the file/formats in column 1, and rotate the sub-command dial to change the image sizes in columns 2, 3, and, 4.) The current file format appears in the top-panel mono-chrome LCD along with the number of exposures possible with the current memory card.

At this point, your camera is set up and ready to shoot. You can move on to Chapter 2, where I show you how to make basic settings.

Table 1.1 File Capacity of 8GB Card

	Large	Medium	Small
JPEG Fine	813	1,400	3,100
JPEG Normal	1,600	2,800	6,000
JPEG Basic	3,100	5,500	11,500
RAW	291	N/A	N/A
RAW+JPEG Fine	191	225	258
RAW+JPEG Normal	231	254	274
RAW+JPEG Basic	258	271	283

2

Nikon D7000 Quick Start

Now it's time to fire up your Nikon D7000 and take some photos. The easy part is turning on the power—the Off-On switch is on the right side, concentric with the shutter release button. Turn on the camera, and, if you mounted a lens and inserted a fresh battery and memory card—as I prompted you in the last chapter—you're ready to begin. You'll need to select a release mode, exposure mode, metering mode, focus mode, and, if need be, elevate the D7000's built-in flash.

Choosing a Release Mode

This section shows you how to choose from Single frame, Continuous mode, Self-timer mode, Remote control mode, "quiet" mode, and a special vibration-damping Mirror Up (Mup) mode. Unless you have need of burst shooting or the self-timer, you can set your camera to Single frame mode and skip ahead to "Selecting an Exposure Mode" (next). Just press the release mode dial lock release button at the 7 o'clock position on the release mode dial (at the top-left edge of the camera) and rotate to the first, or S position, if it's been changed to something else. (See Figure 2.1.)

The shooting mode determines when (and how often) the D7000 makes an exposure. If you're coming to the dSLR world from a point-and-shoot camera, you might have used a model that labels these options as drive modes, dating back to the film era when cameras could be set for single shot or "motor drive" (continuous) shooting modes. Your D7000 has seven release (shooting) modes: Single frame, Continuous low speed, Continuous high speed, Quiet shutter release, Self-timer, Remote control, Mirror Up.

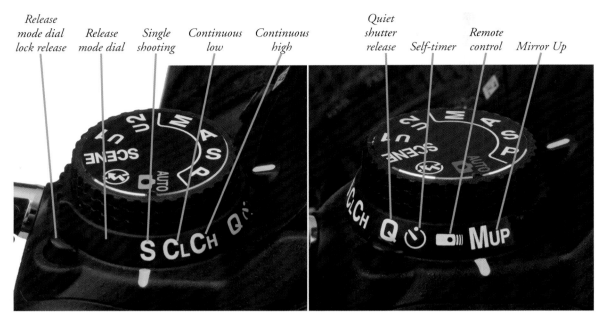

Figure 2.1 Hold down the lock release and rotate the dial to choose a release mode.

I'll explain all these modes in more detail and provide tips for using them in particular situations in Chapter 8. The Shooting modes are as follows:

- **Single frame.** In single shot mode, the D7000 takes one picture each time you press the shutter release button down all the way. If you press the shutter and nothing happens (which is very frustrating!), you may be using a focus mode that requires sharp focus to be achieved before a picture can be taken. This is called focus priority, and is discussed in more detail under "Choosing a Focus Mode," later in this chapter.

- **Continuous low speed (C_L).** This "low speed" shooting mode can be set to produce bursts of 1 to 5 frames per second (the latter hardly qualifies as *low* speed). You can set the frame rate in the Custom Settings menu entry CSM #d6. I use this setting when slicing a scene into tiny fragments of time isn't necessary or desirable (say, I'm bracketing in three shot bursts, or don't want a zillion versions of a scene that really isn't changing that fast).

- **Continuous high speed (C_H).** This mode fires off shots at up to 6 fps. The frame rate can slow down as your D7000's memory buffer fills, which forces the camera to wait until some of the pictures you have already taken are written to the memory card, freeing up more space in the buffer. The frame rate may also decrease at shutter speeds slower than 1/250th second, or when operations like Continuous-servo autofocus (described later in this chapter) force the D7000 to work at a slightly slower interval.

SHOOTING MOVIES

You'll learn more about shooting HDTV movie clips with your D7000 later in Chapter 6. But if you want to get started right away, it's easy. Just select Live View mode by rotating the Live View (Lv) switch located just northwest of the multi selector. When you want to start shooting, press the button in the center of the Live View switch. Press the button again to stop shooting. That's it!

- **Quiet shutter release.** This setting, marked with a Q symbol, activates the D7000's "quiet mode," which silences the camera's beep noise, reduces the sound the mirror makes when it flips back down, and delays that "noise" until you release the shutter button.

- **Self-timer.** You can use the self-timer as a replacement for a remote release, to reduce the effects of camera/user shake when the D7000 is mounted on a tripod or, say, set on a firm surface, or when you want to get in the picture yourself. Use Custom Settings menu choice CSM #c3 to specify delays of 2, 5, 10, or 20 seconds. You can also specify the number of shots taken at the end of the elapsed period, and the interval between those shots (see Chapter 9 for instructions). Any time you use the camera on a tripod (with the self-timer or otherwise) make sure there is no bright light shining on the viewfinder window; if so, cover it or locate that DK-5 eyepiece cap and block the window.

Note

If you plan to dash in front of the camera to join the scene when working with the self-timer, consider using manual focus so the D7000 won't refocus on your fleeing form and produce unintended results. (Nikon really needs to offer an option to autofocus at the *end* of the self-timer cycle.) An alternative is to use the ML-L3 IR remote, because the camera focuses when you press the button (after you've ensconced yourself safely in the frame).

- **Remote control.** No special setting of the release mode is necessary when you plug in the wired MC-DC2 remote into the side of the camera. However, if you want to use the ML-L3 infrared remote, you'll need to change the release mode to this setting. The camera then "looks" for the remote signal for a period of time you specify using Custom Settings menu choice CSM #c5 (select from 1, 5, 10, or 15 minutes). As with the self-timer, make sure there is no bright light shining on the viewfinder window; if so, cover it or locate that DK-5 eyepiece cap and block the window. The remote control can be used in three modes: Delayed Remote (shutter releases two seconds after you press the button on the ML-L3 IR remote); Quick Response Remote (the shutter trips immediately when the button is pressed); and Remote Mirror Up (press once to flip up the mirror, a second time to release the shutter). I'll explain in Chapter 8 how to choose these options with the Remote Control Mode entry in the Shooting menu.

■ **Mirror Up (Mup).** This mode delays the taking of the picture until after the mirror is flipped up out of the way (blanking the viewfinder), producing a short delay that also minimizes the effect of the mirror's movement on a picture taken using a long shutter speed. When shooting with telephoto lenses or during close-up photography, a "long" shutter speed can be anything from 1/125th seconds to several seconds. (Mirror movement has only an imperceptible effect on exposures longer than a second or two.) When Mup is activated, pressing the shutter release down all the way once lifts the mirror; pressing it a second time takes the picture and returns the mirror to its down position. To use Mup to take a picture after a delay, press the shutter just once. About 30 seconds after the mirror is raised, the camera will take the picture automatically, with no further action required on your part.

Note

The Mup facility is an offbeat way of producing a self-timer delay of 30 seconds, rather than the maximum 20 seconds that the D7000's self-timer feature provides.

Selecting an Exposure Mode

This section shows you how to choose an exposure mode. If you'd rather have the D7000 make all of the decisions for you, just rotate the mode dial to Auto or Auto (flash off) and jump to the section titled "Reviewing the Pictures You've Taken." If you'd rather choose one of the Scene modes, tailored to specific types of shooting situations, or try out the camera's semi-automatic modes, continue reading this section.

The Nikon D7000 has three types of shooting modes, advanced modes/exposure modes, auto modes, which include Auto and Auto (flash off), and a third set, which Nikon labels Scene modes. The advanced modes include Programmed-Auto (or Program mode), Shutter-Priority Auto, Aperture-Priority Auto, and Manual exposure mode. These are the modes you'll use most often after you've learned all your D7000's features, because they allow you to specify how the camera chooses its settings when making an exposure, for greater creative control.

The Scene modes take full control of the camera, make all the decisions for you, and don't allow you to override the D7000's settings. They are most useful while you're learning to use the camera, because you can select an appropriate mode (Auto, Auto/No Flash, Portrait, Landscape, Child, Sports, Close Up, or Night Portrait) and fire away. You'll end up with decent photos using appropriate settings, but your opportunities to use a little creativity (say, to overexpose an image to create a silhouette, or to deliberately use a slow shutter speed to add a little blur to an action shot) are minimal.

Choosing a Scene Mode

The 21 Scene and Auto modes can be selected by rotating the mode dial on the top left of the Nikon D7000 to the Scene position, and then rotating the main command dial to select one of the following:

- **Auto.** In this mode, the D7000 makes all the exposure decisions for you, and will pop up the internal flash if necessary under low-light conditions. The camera automatically focuses on the subject closest to the camera (unless you've set the lens to manual focus), and the autofocus assist illuminator lamp on the front of the camera will light up to help the camera focus in low-light conditions.

- **Auto (Flash Off).** Identical to Auto mode, except that the flash will not pop up under any circumstances. You'd want to use this in a museum, during religious ceremonies, concerts, or any environment where flash is forbidden or distracting.

- **Portrait.** Use this mode when you're taking a portrait of a subject standing relatively close to the camera and want to de-emphasize the background, maximize sharpness, and produce flattering skin tones. The built-in flash will pop up if needed.

- **Landscape.** Select this mode when you want extra sharpness and rich colors of distant scenes. The built-in flash and AF-assist illuminator are disabled.

- **Child.** Use this mode to accentuate the vivid colors often found in children's clothing, and to render skin tones with a soft, natural-looking texture. The D7000 focuses on the closest subject to the camera. The built-in flash will pop up if needed.

- **Sports.** Use this mode to freeze fast-moving subjects. The D7000 selects a fast shutter speed to stop action, and focuses continuously on the center focus point while you have the shutter release button pressed halfway. However, you can select one of the other two focus points to the left or right of the center by pressing the multi selector left/right buttons. The built-in electronic flash and focus assist illuminator lamp are disabled.

- **Close Up.** This mode is helpful when you are shooting close-up pictures of a subject from about one foot away or less, such as flowers, bugs, and small items. The D7000 focuses on the closest subject in the center of the frame, but you can use the multi selector right and left buttons to focus on a different point. Use a tripod in this mode, as exposures may be long enough to cause blurring from camera movement. The built-in flash will pop up if needed.

- **Night Portrait.** Choose this mode when you want to illuminate a subject in the foreground with flash (it will pop up automatically, if needed), but still allow the background to be exposed properly by the available light. The camera focuses on the closest main subject. Be prepared to use a tripod or a vibration-resistant lens like the 18-55 VR kit lens to reduce the effects of camera shake.

- **Night Landscape.** Mount your camera on a tripod and use this mode for longer exposure times to produce images with more natural colors and reduced visual noise in scenes with street lights or neon signs.

- **Party/Indoor.** For indoor scenes with typical background lighting.

- **Beach/Snow.** Useful for bright high-contrast scenes with sand or snow.

- **Sunset.** Emphasizes the rich colors at sunset or sunrise, disables the flash, and may use a slow shutter speed, so consider working with a tripod.

- **Dusk/dawn.** Similar to Sunset mode, but preserves the subtle colors in the sky just after sunset, or just prior to dawn.

- **Pet Portrait.** An "action" mode specifically for fast-moving, erratic subjects, such as pets.

- **Candlelight.** Disables your flash to allow photographs by candle; a tripod is recommended.

- **Blossom.** Uses a small f/stop to expand depth-of-field when shooting landscapes with broad expanses of blossoms. This Scene mode may result in longer shutter speeds, so consider using a tripod.

- **Autumn Colors.** Makes reds and yellows in Fall foliage richer.

- **Food.** Boosts saturation to make food look more appetizing in your snaps.

- **Silhouette.** Exposes for bright backgrounds, turning foreground objects into underexposed silhouettes.

- **High Key.** Exposes for bright scenes with lots of highlight areas.

- **Low Key.** Tailors exposure for darker scenes, retaining murky shadows while allowing highlights to remain.

Choosing an Advanced Mode

If you're very new to digital photography, you might want to set the camera to P (Program mode) and start snapping away. That mode will make all the appropriate settings for you for many shooting situations. If you have more photographic experience, you might want to opt for one of the semi-automatic modes. These, too, are described in more detail in Chapter 4. These modes all let you apply a little more creativity to your camera's settings.

- **P (Program).** This mode allows the D7000 to select the basic exposure settings, but you can still override the camera's choices to fine-tune your image, while maintaining metered exposure, as I'll explain in Chapter 4.

- **S (Shutter-priority).** This mode is useful when you want to use a particular shutter speed to stop action or produce creative blur effects. Choose your preferred shutter speed by rotating the main command dial when the meter is active, and the D7000 will select the appropriate f/stop for you.

- **A (Aperture-priority).** Choose when you want to use a particular lens opening, especially to control sharpness or how much of your image is in focus. Specify the f/stop you want using the sub-command dial when the meter is "awake" (tap the shutter release to activate the meter, if necessary), and the D7000 will select the appropriate shutter speed for you.

- **M (Manual).** Select when you want full control over the shutter speed and lens opening, either for creative effects or because you are using a studio flash or other flash unit not compatible with the D7000's automatic flash metering. Use the main command dial and sub-command dial when the exposure meter is active to specify the shutter speed and f/stop (respectively).

Choosing a Metering Mode

> This section shows you how to choose the area the D7000 will use to measure exposure, giving emphasis to the center of the frame; evaluating many different areas of the frame; or measuring light from a small spot in the center of the frame.

The metering mode you select determines how the D7000 calculates exposure. You might want to select a particular metering mode for your first shots, although the default Matrix metering is probably the best choice as you get to know your camera. I'll explain when and how to use each of the three metering modes later. To change metering modes, hold down the metering mode button, located southwest of the shutter release, while rotating the main dial to select from among the choices that are displayed on the LCD in the control panel (See Figure 2.2):

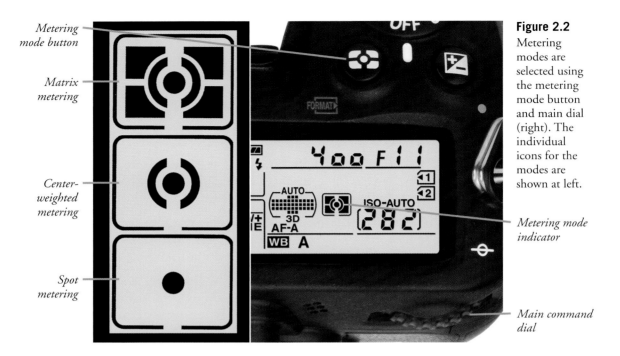

Figure 2.2
Metering modes are selected using the metering mode button and main dial (right). The individual icons for the modes are shown at left.

Metering mode button

Matrix metering

Center-weighted metering

Spot metering

Metering mode indicator

Main command dial

- **Matrix metering.** The standard metering mode; the D7000 attempts to intelligently classify your image and choose the best exposure based on readings from a 2,016-segment color CCD sensor that interprets light reaching the viewfinder using a database of hundreds of thousands of patterns.

- **Center-weighted metering.** The D7000 meters the entire scene, but gives the most emphasis to the central area of the frame, measuring about 8mm.

- **Spot metering.** Exposure is calculated from a smaller 3mm central spot, about 2 percent of the image area.

You'll find a detailed description of each of these modes in Chapter 4.

Choosing a Focus Mode

> This section shows how to select *when* the D7000 calculates focus, either all the time (continuously), only once when you press a control like the shutter release button (single autofocus), or manually when you rotate a focus ring on the lens.

You can easily switch between automatic and manual focus by moving the AF/MF or M-AF/MF switch on the lens mounted on your camera. There is also an AF/MF lever on the camera body. (See Figure 2.3.) When using autofocus, you have additional choices. You can select the autofocus mode (*when* the D7000 measures and locks in

Figure 2.3
Activate auto-
focus mode on
the camera
body.

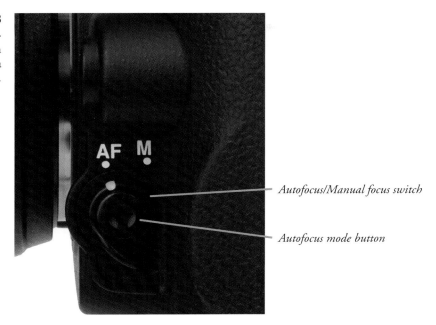

Autofocus/Manual focus switch

Autofocus mode button

focus) and autofocus pattern (*which* of the 39 available autofocus points or zones are used to interpret correct focus). To specify when the D7000 locks in focus, follow these steps:

1. **Activate autofocus.** Make sure the camera is set for autofocus mode by sliding any MA/M or AF/M switch on the lens to the MA or AF position. The camera body AF/M switch (see Figure 2.3) must also be set in the AF position. Note that the autofocus/manual focus switches on the lens and camera body must agree; if either is set to manual focus, then the D7000 defaults to manual focus regardless of how the other switch is set. Nikon, in fact, specifically warns against using autofocus lenses with the lens switch set to M and the camera body switch to AF, saying that doing so could damage the camera.

2. **Enter setting mode.** Press and hold the autofocus mode button in the center of the AF/M switch.

3. **Choose AF mode.** While holding down the AF mode button, rotate the main dial until AF-S, AF-C, or AF-A are shown on the top-panel monochrome LCD, as at left in Figure 2.4, as well as on the back-panel color LCD when the information display screen is visible (press the Info button, located to the immediate right of the LCD, at the bottom, to produce it). (See Figure 2.4, right.) While the button is held down, you'll also see AFS, AFC, or AFA in green at the bottom of the optical viewfinder. If you haven't activated autofocus mode, as described in Step 1, nothing will happen while the button is pressed and the main dial is rotated. The three focus modes are described in more detail next.

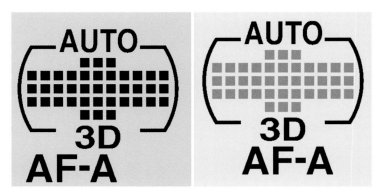

Figure 2.4
The autofocus mode you select is displayed on the top-panel LCD (left) and on the back-panel LCD when the Info button is pressed.

The three autofocus modes are:

- **(AF-C) Continuous-servo autofocus.** This mode, sometimes called *continuous autofocus*, or AF-C, sets focus when you partially depress the shutter button (or other autofocus activation button), but continues to monitor the frame and refocuses if the camera or subject is moved. This is a useful mode for photographing sports and moving subjects. Focus or release priority can be specified for AF-C mode using CSM #a1.

- **(AF-S) Single-servo autofocus.** This mode, sometimes called *single autofocus*, or AF-S, locks in a focus point when the shutter button is pressed down halfway (there are other autofocus activation button options, described in Chapter 9), and the focus confirmation light glows at bottom left in the viewfinder. The focus will remain locked until you release the button or take the picture. This mode is best when your subject is relatively motionless. As you'll learn in Chapter 9, you can set your Nikon D7000 using the Custom Settings menu (CSM #a2) so that the camera will not take a photo unless sharp focus is achieved (*focus priority*), or so that it will go ahead and snap a photo while still adjusting focus (*release priority*).

- **(AF-A) Automatic autofocus.** In this mode, the D7000 will select from AF-S or AF-C, depending on whether your subject is stationary or moving.

Choosing the Focus Area Mode

The Nikon D7000 uses up to 39 different focus points to calculate correct focus, using one or more points you can select yourself, or which the camera can choose. To choose a focus area mode, follow these steps:

1. **Enter setting mode.** Press and hold the autofocus mode button in the center of the AF/M switch.

2. **Rotate sub-command dial.** The dial, on the front of the camera, can be used to select one of the six modes. The current AF area mode chosen will be displayed on

the top panel LCD (see Figure 2.5, left) and an equivalent indicator in the viewfinder (see Figure 2.5, right).

3. **Choose AF-area mode.** For now, you should set to Auto-area AF and allow the D7000 to choose the focus zone for you.

The six AF area modes are as follows.

- **Single-point.** The camera focuses on a point you select, using the multi selector directional buttons, when the AF point lock lever (located just below the multi selector) is not set to the L (lock) position.

- **9-point dynamic-area AF.** You select the focus point, and the camera also uses information from surrounding AF points (nine points, total) to calculate focus.

- **21-point dynamic-area AF.** You select the focus point, and the camera also uses information from surrounding AF points (21 points, total) to calculate focus.

- **39-point dynamic-area AF.** You select the focus point, and the camera also uses information from all 39 focus points to calculate focus.

Figure 2.5

Focus area modes shown on the top-panel LCD (left) and in the viewfinder (right) are, top to bottom, Single-point, 9-point dynamic-area AF, 21-point dynamic-area AF, 39-point dynamic-area AF, 3D-track-ing, and Auto-area AF.

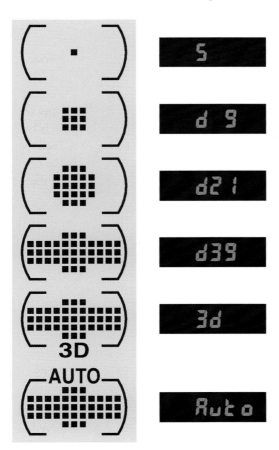

- **3D-tracking.** You select the focus point, and the camera will track your subject, using any of the other focus points, as needed, when using AF-A and AF-C modes. (In AF-S mode, focus tracking is not used, as focus is locked in when you press the shutter release halfway.)

- **Auto-area AF.** The D7000 chooses a focus point.

Other Settings

This section describes some optional features you can select if you feel you need to choose the white balance, change the camera's sensitivity setting, or delay taking a picture with the self-timer.

There are a few other settings you can make if you're feeling ambitious, but don't feel ashamed if you postpone using these features until you've racked up a little more experience with your D7000.

Adjusting White Balance and ISO

If you like, you can custom-tailor your white balance (color balance) and ISO sensitivity settings. To start out, it's best to set white balance (WB) to Auto, and ISO to ISO 200 for daylight photos, and ISO 400 for pictures in dimmer light. (Don't be afraid of ISO 1600 or even higher, however; the D7000 does a *much* better job of producing low-noise photos at higher ISOs than earlier generations.) You can adjust either one now by pressing the WB (for white balance) or ISO buttons on the back of the camera to the left of the LCD, and rotating the main command dial until the setting you want appears on the status LCD on top of the camera.

MAKING SETTINGS UNDER LOW LIGHT

When working under low light levels, you might experience some difficulty seeing the white balance, ISO, or other settings on the top-panel monochrome LCD as you make them. You can always rotate the ON-OFF switch an additional push in the clockwise direction to illuminate the LCD backlight, but there is a better way. Instead, press the Info button (at the bottom of the right side of the camera to the right of the LCD) to show the much larger and easier-to-read shooting information display on the color LCD. Then press the WB or ISO button (or the button for whatever setting you're changing) and rotate the appropriate dial until the value you want appears on the shooting information display. Indeed, you can press the Info button at any time to pop up this information screen, which is especially helpful when working with the camera on a tripod, or under dim illumination.

Using the Self-Timer

If you want to set a short delay before your picture is taken, you can use the self-timer. Press the lock release button to free the release mode dial, and rotate it five clicks clockwise until the self-timer icon appears next to the indicator line. Press the shutter release to lock focus and start the timer. The self-timer lamp on the front of the camera will blink and the beeper will sound (unless you've silenced it in the menus) until the final two seconds, when the lamp remains on and the beeper beeps more rapidly. The default delay is 10 seconds, but you can set it to 2, 5, 10, or 20 seconds using Custom Settings menu option CSM #c3, as described in Chapter 9. As I mentioned earlier, you can also use the Mup release mode to get a 30-second delay.

Reviewing the Images You've Taken

Read this section when you're ready to take a closer look at the images you've taken, and want to know how to review pictures and zoom in.

The Nikon D7000 has a broad range of playback and image review options, and I'll cover them in more detail in Chapter 8. For now, you'll want to learn just the basics. Here is all you really need to know at this time, as shown in Figure 2.6:

- **View image.** Press the Playback button (marked with a white right-pointing triangle) at the upper-left corner of the back of the camera to display the most recent image on the LCD.

- **View additional images.** Press the multi selector left or right to review additional images. Press right to advance to the next image, or left to go back to a previous image.

- **Change information display.** Press the multi selector button up or down to change among overlays of basic image information or detailed shooting information.

- **Change magnification.** Press the Zoom In button repeatedly to zoom in on the image displayed; the Zoom Out button reduces the image. (Both buttons are located to the left of the color LCD.) A thumbnail representation of the whole image appears in the lower-right corner with a yellow rectangle showing the relative level of zoom. At intermediate zoom positions, the yellow rectangle can be moved around within the frame using the multi selector.

- **Exit image review.** Press the Playback button again, or just tap the shutter release button to exit playback view.

You'll find information on viewing thumbnail indexes of images, automated playback, and other options in Chapter 8.

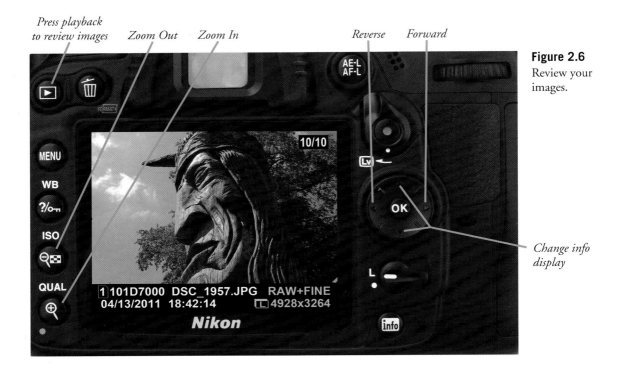

Press playback to review images   Zoom Out   Zoom In   Reverse   Forward

Figure 2.6
Review your images.

Change info display

Using the Built-in Flash

Working with the D7000's built-in flash (as well as external flash units like the Nikon SB-900) deserves detailed coverage, and I'm providing the information you need (see Chapter 12). But the built-in flash is easy enough to work with that you can begin using it right away, either to provide the main lighting of a scene or as supplementary illumination to fill in the shadows. For example, if you choose Matrix or Center-weighted metering (as described earlier), you can even use the flash in full daylight, as the D7000 will even automatically balance the amount of light emitted from the flash so that it illuminates the shadows nicely, without overwhelming the highlights and producing a glaring "flash" look. (Think *Baywatch* when they're using too many reflectors on the lifeguards!)

The D7000's flash has a power rating of 12/39 (meters/feet) at ISO 100, using the GN (guide number) system that dates back to the film era and before electronic flash units had any sort of automatic features. I'll explain guide numbers (which can be a little confusing) in more detail in Chapter 12, but in plain terms, the flash's rating means that the unit is powerful enough to allow proper illumination of a subject that's 10 feet away at f/4 at the ISO 100 (sensitivity) setting of your camera. Boost the ISO (or use a wider f/stop) and you can shoot subjects that are located at a great distance. For example, at ISO 800, the D7000's flash is good enough for a subject at 20 feet using f/5.6

or, alternatively, you can expose that scene at the original 10 feet distance at f/11. Ordinarily, the D7000 takes care of all these calculations for you. If you need a bigger blast of light, you can add an external flash, like the Nikon SB-900, which lets you reach out to 32-45 feet at ISO 200 and f/5.6 (or even farther at larger f/stops).

When using Auto, Portrait, Child, Close Up, Night Portrait, Party/Indoor, or Pet Portrait Scene modes, the flash will pop up when needed. To use the built-in flash, for Program, Shutter-priority, Aperture-priority, Manual modes, or Food Scene mode, just press the flash pop-up button (shown in Figure 2.7). When you're finished using it, you need to push it back down. When the flash is fully charged, a lightning bolt symbol will flash at the right side of the viewfinder display. When using P (Program) or A (Aperture-priority) exposure modes, the D7000 will select a shutter speed for you automatically from the range 1/250th to 1/60th seconds (with a couple exceptions described in Chapter 12). In S (Shutter-priority) and M (Manual) modes, you select the shutter speed from 1/250th to 30 seconds (again, with a couple exceptions that I won't get into here). When using the built-in flash, if you select a shutter speed higher than 1/250th second (which prevents the camera from synchronizing with the shutter; see Chapter 12), the D7000 will set 1/250th second for you automatically.

Figure 2.7
The pop-up electronic flash can be used as the main light source or for supplemental illumination.

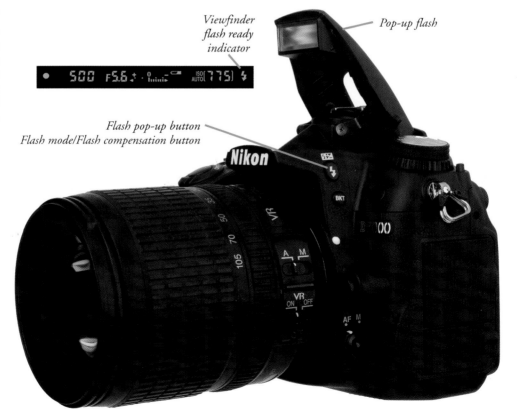

Viewfinder flash ready indicator

Pop-up flash

Flash pop-up button
Flash mode/Flash compensation button

When using PSAM modes, you can preview the effect of your flash visually by pressing the depth-of-field button, which activates a brief, continuous series of bursts (which look to the eye like a single, long flash of light)—unless you've disabled this "modeling light" using Custom Settings menu entry CSM #e4.

You'll also learn in Chapter 12 how to change the flash syncing mode (and why you might want to do so), as well as how to increase/reduce the effects of the flash on your scene using *flash compensation* adjustments.

Transferring Photos to Your Computer

The final step in your picture-taking session will be to transfer the photos you've taken to your computer for printing, further review, or image editing. Your D7000 allows you to print directly to PictBridge-compatible printers and to create print orders right in the camera, plus you can select which images to transfer to your computer. I'll outline those options in Chapter 8.

I always recommend using a card reader attached to your computer to transfer files, because that process is generally a lot faster and doesn't drain the D7000's battery. However, you can also use a cable for direct transfer, which may be your only option when you have the cable and a computer, but no card reader (perhaps you're using the computer of a friend or colleague, or at an Internet café).

To transfer images from the camera to a Mac or PC computer using the USB cable:

1. Turn off the camera.

2. Pry back the rubber cover that protects the D7000's USB port, and plug the USB cable furnished with the camera into the USB port. (See Figure 2.8.)

3. Connect the other end of the USB cable to a USB port on your computer.

4. Turn on the camera. The operating system itself, or installed software such as Nikon Transfer or Adobe Photoshop Elements Transfer usually detects the camera and offers to copy or move the pictures. Or, the camera appears on your desktop as a mass storage device, enabling you to drag and drop the files to your computer.

To transfer images from a memory card to the computer using a card reader, as shown in Figure 2.9:

1. Turn off the camera.

2. Open the memory card door and extract the Secure Digital card.

3. Insert the memory card into your memory card reader. Your installed software detects the files on the card and offers to transfer them. The card can also appear as a mass storage device on your desktop, which you can open and then drag and drop the files to your computer.

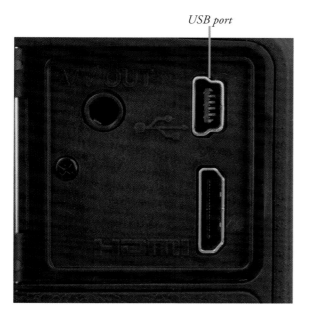

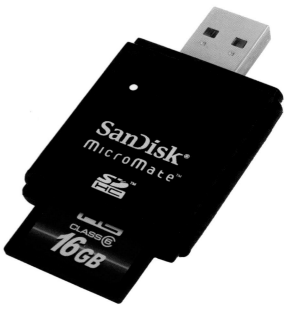

Figure 2.8 Images can be transferred to your computer using a USB cable connected to this port.

Figure 2.9 A card reader is the fastest way to transfer photos. A Secure Digital reader is shown above. Other readers accept both types of cards.

Changing Default Settings

> This section is purely optional, especially for true beginners, who should skip it entirely for now, and return when they've gained some experience with this full-featured camera. This section is for the benefit of those who want to know *now* some of the most common changes I recommend to the default settings of your D7000. Nikon has excellent reasons for using these settings as a default; I have better reasons for changing them.

Even if this is your first experience with a Nikon digital SLR, you can easily make a few changes to the default settings that I'm going to recommend, and then take your time learning *why* I suggest these changes when they're explained in the more detailed chapters of this book. I'm not going to provide step-by-step instructions for changing settings here; I'll give you an overview of how to make any setting adjustment, and leave you to navigate through the fairly intuitive D7000 menu system to make the changes yourself.

Resetting the Nikon D7000

If you want to change from the factory default values, you might think that it would be a good idea to make sure that the Nikon D7000 is set to the factory defaults in the first place. After all, even a brand-new camera might have had its settings changed at the retailer, or during a demo. Unfortunately, Nikon doesn't make it easy to reset *all* settings in the camera to their factory defaults. In fact, there are no fewer than *five* different ways to "reset" the D7000, each of which does slightly different things. Those ways include:

- **Two-button reset.** This type of "rebooting" changes ten of the most basic settings in your camera, and is useful when you want to cancel the most common changes you make when adjusting your camera. It does not affect all Shooting menu settings, or any of the Custom Settings memory banks, described next. I'll show you how to perform the two-button reset shortly.

- **Shooting menu bank reset.** The Shooting menu has a separate Reset Shooting menu option that zeroes out the changes you've made to the default options.

- **Custom Settings menu bank reset.** The Custom Settings menu also has a separate Reset Custom Settings option that zeroes out most of the changes you've made to the default options. A two-button reset does not affect any of the settings in the Custom Settings menu banks.

- **User settings reset.** The mode dial has two slots, labeled U1 and U2, that can be selected to switch the camera to a specific set of settings you've chosen and then registered, using the Setup menu's Save User Settings option. The Setup menu also has a Reset User Options entry that can be used to zero out any changes you've made to U1 and U2, individually.

- **Cold reset.** The only way to reset *all* of the D7000's internal settings is to remove the battery and allow the internal backup battery to run down until the settings are lost, which can take as long as several weeks. You can remove the battery and then turn on the camera briefly to reset *most* settings, but this won't zero out all settings to the factory defaults as long as some juice remains in the backup battery (which is tucked deep inside the camera and not user-accessible). You might want to try a cold reset if your camera is hopelessly locked up, and you'd like to make one last attempt at restoring it to factory operation before sending it in for service.

Two-Button Reset

Just follow these steps to perform a two-button reset of the camera:

1. **Find reset buttons.** Locate the QUAL button on the back left side of the camera, and the EV button on the top panel of the D7000, just southeast of the shutter release button. Each is marked with a green dot. Figure 2.10 shows the two buttons highlighted in yellow.

Figure 2.10
Perform a two-button reset by holding down the QUAL and EV buttons for more than two seconds.

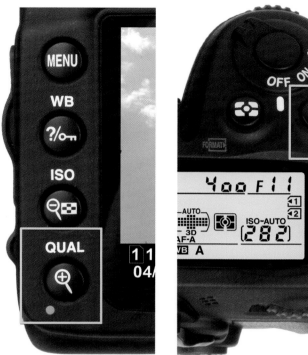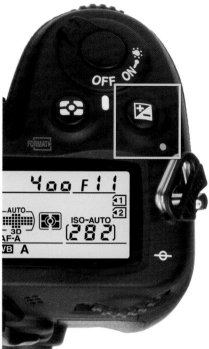

2. **Start reset.** Press and hold the two buttons for more than two seconds. The monochrome LCD control panel switches off momentarily while the settings are reset.

3. **Release the two buttons.** Your camera's settings have been returned to the factory default, as described below.

Once a two-button reset has been performed, the following settings will be restored to their defaults (all these options are described in Chapters 8, 9, and 10):

- **Image quality:** Normal

- **Image Size:** L (Large)

- **White balance:**
  Auto>Normal
  White balance Fine Tuning: 0

- **ISO sensitivity:**
  Auto and Scene modes: Auto
  Program, Shutter-priority, Aperture-priority, Manual modes: 100

- **Autofocus/Viewfinder:**

  Autofocus mode: AF-A

  AF-area mode: Close Up, Candlelight, Food, Beach, High Key, Low Key – Single-point AF

  AF-area mode: Sports, Pet - 39-point dynamic area AF

  AF-area mode: All other - Auto-area AF

- **Autofocus/Live View, Movie:**

  Autofocus mode: AF-S

  AF-area mode: Sports, Night Landscape, Pet Portrait, Beach, High Key, Low Key – Wide-area AF

  AF-area mode: Close Up, Food – Normal-area AF

  AF-area mode: All other – Face Priority AF

- **Focus point:** Center

- **Metering:** Matrix

- **AE/AF lock hold:** Off

- **Active D-Lighting:** Off

- **Bracketing:** Off

- **Picture Control Settings:** Current Picture Control retained

- **Flash compensation:** Off

- **Exposure compensation:** Off

- **Flash mode**

  Auto/Portrait/Child/Close Up/Pet: Auto front-curtain sync

  Party: Auto/Red-eye reduction

  Night Portrait: Auto slow sync

  Food, Program, Shutter-priority, Aperture-priority, Manual: Front-curtain sync

- **FV (Flash value) lock:** Off

- **Multiple exposure:** Off

- **Flexible Program:** Off

Shooting Menu/Custom Settings menu Reset

If you'd like to reset all the options in the Shooting menu and Custom Settings menu individually, follow these steps:

1. **Access menus.** Press the MENU button at the top of the array of five buttons located to the immediate left of the back-panel LCD.

2. **Choose Shooting menu or Custom Settings menu.** Press the multi selector down button to scroll down to either the Shooting menu (represented by a camera icon; the second icon from the top in the left-column of the menus) or the Custom Settings menu (represented by a pencil icon; the third icon from the top). Press the right multi selector button to reveal the Shooting or Custom Settings menus.

3. **Reset menu.** Use the down button to scroll to the Reset Shooting Menu or Reset Custom Settings choices, then press the right button to reveal a screen with Yes and No choices. Press the up button to highlight Yes, and press OK (or the center button of the multi selector) to reset the active bank.

4. **Exit.** Press MENU or tap the shutter release to exit.

Recommended Default Changes

Although I won't be explaining how to use the Nikon D7000's menu system in detail until Chapter 8, you can make some simple changes now. These general instructions will serve you to make any of the default setting changes I recommend next. To change any menu setting, follow these steps:

1. **Access menus.** Press the MENU button at the top of the array of five buttons located to the immediate left of the back-panel LCD.

2. **Choose the main menu you need to access.** Press the multi selector down button to scroll down to the menu containing the entry you want to change. The available menus include (from top to bottom in the left column of the Menu screen: Playback menu (right-pointing triangle icon); Shooting menu (camera icon); Custom Settings menu (pencil icon); Setup menu (wrench icon); Retouch menu (paintbrush icon); My Menu (text page/text page with checkmark icon).

3. **Select main menu.** Press the right multi selector button to choose the menu heading containing the submenu entry you want to change.

4. **Choose menu entry.** Press the down multi selector button to move within the main menu to the entry you want to change. A scroll bar at the right side shows your progress through the menu, as all the main menus except for the Custom Settings menu and My Menu (if it contains fewer than five custom entries) have more items than can fit on a single screen.

5. **Choose options.** Press the right multi selector button to choose the highlighted menu entry, and view a screen with options. Select the options you want, and press OK to confirm. Some menus allow you to confirm by pressing the right button again, or require you to move to a Done selection and choose that before exiting.

6. **Exit menus.** Usually you can exit the menu system by pressing the MENU button. If an option has variations, I'll explain them when I discuss each of the menu choices in Chapters 8, 9, and 10.

Here are some of the changes I recommend you make to the defaults that Nikon sets up for you. (I have no changes to recommend for the Playback, Setup, and My Menu settings, which are fine the way they are for most people, nor for the Retouch menu, which doesn't have parameters that can be stored.) You'll find other settings recommendations at the end of Chapter 7:

Shooting Menu

Make these changes to the Shooting menu entries listed:

- **Image Quality.** Change from JPEG Normal to JPEG Fine, to produce better image quality.

- **High ISO NR.** Change from default Normal to Off, until you've had a chance to evaluate whether the D7000 performs to your liking at high sensitivity settings. Off produces the least amount of noise reduction, but also doesn't degrade the amount of detail as much as any of the On settings.

Custom Settings Menu

Make these changes to the Custom Settings menu entries listed:

- **CSM #a7: Built-in AF-assist illumination.** Change from the default On to Off. This feature doesn't work well, except at close distances and when the lamp isn't blocked by your fingers, and is annoying at other times.

- **CSM #c2: Auto meter-off delay.** If you shoot sports or other events where you don't want the camera going to sleep and delaying your ability to snap off a shot *now*, change from the default 6 seconds to 30 seconds, 1 minute, 5 minutes, or 10 minutes. You'll use more power, but won't lose a shot from a split-second delay while the camera wakes up.

- **CSM #d1: Beep.** Choose the Volume setting and turn to OFF to quiet the camera during self-timer countdowns and single-servo autofocus confirmation. If you decide you need this reminder, you can always turn it back on, but most of the time it's annoying and calls attention to your shooting.

- **CSM #f8: Slot empty release lock.** This controls what happens when you press the shutter release while no memory card is loaded in the camera. Change from the default OK: Enable Release to LOCK: Release Locked. Why would you want to be able to take pictures with no memory card in the camera, other than to demonstrate the camera or a few other reasons? Even though a DEMO label appears on the LCD when you "take" pictures with no memory card inserted, it's easy to overlook. Turn this capability to LOCK.

3

Nikon D7000 Roadmap

Most of the Nikon D7000's key functions and settings that are changed frequently can be accessed directly using the array of dials, buttons, and knobs that populate the camera's surface. With so many dedicated controls available, you'll find that the bulk of your shooting won't be slowed down by a visit to the vast thicket of text options called Menuland. That's a distinct paradigm shift from early point-and-shoot cameras, which had only four or five buttons, and relied on menus to control virtually every setting you might want to make. With the D7000, you can press specific buttons dedicated to image quality, white balance, ISO sensitivity, shooting mode, exposure compensation, and playback options, and then spin a command dial or make adjustments using the multi selector.

While it might take some time to learn the position and function of each of these controls, once you've mastered them, the D7000 camera is remarkably easy to use. That's because dedicated buttons with only one or two functions each are much faster to access than the alternative—a maze of menus that must be navigated every time you want to use a feature. The advantage of menu systems—dating back to early computer user interfaces of the 1980s—is that they are easy to *learn*. The ironic disadvantage of menus is that they are clumsy to *use*.

Imagine that you are familiar with digital SLRs in general, but know virtually nothing about the Nikon D7000. You've decided that you want to format the memory card. A-ha! There's a big ol' MENU button on the left side of the camera. Press it, and you'll see a series of different menu icons, which, when you scroll through them, have titles like Playback menu, Shooting menu, Custom Settings menu, and Setup menu. You might guess that the Setup menu is the likely repository for a Format command, but even if you guess wrong, it takes only a minute or two to check out the other menus and discover the Format command tucked away within the Setup menu. A couple more button presses (you'll need to choose between which of the two SD card slots you want to format—if both contain cards) and you've successfully formatted your memory card.

You didn't really need instructions—the menu system itself led you to the right command. If you don't format another card for weeks and weeks, you can come back to the menus and discover how to perform the task all over again. The main cost to you was the time required to negotiate through all the menus to carry out the function; while menus are easy to learn, the multiple steps they call for (10 or more button presses may be required) can be cumbersome to use. Direct access buttons are the exact opposite: you have to teach yourself how to use them, and then remember what you've learned over time, but once learned, buttons are much faster to use.

For example, simple direct button presses can also format your memory card, as I pointed out in the last chapter. Recall how easy it is to just hold down the metering mode button and the trash can button simultaneously for about two seconds. When the characters For and the exposures remaining displays blink in the viewfinder and top-panel LCD, select the slot containing the memory card you want to format (rotate the main command dial), press the pair of buttons again, and the D7000 formats your card. To cancel the format, press any other button. The sequence may be tricky to learn or remember (although red Format labels appear next to the pair of buttons), but it's much faster to use than threading through a series of menu options.

If you want to operate your D7000 efficiently, you'll need to learn the location, function, and application of all these controls. What you really need is a street-level roadmap that shows where everything is, and how it's used. But what Nikon gives you in the user's manual is akin to a world globe with an overall view and many cross-references to the pages that will tell you what you really need to know. Check out the Getting to Know the Camera pages in Nikon's manual, which offer four tiny black-and-white line drawings of the camera body that show front (see Figure 3.1), back, two sides, and the top and bottom of the D7000. There are about six dozen callouts pointing to various buttons and dials. If you can find the control you want in this cramped layout, you'll still need to flip back and forth among multiple pages (individual buttons can have several different cross-references!) to locate the information.

Most other third-party books follow this format, featuring black-and-white photos or line drawings of front, back, and top views, and many labels. I originated the up-close-and-personal, full-color, street-level roadmap (rather than a satellite view) that I use in this book and my previous camera guidebooks. I provide you with many different views and lots of explanation accompanying each zone of the camera, so that by the time you finish this chapter, you'll have a basic understanding of every control and what it does. I'm not going to delve into menu functions here—you'll find a discussion of your Playback, Shooting, Custom Settings, and Setup options in Chapters 8, 9, and 10. Everything here is devoted to the button pusher and dial twirler in you.

Figure 3.1

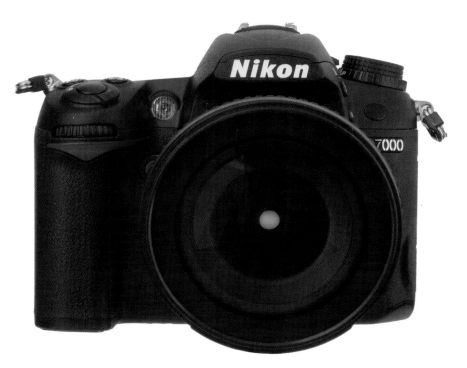

You'll also find this "roadmap" chapter a good guide to the rest of the book, as well. I'll try to provide as much detail here about the use of the main controls as I can, but some topics (such as autofocus and exposure) are too complex to address in depth right away. So, I'll point you to the relevant chapters that discuss things like setup options, exposure, use of electronic flash, and working with lenses with the occasional cross-reference.

Nikon D7000: Full Frontal

This is the side seen by your victims as you snap away. For the photographer, though, the front is the surface your fingers curl around as you hold the camera, and there are really only a few buttons to press, all within easy reach of the fingers of your left and right hands. There are additional controls on the lens itself. You'll need to look at several different views to see everything.

Figure 3.2 shows a view of the left side of the Nikon D7000, as seen from the front. The main components you need to know about are as follows:

■ **Shutter release.** Angled on top of the handgrip is the shutter release button, which has multiple functions. Press this button down halfway to lock exposure and focus. Press it down all the way to actually take a photo or sequence of photos if you've changed the mode dial to either of the continuous shooting modes, C_L or C_H (Continuous shooting low speed and Continuous shooting high speed), or if you've redefined the behavior of the self-timer to take 1 to 9 exposures when its delay has expired. (I'll show you how to take multiple shots with the self-timer in Chapter 9.) Tapping the shutter button when the D7000's exposure meters have turned themselves off reactivates them, and a tap can be used to remove the display of a menu or image from the rear color LCD.

- **On/Off switch.** Rotating this switch to the detent turns the camera on. Continuing to rotate past the detent to the farthest position illuminates the top-panel LCD lamp, so you can read settings in dim lighting.

- **Sub-command dial.** This dial is used to change shooting settings. When settings are available in pairs (such as shutter speed/aperture), this dial will be used to make one type of setting, such as aperture, while the main command dial (on the back of the camera) will be used to make the other, such as aperture setting. Using the Custom Settings menu adjustments in CSM #f6, you can reverse the default rotational direction, swap the functions of the sub-command and main command dials,

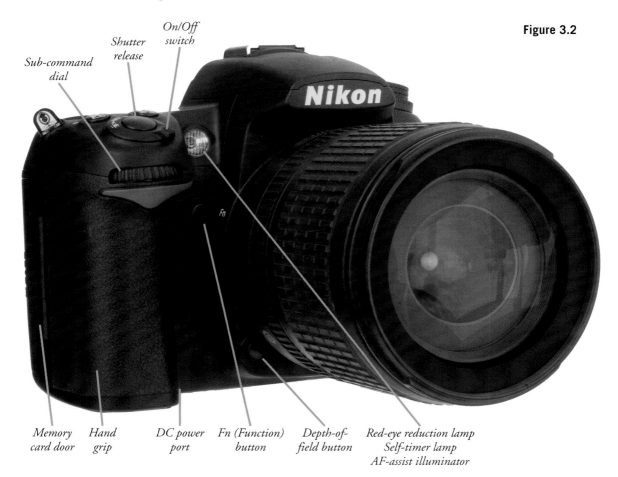

Figure 3.2

Sub-command dial

Shutter release

On/Off switch

Nikon

Fn

Memory card door

Hand grip

DC power port

Fn (Function) button

Depth-of-field button

Red-eye reduction lamp
Self-timer lamp
AF-assist illuminator

control how the sub-command dial is used to set aperture, and tell the D7000 that you want to use the main command dial to scroll through menus and images. All these options are discussed in more detail in Chapter 9.

■ **AF-assist illuminator/Red-eye reduction/Self-timer lamp.** This LED provides a blip of light shortly before a flash exposure to cause the subjects' pupils to close down, reducing the effect of red-eye reflections off their retinas. When using the self-timer, this lamp also flashes to mark the countdown until the photo is taken. It can also illuminate to provide assistance for the D7000's autofocus mechanism at fairly close distances.

■ **Hand grip.** This provides a comfortable hand hold, and also contains the D7000's battery. Unlike some earlier Nikon models, which had their electrical contacts inside the battery compartment, it's not necessary to remove the battery of the D7000 to mount the MB-D11 accessory battery/vertical grip. Its contacts are located on the bottom of the camera.

■ **Fn (Function button).** This conveniently located button has no function by default, but can be programmed to perform any one of 20 different actions, ranging from metering modes (Matrix, Center-weighted, Spot) to flash off or bracketing bursts.

TIP

Note that on some earlier Nikon cameras that have both an Fn button and depth-of-field preview (described next), the position of these two is swapped. If you'd rather have this button (the upper one) act as a DOF button, as on those earlier cameras, you can define it for that function. I'll explain how to define a function using Custom Settings menu entry CSM #f3 in Chapter 9.

■ **Depth-of-field (preview) button.** By default, this button closes down the lens aperture to the opening that will be used to take the picture, as set by the D7000's light meters or by you (when in Manual or Aperture-priority modes). The DOF button can be redefined using the same functions offered for the Fn button. I'll explain how to define a function using Custom Settings menu entry CSM #f4 in Chapter 9.

■ **Memory card door.** Your Secure Digital memory cards can be inserted here when you slide the door towards the rear of the camera to open it.

You'll find more controls on the other side of the D7000, shown in Figure 3.3. In the illustration, you can see the mode dial on top, and the rubber covers on the side that protects the camera's USB, TV, HDMI, microphone ports, and GPS/accessory terminal.

The main points of interest shown include:

- **Bracket button.** Hold down this button and rotate the main command dial to change the number of bracketed exposures to shoot; rotate the sub-command dial to change the exposure increment to be changed between each bracketed shot. When the number of exposures is set to zero, bracketing is turned off.

- **Infrared receiver.** This is one of two IR sensors located on the camera (the other is on the back). You'll use this one when triggering the camera with the Nikon ML-L3 infrared remote control while standing in front of the camera (say, when you want to get in the picture yourself).

- **Lens release button.** Press this button to unlock the lens, then rotate the lens away from the shutter release button to dismount your optics.

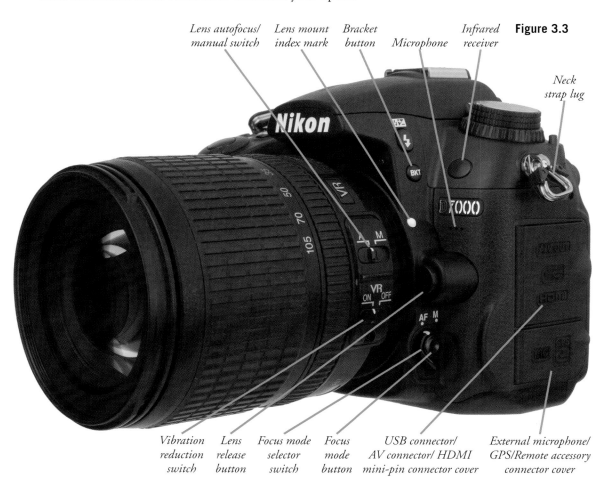

Figure 3.3

■ **Lens autofocus/manual switch.** You can change from Autofocus mode to Manual using this switch, or the switch on the camera body.

■ **Neck strap lug.** It comes with a split-ring attached that can be used to fasten a neck strap to the D7000.

■ **Microphone.** The D7000 has a microphone built into the front of the camera, seen as a trio of holes set in a horizontal line.

■ **Port covers.** These two rubber covers protect the USB, TV, HDMI, microphone ports, and GPS/accessory terminals when not in use.

■ **Focus mode selector switch.** Rotate to change from autofocus to manual focus. You should remember that the modes selected with this switch and the autofocus/manual focus switch on the lens must agree. If you've chosen A (or M/A, which allows for manual fine-tuning of autofocus) on the lens, then the camera body switch must be set to either AF. If either the lens or body switch (or both) are set to M, then the lens must be focused manually.

■ **Focus mode.** Press this button and rotate the main command dial to change from Continuous-servo autofocus (AF-C) to Single-servo autofocus (AF-S) or Manual focus (M). Rotate the sub-command dial to change autofocus area selection modes. Both options were described in Chapter 2, and will be explained in more detail in Chapter 4.

Controls for using the D7000's built-in electronic flash (also called a strobe or speedlight) are shown in Figure 3.4. These components include:

■ **Pop-up flash.** The flash elevates from the top of the camera, theoretically reducing the chances of red-eye reflections, because the higher light source is less likely to reflect back from your subjects' eyes into the camera lens. In practice, the red-eye effect is still possible (and likely), and can be further minimized with the D7000's red-eye reduction lamp (which flashes before the exposure, causing the subjects' pupils to contract, and the after-shot red-eye elimination offered in the Retouch menu. (Your image editor may also have anti-red-eye tools.) Of course, the best strategy is to use an external speedlight that mounts on the accessory shoe on top of the camera (and thus is even higher) or a flash that is off-camera entirely.

■ **Flash pop-up/Flash mode/Flash compensation button.** This button releases the built-in flash so it can flip up and start the charging process. If you decide you do not want to use the flash, you can turn it off by pressing the flash head back down. This button is held down while spinning the main command dial (to choose flash mode) or sub-command dial (to add or subtract exposure using flash compensation). I'll explain how to use the various flash modes (red-eye reduction, front/rear curtain sync, and slow sync) in Chapter 12, along with some tips for adjusting flash exposure.

Figure 3.4

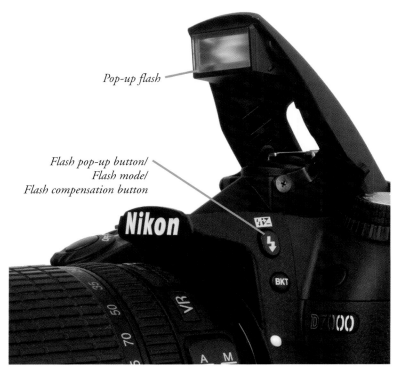

Pop-up flash

Flash pop-up button/
Flash mode/
Flash compensation button

The main feature on the side of the Nikon D7000 is a pair of rubber covers that protect the five connector ports underneath from dust and moisture. The five connectors, shown in Figure 3.5, with the rubber covers removed, are as follows:

- **Audio/Video port.** You can link this connector with a television to view your photos and movies on a large screen. Connect the red/white RCA plugs on the included cable to the audio input jacks of your monitor/TV, and the yellow plug to the video jack.

- **HDMI port.** You need to buy an accessory cable to connect your D7000 to an HDTV, as one to fit this port is not provided with the camera. If you have a high-resolution television, it's worth the expenditure to be able to view your camera's output in all its glory.

- **GPS/Accessory terminal.** Connect the Nikon GP-1 Global Positioning Service device here, or plug in the MC-DC2 wired remote control here, instead. If you want to use both, connect the GP-1 and then plug the remote into a pass-through connector on the GPS device.

Figure 3.5

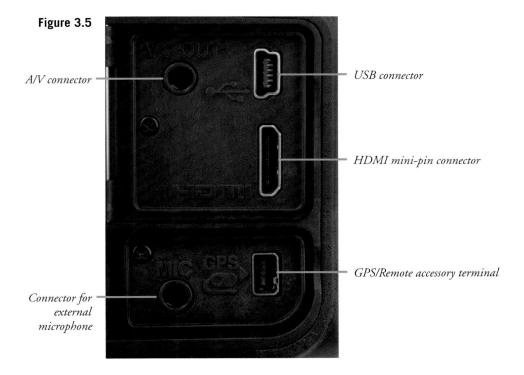

A/V connector

USB connector

HDMI mini-pin connector

GPS/Remote accessory terminal

Connector for external microphone

- **USB port.** Plug in the USB cable furnished with your Nikon D7000 and connect the other end to a USB port in your computer to transfer photos, to upload Picture Control settings, or to upload/download other settings between your camera and computer.

- **Microphone connector.** Although the D7000 has a built-in microphone on the front, if you want better quality (and want to shield your video clip soundtracks from noises emanating from the camera and/or your handling of it), you can plug in an accessory mic here, such as the new Nikon ME-1 stereo microphone (a $179 accessory).

The Nikon D7000's Business End

The back panel of the Nikon D7000 (see Figure 3.6) bristles with more than a dozen different controls, buttons, and knobs. That might seem like a lot of controls to learn, but you'll find, as I noted earlier, that it's a lot easier to press a dedicated button and spin a dial than to jump to a menu every time you want to change a setting.

Figure 3.6

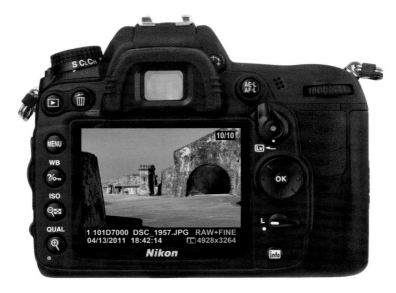

You can see the controls clustered along the top edge of the back panel in Figure 3.7. The key buttons and components and their functions are as follows:

- **Playback button.** Press this button to review images you've taken, using the controls and options I'll explain in the next section. To remove the displayed image, press the Playback button again, or simply tap the shutter release button.

- **Trash/Format #1.** Press to erase the image shown on the LCD. A display will pop up on the LCD asking you to press the Trash button once more to delete the photo, or press the Playback button to cancel. Hold down this button and the metering mode button on the top-right surface of the camera (both are marked with red Format labels). "For" will appear in the monochrome status LCD. Choose which memory card you want to erase (rotate the main command dial). Press the buttons again to begin formatting your memory card.

- **Viewfinder eyepiece.** You can frame your composition by peering into the viewfinder. It's surrounded by a soft rubber frame that seals out extraneous light when pressing your eye tightly up to the viewfinder, and it also protects your eyeglass lenses (if worn) from scratching. It can be removed and replaced by the DK-5 eyepiece cap when you use the camera on a tripod, to ensure that light coming from the back of the camera doesn't venture inside and possibly affect the exposure reading. Shielding the viewfinder with your hand may be more convenient (unless you're using the self-timer to get in the photo yourself).

- **Diopter adjustment wheel.** Rotate this to adjust the diopter correction for your eyesight, as described in Chapter 1.

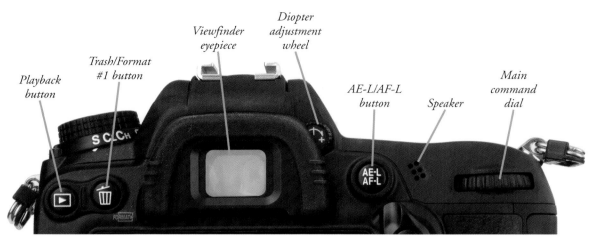

Figure 3.7

- **Speaker.** Your D7000 emits sounds, such as your movie audio track, through this device.

- **AE-L/AF-L (autoexposure/autofocus) lock.** This button can be programmed by you to provide a variety of autoexposure/autofocus locking functions, which I'll explain in Chapter 9. By default, it locks the exposure or focus that the camera sets when you partially depress the shutter button. The exposure lock indication (AE-L icon) appears in the viewfinder. If you want to recalculate exposure or autofocus with the shutter button still partially depressed, press the button again. The exposure/autofocus will be unlocked when you release the shutter button or take the picture. To retain the exposure/autofocus lock for subsequent photos, keep the button pressed while shooting.

- **Main command dial.** This is the main control dial of the D7000, used to set or adjust most functions, such as shutter speed, bracketing sequence, white balance, ISO, and so forth, either alone or when another button is depressed simultaneously. It is often used in conjunction with the sub-command dial on the front of the camera when pairs of settings can be made, such as image formats (main command dial: image format; sub-command dial: resolution); exposure (main: shutter speed; sub: aperture); flash (main: flash mode; sub: flash compensation); or white balance (main: WB preset; sub: fine-tune WB). You can swap functions of the main and sub-command dials, reverse the rotation direction, choose whether the aperture ring on the lens or the sub-command dial will be used to set the f/stop, and activate the main command dials to navigate menus and images. You'll learn about these Custom Settings menu options (CSM #f6) in Chapter 9.

You'll be using the four buttons to the left of the LCD (shown in Figure 3.8) quite frequently, so learn their functions now.

- **MENU button.** Summons/exits the menu displayed on the rear LCD of the D7000. When you're working with submenus, this button also serves to exit a submenu and return to the main menu.

- **Help/Protect/White balance button.** When viewing most menu items on the LCD, pressing this button produces a concise Help screen with tips on how to make the relevant setting. This double-duty button also can be used to protect an image from accidental erasure when reviewing a picture on the LCD. Press once to protect the image, a second time to unprotect it. A key symbol appears when the image is displayed to show that it is protected. (This feature safeguards an image from erasure when deleting or transferring pictures only; when you format a card, protected images are removed along with all the others.) The button also summons the white balance settings.

- **Thumbnail/Zoom Out/ISO button.** Use this button to change from full-screen view to six, nine, or 72 thumbnails, Calendar View, or to zoom out. I'll explain zooming and other playback options in the next section. The button also accesses ISO sensitivity settings.

- **Zoom In button.** Press to zoom in on an image, and to select image quality settings.

More buttons reside on the right side of the back panel, as shown in Figure 3.9. The key controls and their functions are as follows:

- **Live View switch.** Rotate this momentary-contact switch clockwise to turn on Live View and enable movie shooting. Rotate it again to turn Live View/moving shooting off.

- **Movie-record button.** Press the red button to start movie shooting, and again to stop shooting.

- **Multi selector.** This joypad-like button can be shifted up, down, side to side, and diagonally for a total of eight directions, or pressed. It can be used for several functions, including AF point selection, scrolling around a magnified image, trimming a photo, or setting white balance correction. Within menus, pressing the up/down arrows moves the on-screen cursor up or down; pressing towards the right selects the highlighted item and displays its options; pressing left cancels and returns to the previous menu.

- **OK button.** The button in the center of the multi selector can be pressed to choose a highlighted selection in a menu and to confirm choices.

- **Infrared receiver.** This is one of two IR sensors on the camera; the other is located on the front. Both are active at the same time when the release mode dial is set to

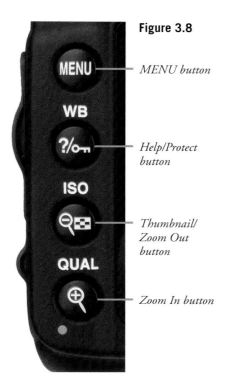

Figure 3.8

MENU button

Help/Protect button

Thumbnail/ Zoom Out button

Zoom In button

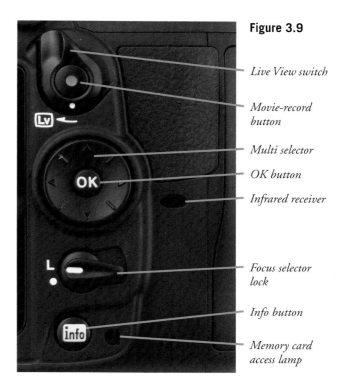

Figure 3.9

Live View switch

Movie-record button

Multi selector

OK button

Infrared receiver

Focus selector lock

Info button

Memory card access lamp

the Remote position. You'd use this receiver to trigger the camera using the ML-L3 infrared remote control when you want to release the shutter while standing behind the camera.

- **Focus selector lock.** Rotate this switch to the L position to disable changing the focus point with the multi selector.

- **Memory card access lamp.** When lit or blinking, this lamp indicates that a memory card is being accessed.

- **LCD.** View your images and navigate through the menus on this screen.

- **Info button.** Press this button to activate the shooting information display. Press again to change any of the parameters in the bottom rows of the display, using the multi selector to highlight the option. Then, press OK to summon a screen that lets you make the changes. Or, press a third time to remove the information display (or simply tap the shutter release button). The display will also clear after the period you've set for LCD display (the default value is 20 seconds). The information display can be set to alternate between modes that are best viewed under bright daylight (see Figure 3.10), as well as in dimmer illumination (see Figure 3.11). I'll describe the use of the shooting information display in more detail later in this chapter.

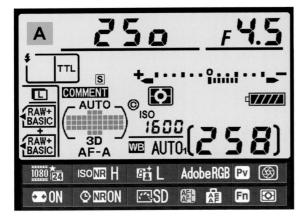

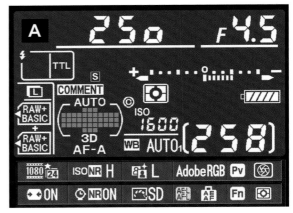

Figure 3.10

Figure 3.11

Playing Back Images

Reviewing images is a joy on the Nikon D7000's big three-inch LCD. The display is big and bright, and there is abundant detail on that 920,000-dot, VGA-resolution screen.

Here are the basics involved in reviewing images on the LCD screen (or on a television/HDTV screen you have connected with a cable). You'll find more details about some of these functions later in this chapter, or, for more complex capabilities, in the chapters that I point you to. This section just lists the must-know information.

- **Start review.** To begin review, press the Playback button at the upper-left corner of the back of the D7000. The most recently viewed image will appear on the LCD.

- **Playback card.** If you have two memory cards installed in your D7000, you can change which card is used for playback by holding down the BKT button (located underneath the Flash button on the front of the camera) and pressing the multi controller up button. A dialog box appears that allows you to highlight and select the slot and folder you want to use. I would have preferred just holding down the BKT button and pressing the left/right keys to swap slots, but the extra step is necessary to allow you to choose a particular folder in addition to the slot to be used for playback.

- **Playback folder.** Image review generally shows you the images in the currently selected folder on your Secure Digital card. A given card can contain several folders (a new one is created anytime you exceed 999 images in the current folder). You can use the Playback folder menu option in the Playback menu (as I'll explain in Chapter 8) to select a specific folder on one of the two memory cards, or direct the D7000 to display images from all the folders on the memory card(s).

■ **View thumbnail images.** To change the view from a single image to four, nine, or 72 thumbnails, follow the instructions in the "Viewing Thumbnails" section that follows.

■ **Zoom in and out.** To zoom in or out, press the Zoom/Thumbnail key, following the instructions in the "Zooming the Nikon D7000 Playback Display" in the next section. (It also shows you how to move the zoomed area around using the multi selector keypad.)

■ **Move back and forth.** To advance to the next image, press the right edge of the multi selector pad; to go back to a previous shot, press the left edge. When you reach the beginning/end of the photos in your folder, the display "wraps around" to the end/beginning of the available shots. (Note that you can change the behavior of the D7000 in Custom Settings entry CSM #f6's Menus and Playback option so that the main command dial can be used to move forward and backward during picture review. I'll show you how to activate this feature in Chapter 9.)

■ **See different types of data.** To change the type of information about the displayed image that is shown, press the up and down portions of the multi selector pad. To learn what data is available, read the "Using Shooting Data" section later in this chapter.

■ **Remove images.** To delete an image that's currently on the screen, press the Trash button once, then press it again to confirm the deletion. To select and delete a group of images, use the Delete option in the Playback menu to specify particular photos to remove, as described in more detail in Chapter 8.

■ **Cancel playback.** To cancel image review, press the Playback button again, or simply tap the shutter release button.

Zooming the Nikon D7000 Playback Display

The Nikon D7000 zooms in and out of preview images using the procedure that follows:

1. When an image is displayed (use the Playback button to start), press the Zoom In button to fill the screen with a slightly magnified version of the image.

2. A navigation window appears in the lower-right corner of the LCD showing the entire image. Keep pressing to continue zooming in to the maximum of 31X enlargement (with a full resolution large image).

3. A yellow box in the navigation window shows the zoomed area within the full image. The entire navigation window vanishes from the screen after a few seconds, leaving you with a full-screen view of the zoomed portion of the image. (See Figure 3.12.)

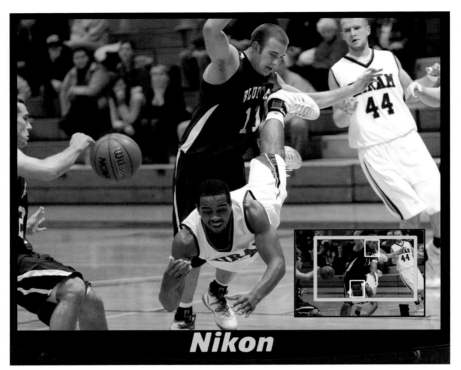

Figure 3.12
The Nikon D7000 incorporates a small thumbnail image with a yellow box showing the current zoom area.

4. To detect faces, rotate the sub-command dial while an image is zoomed. Up to 35 faces will be detected by the D7000, indicated by white borders in the navigation window. Rotate the sub-command dial to move highlighting to the individual faces.

5. Use the main command dial to move to the same zoomed area of the next/ previous image.

6. Use the Zoom Out/Thumbnail button to zoom back out of the image.

7. Use the multi selector buttons to move the zoomed area around within the image. The navigation window will reappear for reference when zooming or scrolling around within the display.

8. To exit zoom in/zoom out display, keep pressing the Zoom Out button until the full screen/full image/information display appears again.

Viewing Thumbnails

The Nikon D7000 provides other options for reviewing images in addition to zooming in and out. You can switch between single image view and either four, nine, or 72 reduced-size thumbnail images on a single LCD screen. There's also a calendar view that shows images grouped by the date they were shot.

Pages of thumbnail images offer a quick way to scroll through a large number of pictures quickly to find the one you want to examine in more detail. The D7000 lets you switch quickly from single- to four- to nine- to 72-image views, with a scroll bar displayed at the right side of the screen to show you the relative position of the displayed thumbnails within the full collection of images in the active folder on your memory card. Figure 3.13 offers a comparison between the three levels of thumbnail views. The Zoom In and Zoom Out/Thumbnail buttons are used.

- **Add thumbnails.** To increase the number of thumbnails on the screen, press the Zoom Out button. The D7000 will switch from single image to four thumbnails to nine thumbnails to 72 thumbnails, and then on to calendar view, described next. (The display doesn't cycle back to single image again.)

- **Reduce number of thumbnails.** To decrease the number of thumbnails on the screen, press the Zoom In button to change from Calendar View to 72 to nine thumbnails to four thumbnails, or from four to single-image display. Continuing to press the Zoom In button once you've returned to single-image display starts the zoom process described in the previous section.

- **Change slot and folder.** When viewing 72 thumbnails, if two memory cards are installed in the D7000, then pressing the Zoom Out button one additional time produces a screen that allows you to choose the memory card slot and folder that contains the images you want to view. Press the Playback button to back out of this option and return to the 72-thumbnail view.

- **Switch between thumbnails and full image.** When viewing thumbnails, you can quickly switch between thumbnail view and full image display by pressing the OK button in the center of the multi selector. Pressing it again brings up the Retouch menu (described in Chapter 10). If you want to return to thumbnail views instead, press the Zoom In button.

- **Change highlighted thumbnail area.** Use the multi selector to move the yellow highlight box around among the thumbnails.

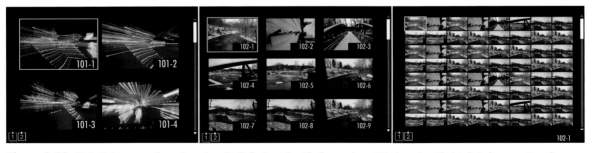

Figure 3.13 Switch between four thumbnails (left thumbnails (center), or 72 thumbnails (right), by pressing the Zoom Out and Zoom In buttons.

- **Protect and delete images.** When viewing thumbnails or a single page image, press the Protect button to preserve the image against accidental deletion (a key icon is overlaid over the full-page image; press Protect again to remove protection).

- **Exit image review.** Tap the shutter release button or press the Playback button to exit image review. You don't have to worry about missing a shot because you were reviewing images; a half-press of shutter release automatically brings back the D7000's exposure meters, the autofocus system, and, unless you've redefined your controls or are using manual focus, cancels image review.

Working with Calendar View

When you're in 72 thumbnail mode, pressing the Zoom Out button one more time takes you to calendar view, where you can sort through images arranged by the date they were taken. This feature is especially useful when you're traveling and want to see only the pictures you took in, say, a particular city on a certain day.

- **View dates and images taken on that date.** A yellow highlight box appears around a selected date in the date list calendar, as shown in Figure 3.14. When there are images available that were taken on that date, a scrolling thumbnail column appears at the right of the screen. The thumbnail column disappears if there are no photos taken on the highlighted date.

- **Change dates.** Use the multi selector keys to move through the date list.

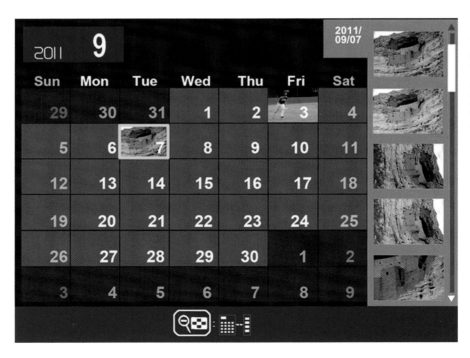

Figure 3.14
Calendar view allows you to browse through all images on your memory card taken on a certain date.

- **View a date's images.** Press the Zoom In button to toggle between the date list to the scrolling thumbnail list of images taken on that date at the right of the screen. When viewing the thumbnail list, you can use the multi selector up/down keys to scroll through the available images. Press the Zoom In button again to return to the date list calendar when you want to select a different date.

- **Preview an image.** In the thumbnail list, when you've highlighted an image you want to look at, press the Zoom In button to see an enlarged view of that image without leaving the calendar view mode. The zoomed image replaces the date list.

- **Delete images.** Pressing the Trash button deletes a highlighted image in the thumbnail list. In the date list view, pressing the Trash button removes all the images taken on that date (use with caution!).

- **Exit calendar view.** In thumbnail list view, if you highlight an image and press the OK button, you'll exit calendar view and the highlighted image will be shown on the LCD in the display mode you've chosen. (See "Working with Photo Information" to learn about the various display modes.) In date list view, pressing the Zoom In button exits calendar view and returns to 72 thumbnails view. You can also exit calendar view by tapping the shutter release (to turn off the LCD to ready the camera for shooting) or by pressing the MENU button.

Working with the Shooting Information/ Photo Data Displays

Your Nikon D7000 can display two types of information on the color LCD as you are reviewing or taking pictures:

- **Shooting information display.** This is the screen of information (illustrated by Figure 3.11 earlier) that provides a readout of various settings for the D7000's shooting parameters. It appears when you press the Info button on the back of the camera, just to the right of the bottom edge of the color LCD. The shooting information display partially duplicates some of the data shown on the top-panel monochrome LCD, but has an additional feature: you can change any of the parameters listed in the bottom two rows of the display, without the need to press a function button or visit the menus. I'll describe exactly how to do this next.

Caution

Nikon calls this screen the information display most of the time in its manual, which is the same name it applies to a quite different series of six data screens that appear when using Live View. To avoid confusion, I will call this screen the *shooting information display*, and the other six the *Live View information display*.

■ **Photo Data.** These are a series of up to eight screens (including GPS data, which appears only if you used a GPS device to take the picture) that provide various types of shooting and other information *about a particular image* that you are reviewing. The data shown applies only to that image, and does not reflect your D7000's current shooting settings (unless you're viewing an image you've just taken). I'll show you each of these screens, too, and explain how you can use them.

Using the Shooting Information Display

The shooting information display appears when you press the Info button to the lower right of the color LCD. This display shows for about 10 seconds by default, but you can change this to a period of up to 10 minutes using Custom Settings CSM #c4, as described in Chapter 9. Hide this display by pressing the Info button twice, or by tapping the shutter release button. (The D7000 will always clear the LCD screen when you depress the shutter release button, and activate the exposure meter at the same time, so you'll be ready to take a shot if you want.)

The shooting information display provides a lot of basic shooting data. Figure 3.15 shows a color-coded version. It does *not* appear colored like this on your LCD, and, for clarity, I'm showing some options that don't appear on the screen at the same time; your display will have only some of the flash information that I've coded in pink in my illustration.

I've applied some labels highlighting the basic kinds of settings you'll find on this screen. I've simplified the labels here; you'll find similar callouts of the individual icons later in this chapter in the section on the top-panel monochrome display, which largely duplicates the information you see here. As I noted, this rendition just provides an overview of the kind of data you'll find on the color LCD; not every readout will appear on your screen, and certainly not all at once.

When the shooting information display is shown, press the Info button a second time, and you'll be able to change the parameters in the bottom two rows, shown in the yellow highlighted area in Figure 3.16. Use the multi selector buttons to navigate to the parameter you want to adjust and press the OK button or the multi selector center button to produce a menu with your options. If you've set Custom Settings CSM #d5 to On (the default), a handy tool tip appears near a highlighted entry, so you can easily tell what each of the parameters does. Once you've learned the functions, you can turn the tool tips off in the Custom Settings menu. The specs you can change include the following. (I'll describe the options for each of them in Chapters 8, 9, and 10.)

■ **Movie Quality.** Select from eight different movie shooting resolutions and frame rates.

■ **Auto Distortion Control.** Switch the D7000's automatic lens distortion control on or off.

Figure 3.15
The shooting information display has this kind of information, color-coded here for simplicity.

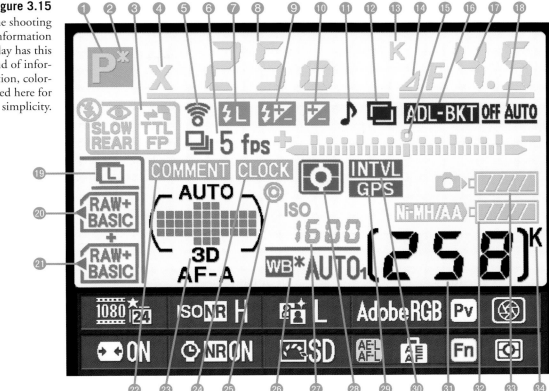

1. Shooting mode
2. Flexible program indicator
3. Flash mode
4. Flash sync indicator
5. Eye-Fi connection
6. Release mode/Continuous shooting speed
7. Value lock indicator
8. Shutter speed/Exposure compensation value/Flash compensation value/Number of shots in bracketing sequence/Focal length (non-CPU lens)/Color temperature

9. Flash compensation
10. Exposure compensation
11. Beep indicator
12. Multiple exposure
13. Color temperature indicator
14. Aperture stop indicator
15. Exposure indicator/Exposure compensation/Exposure, Flash, WB bracketing progress indicator
16. Exposure/Flash bracketing indicator/WB bracketing indicator/Active D-Lighting bracketing indicator

17. f/stop/Number of stops/Bracketing increment/Maximum aperture (non-CPU lens)
18. Active D-Lighting bracketing amount
19. Image quality
20. Mode for card in Slot 1
21. Mode for card in Slot 2
22. Image comment
23. Auto-area AF indicator/Focus points indicator/AF-area mode indicator/3D-tracking indicator
24. Clock Not Set
25. Copyright information

26. White balance/White balance fine-tuning
27. ISO sensitivity
28. Metering mode
29. GPS connection
30. Interval timer
31. Number of exposures remaining/Manual lens numbers
32. MB-D11 battery indicator/Battery type
33. Camera battery indicator
34. Thousands of exposures

- **ISO Noise Reduction/Long Exposure Noise Reduction.** You can turn each of these two types of noise reduction off, or to high, normal, or low settings.

- **Active D-Lighting.** Choose to extend the dynamic range of your image to one of four levels (Low, Normal, High, Extra High), plus Auto or Off. I'll explain the pitfalls/advantages of Active D-Lighting in Chapter 8.

- **Picture Control.** Choose a Picture Control style, or make adjustments to an existing style.

- **Color Space.** Switch between Adobe RGB and sRGB color spaces.

- **AE-L/AF-L button, Function button, Depth-of-field preview button assignment.** Change the function of each of these three buttons, so that pressing them performs a function of your choice (such as locking the flash off, changing metering mode, or triggering a burst of bracketed shots). You'll find out how to use these (seemingly) infinite combinations of useful shortcuts in Chapter 9.

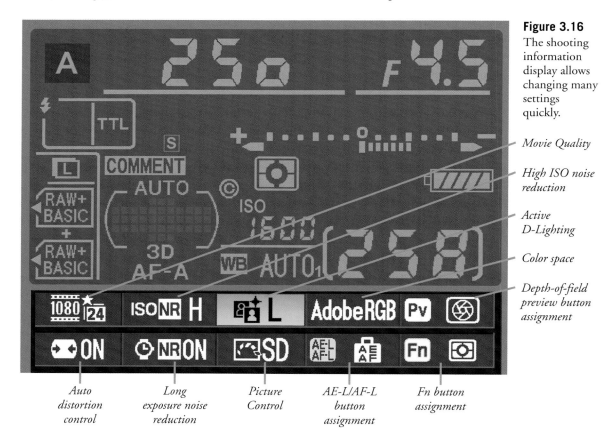

Figure 3.16
The shooting information display allows changing many settings quickly.

Movie Quality

High ISO noise reduction

Active D-Lighting

Color space

Depth-of-field preview button assignment

Auto distortion control

Long exposure noise reduction

Picture Control

AE-L/AF-L button assignment

Fn button assignment

Using the Photo Data Displays

When reviewing an image on the screen, your D7000 can supplement the image itself with a variety of shooting data, ranging from basic information presented at the bottom of the LCD display, to three text overlays that detail virtually every shooting option you've selected. There is also a display for GPS data if you're using a GPS device, and two views of histograms. There's actually a third histogram view that can be summoned when you reprogram the center button of the multi selector. I'll explain how to do that and how to work with histograms in the discussion on achieving optimum exposure in Chapter 4. However, this is a good place to provide an overview of the kind of information you can view when playing back your photos.

You can change the *types* of information displayed using the Display Mode entry in the Playback menu. There you will find checkboxes you can mark for both basic photo information (overexposed highlights and the focus point used when the image was captured) and detailed photo information (which includes an RGB histogram and various data screens). I'll show you how to activate these info options in Chapter 8, and provide more detailed reasons why you might want to see this data when you review your pictures. This section will simply show you the type of information available. Most of the data is self-explanatory, so the labels in the accompanying figures should tell you most of what you need to know. To change to any of these views while an image is on the screen in Playback mode, press the multi selector up/down buttons.

- **File information screen.** The basic full image review display is officially called the file information screen, and looks like Figure 3.17. Press the multi selector down button to advance to the next information screen.

- **Highlights.** When highlights display is active (after being chosen in the Display Mode entry of the Playback menu, as described in Chapter 8), any overexposed areas will be indicated by a flashing black border. As I am unable to make the printed page flash, you'll have to check out this effect for yourself. You can visualize what these "blinkies" look like in Figure 3.18.

- **RGB Histogram.** Another optional screen is the RGB histogram, which you can see in Figure 3.19. I'm going to leave the discussion of histograms for Chapter 4.

- **Shooting Data 1.** This is the first in a series of three screens that collectively provide everything else you might want to know about a picture you've taken. I'm not providing any labels in Figure 3.20, because the information in the first seven lines in the screen should be obvious.

- **Shooting Data 2.** This screen shows white balance data and adjustments, the color space you've selected, and lists any Picture Control tweaks you've entered. (See Figure 3.21.)

- **Shooting Data 3.** The next screen shows any noise reduction you've specified, Active D-Lighting status, and any Retouch menu changes you may have made.

Although none of them apply to the background image shown in Figure 3.22, I've added a few entries to show the kind of changes that can be made. You'll learn more about the Retouch menu in Chapter 10, which also will tell you how to create an image comment, like the one shown in the figure.

- **Shooting Data 4.** This screen appears *only* if you've entered artist and/or copyright information in the Copyright Information setting of the Setup Menu, as described in Chapter 10. I'm not providing an illustration for this screen, because it shows nothing except the name of the photographer (artist) and the copyright.

- **GPS data.** This screen appears *only* if the image was taken using the GPS device. It includes latitude, longitude, altitude, and time information, as shown in Figure 3.23.

- **Overview data.** This screen, shown in Figure 3.24, provides a smaller image of your photo, but more information, including a luminance (brightness) histogram, metering mode used, lens focal length, exposure compensation, flash compensation, and lots of other data that's self-explanatory.

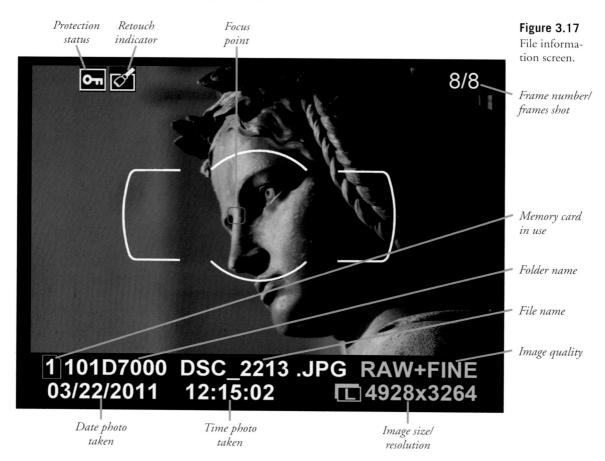

Protection status   *Retouch indicator*   *Focus point*

8/8

Figure 3.17
File information screen.

Frame number/ frames shot

Memory card in use

Folder name

File name

Image quality

1 101D7000 DSC_2213 .JPG RAW+FINE
03/22/2011   12:15:02   4928x3264

Date photo taken   *Time photo taken*   *Image size/ resolution*

Figure 3.18
Highlights
screen.

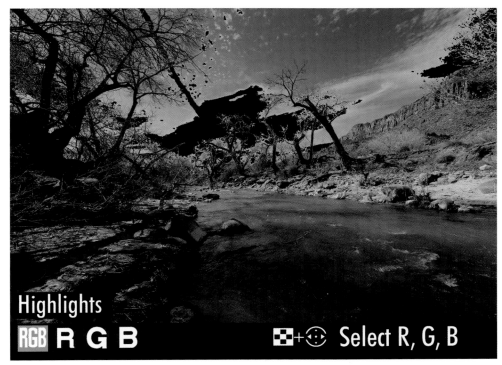

Figure 3.19
RGB histogram
screen.

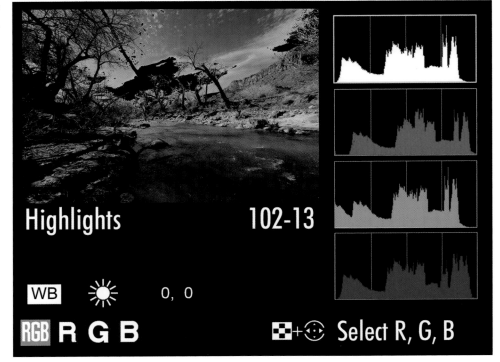

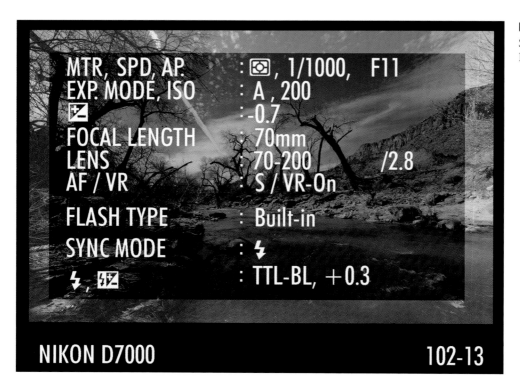

Figure 3.20
Shooting
Data 1 screen.

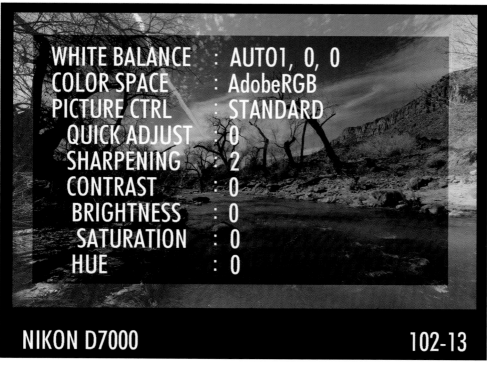

Figure 3.21
Shooting
Data 2 screen.

Figure 3.22
Shooting
Data 3 screen.

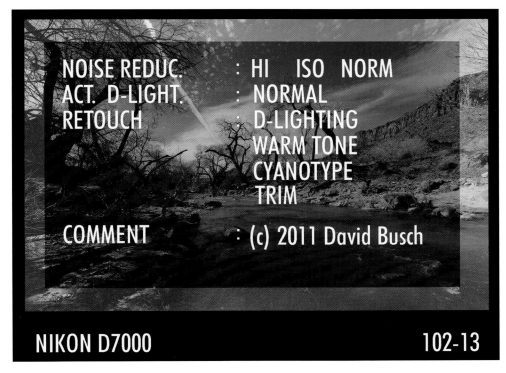

Figure 3.23
GPS data
screen.

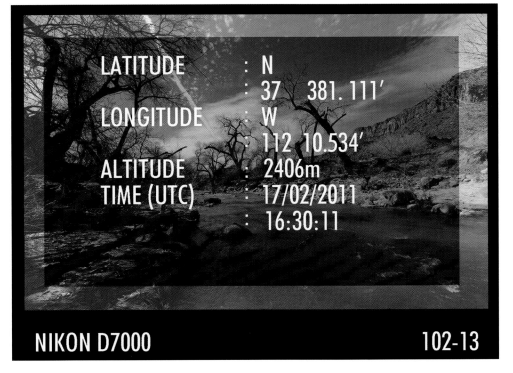

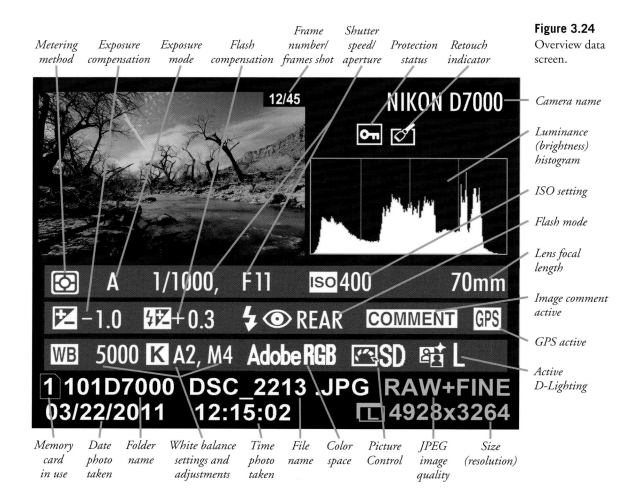

Figure 3.24
Overview data
screen.

Metering method · Exposure compensation · Exposure mode · Flash compensation · Frame number/ frames shot · Shutter speed/ aperture · Protection status · Retouch indicator

Camera name · Luminance (brightness) histogram · ISO setting · Flash mode · Lens focal length · Image comment active · GPS active · Active D-Lighting

Memory card in use · Date photo taken · Folder name · White balance settings and adjustments · Time photo taken · File name · Color space · Picture Control · JPEG image quality · Size (resolution)

Going Topside

The top surface of the Nikon D7000 (see Figure 3.25) has its own set of frequently accessed controls. I'm going to divide them into two parts: those to the left side of the camera, and those on the right side. The left side controls offer some settings that you may change frequently, perhaps even during a shooting session (white balance and ISO sensitivity), and one that you'll probably change once at the beginning: image quality (when you choose whether to shoot RAW, JPEG [and which compression level you want], or a combination of the two). Also on the left side of the camera is the release mode dial itself, which you'll use to flip among Single frame, Continuous shooting, Self-timer, Live View, and other modes. Figure 3.26 shows this side of the D7000's top panel up close.

Figure 3.25

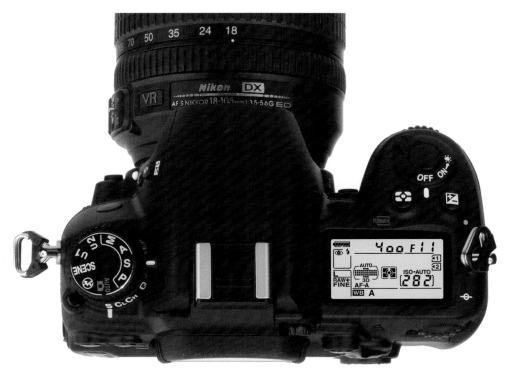

Figure 3.26

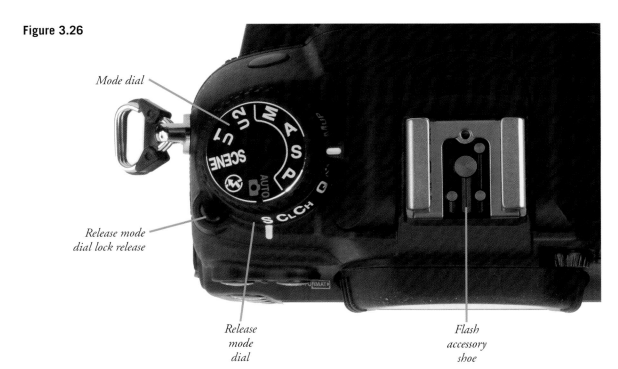

Mode dial

Release mode
dial lock release

Release
mode
dial

Flash
accessory
shoe

- **Mode dial.** Rotate this dial to select from two fully automatic modes (Auto and Auto No Flash), four advanced exposure modes (Manual, Aperture-priority, Shutter-priority, and Program), 19 different Scene modes (first described in Chapter 2, and next in Chapter 4) selected by rotating the main command dial, plus two User Setting positions, U1 and U2 (which each store a selection of settings for quick retrieval).

- **Release mode dial lock release.** Before you can choose any of the release mode dial's settings, you must hold down this button to free the dial so it can rotate.

- **Release mode dial.** Your choices include S (Single frame), C_L (Continuous low speed), C_H (Continuous high speed), Quiet shutter release, Self-timer, Remote control, and Mup (Mirror Up). I'll have more information on using these modes in Chapter 2.

- **Accessory shoe.** Slide an electronic flash into this mount when you need a more powerful speedlight. A dedicated flash unit, like the Nikon SB-900, can use the multiple contact points shown to communicate exposure, zoom setting, white balance information, and other data between the flash and the camera. There's more on using electronic flash in Chapter 12. You can also mount other accessories on this shoe, such as the Nikon GP-1 GPS adapter.

On the right side of the camera is another batch of controls and a display panel, as shown in Figure 3.27:

- **Power switch.** Rotate this switch clockwise to turn on the Nikon D7000 (and virtually all other Nikon dSLRs). Continue past the ON position to illuminate the monochrome LCD control panel's backlight for a few seconds. If you'd rather have the backlight remain on for the length of time the exposure meters are active, you can specify this using the Custom Settings menu CSM #D11 (set to On). For this setting to be useful, you'll need to set the automatic meter-off delay to something other than the default six seconds. If you're carefree about battery usage, you can specify meter-off delays of four seconds to 10 minutes using CSM #c2, as described in Chapter 9.

- **Shutter release button.** Partially depress this button to activate the exposure meter (and the main and sub-command dials that adjust metering settings), lock in exposure, and focus (unless you've redefined the focus activation button, as outlined in Chapter 9). Press all the way to take the picture. Tapping the shutter release when the camera has turned off the autoexposure and autofocus mechanisms reactivates both. When a review image is displayed on the back-panel color LCD, tapping this button removes the image from the display and reactivates the autoexposure and autofocus mechanisms.

Figure 3.27

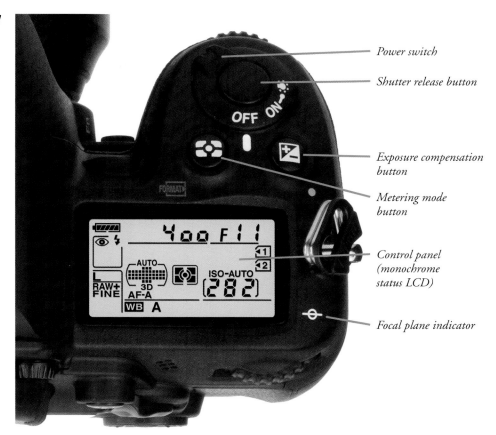

Power switch

Shutter release button

Exposure compensation button

Metering mode button

Control panel (monochrome status LCD)

Focal plane indicator

- **Metering mode button/Format #2.** Press this button and rotate the main command dial while watching the top-panel LCD to change to Center-weighted (top), Matrix (middle), or Spot metering. If you'd like to switch back and forth between one metering mode and another rapidly, set your default mode, such as Matrix metering, with this switch, then program the Fn or DOF preview button to provide your alternate mode (say, Spot metering) with a simple press. You can hold this button down at the same time as the Trash button on the back of the camera (which I call Format #1) to reformat a memory card.

- **Exposure compensation button/Reset #1.** Hold down this button and spin the main command dial to add or subtract exposure when using Program, Aperture-priority, or Shutter-priority modes. (In Manual mode, the exposure remains the same, but the "ideal" exposure shown in the electronic analog display [more on that in the next section] is modified to reflect the extra/reduced exposure you're calling for.) The exposure compensation amount is shown on the monochrome status panel as plus or minus values. This button is also used in conjunction with the QUAL button to provide a quick two-button reset of the camera to many of the factory default settings, as described in Chapter 1. (Any reassignment of the AE-L/AF-L button you made using Custom Settings menu CSM #f6 is unaffected.) Hold down the two buttons, each marked with a green dot, for about two seconds to effect the reset.

- **Focal plane indicator.** This indicator shows the *plane* of the sensor, for use in applications where exact measurement of the distance from the focal plane to the subject is necessary. (These are mostly scientific/close-up applications.)

- **Control panel.** I find Nikon's term for the top monochrome LCD status panel confusing, so control panel is the term I use most of the time. This useful indicator shows the status of many settings. Unfortunately, because it's on top of the camera, you may not be able to *see* those settings when the camera is elevated (especially on a tripod). In that case, use the shooting information display, described earlier in this chapter, which can show much of the same information on the back-panel color LCD when you press the Info button.

LCD Control Panel Readouts

The top panel of the Nikon D7000 (see Figure 3.28) contains a monochrome LCD readout (the "control panel") that displays status information about most of the shooting settings. All of the information segments available are shown in Figures 3.29 and

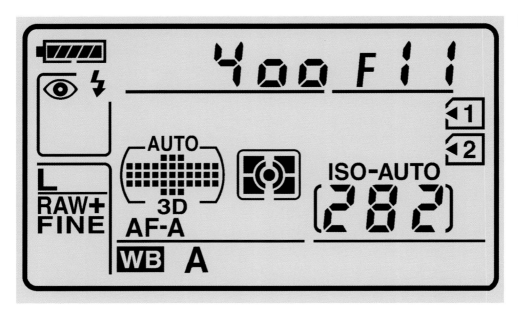

Figure 3.28

3.30. I've color-coded the display and divided the figure into two parts to avoid drowning you in labels for this intensely dense readout. The information does *not* appear in color on the actual D7000, and all of these indicators will not appear at once. Many of the information items are mutually exclusive (that is, in the white balance area at lower right, only one of the possible settings illustrated will appear).

Some of the items on the status LCD also appear in the viewfinder, such as the shutter speed and aperture. This is a thicket of information, but I'll spell out what the categories of data include.

Figure 3.29

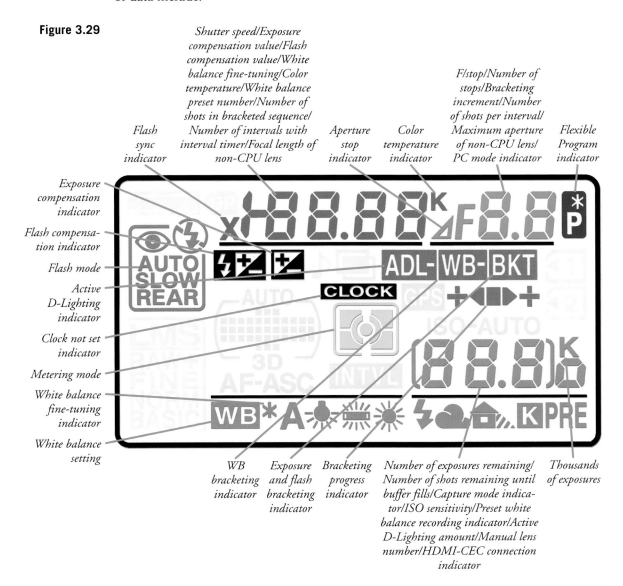

Shutter speed/Exposure compensation value/Flash compensation value/White balance fine-tuning/Color temperature/White balance preset number/Number of shots in bracketed sequence/Number of intervals with interval timer/Focal length of non-CPU lens

F/stop/Number of stops/Bracketing increment/Number of shots per interval/Maximum aperture of non-CPU lens/PC mode indicator

Flash sync indicator

Aperture stop indicator

Color temperature indicator

Flexible Program indicator

Exposure compensation indicator

Flash compensation indicator

Flash mode

Active D-Lighting indicator

Clock not set indicator

Metering mode

White balance fine-tuning indicator

White balance setting

WB bracketing indicator

Exposure and flash bracketing indicator

Bracketing progress indicator

Number of exposures remaining/Number of shots remaining until buffer fills/Capture mode indicator/ISO sensitivity/Preset white balance recording indicator/Active D-Lighting amount/Manual lens number/HDMI-CEC connection indicator

Thousands of exposures

First, in Figure 3.29:

- **Shutter speed/additional functions (magenta).** Here you'll find the shutter speed, exposure compensation values, color temperature, and other useful data.

- **Aperture/additional functions (magenta).** The selected f/stop appears here, along with a lot of other alternate information, as shown in the label in the figure.

- **Flexible program indicator (dark blue).** Appears when you've adjusted the camera's Program mode exposure by spinning the main command dial to change to a different setting that produces the same exposure, but with a different combination of shutter speed and aperture.

- **Electronic flash mode (green).** The current mode for the D7000's built-in electronic flash unit is shown here.

- **Flash compensation active (black).** Reminds you that you've tweaked the D7000's electronic flash exposure system with more or less exposure requested.

- **Exposure compensation active (black).** Appears when you've dialed in exposure compensation. Monitor this indicator, as it's easy to forget that you've told the Nikon D7000 to use more or less exposure than what its (reasonably intelligent) metering system would otherwise select.

- **Clock not set (black).** This indicator is displayed when your clock needs to be reset. You'll see it when your camera is activated for the first time, any time that the internal clock battery runs down (say, when you've removed the main battery for a few days), and when your internal clock battery wears out and will no longer hold a charge.

- **Metering Mode (yellow).** Shows whether you've selected Matrix, Center-weighted, or Spot metering.

- **Active D-Lighting/Exposure/Flash/White balance bracketing indicator (tan).** Shows that ADL, exposure, flash, or white balance bracketing is underway. Underneath this display is an indicator that shows the progress of the bracketing currently underway. There are three symbols, a square flanked by left and right pointing triangles as well as plus or minus signs (depending on what type of bracketing you are doing); after each shot in the bracket set, one of the symbols disappears.

- **Number of exposures/additional functions (orange).** This indicator shows the number of exposures remaining on your memory card, as well as other functions, such as the number of shots remaining until your memory buffer fills.

- **White balance setting (light blue).** One of the white balance settings will appear here, depending on the selection you've made.

In Figure 3.30, you'll find the following readouts highlighted:

- **Battery status (gray).** Five segments show the approximate battery power remaining. A better indicator is the Battery Info entry in the Setup menu.

- **MB-D11 battery indicator (gray).** Appears when the D7000 is being powered by the MB-D11 battery grip.

- **Beep indicator (gray).** Indicates that a helpful beep will sound when using the self-timer or when the D7000 successfully focuses when in Single-servo autofocus mode (AF-S) (as long as release priority hasn't been specified in CSM #a2). You can specify a loud, soft beep, or none at all and select the pitch in CSM #d1.

- **Multiple exposures (gray).** If you're shooting multiple exposures (selected under Multiple Exposures in the Shooting menu) this indicator will be shown. You can dial in a specific number of exposures when you set up the sequence, as I'll describe in Chapter 8.

- **Secure Digital indicator/Slot 1/Slot 2 (gray).** Shows when a card of either type is inserted in the camera.

- **Image Size (dark orange).** Shows whether the D7000 is shooting Large (4,927 × 3,264 pixels), Medium (3,696 × 2,448 pixels), or Small (2,464 × 1,632 pixels) sizes.

Figure 3.30

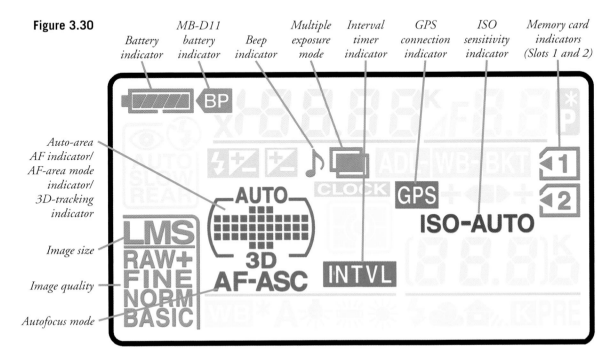

- **Image Quality (dark orange).** Shows current image quality, including JPEG, RAW, and RAW+JPEG Fine, Norm, or Basic.

- **Secure Digital indicator (gray).** Shows when a card of either type is inserted in the camera.

- **Autofocus-area indicator (dark red).** Displays the autofocus area status, with the active focus zone shown from among the 39 available points.

- **Autofocus mode.** Shows whether AF-A, AF-S, or AF-C focus modes are active.

- **ISO indicator (brown).** Displayed when you've set the D7000 to adjust ISO for you automatically.

- **GPS active (pink).** If you have a GPS device attached and working, you'll know it when this indicator shows up.

- **Interval timer active (pink).** When using the D7000's interval timer facility (as described in Chapter 8), this indicator appears.

Lens Components

The lens shown at left in Figure 3.31 is a typical lens that might be mounted on a Nikon dSLR. Unfortunately, this particular lens doesn't include all the common features found on the various Nikon lenses available for your camera, so I am including a second lens (shown at right in the figure) that *does* have more features and components. It's not a typical lens that a D7000 user might work with, however. This 17-35mm zoom is a pricey "pro" lens that costs about half as much as the entire D3100 camera. Nevertheless, it makes a good example. Components found on this pair of lenses include:

- **Filter thread.** Most lenses have a thread on the front for attaching filters and other add-ons. Some, like the 18-55 VR kit lens shown, also use this thread for attaching a lens hood (you screw on the filter first, and then attach the hood to the screw thread on the front of the filter). Some lenses, such as the AF-S Nikkor 14-24mm f/2.8G ED lens, have no front filter thread, either because their front elements are too curved to allow mounting a filter and/or because the front element is so large that huge filters would be prohibitively expensive. Some of these front-filter-hostile lenses allow using smaller filters that drop into a slot at the back of the lens.

- **Lens hood bayonet.** Lenses like the 17-35mm zoom shown in the figure use this bayonet to mount the lens hood. Such lenses generally will have a dot on the edge showing how to align the lens hood with the bayonet mount.

- **Focus ring.** This is the ring you turn when you manually focus the lens, or fine-tune autofocus adjustment. It's a narrow ring at the very front of the lens (on the 18-55mm kit lens), or a wider ring located somewhere else.

Figure 3.31

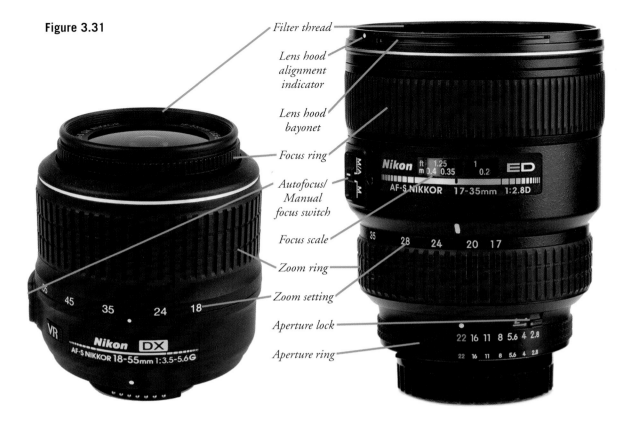

- **Focus scale.** This is a readout found on many lenses that rotates in unison with the lens's focus mechanism to show the distance at which the lens has been focused. It's a useful indicator for double-checking autofocus, roughly evaluating depth-of-field, and for setting manual focus guesstimates. Chapter 11 deals with the mysteries of lenses and their controls in more detail.

- **Zoom setting.** These markings on the lens show the current focal length selected.

- **Zoom ring.** Turn this ring to change the zoom setting.

- **Autofocus/Manual switch.** Allows you to change from automatic focus to manual focus.

- **Aperture ring.** Some lenses have a ring that allows you to set a specific f/stop manually, rather than use the camera's internal electronic aperture control. An aperture ring is useful when a lens is mounted on a non-automatic extension ring, bellows, or other accessory that doesn't couple electronically with the camera. Aperture rings also allow using a lens on an older camera that lacks electronic control. In recent years, Nikon has been replacing lenses that have aperture rings with versions that only allow setting the aperture with camera controls.

- **Aperture lock.** If you want your D7000 (or other Nikon dSLR) to control the aperture electronically, you must set the lens to its smallest aperture (usually f/22 or f/32) and lock it with this control.

- **Focus limit switch.** Some lenses have this switch (shown in Figure 3.32), which limits the focus range of the lens, thus potentially reducing focus seeking when shooting distant subjects. The limiter stops the lens from trying to focus at closer distances (in this case, closer than 2.5 meters).

- **Vibration reduction switch.** Lenses with Nikon's Vibration Reduction (VR) feature include a switch for turning the stabilization feature on and off, and, in some cases, for changing from normal vibration reduction to a more aggressive "active" VR mode useful for, say, shooting from moving vehicles. More on VR and other lens topics in Chapter 11.

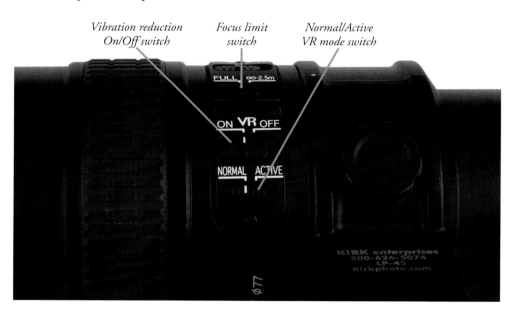

Vibration reduction On/Off switch   *Focus limit switch*   *Normal/Active VR mode switch*

Figure 3.32
Some lenses have focus limit switches and controls for vibration reduction (VR) features.

The back end of a lens intended for use on a Nikon camera has other components that you seldom see (except when you swap lenses), shown in Figure 3.33, but still should know about:

- **Lens bayonet mount.** This is the mounting mechanism that attaches to a matching mount on the camera. Although the lens bayonet is usually metal, some lower-priced lenses use a rugged plastic for this key component.

- **Automatic diaphragm lever.** This lever is moved by a matching lever in the camera to adjust the f/stop from wide open (which makes for the brightest view) to the *taking aperture*, which is the f/stop that will be used to take the picture. The actual

Figure 3.33

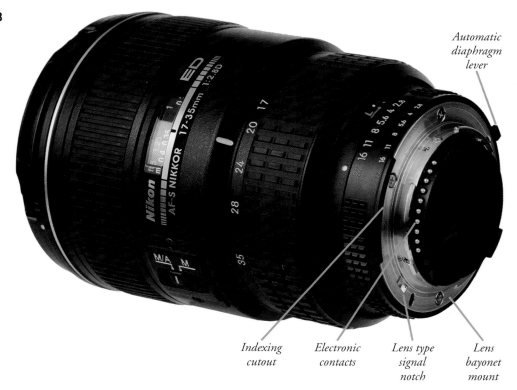

Automatic diaphragm lever

Indexing cutout   *Electronic contacts*   *Lens type signal notch*   *Lens bayonet mount*

taking aperture is determined by the camera's metering system (or by you when the D7000 is in Manual mode), and is communicated to the lens through the electronic contacts described next. (An exception is when the aperture ring on the lens itself is unlocked and used to specify the f/stop.) However, the spring-loaded physical levers are what actually push the aperture to the selected f/stop—even with advanced cameras like the D7000 or D3s. The aperture lever is also activated when you press the DOF button.

■ **Electronic contacts.** These metal contacts pass information to matching contacts located in the camera body allowing a firm electrical connection so that exposure, distance, and other information can be exchanged between the camera and lens.

■ **Lens type signal notch.** This is a machined groove in the lens mount, designed to tell older (non-dSLR) cameras that the aperture stops were linear. Today, this information would be conveyed electronically, except that all current lenses already have linear f/stops.

■ **Indexing cutout.** The base of any Nikon lens made after 1977 that has an aperture ring includes a cutout notch that mates with a ring around the lens mount of Nikon's advanced cameras (D200, D300/D300s, D2x/D2xs/D3/D3s/D3x/D700, and some older pro models). It tells the camera what the maximum aperture is and what f/stop has been set. For a D7000 owner, this means that older manual focus lenses (including pre-1977 lenses that have been converted to this system) can be used for automatic metering with the Aperture-priority exposure mode, and for manual metering in Manual exposure mode.

- **Autofocus drive screw slot.** (Not shown in the figure.) As you'll learn in Chapter 11, older autofocus lenses (given the AF designation in Nikon nomenclature) lack an internal autofocus motor. Focus is set using a screw drive built into the camera body of every Nikon autofocus camera (film or digital) except (at the time I write this) the Nikon D40/D40x, D60, D3000, D3100, D5000, and D5100. Lenses given the AF-S designation lack this connection, because autofocus is achieved internally using a tiny motor.

Looking Inside the Viewfinder

Much of the important shooting status information is shown inside the viewfinder of the Nikon D7000. As with the status LCD up on top, not all of this information will be shown at any one time. Figure 3.34 shows what you can expect to see. These readouts include:

- **Alignment grid.** This optional grid (it can be turned on and off in the Custom Settings menu option CSM #d2) can be useful when aligning horizontal or vertical shapes as you compose your image.

- **Focus points.** Can display the 39 areas used by the D7000 to focus. The camera can select the appropriate focus zone for you, or you can manually select one or all of the zones.

- **Active focus point.** The currently selected focus point can be highlighted with red illumination, depending on focus mode.

- **AF area bracket.** Shows the area covered by the autofocus sensors.

- **No card warning indicator.** Appears when the D7000 doesn't have a memory card installed in either slot. If you find this warning distracting, you can turn it, and the two described next, off with CSM #d4.

- **Black-and-white mode warning indicator.** Reminder that you're shooting JPEGs in monochrome mode.

- **Low battery warning indicator.** Appears when the D7000's battery becomes depleted.

- **Focus indicator.** This green dot stops blinking when the subject covered by the active autofocus zone is in sharp focus, whether focus was achieved by the AF system, or by you using manual focusing. Left and right arrows show whether focus is set ahead of or behind the subject.

- **Autoexposure (AE) lock/Flash value lock indicator.** Shows that exposure or flash exposure has been locked.

- **Flash sync.** Shows that the shutter speed has been locked in S or M modes at the x250 (1/250th second) setting (located, not between 1/125th and 1/500th second, but as the speed *past* bulb and 30 seconds).

- **Shutter speed.** Displays the current shutter speed selected by the camera, or by you in Manual exposure mode.

Figure 3.34

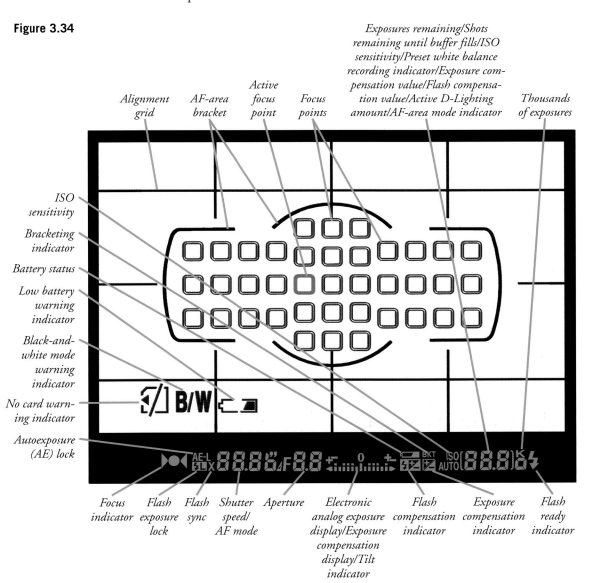

- **Aperture.** Shows the current aperture chosen by the D7000's autoexposure system, or specified by you when using Manual exposure mode.

- **Automatic ISO indicator.** Is shown as a reminder that the D7000 has been set to adjust ISO sensitivity automatically.

- **Flash compensation indicator.** Appears when flash EV changes have been made.

- **Exposure compensation indicator.** This is shown when exposure compensation (EV) changes have been made. It's easy to forget you've dialed in a little more or less exposure, and then shoot a whole series of pictures of a different scene that doesn't require such compensation. Beware!

- **Electronic analog exposure display.** This scale shows the current exposure level, with the bottom indicator centered when the exposure is correct as metered. The indicator may also move to the left or right to indicate over- or underexposure (respectively). The scale is also used to show the amount of exposure compensation dialed in. Also shows exposure compensation and degree of horizontal tilt.

- **Exposures remaining/maximum burst available/other data.** Normally displays the number of exposures remaining on your memory card, but while shooting it changes to show a number that indicates the number of frames that can be taken in continuous shooting mode using the current settings. This indicator also shows other information, such as ISO sensitivity, exposure compensation value, and Active D-Lighting amount.

- **Thousands of exposures.** Displayed when more than 999 exposures remaining; the readout to the left will then show number of shots remaining in thousands.

- **Flash ready indicator.** This icon appears when the flash is fully charged.

- **Battery status.** Shows amount of remaining power.

- **Bracketing indicator.** Shows when Active D-Lighting, exposure, flash, or white balance bracketing is underway.

- **ISO sensitivity.** This useful indicator shows the current ISO setting value. Those who have accidentally taken dozens of shots under bright sunlight at ISO 1600 because they forgot to change the setting back after some indoor shooting will treasure this addition.

Underneath Your Nikon D7000

There's not a lot going on with the bottom panel of your Nikon D7000. You'll find the battery compartment access door, and a tripod socket, which secures the camera to a tripod. The socket accepts other accessories, such as quick release plates that allow rapid attaching and detaching the D7000 from a matching platform affixed to your tripod.

Figure 3.35

Tripod socket

Battery compartment door

MB-D11 port cover

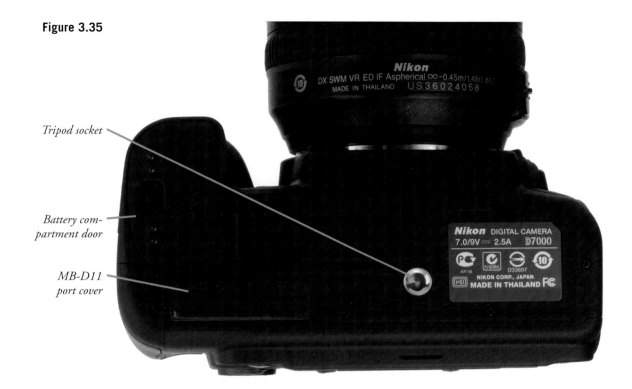

The socket is also used to secure the optional MB-D11 battery grip, which provides more juice to run your camera to take more exposures with a single charge. Figure 3.35 shows the underside view of the camera.

Using the MB-D11 Multi-Power Battery Pack/Vertical Grip

One optional accessory that you might want to consider is the Nikon MB-D11 battery pack/vertical grip, which attaches to the underside of the D7000 and provides extra power for those long shooting sessions. It also adds a vertically oriented shutter release, main command dial, sub-command dial, an AE-L/AF-L button, and a miniature joystick-like version of the multi selector, all arranged for easier shooting when the camera is rotated to a vertical position. There's a terminal connector under a rubber cover to provide a connection between the D7000 and accessories that fasten to the underside.

This accessory (see Figure 3.36 for front and back views) is available for about $250. Recently, Nikon has been making these grips compatible with succeeding cameras, so if you buy one for your D7000, it may be compatible with your next one, too. I used my MB-D10 with my Nikon D300, D300s, and D700, so I consider my purchase to have been a real bargain.

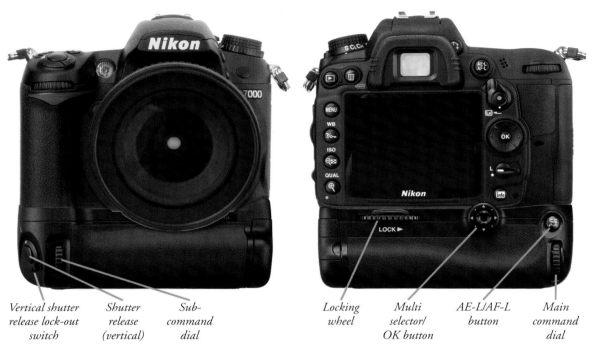

Vertical shutter | Shutter | Sub-   Locking | Multi | AE-L/AF-L | Main
release lock-out | release | command   wheel | selector/ | button | command
switch | (vertical) | dial   OK button | | dial

Figure 3.36 The Nikon MB-D11 Multi-Power Grip can double the length of your battery-powered shooting session, while adding convenient vertically oriented controls.

FALSE ECONOMY

Yes, the MB-D11 costs $250, and serviceable knock-offs are available from several Asian sources for as little as $69.95. I've checked them out carefully. They're made of light-weight plastic, don't look especially durable, and are probably not a serious option for anything other than light-duty use. If you plan on giving your battery/grip a real work-out, I'd recommend springing for the real thing. I don't know what would happen to a D7000 if one of these units shorted out, and don't plan to find out. Keep in mind that the MB-D11 may work with future cameras as well, now that Nikon has stopped giving its grips nomenclature linked to the camera model. But, even if it does not, you'll have a grip that can be re-sold to owners of compatible models, so the resale value is likely to be higher. A battery pack/grip is one place that I recommend not cutting corners.

To use the MB-D11, just follow these steps:

1. **Expose contacts.** Remove the rubber protective cover over the contacts on the bottom of the D7000 body. (See Figure 3.35, earlier.) Don't worry about losing the cover: it fits in a matching well inside the MB-D11. Retrieve the cover from that safe location when you remove the grip. Next, remove the white plastic protective cover from the terminal contacts on the MB-D11.

2. **Line up the camera and grip.** There are two holes on the underside surface of the D7000 that mate with matching pins on the MB-D11. Line up those components, the tripod socket and tripod screw, and the contacts (as shown in Figure 3.37) and slide the MB-D11 onto the underside of the camera.

Figure 3.37
First, remove the rubber gasket covering the contacts.

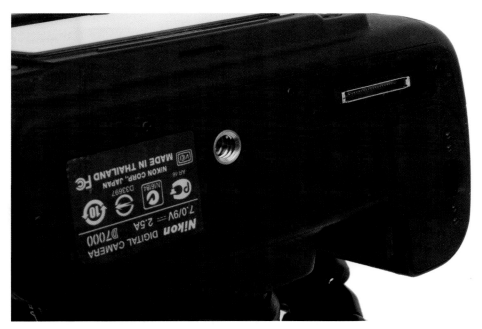

TIP

Unlike some earlier battery grips, you don't need to remove the battery in the camera; the D7000 can use both, in the order you specify (use CSM #d14, described in Chapter 9). I recommend using the battery in the MB-D11 grip first; as it poops out, you can replace it with a fresh EN-EL15 or set of AA batteries without the need to remove the grip. (You do own several back-up batteries, don't you?) Use the D7000's internal battery only when you have no other replacements available.

3. **Tighten the connection.** When the grip and D7000 are fit snugly together, rotate the large wheel under the base of the MB-D11 to lock the device onto the D7000.

4. **Add batteries.** The MB-D11 is furnished with two trays to hold batteries. You can add a second EN-EL15 battery to one tray to double your available power. Or you can use eight AA alkaline, nickel-metal hydride, nickel-manganese, or lithium batteries with the supplied holder. Slide the battery tray inside the base of the grip, and rotate the locking knob. Use CSM #d13 to tell the D7000 which type of AA batteries you are using.

5. **Fire away.** To use the shutter release on the vertical grip, you must turn the rotating switch so the dot aligns with the line on the grip, indicating that the shutter release is unlocked. If you're holding the camera in horizontal orientation and using the regular shutter release, it's easy to accidentally trip the vertical release with the palm of your right hand. (This accounts for the "phantom" shutter releases that mystify new users of this grip.) See Figure 3.36, earlier, for the key controls.

6. **Remove the grip.** To remove the grip, reverse these steps.

Part II

Beyond the Basics

Why do you need the four chapters in Part II: Beyond the Basics? I think you'll find that even if you've mastered the fundamentals and controls of the D7000 there is lots of room to learn more and use the features of the camera to their fullest. Even if you're getting great exposures a high percentage of the time, you can fine-tune tonal values and use your shutter speed, aperture, and ISO controls creatively. Your camera's high performance autofocus system may zero in on your subject in most situations—but you still need to be able to tell the D7000 *what* to focus on, and *when*. Other tools at your disposal let you freeze an instant of time, record a continuous series of instants as a movie, and improve your images in other imaginative ways. The chapters in this part will help you move your photography to the next level by understanding exposure, mastering the mysteries of autofocus, and using the Nikon D7000's advanced features.

4

Getting the Right Exposure

When you bought your Nikon D7000, you probably thought your days of worrying about getting the correct exposure were over. To paraphrase an old Kodak tagline dating back to the 19th Century—the goal is, "you press the button, and the camera does the rest." For the most part, that's a realistic objective. The D7000 is one of the smartest cameras available when it comes to calculating the right exposure for most situations. You can generally choose one of the Scene modes, or press the mode button and spin the main command dial to switch to Program (P), Aperture-priority (A), or Shutter-priority (S) and shoot away.

For example, when you shoot with the main light source behind the subject, you end up with *backlighting*, which can result in an overexposed background and/or an under-exposed subject. The Nikon D7000 recognizes backlit situations nicely, and can properly base exposure on the main subject, producing a decent photo. Features like Active D-Lighting (discussed in Chapter 8) can fine-tune exposure as you take photos, to preserve detail in the highlights and shadows.

But what if you *want* to underexpose the subject, to produce a silhouette effect? Or, perhaps, you might want to flip up the D7000's built-in flash unit to fill in the shadows on your subject. The more you know about how to use your D7000, the more you'll run into situations where you want to creatively tweak the exposure to provide a different look than you'd get with a straight shot.

This chapter shows you the fundamentals of exposure, so you'll be better equipped to override the Nikon D7000's default settings when you want to, or need to. After all, correct exposure is one of the foundations of good photography, along with accurate focus and sharpness, appropriate color balance, freedom from unwanted noise and excessive contrast, as well as pleasing composition.

The Nikon D7000 gives you a great deal of control over all of these, although composition is entirely up to you. You must still frame the photograph to create an interesting arrangement of subject matter, but all the other parameters are basic functions of the camera. You can let your D7000 set them for you automatically, you can fine-tune how the camera applies its automatic settings, or you can make them yourself, manually. The amount of control you have over exposure, sensitivity (ISO settings), color balance, focus, and image parameters like sharpness and contrast make the D7000 a versatile tool for creating images.

In the next few pages I'm going to give you a grounding in one of those foundations, and explain the basics of exposure, either as an introduction or as a refresher course, depending on your current level of expertise. When you finish this chapter, you'll understand most of what you need to know to take well-exposed photographs creatively in a broad range of situations.

Getting a Handle on Exposure

In the most basic sense, exposure is all about light. Exposure can make or break your photo. Correct exposure brings out the detail in the areas you want to picture, providing the range of tones and colors you need to create the desired image. Poor exposure can cloak important details in shadow, or wash them out in glare-filled featureless expanses of white. However, getting the perfect exposure requires some intelligence—either that built into the camera, or the smarts in your head—because digital sensors can't capture all the tones we are able to see. If the range of tones in an image is extensive, embracing both inky black shadows and bright highlights, we often must settle for an exposure that renders most of those tones—but not all—in a way that best suits the photo we want to produce.

For example, look at two bracketed exposures presented in Figure 4.1. For the image at the left, the highlights (chiefly the clouds at upper left and the top left edge of the skyscraper) are well-exposed, but everything else in the shot is seriously underexposed. The version at the right, taken an instant later with the tripod-mounted camera, shows detail in the shadow areas of the buildings, but the highlights are completely washed out. The camera's sensor simply can't capture detail in both dark areas and bright areas in a single shot.

The solution, in this particular case, was to resort to a technique called High Dynamic Range (HDR) photography, in which the two exposures from Figure 4.1 were combined in an image editor such as Photoshop, or a specialized HDR tool like Photomatix (about $100 from www.hdrsoft.com). The resulting shot is shown in Figure 4.2. I'll explain more about HDR photography later in this chapter. For now, though, I'm going to concentrate on showing you how to get the best exposures possible without resorting to such tools, using only the features of your Nikon D7000.

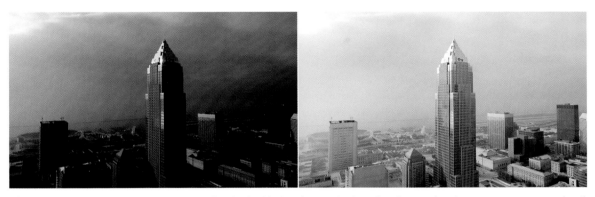

Figure 4.1 At left, the image is exposed for the highlights, losing shadow detail. At right, the exposure captures detail in the shadows, but the highlights are washed out.

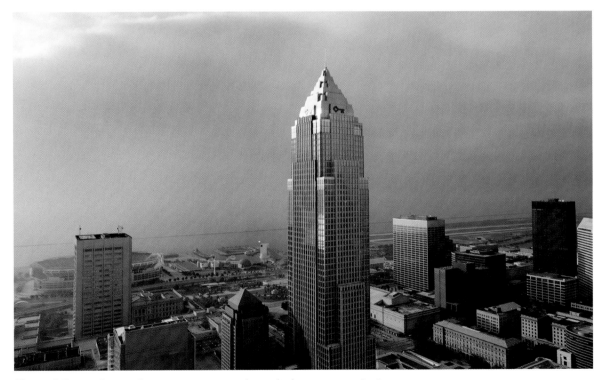

Figure 4.2 Combining the two exposures produces the best compromise image.

To understand exposure, you need to understand the six aspects of light that combine to produce an image. Start with a light source—the sun, an interior lamp, or the glow from a campfire—and trace its path to your camera, through the lens, and finally to the sensor that captures the illumination. Here's a brief review of the things within our control that affect exposure, listed in "chronological" order (that is, as the light moves from the subject to the sensor):

- **Light at its source.** Our eyes and our cameras—film or digital—are most sensitive to that portion of the electromagnetic spectrum we call *visible light*. That light has several important aspects that are relevant to photography, such as color, and harshness (which is determined primarily by the apparent size of the light source as it illuminates a subject). But, in terms of exposure, the important attribute of a light source is its *intensity*. We may have direct control over intensity, which might be the case with an interior light that can be brightened or dimmed. Or, we might have only indirect control over intensity, as with sunlight, which can be made to appear dimmer by introducing translucent light-absorbing or reflective materials in its path.

- **Light's duration.** We tend to think of most light sources as continuous. But, as you'll learn in Chapter 12, the duration of light can change quickly enough to modify the exposure, as when the main illumination in a photograph comes from an intermittent source, such as an electronic flash.

- **Light reflected, transmitted, or emitted.** Once light is produced by its source, either continuously or in a brief burst, we are able to see and photograph objects by the light that is reflected from our subjects towards the camera lens; transmitted (say, from translucent objects that are lit from behind); or emitted (by a candle or television screen). When more or less light reaches the lens from the subject, we need to adjust the exposure. This part of the equation is under our control to the extent we can increase the amount of light falling on or passing through the subject (by adding extra light sources or using reflectors), or by pumping up the light that's emitted (by increasing the brightness of the glowing object).

- **Light passed by the lens.** Not all the illumination that reaches the front of the lens makes it all the way through. Filters can remove some of the light before it enters the lens. Inside the lens barrel is a variable-sized diaphragm that produces an opening called an *aperture* that dilates and contracts to control the amount of light that enters the lens. You, or the D7000's autoexposure system, can control exposure by varying the size of the aperture. The relative size of the aperture is called the *f/stop*. (See Figure 4.3.)

- **Light passing through the shutter.** Once light passes through the lens, the amount of time the sensor receives it is determined by the D7000's shutter, which can remain open for as long as 30 seconds (or even longer if you use the Bulb setting) or as briefly as 1/8,000th second.

■ **Light captured by the sensor.** Not all the light falling onto the sensor is captured. If the number of photons reaching a particular photosite doesn't pass a set threshold, no information is recorded. Similarly, if too much light illuminates a pixel in the sensor, then the excess isn't recorded or, worse, spills over to contaminate adjacent pixels. We can modify the minimum and maximum number of pixels that contribute to image detail by adjusting the ISO setting. At higher ISOs, the incoming light is amplified to boost the effective sensitivity of the sensor.

Figure 4.3
Top row (left to right): f/2, f/2.8, f/4, f/5.6; bottom row, f/8, f/11, f/16, f/22.

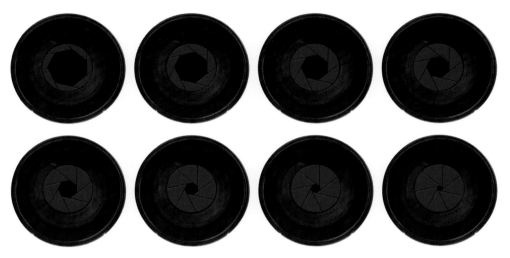

F/STOPS AND SHUTTER SPEEDS

If you're *really* new to more advanced cameras (and I realize that some ambitious amateurs do purchase the D7000 as their first digital SLR), you might need to know that the lens aperture, or f/stop, is a ratio, much like a fraction, which is why f/2 is larger than f/4, just as 1/2 is larger than 1/4. However, f/2 is actually *four times* as large as f/4. (If you remember your high-school geometry, you'll know that to double the area of a circle, you multiply its diameter by the square root of two: 1.4.)

Lenses are usually marked with intermediate f/stops that represent a size that's twice as much/half as much as the previous aperture. So, a lens might be marked: f/2, f/2.8, f/4, f/5.6, f/8, f/11, f/16, f/22, with each larger number representing an aperture that admits half as much light as the one before, as shown in Figure 4.3.

Shutter speeds are actual fractions (of a second), but the numerator is omitted, so that 60, 125, 250, 500, 1,000, and so forth represent 1/60th, 1/125th, 1/250th, 1/500th, and 1/1,000th second. To avoid confusion, Nikon uses quotation marks to signify longer exposures: 2", 2"5, 4", and so forth representing 2.0, 2.5, and 4.0-second exposures, respectively.

These four factors—quantity of light, light passed by the lens, the amount of time the shutter is open, and the sensitivity of the sensor—all work proportionately and reciprocally to produce an exposure. That is, if you double the amount of light, increase the aperture by one stop, make the shutter speed twice as long, or boost the ISO setting 2X, you'll get twice as much exposure. Similarly, you can increase any of these factors while decreasing one of the others by a similar amount to keep the same exposure.

Most commonly, exposure settings are made using the aperture and shutter speed, followed by adjusting the ISO sensitivity, if it's not possible to get the preferred exposure (that is, the one that uses the "best" f/stop or shutter speed for the depth-of-field or action stopping we want). Table 4.1 shows equivalent exposure settings using various shutter speeds and f/stops.

Table 4.1 Equivalent Exposures

Shutter speed	f/stop	Shutter speed	f/stop
1/30th second	f/22	1/1,000th second	f/4
1/60th second	f/16	1/2,000th second	f/2.8
1/125th second	f/11	1/4,000th second	f/2
1/250th second	f/8	1/8,000th second	f/1.4
1/500th second	f/5.6		

When the D7000 is set for P mode, the metering system selects the correct exposure for you automatically, but you can change quickly to an equivalent exposure by spinning the main command dial until the desired equivalent exposure combination is displayed. You can use this Flexible Program feature more easily if you remember that you need to rotate the command dial towards the left when you want to increase the amount of depth-of-field or use a slower shutter speed; rotate to the right when you want to reduce the depth-of-field or use a faster shutter speed. The need for more/less DOF and slower/faster shutter speed are the primary reasons you'd want to use Flexible Program. This program shift mode does not work when you're using flash.

In Aperture-priority (A) and Shutter-priority (S) modes, you can change to an equivalent exposure, but only by either adjusting the aperture (the camera chooses the shutter speed) or shutter speed (the camera selects the aperture). I'll cover all these exposure modes later in the chapter.

F/STOPS VERSUS STOPS

In photography parlance, *f/stop* always means the aperture or lens opening. However, for lack of a current commonly used word for one exposure increment, the term *stop* is often used. (In the past, EV served this purpose, but Exposure Value and its abbreviation have since been inextricably intertwined with its use in describing Exposure Compensation.) In this book, when I say "stop" by itself (no *f/*), I mean one whole unit of exposure, and am not necessarily referring to an actual f/stop or lens aperture. So, adjusting the exposure by "one stop" can mean both changing to the next shutter speed increment (say, from 1/125th second to 1/250th second) or the next aperture (such as f/4 to f/5.6). Similarly, 1/3 stop or 1/2 stop increments can mean either shutter speed or aperture changes, depending on the context. Be forewarned.

How the D7000 Calculates Exposure

Your D7000 calculates exposure by measuring the light that passes through the lens and is bounced up by the mirror to sensors located near the focusing surface, using a pattern you can select (more on that later) and based on the assumption that each area being measured reflects about the same amount of light as a neutral gray card that reflects a "middle" gray of about 12- to 18-percent reflectance. (The photographic "gray cards" you buy at a camera store have an 18-percent gray tone; your camera is calibrated to interpret a somewhat darker 12-percent gray; I'll explain more about this later.) That "average" 12- to 18-percent gray assumption is necessary, because different subjects reflect different amounts of light. In a photo containing, say, a white cat and a dark gray cat, the white cat might reflect five times as much light as the gray cat. An exposure based on the white cat will cause the gray cat to appear to be black, while an exposure based only on the gray cat will make the white cat washed out.

This is more easily understood if you look at some photos of subjects that are dark (they reflect little light), those that have predominantly middle tones, and subjects that are highly reflective. The next few figures show some images of actual cats (actually, the *same* cat rendered in black, gray, and white varieties through the magic of Photoshop), with each of the three strips exposed using a different cat for reference.

Correctly Exposed

The three pictures shown in Figure 4.4 represent how the black, gray, and white cats would appear if the exposure were calculated by measuring the light reflecting from the middle, gray cat, which, for the sake of illustration, we'll assume reflects approximately 12 to 18 percent of the light that strikes it. The exposure meter sees an object that it

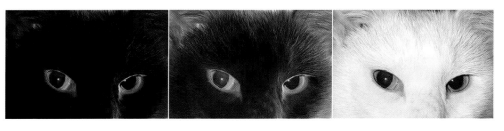

Figure 4.4
When exposure is calculated based on the middle-gray cat in the center, the black and white cats are rendered accurately, too.

thinks is a middle gray, calculates an exposure based on that, and the feline in the center of the strip is rendered at its proper tonal value. Best of all, because the resulting exposure is correct, the black cat at left and white cat at right are rendered properly as well.

When you're shooting pictures with your D7000, and the meter happens to base its exposure on a subject that averages that "ideal" middle gray, then you'll end up with similar (accurate) results. The camera's exposure algorithms are concocted to ensure this kind of result as often as possible, barring any unusual subjects (that is, those that are backlit, or have uneven illumination). The D7000 has three different metering modes (described next), plus Scene modes, each of which is equipped to handle certain types of unusual subjects, as I'll outline.

Overexposed

The strip of three images in Figure 4.5 show what would happen if the exposure were calculated based on metering the leftmost, black cat. The light meter sees less light reflecting from the black cat than it would see from a gray middle-tone subject, and so figures, "Aha! I need to add exposure to brighten this subject up to a middle gray!" That lightens the black cat, so it now appears to be gray.

But now the cat in the middle that was *originally* middle gray is overexposed and becomes light gray. And the white cat at right is now seriously overexposed, and loses detail in the highlights, which have become a featureless white.

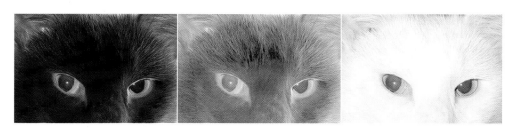

Figure 4.5
When exposure is calculated based on the black cat at the left, the black cat looks gray, the gray cat appears to be a light gray, and the white cat is seriously over-exposed.

Underexposed

The third possibility in this simplified scenario is that the light meter might measure the illumination bouncing off the white cat, and try to render that feline as a middle gray. A lot of light is reflected by the white kitty, so the exposure is *reduced*, bringing that cat closer to a middle gray tone. The cats that were originally gray and black are now rendered too dark. Clearly, measuring the gray cat—or a substitute that reflects about the same amount of light, is the only way to ensure that the exposure is precisely correct. (See Figure 4.6.)

Figure 4.6
When exposure is calculated based on the white cat on the right, the other two cats are underexposed.

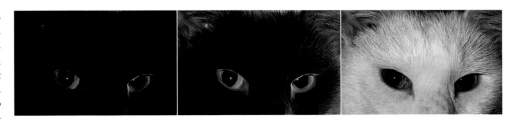

As you can see, the ideal way to measure exposure is to meter from a subject that reflects 12 to 18 percent of the light that reaches it. If you want the most precise exposure calculations, if you don't have a gray cat handy, the solution is to use a stand-in, such as the evenly illuminated gray card I mentioned earlier. But, because the standard Kodak gray card reflects 18 percent of the light that reaches it and, as I said, your camera is calibrated for a somewhat darker 12-percent tone, you would need to add about one-half stop *more* exposure than the value metered from the card.

Another substitute for a gray card is the palm of a human hand (the backside of the hand is too variable). But a human palm, regardless of ethnic group, is even brighter than a standard gray card, so instead of one-half stop more exposure, you need to add one additional stop. That is, if your meter reading is 1/500th of a second at f/11, use 1/500th second at f/8 or 1/250th second at f/11 instead. (Both exposures are equivalent.)

If you actually wanted to use a gray card, place it in your frame near your main subject, facing the camera, and with the exact same even illumination falling on it that is falling on your subject. Then, use the spot metering function (described in the next section) to calculate exposure. Of course, in most situations, it's not necessary to do this. Your camera's light meter will do a good job of calculating the right exposure, especially if you use the exposure tips in the next section. But, I felt that explaining exactly what is going on during exposure calculation would help you understand how your D7000's metering system works.

To meter properly you'll want to choose both the *metering method* (how light is evaluated) and *exposure method* (how the appropriate shutter speeds and apertures are chosen). I'll describe both in the following sections.

WHY THE GRAY CARD CONFUSION?

Why are so many photographers under the impression that cameras and meters are calibrated to the 18-percent "standard," rather than the true value, which may be 12 to 14 percent, depending on the vendor? You'll find this misinformation in an alarming number of places. I've seen the 18-percent "myth" taught in camera classes; I've found it in books, and even been given this wrong information from the technical staff of camera vendors. (They should know better—the same vendors' engineers who design and calibrate the cameras have the right figure.)

The most common explanation is that during a revision of Kodak's instructions for its gray cards in the 1970s, the advice to open up an extra half stop was omitted, and a whole generation of shooters grew up thinking that a measurement off a gray card could be used as-is. The proviso returned to the instructions by 1987, it's said, but by then it was too late. Next to me is a (c)2006 version of the instructions for KODAK Gray Cards, Publication R-27Q, and the current directions read (with a bit of paraphrasing from me in italics):

- For subjects of normal reflectance increase the indicated exposure by 1/2 stop.

- For light subjects use the indicated exposure; for very light subjects, decrease the exposure by 1/2 stop. (*That is, you're measuring a cat that's lighter than middle gray.*)

- If the subject is dark to very dark, increase the indicated exposure by 1 to 1-1/2 stops. (*You're shooting a black cat.*)

MODES, MODES, AND MORE MODES

Call them modes or methods, the Nikon D7000 seems to have a lot of different sets of options that are described using similar terms. Here's how to sort them out:

- **Metering method.** These modes determine the *parts of the image* within the 1,005-segment sensor array that are examined in order to calculate exposure. The D7000 may look at many different points within the image, segregating them by zone (Matrix metering), examine the same number of points, but give greater weight to those located in the middle of the frame (Center-weighted metering), or evaluate only a limited number of points in a limited area (Spot metering).

- **Exposure method.** These modes determine *which* settings are used to expose the image. The D7000 may adjust the shutter speed, the aperture, or both, depending on the method you choose.

Choosing a Metering Method

The D7000 has three different schemes for evaluating the light received by its exposure sensors: Matrix (with several variations, depending on what lens you have attached), Center-weighted, and Spot metering. Select the mode you want to use by holding down the Metering button and twirling the main command dial while noting the symbols shown in the top-panel LCD. Here is what you need to know about each metering method:

Matrix Metering

For its various Matrix metering modes, the D7000 slices up the frame into 2,016 different zones in an RGB (red/green/blue) array that covers most of the sensor area, shown in Figure 4.7. When Matrix metering is active, an icon appears in the monochrome status LCD (enlarged in the upper-left corner of the figure). In all cases, the D7000 evaluates the differences between the zones, and compares them with a built-in database of several hundred thousand images to make an educated guess about what kind of picture you're taking. For example, if the top sections of a picture are much lighter than the bottom portions, the algorithm can assume that the scene is a landscape photo with lots of sky. An image that includes most of the lighter portions in the center area may be a portrait. A typical image suitable for Matrix metering is shown in Figure 4.8.

The Nikon D7000 also uses information other than brightness to make its evaluation:

- **3D Color Matrix metering II.** This metering mode is used by default when the D7000 is equipped with a lens that has a type G or type D designator in its name, such as the AF-S DX Nikkor 16-85mm f/3.5-5.6G ED VR lens. The G after the f/5.6 is the giveaway. (More on lens nomenclature in Chapter 11.) The camera calculates exposure based on brightness, colors of the subject matter (that is, blue pixels in the upper part of the image are probably sky; green pixels in the lower half probably foliage), focus point, and distance information. The D7000 is able to use that additional distance data to better calculate what kind of scene you have framed. For example, if you're shooting a portrait with a longer focal-length lens focused to about 5 to 12 feet from the camera, and the upper half of the scene is very bright, the camera assumes you would prefer to meter for the rest of the image, and discount the bright area. However, if the camera has a wide-angle lens attached and is focused at infinity, the D7000 can assume you're taking a landscape photo and take the bright upper area into account to produce better looking sky and clouds.

- **Color Matrix metering II.** If you have a non-G or non-D lens equipped with a CPU chip (these are generally older lenses, although chips can sometimes be added to optics that lack them), the distance range is not used. Instead, only focus, brightness, and color information is taken into account to calculate an appropriate exposure.

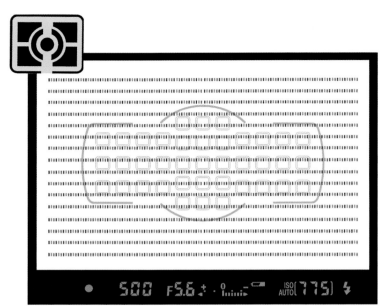

Figure 4.7
Matrix metering calculates exposure based on 2,016 points in the frame.

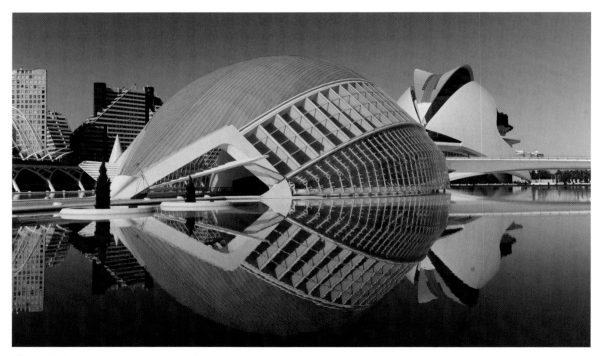

Figure 4.8 Complex scenes lend themselves to the exposure interpretation provided by Matrix metering.

- **Color Matrix metering.** If you're using a non-CPU lens (such as an older manual focus lens) and have specified the focal length and maximum aperture in the Setup menu (as described in Chapter 10), then the D7000 uses plain old color Matrix metering, which evaluates exposure based only on brightness and color information detected in the scene.

- **With other lenses.** If you don't specify focal length or maximum aperture for a non-CPU lens, the D7000 defaults to Center-weighted metering.

Matrix metering is best for most general subjects, because it is able to intelligently analyze a scene and make an excellent guess of what kind of subject you're shooting a great deal of the time. The camera can tell the difference between low-contrast and high-contrast subjects by looking at the range of differences in brightness across the scene. Because the D7000 has a fairly good idea about what kind of subject matter you are shooting, it can underexpose slightly when appropriate to preserve highlight detail when image contrast is high. (It's often possible to pull detail out of shadows that are too dark using an image editor, but once highlights are converted to white pixels, they are gone forever.)

CAUTION

If you're using a strong filter, including a polarizing filter, split-color filter, or neutral-density filter (particularly a graduated neutral-density filter), you should switch from Matrix metering to Center-weighted, because the filter can affect the relationships between the different areas of the frame used to calculate a Matrix exposure. For example, a polarizing filter produces a sky that is darker than usual, hindering the Matrix algorithm's recognition of a landscape photo. Extra dark or colored filters disturb the color relationships used for color Matrix metering, too.

Center-Weighted Metering

In this mode, the exposure meter emphasizes a zone in the center of the frame to calculate exposure, as shown in Figure 4.9. About 75 percent of the exposure is based on that central area, and the remaining exposure is based on the rest of the frame. The theory, here, is that, for most pictures, the main subject will be located in the center. So, if the D7000 reads the center portion and determines that the exposure for that region should be f/8 at 1/250th second, while the outer area, which is a bit darker, calls for f/4 at 1/125th second, the camera will give the center portion the most weight and arrive at a final exposure of f/5.6 at 1/250th second.

Center-weighting works best for portraits, architectural photos, backlit subjects with extra-bright backgrounds (such as snow or sand), and other pictures in which the most important subject is located in the middle of the frame, as in Figure 4.10. As the name

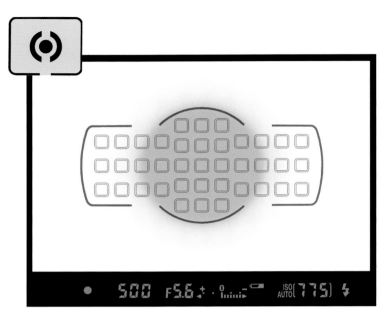

Figure 4.9
Center-weighted metering calculates exposure based on the full frame, but gives 75 percent of the weight to the center area shown; the remaining 25 percent of the exposure is determined by the rest of the image area.

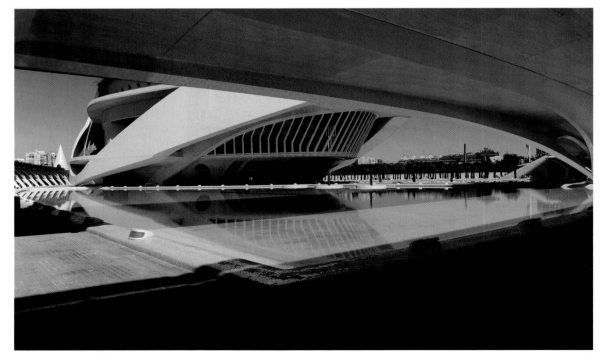

Figure 4.10 Scenes with the main subject in the center, surrounded by areas that are significantly darker or lighter, are perfect for Center-weighted metering.

suggests, the light reading is *weighted* towards the central portion, but information is also used from the rest of the frame. If your main subject is surrounded by very bright or very dark areas, the exposure might not be exactly right. However, this scheme works well in many situations if you don't want to use one of the other modes. This mode can be useful for close-ups of subjects like flowers, or for portraits. You can adjust the size of the center area assigned the greatest weight using CSM #b4, as described in Chapter 9. The available circles include 6mm, 8mm, 10mm, 13mm, and "Average" (which in effect, covers the entire screen to produce what is called Average metering).

Spot Metering

Spot metering is favored by those of us who used a hand-held light meter to measure exposure at various points (such as metering highlights and shadows separately). However, you can use Spot metering in any situation where you want to individually measure the light reflecting from light, midtone, or dark areas of your subject—or any combination of areas.

This mode confines the reading to a limited 3.5mm area in the viewfinder, making up only 2.5 percent of the image, as shown in Figure 4.11. The circle is centered on the *current focus point* (which can be *any* of the 39 focus points, *not* just the center one shown in Figure 4.11), *but is larger than the focus point*, so don't fall into the trap of believing that exposure is being measured only within the brackets that represent the active focus point. This is the only metering method you can use to tell the D7000

Figure 4.11
Spot metering calculates exposure based on a center spot that's only two 2.5 percent of the image area, centered around the current focus point.

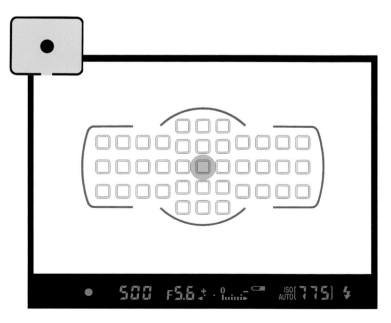

exactly where to measure exposure when using the optical viewfinder. However, if a non-CPU lens is mounted, or you have selected Auto-area AF, only the center focus point is used to spot meter.

You'll find Spot metering useful when you want to base exposure on a small area in the frame. If that area is in the center of the frame, so much the better. If not, you'll have to make your meter reading for an off-center subject using an appropriate focus point, and then lock exposure by pressing the shutter release halfway, or by pressing the AE-L/AF-L button. This mode is best for subjects where the background is significantly brighter or darker, as in Figure 4.12.

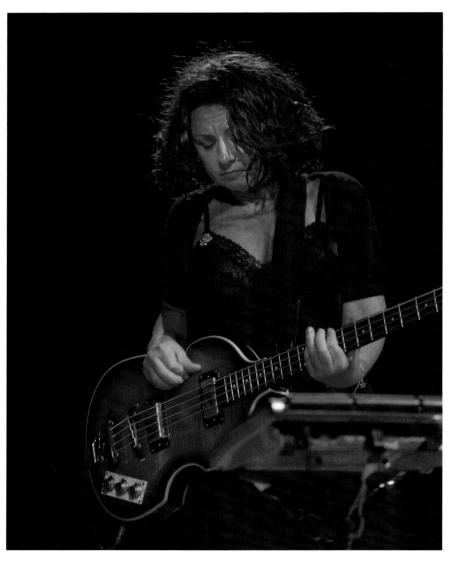

Figure 4.12
Spot metering allowed measuring exposure from this performer's face.

Choosing an Exposure Method

You'll find four methods for choosing the appropriate shutter speed and aperture, when using the semi-automatic/manual modes. (Scene modes, which use their own exposure biases, are described next.) You can choose among Program, Aperture-priority, Shutter-priority, or Manual options by rotating the mode dial on top of the camera. Your choice of which is best for a given shooting situation will depend on things like your need for lots of (or less) depth-of-field, a desire to freeze action or allow motion blur, or how much noise you find acceptable in an image. Each of the D7000's exposure methods emphasizes one aspect of image capture or another. This section introduces you to all four.

Aperture-Priority

In A mode, you specify the lens opening used, and the D7000 selects the shutter speed. Aperture-priority is especially good when you want to use a particular lens opening to achieve a desired effect. Perhaps you'd like to use the smallest f/stop possible to maximize depth-of-field in a close-up picture. Or, you might want to use a large f/stop to throw everything except your main subject out of focus, as in Figure 4.13. Maybe you'd just like to "lock in" a particular f/stop because it's the sharpest available aperture with that lens. Or, you might prefer to use, say, f/2.8 on a lens with a maximum aperture of f/1.4, because you want the best compromise between speed and sharpness.

Aperture-priority can even be used to specify a *range* of shutter speeds you want to use under varying lighting conditions, which seems almost contradictory. But think about it. You're shooting a soccer game outdoors with a telephoto lens and want a relatively high shutter speed, but you don't care if the speed changes a little should the sun duck behind a cloud. Set your D7000 to A, and adjust the aperture until a shutter speed of, say, 1/1,000th second is selected at your current ISO setting. (In bright sunlight at ISO 400, that aperture is likely to be around f/11.) Then, go ahead and shoot, knowing that your D7000 will maintain that f/11 aperture (for sufficient DOF as the soccer players move about the field), but will drop down to 1/750th or 1/500th second if necessary should the lighting change a little.

A Lo or Hi indicator in the viewfinder and the top-panel monochrome LCD indicates that the D7000 is unable to select an appropriate shutter speed at the selected aperture and that over- and underexposure will occur at the current ISO setting. That's the major pitfall of using A: you might select an f/stop that is too small or too large to allow an optimal exposure with the available shutter speeds. For example, if you choose f/2.8 as your aperture and the illumination is quite bright (say, at the beach or in snow), even your camera's fastest shutter speed might not be able to cut down the amount of light reaching the sensor to provide the right exposure. Or, if you select f/8 in a dimly lit room, you might find yourself shooting with a very slow shutter speed that can cause blurring from subject movement or camera shake. Aperture-priority is best used by those

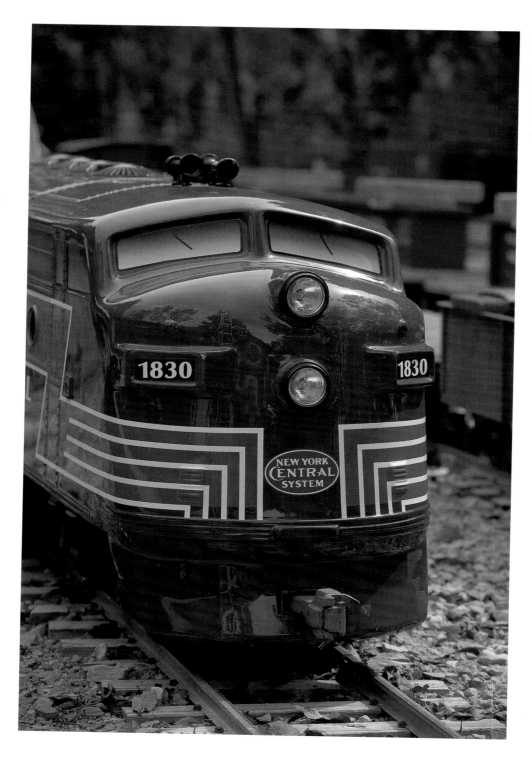

Figure 4.13
Use Aperture-priority to "lock in" a large f/stop when you want to blur the background.

with a bit of experience in choosing settings. Many seasoned photographers leave their D7000 set on A all the time. The exposure indicator scale in the status panel and viewfinder indicate the amount of under- or overexposure.

Shutter-Priority

Shutter-priority (S) is the inverse of Aperture-priority: you choose the shutter speed you'd like to use, and the camera's metering system selects the appropriate f/stop. Perhaps you're shooting action photos and you want to use the absolute fastest shutter speed available with your camera; in other cases, you might want to use a slow shutter speed to add some blur to a sports photo that would be mundane if the action were completely frozen. (See the ends of the hockey sticks in Figure 4.14.) Shutter-priority mode gives you some control over how much action-freezing capability your digital camera brings to bear in a particular situation.

You'll also encounter the same problem as with Aperture-priority when you select a shutter speed that's too long or too short for correct exposure under some conditions. I've

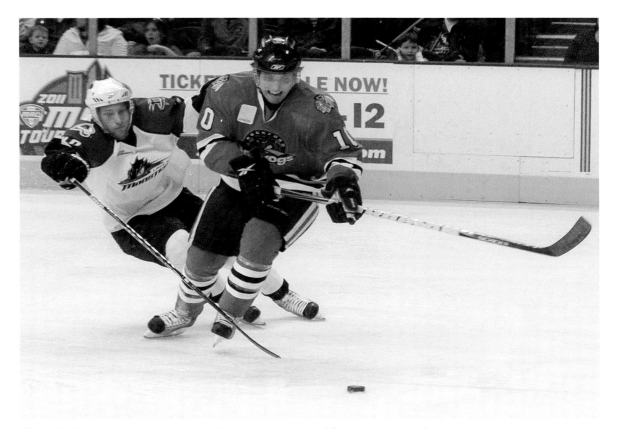

Figure 4.14 Lock the shutter at a specific speed to introduce blur into an action shot.

shot outdoor soccer games on sunny Fall evenings and used Shutter-priority mode to lock in a 1/1,000th second shutter speed, and was unable to continue when the sun dipped behind some trees and there was no longer enough light to shoot at that speed, even with the lens wide open.

Like A mode, it's possible to choose an inappropriate shutter speed. If that's the case, the displays will flash.

Program Mode

Program mode (P) uses the D7000's built-in smarts to select the correct f/stop and shutter speed using a database of picture information that tells it which combination of shutter speed and aperture will work best for a particular photo. If the correct exposure cannot be achieved at the current ISO setting, the Lo or Hi indicator in the viewfinder and monochrome LCD will appear. You can then boost or reduce the ISO to increase or decrease sensitivity.

The D7000's recommended exposure can be overridden if you want. Use the EV (exposure value) setting feature (described later, because it also applies to S and A modes) to add or subtract exposure from the metered value. And, as I mentioned earlier in this chapter, in Program mode you can rotate the main command dial to change from the recommended setting to an equivalent setting (as shown in Table 6.1) that produces the same exposure, but using a different combination of f/stop and shutter speed.

This is called "Flexible Program" by Nikon. Rotate the main command dial counter-clockwise to reduce the size of the aperture (going from, say, f/4 to f/5.6), so that the D7000 will automatically use a slower shutter speed (going from, say, 1/250th second to 1/125th second). Rotate the main command dial clockwise to use a larger f/stop,

MAKING EV CHANGES

Sometimes you'll want more or less exposure than indicated by the D7000's metering system. Perhaps you want to underexpose to create a silhouette effect, or overexpose to produce a high key look. It's easy to use the D7000's exposure compensation system to override the exposure recommendations. Press the EV button on the top of the camera (just southeast of the shutter release). Then rotate the main command dial counterclockwise to add exposure, and clockwise to subtract exposure. The EV change you've made remains for the exposures that follow, until you manually zero out the EV setting. The EV plus/minus icon appears in the viewfinder and monochrome status panel to warn you that an exposure compensation change has been entered. You can increase or decrease exposure over a range of plus or minus five stops. (If you've activated Easy Exposure Compensation using CSM #b3, as described in Chapter 9, you don't have to hold down the EV button; rotating the main or sub-command dials alone changes the EV value when using Program, Aperture-priority, Shutter-priority, or Manual exposure modes.)

while automatically producing a shorter shutter speed that provides the same equivalent exposure as metered in P mode. An asterisk appears next to the P in the monochrome LCD so you'll know you've overridden the D7000's default program setting. Your adjustment remains in force until you rotate the main command dial until the asterisk disappears, or you switch to a different exposure mode, or turn the D7000 off.

Manual Exposure

Part of being an experienced photographer comes from knowing when to rely on your D7000's automation (with P mode), when to go semiautomatic (with S or A), and when to set exposure manually (using M). Some photographers actually prefer to set their exposure manually, as the D7000 will be happy to provide an indication of when its metering system judges your manual settings provide the proper exposure, using the analog exposure scale at the bottom of the viewfinder.

Manual exposure can come in handy in some situations. You might be taking a silhouette photo and find that none of the exposure modes or EV correction features give you exactly the effect you want. Set the exposure manually to use the exact shutter speed and f/stop you need. Or, you might be working in a studio environment using multiple flash units. The additional flash are triggered by slave devices (gadgets that set off the flash when they sense the light from another flash unit, or, perhaps from a radio or infrared remote control). Your camera's exposure meter doesn't compensate for the extra illumination, so you need to set the aperture manually.

Because, depending on your proclivities, you might not need to set exposure manually very often, you should still make sure you understand how it works. Fortunately, the D7000 makes setting exposure manually very easy. Just press the mode button and rotate

METERING WITH OLDER LENSES

Older lenses that lack the CPU chip that tells the Nikon D7000 what kind of lens is mounted can be used with Aperture-priority and Manual exposure modes only, assuming you've entered the Non-CPU Lens information in the Setup menu, as described in Chapter 10. If the D7000 knows the maximum aperture of the lens, you can set the aperture using the lens's aperture ring, and, in A mode, the camera will automatically select an appropriate shutter speed. In Manual mode, you can set the aperture, and the analog exposure scale in the viewfinder will indicate when you've set the correct shutter speed manually. If a non-CPU lens is mounted and you try to set Program or Shutter-priority modes, the D7000 switches to Aperture-priority automatically. The process works because the D7000 camera body and other advanced Nikon models (from the old D200 on up through the D3x) have a mechanical linkage built into the lens mount that tells the camera when the f/stop has been changed. Less advanced Nikon digital cameras, including the D5100 and D3100, lack this linkage and cannot meter with non-CPU lenses.

the main command dial to change to Manual mode, and then turn the main command dial to set the shutter speed, and the sub-command dial to adjust the aperture. Press the shutter release halfway or press the AE lock button, and the exposure scale in the viewfinder shows you how far your chosen setting diverges from the metered exposure.

Using Scene Modes

As described in Chapter 2, the D7000 retains the "quickie" exposure modes found in Nikon's entry-level cameras (like the D5100 and D3100), but absent from the company's "pro" and "semi-pro" models. Of course, anyone who uses a D7000 for more than a day will see that it is just as advanced as many cameras (from Nikon or other vendors) that cost hundreds of dollars more. But because the D7000 is an intermediate model, it includes Scene modes.

As an avid photographer, you probably won't use Scene modes much, except when you're in a hurry to capture a grab shot and don't have time to make any decisions about what advanced exposure mode to use. You're on a beach, so you rotate the mode dial on the top left of the camera to SCENE, then use the main command dial to select Beach/Snow, and you're all set. Nothing could be easier and—surprise, surprise—you will probably end up with some nice snapshots. You don't have all the creative control you might need for a more studied image, but a grab shot that's not perfect trumps any photo you don't take because you're fiddling with settings.

Scene modes are also useful when you loan your camera to someone and don't want to explain to them how to use the D7000. Scene modes not only make decisions about basic exposure, but they select some focusing options, whether or not to use flash, and what shutter speeds/apertures are best for a particular type of subject. Nearly anyone can make the right choice based on the 19 different Scene modes (plus two Auto modes) available at the spin of the main control dial. I'll recap the descriptions of these modes that I originally provided in Chapter 2:

- **Auto.** In this mode, the D7000 makes all the exposure decisions for you, and will pop up the internal flash if necessary under low-light conditions. The camera automatically focuses on the subject closest to the camera (unless you've set the lens to manual focus), and the autofocus assist illuminator lamp on the front of the camera will light up to help the camera focus in low-light conditions.

- **Auto (Flash Off).** Identical to Auto mode, except that the flash will not pop up under any circumstances. You'd want to use this in a museum, during religious ceremonies, concerts, or any environment where flash is forbidden or distracting.

- **Portrait.** Use this mode when you're taking a portrait of a subject standing relatively close to the camera and want to de-emphasize the background, maximize sharpness, and produce flattering skin tones. The built-in flash will pop up if needed.

■ **Landscape.** Select this mode when you want extra sharpness and rich colors of distant scenes. The built-in flash and AF-assist illuminator are disabled.

■ **Child.** Use this mode to accentuate the vivid colors often found in children's clothing, and to render skin tones with a soft, natural looking texture. The D7000 focuses on the closest subject to the camera. The built-in flash will pop up if needed.

■ **Sports.** Use this mode to freeze fast moving subjects. The D7000 selects a fast shutter speed to stop action, and focuses continuously on the center focus point while you have the shutter release button pressed halfway. However, you can select one of the other two focus points to the left or right of the center by pressing the multi selector left/right buttons. The built-in electronic flash and focus assist illuminator lamp are disabled.

■ **Close-Up.** This mode is helpful when you are shooting close-up pictures of a subject from about one foot away or less, such as flowers, bugs, and small items. The D7000 focuses on the closest subject in the center of the frame, but you can use the multi selector right and left buttons to focus on a different point. Use a tripod in this mode, as exposures may be long enough to cause blurring from camera movement. The built-in flash will pop up if needed.

■ **Night Portrait.** Choose this mode when you want to illuminate a subject in the foreground with flash (it will pop up automatically, if needed), but still allow the background to be exposed properly by the available light. The camera focuses on the closest main subject. Be prepared to use a tripod or a vibration-resistant lens like the 18-55 VR kit lens to reduce the effects of camera shake. (You'll find more about VR and camera shake in Chapter 11.)

■ **Night Landscape.** Mount your camera on a tripod and use this mode for longer exposure times to produce images with more natural colors and reduced visual noise in scenes with street lights or neon signs.

■ **Party/Indoor.** For indoor scenes with typical background lighting.

■ **Beach/Snow.** Useful for bright high-contrast scenes with sand or snow.

■ **Sunset.** Emphasizes the rich colors at sunset or sunrise, disables the flash, and may use a slow shutter speed, so consider working with a tripod.

■ **Dusk/dawn.** Similar to Sunset mode, but preserves the subtle colors in the sky just after sunset, or just prior to dawn.

■ **Pet Portrait.** An "action" mode specifically for fast-moving, erratic subjects, such as pets.

■ **Candlelight.** Disables your flash to allow photographs by candle; a tripod is recommended.

- **Blossom.** Uses a small f/stop to expand depth-of-field when shooting landscapes with broad expanses of blossoms. This Scene mode may result in longer shutter speeds, so consider using a tripod.

- **Autumn colors.** Makes reds and yellows in Fall foliage richer.

- **Food.** Boosts saturation to make food look more appetizing in your snaps.

- **Silhouette.** Exposes for bright backgrounds, turning foreground objects into under-exposed silhouettes.

- **High Key.** Exposes for bright scenes with lots of highlight areas.

- **Low Key.** Tailors exposure for darker scenes, retaining murky shadows while allowing highlights to remain.

Adjusting Exposure with ISO Settings

Another way of adjusting exposures is by changing the ISO sensitivity setting. Sometimes photographers forget about this option, because the common practice is to set the ISO once for a particular shooting session (say, at ISO 200 for bright sunlight outdoors, or ISO 800 when shooting indoors) and then forget about ISO. ISOs higher than ISO 200 or 400 are seen as "bad" or "necessary evils." However, changing the ISO is a valid way of adjusting exposure settings, particularly with the Nikon D7000, which produces good results at ISO settings that create grainy, unusable pictures with some other camera models.

Indeed, I find myself using ISO adjustment as a convenient alternate way of adding or subtracting EV when shooting in Manual mode, and as a quick way of choosing equivalent exposures when in Program or Shutter-priority or Aperture-priority modes. For example, I've selected a Manual exposure with both f/stop and shutter speed suitable for my image using, say, ISO 200. I can change the exposure in 1/3 stop increments by holding down the ISO button located on the left side of the camera next to the LCD, and spinning the main command dial one click at a time. The difference in image quality/noise at ISO 200 is negligible if I dial in ISO 160 or ISO 125 to reduce exposure a little, or change to ISO 250 or 320 to increase exposure. I keep my preferred f/stop and shutter speed, but still adjust the exposure.

Or, perhaps, I am using S mode and the metered exposure at ISO 200 is 1/500th second at f/11. If I decide on the spur of the moment I'd rather use 1/500th second at f/8, I can press the ISO button and spin the main command dial three clicks counterclockwise to switch to ISO 100. Of course, it's a good idea to monitor your ISO changes, so you don't end up at ISO 6400 accidentally. An ISO indicator appears in the monochrome control panel and in the viewfinder to remind you what sensitivity setting has been dialed in.

ISO settings can, of course, also be used to boost or reduce sensitivity in particular shooting situations. The D7000 can use ISO settings from ISO 100 up to ISO 6400, plus H 1.0 and H 2.0 (ISO 12800 and 25600 equivalent). The camera can also adjust the ISO automatically as appropriate for various lighting conditions. When you choose the Auto ISO setting in the Shooting menu, as described in Chapter 8, the D7000 adjusts the sensitivity dynamically to suit the subject matter, based on minimum shutter speed and ISO limits you have prescribed. As I noted in Chapter 8, you should use Auto ISO cautiously if you don't want the D7000 to use an ISO higher than you might otherwise have selected.

Dealing with Noise

Visual image noise is that random grainy effect that some like to use as a special effect, but which, most of the time, is objectionable because it robs your image of detail even as it adds that "interesting" texture. Noise is caused by two different phenomena: high ISO settings and long exposures.

High ISO noise commonly appears when you raise your camera's sensitivity setting above ISO 400. With the Nikon D7000, noise may become visible at ISO 1600, and is often fairly noticeable at ISO 3200. At ISO 6400 and above, noise is usually quite bothersome. Nikon tips you off that ISO 12800 and 25600 may be tools used in special circumstances only by labeling them H1.0 and H2.0. You can expect noise and increase in contrast in any pictures taken at these lofty ratings. High ISO noise appears as a result of the amplification needed to increase the sensitivity of the sensor. While higher ISOs do pull details out of dark areas, they also amplify non-signal information randomly, creating noise. You'll find a High ISO NR choice in the Shooting menu, where you can specify High, Norm, or Low noise reduction, or turn the feature off entirely. Because noise reduction tends to soften the grainy look while robbing an image of detail, you may want to disable the feature if you're willing to accept a little noise in exchange for more details.

A similar noisy phenomenon occurs during long time exposures, which allow more photons to reach the sensor, increasing your ability to capture a picture under low light conditions. However, the longer exposures also increase the likelihood that some pixels will register random phantom photons, often because the longer an imager is "hot," the warmer it gets, and that heat can be mistaken for photons. There's also a special kind of noise that CMOS sensors like the one used in the D7000 are potentially susceptible to. With a CCD, the entire signal is conveyed off the chip and funneled through a single amplifier and analog-to-digital conversion circuit. Any noise introduced there is, at least, consistent. CMOS imagers, on the other hand, contain millions of individual amplifiers and A/D converters, all working in unison. Because these circuits don't necessarily all process in precisely the same way all the time, they can introduce something called fixed-pattern noise into the image data.

Fortunately, Nikon's electronics geniuses have done an exceptional job minimizing noise from all causes in the D7000. Even so, you might still want to apply the optional long exposure noise reduction that can be activated using Long Exp. NR in the Shooting menu, where the feature can be turned On or Off. This type of noise reduction involves the D7000 taking a second, blank exposure, and comparing the random pixels in that image with the photograph you just took. Pixels that coincide in the two represent noise and can safely be suppressed. This noise reduction system, called *dark frame subtraction,* effectively doubles the amount of time required to take a picture, and is used only for exposures longer than one second. Noise reduction can reduce the amount of detail in your picture, as some image information may be removed along with the noise. So, you might want to use this feature with moderation.

You can also apply noise reduction to a lesser extent using Photoshop, and when converting RAW files to some other format, using your favorite RAW converter, or an industrial-strength product like Noise Ninja (www.picturecode.com) to wipe out noise after you've already taken the picture.

Bracketing

Bracketing is a method for shooting several consecutive exposures using different settings, as a way of improving the odds that one will be exactly right. Alternatively, bracketing can be used to create a series of photos with slightly different exposures (or white balances) in anticipation that one of the exposures will be "better" from a creative standpoint. For example, bracketing can supply you with a normal exposure of a backlit subject, one that's "underexposed," producing a silhouette effect, and a third that's "overexposed" to create still another look.

Before digital cameras took over the universe, it was common to bracket exposures, shooting, say, a series of three photos at 1/125th second, but varying the f/stop from f/8 to f/11 to f/16. In practice, smaller than whole-stop increments were used for greater precision, and lenses with apertures that were set manually commonly had half-stop detents on their aperture rings, or could easily be set to a mid-way position between whole f/stops. It was just as common to keep the same aperture and vary the shutter speed, although in the days before electronic shutters, film cameras often had only whole increment shutter speeds available.

Today, cameras like the D7000 can bracket exposures much more precisely, and bracket white balance and Active D-Lighting (ADL) as well. While WB bracketing is sometimes used when getting color absolutely correct in the camera is important, and ADL bracketing allows you to have the camera adjust the contrast of difficult images as they are exposed, autoexposure bracketing (AEB) is used much more often.

When AEB is activated, the D7000 takes three consecutive photos: one at the metered "correct" exposure, one with less exposure, and one with more exposure, using an increment of your choice up to +2/–2 stops. (Choose between increments by setting Custom Function CSM #b2.) In S mode, the aperture will change, while in A mode, the shutter speed will change.

Using autoexposure bracketing is trickier than it needs to be, but you can follow these steps to get results like those shown in Figure 4.15:

1. **Choose type of bracketing.** First, select the type of bracketing you want to do, using CSM #e5, as explained in Chapter 9. You can select autoexposure and flash, autoexposure only, flash only, white balance, and ADL bracketing.

2. **Press bracketing setting button.** Press the BKT button (on the left side of the camera under the Flash button) or another button you defined as the bracketing setting button, either in CSM #f3 (Fn button) or CSM #f4 (Preview button), as described in Chapter 9.

3. **Select number of bracketed exposures.** With the setting button held down, rotate the main command dial to choose the number of shots in the sequence, either 0 (which turns bracketing off), or 2 or 3 bracketed shots. An indicator appears on the top LCD: either 3F (three shots, normal exposure, underexposure, overexposure), +2F (normal exposure, overexposure), or –2F (normal exposure, underexposure). You can change the order in which these exposures are made using CSM #e6, as described in Chapter 9.

Figure 4.15
Bracketing can give you three different exposures of the same subject.

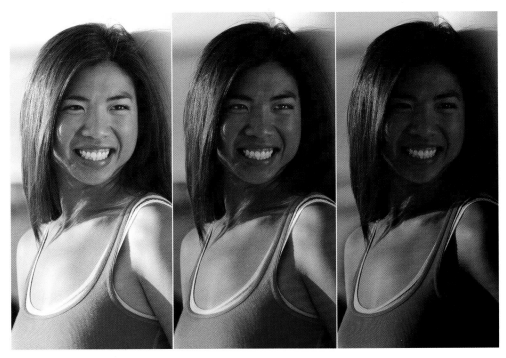

4. **Choose bracket increment.** With the setting button still held down, rotate the sub-command dial to choose the exposure increment, 0.3, 0.7, 1.0, 1.3, 1.7, or 2.0 EV (unless you've redefined the exposure compensation increment in CSM #b2). BKT will be displayed in the viewfinder and top-panel LCD.

5. **Frame and shoot.** As you take your photos, the camera will vary exposure, flash level, or white balance for each image, based on the bracketing "program" you selected, and in the order you specified in CSM #e6. In Single frame mode, you'll need to press the shutter release button the number of times you specified for the exposures in your bracketed burst (2 or 3 shots). I've found it easy to forget that I am shooting bracketed pictures, stop taking my sequence, and then wonder why the remaining pictures in my defined burst are "incorrectly" exposed. To avoid that, I often set the D7000 to one of the two continuous shooting modes, so that all my bracketed pictures are taken at once. The D7000 does provide those indicators on the monochrome LCD (a BKT indicator as well as a bracketing progress indicator), but they may be overlooked.

6. **Turn bracketing off.** When you're finished bracketing shots, remember to press the bracket setting button and rotate the main command dial until the number of shots in the sequence is 0F, and the BKT indicator is no longer displayed.

White Balance Bracketing

When you choose white balance bracketing, the D7000 does not take three different exposures. There's no need, if you think about it. The camera always takes a RAW exposure first, no matter whether the camera is set to JPEG, RAW, or RAW+JPEG. If you've selected JPEG-only mode, the camera converts the initial RAW exposure to JPEG format using the settings you've opted for in the camera, and then discards the RAW data. In RAW mode, the camera stores the RAW data as an NEF file, and also creates a Basic JPEG version of the image that is embedded in the RAW file as a thumbnail. That thumbnail is what you're actually looking at on the back-panel LCD when you review your pictures; you never actually see the RAW file itself until you import it into your image editor. Your computer may also use the embedded JPEG file, when it displays a RAW image. Finally, if you save in RAW+JPEG, you end up with two files: the NEF RAW file (with its embedded JPEG image) and a separate JPEG file at the quality level you specify (Fine, Normal, or Basic).

Since the RAW file that the camera initially captures contains all the digital information captured during exposure, when you specify white balance bracketing, the D7000 needs to take only one picture—and then save a JPEG file at each of the required white balance settings. One snap, and you get either two or three JPEG files at the quality level you specified, bracketed as you directed. Very slick. As you might guess, WB bracketing is applied only to JPEG files; you can't specify WB bracketing if you've chosen RAW or RAW+JPEG. RAW files created are always unmodified, and will be converted according to the white balance settings you opted for in the camera when the photo is imported into your image editor (if you make no white balance changes during importation).

White balance bracketing produces JPEG files that vary, not by f/stops (which is the case with exposure bracketing), but by units called *mireds* (micro reciprocal degrees) that are used to specify color temperature. You don't really need to understand mireds at all, other than to know that WB bracketing varies the color temperature of your images by 5, 10, or 15 mireds when you select increments of 1, 2, or 3, respectively. Changes are made only in the amber-blue range; bracketing isn't applied to the green-magenta color bias.

As with exposure bracketing, hold down the bracket button and spin the main command dial to select the WB program (off, two shots/amber bias, two shots/blue bias, three shots, amber/+blue bias, and the sub-command dial to choose the increment). The whole process can be a little non-intuitive, so Table 4.2 might be a help.

Table 4.2 White Balance Bracketing Programs

Rotate main command dial to select program	Rotate sub-command dial to select increment	Number of exposures saved	Bias	Bracket order
0F		WB bracketing off	N/A	N/A
b2F	1/2/3 (5/10/15 mireds)	2	Blue	None->1 increment blue
A2F	1/2/3 (5/10/15 mireds)	2	Amber	None->1 increment amber
3F	1/2/3 (5/10/15 mireds)	3	Amber /Blue	None->1 increment amber->1 increment blue

ADL Bracketing

To initiate Active D-Lighting bracketing, select it from the CSM #e5 Auto Bracketing Set menu entry. Hold the bracketing button you've specified, and rotate the main command dial to select the number of shots in the bracketing sequence: 0 (off), 2, or 3 shots. Here's how it works:

■ **0.** Active D-Lighting bracketing is disabled. Only *bracketing* is turned off. If you've turned basic Active D-Lighting on in the Shooting menu, then each shot you take will have the amount of ADL applied that you specified (Auto, Extra High, High, Normal, or Low).

■ **2.** A pair of shots will be taken, one with ADL turned off (your "control", so to speak), and a second shot with ADL applied at the setting you specified in the Shooting menu (Auto, Extra High, High, Normal, or Low). *However,* if you have turned ADL off in the Shooting menu, the D7000 will take the second shot using Auto, in effect overriding the Off setting you made. Confusing, but this provision allows you to keep ADL turned off, and then temporarily activate it in Auto mode just by selecting an ADL bracket burst.

■ **3.** Three shots will be taken in the bracket sequence, one with ADL Off, a second using Normal ADL, and a third at the High setting.

As with exposure, flash, and WB bracketing, remember to turn off ADL bracketing when you no longer want to use it.

Bracketing and Merge to HDR

While my goal in this book is to show you how to take great photos *in the camera* rather than how to fix your errors in Photoshop, the Merge to HDR (high dynamic range) feature in Adobe's flagship image editor is too cool to ignore. The ability to have a bracketed set of exposures that are identical except for exposure is key to getting good results with this Photoshop feature, which allows you to produce images with a full, rich dynamic range that includes a level of detail in the highlights and shadows that is almost impossible to achieve with digital cameras. In contrasty lighting situations, even the Nikon D7000 has a tendency to blow out highlights when you expose solely for the shadows or midtones.

Suppose you wanted to photograph a dimly lit room that had a bright window showing an outdoors scene. Proper exposure for the room might be on the order of 1/60th second at f/2.8 at ISO 200, while the outdoors scene probably would require f/11 at 1/400th second. That's almost a 7 EV step difference (approximately 7 f/stops) and well beyond the dynamic range of any digital camera, including the Nikon D7000.

When you're using Merge to HDR, you'd take two to three pictures, one for the shadows, one for the highlights, and perhaps one for the midtones. Then, you'd use the Merge to HDR command to combine all of the images into one HDR image that integrates the well-exposed sections of each version. You can use the Nikon D7000's bracketing feature to produce those images.

The images should be as identical as possible, except for exposure. So, it's a good idea to mount the D7000 on a tripod, use a remote release like the Nikon MC-DC2, and take all the exposures in one burst. Just follow these steps:

1. Mount the D7000 on a tripod and connect the remote release cable.

2. Press the bracketing setting button and rotate the sub-command dial to set the increment to 2EV. Merge to HDR works best with a significant difference in exposure between the bracketed shots; subtle changes are not better here.

3. Still holding down the bracketing setting button, rotate the main dial until the 3F setting is made. This will take a total of three exposures, one at the metered exposure, one 1 stop under, and one 1 stop over.

4. Rotate the release mode dial to one of the continuous shooting modes. This will ensure that all three bracketed shots are taken consecutively once you've triggered the shutter with the remote release.

5. Set the D7000 to S (Shutter-priority). This forces the D7000 to bracket the exposures by changing the shutter speed. You don't want the bracketed exposures to have different aperture settings, because the depth-of-field will change, perhaps enough to disturb a smooth merger of the final shots.

6. Hold down the QUAL button and choose RAW exposures. You'll need RAW files to give you the 16-bit high dynamic range images that the Merge to HDR feature processes best.

7. Manually focus or autofocus the D7000.

8. Trigger the remote release to take all the exposures in the bracketed set. Repeat if you like.

9. Copy your images to your computer and continue with the Merge to HDR steps listed next.

The next steps show you how to combine the separate exposures into one merged high dynamic range image. The sample images in Figure 4.16 show the results you can get from a three-shot bracketed sequence.

1. If you use an application to transfer the files to your computer, make sure it does not make any adjustments to brightness, contrast, or exposure. You want the real raw information for Merge to HDR to work with. If you do everything correctly, you'll end up with at least three photos like the ones shown in Figures 4.16.

2. Load the images into Photoshop using your preferred RAW converter. Make sure the 16-bits-per-channel depth is retained (don't reduce them to 8-bit files). You can load them ahead of time and save as 16-bit Photoshop PSD files, as I did for my example photos.

3. Activate Merge to HDR by choosing File > Automate > Merge to HDR Pro.

4. Select the photos to be merged, as shown in Figure 4.17, where I have specified the three 16-bit NEF files. You'll note a checkbox that can be used to automatically align the images if they were not taken with the D7000 mounted on a rock-steady support.

5. Once HDR merge has done its thing, you must save in PSD, PFM, TIFF, or EXR formats to retain the 16-bit file's floating-point data, in case you want to work with the HDR image later. Otherwise, you can convert to a normal 24-bit file and save in any compatible format.

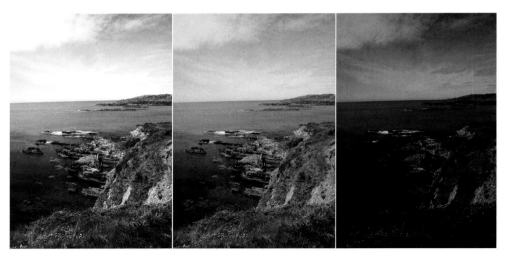

Figure 4.16
Make three
exposures for
the highlights,
midtones, and
shadow areas.

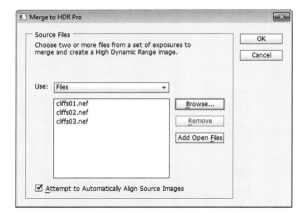

Figure 4.17
Use the Merge
to HDR com-
mand in
Photoshop to
combine the
two images.

If you do everything correctly, you'll end up with a photo like the one shown in Figure 4.18, which has the properly exposed foreground of the first shot, and the well-exposed rocks of the second and third images. Note that, ideally, nothing should move between shots. In the example pictures, the ocean waves are moving, but the exposures were made so close together that, after the merger, you can't really tell.

What if you don't have the opportunity, inclination, or skills to create several images at different exposures, as described? If you shoot in RAW format, you can still use Merge to HDR, working with a *single* original image file. What you do is import the image into Photoshop several times, using Adobe Camera Raw to create multiple copies of the file at different exposure levels.

For example, you'd create one copy that's too dark, so the shadows lose detail, but the highlights are preserved. Create another copy with the shadows intact and allow the highlights to wash out. Then, you can use Merge to HDR to combine the two and end

Figure 4.18
You'll end up with an extended dynamic range photo like this one.

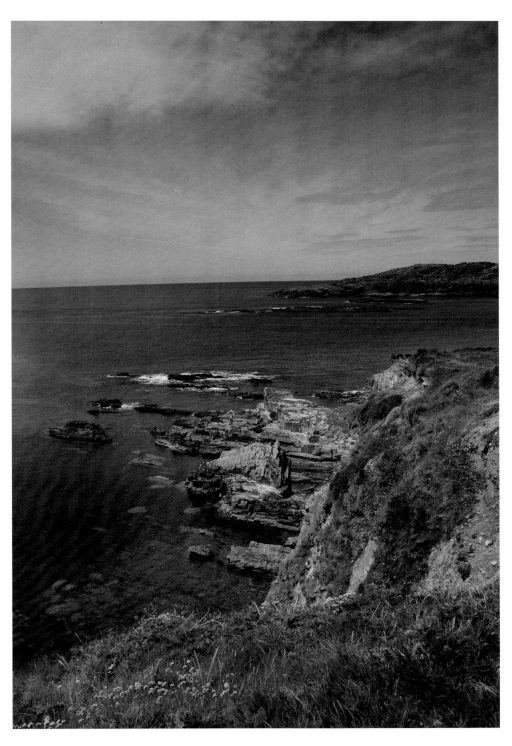

up with a finished image that has the extended dynamic range you're looking for. (This concludes the image editing portion of the chapter. We now return you to our alternate sponsor: photography.)

Fixing Exposures with Histograms

While you can often recover poorly exposed photos in your image editor, your best bet is to arrive at the correct exposure in the camera, minimizing the tweaks that you have to make in post-processing. However, you can't always judge exposure just by viewing the image on your D7000's LCD after the shot is made. Nor can you get a 100 percent accurately exposed picture by using the D7000's Live View feature. Ambient light may make the LCD difficult to see, and the brightness level you've set can affect the appearance of the playback image.

Instead, you can use a histogram, which is a chart displayed on the D7000's LCD that shows the number of tones being captured at each brightness level. You can use the information to provide correction for the next shot you take. The D7000 offers four histogram variations in three screens: three histograms that show overall brightness levels for an image and an alternate version that separates the red, green, and blue channels of your image into separate histograms.

DISPLAYING HISTOGRAMS

To view all the available histograms on your screen, you must have the D7000 set up properly. First, you'll need to mark Histograms using the Display Mode entry in the Playback menu, as described in Chapter 8. That will make the Histograms screen visible when you cycle among the informational screens while pressing the multi selector up/down buttons while an image is displayed.

The most basic histogram is displayed during playback when you press the multi selector up/down buttons to produce the Overview Data screen, as described briefly in Chapter 3, and shown in Figure 3.24. This screen provides a small histogram at the right side that displays the distribution of luminance or brightness. The most useful histogram screen is the one shown in Figure 4.19, which displays both a luminance chart and separate red, green, and blue charts.

Both luminance and RGB histograms are charts that include a representation of up to 256 vertical lines on a horizontal axis that show the number of pixels in the image at each brightness level, from 0 (black) on the left side to 255 (white) on the right. (The three-inch LCD doesn't have enough pixels to show each and every one of the 256 lines, but, instead provides a representation of the shape of the curve formed.) The more

Figure 4.19
The D7000's most complete histogram screen shows both luminance and separate red, green, and blue histograms.

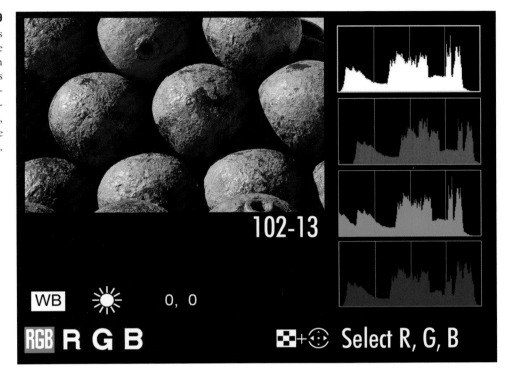

pixels at a given level, the taller the bar at that position. If no bar appears at a particular position on the scale from left to right, there are no pixels at that particular brightness level.

As you can see, a typical histogram produces a mountain-like shape, with most of the pixels bunched in the middle tones, with fewer pixels at the dark and light ends of the scale. Ideally, though, there will be at least some pixels at either extreme, so that your image has both a true black and a true white representing some details. Learn to spot histograms that represent over- and underexposure, and add or subtract exposure using an EV modification to compensate.

For example, Figure 4.20 shows the histogram (in the inset) for an image that is badly underexposed. You can guess from the shape of the histogram that many of the dark tones to the left of the graph have been clipped off. There's plenty of room on the right side for additional pixels to reside without having them become overexposed. Or, a histogram might look like the insert in Figure 4.21, which is overexposed. In either case, you can increase or decrease the exposure (either by changing the f/stop or shutter speed in Manual mode or by adding or subtracting an EV value in A or S modes) to produce the corrected histogram shown inset in Figure 4.22, in which the tones "hug" the right side of the histogram to produce as many highlight details as possible. See "Making EV Changes," above for information on dialing in exposure compensation.

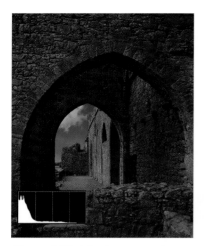

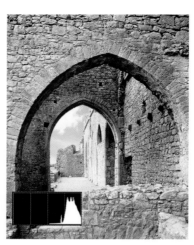

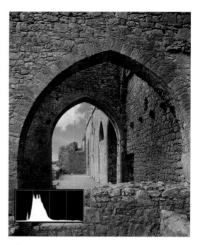

Figure 4.20 This histogram shows an underexposed image.

Figure 4.21 This histogram reveals that the image is overexposed.

Figure 4.22 A histogram for a properly exposed image should look like this.

The histogram can also be used to aid in fixing the contrast of an image, although gauging incorrect contrast is more difficult. For example, if the histogram shows all the tones bunched up in one place in the image, the photo will be low in contrast. If the tones are spread out more or less evenly, the image is probably high in contrast. In either case, your best bet may be to switch to RAW (if you're not already using that format) so you can adjust contrast in post processing. However, you can also change to a user-defined Picture Control with contrast set lower (–3 to -3) or higher (+1 to +3) as required. You'll find instructions for creating Picture Controls in Chapter 8.

One useful, but often overlooked tool in evaluating histograms is the Highlights display, which shows blown out highlights with a black blinking border for the selected active channel. Highlights can give you a better picture of what information is being lost to overexposure. By default, the Highlights display shows "blinkies" for the luminance channel, but you can separately view highlights for the red, green, and blue channels. Just follow these steps:

1. With an image displayed, and the highlights/histogram screen shown, hold down the Thumbnail/Zoom In button.

2. Press the multi selector left/right buttons to cycle among RGB (all channels), R, G, and B.

3. When a channel is framed in an orange outline, the highlight information for that channel is shown in the thumbnail image in the upper-left corner. At the bottom left of the screen, either RGB, R, G, or B will be highlighted to show the currently active channel.

In working with histograms, your goal should be to have all the tones in an image spread out between the edges, with none clipped off at the left and right sides. Underexposing (to preserve highlights) should be done only as a last resort, because retrieving the underexposed shadows in your image editor will frequently increase the noise, even if you're working with RAW files. A better course of action is to expose for the highlights, but, when the subject matter makes it practical, fill in the shadows with additional light, using reflectors, fill flash, or other techniques rather than allowing them to be seriously underexposed.

The more you work with histograms, the more useful they become. One of the first things that histogram veterans notice is that it's possible to overexpose one channel even if the overall exposure appears to be correct. For example, flower photographers soon discover that it's really, really difficult to get a good picture of a rose, like the one shown in Figure 4.23. The exposure looks okay—but there's no detail in the rose's petals. Looking at the histogram (see Figure 4.24) shows why: the red channel is blown out. If you look at the red histogram, there's a peak at the right edge that indicates that highlight information has been lost. In fact, the green channel has been blown, too, and so the green parts of the flower also lack detail. Only the blue channel's histogram is entirely contained within the boundaries of the chart, and, on first glance, the white luminance histogram at top of the column of graphs seems fairly normal.

Any of the primary channels, red, green, or blue, can blow out all by themselves, although bright reds seem to be the most common problem area. More difficult to diagnose are overexposed tones in one of the "in-between" hues on the color wheel.

Figure 4.23
It's common to lose detail in bright red flowers because the red channel becomes overexposed even when the other channels are properly exposed.

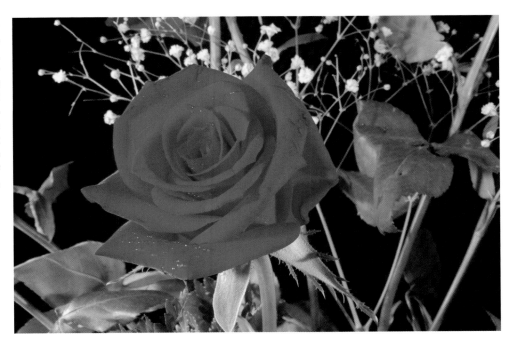

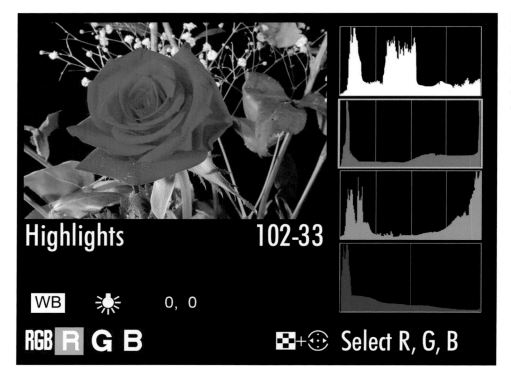

Figure 4.24
The RGB histograms show that both the red and green channels are overexposed.

Overexposed yellows (which are very common) will be shown by blowouts in *both* the red and green channels. Too-bright cyans will manifest as excessive blue and green highlights, while overexposure in the red and blue channels reduces detail in magenta colors. As you gain experience, you'll be able to see exactly how anomalies in the RGB channels translate into poor highlights and murky shadows.

The only way to correct for color channel blowouts is to reduce exposure. As I mentioned earlier, you might want to consider filling in the shadows with additional light to keep them from becoming too dark when you decrease exposure. In practice, you'll want to monitor the red channel most closely, followed by the blue channel, and slightly decrease exposure to see if that helps. Because of the way our eyes perceive color, we are more sensitive to variations in green, so green channel blowouts are less of a problem, unless your main subject is heavily colored in that hue. If you plan on photographing a frog hopping around on your front lawn, you'll want to be extra careful to preserve detail in the green channel, using bracketing or other exposure techniques outlined in this chapter.

5

Mastering Autofocus Options

One of the most useful and powerful features of modern digital SLR cameras is their ability to lock in sharp focus faster than the blink of an eye. Sometimes. Although autofocus has been with us for more than 20 years, it continues to be problematic. While vendors like Nikon are giving us faster and more precise autofocus systems, with many more options, it's common for the sheer number of options to confuse even the most advanced photographers.

One key problem is that the camera doesn't really know, for certain, what subject you want to be in sharp focus. It may select an object and lock in focus with lightning speed—even though the subject is not the one that's the center of interest of your photograph. Or, the camera may lock focus too soon, or too late. This chapter will help you choose the options available with your Nikon D7000 that will help the camera understand what you want to focus, when, and maybe even why.

How Focus Works

Although Nikon added autofocus capabilities in the 1980s, back in the day of film cameras, prior to that focusing was always done manually. Honest. Even though viewfinders were bigger and brighter than they are today, special focusing screens, magnifiers, and other gadgets were often used to help the photographer achieve correct focus. Imagine what it must have been like to focus manually under demanding, fast-moving conditions such as sports photography.

Focusing was problematic because our eyes and brains have poor memory for correct focus, which is why your eye doctor must shift back and forth between sets of lenses and ask "Does that look sharper—or was it sharper before?" in determining your correct prescription. Similarly, manual focusing involves jogging the focus ring back and forth as you go from almost in focus, to sharp focus, to almost focused again. The little clockwise and counterclockwise arcs decrease in size until you've zeroed in on the point of correct focus. What you're looking for is the image with the most contrast between the edges of elements in the image.

The camera also looks for these contrast differences among pixels to determine relative sharpness. There are two ways that sharp focus is determined: Phase Detection (used when framing your image through the optical viewfinder) and Contrast Detection (used when shooting stills and movies with Live View).

Phase Detection

The 39 autofocus sensors of Nikon's new Multi-CAM 4800DX autofocus module are located in the "floor" of the mirror box, just under the flip-up mirror, which is partially silvered so that most of the light reaching it from the lens is bounced upwards to the viewfinder, while some light is directed downward towards the focus sensors. If you lock up the mirror of your camera (using the Lock Mirror Up for Cleaning option in the Setup menu), you can see where these sensors are located. The focus zones cover an area on the center of the viewing frame, as shown in Figure 5.1.

In Phase Detection mode, the autofocus sampling area for each autofocus sensor is divided into two halves by a prism-like optical component in front of the focus sensor. The two halves are compared, much like (actually, *exactly* like) a two-window rangefinder used in surveying, weaponry—and non-SLR cameras like the venerable Leica M film models. The relative positions between the two images change as focus is moved in or out, until sharp focus is achieved when the images are "in phase," or lined up.

You can visualize how Phase Detection autofocus works if you look at Figures 5.2 and 5.3. (However, the action of your camera's actual autofocus sensors don't look *anything* like this; I'm providing a greatly simplified view just for illustration.) In Figure 5.2, a typical horizontally oriented focus sensor is looking at a series of parallel vertical lines in a weathered piece of wood. The lines are broken into two halves by the sensor's rangefinder prism, and you can see that they don't line up exactly; the image is slightly out of focus.

Fortunately, the rangefinder approach of Phase Detection tells the D7000 exactly how out of focus the image is, and in which direction (focus is too near, or too far) thanks to the amount and direction of the displacement of the split image. The camera can

Figure 5.1
The D7000's focus sensors cover an area in the center of the frame.

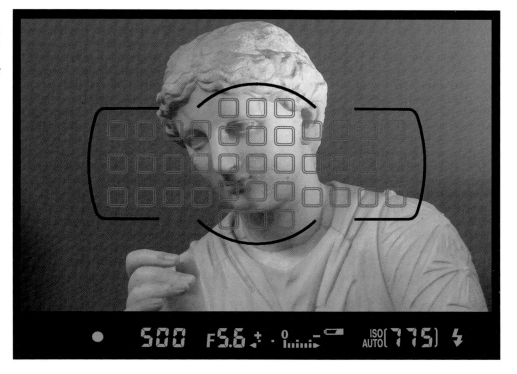

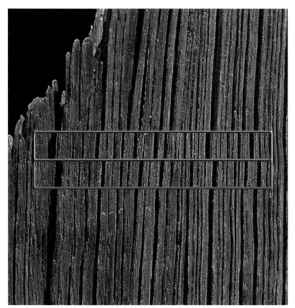

Figure 5.2 When an image is out of focus, the split lines don't align precisely.

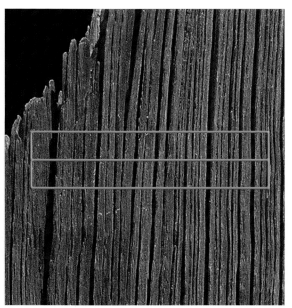

Figure 5.3 Using Phase Detection, the D7000 is able to align the features of the image and achieve sharp focus quickly.

quickly and precisely snap the image into sharp focus and line up the vertical lines, as shown in Figure 5.3. Of course, this scenario—vertical lines being interpreted by a horizontally oriented sensor—is ideal. When the same sensor is asked to measure focus for, say, horizontal lines that don't split up quite so conveniently, or, in the worst case, subjects such as the sky (which may have neither vertical nor horizontal lines), focus can slow down drastically, or even become impossible.

Phase Detection is the normal mode used by the D7000. As with any rangefinder-like function, accuracy is better when the "base length" between the two images is larger. (Think back to your high-school trigonometry; you could calculate a distance more accurately when the separation between the two points where the angles were measured was greater.) For that reason, Phase Detection autofocus is more accurate with larger (wider) lens openings—especially those with maximum f/stops of f/2.8 or better—than with smaller lens openings, and may not work at all when the f/stop is smaller than f/5.6. As I noted, the D7000 is able to perform these comparisons very quickly.

Improved Cross-Type Focus Point

One improvement that Nikon D7000 owners sometimes overlook is the upgrade to a cross-type focus point at 9 of the 39 center positions. Why is this important? It helps to take a closer look at the Phase Detection system when presented with a non-ideal subject.

Figure 5.4 shows the same weathered wood pictured earlier, except in this case we've chosen to rotate the camera 90 degrees (say, because we want a vertically oriented composition). In the illustration, the image within the focus sensor's area is split in two and displaced slightly side-to-side, but the amount and direction of the misalignment is far from obvious. A horizontally oriented focus sensor will be forced to look for less obvious vertical lines to match up. Our best-case subject has been transformed into a worst--case subject for a horizontal focus sensor.

The value of the cross-type focus sensor, which can interpret contrast in both horizontal and vertical directions, can be seen in Figure 5.5. The horizontal lines are still giving the horizontal portion of the cross sensor fits, but the vertical bar can easily split and align the subject to achieve optimum focus. Cross-type sensors can handle horizontal and vertical lines with equal aplomb and, if you think about it, lines at any diagonal angle as well. In lower light levels, with subjects that were moving, or with subjects that have no pattern and less contrast to begin with, the cross-type sensor not only works faster but can focus subjects that a horizontal- or vertical-only sensor can't handle at all.

So, you can see that having a center cross-type focus sensor that is extra-sensitive with faster lenses is a definite advantage. The location of the D7000's cross-type focus sensors is shown in Figure 5.6.

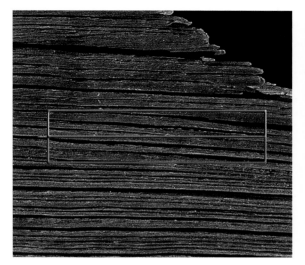

Figure 5.4 A horizontal focus censor doesn't handle horizontal lines very well.

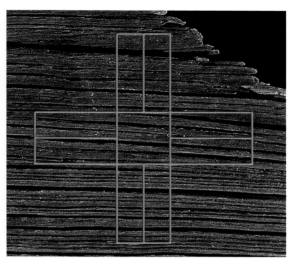

Figure 5.5 Cross-type sensors can evaluate contrast in both horizontal and vertical directions, as well as diagonally.

Figure 5.6
The D7000's cross-type sensors are located in the middle of the frame.

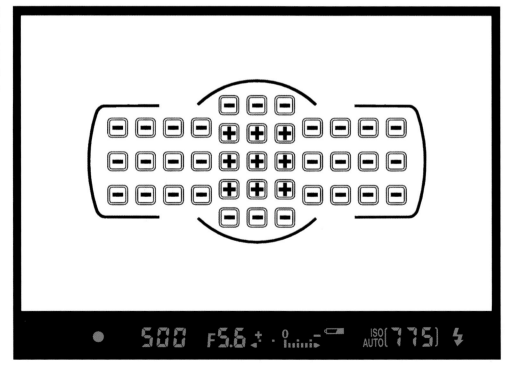

Contrast Detection

This is a slower mode, suitable for static subjects, and used by the D7000 in Live View and Movie modes. It's a bit easier to understand, and is illustrated by Figure 5.7. At top in the figure, the transitions between the edges found in the image are soft and blurred because of the low contrast between them. Although the illustration uses the same vertical lines used with the Phase Detection example, the orientation of the features doesn't matter. The focus system looks only for contrast between edges, and those edges can run in any direction.

At the bottom of Figure 5.7, the image has been brought into sharp focus, and the edges have much more contrast; the transitions are sharp and clear. Although this example is a bit exaggerated so you can see the results on the printed page, it's easy to understand that when maximum contrast in a subject is achieved, it can be deemed to be in sharp focus. Although achieving focus with Contrast Detection is generally quite a bit slower, there are several advantages to this method:

- **Works with more image types.** Contrast Detection doesn't require subject matter rotated 90 degrees from the sensor's orientation to operate optimally. Any subject that has edges will work.

- **Focus on any point.** While Phase Detection focus can be achieved *only* at the points that fall under one of the nine autofocus sensors, with Contrast Detection, any portion of the image can be used. Focus is achieved with the actual sensor image, so focus point selection is simply a matter of choosing which part of the sensor image to use. As you'll learn in Chapter 6, you can move the focus frame around on the screen when working with Live View.

- **Potentially more accurate.** Phase Detection can fall prey to the vagaries of uncooperative subject matter: if suitable lines aren't available, the system may have to hunt for focus or achieve less than optimal focus. Contrast Detection is more clearcut. The camera can clearly see when the highest contrast has been achieved, as long as there is sufficient light to allow the camera to examine the image produced by the sensor. (The focus assist lamp can help when shooting subjects close enough to the camera for the focus assist illumination to provide extra contrast.)

The D7000's autofocus mechanism, like all such systems found in SLR cameras, evaluates the degree of focus, but, unlike the human eye, it is able to remember the progression perfectly, so that autofocus can lock in much more quickly and, with an image that has sufficient contrast, more precisely. Unfortunately, while the D7000's focus system finds it easy to measure degrees of apparent focus at each of the focus points in the viewfinder, it doesn't really know with any certainty *which* object should be in sharpest focus. Is it the closest object? The subject in the center? Something lurking *behind* the closest subject? A person standing over at the side of the picture? Many of the techniques for using autofocus effectively involve telling the Nikon D7000 exactly what it should

Figure 5.7
Focus in Contrast Detection mode evaluates the increase in contrast in the edges of subjects, starting with a blurry image (top) and producing a sharp, contrasty image (bottom).

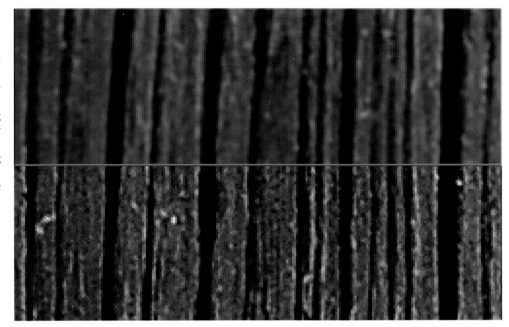

be focusing on, by choosing a focus zone or by allowing the camera to choose a focus zone for you. I'll address that topic shortly.

As the camera collects focus information from the sensors, it then evaluates it to determine whether the desired sharp focus has been achieved. The calculations may include whether the subject is moving, and whether the camera needs to "predict" where the subject will be when the shutter release button is fully depressed and the picture is taken. The speed with which the camera is able to evaluate focus and then move the lens elements into the proper position to achieve the sharpest focus determines how fast the autofocus mechanism is. Although your D7000 will almost always focus more quickly than a human, there are types of shooting situations where that's not fast enough. For example, if you're having problems shooting sports because the D7000's autofocus system manically follows each moving subject, a better choice might be to switch Autofocus modes or shift into Manual and prefocus on a spot where you anticipate the action will be, such as a goal line or soccer net.

Adding Circles of Confusion

But there are other factors in play, as well. You know that increased depth-of-field brings more of your subject into focus. But more depth-of-field also makes autofocusing (or manual focusing) more difficult because the contrast is lower between objects at different distances. So, autofocus with a 200mm lens (or zoom setting) may be easier than at a 28mm focal length (or zoom setting) because the longer lens has less apparent depth-of-field. By the same token, a lens with a maximum aperture of f/1.8 will be easier to autofocus (or manually focus) than one of the same focal length with an f/4 maximum aperture, because the f/4 lens has more depth-of-field *and* a dimmer view. That's why lenses with a maximum aperture smaller than f/5.6 can give your D7000's autofocus system fits.

To make things even more complicated, many subjects aren't polite enough to remain still. They move around in the frame, so that even if the D7000 is sharply focused on your main subject, it may change position and require refocusing. An intervening subject may pop into the frame and pass between you and the subject you meant to photograph. You (or the D7000) have to decide whether to lock focus on this new subject, or remain focused on the original subject. Finally, there are some kinds of subjects that are difficult to bring into sharp focus because they lack enough contrast to allow the D7000's AF system (or our eyes) to lock in. Blank walls, a clear blue sky, or other subject matter may make focusing difficult.

If you find all these focus factors confusing, you're on the right track. Focus is, in fact, measured using something called a *circle of confusion*. An ideal image consists of zillions of tiny little points, which, like all points, theoretically have no height or width. There is perfect contrast between the point and its surroundings. You can think of each point as a pinpoint of light in a darkened room. When a given point is out of focus, its edges decrease in contrast and it changes from a perfect point to a tiny disc with blurry edges (remember, blur is the lack of contrast between boundaries in an image). (See Figure 5.8.)

If this blurry disc—the circle of confusion—is small enough, our eye still perceives it as a point. It's only when the disc grows large enough that we can see it as a blur rather than a sharp point that a given point is viewed as out of focus. You can see, then, that enlarging an image, either by displaying it larger on your computer monitor or by making a large print, also enlarges the size of each circle of confusion. Moving closer to the image does the same thing. So, parts of an image that may look perfectly sharp in a

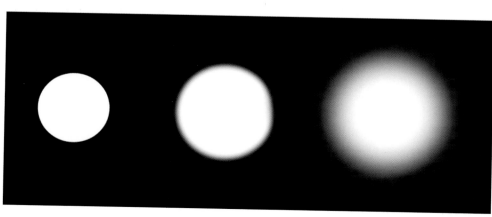

Figure 5.8
When a pinpoint of light (left) goes out of focus, its blurry edges form a circle of confusion (center and right).

5 × 7-inch print viewed at arm's length, might appear blurry when blown up to 11 × 14 and examined at the same distance. Take a few steps back, however, and it may look sharp again.

To a lesser extent, the viewer also affects the apparent size of these circles of confusion. Some people see details better at a given distance and may perceive smaller circles of confusion than someone standing next to them. For the most part, however, such differences are small. Truly blurry images will look blurry to just about everyone under the same conditions.

Technically, there is just one plane within your picture area, parallel to the back of the camera (or sensor, in the case of a digital camera), that is in sharp focus. That's the plane in which the points of the image are rendered as precise points. At every other plane in front of or behind the focus plane, the points show up as discs that range from slightly blurry to extremely blurry (see Figure 5.9). In practice, the discs in many of these planes will still be so small that we see them as points, and that's where we get depth-of-field. Depth-of-field is just the range of planes that include discs that we perceive as points rather than blurred splotches. The size of this range increases as the aperture is reduced in size and is allocated roughly one-third in front of the plane of sharpest focus, and two-thirds behind it. The range of sharp focus is always greater behind your subject than in front of it.

Figure 5.9
Only the blossoms in the foreground are in focus—the area behind them appears blurry because the depth-of-field is limited.

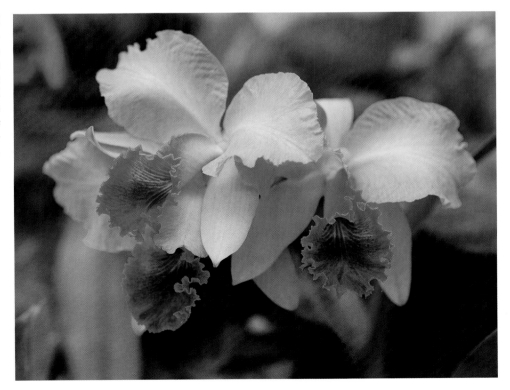

Using Autofocus with the Nikon D7000

Autofocus can sometimes be frustrating for the new digital SLR photographer, especially those coming from the point-and-shoot world. That's because correct focus plays a greater role among your creative options with a dSLR, even when photographing the same subjects. Most non-dSLR digital cameras have sensors that are much tinier than the sensor in the D7000. Those smaller sensors require shorter focal lengths, which have, effectively, more depth-of-field.

The bottom line is that with the average point-and-shoot camera, *everything* is in focus from about one foot to infinity and at virtually every f/stop. Unless you're shooting close-up photos a few inches from the camera, the depth-of-field is prodigious, and autofocus is almost a non-factor. The D7000, on the other hand, uses longer focal length lenses to achieve the same field of view with its larger sensor, so there is less depth-of-field. That's a *good* thing, creatively, because you have the choice to use selective focus to isolate subjects. But it does make the correct use of autofocus more critical. To maintain the most creative control, you have to choose three attributes:

- **How much is in focus.** Generally, by choosing the f/stop used, you'll determine the *range* of sharpness/amount of depth-of-field. The larger the DOF, the "easier" it is for the autofocus system's locked-in focus point to be appropriate (even though, strictly speaking, there is only one actual plane of sharp focus). With less depth-of-field, the accuracy of the focus point becomes more critical, because even a small error will result in an out-of-focus shot.

- **What subject is in focus.** The portion of your subject that is zeroed in for autofocus is determined by the autofocus zone that is active, and which is chosen either by you or by the Nikon D7000 (as described next). For example, when shooting portraits, it's actually okay for part of the subject—or even part of the subject's face—to be slightly out of focus as long as the eyes (or even just the *nearest* eye) appear sharp.

- **When focus is applied.** For static shots of objects that aren't moving, *when* focus is applied doesn't matter much. But when you're shooting sports, or birds in flight, or children, the subject may move within the viewfinder as you're framing the image. Whether that movement is across the frame or headed right towards you, timing the instant when autofocus is applied can be important.

Autofocus Simplifies Our Lives... Doesn't It?

Manual focus is tricky, requires judgment, and fast reflexes. So, we're all better off now that autofocus has become almost universal, right? On the one hand, AF does save time and allows us to capture subjects (particularly fast-moving sports) that are difficult to image sharply using manual focusing (unless you have training and know certain techniques). On the other hand, learning to apply the Nikon D7000's autofocus system most effectively requires a bit of study and some practice. Then, once you're comfortable with autofocus, you'll know when it's appropriate to use the manual focus option, too.

The important thing to remember is that focus isn't absolute. For example, some things that look in sharp focus at a given viewing size and distance might not be in focus at a larger size and/or closer distance. In addition, the goal of optimum focus isn't always to make things look sharp. Not all of an image will be or should be sharp. Controlling exactly what is sharp and what is not is part of your creative palette. Use of depth-of-field characteristics to throw part of an image out of focus while other parts are sharply focused is one of the most valuable tools available to a photographer. But selective focus works only when the desired areas of an image are in focus properly. For the digital SLR photographer, correct focus can be one of the trickiest parts of the technical and creative process.

The D7000 now uses Nikon's new 39-zone Multi-CAM 4800DX autofocus system, similar in many ways to the 51-zone system used in the company's higher-end cameras. The D7000's DX AF sensor actually covers a larger percentage of the frame than Nikon's full-frame cameras, which have their sensors more concentrated in the center of the frame. That's actually an advantage for D7000 owners; there is less chance that an important subject will fall outside the larger focus area.

As mentioned previously, the D7000 deploys an intelligent array of 9 cross-type sensors and 30 horizontal sensors in the viewing system. All 39 autofocus sensors can be used individually or in groups of 9, 21, or all 39 focus zones. The AF system uses the color and light values found in the focus zone array to accurately track moving objects, and to classify subjects into what Nikon calls a "scene recognition system." The new autofocus system uses a separate sensor in the viewing system to measure the focus of the image. That's Nikon's autofocus system in a nutshell.

Like all camera autofocus sensors, those in your D7000 require a minimum amount of light as well as a minimum aperture size to operate, which is why autofocus capabilities are possible only with lenses having an f/5.6 or larger maximum aperture. While there's not a lot you can do to "fix" a lens that has a maximum aperture that's too small, if your subject's focus is difficult to evaluate because of waning light levels, the AF assist beam built into the D7000 (usually of minimal aid because it is relatively weak) and the assist beams of Nikon's dedicated flash units provide additional light that helps assure enough illumination for autofocus under some circumstances.

Bringing the Multi-CAM 4800DX AF System into Focus

I've explained individual bits and pieces of the Nikon D7000's autofocus system earlier in this book, particularly in the "roadmap" sections that showed you where all the controls were located, and the "setup" chapters that explained the key autofocus options. Now it's time to round out the coverage as we tie everything together. There are three aspects of autofocus that you need to understand to use this essential feature productively. They apply—in slightly different ways—to both autofocus when using the optical viewfinder, and in Live View. In this chapter, I'm going to emphasize the optical viewfinder/Phase Detection system, and explore autofocus in Live View in more detail in Chapter 6.

- **Autofocus point selection.** This aspect controls how the D7000 selects which areas of the frame are used to evaluate focus. Point selection allows the camera (or you) to specify a subject and lock focus in on that subject.

- **Autofocus mode and priority.** This governs *when* during the framing and shooting process autofocus is achieved. Should the camera focus once when activated, or continue to monitor your subject and refocus should the subject move? Is it okay to take a picture even if sharp focus isn't yet achieved, or should the camera lock out the shutter release until the image is sharp?

- **Autofocus activation.** When should the autofocus process begin, and when should it be locked? This aspect is related to the autofocus mode, but uses controls that you can specify to activate and/or lock the autofocus process.

Autofocus Point Selection Overview

I'm discussing this aspect of autofocus first, because, in many ways, it is the most important. If your D7000 isn't focusing on the correct subject, autofocus speed and activation are pretty much wasted effort. As you've learned, the D7000 has up to 39 different points on the screen that can be individually selected by you or the camera as the active focus zone.

The number and type of autofocus sensors in use can affect how well the system operates. The focus sensors can consist of lines of pixels, cross-shapes, and/or a mixture of these types within a single camera, as with the D7000. The more AF points available, the more easily the camera can differentiate among areas of the frame, and the more precisely you can specify the area you want to be in focus if you're manually choosing a focus spot.

But, there's another side of the coin. There is such a thing as *too many* focus zones for some types of subjects. For example, when using 39 focus points to select a zone for large, evenly illuminated subjects, you can waste a lot of time thumbing the multi

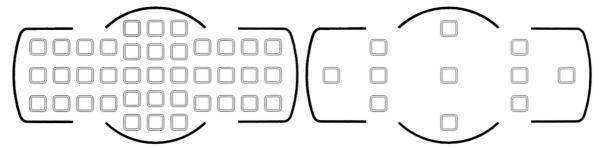

Figure 5.10 The D7000 can use a dense set of 39 focus points (left), or a wider array of 11 points (right).

selector among the three-dozen (plus) focus points. That's why CSM #a6 lets you switch the D7000 to a more widely spaced set of 11 focus zones that you can select quickly. (Learn how to do that in Chapter 9.) Figure 5.10 shows the distribution of the active focus points when in 39-point mode (left) or 11-point mode (right).

As the camera collects contrast information from the sensors, it then evaluates the data to determine whether the desired sharp focus has been achieved. The calculations may include whether the subject is moving, and whether the camera needs to "predict" where the subject will be when the shutter release button is fully depressed and the picture is taken. (Predictive focus tracking kicks in when the camera is set to AF-C continuous autofocus, or when you're using AF-A and the D7000 shifts from AF-S to AF-C. I'll explain these modes in more detail in the next section.)

The speed with which the camera is able to evaluate focus and then move the lens elements into the proper position to achieve the sharpest focus determines how fast the autofocus mechanism is. Although your D7000 will almost always focus more quickly than a human, there are types of shooting situations where that's not fast enough. For example, if you're having problems shooting sports because the D7000's autofocus system manically follows each moving subject, a better choice might be to switch autofocus modes or shift into manual and prefocus on a spot where you anticipate the action will be, such as a goal line or soccer net. At night football games, for example, when I am shooting with a telephoto lens almost wide open, I often focus manually on one of the referees who happens to be standing where I expect the action to be taking place (say, a halfback run or a pass reception). I also use *trap focus*, which is a technique discussed in a sidebar later in this chapter.

Choosing Autofocus Point Selection Mode

The D7000 has only three different focus point selection modes. I'm going to describe each of the three modes, and explain how to use them. You can set any of the three point selection modes: hold down the center button of the focus mode selector switch on the front of the camera (under the lens release button) to the AF position. Then, hold down

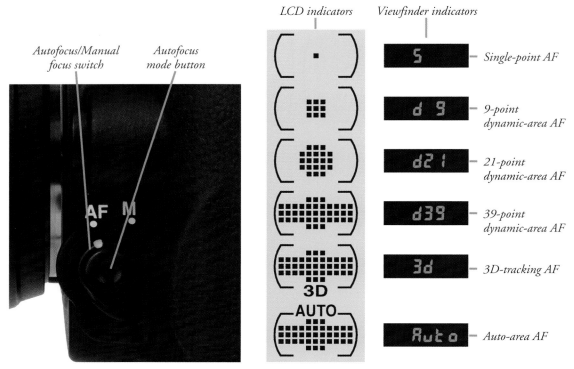

Figure 5.11 Autofocus mode selector switch is used to choose autofocus settings.

Figure 5.12 Autofocus point selection modes.

the button in the center of that switch (seen in Figure 5.11) and rotate the sub-command dial. The selected AF mode will appear in the viewfinder briefly as you make your selection, and on top of the camera in the monochrome LCD panel. It will also be shown on the back-panel LCD when the shooting settings screen is active. (See Figure 5.12.)

Single-Point AF

In this mode, you always select the focus point manually, using the multi selector button (which, helpfully, will respond to your thumb-presses not only in the left/right and up/down directions, but diagonally, as well). The D7000 evaluates focus based solely on the point you select, making this a good choice for subjects that don't move much. As I mentioned earlier, you can use CSM #a6 to choose whether the selected focus point resides in an 11-point widely spaced distribution, or within the full 39-point array. In either Single-point AF or Dynamic AF, if you want to lock the focus point you've selected for a series of shots, rotate the focus selector lock lever back to the L position. You can also temporarily lock the focus point by partially depressing the shutter release, or pressing the AE-L/AF-L button (unless you've redefined this behavior to some other controls in the Custom Settings menu).

Dynamic-Area AF

In this mode, you still select the focus point yourself using the multi selector button, and when using Single-servo autofocus (AF-S, discussed later), the D7000 will evaluate focus solely based on that point. In that respect, the D7000 behaves exactly as it does in Single-point AF mode. However, if you have chosen Continuous-servo autofocus (AF-C) or are using Automatic autofocus (AF-A) and the camera shifts from AF-S to AF-C, the D7000's "smarts" spring to life if your subject leaves the selected focus zone. When that happens, the camera re-evaluates focus based on the other focus points surrounding the one you chose. To recap, you can set the D7000 so that it will use 9, 21, or 39 points. You can view what pattern is currently being used by pressing the Info button and viewing the autofocus array representation in the screen that pops up.

- **9 points.** Only eight surrounding focus points will be used, allowing the D7000 to respond quickly to subjects that are moving in a predictable way.

- **21 points.** Should the subject leave the selected focus point, the D7000 will refocus based on information from 20 surrounding focus points. This mode is best for subjects that are moving erratically. Autofocus may take slightly longer because more points are considered. I prefer this mode most of the time.

Note

The active focus points surrounding the red highlighted focus zone will shift around the array as you move the manually chosen focus point. The highlighting applies to the 9-point and 21-point options *only* when the center point is selected as the active focus point.

- **39 points.** Should the subject leave your selected focus point, the camera will refocus based on information from all surrounding focus points, which may be best for fast moving subjects.

3D-tracking

All 39 points are used, and you can select the focus point as described for the other modes. Should the subject leave your selected focus zone, the D7000 uses distance information to calculate the path of the subject and select a new focus point. Nikon recommends using this setting to focus subjects that move erratically from side to side, because the camera can use the distance information to differentiate the original subject from objects that are closer or farther away. Tracking will abort if your subject leaves the viewfinder entirely; in that case, release the shutter button and reframe your image with your subject in the selected focus point.

Automatic-Area AF

In this mode, autofocus point selection is out of your hands; the D7000 performs the task for you using its own intelligence. If you are using a type G or D lens, the camera can even work with the supplied distance information to distinguish humans from their background, so a person standing at the side of the frame will be detected and used to evaluate focus, while the camera ignores the background area in the frame.

The D7000 tends to keep the active focus point somewhat of a mystery (although it will be displayed during picture review if you've activated that option). In AF-S mode, the active focus point is highlighted in the viewfinder for about one second after focus is achieved. In AF-C mode, the active focus point is not shown.

Autofocus Mode and Priority

Choosing the right autofocus mode (AF-S, AF-C, or Manual) is another key to focusing success. To save battery power, your D7000 doesn't start to focus the lens until you partially depress the shutter release or press the AE-L/AF-L button on the back of the camera or on the MB-D11 battery pack/grip (unless you've reprogrammed the button for some other function or have specified another control to activate autofocus, as described in Chapter 9). But, autofocus isn't some mindless beast out there snapping your pictures in and out of focus with no feedback from you after you press that button. There are several settings you can modify that return at least a modicum of control to you. Your first decision should be whether you set the D7000 to AF-S, AF-C, or Manual.

You can set any of the three modes, with the AF mode switch in the AF position, hold down the center button of the focus mode selector switch on the front of the camera (under the lens release button, and seen in Figure 5.11) and rotate the main command dial. The selected AF mode will appear in the viewfinder briefly as you make your selection, and on top of the camera in the monochrome LCD panel. It will also be shown on the back-panel LCD when the shooting settings screen is active.

Autofocus Mode

This choice determines *when* your D7000 starts to autofocus, and what it does when focus is achieved. Automatic focus is not something that happens all the time when your camera is turned on. To save battery power, your D7000 generally doesn't start to focus the lens until you partially depress the shutter release. (You can also use the AE/AL Lock button to start autofocus, as described in Chapter 9.)

Single-Servo Autofocus (AF-S)

In this mode, also called *AF-S*, focus is set once and remains at that setting until the button is fully depressed, taking the picture, or until you release the shutter button without taking a shot. For non-action photography, this setting is usually your best choice, as it minimizes out-of-focus pictures (at the expense of spontaneity). The drawback here is that you might not be able to take a picture at all while the camera is seeking focus; you're locked out until the autofocus mechanism is happy with the current setting. As described in Chapter 9, you can set AF-S mode to use either focus priority (the default) or release priority using CSM #a2.

When sharp focus is achieved, the selected focus point will flash red in the viewfinder, and the focus confirmation light at the lower left will flash green. If you're using Matrix metering, the exposure will be locked at the same time. By keeping the shutter button depressed halfway, you'll find you can reframe the image while retaining the focus (and exposure) that's been set. You can also use the AE-L/AF-L button, as described in Chapter 9, if you've set that button to lock focus when pressed. Because of the small delay while the camera zeroes in on correct focus, you might experience slightly more shutter lag. This mode uses less battery power.

Continuous-Servo Autofocus (AF-C)

This mode, also known as *AF-C* is the mode to use for sports and other fast-moving subjects. In this mode, once the shutter release is partially depressed, the camera sets the focus but continues to monitor the subject, so that if it moves or you move, the lens will be refocused to suit. Focus and exposure aren't really locked until you press the shutter release down all the way to take the picture. You'll find that AF-C produces the least amount of shutter lag of any autofocus mode when set to release priority: press the button and the camera fires. It also uses the most battery power, because the autofocus system operates as long as the shutter release button is partially depressed.

Continuous-servo autofocus uses a technology called *predictive tracking AF*, which allows the D7000 to calculate the correct focus if the subject is moving toward or away from the camera at a constant rate. (Automatic autofocus, AF-A, described next, also uses predictive tracking when operating in AF-C mode.) It uses either the automatically selected AF point or the point you select manually to set focus. As described in Chapter 9, you can set AF-C mode to use release priority (the default), or focus priority using CSM #a1.

If you want to lock the focus point you've selected for a series of shots, rotate the focus selector lock lever up to the L position. You can also temporarily lock the focus point by partially depressing the shutter release, or pressing the AE-L/AF-L button (unless you've redefined this behavior to some other controls in the Custom Settings menu).

Automatic Autofocus (AF-A)

This setting is actually a combination of the first two. When selected, the camera focuses using AF-S and locks in the focus setting. But, if the subject begins moving, it will switch automatically to AF-C and change the focus to keep the subject sharp. AF-A is a good choice when you're shooting a mixture of action pictures and less dynamic shots and want to use AF-S when possible. The camera will default to that mode, yet switch automatically to AF-C when it would be useful for subjects that might begin moving unexpectedly. However, as with AF-S, the shutter can be released only when the subject at the selected focus point is in focus.

Manual Focus

With manual focus activated by sliding the switch on the lens to the M position, or the rotating switch on the camera body near the lens mount set to M, your D7000 lets you set the focus yourself. (Both the camera and lens settings must agree if you want to use an autofocus mode; when either is set to Manual, then only manual focus is possible.) There are some advantages and disadvantages to this approach. While your batteries will last longer in manual focus mode, it will take you longer to focus the camera for each photo, a process that can be difficult. Modern digital cameras, even dSLRs, depend so much on autofocus that the viewfinders of models that have less than full-frame-sized sensors are no longer designed for optimum manual focus. Pick up any film camera and you'll see a bigger, brighter viewfinder with a focusing screen that's a joy to focus on manually.

WARNING

Do not use a lens marked AF (rather than AF-S) when the focus mode switch on the lens is set to M and the switch on the camera is set to AF. As you'll learn in Chapter 11, non-AF-S lenses do not have a built-in focus motor, and are focused by a motor in the camera body instead. When you set up the lens/camera in this conflicting configuration, it's possible the camera's internal motor may try to focus the lens (which has been set for manual focus only) and, with some lenses, damage can occur to the camera's focus motor. With AF-S lenses, the lens and body switches should agree, but no damage should occur if you have a mismatch; if *either* switch is set to M, then manual focus is what you will get.

If the lens mounted on your camera has a maximum f/stop of f/5.6 or larger, you can use the D7000's *electronic rangefinder* feature to assist in focusing manually.

Just follow these steps:

1. **Activate manual focus.** Set the lens *and* camera focus mode to M (see the warning above). If you happen to be using an old non-autofocus (manual focus) lens, you're all set—it won't autofocus under any circumstances.

2. **Select a focus point.** With the focus point selector lock off, select one of the 39 focus points using the multi selector.

3. **Press the shutter release button halfway.** This activates the D7000's autofocus system, which continues to function even though the camera's ability to adjust the focus of the lens has been disabled.

4. **Rotate the lens's focus ring.** Adjust until the in-focus indicator at the lower left of the viewfinder display illuminates continually.

5. **Confirm.** Visually evaluate whether you're actually in sharp focus—the in-focus indicator is sometimes wrong!

Autofocus Activation… and More

The final considerations in using autofocus are the control or controls used to activate and lock autofocus, plus a few odds and ends. I'll cover them in ample detail in Chapter 9, which explains all the options, but here are some cross references if you feel you need some review. I'm going to continue the discussion of focusing in the next chapter, which explains Live View and movie making, and some special focus options the D7000 has when using those two modes.

- **Focus tracking with lock on.** Intervening subjects passing in front of your main area of interest can interfere with autofocus. Set a delay time before the camera refocuses using CSM #a3, as described in Chapter 9.

- **AF point illumination.** Do you want the active autofocus point illuminated when that is an option? Look up CSM #a4 in Chapter 9.

- **Focus point wrap around.** Do you want the focus point to wrap around to the opposite side during manual selection? Use CSM #a5.

- **AF illuminator.** Need to turn off the autofocus assist illuminator on your camera, flash, or SC-29 connecting cable? Use CSM #a7.

- **Which controls activate/lock autofocus.** You can use a half-press of the shutter release or a press of the AE-L/AF-L button (or both), or another button. See the instructions for CSM #f3, f4, and f5 in Chapter 9 for your options.

- **Center/show focus point.** You can program the multi selector center button to either jump the active focus point to the center or to highlight the active focus point, using CSM #f2, as described in Chapter 9.

TRAP (AUTO) FOCUS

This technique comes in handy when you know where the action is going to take place (such as at the finish line of a horse race), but you don't know exactly *when*. The solution is to prefocus on the point where the action will occur, and then tell your D7000 not to actually take the photo until something moves into the prefocus spot. That's not as difficult as you might think. The key is to decouple the focusing operation from the shutter release function. Just follow these steps:

1. Set CSM #f5 to AF-ON. At that setting, pressing the shutter release halfway down does *not* activate autofocus. That happens *only* when you press the AF-ON button.

2. Set CSM #a2 to Focus Priority. The shutter will trip only when your subject is in focus.

3. Set your point selection mode to Single Area.

4. Make sure your lens is set to autofocus (either A or M/A).

5. Prefocus on the spot where the action will occur, or an equivalent distance. You can use the AE-L/AF-L button to activate focus.

6. Reframe your picture, if necessary, so that nothing is at the prefocused distance. (If an object occupies that spot, the D7000 will take the photo immediately when you press the shutter release.)

7. Press and hold down the shutter release. The camera will not refocus, because you've disconnected the autofocus function from the shutter release.

8. The picture will be taken when a subject moves into the prefocused area.

6

Live View and D-Movies

I've saved some advanced techniques for this chapter, which devotes a little extra space to some special features of the Nikon D7000. This chapter covers Live View and shooting HDTV movies.

The New Perspective of Live View

Live View is one of those features that experienced SLR users (especially those dating from the film era) sometimes think they don't need—until they try it. It's also one of those features (like truly "silent" shooting, without any shutter click) that point-and-shoot refugees are surprised that digital SLRs (until recently) have lacked. As I noted earlier, SLRs have actual, mechanical shutters that can't be completely silenced, as can be done with point-and-shoot cameras. I've fielded almost as many queries from those who want to know how to preview their images on the LCD—just as they did with their point-and-shoot cameras. Indeed, many P & S models don't even *have* optical viewfinders, engendering a whole generation of amateur photographers who think the only way to frame and compose an image is to hold the camera out at arm's length so the back-panel LCD can be viewed more easily.

While dSLR veterans didn't really miss what we've come to know as Live View, it was at least, in part, because they didn't have it and couldn't miss what they never had. After all, why would you eschew a big, bright, magnified through-the-lens optical view that showed depth-of-field fairly well, and which was easily visible under virtually all ambient light conditions? LCD displays, after all, were small, tended to wash out in bright light, and didn't really provide you with an accurate view of what your picture was going to look like.

There were technical problems, as well. Real-time previews theoretically disabled a dSLR's autofocus system, as focus was achieved by measuring contrast through the optical viewfinder, which is blocked when the mirror is flipped up for a live view. Extensive previewing had the same effect on the sensor as long exposures: the sensor heated up, producing excess noise. Pointing the camera at a bright light source when using a real-time view could damage the sensor. The list of potential problems goes on and on.

That was then. This is now.

The Nikon D7000 has a gorgeous three-inch LCD that can be viewed under a variety of lighting conditions and from wide-ranging angles, so you don't have to be exactly behind the display to see it clearly. It offers a 100-percent view of the sensor's capture area, the same as the D7000's optical viewfinder. It's large enough to allow manual focusing—but there is an automatic focus option, too. You still have to avoid pointing your D7000 at bright light sources (especially the Sun) when using Live View, but the real-time preview can be used for fairly long periods without frying the sensor. Nikon's system works just like you'd want it to: the mirror flips up, the shutter opens, and what the sensor sees is displayed in full color on the LCD on the back of the camera, as shown in Figure 6.1.

What You Can Do with Live View

You may not have considered just what you can do with Live View, because the capability is so novel. But once you've played with it, you'll discover dozens of applications for this capability, as well as a few things that you can't do. Here's a list of Live View Do's/Don'ts/Cans/Can'ts.

- **Preview your images on a TV.** Connect your D7000 to a standard definition or high-definition television using a video or (optional) HDMI cable, and you can preview your image on a large screen. Because you're viewing the actual image that will be captured, you can check things like focus or white balance in real time, on a larger display. You can preview exposure with Live View, because the camera adjusts the LCD display to approximate the metered exposure. However, if you make EV changes that exceed +3/–3EV (you can set up to +/–5EV), the LCD will not reflect the actual exposure. In addition, Nikon neglected to provide live histograms with this feature.

- **Preview remotely.** Extend the cable between the camera and TV screen, and you can preview your images some distance away from the camera.

- **Improve your point of view.** If looking through the viewfinder to frame your subject is awkward (say, you have to hold the D7000 over your head to clear obstructions such as a crowd of people), Live View lets you see what you're going to shoot before you snap the shutter. (A remote release is a good idea in this mode.)

■ **Shoot from your computer.** With Camera Control Pro 2 (an extra cost option), you can control your camera from your computer, so you can preview images and take pictures without physically touching the D7000.

■ **Continuous shooting.** You can shoot bursts of images using Live View.

■ **Shoot from tripod or hand-held.** Of course, holding the camera out at arm's length to preview an image is poor technique, and will introduce a lot of camera shake. If you want to use Live View for hand-held images, use an image-stabilized lens and/or a high shutter speed. A tripod is a better choice if you can use one.

■ **Watch your power.** Live View uses a lot of juice and will deplete your battery rapidly. The optional AC adapter is a useful accessory.

■ **Beware exposure snags.** If the camera is mounted on a tripod, you really should consider covering the viewfinder window to avoid light coming from the back affecting your meter reading in automatic exposure modes.

■ **Watch your usage times.** Nikon says Live View can be used continuously for as long as one hour, but notes that after periods of more than a few minutes, the sensor warms up and increases image noise and color artifacts. Your D7000 will shut down before your camera seriously overheats, and will give you a warning on the monitor 30 seconds before shut off.

Beginning Live View

Activate Live View by rotating the Live View switch on the back of the camera (just to the right of the LCD) clockwise until the mirror flips up and the Live View preview is shown on the display. (See Figure 6.1.) Rotate the switch again to turn Live View off. The first thing to do when entering Live View is to double-check three settings that affect how your image or movie is taken. These settings include:

Metering Mode

While using Live View, you can press the metering mode button on top of the camera (just to the southwest of the shutter release), and rotate the main command dial to select Matrix, Center-weighted, or Spot metering.

Focus Mode

Focus mode is chosen using the same controls when using the optical viewfinder. Set the focus mode selector on the side of the camera under the lens release button to AF (and set the lens focus mode switch to AF, as well). Then press the AF mode button and rotate the main command dial until either AF-S or AF-F is displayed on the back-panel

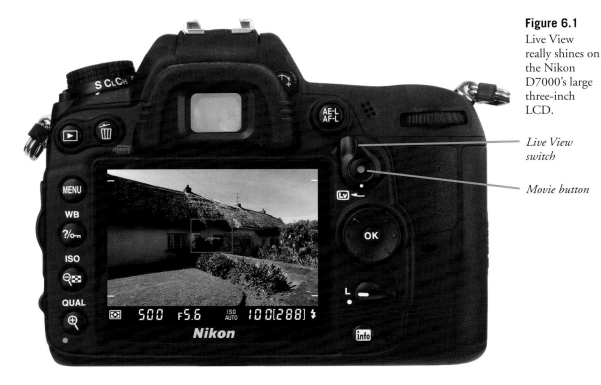

Figure 6.1
Live View really shines on the Nikon D7000's large three-inch LCD.

Live View switch

Movie button

LCD. The available modes differ slightly from those possible when not shooting in Live View. To use manual focus, set the focus mode selector switch to M. You can also choose AF-S or AF-F using Custom Settings menu CSM #a8.

- **AF-S.** This single autofocus mode, which Nikon calls Single-servo AF, locks focus when the shutter release is pressed halfway. This mode uses *focus priority;* the shutter can be fully released to take a picture only if the D7000 is able to achieve sharp focus.

- **AF-F.** This new mode is roughly the equivalent of AF-C. Nikon calls it Full-time servo AF. The D7000 focuses and refocuses continually as you shoot stills in Live View modes or record movies. Unlike AF-C, this mode also uses focus priority. You can't release the shutter unless the camera has achieved sharp focus.

- **MF.** Manual focus. You focus the image by rotating the focus ring on the camera.

Focus Area

With the focus mode selector button pressed, rotate the sub-command dial to choose one of the following focus area modes. You can also choose any of these modes using Custom Settings menu CSM #a8.

Your choices are as follows:

■ **Face-priority AF.** The camera automatically detects faces, and focuses on subjects facing the camera, as when you're shooting a portrait. You can't select the focus zone yourself. Instead, a double yellow border will be displayed on the LCD when the camera detects a face. You don't need to press the shutter release to activate this behavior. (Up to five faces may be detected; the D7000 focuses on the face that is closest to the camera.) When you press down the shutter release halfway, the camera attempts to focus the face. As sharp focus is achieved, the border turns green. (See Figure 6.2.) If the camera is unable to focus, the border blinks red. Focus may also be lost if the subject turns away from the camera and is no longer detectable by Face-priority.

■ **Wide-area AF.** This is the mode to use for non-portrait subjects, such as landscapes, as you can select the focus zone to be used manually. It's good for shooting hand-held, because the subjects may change as you reframe the image with a hand-held camera, and the wide-area zones are forgiving of these changes. The focus zone will be outlined in red. You can move the focus zone around the screen with the multi selector buttons. When sharp focus is achieved, the focus zone box will turn green. (See Figure 6.3.)

Figure 6.2
Face-priority AF attempts to focus on the face that's closest to the camera.

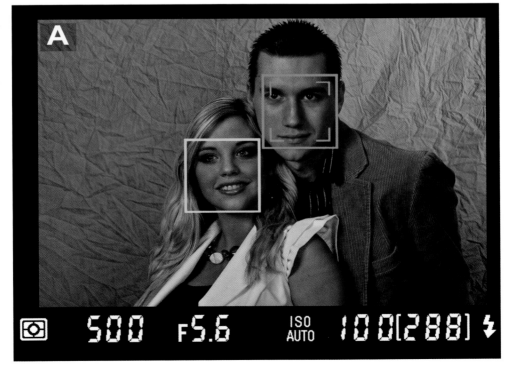

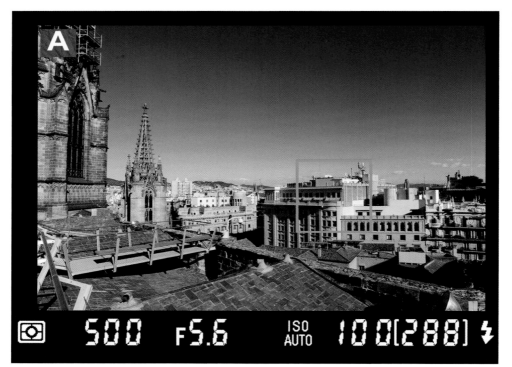

Figure 6.3
Wide-area AF
is best for land-
scapes and
other subjects
with large ele-
ments.

- **Normal-area AF.** This mode uses smaller focus zones, and so is best suited for tri-pod-mounted images where the camera is held fairly steady. As with Wide-area AF, the focus zone will be outlined in red. You can move the focus zone around the screen with the multi selector buttons. When sharp focus is achieved, the focus zone box will turn green. (See Figure 6.4.)

- **Subject-tracking AF.** This mode allows the camera to "grab" a subject, focus, and then follow the subject as it moves within the frame. You can use this mode for sub-jects that don't remain stationary, such as small children. When using Subject-track-ing AF, a white border appears in the center of the frame, and turns yellow when focus is locked in (as described in the section that follows). To activate focus or refo-cus, press the multi selector up button. I'll explain Subject-tracking in more detail next. (See Figure 6.5.)

- **Manual focus.** In this non-automatic focus mode, you can move the focus area around the frame with the multi selector buttons, press the shutter release halfway, and then adjust focus manually by rotating the focus ring on the lens. When sharp focus is achieved, the red focus zone box will turn green, and the camera's beeper, if enabled, will sound.

Figure 6.4
Normal-area
AF allows you
to zero in on a
specific point
of focus.

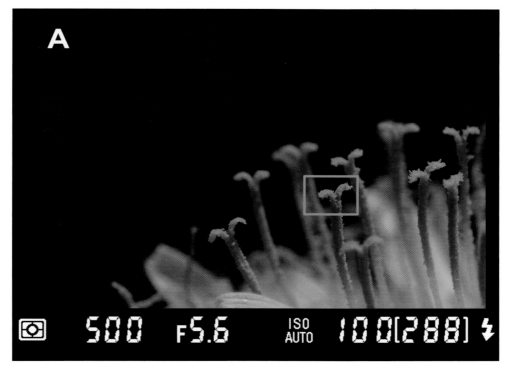

Figure 6.5
Subject-track-
ing can keep
focus as it fol-
lows your sub-
ject around in
the frame.

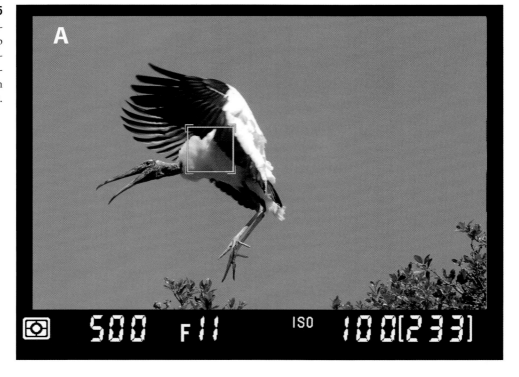

Introducing Subject-Tracking

The useful Subject-tracking autofocus feature is one of those features that can be confusing at first, but once you get the hang of it, it's remarkably easy to use. Face-priority, in comparison, is almost intuitive to learn. Here's the quick introduction you need to Subject-tracking.

■ **Ready, aim…** When you've activated Subject-tracking, a white border appears in the center of the frame. Use that border to "aim" the camera until the subject you want to focus on and track is located within the border.

■ **…Focus.** When you've pinpointed your subject, press the OK button to activate the D7000's Contrast Detection autofocus feature. The focus frame will turn yellow and the camera will emit a beep (unless you've disabled the beep within the Setup menu) when locked in.

■ **Reframe as desired.** Once the focus frame has turned yellow, it seemingly takes on a life of its own, and will "follow" your subject around on the LCD as you reframe your image. (See Figure 6.5.) (In other words, the subject being tracked doesn't have to be in the center of the frame for the actual photo.) Best of all, if your subject moves, the D7000 will follow it and keep focus as required.

■ **Tracking continues.** The only glitches that may pop up might occur if your subject is small and difficult to track, or is too close in tonal value to its background, or if the subject approaches the camera or recedes sufficiently to change its relative size on the LCD significantly.

■ **Grab a new subject.** If you want to refocus or grab a new subject, press the OK button again.

Viewing Live View Information

Once you've activated Live View, a display like the one shown in Figure 6.6 appears. Not all of the information appears all the time. For example, the Time Remaining indicator shows only when there are 30 seconds or less remaining for Live View shooting. The indicators overlaid on the image can be displayed or suppressed by pressing the Info button (that's to the lower right of the LCD). As you press the button, the LCD cycles among these screen variations:

■ Live View screen overlaid with shooting information, as shown in Figure 6.6.

■ Live View screen overlaid with only minimal information. (See Figure 6.7.)

■ Live View screen overlaid with basic information, plus a 16-segment alignment grid. (See Figure 6.8.)

■ Live View screen overlaid with a virtual horizon leveling aid. (See Figure 6.9.)

■ Live View shooting information screen with 16:9 aspect ratio of HD movie format indicated. (See Figure 6.10.)

Figure 6.6
The Live View display includes a lot of information, some of which can be hidden.

Shooting mode

No movies possible

Audio recording indicator

Current AF mode

AF-area mode

Active D-Lighting status

Image size

Image quality

White balance

Live View time remaining

Movie time remaining

Movie frame size

Focus point

Monitor brightness

Action icons

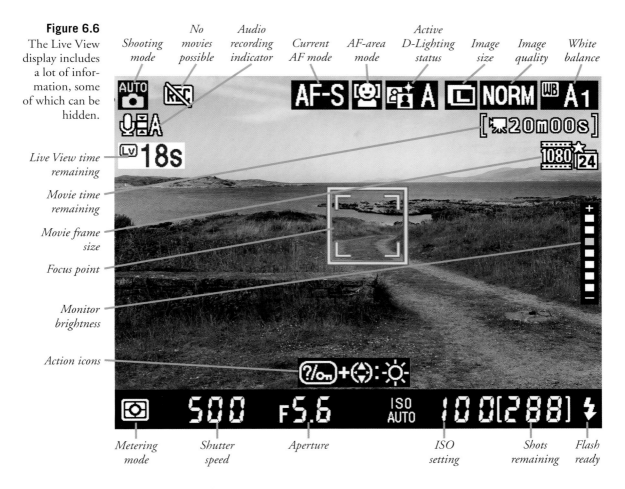

Metering mode

Shutter speed

Aperture

ISO setting

Shots remaining

Flash ready

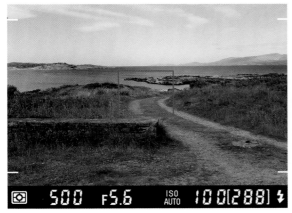

Figure 6.7 The Live View display with minimal information.

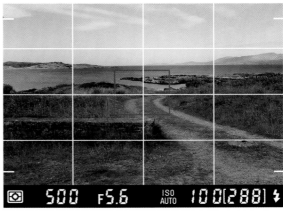

Figure 6.8 The Live View display with alignment grid.

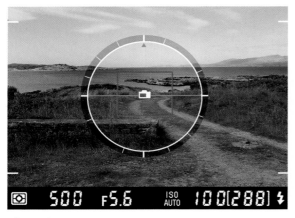

Figure 6.9 The Live View display with virtual horizon.

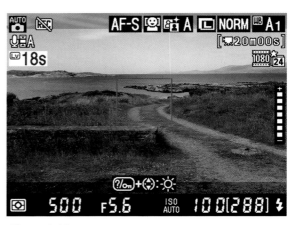

Figure 6.10 The Live View display with 16:9 HDTV frame shown.

The overlaid indicators include:

- **Shooting mode.** This indicator shows the mode dial position you've selected, including any of the PASM (Program, Aperture-priority, Shutter-priority, and Manual) modes, as well as one of the Scene modes. You can change modes while Live View is active. This indicator appears on the LCD even when shooting information is turned off.

- **Audio recording indicator.** Shows when a microphone is being used.

- **No Movies Possible.** This shows that it is not possible to shoot movies, because there is not enough space remaining on your memory card.

- **Live View time remaining.** This is displayed when the amount of shooting time in Live View mode is 30 seconds or less. Although Live View is possible for 60 minutes, if the D7000 overheats, this countdown display appears and the camera exits Live View before damage is done.

- **Current AF mode.** Shows AF-S, AF-F, or M focus.

- **Current AF-area.** Shows whether Face-priority, Wide-area, Normal-area, or Subject-tracking autofocus will be used. This indicator still appears when the alignment grid is displayed, even when other shooting information is turned off.

- **Active D-Lighting status.** Shows the D-Lighting that will be applied.

- **Focus point.** Shows the appropriate focus indicator for the AF-area mode in use.

- **Image Size.** Displays the current resolution, L (Large), M (Medium), or S (Small).

- **Image Quality.** Shows JPEG Image Quality: Fine, Norm, or Basic.

- **White balance.** Displays the current white balance preset or WB Auto.
- **Movie time remaining.** Indicates the number of minutes and seconds remaining for movie shooting.
- **Movie frame size.** Displays the resolution of the movie frame and frames per second rate, from 1920 × 1080 pixels to 1280 × 720, down to 640 × 424, at either 24 or 30 fps (depending on what you've selected in the Movie Settings entry in the Shooting menu). (See Chapter 8.)
- **Alignment grid.** (Shown in Figure 6.8.) This set of guides can be used to help line up horizontal or vertical lines.
- **Self-timer.** (Not shown in figure.) A self-timer icon appears at right when the self-timer is active.
- **Action icons.** These icons are a reminder that you can adjust the screen brightness by pressing the WB/Help/Protect button and using the up/down directional buttons.
- **Monitor brightness.** This indicator shows the relative brightness of the back-panel LCD during Live View as you make adjustments using the WB/Help/Protect button and up/down directional buttons.

Additional information is arrayed along the bottom of the LCD image, more or less duplicating much of the data in the LED display that is seen through the viewfinder when not using Live View. These indicators include:

- **Metering method.** Shows whether Matrix, Center-weighted, or Spot metering is selected. Choose before entering Live View.
- **Shutter speed.** The currently selected shutter speed.
- **F/stop.** The current f/stop.
- **ISO value.** Shows the ISO sensitivity setting, or ISO Auto.
- **Shots remaining.** Indicates the number of images remaining on your memory card at the current Image Size and Image Quality settings.
- **Flash ready.** Shows the electronic flash is fully charged and ready to shoot.

Shooting in Live View

Shooting stills and movies in Live View is easy. Just follow these steps:

1. **Rotate LV switch.** Activate Live View by rotating the switch. (See Figure 6.1.) The D7000 can be hand-held or mounted on a tripod. (Using a tripod mode makes it easier to obtain and keep sharp focus.) You can exit Live View at any time by rotating the LV button again.

2. **Zoom in/out.** Check your view by pressing the Zoom In and Zoom Out buttons (located to the left of the color LCD). Five levels of magnification are available, up to 6.7X zoom. A navigation box appears in the lower right of the LCD with a yellow box representing the portion of the image zoomed, just as when you're reviewing photos you've already taken using Playback mode. Use the multi selector keys to change the zoomed area within the full frame. Press the Zoom Out button to zoom out again.

3. **Make exposure adjustments.** While using an automatic exposure mode, you can add or subtract exposure using the EV settings, as described in Chapter 4. Hold down the EV button (just southeast of the shutter release) and rotate the main command dial to add or subtract exposure when using P, S, and A modes. The back-panel color LCD will brighten or darken to represent the exposure change you make.

4. **Shoot.** Press the shutter release all the way down to take a still picture, or press the red movie button to start motion picture filming. Stop filming by pressing the movie button again. Movies up to 4GB in size can be taken (assuming there is sufficient room on your memory card), which limits you to 20 minutes for an HDTV clip.

Shooting Movies with the D7000

As you've probably gathered, movie making is an extension of the Live View concept. Once you've directed the output of the sensor to the LCD, capturing it as a video file—with audio—is relatively easy. All the focus modes and AF-area modes described for plain old Live View mode can be applied to movie making. Here are some considerations to think about:

- **Stills, too.** You can take a still photograph even while you're shooting a movie clip by pressing the shutter release all the way down. You won't miss a still shot because you're shooting video. However, movie shooting will cease after you take the still, and must be re-activated by pressing the red movie button again.

- **Exposure compensation.** When shooting movies, exposure compensation is available in plus/minus 3EV steps in 1/3 EV increments.

- **Size matters.** Individual movie files can be up to 4GB in size (this will vary according to the resolution you select), and no more than 20 minutes in length. The speed and capacity of your memory card may provide additional restrictions on size/length.

WHAT FRAME RATE: 24 fps or 30 fps?

Even intermediate movie shooters can be confused by the choice between 24 fps and 30 fps, especially since those are only nominal figures (with the D7000, the 24 fps setting actually yields 23.976 frames per second; 30 fps gives you 29.97 actual "frames" per second).

The difference lies in the two "worlds" of motion images, film and video. The standard frame rate for motion picture film is 24 fps, while the video rate, at least in the United States, Japan, and other places using the NTSC standard is 30 fps (actually 60 interlaced *fields* per second). Computer editing software can handle either type, and convert between them. The choice between 24 fps and 30 fps is determined by what you plan to do with your video.

The short explanation is that, for technical reasons I won't go into here, shooting at 24 fps gives your movie a "film" look, excellent for showing fine detail. However, if your clip has moving subjects, or you pan the camera, 24 fps can produce a jerky effect called "judder." A 30 fps rate produces a home-video look that some feel is less desirable, but which is smoother and less jittery when displayed on an electronic monitor. I suggest you try both and use the frame rate that best suits your tastes and video editing software.

In the Movie Settings entry of the Shooting menu, you can make the following choices:

■ **Movie Quality.** Choose your resolution. Use the Movie Settings entry in the Shooting menu. Or, when Live View is activated, and before you start shooting your video clip, you can select the resolution/frame rate of your movie. Your choices are as follows:

- 1920 × 1080 at 24 fps, high quality, low compression.
- 1920 × 1080 at 24 fps, normal quality, medium compression.
- 1280 × 720 at 30 fps, high quality, low compression.
- 1280 × 720 at 30 fps, normal quality, medium compression.
- 1280 × 720 at 24 fps, high quality, low compression.
- 1280 × 720 at 24fps, normal quality, medium compression.
- 640 × 424 at 30 fps, high quality, low compression. (Useful for video clips displayed on web pages)
- 640 × 424 at 30 fps, normal quality, medium compression. (Useful for video clips displayed on web pages)

- **Microphone.** Here you can set audio sensitivity. Choose from Auto, High Sensitivity, Medium Sensitivity, Low Sensitivity, or Off.

- **Destination.** Select Slot 1 or Slot 2. The display will show how much recording time is available with the memory cards currently installed in each slot.

- **Manual movie settings.** Turn On or Off to enable/disable manually changing shutter speed (in the range 1/30th second to 1/8,000th second) and ISO settings (fixed settings only; ISO Auto can't be used while shooting movies).

NOT MUCH OF A LIMITATION

Unless you are shooting an entire performance from a fixed position, such as a stage play, the 20-minute limitation on HDTV movie duration won't put much of a crimp in your style. Good motion picture practice calls for each production to consist of a series of relatively *short* clips, with 10 to 20 seconds a good average. You can assemble and edit your D7000 movies into one long, finished production using one of the many movie-editing software packages available. Andy Warhol might have been successful with his 1963 five-hour epic *Sleep*, but the rest of us will do better with short sequences of the type produced by the Nikon D7000.

To shoot your movies, follow these steps, which are similar to those for using Live View:

1. **Plug in microphone.** If you want to use an external monaural or stereo microphone with a 3.5mm stereo mini plug, attach it to the microphone jack on the left side of the camera.

2. **Start Live View.** Activate Live View by rotating the Live View switch.

3. **Choose a focus mode.** Select from AF-S, AF-F, or M, as described earlier.

4. **Choose an AF-area mode.** Choices include Face-priority AF, Wide-area AF, Normal-area AF, Subject-tracking AF, or Manual focus, as described earlier.

5. **Activate and lock in focus.** This was also described under the Live View instructions.

6. **Start/Stop recording.** Press the red movie recording button. Press again to stop recording.

Viewing Your Movies

Once you've finished recording your movies, they are available for review. Film clips show up during picture review, the same as still photos, but they are differentiated by a movie camera icon overlay. Press the OK button to start playback.

During playback, you can perform the following functions:

- **Pause.** Press the multi selector down button to pause the clip during playback. Press the multi selector center button to resume playback.

- **Rewind/Advance.** Press the left/right multi selector buttons to rewind or advance (respectively). Press once for 2X speed, twice for 8X speed, or three times for 16X speed. Hold down the left/right buttons to move to the end or beginning of the clip.

- **Single Frame Rewind/Advance.** Press the multi selector down key to pause the clip, then use the left/right buttons to rewind or advance one frame at a time.

- **Change volume.** Press the Zoom In and Zoom Out buttons to increase/decrease volume.

- **Trim movie.** Press the AE-L/AF-L button while the movie is paused.

- **Exit Playback.** Press the multi selector up button to exit playback.

- **View menus.** Press the MENU button to interrupt playback to access menus.

Editing Your Movies

In-camera editing is limited to trimming the beginning or end from a clip, and the clip must be at least two seconds long. For more advanced editing, you'll need an application capable of editing AVI movie clips. Google "AVI Editor" to locate any of the hundreds of free video editors available, or use a commercial product like Corel Video Studio, Adobe Premiere Elements, or Pinnacle Studio. These will let you combine several clips into one movie, add titles, special effects, and transitions between scenes.

To do in-camera editing/trimming, follow these steps:

1. **Start movie clip.** Use the Playback button to start image review, and press OK when you see a clip you want to edit. It will begin playing.

2. **Activate edit.** To remove video from the beginning of a clip, view the movie until you reach the first frame you want to keep, and then press the down button to pause. To trim video from the end of a clip, watch the movie until you reach the last frame you want to keep and then press the down button to pause.

3. **Access edit screen.** Press the White Balance/Help/Protect button to display the Edit Movie prompt. (See Figure 6.11.)

4. **Select start/end point.** To remove video from the beginning of the clip, press the up/down multi selector button and highlight either Choose Start Point or Choose End Point, and press OK.

5. **Resume playback.** Press the center button of the multi selector to start or resume playback. You can use the Pause, Rewind, Advance, and Single frame controls described previously to move around within your clip.

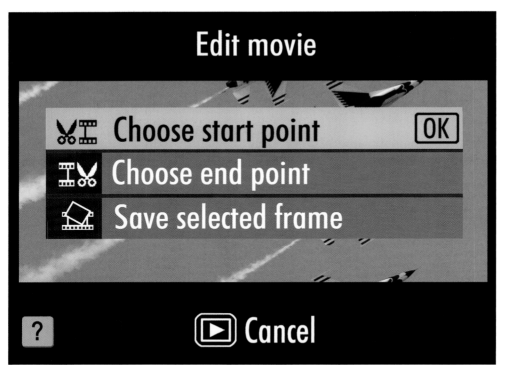

Figure 6.11
Choose editing
options from
this menu.

6. **Mark trim point.** When you reach the point where you want to trim, press the
   Pause button (if the movie is not already paused), and then press the multi selector
   up button. All frames prior to the pause will be deleted if you're in Choose Start
   Point mode; all frames *after* the pause will be deleted if you're in Choose End Point
   mode. Your trimmed movie must be at least two seconds long.

7. **Confirm trim.** A Proceed? prompt appears. Choose Yes or No, and press OK.

8. **Save movie.** You'll see a Saving Movie message and a green progress bar as the
   D7000 stores the trimmed clip to your memory card. Storage takes some time, and
   you don't want to interrupt it to avoid losing your saved clip. So, make sure your
   camera has a fully charged battery before you start to edit a clip.

Saving a Frame

You can store any frame from one of your movies as a JPEG still, using the resolution
of the video format. Just follow these steps:

1. Pause your movie at the frame you want to save. Press the WB/Help/Protect button to access the Edit Movie screen.

2. Choose Save Selected Frame and press OK.

3. Choose Proceed to confirm.

4. Your frame will be stored on the memory card, and will be marked with a scissors icon.

Tips for Shooting Better Movies

Producing high-quality movies can be a real challenge for amateur photographers. After all, by comparison we're used to watching the best productions that television, video, and motion pictures can offer. Whether it's fair or not, our efforts are compared to what we're used to seeing produced by experts. While this chapter can't make you into a pro videographer, it can help you improve your efforts.

There are a number of different things to consider when planning a video shoot, and when possible, a shooting script and storyboard can help you produce a higher quality video.

Make a Shooting Script

A shooting script is nothing more than a coordinated plan that covers both audio and video and provides order and structure for your video. A detailed script will cover what types of shots you're going after, what dialogue you're going to use, audio effects, transitions, and graphics. When you first begin shooting movies, your shooting scripts will be very simple. As you gain experience, you'll learn how to tell stories with video, and will map out your script in more detail before you even begin to capture the first sequence.

A shooting script will also help you if you need to shoot out of sequence. For example, you may have several scenes that take place on different days at the same location. It probably will make sense to shoot all those scenes at one time, rather than in the movie's chronological order. You can check the shooting script to see what types of video and audio you need for the separate scenes, as well as what dialogue your "actors" need to deliver (even, if, as is the case for most informal videos, the "lines" are ad-libbed as you shoot).

Use Storyboards

A storyboard is a series of panels providing visuals of what each scene should look like. While the ones produced by Hollywood are generally of very high quality, there's nothing that says drawing skills are important for this step. Stick figures work just fine if that's the best you can do. The storyboard just helps you visualize locations, placement of actors/actresses, props and furniture, and also helps everyone involved get an idea of what you're trying to show. It also helps show how you want to frame or compose a shot. You can even shoot a series of still photos and transform them into a "storyboard" if you

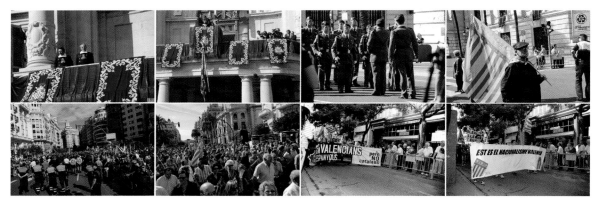

Figure 6.12 A storyboard is a series of simple sketches or photos to help visualize a segment of video.

want, as I did in Figure 6.12. In this case, I took pictures of a parade, and then used them to assemble a storyboard to follow when I shot video at a similar parade on a later date.

Storytelling in Video

Today's audience is accustomed to fast-paced, short scene storytelling. In order to produce interesting video for such viewers, it's important to view video storytelling as a kind of shorthand code for the more leisurely efforts print media offers. Audio and video should always be advancing the story. While it's okay to let the camera linger from time to time, it should only be for a compelling reason and only briefly.

Composition is one of the most important tools available to you for telling a story in video. However, while you can crop a still frame any old way you like, in movie shooting, several factors restrict your composition, and impose requirements you just don't always have in still photography (although other rules of good composition do apply). Here are some of the key differences to keep in mind when composing movie frames:

■ **Horizontal compositions only.** Some subjects, such as basketball players and tall buildings, just lend themselves to vertical compositions. But movies are shown in horizontal format only. So if you're interviewing a local basketball star, you can end up with a worst-case situation like the one shown in Figure 6.13. Using the D7000's FH (1920 × 1080) format, or 1280 × 720 formats, you are limited to relatively wide frames. If you want to show how tall your subject is, it's often impractical to move back far enough to show him full-length. You really can't capture a vertical composition. Tricks like getting down on the floor and shooting up at your subject can exaggerate the perspective, but aren't a perfect solution.

Figure 6.13
Movie shooting requires you to fit all your subjects into a horizontally oriented frame.

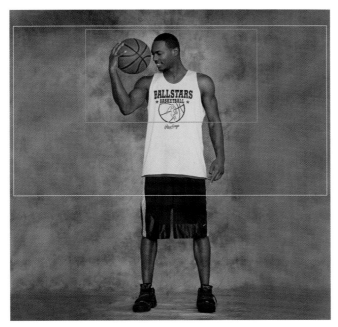

- **Wasted space at the sides.** Moving in to frame the basketball player as outlined by the yellow box in Figure 6.13, means that you're still forced to leave a lot of empty space on either side. (Of course, you can fill that space with other people and/or interesting stuff, but that defeats your intent of concentrating on your main subject.) So when faced with some types of subjects in a horizontal frame, you can be creative, or move in *really* tight. For example, if I was willing to give up the "height" aspect of my composition, I could have framed the shot as shown by the green box in the figure, and wasted less of the image area at either side of the model. The least attractive option is to switch to a movie recording format that has less "wide-screen" perspective, specifically 640 × 424 pixels, in which case you lose the resolution advantage of the HD aspect ratio.

- **Seamless (or seamed) transitions.** Unless you're telling a picture story with a photo essay, still pictures often stand alone. But with movies, each of your compositions must relate to the shot that preceded it, and the one that follows. It can be jarring to jump from a long shot to a tight close-up unless the director—you—is very creative. Another common error is the "jump cut" in which successive shots vary only slightly in camera angle, making it appear that the main subject has "jumped" from one place to another. (Although everyone from French New Wave director Jean-Luc Goddard to Guy Ritchie—Madonna's ex—have used jump cuts effectively in their films.) The rule of thumb is to vary the camera angle by at least 30 degrees between shots to make it appear to be seamless. Unless you prefer that your images flaunt convention and appear to be "seamy."

- **The time dimension.** Unlike still photography, with motion pictures there's a lot more emphasis on using a series of images to build on each other to tell a story. Static shots where the camera is mounted on a tripod and everything is shot from the same distance are a recipe for dull videos. Watch a television program sometime and notice how often camera shots change distances and directions. Viewers are used to this variety and have come to expect it. Professional video productions are often done with multiple cameras shooting from different angles and positions. But many professional productions are shot with just one camera and careful planning, and you can do just fine with your camera.

Within those compositional restraints, you still have a great deal of flexibility. It only takes a second or two for an establishing shot to impart the necessary information. For example, many of the scenes for a video documenting a model being photographed in a Rock and Roll music setting might be close-ups and talking heads, but an establishing shot showing the studio where the video was captured helps set the scene.

Provide variety too. Change camera angles and perspectives often and never leave a static scene on the screen for a long period of time. (You can record a static scene for a reasonably long period and then edit in other shots that cut away and back to the longer scene with close-ups that show each person talking.)

When editing, keep transitions basic! I can't stress this one enough. Watch a television program or movie. The action "jumps" from one scene or person to the next. Fancy transitions that involve exotic "wipes," dissolves, or cross fades take too long for the average viewer and make your video ponderous.

Here's a look at the different types of commonly used compositional tools:

- **Establishing shot.** Much like it sounds, this type of composition, as shown in Figure 6.14, establishes the scene and tells the viewer where the action is taking place. Let's say you're shooting a video of your offspring's move to college; the establishing shot could be a wide shot of the campus with a sign welcoming you to the school in the foreground. Another example would be for a child's birthday party; the establishing shot could be the front of the house decorated with birthday signs and streamers or a shot of the dining room table decked out with party favors and a candle-covered birthday cake. Or, in Figure 6.14, I wanted to show the studio where the video was shot.

- **Medium shot.** This shot is composed from about waist to head room (some space above the subject's head). It's useful for providing variety from a series of close-ups and also makes for a useful first look at a speaker. (See Figure 6.15.)

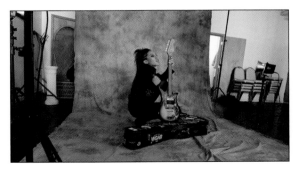

Figure 6.14 An establishing shot from a distance sets the stage for closer views.

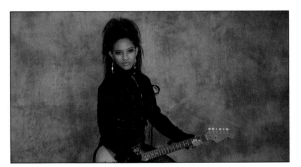

Figure 6.15 A medium shot is used to bring the viewer into a scene without shocking them. It can be used to introduce a character and provide context via their surroundings.

- **Close-up.** The close-up, usually described as "from shirt pocket to head room," provides a good composition for someone talking directly to the camera. Although it's common to have your talking head centered in the shot, that's not a requirement. In Figure 6.16 the subject was offset to the right. This would allow other images, especially graphics or titles, to be superimposed in the frame in a "real" (professional) production. But the compositional technique can be used with your videos, too, even if special effects are not going to be added.

- **Extreme close-up.** When I went through broadcast training back in the '70s, this shot was described as the "big talking face" shot and we were actively discouraged from employing it. Styles and tastes change over the years and now the big talking face is much more commonly used (maybe people are better looking these days?) and so this view may be appropriate. Just remember, your camera is capable of

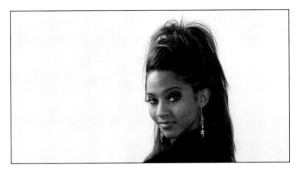

Figure 6.16 A close up generally shows the full face with a little head room at the top and down to the shoulders at the bottom of the frame.

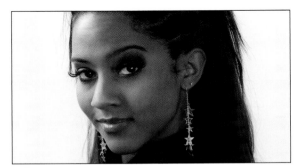

Figure 6.17 An extreme close-up is a very tight shot that cuts off everything above the top of the head and below the chin (or even closer!). Be careful using this shot since many of us look better from a distance!

shooting in high-definition video and you may be playing the video on a high-def TV; be careful that you use this composition on a face that can stand up to high definition. (See Figure 6.17.)

- **"Two" shot.** A two shot shows a pair of subjects in one frame. They can be side by side or one in the foreground and one in the background. This does not have to be a head to ground composition. Subjects can be standing or seated. A "three shot" is the same principle except that three people are in the frame. (See Figure 6.18.)

- **Over the shoulder shot.** Long a composition of interview programs, the "over the shoulder shot" uses the rear of one person's head and shoulder to serve as a frame for the other person. This puts the viewer's perspective as that of the person facing away from the camera. (See Figure 6.19.)

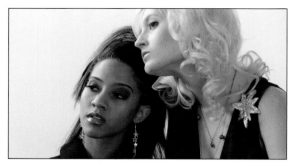

Figure 6.18 A "two-shot" features two people in the frame. This version can be framed at various distances such as medium or close up.

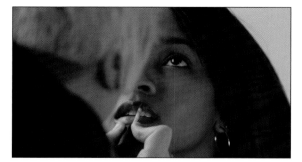

Figure 6.19 An "over-the-shoulder" shot is a popular shot for interview programs. It helps make the viewers feel like they're asking the questions.

Lighting for Video

Much like in still photography, how you handle light pretty much can make or break your videography. Lighting for video though can be more complicated than lighting for still photography, since both subject and camera movement are often part of the process.

Lighting for video presents several concerns. First off, you want enough illumination to create a useable video. Beyond that, you want to use light to help tell your story or increase drama. Let's take a better look at both.

Illumination

You can significantly improve the quality of your video by increasing the light falling in the scene. This is true indoors or out, by the way. While it may seem like sunlight is more than enough, it depends on how much contrast you're dealing with. If your subject is in shadow (which can help them from squinting) or wearing a ball cap, a video light can help make them look a lot better.

Lighting choices for amateur videographers are a lot better these days than they were a decade or two ago. An inexpensive shoe mount video light, which will easily fit in a camera bag, can be found for $15 or $20. You can even get a good quality LED video light for less than $100. Work lights sold at many home improvement stores can also serve as video lights since you can set the camera's white balance to correct for any colorcasts.

Much of the challenge depends upon whether you're just trying to add some fill light on your subject versus trying to boost the light on an entire scene. A small video light in the camera's hot shoe mount or on a flash bracket will do just fine for the former. It won't handle the latter.

Creative Lighting

While ramping up the light intensity will produce better technical quality in your video, it won't necessarily improve the artistic quality of it. Whether we're outdoors or indoors, we're used to seeing light come from above. Videographers need to consider how they position their lights to provide even illumination while up high enough to angle shadows down low and out of sight of the camera.

When considering lighting for video, there are several factors. One is the quality of the light. It can either be hard (direct) light or soft (diffused). Hard light is good for showing detail, but can also be very harsh and unforgiving. "Softening" the light, but diffusing it somehow, can reduce the intensity of the light but make for a kinder, gentler light as well.

While mixing light sources isn't always a good idea, one approach is to combine window light with supplemental lighting. Position your subject with the window to one side and bring in either a supplemental light or a reflector to the other side for reasonably even lighting.

Lighting Styles

Some lighting styles are more heavily used than others. Some forms are used for special effects, while others are designed to be invisible. At its most basic, lighting just illuminates the scene, but when used properly it can also create drama. Let's look at some types of lighting styles:

- **Three-point lighting.** This is a basic lighting setup for one person. A main light illuminates the strong side of a person's face, while a fill light lights up the other side. A third light is then positioned above and behind the subject to light the back of the head and shoulders.

- **Flat lighting.** Use this type of lighting to provide illumination and nothing more. It calls for a variety of lights and diffusers set to raise the light level in a space enough for good video reproduction, but not to create a particular mood or emphasize a particular scene or individual. With flat lighting, you're trying to create even lighting levels throughout the video space and minimizing any shadows. Generally, the lights are placed up high and angled downward (or possibly pointed straight up to bounce off of a white ceiling).

■ **"Ghoul lighting."** This is the style of lighting used for old horror movies. The idea is to position the light down low, pointed upwards. It's such an unnatural style of lighting that it makes its targets seem weird.

■ **Outdoor lighting.** While shooting outdoors may seem easier because the sun provides more light, it also presents its own problems. As a general rule of thumb, keep the sun behind you when you're shooting video outdoors, except when shooting faces (anything from a medium shot and closer) since the viewer won't want to see a squinting subject. When shooting another human this way, put the sun behind him and use a video light to balance light levels between the foreground and background. If the sun is simply too bright, position the subject in the shade and use the video light for your main illumination. Using reflectors (white board panels or aluminum foil covered cardboard panels are cheap options) can also help balance light effectively.

■ **On-camera lighting.** While not "technically" a lighting style, this method is commonly used. A hot shoe mounted light provides direct lighting in the same direction the lens is pointing. It's commonly used at weddings, events, and in photojournalism since it's easy and portable. LED video lights are all the rage these days and a wide variety of these lights are available at various price points. At the low end, these lights tend to be small and produce minimal light (but useful for fill work). More expensive versions offer greater light output and come with built-in barn doors (panels that help you control and shape the light) and diffusers and filters.

Audio

When it comes to making a successful video, audio quality is one of those things that separates the professionals from the amateurs. We're used to watching top-quality productions on television and in the movies, yet the average person has no idea how much effort goes in to producing what seems to be "natural" sound. Much of the sound you hear in such productions is actually recorded on carefully controlled sound stages and "sweetened" with a variety of sound effects and other recordings of "natural" sound.

Tips for Better Audio

Since recording high-quality audio is such a challenge, it's a good idea to do everything possible to maximize recording quality. Here are some ideas for improving the quality of the audio your camera records:

■ **Get the camera and its microphone close to the speaker.** The farther the microphone is from the audio source, the less effective it will be in picking up that sound. While having to position the camera and microphone closer to the subject affects your lens choices and lens perspective options, it will make the most of your audio source. Of course, if you're using a very wide-angle lens, getting too close to your subject can have unflattering results, so don't take this advice too far.

■ **Use an external microphone.** Plug a stereo or monaural mic into the jack on the side of the D7000, and you'll immediately enjoy better sound, because you won't be recording noises including autofocus motors or your own breathing. If you plan to do a lot of movie shooting, you might want to invest in the new Nikon ME-1 stereo microphone, introduced in early 2011 at the same time as the Nikon D5100 Although not inexpensive at $179.95, the ME-1 slips on the D7000's hot shoe and is powered through the camera. It's engineered to reduce or eliminate noise from unintentional contact, has a wind screen, and dampens sound pickup from the camera's autofocus operation. It includes a cable stop to keep the connecting cable out of the way during use.

■ **Turn off any sound makers you can.** Little things like fans and air handling units aren't obvious to the human ear, but will be picked up by the microphone. Turn off any machinery or devices that you can plus make sure cell phones are set to silent mode. Also, do what you can to minimize sounds such as wind, radio, television, or people talking in the background.

■ **Make sure to record some "natural" sound.** If you're shooting video at an event of some kind, make sure you get some background sound that you can add to your audio as desired in postproduction.

■ **Consider recording audio separately.** Lip-syncing is probably beyond most of the people you're going to be shooting, but there's nothing that says you can't record narration separately and add it later. It's relatively easy if you learn how to use simple software video-editing programs like iMovie (for the Macintosh) or Windows Movie Maker (for Windows PCs). Any time the speaker is off-camera, you can work with separately recorded narration rather than recording the speaker on-camera. This can produce much cleaner sound.

7

Advanced Techniques

I've saved some advanced techniques for this chapter, which devotes a little extra space to some special features of the Nikon D7000. This chapter covers GPS techniques and special exposure options, including time-lapse photography, very long, and very short exposures. I wind up this section with a list of recommended settings for your Shooting menu and Custom Settings menu banks.

Continuous Shooting

The Nikon D7000's pair of continuous shooting modes reminds me how far digital photography has brought us. The first accessory I purchased when I worked as a sports photographer some years ago was a motor drive for my film SLR. It enabled me to snap off a series of shots in rapid succession, which came in very handy when a fullback broke through the line and headed for the end zone. Even a seasoned action photographer can miss the decisive instant when a crucial block is made, or a baseball superstar's bat shatters and pieces of cork fly out. Continuous shooting simplifies taking a series of pictures, either to ensure that one has more or less the exact moment you want to capture or to capture a sequence that is interesting as a collection of successive images.

The D7000's "motor drive" capabilities are, in many ways, much superior to what you get with a film camera. For one thing, a motor-driven film camera can eat up film at an incredible pace, which is why many of them are used with cassettes that hold hundreds of feet of film stock. At three frames per second (typical of film cameras), a short burst of a few seconds can burn up as much as half of an ordinary 36 exposure roll of film. Digital cameras, in contrast, have reusable "film," so if you waste a few dozen shots on non-decisive moments, you can erase them and shoot more.

The increased capacity of digital memory cards gives you a prodigious number of frames to work with. At a basketball game I covered earlier this year, I took more than 1,000 images in a couple hours. Yet, even shooting RAW+JPEG Fine I could fit more than 700 images on a single 32GB Secure Digital card. If I'd switched to JPEG only (which is more typical for sports), I could have taken about 3,000 different images without switching cards or using the second card in my D7000, in Overflow mode. Even at the top speed of 6 frames per second that the D7000 is capable of, that's a lot of shooting. Given an average burst of about eight frames per sequence (nobody really takes 15-20 shots or more of one play in a basketball game), I was able to capture hundreds of different sequences before I needed to swap cards. Even simple plays, like a layup, seemed more exciting when captured in a sequence of shots, as in Figure 7.1.

To use the D7000's continuous shooting modes, hold down the release mode dial's unlock button and rotate the dial until either C_L or C_H appear. When you partially depress the shutter button, the viewfinder will display at the right side a number representing the maximum number of shots you can take at the current quality settings. The large buffer in the D7000 will generally allow you to take as many as 31 JPEG shots in a single burst, or 10 RAW photos.

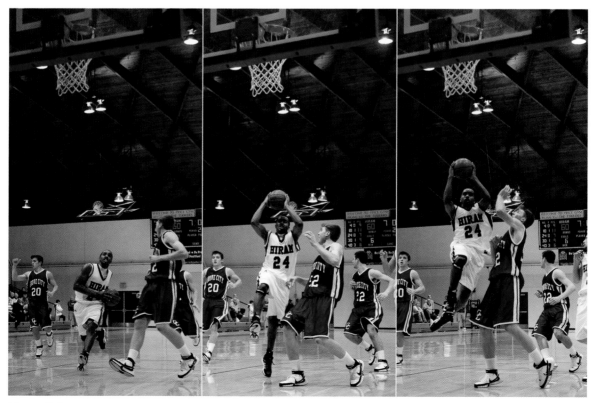

Figure 7.1 Continuous shooting allows you to capture an entire sequence of exciting moments as they unfold.

To increase this number, reduce the image-quality setting by switching to JPEG only (from JPEG+RAW), to a lower JPEG quality setting, such as JPEG Normal, or by reducing the D7000's resolution from L to M or S. The reason the size of your bursts is limited is that continuous images are first shuttled into the D7000's internal memory buffer, then doled out to the Secure Digital card as quickly as they can be written to the card. Technically, the D7000 takes the RAW data received from the digital image processor and converts it to the output format you've selected—either JPG or NEF (RAW)—and deposits it in the buffer ready to store on the card.

This internal "smart" buffer can suck up photos much more quickly than the SD card and, indeed, some memory cards are significantly faster or slower than others. When the buffer fills, you can't take any more continuous shots until the D7000 has written some of them to the card, making more room in the buffer. You should keep in mind that faster SD cards write images more quickly, freeing up buffer space faster. Today, SD cards are speed-rated using a "Class" figure, with Class 4 (4 megabits per second transfer speed) being the slowest units commonly available. Most SD cards on the market are at least Class 6 (6 megabits per second), with the most common "speedy" cards rated as Class 10 (at least 10 megabits per second). We're starting to see SDXC memory cards given a Class 10 designation, but with read/write speeds that actually top out at 20 megabits per second. (Theoretically, SDXC cards could eventually have speeds that are 10 to 20 times faster.)

The frame rate you select will depend on the kind of shooting you want to do. Here are some guidelines:

- **6 fps.** The max rate of 6 fps is available when using Continuous High mode. Use this for sports and other subjects where you want to optimize your chances of capturing the decisive moment. Perhaps you're shooting some active kids and want to grab their most appealing expressions. This fast frame rate can improve the odds. However, there is no guarantee that even at 6 fps the crucial instant won't occur *between* frames. (A ball pitched at 90 miles per hour travels 15 feet between each frame when you're shooting at 6 fps.) For example, when shooting major league baseball games, if I want to shoot a batter, I keep both eyes open, and keep one of them on the pitcher. Then, I start taking my sequence just as the pitcher releases the ball. My goal is to capture the batter making contact with the ball. But even at 6 fps, I find that a hitter connects between frames. I usually must take pictures of a couple dozen at-bats to get a shot of bat and ball connecting.

- **4.0-5.0 fps.** When using Continuous L, you can choose the frame rate from 1 to 5 fps, using CSM #d6. A slower rate can be useful for activities that aren't quite so fast moving. But, there's another benefit. Using the fastest frame rate means that your camera may fill up its buffer and won't be ready for the next sequence. If you don't want to miss any sequences, using a slightly slower frame rate can help prevent buffer overload.

- **1.0-3.0 fps.** You can set Continuous L mode to use a relatively pokey frame rate, too. Use these rates when you just want to be able to take pictures quickly, and aren't interested in filling up your memory card with mostly duplicated images. At 1 fps you can hold down the shutter release and fire away, or ease up when you want to pause. At higher frame rates, by the time you've decided to stop shooting, you may have taken an extra three or four shots that you really don't want. Slow frame rates are good for bracketing, too. Set the D7000 to take a three-frame bracket burst, and you can take all three with one press of the shutter release. You'll find that slower frame rates also come in handy for subjects that are moving around in interesting ways (photographic models come to mind) but don't change their looks or poses quickly enough to merit a 6 fps burst.

A Tiny Slice of Time

Exposures that seem impossibly brief can reveal a world we didn't know existed. In the 1930s, Dr. Harold Edgerton, a professor of electrical engineering at MIT, pioneered high-speed photography using a repeating electronic flash unit he patented called the *stroboscope*. As the inventor of the electronic flash, he popularized its use to freeze objects in motion, and you've probably seen his photographs of bullets piercing balloons and drops of milk forming a coronet-shaped splash.

Electronic flash freezes action by virtue of its extremely short duration—as brief as 1/50,000th second or less. Although the D7000's built-in flash unit can give you these ultra-quick glimpses of moving subjects, an external flash, such as one of the Nikon Speedlights, offers even more versatility. You can read more about using electronic flash to stop action in Chapter 12.

Of course, the D7000 is fully capable of immobilizing all but the fastest movement using only its shutter speeds, which range all the way up to an astonishing 1/8,000th second. Indeed, you'll rarely have need for such a brief shutter speed in ordinary shooting. (For the record, I don't believe I've *ever* used a shutter speed of 1/8,000th second.) But if you wanted to use an aperture of f/1.8 at ISO 200 outdoors in bright sunlight, for some reason, a shutter speed of 1/8,000th second would more than do the job. You'd need a faster shutter speed only if you moved the ISO setting to a higher sensitivity (but why would you do that?). Under less than full sunlight, 1/8,000th second is more than fast enough for any conditions you're likely to encounter.

Most sports action can be frozen at 1/2,000th second or slower, and for many sports a slower shutter speed is actually preferable—for example, to allow the wheels of a racing automobile or motorcycle, or the rotors on a helicopter to blur realistically, as shown in Figure 7.2. At top, a 1/1,000th second shutter speed effectively stopped the rotors of the helicopter, making it look like a crash was impending. At bottom, I used a slower 1/250th second shutter speed to allow enough blur to make this a true action picture.

Figure 7.2
A little blur can be a good thing, as these shots of a helicopter at 1/1,000th second (top) and 1/250th second (bottom) show.

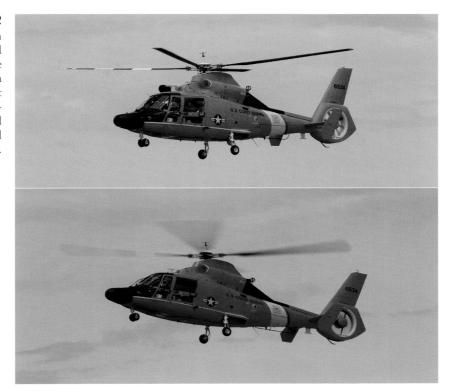

But if you want to do some exotic action-freezing photography without resorting to electronic flash, the D7000's top shutter speed is at your disposal. Here are some things to think about when exploring this type of high-speed photography:

- **You'll need a lot of light.** High shutter speeds cut very fine slices of time and sharply reduce the amount of illumination that reaches your sensor. To use 1/8,000th second at an aperture of f/6.3, you'd need an ISO setting of 1600—even in full daylight. To use an f/stop smaller than f/6.3 or an ISO setting lower than 1600, you'd need *more* light than full daylight provides. (That's why electronic flash units work so well for high-speed photography when used as the sole illumination; they provide both the effect of a brief shutter speed and the high levels of illumination needed.)

- **Forget about reciprocity failure.** If you're an old-time film shooter, you might recall that very brief shutter speeds (as well as very high light levels and very *long* exposures) produced an effect called *reciprocity failure,* in which given exposures ended up providing less than the calculated value because of the way film responded to very short, very intense, or very long exposures of light. Solid-state sensors don't suffer from this defect, so you don't need to make an adjustment when using high shutter speeds (or brief flash bursts).

■ **High shutter speeds with electronic flash.** You might be tempted to use an electronic flash with a high shutter speed. Perhaps you want to stop some action in daylight with a brief shutter speed and use electronic flash only as supplemental illumination to fill in the shadows. Unfortunately, under most conditions you can't use flash in subdued illumination with your D7000 at any shutter speed faster than 1/250th second. That's the fastest speed at which the camera's focal plane shutter is fully open: at shorter speeds, the "slit" described above comes into play, so that the flash will expose only the small portion of the sensor exposed by the slit throughout its duration. (Check out "High Speed Sync" in Chapter 12 if you want to see how you *can* use shutter speeds shorter than 1/250th second, albeit at much-reduced effective power levels.)

Working with Short Exposures

You can have a lot of fun exploring the kinds of pictures you can take using very brief exposure times, whether you decide to take advantage of the action-stopping capabilities of your built-in or external electronic flash or work with the Nikon D7000's faster shutter speeds. Here are a few ideas to get you started:

■ **Take revealing images.** Fast shutter speeds can help you reveal the real subject behind the façade, by freezing constant motion to capture an enlightening moment in time. Legendary fashion/portrait photographer Philippe Halsman used leaping photos of famous people, such as the Duke and Duchess of Windsor, Richard Nixon, and Salvador Dali to illuminate their real selves. Halsman said, "*When you ask a person to jump, his attention is mostly directed toward the act of jumping and the mask falls so that the real person appears.*" Try some high-speed portraits of people you know in motion to see how they appear when concentrating on something other than the portrait.

■ **Create unreal images.** High-speed photography can also produce photographs that show your subjects in ways that are quite unreal. A motocross cyclist leaping over a ramp, but with all motion stopped so that the rider and machine look as if they were frozen in mid-air, make for an unusual picture. When we're accustomed to seeing subjects in motion, seeing them stopped in time can verge on the surreal.

■ **Capture unseen perspectives.** Some things are *never* seen in real life, except when viewed in a stop-action photograph. Edgerton's balloon bursts were only a starting point. Freeze a hummingbird in flight for a view of wings that never seem to stop. Or, capture the splashes as liquid falls into a bowl, as shown in Figure 7.3. No electronic flash was required for this image (and wouldn't have illuminated the water in the bowl as evenly). Instead, a clutch of high intensity lamps and an ISO setting of 1600 allowed the camera to capture this image at 1/2,000th second.

Figure 7.3
A large amount of artificial illumination and an ISO 1600 sensitivity setting allowed capturing this shot at 1/2,000th second without use of an electronic flash.

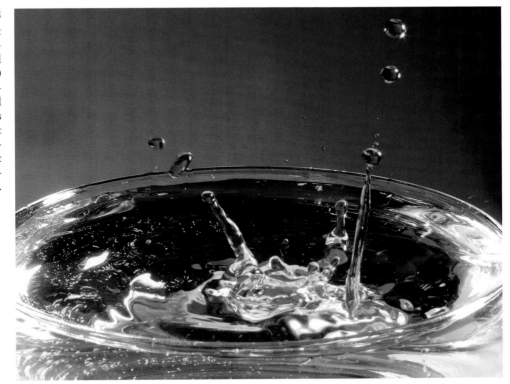

■ **Vanquish camera shake and gain new angles.** Here's an idea that's so obvious it isn't always explored to its fullest extent. A high enough shutter speed can free you from the tyranny of a tripod, making it easier to capture new angles, or to shoot quickly while moving around, especially with longer lenses. I tend to use a monopod or tripod for almost everything when I'm not using an image-stabilized lens, and I end up missing some shots because of a reluctance to adjust my camera support to get a higher, lower, or different angle. If you have enough light and can use an f/stop wide enough to permit a high shutter speed, you'll find a new freedom to choose your shots (see Figure 7.4). I have a favored 170mm-500mm lens that I use for sports and wildlife photography, almost invariably with a tripod, as I don't find the "reciprocal of the focal length" rule particularly helpful in most cases. I would *not* hand-hold this hefty lens at its 500mm setting with a 1/500th second shutter speed under most circumstances. Nor, if you want to account for the crop factor, would I use 1/750th second. However, at 1/2,000th second or faster, it's entirely possible for a steady hand to use this lens without a tripod or monopod's extra support, and I've found that my whole approach to shooting animals and other elusive subjects changes in high-speed mode. Selective focus allows dramatically isolating my prey wide open at f/6.3, too. Of course, at such a high shutter speed, you may need to boost your ISO setting—even when shooting outdoors.

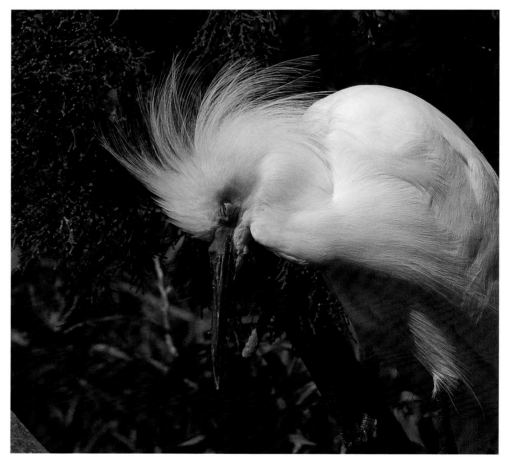

Figure 7.4
Outdoors, you may need a shutter speed of 1/2,000th second to hand-hold a 500mm lens to capture distant wildlife.

Long Exposures

Longer exposures are a doorway into another world, showing us how even familiar scenes can look much different when photographed over periods measured in seconds. At night, long exposures produce streaks of light from moving, illuminated subjects like automobiles or amusement park rides. Extra-long exposures of seemingly pitch-dark subjects can reveal interesting views using light levels barely bright enough to see by. At any time of day, including daytime (in which case you'll often need the help of neutral-density filters to make the long exposure practical), long exposures can cause moving objects to vanish entirely, because they don't remain stationary long enough to register in a photograph.

Three Ways to Take Long Exposures

There are actually three common types of lengthy exposures: *timed exposures*, *bulb exposures*, and *time exposures*. The D7000 offers only the first two, but once you understand all three, you'll see why Nikon made the choices it did. Because of the length of the exposure, all of the following techniques should be used with a tripod to hold the camera steady.

- **Timed exposures.** These are long exposures from 1 second to 30 seconds, measured by the camera itself. To take a picture in this range, simply use Manual or S modes and use the main command dial to set the shutter speed to the length of time you want, choosing from preset speeds of 1.0, 1.5, 2.0, 3.0, 4.0, 6.0, 8.0, 10.0, 15.0, 20.0, or 30.0 seconds (if you've specified 1/2 stop increments for exposure adjustments), or 1.0, 1.3, 1.6, 2.0, 2.5, 3.2, 4.0, 5.0, 6.0, 8.0, 10.0, 13.0, 15.0, 20.0, 25.0, and 30.0 seconds (if you're using 1/3 stop increments). The advantage of timed exposures is that the camera does all the calculating for you. There's no need for a stop-watch. If you review your image on the LCD and decide to try again with the exposure doubled or halved, you can dial in the correct exposure with precision. The disadvantage of timed exposures is that you can't take a photo for longer than 30 seconds.

- **Bulb exposures.** This type of exposure is so-called because in the olden days the photographer squeezed and held an air bulb attached to a tube that provided the force necessary to keep the shutter open. Traditionally, a bulb exposure is one that lasts as long as the shutter release button is pressed; when you release the button, the exposure ends. To make a bulb exposure with the D7000, set the camera on Manual mode and use the main command dial to select the shutter speed immediately after 30 seconds—buLb. Then, press the shutter to start the exposure, and press it again to close the shutter. If you'd like to simulate a time exposure (described below), you can use the Nikon MC-DC2 remote control cable or ML-L3 wireless remote control.

- **Time exposures.** This is a setting found on some cameras to produce longer exposures. With cameras that implement this option, the shutter opens when you press the shutter release button, and remains open until you press the button again. With the Nikon D7000, you can produce this effect with a locking cable release, as I did for the shot in San Juan, Puerto Rico shown in Figure 7.5. You can press the shutter release button, go off for a few minutes, and come back to close the shutter (assuming your camera is still there). The disadvantages of this mode are exposures must be timed manually, and with shorter exposures it's possible for the vibration of manually opening and closing the shutter to register in the photo. For longer exposures, the period of vibration is relatively brief and not usually a problem.

Figure 7.5
A locking cable release can give you long time exposures, such as this 60 second shot in San Juan, Puerto Rico.

Working with Long Exposures

Because the D7000 produces such good images at longer exposures, and there are so many creative things you can do with long exposure techniques, you'll want to do some experimenting. Get yourself a tripod or another firm support and take some test shots with long exposure noise reduction both enabled and disabled (to see whether you prefer low noise or high detail) and get started. Here are some things to try:

- **Make people invisible.** One very cool thing about long exposures is that objects that move rapidly enough won't register at all in a photograph, while the subjects that remain stationary are portrayed in the normal way. That makes it easy to produce people-free landscape photos and architectural photos at night or, even, in full daylight if you use a neutral-density filter (or two) (or three) to allow an exposure of at least a few seconds. At ISO 100, f/22, and a pair of 8X (three-stop) neutral-density filters, you can use exposures of nearly two seconds; overcast days and/or even more neutral-density filtration would work even better if daylight people-vanishing is your goal. They'll have to be walking *very* briskly and across the field of view (rather than directly toward the camera) for this to work. At night, it's much easier to achieve this effect with the 20- to 30-second exposures that are possible, as you can see in Figure 7.6.

- **Create streaks.** If you aren't shooting for total invisibility, long exposures with the camera on a tripod can produce some interesting streaky effects. Even a single 8X ND filter will let you shoot at f/22 and 1/6th second in daylight.

Figure 7.6
This European alleyway is thronged with people, but with the camera on a tripod, a 30-second exposure rendered the passersby almost invisible.

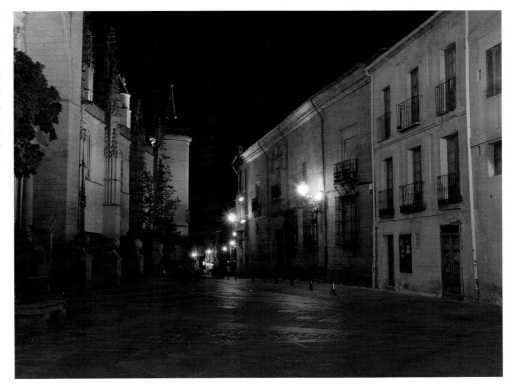

- **Produce light trails.** At night, car headlights and taillights and other moving sources of illumination can generate interesting light trails, as shown in Figure 7.7. Your camera doesn't even need to be mounted on a tripod; hand-holding the D7000 for longer exposures adds movement and patterns to your streaky trails. If you're shooting fireworks, a longer exposure may allow you to combine several bursts into one picture.

- **Blur waterfalls, etc.** You'll find that waterfalls and other sources of moving liquid produce a special type of long-exposure blur, because the water merges into a fantasy-like veil that looks different at different exposure times, and with different waterfalls. Cascades with turbulent flow produce a rougher look at a given longer exposure than falls that flow smoothly. Although blurred waterfalls have become almost a cliché, there are still plenty of variations for a creative photographer to explore. (See Figure 7.8.)

- **Show total darkness in new ways.** Even on the darkest, moonless nights, there is enough starlight or glow from distant illumination sources to see by, and, if you use a long exposure, there is enough light to take a picture, too.

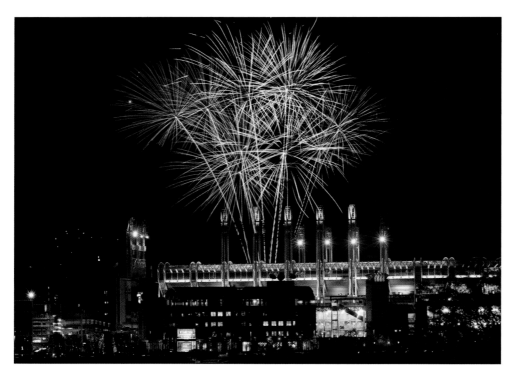

Figure 7.7
Long exposures
can capture
several bursts of
fireworks in
one frame.

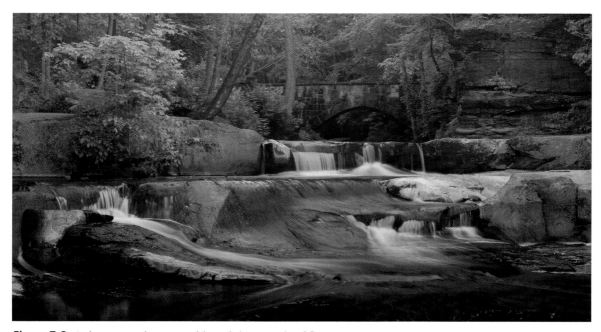

Figure 7.8 A three-second exposure blurred this cascade of flowing water.

Delayed Exposures

Sometimes it's desirable to have a delay of some sort before a picture is actually taken. Perhaps you'd like to get in the picture yourself, and would appreciate it if the camera waited 10 seconds after you press the shutter release to actually take the picture. Maybe you want to give a tripod-mounted camera time to settle down and damp any residual vibration after the release is pressed to improve sharpness for an exposure with a relatively slow shutter speed. It's possible you want to explore the world of time-lapse photography. The next sections present your delayed exposure options.

Self-Timer

The D7000 has a built-in self-timer with a user-selectable delay. Activate the timer by rotating the release mode dial to the self-timer icon. Press the shutter release button halfway to lock in focus on your subjects (if you're taking a self-portrait, focus on an object at a similar distance and use focus lock). When you're ready to take the photo, continue pressing the shutter release the rest of the way. The lamp on the front of the camera will blink slowly for eight seconds (when using the 10-second timer) and the beeper will chirp (if you haven't disabled it in the Custom Settings menu, as described in Chapter 9). During the final two seconds, the beeper sounds more rapidly and the lamp remains on until the picture is taken.

Another way to simulate a longer self-timer is with the Mup mirror lockup. This is something you might want to do if you're shooting close-ups, landscapes, or other types of pictures using the self-timer only to trip the shutter in the most vibration-free way possible. Forget to bring along your tripod, but still want to take a close-up picture with a precise focus setting? That happened to me when I encountered this colorful plant (see Figure 7.9) in a greenhouse when picking up some potted plants. I wheeled a planting cart over to the blossom, rested the camera on a soft bag of potting soil (a beanbag would have been better!), carefully focused, and let the self-timer trip the shutter at the appropriate moment. In such situations, the camera might teeter back and forth for a second or two, but it will settle back to its original position before the self-timer activates the shutter. The self-timer remains the active mode until you turn it off—even if you power down the D7000—so remember to turn the release mode dial back to Single frame mode when you're finished.

Time-Lapse/Interval Photography

Who hasn't marveled at a time-lapse photograph of a flower opening, a series of shots of the moon marching across the sky, or one of those extreme time-lapse picture sets showing something that takes a very, very long time, such as a building under construction.

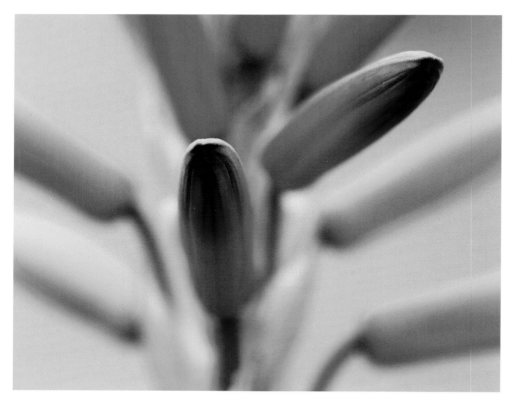

Figure 7.9
With the camera resting on a bag of potting soil on a cart, the self-timer triggered this vibration-free image of a bud about to open.

You probably won't be shooting such construction shots, unless you have a spare D7000 you don't need for a few months (or are willing to go through the rigmarole of figuring out how to set up your camera in precisely the same position using the same lens settings to shoot a series of pictures at intervals). However, other kinds of time-lapse photography are entirely within reach.

The D7000 can take time-lapse/interval photographs all by itself, using the Interval Timer Shooting entry found in the Shooting menu. You'll find step-by-step instructions for using this feature in Chapter 8. If you're willing to tether the camera to a computer (a laptop will do) using the USB cable, you can take time-lapse photos using the optional extra-cost Nikon Camera Control Pro.

Here is a recap of essential tips for effective time-lapse photography:

- **Use AC power.** If you're shooting a long sequence, consider connecting your camera to an AC adapter, as leaving the D7000 on for long periods of time will rapidly deplete the battery.

- **Make sure you have enough storage space.** Unless your memory card has enough capacity to hold all the images you'll be taking, you might want to change to a higher compression rate or reduced resolution to maximize the image count.

- **Make a movie.** While time-lapse stills are interesting, you can increase your fun factor by compiling all your shots into a motion picture using your favorite desktop movie-making software.

- **Protect your camera.** Make sure your camera is protected from weather, earthquakes, animals, young children, innocent bystanders, and theft.

- **Vary intervals.** Experiment with different time intervals. You don't want to take pictures too often or less often than necessary to capture the changes you hope to image.

Geotagging with the Nikon GP-1

The Nikon product line gained a lot of credibility as a tool for serious photographers when Nikon introduced the compact Nikon GP-1 Global Positioning System device. The unit makes it easy to tag your images with the same kind of longitude, latitude, altitude, and time stamp information that is supplied by the GPS unit you use in your car. (Don't have a GPS? Photographers who get lost in the boonies as easily as I do *must* have one of these!) The geotagging information is stored in the metadata space within your image files, and can be accessed by Nikon View NX2, or by online photo services such as mypicturetown.com and Flickr.

Geotagging can also be done by attaching geographic information to the photo after it's already been taken. This is often done with online sharing services, such as Flickr, which allow you to associate your uploaded photographs with a map, city, street address, or postal code. When properly geotagged and uploaded to sites like Flickr, users can browse through your photos using a map, finding pictures you've taken in a given area, or even searching through photos taken at the same location by other users. Of course, in this day and age it's probably wise not to include GPS information in photos of your home, especially if your photos can be viewed by an unrestricted audience.

Having this information available makes it easier to track where your pictures are taken. That can be essential, as I learned from a trip out West this Spring, where I found the red rocks, canyons, and arroyos of Nevada, Utah, Arizona, and Colorado all pretty much look alike to my untrained eye.

Like all GPS units, the Nikon GP-1 obtains its data by triangulating signals from satellites orbiting the Earth. It works with the Nikon D7000, as well as many other Nikon cameras. At about $225, it's not cheap, but those who need geotagging—especially for professional mapping or location applications—will find it to be a bargain.

The GP-1 (see Figure 7.10) slips onto the accessory shoe on top of the Nikon D7000. It connects to the GPS port on the camera using the Nikon GP1-CA90 cable, which plugs into the connector marked CAMERA on the GP-1. The device also has a port

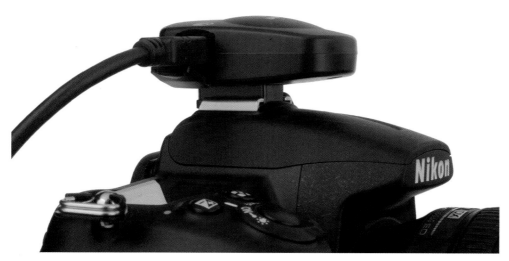

Figure 7.10
Nikon GP-1
geotagging
unit.

labeled with a remote control icon, so you can plug in the Nikon MC-DC2 remote
cable release, which would otherwise attach to the GPS port when you're not using the
geotagging unit.

A third connector connects the GP-1 to your computer using a USB cable. Nikon has
released a utility for Windows and Mac operating systems that allows you to read GPS
data from the GP-1 directly in your computer—no camera required. I tried the driver,
and discovered that the GP-1 couldn't "see" any satellites from inside my office. I plan
on trying it with my netbook outdoors, in a car, or in some other more satellite-acces-
sible location. Once attached, the device is very easy to use. You need to activate the
Nikon D7000's GPS capabilities in the GPS choice within the Setup menu, as described
in Chapter 10.

The first step is to allow the GP-1 to acquire signals from at least three satellites. If you've
used a GPS in your car, you'll know that satellite acquisition works best outdoors under
a clear sky and out of the "shadow" of tall buildings, and the Nikon unit is no exception. It takes about 40-60 seconds for the GP-1 to "connect." A red blinking LED means
that GPS data is not being recorded; a green blinking LED signifies that the unit has
acquired three satellites and is recording data. When the LED is solid green, the unit
has connected to four or more satellites, and is recording data with optimum accuracy.

Next, set up the camera by selecting the GPS option found under the Setup menu on
the Nikon D7000. Then, select Auto Meter Off to disable automatic shutoff of the
D7000's exposure meters. That will assure that the camera doesn't go to sleep while
you're using the GPS unit. Of course, in this mode the camera will use more power (the
meters never go off, and the GPS draws power constantly), but you don't want to go
through the 40-60-second satellite acquisition step each time you take a picture. Next,
use the Position option in the GPS menu to activate the unit.

Figure 7.11
Captured GPS information can be displayed when you review the image.

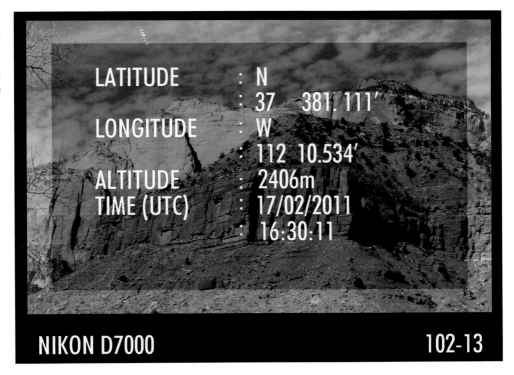

LATITUDE   : N
              : 37   381. 111'
LONGITUDE   : W
              : 112 10.534'
ALTITUDE   : 2406m
TIME (UTC)   : 17/02/2011
              : 16:30:11

NIKON D7000   102-13

You're all set. Once the unit is up and running, you can view GPS information using photo information screens available on the color LCD (and described in Chapter 3). The GPS screen, which appears only when a photo has been taken using the GPS unit, looks something like Figure 7.11.

WiFi

These days, GPS and WiFi capabilities work together with your D7000 in interesting new ways. Wireless capabilities allow you to upload photos directly from your D7000 to your computer at home or in your studio, or, through a hotspot at your hotel or coffee shop back to your home computer or to a photo sharing service like Facebook or Flickr. A special WiFi-enabled memory card that you slip in the SD slot of your camera performs the magic. GPS capabilities—built right into some of those WiFi cards—allow you to mark your photographs with location information, so you don't have to guess where a picture was taken.

Both capabilities are very cool. WiFi uploads can provide instant backup of important shots and sharing. And, as noted in the previous section, geotagging is most important as a way to associate the geographical location where the photographer was when a picture was taken, with the actual photograph itself. It can be done with the location-mapping capabilities of the WiFi card, or through add-on devices that third parties make available for your D7000.

A relatively affordable solution is offered by Eye-Fi (www.eye.fi). The Eye-Fi card is an SDHC memory card with a wireless transmitter built in. You insert it in your camera just as with any ordinary card, and then specify which networks to use. You can add as many as 32 different networks. The next time your camera is on within range of a specified network, your photos and videos can be uploaded to your computer and/or to your favorite sharing site. During setup, you can customize where you want your images uploaded. The Eye-Fi card will only send them to the computer and to the sharing site you choose. Upload to any of 25 popular sharing websites, including Flickr, Facebook, Picasa, Kodak Gallery, MobileMe, Costco, Adorama, Smugmug, YouTube, Shutterfly, or Walmart. Online Sharing is included as a lifetime, unlimited service with all X2 cards.

When uploading to online sites, you can specify not just where your images are sent, but how they are organized, by specifying preset album names, tags, descriptions, and even privacy preferences on certain sharing sites. Some Eye-Fi cards also include geotagging service, which helps you view uploaded photos on a map, and sort them by location. Eye-Fi's geotagging uses Wi-Fi Positioning System (WPS) technology. Using built-in Wi-Fi, the Eye-Fi card senses surrounding Wi-Fi networks as you take pictures. When photos are uploaded, the Eye-Fi service then adds the geotags to your photos. You don't need to have the password or a subscription for the Wi-Fi networks the card accesses; it can grab the location information directly without the need to "log in." You don't need to set up or control the Eye-Fi card from your camera. Software on your computer manages all the parameters. (See Figure 7.12.)

Your D7000 has an Eye-Fi Upload entry in the Setup menu that allows you to enable or disable this capability. You'll want to turn off Eye-Fi when traveling on an airplane (just as you disable your cell phone, tablet, or laptop's wireless capabilities when required to do so). In addition, use of Wi-Fi cards may be restricted or banned outside the United States, because the telecommunications laws differ in other countries. You'll find more about setting up an Eye-Fi card in Chapter 10.

If you frequently travel outside the range of your home (or business) WiFi network, an optional service called Hotspot Access is available, allowing you to connect to any AT&T WiFi hotspot in the USA. In addition, you can use your own WiFi accounts from commercial network providers, your city, even organizations you belong to such as your university.

The card has another interesting feature called Endless Memory. When pictures have been safely uploaded to an external site, the card can be set to automatically erase the oldest images to free up space for new pictures. You choose the threshold where the card starts zapping your old pictures to make room.

Figure 7.12
Functions of
the Eye-Fi card
can be con-
trolled from
your computer.

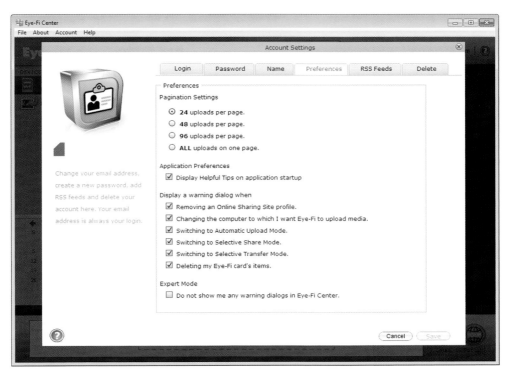

Eye-Fi currently offer four models, including the basic Eye-Fi Home (about $50), which can be used to transmit your photos from the dSLR to a computer on your home network (or any other network you set up somewhere, say, at a family reunion). Eye-Fi Share and Eye-Fi Share Video (about $60 and $80, respectively) are basically exactly the same (Share Video is 4GB instead of 2GB in capacity), but include software to allow you to upload your images from your camera through your computer network directly to websites and digital printing services already mentioned. The most sophisticated option is Eye-Fi Explore, a 4GB SDHC card that adds geographic location labels to your photo (so you'll know where you took it), and frees you from your own computer network by allowing uploads from more than 10,000 WiFi hotspots around the USA. Very cool, and the ultimate in picture backup.

Focus Stacking

If you are doing macro (close-up) photography of flowers, or other small objects at short distances, the depth-of-field often will be extremely narrow. In some cases, it will be so narrow that it will be impossible to keep the entire subject in focus in one photograph. Although having part of the image out of focus can be a pleasing effect for a portrait of a person, it is likely to be a hindrance when you are trying to make an accurate photographic record of a flower, or small piece of precision equipment. One solution to this problem is focus stacking, a procedure that can be considered like HDR translated for the world of focus—taking multiple shots with different settings, and, using software as explained below, combining the best parts from each image in order to make a whole that is better than the sum of the parts. Focus stacking requires a non-moving object, so some subjects, such as flowers, are best photographed in a breezeless environment, such as indoors.

For example, see Figures 7.13 through 7.15, in which I took photographs of three colorful jacks using a macro lens. As you can see from these images, the depth-of-field was extremely narrow, and only a small part of the subject was in focus for each shot.

Now look at Figure 7.16, in which the entire subject is in reasonably sharp focus. This image is a composite, made up of the three shots above, as well as 10 others, each one focused on the same scene, but at very gradually increasing distances from the camera's lens. All 13 images were then combined in Adobe Photoshop CS5 using the focus stacking procedure. Here are the steps you can take to combine shots for the purpose of achieving sharp focus in this sort of situation:

1. Set the camera firmly on a solid tripod. A tripod or other equally firm support is absolutely essential for this procedure.

2. Connect a wired remote control or use an infrared remote control if possible. If not, consider using the self-timer to avoid any movement of the camera when images are captured.

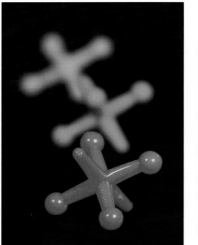 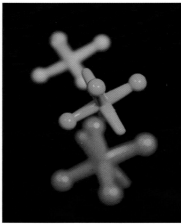 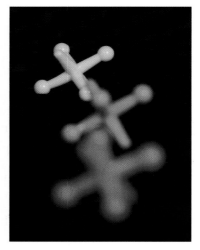

Figures 7.13, 7.14, and 7.15 These three shots were all focused on different distances within the same scene. No single shot could bring the entire subject into sharp focus.

Figure 7.16
Three partially out-of-focus shots have been merged, along with ten others, through a focus stacking procedure in Adobe Photoshop CS5, to produce a single image with the entire subject in focus.

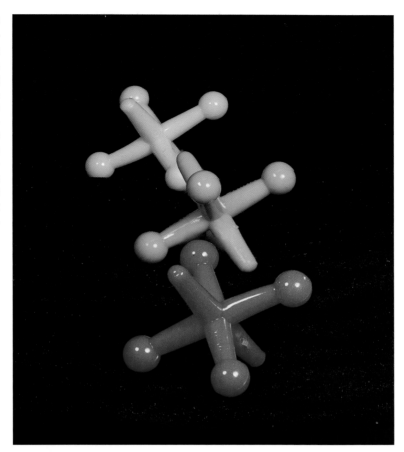

3. Set the camera to manual focus mode.

4. Set the exposure, ISO, and white balance manually, using test shots if necessary to determine the best values. This step will help prevent visible variations from arising among the multiple shots that you'll be taking.

5. Set the quality of the images to RAW & JPEG FINE.

6. Focus manually on the very closest point of the subject to the lens. Trip the shutter, using the remote control or self-timer.

7. Focus on a point slightly farther away from the lens and trip the shutter again.

8. Continue taking photographs in this way until you have covered the entire subject with in-focus shots.

9. In Photoshop CS4 or CS5, select File > Scripts > Load Files into Stack. In the dialog box that then appears, navigate on your computer to find the files for the photographs you have taken, and highlight them all.

10. At the bottom of the next dialog box that appears, check the box that says, "Attempt to Automatically Align Source Images," then click OK. The images will load; it may take several minutes for the program to load the images and attempt to arrange them into layers that are aligned based on their content.

11. Once the program has finished processing the images, go to the Layers panel and select all of the layers. You can do this by clicking on the top layer and then Shift-clicking on the bottom one.

12. While the layers are all selected, in Photoshop go to Edit > Auto-Blend Layers. In the dialog box that appears, select the two options, Stack Images and Seamless Tones and Colors, then click OK. The program will process the images, possibly for a considerable length of time.

13. If the procedure worked well, the result will be a single image made up of numerous layers that have been processed to produce a sharply focused rendering of your subject. If it did not work well, you may have to take additional images the next time, focusing very carefully on small slices of the subject as you move progressively farther away from the lens.

Although this procedure can work very well in Photoshop CS4 and CS5, you also may want to try it with programs that were developed more specifically for focus stacking and related procedures, such as Helicon Focus (www.heliconsoft.com), PhotoAcute (www.photoacute.com), or CombineZM (www.hadleyweb.pwp.blueyonder.co.uk).

Recommended Customized Settings

I'm going to finish off this chapter with some tables listing recommended settings for your Shooting and Custom Settings menus. I've divided the recommended settings into a group of tables, rather than one or two huge tables that would be more difficult to read. The tables show the "default" settings for the Shooting banks and Custom Settings menus, as they come from the factory, plus eight groups intended for Basic, Studio Flash, Portrait, Long Exposure, Sports—Indoors, Sports—Outdoors, Landscapes, and Portraits. For the Custom Settings menu, I add one more group of settings, for exposure bracketing.

Each setting includes options that I consider best-suited for their particular shooting situations. For example, when I am bracketing exposures, I like to shoot off a single bracket burst fairly quickly, so I choose C_L release mode, with the shooting speed set to 4 frames per second. When I press the shutter release, all the exposures are taken consecutively in a brief period of time. Similarly, when I am shooting indoor sports, I like to use ISO 1600 and set my autofocus priority to Release. That lets me shoot bursts of pictures with minimal shutter lag when I press the shutter release button, but still gives the D7000 a little extra time to get that first picture in sharp focus. I understand that the continuous shooting speed may be a little slower in that mode, but it works for me.

You can set up three "banks" of most of these settings simultaneously. Install one set of recommendations as your default set that your camera uses normally. Then switch to U1 or U2 and make alternate settings and register them as described in Chapter 10. That gives you three banks you can select with a spin of the mode dial. I also suggest further customizing these settings to best suit your own habits and needs. In addition, there are some settings that I do not suggest changes for, but which can easily be modified by you, if you like.

Shooting Menu Recommendations

I'll list my Shooting menu suggestions first. The Custom Settings menu recommendations are divided into the exact same categories but, of course, deal with different options. In the first table, the second column shows the default settings, as the D7000 comes from the factory.

Table 7.1 Shooting Menu Recommendations #1

Option	Camera Default	Basic Setting	Studio Flash	Portrait
File Naming	DSC/_DSC	D7K/_D7K or your choice	D7K/_D7K or your choice	D7K/_D7K or your choice
Role played by card in Slot 2	Overflow	Overflow	Backup	Backup
Image Format/Quality	JPEG Normal	NEF(RAW)+ JPEG Fine	NEF	NEF+ JPEG Fine
Image Size	Large	Large	Large	Large
JPEG Compression	Size Priority	Optimal Quality	Optimal Quality	Optimal Quality
NEF (RAW) recording:				
>Type	Lossless Compressed	Lossless Compressed	Lossless Compressed	Lossless Compressed
>NEF(RAW) bit depth	14-bit	14-bit	14-bit	14-bit
White Balance	Auto	Auto	Preset Manual	Auto
Set Picture Control	Standard	C-1 (Standard+ Sharp 7)	Standard	C-3 (Neutral + Sharp −2)
Color Space	sRGB	Adobe RGB	Adobe RGB	Adobe RGB
Auto distortion control	Off	Off	Off	Off
Active D-Lighting	Off	Off	Off	Off

Table 7.1 Shooting Menu Recommendations #1 (continued)

Option	Camera Default	Basic Setting	Studio Flash	Portrait
Long Exp. NR	Off	Off	Off	Off
High ISO NR	Normal	Low	Low	Low
ISO sensitivity settings:				
>ISO sensitivity	200	200	200	200
> ISO sensitivity auto control:	Off	On	Off	Off
Maximum sensitivity	3200	800	1600	1600
Minimum shutter speed	1/30 s	1/60 s	1/60 s	1/60 s
Movie Settings				
Quality	1920 × 1080/ 24 fps, high quality	1920 × 1080/ 24 fps, high quality	1920 × 1080/ 24 fps, high quality	1920 × 1080/ 24 fps, high quality
Microphone	Auto sensitivity (A)	Auto sensitivity (A)	Auto sensitivity (A)	Auto sensitivity (A)
Destination	SD card slot 1	Slot with fastest card	Slot with fastest card	Slot with fastest card
Manual movie settings	Off	Off	Off	Off

Table 7.2 Shooting Menu Recommendations #2

Option	Long Exposure	Sports Indoors	Sports Outdoors	Landscape
File Naming	D7K/_D7K or your choice	D7K/_D7K or your choice	D7K/_D7K or your choice	D7K/_D7K or your choice
Role played by card in Slot 2	Overflow	Overflow	Overflow	Backup
Image Format/Quality	NEF	JPEG Fine	JPEG Fine	NEF+JPEG Fine
Image Size	Large	Large	Large	Large
JPEG Compression	Optimal Quality	Optimal Quality	Optimal Quality	Optimal Quality
NEF (RAW) recording:				
>Type	Lossless Compressed	Lossless Compressed	Lossless Compressed	Lossless Compressed
>NEF(RAW) bit depth	14-bit	12-bit	12-bit	14-bit

Table 7.2 Shooting Menu Recommendations #2 (continued)

Option	Long Exposure	Sports Indoors	Sports Outdoors	Landscape
White Balance	Auto	Auto	Auto	Auto
Set Picture Control	Standard	Standard	Standard	C-2 (Vivid+Sharp 5)
Color Space	Adobe RGB	Adobe RGB	Adobe RGB	Adobe RGB
Auto distortion control	Off	Off	Off	On
Active D-Lighting	Off	Off	Off	Off
Long Exp. NR	On	Off	Off	Off
High ISO NR – ISO	Low	Normal	Low	Low
ISO sensitivity settings:				
>ISO Sensitivity	400	1600	400	200
> ISO sensitivity auto control:	Off	Off	Off	Off
Maximum sensitivity	1600	1600	1600	1600
Minimum shutter speed	1/60 s	1/60 s	1/60 s	1/60 s
Movie Settings				
Quality	1920 × 1080/ 24 fps, high quality	1280 × 720/ 30 fps, normal quality	1280 × 720/ 30 fps, normal quality	1920 × 1080/ 24 fps, high quality
Microphone	Auto sensitivity (A)	Auto sensitivity (A)	Auto sensitivity (A)	Auto sensitivity (A)
Destination	Slot with fastest card	Slot with fastest card	Slot with fastest card	Slot with fastest card
Manual movie settings	Off	Off	Off	Off

Custom Settings Menu Recommendations

Next come the Custom Settings menu recommendations. They are divided into the exact same categories, but with the addition of a new category for bracketed shots. And, of course, they all deal with different options.

Table 7.3 Custom Settings Menu Recommendations #1

Item	Option	Camera Default	Basic Setting	Studio Flash	Portrait	Long Exposure
	Autofocus					
a1	AF-C priority selection	Release	Release	Release	Release	Release
a2	AF-S priority selection	Focus	Focus	Focus	Focus	Focus
a3	Focus tracking with lock-on	Normal	Normal	Normal	Normal	Normal
a4	AF point illumination	Auto	Auto	Auto	Auto	Auto
a5	Focus point wrap-around	No wrap (OFF)	No wrap (OFF)	No wrap (OFF)	No wrap (OFF)	No wrap (OFF)
a6	Number of focus points	39 points	39 points	39 points	39 points	39 points
a7	AF assist illuminator	On	On	Off	Off	On
a8	Live view/movie AF					
	>*Autofocus mode*	Single-servo AF	Single-servo AF	Single-servo AF	Single-servo AF	Single-servo AF
	>*AF-area mode: Sports, Night Portrait, Pet, Beach, High Key, Low Key*	Wide-area AF	Wide-area AF	Wide-area AF	Wide-area AF	Wide-area AF
	>*AF-area mode: Close-up, Food*	Normal-area AF	Normal-area AF	Normal-area AF	Normal-area AF	Normal-area AF
	>*AF-area mode: All other modes*	Face-priority AF	Face-priority AF	Face-priority AF	Face-priority AF	Wide-area AF
	Metering/exposure					
b1	ISO sensitivity step value	1/3 step	1/3 step	1/3 step	1/3 step	1/3 step
b2	EV steps for exposure control	1/3 step	1/3 step	1/3 step	1/3 step	1/3 step
b3	Easy exposure compensation	Off	Off	Off	Off	Off
b4	Center-weighted area	8mm	8mm	8mm	8mm	8mm
b5	Fine-tune optimal exposure:					
	> *Matrix metering*	0	0	0	0	0
	> *Center-Weighted*	0	0	0	0	0
	> *Spot metering*	0	0	0	0	0

Table 7.3 Custom Settings Menu Recommendations #1 (continued)

Item	Option	Camera Default	Basic Setting	Studio Flash	Portrait	Long Exposure
	Timers/AE Lock					
c1	Shutter-release button AE-L	Off	Off	Off	Off	Off
c2	Auto meter-off delay	6 sec.	6 sec.	6 sec.	6 sec.	6 sec.
c3	Self-timer	10 sec.	20 sec.	10 sec.	10 sec.	2 sec.
	>*Self-timer delay*	10s	10s	10s	20s	10s
	>*Number of shots*	1	1	1	3	1
	>*Interval between shots*	0.5s	0.5s	3s	0.5s	0.5s
c4	Monitor off delay					
	>*Playback*	10 sec.	10 sec.	10 sec.	10 sec.	20 sec.
	>*Menus*	20 sec.	20 sec.	20 sec.	20 sec.	20 sec.
	>*Information display*	10 sec.	10 sec.	20 sec.	20 sec.	20 sec.
	>*Image review*	4 sec.	10 sec.	4 sec.	4 sec.	4 sec.
	>*Live view*	10 min.	10 min.	10 min.	10 min.	10 min.
c5	Remote on duration					
	Shooting/display					
d1	Beep					
	>*Volume*	Off	Off	Off	Off	On
	>*Pitch*	High	Low	Low	Low	High
d2	Viewfinder grid display	Off	Off	Off	On	Off
d3	ISO display and adjustment	Show frame count	Show frame count	Show frame count	Show frame count	Display ISO
d4	Viewfinder warning display	On	On	On	On	On
d5	Screen tips	On	On	Off	Off	Off
d6	CL mode shooting speed	3 fps	3 fps	3 fps	3 fps	3 fps
d7	Max. continuous release	100	20	20	20	20
d8	File No. Sequence	On	On	On	On	On
d9	Information Display	Auto	Auto	Auto	Auto	Auto

Table 7.3 Custom Settings Menu Recommendations #1 (continued)

Item	Option	Camera Default	Basic Setting	Studio Flash	Portrait	Long Exposure
d10	LCD Illumination	Off	Off	Off	Off	Off
d11	Exposure Delay Mode	Off	Off	Off	Off	Off
d12	MB-D11 Battery Type	AA Alkaline	AA Alkaline	AA Alkaline	AA Alkaline	AA Alkaline
d13	Flash Warning	On	On	Off	Off	Off
d14	Battery Order	MB-D11 First	MB-D11 First	MB-D11 First	MB-D11 First	MB-D11 First
	Bracketing/Flash					
e1	Flash sync speed	1/250	1/250	1/250	1/250	1/250
e2	Flash shutter speed	1/60	1/60	1/60	1/60	1/60
e3	Flash control for built-in flash	TTL	TTL	Commander	Commander	TTL
	> *Commander Only - Built In*	TTL 0	TTL 0	TTL 0	TTL 0	TTL 0
	> *Commander Only - Group A*	TTL 0	TTL 0	TTL 0	TTL 0	TTL 0
	> *Commander Only - Group B*	TTL 0	TTL 0	TTL 0	TTL 0	TTL 0
	> *Commander Only - Channel#*	1	1	1	1	1
e4	Modeling Flash	ON	ON	OFF	ON	ON
e5	Auto Bracketing Set	AE & Flash	AE & Flash	AE & Flash	AE & Flash	AE & Flash
e6	Bracketing Order	Meter>Under >Over	Meter>Under >Over	Meter>Under >Over	Meter>Under >Over	Meter>Under >Over
	Controls					
f1	Illuminator switch	LCD backlight	LCD backlight	LCD backlight	LCD backlight	LCD backlight
f2	OK button	Select center focus point	Select center focus point	Select center focus point	Select center focus point	Select center focus point
f3	Assign Fn Button	FV lock	Flash Off	FV Lock	FV Lock	FV Lock
f4	Assign Preview Button	Preview	Preview	Preview	Preview	Preview
f5	Assign AE-L/ AF-L Button	AE-AF lock	AE-AF lock	AE-AF lock	AE-AF lock	AE-AF lock

Table 7.3 Custom Settings Menu Recommendations #1 (continued)

Item	Option	Camera Default	Basic Setting	Studio Flash	Portrait	Long Exposure
f6	Customize Command Dials					
	> *Reverse rotation*	No (OFF)	No (OFF)	No (OFF)	No (OFF)	No (OFF)
	> *Change main/sub*	No (OFF)	No (OFF)	No (OFF)	No (OFF)	No (OFF)
	> *Aperture setting*	ON (Sub-command Dial)	ON (Sub-command Dial)	ON (Sub-command Dial)	ON (Sub-command Dial)	ON (Sub-command Dial)
	> *Menus and playback*	Off	Off	Off	Off	Off
f7	Release Button to Use Dial	No (OFF)	No (OFF)	No (OFF)	No (OFF)	No (OFF)
f8	Slot empty release lock	Enable Release	Release locked	Release locked	Release locked	Release locked
f9	Reverse Indicators	+ 0 -	+ 0 -	+ 0 -	+ 0 -	+ 0 -
f10	Assign MB-D11 AE-L/AF-L Button	AE/AF Lock	AE/AF Lock	AE/AF Lock	AE/AF Lock	AE/AF Lock

Table 7.4 Custom Settings Menu Recommendations #2

Item	Option	Sports Indoors	Sports Outdoors	Landscape	Bracketing
	Autofocus				
a1	AF-C priority selection	Release	Release	Release	Release
a2	AF-S priority selection	Focus	Focus	Focus	Focus
a3	Focus tracking with lock-on	Normal	Normal	Normal	Normal
a4	AF point illumination	Auto	Auto	Auto	Auto
a5	Focus point wrap-around	No wrap (OFF)	No wrap (OFF)	No wrap (OFF)	No wrap (OFF)
a6	Number of focus points	11 points	11 points	39 points	39 points
a7	AF assist illuminator	Off	Off	Off	Off
a8	Live view/movie AF				
	>*Autofocus mode*	Single-servo AF	Single-servo AF	Single-servo AF	Single-servo AF
	>*AF-area mode: Sports, Night Portrait, Pet, Beach, High Key, Low Key*	Wide-area AF	Wide-area AF	Wide-area AF	Wide-area AF

Table 7.4 Custom Settings Menu Recommendations #2 (continued)

Item	Option	Sports Indoors	Sports Outdoors	Landscape	Bracketing
	>AF-area mode: Close-up, Food	Normal-area AF	Normal-area AF	Normal-area AF	Normal-area AF
	>AF-area mode: All other modes	Face-priority AF	Face-priority AF	Face-priority AF	Face-priority AF
	Metering/exposure				
b1	ISO sensitivity step value	1/3 step	1/3 step	1/3 step	1/3 step
b2	EV steps for exposure control	1/3 step	1/3 step	1/3 step	1/3 step
b3	Easy exposure compensation	Off	Off	Off	Off
b4	Center-weighted area	8mm	8mm	8mm	8mm
b5	Fine-tune optimal exposure:				
	> Matrix metering	0	0	0	0
	> Center-Weighted	0	0	0	0
	> Spot metering	0	0	0	0
	Timers/AE Lock				
c1	Shutter-release button AE-L	Off	Off	Off	Off
c2	Auto meter-off delay	6 sec.	6 sec.	6 sec.	6 sec.
c3	Self-timer	10 sec.	20 sec.	10 sec.	10 sec.
	>Self-timer delay	10s	10s	10s	20s
	>Number of shots	1	1	1	3
	>Interval between shots	0.5s	0.5s	3s	0.5s
c4	Monitor off delay				
	>Playback	6 sec.	6 sec.	10 sec.	10 sec.
	>Menus	20 sec.	20 sec.	20 sec.	20 sec.
	>Information display	10 sec.	10 sec.	20 sec.	20 sec.
	>Image review	4 sec.	4 sec.	4 sec.	4 sec.
	>Live view	10 min.	10 min.	10 min.	10 min.
c5	Remote on duration				

Table 7.4 Custom Settings Menu Recommendations #2 (continued)

Item	Option	Sports Indoors	Sports Outdoors	Landscape	Bracketing
	Shooting/display				
d1	Beep				
	>*Volume*	Off	Off	Off	Off
	>*Pitch*	High	Low	Low	Low
d2	Viewfinder grid display	Off	Off	Off	On
d3	ISO display and adjustment	Show frame count	Show frame count	Show frame count	Show frame count
d4	Viewfinder warning display	On	On	On	On
d5	Screen tips	On	On	Off	Off
d6	CL mode shooting speed	4 fps	4 fps	3 fps	3 fps
d7	Max. continuous release	100	20	20	20
d8	File No. Sequence	On	On	On	On
d9	Information Display	Auto	Auto	Auto	Auto
d10	LCD Illumination	Off	Off	Off	Off
d11	Exposure Delay Mode	Off	Off	Off	Off
d12	MB-D11 Battery Type	AA Alkaline	AA Alkaline	AA Alkaline	AA Alkaline
d13	Flash Warning	On	On	Off	Off
d14	Battery Order	MB-D11 First	MB-D11 First	MB-D11 First	MB-D11 First
	Bracketing/Flash				
e1	Flash sync speed	1/250	1/250	1/250	1/250
e2	Flash shutter speed	1/60	1/60	1/60	1/60
e3	Flash control for built-in flash	TTL	TTL	Commander	Commander
	> *Commander Only - Built In*	TTL 0	TTL 0	TTL 0	TTL 0
	> *Commander Only - Group A*	TTL 0	TTL 0	TTL 0	TTL 0
	> *Commander Only - Group B*	TTL 0	TTL 0	TTL 0	TTL 0
	> *Commander Only - Channel#*	1	1	1	1

Table 7.4 Custom Settings Menu Recommendations #2 (continued)

Item	Option	Sports Indoors	Sports Outdoors	Landscape	Bracketing
e4	Modeling Flash	Off	Off	On	Off
e5	Auto Bracketing Set	AE & Flash	AE & Flash	AE & Flash	Your choice
e6	Bracketing Order	Meter>Under>Over	Meter>Under>Over	Meter>Under>Over	Under>Meter>Over
	Controls				
f1	Illuminator switch	LCD backlight	LCD backlight	LCD backlight	LCD backlight
f2	OK button	Select center focus point	Select center focus point	Select center focus point	Select center focus point
f3	Assign Fn Button	FV lock	Flash Off	FV Lock	FV Lock
f4	Assign Preview Button	Preview	Preview	Preview	Preview
f5	Assign AE-L/AF-L Button	AE-AF lock	AE-AF lock	AE-AF lock	AE-AF lock
f6	Customize Command Dials				
	> *Reverse rotation*	No (OFF)	No (OFF)	No (OFF)	No (OFF)
	> *Change main/sub*	No (OFF)	No (OFF)	No (OFF)	No (OFF)
	> *Aperture setting*	ON (Sub-command Dial)	ON (Sub-command Dial)	ON (Sub-command Dial)	ON (Sub-command Dial)
	> *Menus and playback*	Off	Off	Off	Off
f7	Release Button to Use Dial	No (OFF)	No (OFF)	No (OFF)	No (OFF)
f8	Slot empty release lock	Enable Release	Release locked	Release locked	Release locked
f9	Reverse Indicators	+ 0 -	+ 0 -	+ 0 -	+ 0 -
f10	Assign MB-D11 AE-L/AF-L Button	AE/AF Lock	AE/AF Lock	AE/AF Lock	AE/AF Lock

Part III

Advanced Tools

The next five chapters are devoted to helping you dig deeper into the capabilities of your Nikon D7000, so you can exploit all those cool features that your previous camera lacked. Chapters 8, 9, and 10 list every setting and option found in the Playback, Shooting, Custom Settings, Setup, Retouch, and My Menus. I'll not only tell you what each menu item does, I'll explain exactly when and why you should use every option. Then, in Chapter 11, I'll show you how to select the best lenses for the kinds of photography you want to do, with my recommendations for starter lenses as well as more advanced optics for specialized applications.

Chapter 12 is devoted to the magic of light—your fundamental tool in creating any photograph. There are entire books devoted to working with electronic flash, but I hope to get you started with plenty of coverage of the Nikon D7000's capabilities. I'll show you how to master your camera's built-in flash—and avoid that "built-in flash" look, and offer an introduction to the use of external flash units, including the Nikon SB-900. By the time you finish these essential chapters, you'll be well on the way to mastering your Nikon D7000.

8

Setup: Playback and Shooting Menus

The Nikon D7000 is undoubtedly one of the most customizable, tweakable, fine-tunable cameras Nikon has ever offered, and provides an amazing degree of adjustments for a camera in its price range. This versatility has made the D7000 popular among professional photographers as well as advanced amateurs. On a recent trip to Old San Juan, Puerto Rico, I didn't hesitate to leave my Nikon D3s at home, and travel with the lightweight—but highly capable—D7000.

You can enjoy this flexibility, too. If your camera doesn't behave in exactly the way you'd like, chances are you can make a small change in the Playback, Shooting, Custom Settings, and Setup menus that will tailor the D7000 to your needs. In fact, if you don't like the *menus* you can create your own using the clever My Menu system.

This chapter will help you sort out the settings for the Playback and Shooting menus, which determine how the D7000 displays images on review, and how it uses many of its shooting features to take a photo. The following chapters will focus on the Custom Settings menu (Chapter 9), and Setup, Retouch, and My Menu options (Chapter 10).

As I've mentioned before, this book isn't intended to replace the manual you received with your D7000, nor have I any interest in rehashing its contents. You'll still find the original manual useful as a standby reference that lists every possible option in exhaustive (if mind-numbing) detail—without really telling you how to use those options to take better pictures. There is, however, some unavoidable duplication between the Nikon manual and the next three chapters, because I'm going to explain all the key menu choices and the options you may have in using them. You should find, though, that I will give you the information you need in a much more helpful format, with plenty of detail on why you should make some settings that are particularly cryptic.

I'm not going to waste a lot of space on some of the more obvious menu choices in these chapters. For example, you can probably figure out that the Beep option in Custom Settings menu CSM #d1 deals with the solid-state beeper in your camera that sounds off during various activities (such as the self-timer countdown). You can certainly decipher the import of the three options available for the Beep entry (High, Low, and Off). In this chapter, I'll devote no more than a sentence or two to the blatantly obvious settings and concentrate on the more confusing aspects of the D7000 setup, such as automatic exposure bracketing. I'll start with an overview of using the D7000's menus themselves.

Anatomy of the Nikon D7000's Menus

If you used any Nikon digital SLR before you purchased your Nikon D7000, you're probably already familiar with the basic menu system. The menus consist of a series of screens with entries, as shown in Figure 8.1. Navigating among the various menus is easy and follows a consistent set of rules:

- Press the MENU button to display the main menu screens.

- Use the multi selector's left/right/up/down buttons to navigate among the menu entries to highlight your choice. Moving the highlighting to the left column lets you scroll up and down among the six top-level menus. From the top in Figure 8.1, they are Playback, Shooting, Custom Settings, Setup, Retouch, and My Menu, with Help access represented by a question mark at the bottom of the column.

- A highlighted top-level menu's icon will change from black and white to yellow highlighting. Use the multi selector's right button to move into the column containing that menu's choices, and the up/down buttons to scroll among the entries. If more than one screen full of choices is available, a scroll bar appears at the far right of the screen, with a position slider showing the relative position of the currently highlighted entry.

- To work with a highlighted menu entry, press the OK button in the center of the multi selector, or just press the right button on the multi selector. Any additional screens of choices will appear. You can move among them using the same multi selector movements.

- You can confirm a selection by pressing the OK button or, frequently, by pressing the right button on the multi selector once again. Some functions require scrolling to a Done menu choice, or include an instruction to set a choice using some other button.

Figure 8.1
The multi selector's navigational buttons are used to move among the various menu entries.

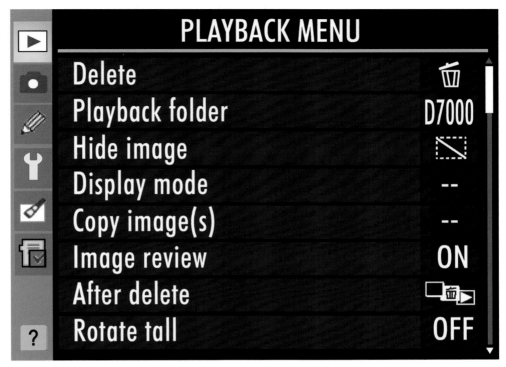

- Pressing the multi selector left button usually backs you out of the current screen, and pressing the MENU button again usually does the same thing. You can exit the menu system at any time by tapping the shutter release button.

- The Nikon D7000 "remembers" the top-level menu and specific menu entry you were using (but not any submenus) the last time the menu system was accessed, so pressing the MENU button brings you back to where you left off. So, if you were working with an entry in the Custom Settings menu's Metering/Exposure section, then decided to take a photo, the next time you press the MENU button the Custom Settings menu and the Metering/Exposure entry will be highlighted, but not the specific submenu (b1 through b5) that you might have selected.

The top-level menus are color-coded, and a bar in that color is displayed underneath the menu title when one of those menus is highlighted. The colors are: Playback menu (blue); Shooting menu (green); Custom Settings menu (red); Setup menu (orange); Retouch menu (purple); and My Menu (gray). The Custom Settings menu has six sub-menus that are themselves color-coded to help you keep track of where you are located in the menu system. You'll learn about the Custom Settings, Setup, Retouch, and My Menu options in Chapters 9 and 10.

Playback Menu Options

The blue-coded Playback menu has ten entries where you select options related to the display, review, transfer, and printing of the photos you've taken. The choices you'll find include the following entries (the last two, Slide Show and Print Set [DPOF] are not pictured in Figure 8.1, and don't appear until you scroll the listing to the bottom):

- Delete
- Playback folder
- Hide image
- Display mode
- Copy image(s)
- Image review
- After delete
- Rotate tall
- Slide show
- Print set (DPOF)

Delete

Choose this menu entry and you'll be given three choices: Selected, Select Date, and All. If you choose All, then all the pictures in the folder currently selected for playback (as described next) will be removed. When two memory cards are in the camera and have photos, you can choose which card to use to select images for removal. To delete only some pictures from a folder, choose Selected; you'll see an image selection screen like the one shown in Figure 8.2. Then, follow these instructions:

1. Use the multi selector cursor keys to scroll among the available images.

2. When you highlight an image you think you might like to delete, press the Playback button to temporarily enlarge that image so you can evaluate it further. When you release the button, the selection screen returns. To examine images on a card in the other slot, press and hold the BKT button and press the multi selector up button.

3. To mark an image for deletion, press the Zoom In/Thumbnail button (*not* the Trash button). A trash can icon will appear overlaid on that image's thumbnail. To unmark an image, press the Zoom In/Thumbnail button again.

4. When you've finished marking images to delete, press OK. A final screen will appear asking you to confirm the removal of the image(s). Choose Yes to delete the image(s) or No to cancel deletion, and then press OK. If you selected Yes, then you'll return to the Playback menu; if you chose No, you'll be taken back to the selection screen to mark/unmark images.

5. To back out of the selection screen, press the MENU button.

In the main Delete screen you can also choose Select Date. Highlight any of the available dates that have pictures, and press the multi selector right button to add a check

Figure 8.2
Select images
to delete.

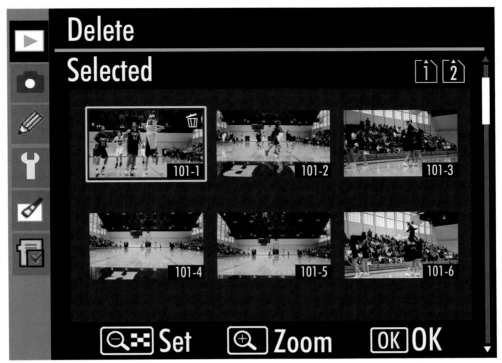

mark to that date. Press the Zoom Out/Index button to view/confirm that the images for the date you've marked are those you want to delete, and press the button again to return to the Select Date screen. When you're finished choosing dates, press OK to delete the images from the confirmation screen.

Your final choice from the main Delete screen is All, which removes all the images from your memory card, except for those marked as Protected. Keep in mind that deleting images through the Delete process is slower than just wiping out the whole card with the Format command, so using Format is generally much faster than choosing Delete: All, and also is a safer way of returning your memory card to a fresh, blank state.

Playback Folder

Your Nikon D7000 will create folders on your memory card to store the images that it creates. It assigns the first folder a number, like 100D7000, and when that folder fills with 999 images, the camera automatically creates a new folder numbered one higher, such as 101D7000. If you use the same memory card in another camera, that camera will also create its own folder. Thus you can end up with several folders on the same memory card, until you eventually reformat the card and folder creation starts anew.

This menu item allows you to choose which folders are accessed when displaying images using the D7000's Playback facility. Your choices are as follows:

- **D7000.** The camera will use only the folders on your memory card created by the D7000 and ignore those created by other cameras. Images in all the D7000's folders will be displayed. This is the default setting.

- **All.** All folders containing images that the D7000 can read will be accessed, regardless of which camera created them. You might want to use this setting if you swap memory cards among several cameras and want to be able to review all the photos (especially when considering reformatting the memory card). You will be able to view images even if they were created by a non-Nikon camera if those images conform to the Design Rule for Camera File system (DCF) specifications.

- **Current.** The D7000 will display only images in the current folder. For example, if you have been shooting heavily at an event and have already accumulated more than 999 shots in one folder and the D7000 has created a new folder for the overflow, you'd use this setting to view only the most recent photos, which reside in the current folder. You can change the current folder to any other folder on your memory card using the Active Folder option in the Shooting menu, described later in this chapter.

Hide Image

Use this menu option to protect *and* hide images. When you choose Hide Image, you'll be given a choice to select/set images (using a selection screen almost identical to the one used to delete images, as shown in Figure 8.2); the choice of selecting by date (as with deleting images); or the option of deselecting all hidden images.

Unlike the Protect option, which just marks images to keep them from accidental deletion, this selection also hides them from view using the regular Playback functions. Pictures that have been hidden can only be viewed from the selection screen. I use this facility in two different ways:

- Sometimes I have a memory card filled with images and I want to show some of the images, perhaps as a slideshow, or sometimes just by handing the camera to someone and asking them to browse through the photos. I can hide the non-relevant images so only the relevant pictures appear.

- Hiding images is a good way to make your real stinkers invisible if you haven't quite made up your mind to delete them.

Remember that if you "unhide" an image you are also removing the Protect attribute. If you want the photo to be visible, but still protected, press the Protect button (it has a key icon as a label) while viewing the image on the LCD. The key icon will be superimposed on the image, showing you that it is now protected from accidental erasure. Reformatting the card removes the Hidden and Protected attributes, of course—because it removes those images as well!

Display Mode

You'll recall from Chapter 3 that a great deal of information, available on multiple screens, can be displayed when reviewing images. This menu item helps you reduce/increase the clutter by specifying which information and screens will be available. To activate or deactivate an info option, scroll to that option and press the OK button or right multi selector button to add a check mark to the box next to that item. Press the OK button or right multi selector button to unmark an item that has previously been checked. Important: when you're finished, you must scroll up to Done and press OK or the right multi selector button to confirm your choices. Exiting the Display mode menu any other way will cause any changes you may have made to be ignored. Your info options include:

■ **Focus point.** Activate this option to display the active focus point(s) with red highlighting.

Figure 8.3
Use the Display mode menu entry to activate data display, like the focus point shown in this reviewed image.

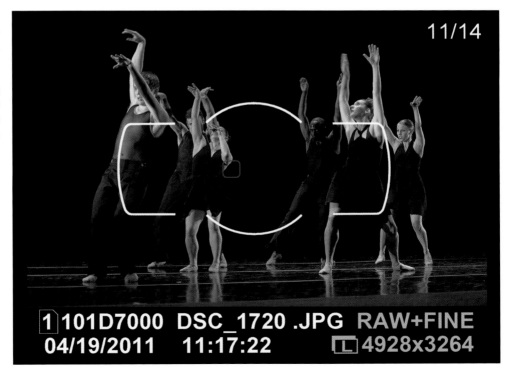

- **Highlights.** When enabled, overexposed highlight areas in your image will blink with a black border during picture review. That's your cue to consider using exposure compensation to reduce exposure, unless a minus-EV setting will cause loss of shadow detail that you want to preserve. You can read more about correcting exposure in Chapter 4.

- **RGB histogram.** Displays both luminance (brightness) and RGB histograms on a screen that can be displayed using the up/down multi selector buttons, as shown in Chapter 2. If you're viewing this histogram with the Highlights display enabled, you can change the Highlights focus from the luminance histogram to any of the three RGB channels by holding down the Thumbnail button and pressing the multi selector right button until the channel you want is selected. I explain the use of this feature in more detail in Chapter 4.

- **Data.** Activates the four pages of shooting data shown in Chapter 3. (Flip back to Figures 3.20 through 3.23 if you need a refresher.)

Copy Image(s)

The ability to work with two memory cards simultaneously ranks as my absolutely favorite feature of the Nikon D7000, way ahead of movie making by a long shot. One of the best uses for two cards is to make back-up images while traveling, or at any other time that your computer isn't easily accessible. Here are some examples of what I do:

- **Shoot to two cards simultaneously.** This gives you an instant backup in case pictures on your primary card become corrupt or are erased. Ideally, your two cards should be equal in size.

- **Make a copy.** Use this Copy Image(s) facility to make a copy of images you shot on one card to your second card. Instead of shooting on two cards at once (which does slow down the D7000 a bit), use only one card when you take photos, then make a backup onto a second card at the end of the day. You can copy all or only some of the photos you've shot.

- **Make copies to distribute.** I bought a bunch of 2GB SD cards for $4.98 each, and find it's quick and easy to make multiple copies of photos, not for backup, but for distribution either on the spot, say, to provide models I've hired with some raw (not RAW) images, or to send by snail mail to colleagues, friends, or family that I want to share photos with. No computer required!

- **Leave your PSD at home.** Since I've begun using Nikon cameras with dual memory card slots, I leave my hard disk/personal storage device with its built-in reader at home more often. If I am going to be gone for only a day or two, it's easier to just make copies in the camera, and not bother with another external device.

To copy images from one card to another, just follow these steps (which are available only when two memory cards are present in the camera):

1. **Access copy menus.** Choose Copy Image(s) from the Playback menu. There are four choices that may be available to you: Select Source; Select Image(s); Select Destination Folder; and Copy Image(s)?.

   - If you have images on only one card, all other choices will be grayed out, and the card containing images will be selected. In the Copy Image(s) menu, Select Image(s) will be pre-selected for you, as shown at left in Figure 8.4.

   - If there are images on both cards already, you can choose Select Source to specify either Slot 1 or Slot 2 as the source to copy from or you can Select Image(s) if the source displayed is satisfactory.

   - If you have already marked some images previously, then all four choices will be available.

2. **Select Source or copy.** Press the right button on the multi selector to perform the task of your choice:

   - Choose Select Source, then highlight Slot 1 or Slot 2 and press OK. (See Figure 8.4, right.)

   - Choose Select Image(s) and continue to Step 3.

   - Choose Select Destination Folder and continue to Step 3.

   - If you've chosen source, destination, and images, choose Copy Image(s)? and skip to Step 4.

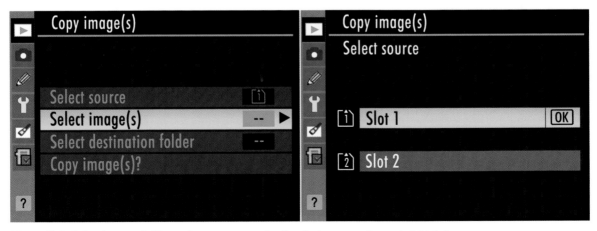

Figure 8.4 Select images (left), or choose a source slot for the images to be copied (right).

3. **Select destination folder or images.** Perform one or both of these tasks.

   ■ If you are choosing a destination folder, you can select by folder number (either a current folder number or one you create by specifying a number for the new folder), or choose from a list of existing folders. (See Figure 8.5, left.) Press OK when finished to return to the Copy Image(s) menu.

   ■ If you are selecting images (as shown in Figure 8.5, right), you can either Deselect All images to cancel previous selections (and then proceed to mark individual images with the Thumbnail/Zoom Out button); Select All Images to view a screen similar to the one shown previously in Figure 8.2, where you can mark and unmark specific thumbnails (hidden images cannot be copied); or Select Protected Images to choose from among images you've previously marked with the Protect key (located just under the MENU button). Press OK when finished to return to the Copy Image(s) menu.

4. **Start copying.** When you choose Copy Image(s)? you'll see a confirmation screen. Highlight Yes, press OK, and a progress screen with a green progress bar appears while the copying is underway. You'll see a Copy Complete message when the task is finished. Press OK, and then the MENU button twice to back out of the menus; or just tap the shutter release button.

Tip

The Copy command will ask for confirmation before overwriting images on the destination card that have the same name as the source images. You can choose Replace Existing Image, Replace All, Skip, or Cancel the rest of the copying operation.

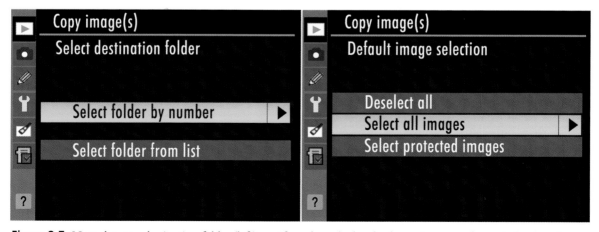

Figure 8.5 Next choose a destination folder (left), or, if you haven't already chosen images to be copied, select them (right).

Image Review

There are certain shooting situations in which it's useful to have the picture you've just shot pop up on the LCD automatically for review. Perhaps you're fine-tuning exposure or autofocus and want to be able to see whether your most recent image is acceptable. Or, maybe you're the nervous type and just want confirmation that you actually took a picture. Instant review has saved my bacon a few times; for example, when I was shooting with studio flash in Manual mode and didn't notice that the shutter speed had been set to a (non-syncing) 1/500th second by mistake.

A lot of the time, however, it's a better idea to *not* automatically review your shots in order to conserve battery power (the LCD is one of the major juice drains in the camera) or to speed up or simplify operations. For example, if you've just fired off a burst of eight shots at 6 fps during a football game, do you *really* need to have each and every frame display as the D7000 clears its buffer and stores the photos on your memory card? This menu operation allows you to choose which mode to use:

- **On.** Image review is automatic after every shot is taken.
- **Off.** Images are displayed only when you press the Playback button. Nikon, in its wisdom, has made this the default setting.

After Delete

When you've deleted an image, you probably will want to do one of three things: have the D7000 display the next picture (in the order shot); show the *previous* picture; or show either the next *or* previous picture, depending on which way you were scrolling during picture review. Your D7000 lets you select which action to take:

- **Show next.** It's likely that you'll want to look at the picture taken after the one you just deleted, so Nikon makes this the default action.
- **Show previous.** I use this setting a lot when shooting sports with a continuous shooting setting. After the sequence is taken, I press the Playback button to see the last picture in the series and sometimes discover that the whole sequence missed the boat. I sometimes go ahead and press the Trash button twice to delete the offending image, then continue moving backwards to delete the five or six or eleven other pictures in the wasted sequence. You'll often find yourself with time on your hands at football games, and the urge to delete some stinker series to save your time reviewing back at the computer, while freeing up a little space on your card.
- **Continue as before.** This setting actually makes a lot of sense: if you were scrolling backwards or forwards and deleting photos as you go, you might want to continue in the same direction weeding out bad shots. Use this setting to set your Nikon D7000 to behave that way.

Rotate Tall

When you rotate the D7000 to photograph vertical subjects in portrait (tall), rather than landscape (wide) orientation, you probably don't want to view them tilted onto their sides later on, either on the camera LCD or within your image viewing/editing application on your computer. The D7000 is way ahead of you. It has a directional sensor built in that can detect whether the camera was rotated when the photo was taken and hide this information in the image file itself.

The orientation data is applied in two different ways. It can be used by the D7000 to automatically rotate images when they are displayed on the camera's LCD monitor, or you can ignore the data and let the images display in non-rotated fashion (so you have to rotate the camera to view them in their proper orientation). Your image editing application, such as Adobe Photoshop Elements, can also use the embedded file data to automatically rotate images on your computer screen.

Rotation works only if you've set Auto Image Rotation to On in the Setup menu (I'll show you how to do that later in this chapter). Once you've done that, the D7000 will embed information about orientation in the image file, and your image editor (such as Adobe Photoshop or Photoshop Elements) will rotate the images for you as the files are loaded.

This menu choice deals only with whether the image should be rotated when displayed on the *camera LCD monitor*. (If you de-activate this option, your image editing software can still read the embedded rotation data and properly display your images.) When Rotate Tall is turned off, the Nikon D7000 does not rotate pictures taken in vertical orientation, displaying them as shown at left in Figure 8.6. The image is large on your LCD screen, but you must rotate the camera to view it upright.

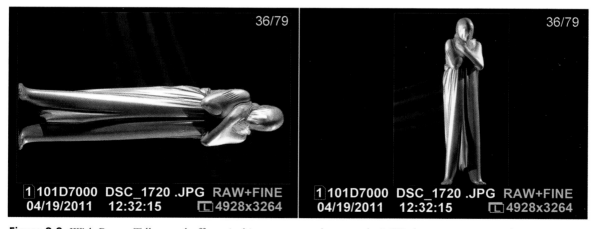

Figure 8.6 With Rotate Tall turned off, vertical images appear large on the LCD, but you must turn the camera to view them upright. With Rotate Tall turned on, vertical images are shown in a smaller size, but oriented for viewing without turning the camera.

When Rotate Tall is turned on, the D7000 rotates pictures taken in vertical orientation on the LCD screen so you don't have to turn the camera to view them comfortably. However, this orientation also means that the longest dimension of the image is shown using the shortest dimension of the LCD, so the picture is reduced in size, as you can see at right in Figure 8.6.

So, turn this feature On (as well as Auto Image Rotation in the Setup menu), if you'd rather not turn your camera to view vertical shots in their natural orientation, and don't mind the smaller image. Turn the feature Off if, as I do, you'd rather see a larger image and are willing to rotate the camera to do so.

Slide Show

The D7000's Slide Show feature is a convenient way to review images in the current playback folder one after another, without the need to manually switch between them.

To activate a slide show, just choose Start from this entry in the Playback menu. If you like, you can choose Frame Interval before commencing the show in order to select an interval of either 2, 3, 5, or 10 seconds between "slides." During playback, you can press the OK button to pause the "slide show." When the show is paused, a menu pops up, as shown in Figure 8.7, with choices to restart the show (by pressing the OK button again); change the interval between frames; or to exit the show entirely.

Figure 8.7
Press the OK button to pause the slide show, change the interval between slides, or to exit the presentation.

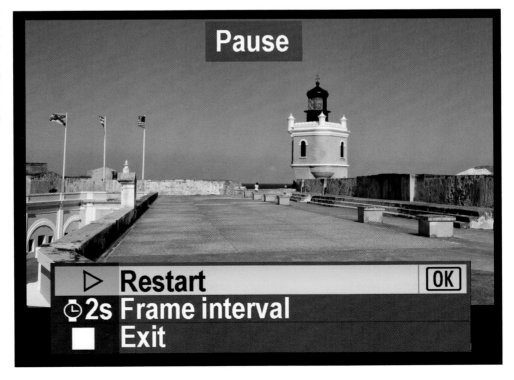

As the images are displayed, press the up/down multi selector buttons to change the amount of information presented on the screen with each image. For example, you might want to review a set of images and the settings used to shoot them. At any time during the show, press the up/down buttons until the informational screen you want is overlaid on the images.

As the slide show progresses, you can press the left/right multi selector buttons to move back to a previous frame or jump ahead to the next one. The slide show will then proceed as before. Press the MENU button to exit the slide show and return to the menu, or press the Playback button to exit the menu system totally. As always, while reviewing images you can tap the MENU button to exit the show and return to the menus, or tap the shutter release button if you want to remove everything from the screen and return to shooting mode.

At the end of the slide show, as when you've paused it, you'll be offered the choice of restarting the sequence, changing the frame interval, or exiting the Slide Show feature completely.

Print Set (DPOF)

The Nikon D7000 supports the DPOF (Digital Print Order Format) that is now almost universally used by digital cameras to specify which images on your memory card should be printed, and the number of prints desired of each image. This information is recorded on the memory card and can be interpreted by a compatible printer when the camera is linked to the printer using the USB cable, or when the memory card is inserted into a card reader slot on the printer itself. Photo labs are also equipped to read this data and make prints when you supply your memory card to them.

When you choose this menu item, you're presented with a set of screens that look very much like the Delete Photos screens described earlier, only you're selecting pictures for printing rather than deleting them. The button sequences are slightly different, however:

1. Use the multi selector cursor keys to scroll among the available images.

2. When you highlight an image you might want to print, press the Playback Zoom In button to temporarily enlarge that image so you can evaluate it further. When you release the button, the selection screen returns.

3. To mark an image for printing, press and hold the Thumbnail/Zoom Out button while pressing the multi selector up buttons to choose the number of prints you want, up to 99 per image. To deselect an image, hold the Thumbnail/Zoom Out button while pressing the multi selector down button. A printer icon and the number specified will appear overlaid on that image's thumbnail. (See Figure 8.8.)

Figure 8.8
Select images
for printing.

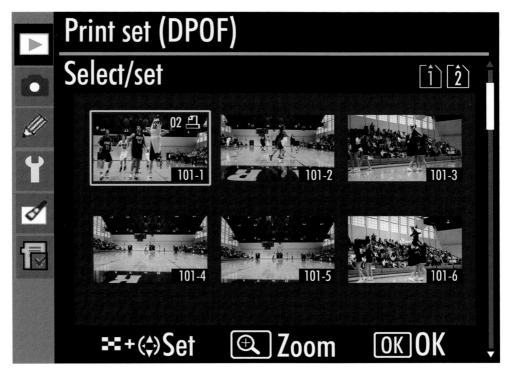

4. To unmark an image for printing, highlight and hold down the Protect/Info button while pressing the down button until the number of prints reaches zero. The printer icon will vanish.

5. When you've finished marking images to print, press OK.

6. A final screen will appear in which you can request a data imprint (shutter speed and aperture) or imprint date (the date the photos were taken). Use the up/down buttons to select one or both of these options, if desired, and press the left/right buttons to mark or unmark the check boxes. When a box is marked, the imprint information for that option will be included on *all* prints in the print order.

7. Scroll up to Done when finished, and press OK or the right cursor button.

Shooting Menu Options

The various direct setting buttons and dials on the D7000, for image quality, autofocus mode, white balance, release mode, ISO sensitivity, metering mode, and flash, along with exposure compensation (EV) adjustments, are likely to be the most frequent settings changes you make, with changes during a particular session fairly common. You'll find some of these duplicated in the Shooting menu (see Figure 8.9), along with options that you access second-most frequently when you're using your Nikon D7000, such as

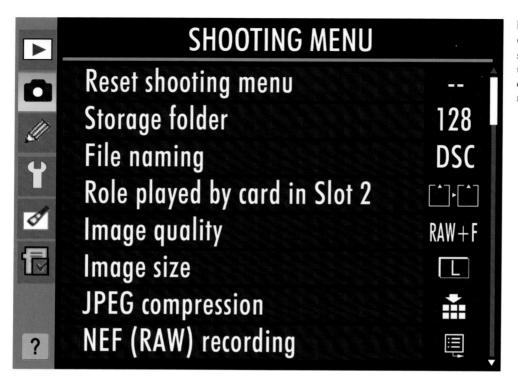

Figure 8.9
Common shooting settings can be changed in this menu.

specifying noise reduction for long exposures or high ISO settings. You might make such adjustments as you begin a shooting session, or when you move from one type of subject to another. Nikon makes accessing these changes very easy.

This section explains the options of the Shooting menu and how to use them. The options you'll find in these green-coded menus include:

- Reset shooting menu
- Storage folder
- File naming
- Role played by card in Slot 2
- Image quality
- Image size
- JPEG compression
- NEF (RAW) recording
- White balance
- Set Picture Control
- Manage Picture Control

- Auto distortion control
- Color space
- Active D-Lighting
- Long exp. NR
- High ISO NR
- ISO sensitivity settings
- Multiple exposure
- Movie settings
- Interval timer shooting
- Remote control mode

Reset Shooting Menu

Don't feel bad over being confused about what this menu item does. The Nikon D7000 has, in effect, *three* different kinds of resets. This is one of them.

- **Shooting menu reset.** Use this option to reset the values of the currently selected Shooting menu bank *except for image quality, image size, white balance, and ISO sensitivity* to their default values. When you select this menu item, your choices are Yes and No.

- **Custom Settings menu reset.** This option is used to reset the four Custom Settings values. It has no effect on camera settings or Shooting menu banks.

- **Two-button reset.** The Nikon D7000's two-button reset (holding down the Exposure Value and QUAL buttons simultaneously for more than two seconds) will *not* reset your Shooting menu banks or Custom Settings menu banks. This particular reset is for basic settings, such as focus point, exposure mode, flexible program, exposure/flash compensation, bracketing, flash mode, flash value lock, and multiple exposure settings.

Table 8.1 shows the default values that are set using the Reset Shooting menu option. If you don't know what some of these settings are, I'll explain them later in this section.

Storage Folder

If you want to store images in a folder other than the one created and selected by the Nikon D7000, you can switch among available folders on your Secure Digital card, or create your own folder. Remember that any folders you create will be deleted when you reformat your memory card.

To change the currently active folder:

1. Choose Storage Folder in the Shooting menu.

2. Scroll down to Select Folder and press the multi selector right button.

3. From among the available folders shown, scroll to the one that you want to become active for image storage and playback. (Handy when displaying slide shows.)

4. Press the OK button to confirm your choice, or press the multi selector right button to return to the Shooting menu.

Why create your own folders? Perhaps you're traveling and have a high-capacity memory card and want to store the images for each day (or for each city that you visit) in a separate folder. When I'm shooting images on the same card on consecutive days, I change the folder number so I can copy only that day's new pictures to my backup media back in my hotel room. The photos I shoot on January 25 go in a folder numbered 125; those shot on January 26 go in 126; and so forth. (Use some other system in October, November, and December, as folders can have only three-digit prefixes.)

Table 8.1 Default Shooting Menu Values

Function	Value
File Naming	*DSC*
Role played by card in Slot 2	*Overflow*
Image Quality	*JPEG Normal*
Image Size	*Large*
JPEG Compression	*Size priority*
NEF (RAW Recording)	
Type	*Lossless compressed*
Bit Depth	*14-bit*
White Balance	*Auto>Normal*
Fine tuning	*Off*
Color temperature	*5,000K*
Set Picture Control	*Standard*
Auto distortion control	*Off*
Color Space	*sRGB*
Active D-Lighting	*Off*
Long exp. NR	*Off*
High ISO NR	*Normal*
ISO sensitivity	
P, S, A, M modes	*100*
Other modes	*Auto*
Auto ISO sensitivity control	*Reset*
Multiple exposure	*Reset*
Movie settings	
Movie Quality	*1920x1080; 24 fps; high quality*
Microphone	*Auto sensitivity (A)*
Destination	*Slot 1*
Manual Movie Settings	*Off*
Interval timer shooting	*Reset*
Remote-control mode	*Delayed remote*

Or, maybe you'd like to separate those wedding photos you snapped at the ceremony from those taken at the reception. As I mentioned earlier, the Nikon D7000 automatically creates a folder on a newly formatted memory card with a name like 100D7000, and when it fills with 999 images, it will automatically create a new folder with a number incremented by one (such as 101D7000). To create your own folder:

1. Choose Active Folder in the Shooting menu.

2. Scroll down to New Folder Number and press the multi selector right button.

3. A three-number value, such as 101, appears. Use the left/right multi selector buttons to change from one column to the next to modify the hundreds, tens, or single digits from 100 up to 999. Use the up/down multi selector buttons to increment or decrement the values in the currently selected column.

4. Press OK when finished to create and activate the new folder.

File Naming

The D7000, like other cameras in the Nikon product line, automatically applies a name like _DSC0001.jpg or DSC_0001.nef to your image files as they are created. You can use this menu option to change the names applied to your photos—but only within certain strict limitations. In practice, you can change only three of the eight characters, the *DSC* portion of the file name. The other five are mandated either by the Design Rule for Camera File System (DCF) specification that all digital camera makers adhere to or to industry conventions.

DCF limits file names created by conforming digital cameras to a maximum of eight characters, plus a three-character extension (such as JPG or NEF) that represents the file format of the image. The eight-plus-three (usually called 8.3) length limitation dates back to an evil and frustrating computer operating system that we older photographers would like to forget (its initials are D.O.S), but which, unhappily, lives on as the wraith of a file-naming convention.

Of the eight available characters, four are used to represent, in a general sense, the type of camera used to create the image. By convention, one of those characters is an underline, placed in the first position (as in _DSCxxxx.xxx) when the image uses the Adobe RGB color space (more on color spaces later), and in the fourth position (as in DSC_xxxx.xxx) for sRGB and RAW (NEF) files. That leaves just three characters for the manufacturer (and you) to use. Nikon, Sony, and some other vendors use DSC (which may or may not stand for Digital Still Camera, depending on who you ask), while Canon prefers IMG. The remaining four characters are used for numbers from 0000 to 9999, which is why your D7000 "rolls over" to DSC_0000 again when the 9999 number limitation is reached.

When you select File Naming in the Shooting menu, you'll be shown the current settings for both sRGB (and RAW) and Adobe RGB. Press the right multi selector button, and you'll be taken to the (mostly) standard Nikon text entry screen, like the one shown in Figure 8.10, and allowed to change the DSC value to something else. In this version of the text entry screen, however, only the numbers from 0 to 9 and characters A-Z are available; the file name cannot contain other characters. As always, press the OK button to confirm your new setting.

Because the default DSC characters don't tell you much, don't hesitate to change them to something else. I own, or used to own, a whole collection of Nikon digital cameras, so I've used D40_, D50_, D70_, and D80_ as my templates over the years. Because only three digits are available, I use D7K for my D7000, to differentiate it from my older Nikon D700, which uses the 700 "code."

If you don't need to differentiate between different camera models, you can change the three characters to anything else that suits your purposes, including your initials (DDB_ or JFK_ for example) or even customize for particular shooting sessions (EUR_, GER_, FRA_, and JAP_ when taking vacation trips). You can also use the file name flexibility to partially overcome the 9999 numbering limitation. You could, for example, use the template D71_ to represent the first 10,000 pictures you take with your D7000, and then D72_ for the next 10,000, and D73_ for the 10,000 after that.

That's assuming that you don't rename your image files in your computer. In a way, file naming verges on a moot consideration, because, they apply *only* to the images as they exist in your camera. After (or during) transfer to your computer you can change the names to anything you want, completely disregarding the 8.3 limitations (although it's a good idea to retain the default extensions). If you shot an image file named DSC_4832.jpg in your camera, you could change it to Paris_EiffelTower_32.jpg later on. Indeed, virtually all photo transfer programs, including Nikon Transfer and Photoshop Elements Transfer, allow you to specify a template and rename your photos as they are moved or copied to your computer from your camera or memory card.

I usually don't go to that bother (I generally don't use transfer software; I just drag and drop images from my memory card to folders I have set up), but renaming can be useful for those willing to take the time to do it.

Entering Text on the Nikon D7000

Now is a good time to master text entry, because you can use it to enter comments, rename folders, and perform other functions. The Nikon D7000 uses a fairly standardized text entry screen to name files, Picture Controls, create new folder names, enter image comments, and other text. You'll be using text entry with other functions that I'll describe later in this book. The screen looks like the one shown in Figure 8.10, with some variations (for example, some functions have a less diverse character set, or offer more or fewer spaces for your entries). To name a Picture Control, first select File

Figure 8.10
Use this
D7000 screen
to enter text.

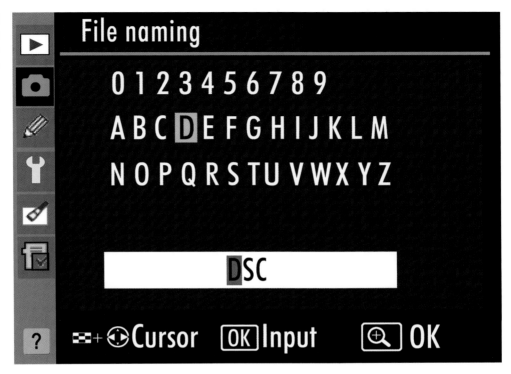

Naming, then use the right multi selector button to reveal the text entry screen. After that, you can use the multi selector navigational buttons to scroll around within the array of alphanumerics, and enter your text:

- **Highlight a character.** Use the multi selector keys to scroll around within the array of characters.

- **Insert highlighted character.** Press the multi selector center button to insert the highlighted character. The cursor will move one place to the right to accept the next character.

- **Non-destructively backspace.** Hold down the Thumbnail/Zoom Out button and use the left/right buttons to move the cursor within the line of characters you've entered. This allows you to backspace and replace a character without disturbing the others you've entered.

- **Erase a highlighted character.** To remove a character you've already input, move the cursor to highlight that character, and then press the Trash button.

- **Confirm your entry.** When you're finished entering text, press the OK button to confirm your entry, then press the left button twice to return to the Shooting menu, or just tap the shutter release to exit the menu system entirely.

Role Played by Card in Slot 2

You can specify how you want that handy second slot used. You have three choices:

- **Overflow.** Use this default function when you want to create one larger virtual memory card. Images will be stored to the primary card in Slot 1 until that card is full, and then the D7000 will save any additional photos to the secondary slot. The Overflow option is of particular use to those who own smaller memory cards (a 2GB card will fill up rather quickly), and sports/photojournalism photographers, who typically swap out memory cards when they are 80-90 percent full, to avoid losing an important shot during a changeover. The Overflow setting allows using the primary card to its full capacity, with the secondary card taking over seamlessly. The Slot 1 card can then be changed during a lull in your picture taking activities.

- **Backup.** Images are recorded to both the Slot 1 and Slot 2 memory cards simultaneously. This setting is a godsend for event photographers who can't risk losing even a single shot, and for folks like me who travel extensively specifically to take photographs. When I'm going to be away from my main computer for more than a day, I always shoot in Backup mode, so I can create an instant copy of the images on my main card. On short trips, I can even leave my netbook and PSD (personal storage device) at home. Keep in mind that writing to a pair of cards simultaneously slows your D7000 down a bit, so you probably don't want to use this option for sports photography, unless you're willing to take a performance hit.

- **RAW Slot 1, JPEG Slot 2.** In this mode, the RAW images are stored on the primary memory card in Slot 1 and the JPEG files relegated to the secondary card in Slot 2. This is another way of giving you an automatic backup of your images, and is especially useful if you typically shoot RAW+JPEG. Your JPEG images, with the camera settings you selected applied, are available on one card, while the RAW versions, ready for image processing if you want to tweak some settings, are stored on a second card. Writing both RAW and JPEG files to a pair of cards is even slower than dual JPEG backups, so this option is not your best choice for sports. Keep in mind that RAW files take up more space than JPEG files, so if your cards are the same size, the primary card will fill up more quickly. (A partial solution is to use a larger card as your primary, and a smaller one for the secondary.) When using this mode, the D7000 reports the number of shots remaining for the card with the least amount of space left, and if either card fills, the shutter release locks.

Image Quality

As I noted in Chapter 1, you can choose the image quality settings used by the D7000 to store its files. The quickest way to do that is to hold down the QUAL button on the bottom-left side of the camera and spin the main command and sub-command dials until the quality/image size settings (respectively) that you want are shown in the top-side monochrome status LCD. You can also use this menu option to make the quality settings using the bigger, brighter three-inch color LCD. You might want to do that when the D7000 is mounted on a tripod and the top-panel LCD is above eyelevel, or you simply might prefer the color LCD's display, which can be easier to read. You have two choices to make:

- **JPEG compression.** To reduce the size of your image files and allow more photos to be stored on a given memory card, the D7000 uses JPEG compression to squeeze the images down to a smaller size. This compacting reduces the image quality a little, so you're offered your choice of Fine (a 1:4 reduction), Normal (1:8 reduction), and Basic (1:16) compression. You can see an exaggerated version of the effects of JPEG compression in Figure 8.11. There is a further tweak you can make, specifying whether JPEG compression should be optimized for the smallest possible image size at a given compression level, or whether you'd prefer to sacrifice some compression for optimal quality. You won't find those options in this menu entry; instead, use the JPEG Compression menu item, described later in this section.

- **JPEG, RAW, or both.** You can elect to store only JPEG versions of the images you shoot, or you can save your photos as RAW files, which consume more than twice as much space on your memory card. Or, you can store both at once as you shoot. Many photographers elect to save *both* JPEG and a RAW, so they'll have a JPEG version that might be usable as-is, as well as the original "digital negative" RAW file in case they want to do some processing of the image later. You'll end up with two different versions of the same file: one with a JPG extension, and one with the NEF extension that signifies a Nikon RAW file.

Figure 8.11
At low levels of JPEG compression the image looks sharp even when you enlarge it enough to see the actual pixels (top); when using extreme JPEG compression (bottom) an image obviously loses quality.

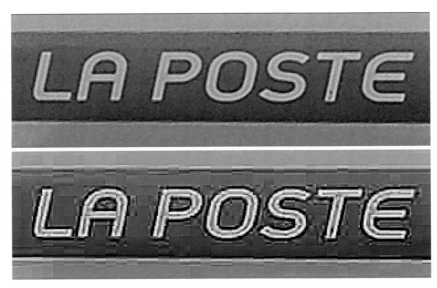

> **Tip**
>
> The D7000 always saves a full-resolution 4928 × 3264 pixel RAW image even if you choose a smaller image size (resolution) for the JPEG version (such as Medium (M) or Small (S)).

To choose the combination you want, access the Shooting menu, scroll to Image Quality, and select it. A screen similar to the one shown in Figure 8.12 will appear. Scroll to highlight the setting you want, and either press OK or push the multi selector right button to confirm your selection.

In practice, you'll probably use the JPEG Fine, RAW+JPEG Fine selections most often. Why so many choices, then? There are some limited advantages to using the JPEG Normal and JPEG Basic settings, either at full resolution (Large) or when using the Medium and Small resolution settings. Settings that are less than max allow stretching the capacity of your memory card so you can shoehorn quite a few more pictures onto a single memory card. That can come in useful when on vacation and you're running out of storage, or when you're shooting non-critical work that doesn't require 16 megapixels of resolution (such as photos taken for real estate listings, web page display, photo ID cards, or similar applications). Some photographers like to record RAW+JPEG

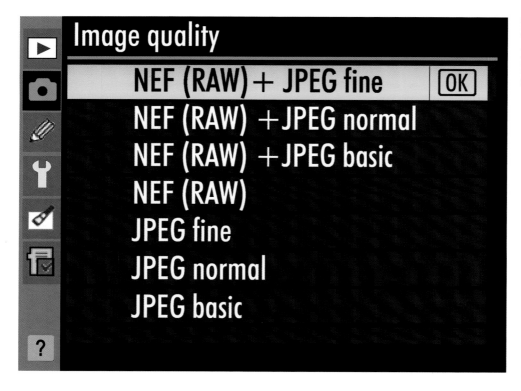

Figure 8.12
You can choose RAW, JPEG, or RAW+JPEG formats here.

Normal so they'll have a moderate quality JPEG file for review only and no intention of using for editing purposes, while retaining access to the original RAW file for serious editing.

For most work, using lower resolution and extra compression is false economy. You never know when you might actually need that extra bit of picture detail. Your best bet is to have enough memory cards to handle all the shooting you want to do until you have the chance to transfer your photos to your computer or a personal storage device.

However, reduced image quality can sometimes be beneficial if you're shooting sequences of photos rapidly, as the D7000 is able to hold more of them in its internal memory buffer before transferring to the memory card. Still, for most sports and other applications, you'd probably rather have better, sharper pictures than longer periods of continuous shooting. Do you really need 20 or 30 shots of a pass reception in a football game, or a dozen or two slightly different versions of your local basketball star driving in for a lay-up?

JPEG vs. RAW

You'll sometimes be told that RAW files are the "unprocessed" image information your camera produces, before it's been modified. That's nonsense. RAW files are no more unprocessed than your camera film is after it's been through the chemicals to produce a negative or transparency. A lot can happen in the developer that can affect the quality of a film image—positively and negatively—and, similarly, your digital image undergoes a significant amount of processing before it is saved as a RAW file. Nikon even applies a name (EXPEED) to the digital image processing (DIP) chip used to perform this magic.

A RAW file is more similar to a film camera's processed negative. It contains all the information, captured in 12-bit or 14-bit channels per color (and stored in a 16-bit space), with no sharpening and no application of any special filters or other settings you might have specified when you took the picture. Those settings are *stored* with the RAW file so they can be applied when the image is converted to a form compatible with your favorite image editor. However, using RAW conversion software such as Adobe Camera Raw or Nikon Capture NX, you can override those settings and apply settings of your own. You can select essentially the same changes there that you might have specified in your camera's picture taking options.

RAW exists because sometimes we want to have access to all the information captured by the camera, before the camera's internal logic has processed it and converted the image to a standard file format. Even Compressed RAW doesn't save as much space as JPEG. What it does do is preserve all the information captured by your camera after it's been converted from analog to digital form.

So, why don't we always use RAW? Some photographers avoid using Nikon's RAW NEF files on the misguided conviction that they don't want to spend time in post-processing, forgetting that, if the camera settings you would have used for JPEG are correct, each RAW image's default attributes will use those settings and the RAW image will not need much manipulation. Post-processing in such cases is *optional*, and overwhelmingly helpful when an image needs to be fine-tuned.

Although some photographers do save *only* in RAW format, it's more common (and frequently more convenient) to use RAW plus one of the JPEG options, or, if you're confident about your settings, just shoot JPEG and eschew RAW altogether. In some situations, working with a RAW file can slow you down a little. RAW images take longer to store on the memory card, and must be converted from RAW to a format your image editor can handle, whether you elect to go with the default settings in force when the picture was taken, or make minor adjustments to the settings you specified in the camera.

As a result, those who depend on speedy access to images or who shoot large numbers of photos at once may prefer JPEG over RAW. Wedding photographers, for example, might expose several thousand photos during a bridal affair and offer hundreds to clients as electronic proofs for inclusion in an album. Wedding shooters take the time to make sure that their in-camera settings are correct, minimizing the need to post-process photos after the event. Given that their JPEGs are so good, there is little need to get bogged down shooting RAW.

Sports photographers also avoid RAW files. I visited a local Division III college one sunny September afternoon. I covered the first half of a football game, trotted down a hill to shoot a women's soccer match later that afternoon, and ended up in the adjacent field house shooting a volleyball invitational tournament an hour later. I managed to shoot 1,920 photos, most of them at a 6 fps clip, in about four hours. I certainly didn't have any plans to do post-processing on very many of those shots, and firing the camera at its maximum frame rate didn't allow RAW shooting, so carefully exposed and precisely focused JPEG images were my file format of choice that day.

JPEG was invented as a more compact file format that can store most of the information in a digital image, but in a much smaller size. JPEG predates most digital SLRs and was initially used to squeeze down files for transmission over slow dial-up connections. Even if you were using an early dSLR with 1.3 megapixel files for news photography, you didn't want to send them back to the office over a modem at 1,200 bps.

But, as I noted, JPEG provides smaller files by compressing the information in a way that loses some image data. JPEG remains a viable alternative because it offers several different quality levels. At the highest quality Fine level, you might not be able to tell the difference between the original RAW file and the JPEG version, even though a lossless compressed, 14-bit RAW file (I'll explain the bit-business later in this chapter) occupies, by Nikon's estimate, 19.4MB on your memory card, while the Fine JPEG takes up only 7.8MB of space. You've squeezed the image by more than 70 percent without losing much visual information at all. If you don't mind losing some quality, you can use more aggressive Normal compression with JPEG to cut the size in half again, to 2.9MB.

In my case, I shoot virtually everything at RAW+JPEG Fine. Most of the time, I'm not concerned about filling up my memory cards, as I usually have a minimum of five 32GB memory cards with me. If I know I may fill up all those cards, I have a tiny battery-operated personal storage device that can copy 8GB worth of images (a typical day's shooting) in about 15 minutes. Although it's a bit slower, I often copy shots to my Apple iPad because, thanks to its 3G connectivity, I can e-mail them immediately or post them on Facebook or Flickr, no matter where I happen to be.

I also use a netbook with an external 320GB hard drive, and, most recently, a tiny MacBook Air with an 11.6 inch screen (it's not much bigger than my iPad). For short trips, I rely on my D7000's capability of copying directly from one memory card to the other in the camera. As I mentioned earlier, when shooting sports I'll shift to JPEG FINE (with no RAW file) to squeeze a little extra speed out of my camera's continuous shooting mode, and to reduce the need to wade through eight-photo bursts taken in RAW format.

HIDDEN JPEGS

You may not be aware that your RAW file contains an embedded JPEG file, hidden inside in the JPEG Basic format. It's used to provide thumbnail previews of JPEG files, and to display images you've shot during picture review on the D7000's built-in screen. That's right, even if you're shooting RAW (only), the D7000 still creates a JPEG version, and that—not your RAW image—is displayed on the color LCD.

This is also why you may notice an interesting phenomenon when loading a RAW image into a program like Nikon Capture NX2 or Adobe Lightroom. When the software first starts interpreting the RAW image, it may immediately display this hidden JPEG view which has, as you might expect, all the settings applied that you dialed into the camera. Then, as it finishes loading the RAW file, the application (Lightroom in particular) uses its own intelligence to fine-tune the image and display what it thinks is a decent version of the image, replacing the embedded JPEG. That's why you may see complaints that Lightroom or another program is behaving oddly: the initial embedded JPEG may look better than the final version, so it looks as if the application is degrading the image quality as the file loads. Of course, in all cases, once the RAW file is available, you can make your own changes to optimize it to your taste.

There is a second use for these hidden JPEG files. If you shoot RAW without creating JPEG files and later decide you want a JPEG version, there are dozens of utility programs that will extract the embedded JPEG and save it as a separate file. (Google "JPEG extractor" to locate a freeware program that will perform this step for your Mac, PC, or other computer.)

Image Size

The next menu command in the Shooting menu lets you select the resolution, or number of pixels captured as you shoot with your Nikon D7000. Your choices range from Large (L—4928 × 3264 pixels, 16.1 megapixels), Medium (M—3696 × 2448 pixels, 9.0 megapixels), and Small (S—2464 × 1632 pixels, 4.0 megapixels). Personally, I think it's pretty cool that after using a Nikon D70 (with 6MP) and a Nikon D200 (with 10MP) for several years, my D7000 has a *medium* resolution that exceeds or nearly matches both of them.

You can select image sizes by holding down the QUAL button on the back left panel of the D7000, while spinning the sub-command dial until the resolution you want appears on the monochrome LCD status screen. (This provides you with a status panel estimate of the number of exposures available at each setting.) Or, you can use this menu to perform the task (usually because you find the color LCD easier to view under the particular circumstances). There are no additional options available from the Image Size menu screen.

JPEG Compression

This menu entry is a simple one, offering you the choice of specifying either Size Priority (variable compression) or Optimal Quality (minimal compression) when the D7000 creates JPEG files. I'll explain image compression in more detail in the next section.

- **Size priority.** When this option is selected, the D7000 will create files that are fairly uniformly sized at about 7.8MB for a JPEG Fine image. Because some photos have content that is more easily compressible (for example, plain areas of sky can be squeezed down more than areas filled with detail), to maintain the standard file size the camera must apply more compression to some images, and less to others. As a result, there may be a barely noticeable loss of detail in the more heavily compressed images. The uniform file size also means that the D7000's buffer will hold the maximum number of shots during continuous shooting, allowing you to shoot longer sequences without the need to pause and wait for some images to be written to the memory card.

- **Optimal quality.** Choose this option if you want to maintain the best image quality possible at a particular JPEG setting (Fine, Normal, or Basic) and don't care if the file size varies. Because the D7000 will use only the minimum amount of compression required at each JPEG setting, file size will vary depending on scene content, and your buffer may hold fewer images during continuous shooting.

NEF (RAW) Recording

You can choose the type (amount) of compression applied to NEF (RAW) files as they are stored on your memory card, and whether the images are stored using 12-bit or

14-bit depth. The default values for type (Lossless compressed) and color depth (14-bit) work best for most situations, but there are times when you might want to use one of the other choices.

Compression is a mathematical technique for reducing the size of a collection of information (such as an image; but other types of data or even programs can be compressed, too) in order to reduce the storage requirements and/or time required to transmit or transfer the information. Some compression algorithms arrange strings of bits that are most frequently used into a table, so that a binary number like, say, 1001011011100111 (16 digits long) doesn't have to be stored as two 8-bit bytes every time it appears in the image file. Instead, a smaller number that points to that position in the table can be used. The more times the pointer is used rather than the full number, the more space is saved in the file. Such a compression scheme can be used to reproduce exactly the original string of numbers, and so is called *lossless* compression.

Other types of compression are more aggressive and actually discard some of the information deemed to be redundant from a visual standpoint, so that, theoretically, you won't *notice* that details are missing, and the file can be made even more compact. The Nikon D7000's RAW storage routines can use this kind of size reduction, which is called *lossy* compression, to reduce file size by up to about half with very little effect on image quality. JPEG compression can be even more enthusiastic, resulting in images that are 15X smaller (or more) and which display noticeable loss of image quality.

Under Type in the NEF (RAW) recording menu, you can select from:

- **Lossless compressed.** This is the default setting, and uses what you might think of as reversible algorithms that discard no image information, so that the image can be compressed from 20-40 percent for a significantly smaller file size. Typically, you'll get up to 200-250 RAW images on a single 8GB memory card at this setting. The squeezed file can always be restored to its original size precisely, with no effect on image quality.

- **Compressed.** Use this setting if you want to store more images on your memory card and are willing to accept a tiny potential loss in image quality in the highlights, after significant editing (I've never been able to detect any effect at all). The D7000 can achieve from 40-55 percent compression with this option, giving you 330 or more RAW exposures on an 8GB Secure Digital card. It uses a two-step process, first grouping some very similar tonal values in the mid-tone and lighter areas of the image together, and then storing each group as a single value, followed by a lossless compression scheme that is applied to the dark tones, further reducing the file size. The process does a good job of preserving tones in shadow areas of an image, with only small losses in the midtone and lighter areas. The differences may show up only if you perform certain types of extensive post-processing on an image, such as image sharpening or some tonal corrections.

The Bit Depth setting is another option that looks good on paper but, in the real world, is less useful than you might think. For most applications, the default value that produces 14-bit image files is probably your best choice, especially if you're exposing images that will be combined using HDR (High Dynamic Range) software later on. In that case, you can definitely gain some extra exposure "headroom" using 14-bit processing.

As you may know, bit depth is a way of measuring the amount of color data that an image file can contain. What we call "24-bit color" actually consists of three channels of information—red, green, and blue—with one 8-bit bit assigned to each channel, so a 24-bit image contains three 8-bit channels (each with 256 different shades of red, green, or blue). A 24-bit color image can contain up to 16.8 million different colors ($256 \times 256 \times 256$; you do the math). Because each of the red, green, and blue channels always is stored using the same number of bits, it's become the custom to refer only to the channel bit depth to describe the amount of color information that can be collected.

So, when we're talking about 12-bit color, what we really mean are three 12-bit RGB channels, each capable of recording colors from 000000000000 to 111111111111 hues in a particular channel (in binary), or 4,096 colors per channel (decimal) and a total of 68,719,476,736 (68.7 billion) different hues. By comparison, 14-bit color offers 16,384 colors per channel and a total of 4,398,046,511,104 (4.4 trillion) colors.

The advantage of having such a humongous number of colors for an image that will, in the end, be boiled down to 16.8 million hues in Photoshop or another image editor is that, to simplify things a little, there is a better chance that the mere millions of colors you end up with have a better chance of being the *right* colors to accurately represent the image. For example, if there are subtle differences in the colors of a certain range of tones that represent only, say, 10 percent of a channel's colors, there would be only 26 colors to choose from in an 8-bit channel, but 410 colors in a 12-bit channel, and a whopping 1,638 colors in a 14-bit channel. The larger number of colors improves the odds of ending up with accurate hues.

It's not quite that simple, of course, because bit depth also improves the chances of having the right number of colors to choose from after the inevitable loss of some information due to noise and other factors. But in the real world, the difference between 26 colors and 410 colors is significant (which is why digital cameras always capture at least 12 bits per channel), and the difference between 12 bits and 14 bits (410 and 1,638 colors, respectively in our example) is less significant. Even though there is a penalty in terms of file size and the amount of time needed to process the image as it is recorded to your memory card, Nikon has set the D7000 to default to 14-bit capture, because it does improve the dynamic range for which the camera is so prized.

Your two choices look like this:

■ **12 bit.** This is an optional bit depth for the Nikon D7000. Images are recorded at 12-bits per channel in the RAW file, and end up with 12 bits of information per channel that is translated during conversion for your image editor either into 12 bits within a 16-bits-per-channel space or interpreted down to 8 bits per channel.

■ **14 bit.** At this default setting, the D7000 grabs 16,384 colors per channel instead of 4,096, ending up as 14 bits in a 16-channel space or reduced to 256 colors by the RAW conversion software that translates the image for your image editor. You'll find that such 14-bit files end up almost one-third larger than 12-bit files, and that your camera's continuous shooting rate may be reduced (which alone is a good argument for not using the 14-bit setting any time you may need to shoot bursts of images). 14-bit images are unmatched for HDR photography, however.

White Balance

This menu entry, the first in the second page of Shooting menu entries (see Figure 8.13) allows you to choose one of the white balance values from among Auto, incandescent, seven varieties of fluorescent illumination, direct sunlight, flash, cloudy, shade, a specific color temperature of your choice, or a preset value taken from an existing photograph, or a measurement you make. Some of the settings you make here can be

Figure 8.13
White Balance is the first entry on the second page of the Shooting menu.

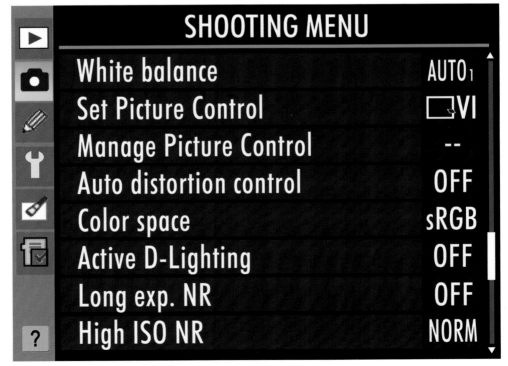

duplicated using the WB button located second from the top to the left of the camera's color LCD, but the menus offer even more choices, as you'll see. Your white balance settings can have a significant impact on the color rendition of your images, as you can see in Figure 8.14.

In this section I'm going to describe only the menu commands at your disposal for setting white balance. To learn more about the theory behind why and when you should make white balance adjustments, check out the more complete description of white balance bracketing in Chapter 4.

When you select the White Balance entry on the Shooting menu, you'll see an array of choices like those shown in Figure 8.15. (One additional choice, PRE Preset Manual is not visible until you scroll down to it.) If you choose Fluorescent, you'll be taken to another screen that presents seven different types of lamps, from sodium-vapor through warm-white fluorescent down to high temperature mercury-vapor. If you know the exact type of non-incandescent lighting being used, you can select it, or settle on a likely compromise.

The Choose Color Temp. selection allows you to select from an array of color temperatures in degrees Kelvin from 2,500K to 10,000K, and then further fine-tune the color bias using the fine-tuning feature described below. Select Preset Manual to record or

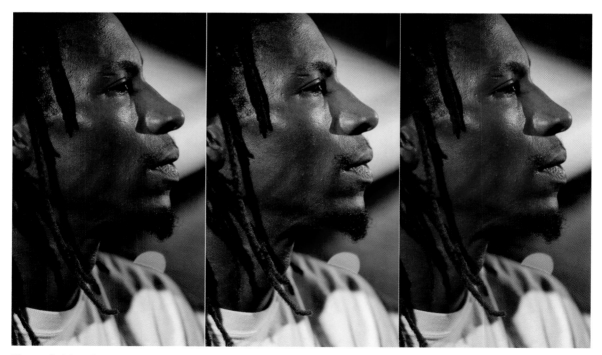

Figure 8.14 Adjusting color temperature can provide different results of the same subject at settings of 3,400K (left), 5,000K (middle), and 2,800K (right).

Figure 8.15
The White
Balance menu
has predefined
values, plus
the option of
setting color
temperature
and presets
you measure
yourself.

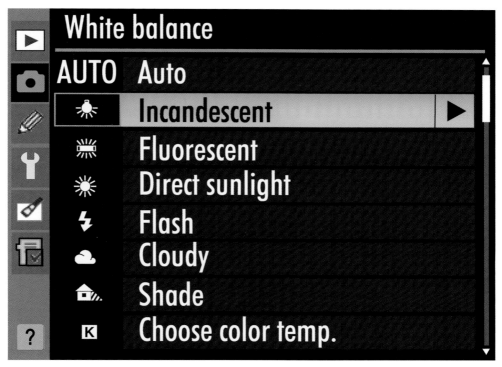

recall custom white balance settings suitable for environments with unusual lighting or mixed lighting, as described later in this section.

For all other settings (Auto, Incandescent, Direct Sunlight, Flash, Cloudy, or Shade), highlight the white balance option you want, then press the multi selector right button (or press OK) to view the fine-tuning screen shown in Figure 8.16 (and which uses the Incandescent setting as an example). The screen shows a grid with two axes, a blue/amber axis extending left/right, and a green/magenta axis extending up and down the grid. By default, the grid's cursor is positioned in the middle, and a readout to the right of grid shows the cursor's coordinates on the A-B axis (yes, I know the display has the end points reversed) and G-M axis at 0,0.

You can use the multi selector's up/down and right/left buttons to move the cursor to any coordinate in the grid, thereby biasing the white balance in the direction(s) you choose. The amber-blue axis makes the image warmer or colder (but not actually yellow or blue). Similarly, the green-magenta axis preserves all the colors in the original image, but gives them a tinge biased toward green or magenta. Each increment equals about five mired units, but you should know that mired values aren't linear; five mireds at 2,500K produces a much stronger effect than five mireds at 6,000K. If you really want to fine-tune your color balance, you're better off experimenting and evaluating the results of a particular change.

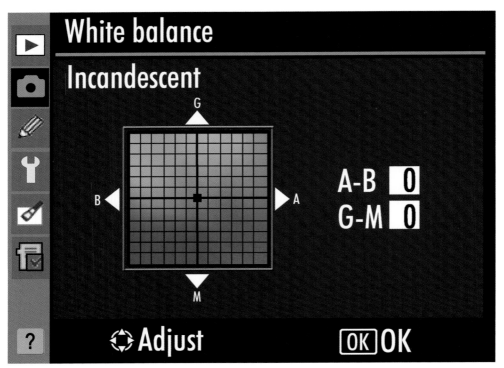

Figure 8.16
Specific white balance settings can be fine-tuned by changing their bias in the amber/blue, magenta/green directions—or along both axes simultaneously.

When you've fine-tuned white balance, either using the Shooting menu options or the WB button, left/right triangles appear in the white balance section of the monochrome LCD at lower right to remind you that this tweaking has taken place.

Using Preset Manual White Balance

If automatic white balance or one of the predefined settings available aren't suitable, you can set a custom white balance using the Preset Manual menu option. You can apply the white balance from a scene, either by shooting a new picture on the spot and using the resulting white balance (Direct Measurement), or using an image you have already shot (Copy from Existing Photograph). To perform direct measurement from your current scene using a reference object (preferably a neutral gray or white object), follow these steps:

1. **Position reference subject.** Place the neutral reference under the lighting you want to measure.

2. **Change to Preset white balance.** Hold down the WB button on the back left panel of the camera and rotate the main command dial until you see PRE and d-0 displayed in the monochrome LCD.

3. **Activate capture mode.** Release the WB button for a moment, then press and hold it again until the PRE icon on the monochrome LCD begins a flashing cycle of about six seconds.

4. **Capture white balance of reference.** While the PRE icon is flashing, take a picture of the reference object. The white balance will be stored in a preset menu slot numbered d-0, as shown in Figure 8.17.

5. **Confirm successful capture of white balance.** If the camera successfully measured white balance, Good will flash on the monochrome LCD for about six seconds, and Gd will appear in the bottom line of the viewfinder. Otherwise, you'll see no Gd on the LCD and viewfinder. White balance measurement can fail when the reference object is too brightly or poorly illuminated. In that case, repeat steps 2-5 until the measurement is successful.

6. **Use captured white balance.** You can immediately begin taking pictures using the captured white balance, until you hold down the WB button again and switch to one of the other white balance settings, such as Tungsten, or Fluorescent. The next time you switch to Pre, the white balance you just captured will be used again, unless you manually switch to one of the other captured settings, which are stored in "slots" labeled d-1 to d-4, as described next.

Figure 8.17
When you capture a scene's white balance, it will be stored in slot d-0.

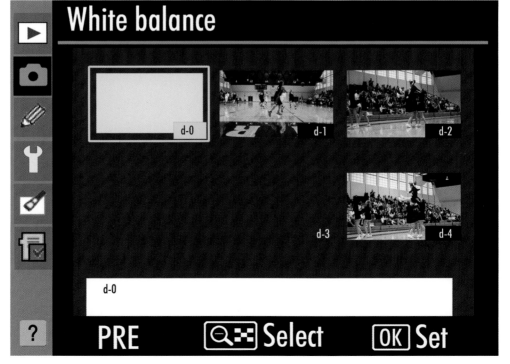

Storing and Retrieving White Balance Settings

A memory slot, labeled d-0, always stores the last white balance captured. When you capture a new white balance, the old value in d-0 is replaced with the new captured value. The value in slot d-0 can be summoned at any time (press the WB button on the top left of the camera and dial it in by rotating the sub-command dial until d-0 is displayed on the monochrome LCD).

But if you want to preserve the captured white balance in d-0, you must copy it to one of the four additional slots, numbered d-1 to d-4. You can also use those four slots to store white balance information from a picture you've already taken, using the Copy from Existing Photograph option, as described next:

1. **Switch to Pre.** Access the White Balance menu and choose Preset Manual.

2. **View available white balances.** A screen of thumbnails appears, showing the additional four "slots" numbered d-1 to d-4, which you can use to store information from slot d-0, or from images that contain the white balance information you want to apply. Use the multi selector buttons to highlight one of the four thumbnail slots, and press the Thumbnail/Zoom Out button to select the value stored in that slot.

3. **Choose a function.** The next screen that appears (see Figure 8.18) has five options: Slot Number, Set, Edit Comment, Select Image, and Copy d-0.

    - **Slot number.** If you highlight the slot number you just selected, you can press the right multi selector button to change to a different white balance slot.

    - **Set.** Choose Set to fine-tune the amber/blue/magenta/green white balance of an image already stored in the selected slot, either d-0 or one of the other four user slots. You'll use the same adjustment screen shown earlier in Figure 8.16.

    - **Edit Comment.** Choose this option to add or change the comment applied to d-0 to d-4. The comment can be used as a label to better identify the white balance information in the slot, with terms like Gymnasium or Rumpus Room. (A variation of the standard D7000 Edit Comment screen, as in Figure 8.19, appears.)

    - **Select Image.** Choose this option to view the D7000's standard image selection screen and highlight and choose the existing image slot you want to use. Press the multi selector center button to confirm your choice and copy the white balance of the selected image to the slot you selected in Step 2.

    - **Copy d-0.** Use this option to copy the white balance setting currently stored in slot d-0 to the slot you selected in Step 2. Use this to preserve a captured white balance setting, freeing d-0 for a new capture.

4. **Confirm.** Press OK to confirm your white balance setting.

Figure 8.18
The Preset Manual screen lets you fine-tune preset white balance settings, label them with a comment, select an image to use as a white balance reference, and copy captured settings.

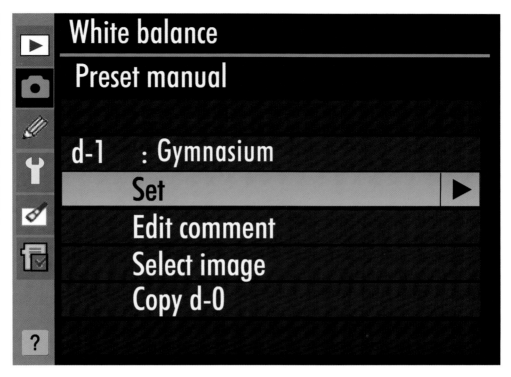

Figure 8.19
Add a comment to your white balance setting.

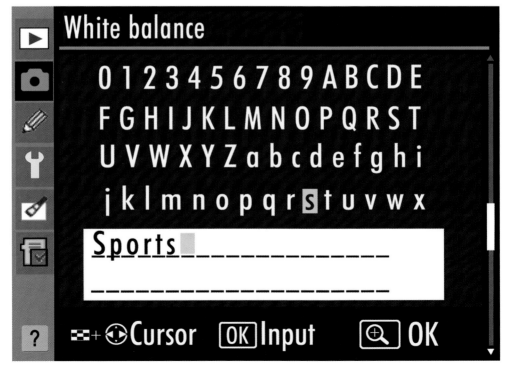

A WHITE BALANCE LIBRARY

Consider dedicating a low-capacity memory card to stow a selection of images taken under a variety of lighting conditions. If you want to "recycle" one of the color temperatures you've stored, insert the card and load one of those images into your choice of preset slots d-1 to d-4, as described above.

Set Picture Control

Nikon's Picture Control styles allow you to choose your own sharpness, contrast, color saturation, and hue settings and apply them to your images as they are taken. If you have used an older Nikon camera with the Optimize Image option, you'll recall that it offered five fixed settings to choose from (Normal, Softer, Vivid, More Vivid, Portrait), plus Black-and-White, and a single Custom entry that allowed you to specify sharpening, tone compensation (contrast), color mode, saturation, and hue. Yes, that's right—you got *one* Custom Settings slot, and although you could create your own custom settings on your computer and upload them to the camera, the five predefined settings and single set of custom parameters was quite a limitation.

Happily, the Nikon D7000 sweeps those limitations aside with the Picture Control styles. There are only six predefined styles offered, which Nikon calls Original Picture Controls: Standard, Neutral, Vivid, Monochrome, Portrait, and Landscape. However, you can *edit* the settings of any of those styles so they better suit your taste. But that's only the beginning; the D7000 also offers *nine* (count 'em) user-definable Picture Control styles, which you can edit to your heart's content, assign descriptive names, and deploy at the press of a few buttons. Even better, you can *copy* these styles to a memory card, edit them on your computer, and reload them into your camera at any time. So, effectively, you can have a lot more than nine custom Picture Control styles available: the nine in your camera, as well as a virtually unlimited library of user-defined styles that you have stored on memory cards.

Moreover, Nikon insists that these styles have been standardized to the extent that if you re-use a style created for one camera (say, your D7000) and load it into a different compatible camera (such as a Nikon D3s), you'll get substantially the same rendition. In a way, Picture Control styles are a bit like using a particular film. Do you want the look of Kodak Ektachrome or Fujifilm Velvia? Load the appropriate style created by you—or anyone else.

Using and managing Picture Control styles is accomplished using two different menu entries, Set Picture Control, which allows you to choose an existing style and to edit the predefined styles that Nikon provides, and Manage Picture Control, discussed in the next section, which gives you the capability of creating and editing user-defined styles.

Choosing a Picture Control Style

To choose from one of the predefined styles (Standard, Neutral, Vivid, Monochrome, Portrait, or Landscape) or select a user-defined style (numbered C-1 to C-9), follow these steps:

1. **Choose Set Picture Control.** This option is located in the Shooting menu. The screen shown in Figure 8.20 appears. Note that Picture Controls that have been modified from their standard settings have an asterisk next to their name.

2. **Select style.** Scroll down to the Picture Control you'd like to use.

3. **Activate Picture Control.** Press OK to activate the highlighted style. (Although you can usually select a menu item by pressing the multi selector right button; in this case, that button activates editing instead.)

4. **Exit menu.** Press the MENU button or tap the shutter release to exit the menu system.

Figure 8.20
You can choose from six predefined Picture Controls, or select a user-defined style, such as *C-1 Concerts* shown here.

Indicates Custom Setting

Original Picture Controls

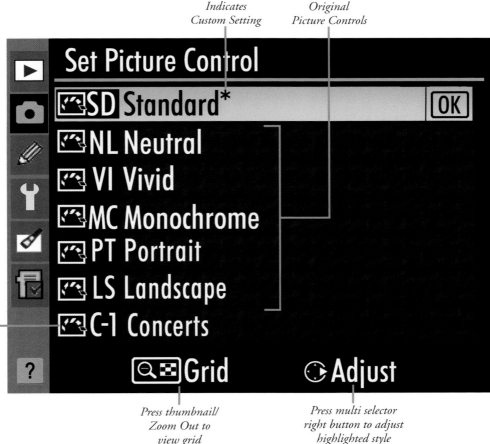

User-defined Picture Control

Press thumbnail/ Zoom Out to view grid

Press multi selector right button to adjust highlighted style

Editing a Picture Control Style

You can change the parameters of any of Nikon's predefined Picture Controls in P, S, A, and M modes, or any of the nine user-defined styles you create. In other modes, the camera selects a Picture Control automatically. You are given the choice of using the quick adjust/fine-tune facility to modify a Picture Control with a few sliders, or to view the relationship of your Picture Controls on a grid. To make quick adjustments to any Picture Control except the Monochrome style, follow these steps:

1. **Access menu.** Choose Set Picture Control from the Shooting menu.

2. **Select style.** Scroll down to the Picture Control you'd like to edit.

3. **Access adjustment screen.** Press the multi selector right button to produce the adjustment screen shown in Figure 8.21.

4. **Make fast changes.** Use the Quick Adjust slider to exaggerate the attributes of the Standard or Vivid styles (Quick Adjustments are not available with other styles).

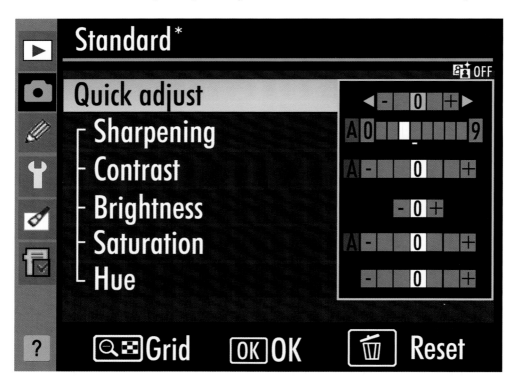

Figure 8.21
Sliders can be used to make quick adjustments to your Picture Control styles.

5. **Change other attributes.** Scroll down to the Sharpening, Contrast, Brightness, Saturation, and Hue sliders with the multi selector up/down buttons, then use the left/right buttons to decrease or increase the effects. A line will appear under the original setting in the slider whenever you've made a change from the defaults. **Note:** You can't adjust contrast and brightness when Active D-Lighting (discussed later in this chapter) is active. Turn it off to make those Picture Control adjustments. An icon at the upper right of the screen shows whether Active D-Lighting is on or off.

6. **Or use auto adjustments.** Instead of making changes with the slider's scale, you can move the cursor to the far left and choose A (for auto) instead when working with the Sharpening, Contrast, and Saturation sliders. The D7000 will adjust these parameters automatically, depending on the type of scene it detects.

7. **To Reset Values.** Press the Trash button to reset the values to their defaults.

8. **View adjustment grid.** Press the Thumbnail/Zoom Out button to view an adjustment grid (discussed next).

9. **Confirm changes.** Press OK when you're finished making adjustments.

The changes Picture Controls make to your images are more subtle than you realize, because the values that are applied among the various Picture Controls aren't absolute. Adjustments you make to, say, the Standard or Vivid styles are relative to the base values of those styles themselves. For example, the Standard style is inherently less saturated than the Vivid style, so if you move the Saturation slider two notches to the right, you'll end up with a modified Standard style that is *still* less saturated than the Vivid style's default. You'll want to learn exactly what happens to your images when you adjust each individual Picture Control, and, moreover, use the right Picture Control as your base or "parent" style when creating Picture Controls of your own. If you wanted a very, very saturated Picture Control, you'd start with the Vivid style, then adjust that and save it as Super Vivid (or something along those lines). Figure 8.22 shows pairs of images that compare four of the most frequently adjusted attributes.

Editing the Monochrome style is similar to modifying the other styles, except that the parameters differ slightly. Sharpening, Contrast, and Brightness are available, but, instead of Saturation and Hue, you can choose a filter effect (Yellow, Orange, Red, Green, or none) and a toning effect (black-and-white, plus seven levels of Sepia, Cyanotype, Red, Yellow, Green, Blue Green, Blue, Purple Blue, and Red Purple). (Keep in mind that once you've taken a JPEG photo using a Monochrome style, you can't convert the image back to full color.)

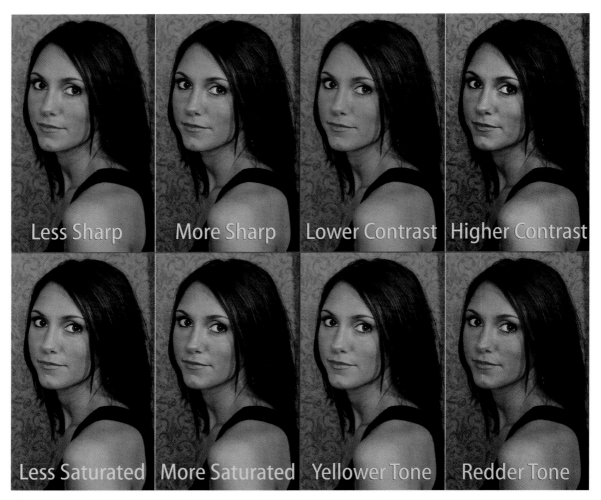

Figure 8.22 Picture Controls allow you to adjust attributes like sharpness (upper-left pair); contrast (upper-right pair); saturation (lower-left pair); and hue (lower-right pair).

FILTERS VS. TONING

Although some of the color choices seem to overlap, you'll get very different looks when choosing between Filter Effects and Toning. Filter Effects add no color to the mono-chrome image. Instead, they reproduce the look of black-and-white film that has been shot through a color filter. That is, Yellow will make the sky darker and the clouds will stand out more, while Orange makes the sky even darker and sunsets more full of detail.

The Red filter produces the darkest sky of all and darkens green objects, such as leaves. Human skin may appear lighter than normal. The Green filter has the opposite effect on leaves, making them appear lighter in tone. Figure 8.23 shows a landscape scene shot with no filter, then Yellow, Green, and Red filters.

The Sepia, Blue, Green, and other toning effects, on the other hand, all add a color cast to your monochrome image. Use these when you want an old-time look or a special effect, without bothering to recolor your shots in an image editor. Several toning effects are shown in Figure 8.24.

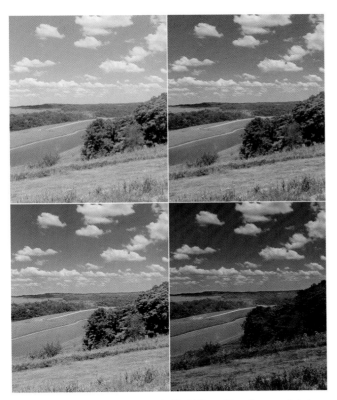

Figure 8.23 No filter (upper left); Yellow filter (upper right); Green filter (lower left); and Red filter (lower right).

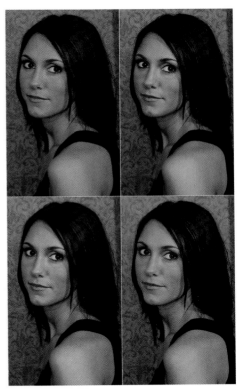

Figure 8.24 Toning effects: Sepia (upper left); Purple Blue (upper right); Red Purple (lower left); and Green (lower right).

When you press the Thumbnail/Zoom Out button, a grid display, like the one shown in Figure 8.25, appears, showing the relative contrast and saturation of each of the predefined Picture Controls. If you've created your own custom Picture Controls, they will appear on this grid, too, represented by the numbers 1-9. Because the values for auto-contrast and autosaturation may vary, the icons for any Picture Control that uses the Auto feature will be shown on the grid in green, with lines extending up and down from the icon to tip you off that the position within the coordinates may vary from the one shown.

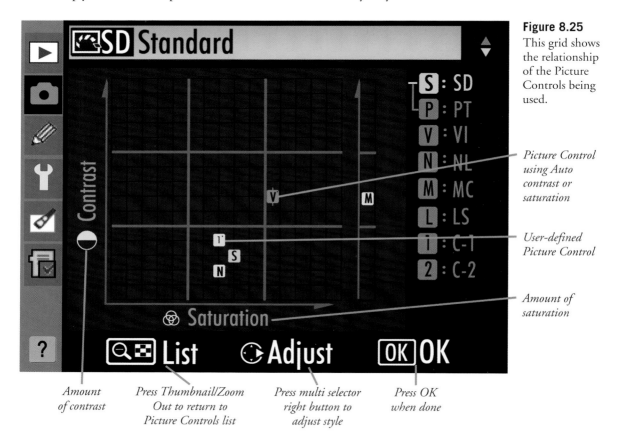

Figure 8.25
This grid shows the relationship of the Picture Controls being used.

Picture Control using Auto contrast or saturation

User-defined Picture Control

Amount of saturation

Amount of contrast

Press Thumbnail/Zoom Out to return to Picture Controls list

Press multi selector right button to adjust style

Press OK when done

Manage Picture Control

The Manage Picture Control menu entry can be used to create new styles, edit existing styles, rename or delete them, and store/retrieve them from the memory card. Here are the basic functions of this menu item, which can be found on the Shooting menu directly below the Set Picture Control entry:

■ **Make a copy.** Choose Save/Edit, select from the list of available Picture Controls, and press OK to store that style in one of the user-defined slots C-1 to C-9 (with slots C1 to C7 shown in Figure 8.26).

Figure 8.26
Picture Controls that you define can be stored in your D7000's settings.

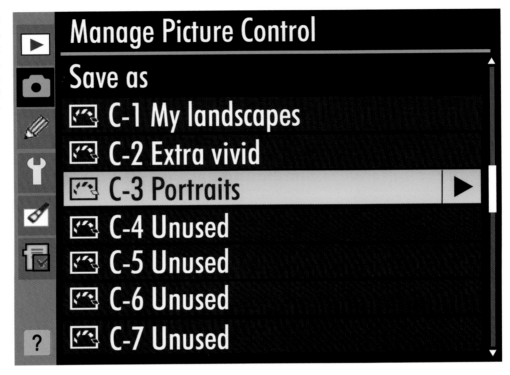

- **Save an edited copy.** Choose Save/Edit, select from the list of available Picture Controls, and then press the multi selector right button to edit the style, as described in the previous section. Press OK when finished editing, and then save the modified style in one of the user-defined slots C-1 to C-9.

- **Rename a style.** Choose Rename, select from the list of user-defined Picture Controls (you cannot rename the default styles), and then enter the text used as the new label for the style, using the standard D7000 text entry screen like those shown earlier in this chapter. You may use up to 19 characters for the name.

- **Remove a style.** Select Delete, choose from the list of user-defined Picture Controls (you can't remove one of the default styles), press the multi selector right button, then highlight Yes in the screen that follows, and press OK to remove that Picture Control.

- **Store/retrieve style on card.** Choose Load/Save, then select Copy to Camera to locate a Picture Control on your Secure Digital card and copy it to the D7000; Delete from Card to select a Picture Control on your memory card and remove it; or Copy to Card to duplicate a style currently in your camera onto the Secure Digital card. This last option allows you to create and save Picture Controls in excess of the nine that can be loaded into the camera at one time. Once you've copied a style to your memory card, you can modify the version in the camera, give it a new name, and, in effect, create a whole new Picture Control.

Auto Distortion Control

This option can correct barrel distortion (outward bowing of lines that should be straight) that sometimes occurs with telephoto lenses, and pin-cushion distortion (lines that curve inwards, towards the center of the frame) that can appear when using wide-angle lenses. When turned on, the D7000 uses information about your Nikon-brand lens that is stored in the third (L) firmware module (and which can be updated with new firmware releases as lenses are introduced). Because this correction can result in cropping out part of your image, you may want to turn it off and use it only if you find the distortion produced by your lens is particularly bad.

Nikon recommends using this feature only with type G and D lenses (that is, lenses that have those designations as part of their names). Auto Distortion Control operates as you take the picture; you can also apply distortion control after a picture is taken using the Retouch menu (discussed in Chapter 10). Barrel and pincushion distortion can also be fully or partially corrected using an image editor like Photoshop. The in-camera feature is faster when you have lots of photos to process, because it performs its magic as the photo is saved to your memory card. You'll find more information about the L firmware module in Chapter 14.

Color Space

The Nikon D7000's Color Space option gives you two different color spaces (also called *color gamuts*), named Adobe RGB (because it was developed by Adobe Systems in 1998), and sRGB (supposedly because it is the *standard* RGB color space). These two color gamuts define a specific set of colors that can be applied to the images your D7000 captures.

You're probably surprised that the Nikon D7000 doesn't automatically capture *all* the colors we see. Unfortunately, that's impossible because of the limitations of the sensor and the filters used to capture the fundamental red, green, and blue colors, as well as that of the phosphors used to display those colors on your camera and computer monitors. Nor is it possible to *print* every color our eyes detect, because the inks or pigments used don't absorb and reflect colors perfectly.

On the other hand, the D7000 does capture quite a few more colors than we need. Even if you use 12-bit capture instead of the default 14-bit capture, an original 12-bit RAW image contains a possible 68 *billion* different hues, which are condensed down to a mere 16.8 million possible colors when converted to a 24-bit (eight bits per channel) image. While 16.8 million colors may seem like a lot, it's a small subset of 68 billion captured, and an even smaller subset of all the possible colors we can see.

The set of colors, or gamut, that can be reproduced or captured by a given device (scanner, digital camera, monitor, printer, or some other piece of equipment) is represented as a color space that exists within the larger full range of colors. That full range is represented by the odd-shaped splotch of color shown in Figure 8.27, as defined by scientists at an international organization back in 1931. The colors possible with Adobe RGB are represented by the larger, black triangle in the figure, while the sRGB gamut is represented by the smaller white triangle.

Regardless of which triangle—or color space—is used by the D7000, you end up with some combination of 16.8 million different colors that can be used in your photograph. (No one image will contain all 16.8 million! If each and every pixel in a D7000's 16-megapixel image were a different color—which is extremely unlikely—you'd need only 16 million different colors.) But, as you can see from the figure, the colors available will be *different.*

Adobe RGB is an expanded color space useful for commercial and professional printing, and it can reproduce a wider range of colors. It can also come in useful if an image is going to be extensively retouched, especially within an advanced image editor, like Adobe Photoshop, which has sophisticated color management capabilities that can be tailored to specific color spaces. As an advanced user, you don't need to automatically "upgrade" your D7000 to Adobe RGB, because images tend to look less saturated on your monitor and, it is likely, significantly different from what you will get if you output the photo to your personal inkjet. (You can *profile* your monitor for the Adobe RGB color space to improve your on-screen rendition, as I'll describe shortly.)

Figure 8.27
The outer figure shows all the colors we can see; the two inner outlines show the boundaries of Adobe RGB (black triangle) and sRGB (white triangle).

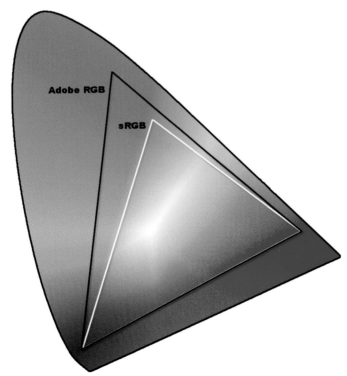

While both Adobe RGB and sRGB can reproduce the exact same 16.8 million absolute colors, Adobe RGB spreads those colors over a larger portion of the visible spectrum. Think of a box of crayons (the jumbo 16.8 million crayon variety). Some of the basic crayons from the original sRGB set have been removed and replaced with new hues not contained in the original box. Your "new" box contains colors that can't be reproduced by your computer monitor, but which work just fine with a commercial printing press. For example, Adobe RGB has more "crayons" available in the cyan-green portion of the box, compared to sRGB, which is unlikely to be an advantage unless your image's final destination is the cyan, magenta, yellow, and black inks of a printing press.

The other color space, sRGB, is recommended for images that will be output locally on the user's own printer, as this color space matches that of the typical inkjet printer fairly closely. You might prefer sRGB, which is the default for the Nikon D7000 and most other cameras, as it is well suited for the range of colors that can be displayed on a computer screen and viewed over the Internet. If you plan to take your image file to a retailer's kiosk for printing, sRGB is your best choice, because those automated output devices are calibrated for the sRGB color space that consumers use.

Of course, choosing the right color space doesn't solve the problems that result from having each device in the image chain manipulating or producing a slightly different set of colors. To that end, you'll need to investigate the wonderful world of *color management*, which uses hardware and software tools to match or *calibrate* all your devices, as closely as possible, so that what you see more closely resembles what you capture, what you see on your computer display, and what ends up on a printed hardcopy. Entire books have been devoted to color management, and most of what you need to know doesn't directly involve your Nikon D7000, so I won't detail the nuts and bolts here.

To manage your color, you'll need, at the bare minimum, some sort of calibration system for your computer display, so that your monitor can be adjusted to show a standardized set of colors that is repeatable over time. (What you see on the screen can vary as the monitor ages, or even when the room light changes.) I use Pantone's Huey monitor color correction system for my computer's main 26-inch wide-screen LCD display, as well as for my matching 26-inch wide-screen secondary display that flanks it. The Huey checks room light levels every five minutes, and reminds me to recalibrate every week or two, using the small sensor device shown in Figure 8.28, which attaches temporarily to the front of screen with tiny suction cups, and interprets test patches that the Huey software displays during calibration. The rest of the time, the Huey sensor sits in the stand shown, measuring the room illumination and adjusting my monitors for higher or lower ambient light levels.

The Huey (www.pantone.com) is an inexpensive (under $100) system that does a good job of calibrating a single monitor. You can upgrade it, as I did, for use with multiple monitors using a $40 software download. If you're serious about accurate color

Figure 8.28
Pantone's Huey monitor color correction system is an inexpensive device for calibrating your display.

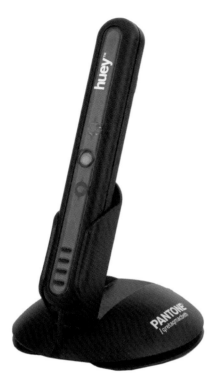

and making prints, you'll want a more advanced system (up to $500) like the various Spyder products from Datacolor (www.datacolor.com), or Colormunki from X-Rite (www.colormunki.com).

Active D-Lighting

Active D-Lighting is a feature that improves the rendition of detail in highlights and shadows when you're photographing high contrast scenes. It's been available as an internal retouching option in Nikon's lower-end cameras (by that I mean the CoolPix point-and-shoot line) for some time, and has gradually worked its way up through the company's dSLR products, eventually reaching the more advanced cameras, including the D7000. You'll find the "non-active" D-Lighting feature in the Retouch menu, which I'll describe in Chapter 10.

A new wrinkle, however, is the Active D-Lighting capability introduced with Nikon's new higher-end models, which, unlike the Retouch menu post-processing feature, applies its tonal improvements *while you are actually taking the photo*. That's good news and bad news. It means that, if you're taking photos in a contrasty environment, Active D-Lighting can automatically improve the apparent dynamic range of your image as you shoot, without additional effort on your part. However, you'll need to disable the feature once you leave the high contrast lighting behind, and the process does take some time. You wouldn't want to use Active D-Lighting for continuous shooting of sports subjects, for example. There are many situations in which the selective application of D-Lighting using the Retouch menu is a better choice.

You have six choices: Auto, Extra High, High, Normal, Low, and Off. You may need to experiment with the feature a little to discover how much D-Lighting you can apply to a high contrast image before the shadows start to darken objectionably. Note that when this feature is activated, brightness and contrast Picture Control settings cannot be changed. Figure 8.29 shows some examples of Active D-Light applied. By the time the

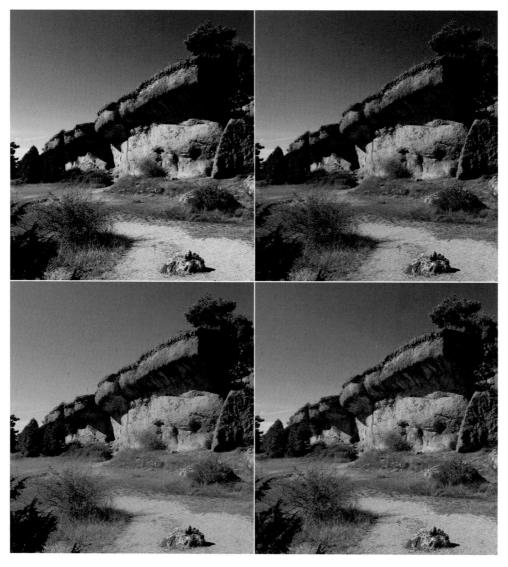

Figure 8.29
No D-Lighting (upper left); low (upper right); normal (lower left); and high (lower right).

sample images shown have been half-toned and rendered to the printed page, the differences may be fairly subtle. For that reason, I'm not illustrating the effects of the Auto setting (which varies, of course, depending on the scene) and Extra High, which is difficult to distinguish from High under normal circumstances. Look at the amount of detail in the overhanging rock in the upper-right area of each version.

For best results, use your D7000's Matrix metering mode, so the Active D-Lighting feature can work with a full range of exposure information from multiple points in the image. Active D-Lighting works its magic by subtly *underexposing* your image so that details in the highlights (which would normally be overexposed and become featureless white pixels) are not lost. At the same time, it adjusts the values of pixels located in midtone and shadow areas so they don't become too dark because of the underexposure. Highlight tones will be preserved, while shadows will eventually be allowed to go dark more readily. Bright beach or snow scenes, especially those with few shadows (think high noon, when the shadows are smaller) can benefit from using Active D-Lighting.

It's important to *always* keep in mind that Active D-Lighting not only adjusts the contrast automatically of your image (that's why you can't adjust the brightness/contrast of a Picture Control when Active D-Lighting is turned on), it modifies exposure for both existing light and flash as well, as I've noted. Exposure for both is reduced from about 1/3 stop (at the Low setting) to as much as 1 full stop less at the Extra High setting.

Tip

In Manual exposure mode, Active D-Lighting does not adjust the exposure of your image; it simply shifts the center (zero) point of the analog exposure indicator in the viewfinder/LCD.

Nikon gives you a lot of flexibility in using Active D-Lighting. You can choose the setting yourself, or let the camera *vary* the amount of tweaking by using Active D-Lighting Bracketing, which I explained in the general bracketing discussion in Chapter 4. You'll find this is a useful feature, if used with caution.

Long Exp. NR

Visual noise is that awful graininess caused by long exposures and high ISO settings, and which shows up as multicolored specks in images. This setting helps you manage the kind of noise caused by lengthy exposure times. In some ways, noise is like the excessive grain found in some high-speed photographic films. However, while photographic grain is sometimes used as a special effect, it's rarely desirable in a digital photograph. There are easier ways to add texture to your photos.

Some noise is created when you're using shutter speeds longer than eight seconds to create a longer exposure. Extended exposure times allow more photons to reach the sensor, but increase the likelihood that some photosites will react randomly even though not struck by a particle of light. Moreover, as the sensor remains switched on for the longer exposure, it heats, and this heat can be mistakenly recorded as if it were a barrage of photons. This menu setting can be used to activate the D7000's long exposure noise-canceling operation performed by the EXPEED digital signal processor.

- **Off.** This default setting disables long exposure noise reduction. Use it when you want the maximum amount of detail present in your photograph, even though higher noise levels will result. This setting also eliminates the extra time needed to take a picture caused by the noise reduction process. If you plan to use only lower ISO settings (thereby reducing the noise caused by ISO amplification), the noise levels produced by longer exposures may be acceptable. For example, you might be shooting a waterfall at ISO 100 with the camera mounted on a tripod, using a neutral-density filter and a long exposure to cause the water to blur. (Try exposures of 2 to 16 seconds, depending on the intensity of the light and how much blur you want.) (See Figure 8.30.) To maximize detail in the non-moving portions of your photos for the exposures that are eight seconds or longer, you can switch off long exposure noise reduction.

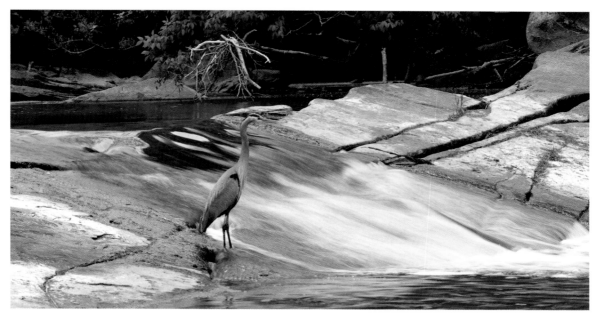

Figure 8.30 A long exposure with the camera mounted on a tripod produces this traditional moving water photo.

■ **On.** When exposures are eight seconds or longer, the Nikon D7000 takes a second, blank exposure to compare that to the first image. (While the second image is taken, the warning Job nr appears on the monochrome LCD panel and in the viewfinder.) Noise (pixels that are bright in a frame that *should* be completely black) in the "dark frame" image is subtracted from your original picture, and only the noise-corrected image is saved to your memory card. Because the noise-reduction process effectively doubles the time required to take a picture, you won't want to use this setting when you're rushed. Some noise can be removed later on, using tools like the noise reduction features built into Bibble Pro, many image editors, or Nikon Capture NX2.

High ISO NR

Noise can also be caused by higher ISO sensitivity settings, and the Nikon D7000, which offers settings up to ISO 6400 (and thence up to the equivalent of ISO 12800 and 25600 with the Hi 1.0 and Hi 2.0 settings) has a loftier ISO ceiling than many cameras. Even so, high ISO noise reduction, which can be set with this menu option, may be a good option in many cases. You can choose Off when you want to preserve detail at the cost of some noise graininess, and the D7000 will apply high ISO NR only at the "boosted" settings of Hi 0.3 and above. Or, you can select On, which is applied when ISO sensitivity has been set to ISO 800 or higher.

The effects of high ISO noise are something like listening to a CD in your car, and then rolling down all the windows. You're adding sonic noise to the audio signal, and while increasing the CD player's volume may help a bit, you're still contending with an unfavorable signal to noise ratio that probably mutes tones (especially higher treble notes) that you really want to hear.

The same thing happens when the analog image signal is amplified: You're increasing the image information in the signal, but boosting the background fuzziness at the same time. Tune in a very faint or distant AM radio station on your car stereo. Then turn up the volume. After a certain point, turning up the volume further no longer helps you hear better. There's a similar point of diminishing returns for digital sensor ISO increases and signal amplification as well.

As the captured information is amplified to produce higher ISO sensitivities, some random noise in the signal is amplified along with the photon information. Increasing the ISO setting of your camera raises the threshold of sensitivity so that fewer and fewer photons are needed to register as an exposed pixel. Yet, that also increases the chances of one of those phantom photons being counted among the real-life light particles, too.

Fortunately, the Nikon D7000's CMOS sensor and its EXPEED digital processing chip are optimized to produce the low noise levels, so ratings as high as ISO 1600 to ISO 3200 can be used routinely (although there will be some noise, of course), and even

ISO 6400 can generate good results. Some kinds of subjects may not require this kind of noise cancellation, such as those that have a texture of their own that tends to hide or mask the noise.

ISO Sensitivity Settings

You'll have to scroll down the Shooting menu to see the final five options, including this one. (See Figure 8.31.) This menu entry has two parts, ISO Sensitivity and ISO Sensitivity Auto Control. The former is simply a screen that allows you to specify the ISO setting, just as you would by spinning the main command dial while holding down the ISO button, located second from the bottom to the left of the color LCD. The available settings range from Auto and ISO 100 through ISO 6400 to Hi 1 (ISO 12800 equivalent) and Hi 2 (ISO 25600 equivalent). The available settings are determined by the size of the increment you've specified in Custom Settings menu CSM #b1: 1/3 or 1/2 step values. Use the ISO sensitivity menu when you find it more convenient to set ISO using the top-panel monochrome display.

The ISO Sensitivity Auto Control menu entry lets you specify how and when the D7000 will adjust the ISO value for you automatically under certain conditions. This capability can be potentially useful, although experienced photographers tend to shy away from any feature that allows the camera to change basic settings like ISO that have

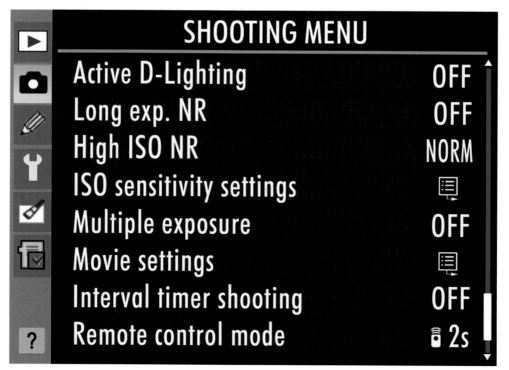

Figure 8.31
Scroll down to see the last five entries in the Shooting menu.

been carefully selected. Fortunately, you can set some boundaries so the D7000 will use this adjustment in a fairly intelligent way.

When Auto ISO is activated, the camera can bump up the ISO sensitivity, if necessary, whenever an optimal exposure cannot be achieved at the current ISO setting. Of course, it can be disconcerting to think you're shooting at ISO 400 and then see a grainier ISO 1600 shot during LCD review. While the D7000 provides a flashing ISO-Auto alert in the viewfinder and top-panel status LCD, the warning is easy to miss. Here are the important considerations to keep in mind when using the options available for this feature:

- **Off.** Set ISO Sensitivity Auto Control to off, and the ISO setting will not budge from whatever value you have specified. Use this setting when you don't want any ISO surprises, or when ISO increases are not needed to counter slow shutter speeds. For example, if the D7000 is mounted on a tripod, you can safely use slower shutter speeds at a relatively low ISO setting, so there is no need for a speed bump. On the other hand, if you're hand-holding the camera and the D7000 set for Program (P) or Aperture-priority (A) mode wants to use a shutter speed slower than, say, 1/30th second, it's probably a good idea to increase the ISO to avoid the effects of camera shake. If you're using a longer lens, a shutter speed of 1/125th second or higher might be the point where an ISO bump would be a good idea. In that case, you can turn the ISO Sensitivity Auto Control on, or remember to boost the ISO setting yourself.

- **Maximum sensitivity.** Use this parameter to indicate the highest ISO setting you're comfortable having the D7000 set on its own. You can choose from ISO 400, 800, 1600, 3200, 6400 and Hi 1 and Hi 2 as the max ISO setting the camera will use. (Note that the increments are fixed at those listed, regardless of how CSM #b1 is set.) Use a low number if you'd rather not take any photos at a high ISO without manually setting that value yourself. Dial in a higher ISO number if getting the photo at any sensitivity setting is more important than worrying about noise.

- **Minimum shutter speed.** This setting allows you to tell the D7000 how slow the shutter speed must be before the ISO boost kicks in, within the range 1 second to 1/4,000th second. The default value is 1/30th second, because for most shooters in most situations, any shutter speed longer than 1/30 is to be avoided, unless you're using a tripod, monopod, or looking for a special effect. If you have steady hands, or the camera is partially braced against movement (say, you're using that monopod), a slower shutter speed, down to 1 full second, can be specified. Similarly, if you're working with a telephoto lens and find even a relatively brief shutter speed "dangerous," you can set a minimum shutter speed threshold of, say, 1/250th second. When the shutter speed is faster than the minimum you enter, Auto ISO will not take effect.

Multiple Exposure

This option lets you combine two exposures into one image without the need for an image editor like Photoshop and can be an entertaining way to return to those thrilling days of yesteryear, when complex photos were created in the camera itself. In truth, prior to the digital age, multiple exposures were a cool, groovy, far-out, hep/hip, phat, sick, fabulous way of producing composite images. Today, it's more common to take the lazy way out, snap two or more pictures, and then assemble them in an image editor like Photoshop.

However, if you're willing to spend the time planning a multiple exposure (or are open to some happy accidents), there is a lot to recommend the multiple exposure capability that Nikon has bestowed on the D7000. For one thing, the camera is able to combine two or more images using the RAW data from the sensor, producing photos that are blended together more smoothly than is likely for anyone who's not a Photoshop guru. To take your own multiple exposures, just follow these steps (although it's probably a good idea to do a little planning and maybe even some sketching on paper first):

1. **Access Multiple Exposure setting.** Navigate to the option in the Shooting menu.

2. **Select Number of shots.** Choose a value from 2 to 3 with the multi selector up/down buttons, and press OK.

3. **Choose Auto gain.** Specify either On (the default) or Off. When On is selected, the D7000 will divide the total exposure of the image by the number of shots specified; for example, applying 1/3 of the exposure time to each shot in a three-image series. Choose Off, and the full exposure is applied to each picture. You'd want to use Off when using a dark background that would allow successive exposures to add details, and On to avoid the risk of overlapping images washing each other out. Press OK to set the gain.

4. **Finish.** Move the cursor up to Done and press OK. The multiple exposure icon appears in the monochrome LCD status panel.

5. **Take the multiple exposures.** Press the shutter release button multiple times until all the exposures in the series have been taken. (In continuous shooting mode, the entire series will be shot in a single burst.) The blinking multiple exposure icon vanishes when the series is finished. Note: you'll need to reactivate the Multiple Exposure feature once you've finished taking a series; it shuts off automatically.

Keep in mind if you wait longer than 30 seconds between any two photos in the series, the sequence will terminate and combine the images taken so far. If you want a longer elapsed time between exposures, go to the Playback menu and make sure On has been specified for Image Review, and then extend the monitor display time using CSM #c4 to an appropriate maximum interval. The Multiple Exposure feature will then use the monitor-off delay as its maximum interval between shots. Figure 8.32 shows double exposure created at a ballet performance.

Figure 8.32
The D7000's Multiple Exposure capability allows combining images without an image editor.

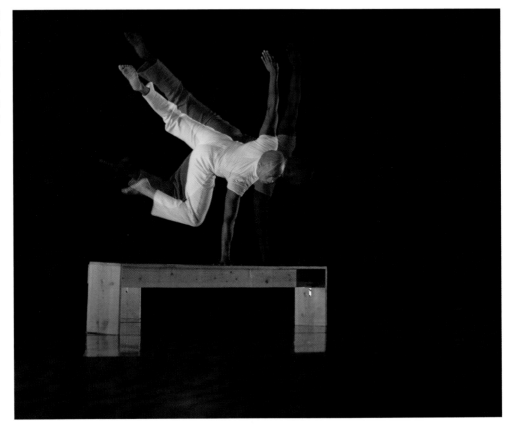

Movie Settings

This menu entry allows you to choose three movie making parameters, which I discussed in Chapter 6. To begin shooting, rotate the Live View switch, and then push the red Movie button. Your three options are:

- **Movie Quality.** Choose from 1920 × 1080 pixels/24 fps; 1280 × 720 pixels at 24 fps or 30 fps; or 640 × 424/30 fps. I explained why you'd select each of these in Chapter 6.

- **Microphone.** Select from Low, Medium, High sensitivity microphones, Auto sensitivity, or Off.

- **Destination.** Select either Slot 1 or Slot 2 to specify where your movies will be stored. As a practical matter, you should choose the slot containing the faster of the two SD cards, because movie shooting benefits from having a fast card. (At least a Class 6 card; preferably a Class 10 card.)

■ **Manual movie settings.** Select On if you want to adjust shutter speed and ISO sensitivity while shooting movies with the D7000 in Manual exposure mode. Note that, due to the interval required between frames, shutter speeds no slower than 1/30th second can be used. Speeds up to 1/8000th second are possible, and ISO settings from ISO 100 to Hi 2 can be used. Exposure compensation cannot be used.

Interval Timer Shooting

Nikon D7000's built-in time-lapse photography feature allows you to take pictures for up to 999 intervals in bursts of as many as nine shots, with a delay of up to 23 hours and 59 minutes between shots/bursts, and an initial start-up time of as long as 23 hours and 59 minutes from the time you activate the feature. That means that if you want to photograph a rosebud opening and would like to photograph the flower once every two minutes over the next 16 hours, you can do that easily. If you like, you can delay the first photo taken by a couple hours so you don't have to stand there by the D7000 waiting for the right moment.

Or, you might want to photograph a particular scene every hour for 24 hours to capture, say, a landscape from sunrise to sunset to the following day's sunrise again. The D7000 can do that, too, and, in fact, offers most of the features of the expensive ($130) Nikon MC-36 Multi-Function Remote control. Nikon has done us all a huge favor by including this functionality essentially for free! I will offer two practical tips right now, in case you want to run out and try interval timer shooting immediately: *use a tripod, and for best results over longer time periods, plan on connecting your D7000 to an external power source!*

The Interval Timer Shooting screen (see Figure 8.33) is confusingly designed, in my opinion. It's needlessly complex; the display changes in a quirky way depending on what information you're entering, and some portions of the screen aren't accessible until you've performed a prerequisite function. I would have set up this menu with nothing more than five entries, each with their own screen of options: On/Off, Start Time, interval delay, total number of shots to expose, and the number of shots in the burst per interval (if more than one image per interval is desired).

To set up interval timer shooting, just follow these steps.

Before you start:

1. **Set your clock.** The D7000 uses its internal World Time clock to activate, so make sure the time has been set accurately in the Setup menu before you begin.

2. **Select release mode.** If you want to shoot bursts of images each time an interval elapses, set the release mode dial to C$_L$ (Continuous low speed; pictures will be taken at the rate specified in CSM #d6) or C$_H$ (Continuous high speed; pictures will be taken at a rate of up to 6 fps). If you prefer to take one picture per interval,

Figure 8.33
The Interval Timer Shooting main screen.

Select time to begin shooting sequence

Now has been selected

Specific time has been selected

Starting time

Interval between shots

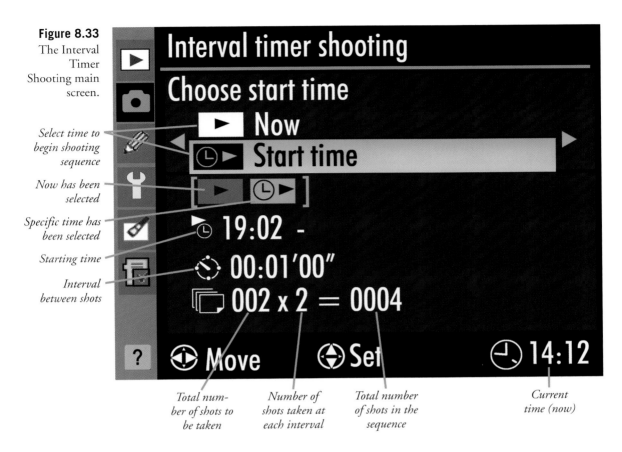

Interval timer shooting

Choose start time

▶ Now

🕐▶ Start time

[▶ 🕐▶]

🕐 19:02 -

⏱ 00:01′00″

002 x 2 = 0004

✛ Move   ✛ Set   🕐 14:12

Total number of shots to be taken

Number of shots taken at each interval

Total number of shots in the sequence

Current time (now)

set the release mode dial to S. However, you can still specify multiple shots per interval when using S; the D7000 will use the frame rate specified in CSM #d6 just as if you had set the release mode to C$_L$.

3. **Bracket, if desired.** If you'd like to bracket exposures during interval shooting, set up bracketing prior to beginning. (You'll learn how to bracket in Chapter 4.)

4. **Secure camera.** Mount the camera on a tripod or other secure support.

5. **Fully charge the battery.** You might want to mount the MB-D11 battery grip if you have one, or connect the D7000 to the Nikon AC Adapter EH-5a or EH-5 if you plan to shoot long sequences. Although the camera more or less goes to sleep between intervals, some power is drawn, and long sequences with bursts of shots can drain power even when you're not using the interval timer feature.

6. **Protect your camera.** Make sure the camera is shielded from the elements, accidents, and theft, and that the viewfinder is covered (using the DK-5 eyepiece cap if necessary) if you need to keep strong ambient light from entering the viewfinder and affecting exposure.

When you're ready to go, set up the D7000 for interval shooting:

1. **Select timer.** Choose Interval Timer Shooting from the Shooting menu.

2. **Specify a starting time.** You must do this before the D7000 will let you set other parameters. Highlight either Now or Start Time and press the multi selector right button. If you choose Now, the interval shooting will begin approximately three seconds after you've finished setting the parameters beginning with Step 5. If you select Start Time, you'll be able to enter a specific time, as described in Steps 3 and 4.

3. **Choose start time.** When the Start Time sub-screen appears, use the multi selector left/right buttons to highlight the hours or minutes, and the up/down buttons to increase or decrease the hours/minutes entry. The 24-hour clock is used, so you can specify a time from 00:00 (midnight) to 23:59 (one minute to midnight). When both hours and minutes have been set, press the multi selector right button to move the highlighting to the Interval section of the sub-screen.

4. **Set the interval between exposures.** You can use the left/right buttons to move among hours, minutes, and seconds, and use the up/down buttons to choose an interval from one second to 24 hours. Press the right button when finished to move down to the number of intervals/shots per interval sub-screen.

> **Tip**
>
> The interval cannot be shorter than the shutter speed; for example, you cannot set one second as the interval if the images will be taken at two seconds or longer.

5. **Set number of intervals and shots per interval.** Use the left/right buttons to highlight the number of intervals, the number of shots taken after each interval has elapsed, and the total number of shots to be exposed overall. You can highlight each number column separately, so that to enter, say, 250 intervals you can set the 100s, 10s, and 1s columns individually (rather than press the up button 250 times!). You can select up to 999 intervals, and 9 shots per interval for a maximum of 8991 exposures with one interval shooting cycle.

6. **Start.** When all the parameters have been entered, press the multi selector right button once more, and the Start subscreen appears, with the choices On or Off. Choose either one and press OK. If you activate interval shooting, a message is displayed on the monitor one minute before each series of shots begins.

PAUSE OR CANCEL INTERVAL SHOOTING

Press the MENU button between intervals (but not when images are still being recorded to the memory card), choose the Interval Timer Shooting menu entry, and select Pause. Interval shooting can also be paused by turning the camera on or off, or by rotating the release mode dial to Live View, self-timer, or Mup positions. To resume the Interval Timer Shooting menu again, press the multi selector left button, and choose Restart. You may also select Off to stop the shooting entirely.

Remote Control Mode

This option lets you select how you want the D7000 to respond to the optional ML-L3 infrared remote control. I really like how this camera has IR sensors on both front and back, which makes this remote much more useful. It's smaller than the MC-D10 wired remote, and doesn't need to be "plugged in" to use. You have three choices in this menu entry:

- **2s Delayed remote.** When you press the button on the remote, the shutter is triggered two seconds later. Use this mode when you want a short delay before the picture is taken, say, for any camera movement to subside after you've adjusted one of the other controls.

- **Quick response remote.** When you press the button on the remote, the shutter is triggered instantly. This mode is useful when you want to control the exact time the picture is taken, say, when some wildlife appears in the frame, or when you're shooting remotely at a sports event.

- **Remote mirror up.** When you press the button on the remote once, the mirror is raised. Once all the vibration from the mirror flip has subsided, press the remote button a second time to take the actual picture.

9

Setup: The Custom Settings Menu

Unlike the Shooting menu options, which you are likely to modify frequently as your picture-taking environment changes, Custom Settings are slightly more stable sets of preferences that let you tailor the behavior of your camera in a variety of different ways for longer-term use.

Some options are minor tweaks useful for specific shooting situations. You can turn off the autofocus assist lamp, the back-panel LCD's shooting information display, and the D7000's built-in beeper when you are shooting an acoustic music concert, when you'd rather not disrupt the environment. Others make the camera more convenient to use. Perhaps you'd like to assign a frequently used feature to the Fn button, or turn on the viewfinder grid display to make it easier to align vertical or horizontal shapes.

Best of all are the settings that actually *improve* the way the D7000 operates. CSM #b5, for example, provides a way to fine-tune the exposures your camera calculates for each of the metering modes: Matrix, Center-weighted, and Spot. If you find that one or the other consistently over- or underexposes more than you like, it's easy to dial in a permanent correction. Should you feel that the D7000 is taking a few pictures that are out of focus, you can tell it not to fire until optimum focus is achieved.

This chapter concentrates on explaining all the options of the Custom Settings menu and, most importantly, when and why you might want to use each setting.

Custom Settings Menu Layout

There are 48 different Custom Settings, arranged in six different categories, as shown in Figure 9.1: Autofocus, Metering/Exposure, Timers/AE Lock, Shooting/Display, Bracketing/Flash, and Controls. Some of those may seem to be an odd match. What does bracketing have to do with flash? Oh, wait! You can *bracket* flash (as well as non-flash) exposures. The category system does have an advantage. Once you've learned what settings are available within each category, you can select the Custom Settings menu, scroll down to the specific category you want, and enter the CSM system at that point, skipping the other entries.

However, once you get past the main CSM screen, the entries are one long scrolling list, so if you've guessed wrong about where you want to start, you can enter the list at any point and then scroll up or down until you find the entry you want. The CSM menu items are all color- and letter-coded: **a** (red) for autofocus functions; **b** (orange) for metering/exposure; **c** (green) for timers and AE/Lock features; **d** (light blue) for shooting/display functions; **e** (dark blue) for bracketing/flash; and **f** (purple) for adjustments to the D7000's controls.

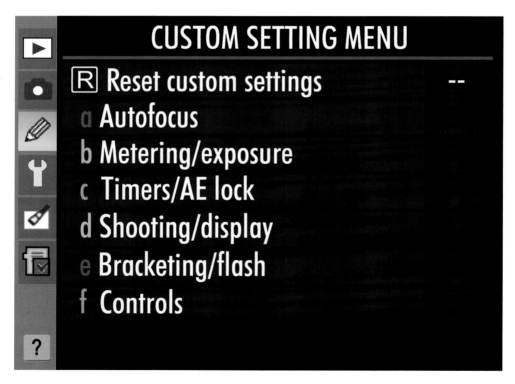

Figure 9.1
These six categories include 48 different entries in the Custom Settings menu.

For simplicity, in this book I have been consistently referring to the Custom Settings menu entries by their letter/names, so that you always know that when I mention CSM #a6, I am describing the sixth entry in the Autofocus menu, Number of Focus Points. That terminology makes it easy to jump quickly to the specific entry.

You can select a CSM function as you do any menu entry, by pressing the multi selector right button, and navigating through the screen that appears with the up/down (and sometimes left/right) buttons. Confirming an option is usually done by pressing the OK button, pushing the multi selector right button, or sometimes by choosing Done when a series of related options have been chosen.

At the top level, you'll see these entries:

- Reset custom settings
- a. Autofocus
- b. Metering/exposure
- c. Timers/AE Lock
- d. Shooting/display
- e. Bracketing/flash
- f. Controls

Reset Custom Settings

You can restore the settings of the Custom Settings banks to their default values by choosing this menu entry and selecting Yes or No. In Chapter 7, I provided a list of recommended Custom Settings menu settings for typical photo environments. Tables 9.1 to 9.6 show the default values as the Nikon D7000 comes from the factory, and after a reset. If you don't know what some of these settings are, I'll explain them later in this chapter. Be careful when changing any of your carefully tailored customized settings back to the defaults.

Table 9.1 Default Custom Settings Values: Autofocus

Function	Option	Default
a1	AF-C priority selection	Release
a2	AF-S priority selection	Focus
a3	Focus tracking with lock-on	3 (Normal)
a4	AF point illumination	Auto
a5	Focus point wrap-around	No wrap
a6	Number of focus points	39 points
a7	Built-in AF-assist illuminator	On

Table 9.1 (continued)

Function	Option	Default
a8	Live view/movie AF	
	Autofocus mode	Single-servo AF
	AF-area mode:	
	Sport, Night Portrait, Pets, Beach, Hi Key, Low Key	Wide-area AF
	Close-Up, Food	Normal-area AF
	Other shooting modes	Face-priority AF

Table 9.2 Default Custom Settings Bank Values: Metering/Exposure

Function	Option	Default
b1	ISO sensitivity step value	1/3 step
b2	EV steps for exposure cntrl.	1/3 step
b3	Easy exposure compensation	Off
b4	Center-weighted area	8mm
b5	Fine-tune optimal exposure	
	Matrix metering	0
	Center-weighted metering	0
	Spot metering	0

Table 9.3 Default Custom Settings Bank Values: Timers/AE Lock

Function	Option	Default
c1	Shutter release button AE-L	Off
c2	Auto meter-off delay	6 seconds
c3	Self-timer	
	Self-timer delay	10 seconds
	Number of Shots	0
	Interval between shots	0.5 seconds

Table 9.3 (continued)

Function	Option	Default
c4	Monitor off delay	
	Playback	10 seconds
	Menus	20 seconds
	Information display	10 seconds
	Image review	4 seconds
	Live view	10 minutes
c5	Remote on duration	1 minute

Table 9.4 Default Custom Settings Bank Values: Shooting/Display

Function	Option	Default
d1	Beep	
	Volume	Off
	Pitch	High
d2	Viewfinder grid display	Off
d3	ISO display and adjustment	Show frame count
d4	Viewfinder warning display	On
d5	Screen tips	On
d6	CL mode shooting speed	3 fps
d7	Max. continuous release	100
d8	File number sequence	On
d9	Information display	Auto
d10	LCD illumination	Off
d11	Exposure delay mode	Off
d12	Flash warning	On
d13	MB-D11 battery type	LR6 (AA Alkaline)
d14	Battery order	Use MB-D11 batteries first

Table 9.5 Default Custom Settings Bank Values: Bracketing/Flash

Function	Option	Default
e1	Flash sync speed	1/250 second
e2	Flash shutter speed	1/60 second
e3	Flash control for built-in flash	TTL
e4	Modeling flash	On
e5	Auto bracketing set	AE & Flash
e6	Bracketing order	MTR>under>over

Table 9.6 Default Custom Settings Bank Values: Controls

Function	Option	Default
f1	Illuminator switch	LCD backlight
f2	OK button (Shooting mode)	Select center focus point
f3	Assign Fn. Button	FV lock
f4	Assign preview button	Preview
f5	Assign AE-L/AF-L button	AE/AF lock
f6	Customize command dials	
	Reverse rotation	No
	Change main/sub	Off
	Aperture setting	Sub-command dial
	Menus and playback	Off
f7	Release button to use dial	No
f8	Slot empty release lock	Enable release
f9	Reverse indicators	+ 0 -
f10	Assign MB-D11 AE-L/AF-L button	AE/AF lock

a. Autofocus

The red-coded Autofocus options (see Figure 9.2, which shows all but the last two entries) deal with some of the potentially most vexing settings available with the Nikon D7000. After all, incorrect focus is one of the most damaging picture-killers of all the attributes in an image. You may be able to compensate for bad exposure, partially fix errant color balance, and perhaps even incorporate motion blur into an image as a creative element. But if focus is wrong, the photograph doesn't look right, and no amount of "I meant to do that!" pleas are likely to work. The D7000's autofocus options enable you to choose how and when focus is applied (using the AF-S or AF-C focus mode you selected on the camera body), the controls used to activate the feature, and the way focus points are selected from the available 39 zones.

Figure 9.2
The first eight entries in the Autofocus options menu.

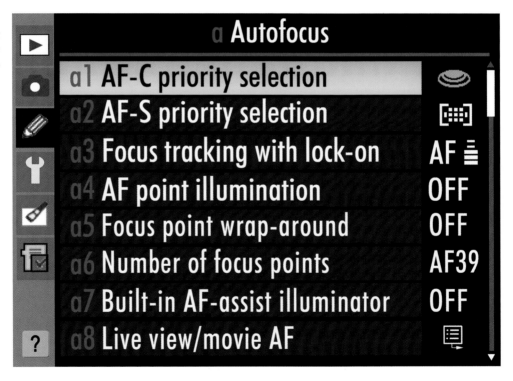

a1 AF-C Priority Selection

As you learned in Chapter 5, the Nikon D7000 has three primary autofocus modes when using the optical viewfinder: Continuous-servo autofocus (AF-C) and Single-servo autofocus (AF-S)—plus AF-A, which, in effect, flips between the two main modes as appropriate. (Live View has two similar modes, AF-S and AF-F.) This menu entry allows you to specify what takes precedence in optical viewfinder modes when you press the shutter release all the way down to take a picture. You can give precedence to focus (called *focus priority*) or to the release button (called *release priority*). You can choose from:

- **Release.** When this option is selected (the default), the shutter is activated when the release button is pushed down all the way, even if sharp focus has not yet been achieved. Because AF-C focuses and refocuses constantly when autofocus is active, you may find that an image is not quite in sharpest focus. Use this option when taking a picture is more important than absolute best focus, such as fast action or photojournalism applications. (You don't want to miss that record-setting home run, or the protestor's pie smashing into the Governor's face.) Using this setting doesn't mean that your image won't be sharply focused; it just means that you'll get a picture even if autofocusing isn't quite complete. If you've been poised with the shutter release pressed halfway, the D7000 probably has been tracking the focus of your image.

- **Focus.** The shutter is not activated until sharp focus is achieved. This is best for subjects that are not moving rapidly. AF-C will continue to track your subjects' movement, but the D7000 won't take a picture until focus is locked in. You might miss a few shots, but you will have fewer out-of-focus images.

a2 AF-S Priority Selection

This is the counterpart setting for Single-servo Autofocus mode.

- **Release.** The shutter is activated when the button is depressed all the way, even if sharp focus is not quite achieved. Keep in mind that, unlike AF-C, the D7000 focuses only *once* when AF-S mode is used. So, if you've partially depressed the shutter release, paused, and then pressed the button down all the way, it's possible that the subject has moved and Release Priority will yield more out-of-focus shots than Release Priority with AF-C. This setting is most viable if you're using a fast lens with a speedy internal focus motor (designated AF-S, which is *not* the same as the AF-S focus mode).

- **Focus.** This default prevents the D7000 from taking a picture until focus is achieved and the in-focus indicator in the viewfinder glows a steady green. If you're using Single-servo autofocus mode, this is probably the best setting. Moving subjects really call for AF-C mode in most cases.

a3 Focus Tracking with Lock-on

Sometimes new subjects interject themselves in the frame temporarily. Perhaps you're shooting an architectural photo from across the street and a car passes in front of the camera. Or, at a football game, a referee dashes past just as a receiver is about to make a catch. This setting lets you specify how quickly the D7000 reacts to these transient interruptions that would cause relatively large changes in focus before refocusing on the "new" subject matter. You can specify a long delay, so that the interloper is ignored, a shorter delay, or turn lock-on off completely so that the D7000 immediately refocuses when a new subject moves into the frame. Your options are:

- **AF 5 (Long).** The longest delay causes the D7000 to ignore the intervening subject matter for a significant period of time. Use this setting when shooting subjects, such as sports, in which focus interruptions are likely to be frequent and significant.

- **AF 4.** The second-longest delay causes the D7000 to ignore the intervening subject matter for a slightly less lengthy period of time. Use this setting when shooting subjects, such as sports, in which focus interruptions are likely to be fairly frequent.

- **AF 3 (Normal).** This default setting provides an intermediate delay before the camera refocuses on the new subject. It's usually the best choice when shooting sports in either of the continuous shooting modes, as the long delay can throw off autofocus accuracy at higher fps settings.

- **AF 2.** Provides slightly less delay.

- **AF 1 (Short).** Choose this setting to tell the D7000 to wait only a moment before refocusing. Very high continuous shooting frame rates may work better when you allow refocusing to take place rapidly, without a lock-on delay.

- **Off.** Turn off focus lock-on if you want the D7000 to refocus immediately. This may be the best choice for general subjects, because it allows the camera to smoothly follow focus on a moving subject with no delay.

a4 AF Point Illumination

It's usually helpful to have the active focus point highlighted in red in the viewfinder, although the flashing indicator does use a minuscule amount of power. This setting lets you specify when/if this highlighting happens. Your choices include:

- **Auto.** With this default setting, the D7000 will illuminate the selected focus point if it determines that highlighting is needed to sufficiently contrast the focus zone from the background.

- **On.** The selected focus point is always highlighted.

- **Off.** The selected focus point is never highlighted in red.

a5 Focus Point Wrap-Around

This setting is purely a personal preference parameter. When you press the multi selector left/right and up/down buttons to choose a focus point, the D7000 can be told to stop when the selection reaches the edge of the 39-point array—or, it can continue, wrapping around to the opposite edge, like Pac-Man leaving the playing area on one side or top/bottom to re-emerge on the other. (I hope I'm not revealing my age, here.)

- **Wrap.** Pressing the left/right or up/down buttons when you've reached the edge of the focus point display wraps the selection to the opposite side, still moving in the same direction.

- **No Wrap.** The focus point selection stops at the edge of the focus zone array.

a6 Number of Focus Points

You can choose the number of focus points available when you *manually* select a zone using the multi selector up/down and left/right buttons. (Note that this option is different from the 9, 21, or 39 points that may be selected *automatically* [dynamically] when using Dynamic-area AF, as described in Chapter 5.) Your choices, shown in Figure 9.3, are as follows:

- **39 points.** This is the default. All 39 focus points can be selected.

- **11 points.** A more widely spaced array of points is available. This can be the best choice for faster focus point selection when taking pictures of relatively large, evenly illuminated subject matter such that choosing precise focus zones is not particularly beneficial. I often use the 11-point option when photographing basketball games.

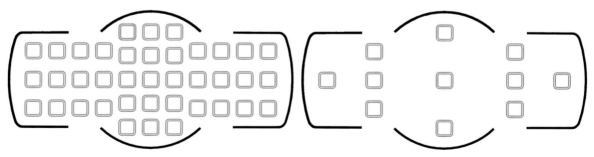

Figure 9.3 Select from all 39 focus points (left), or 11 more widely spaced points (right).

a7 Built-in AF-Assist Illuminator

Use this setting to control whether to use the AF-assist lamp built into the Nikon D7000, or rely on the more powerful AF-assist lamp built into Nikon electronic flash units (like the Nikon SB-900) and the Nikon SC-29 coiled remote flash cord (for firing the flash when not mounted on the camera).

- **On.** This default value will cause the AF-assist illuminator lamp to fire when lighting is poor, but only if Single-servo autofocus (AF-S) is active, or you have selected the center focus point manually and either Single-point or Dynamic-area autofocus (rather than Auto-area autofocus) has been chosen.

- **Off.** Use this to disable the AF-assist illuminator. You'd find that useful when the lamp might be distracting or discourteous (say, at a religious ceremony or acoustic music concert), or your subject is located closer than one foot, eight inches or farther than about 10 feet.

a8 Live View/Movie AF

Use this entry to set the focus mode when using Live View and when shooting movies. You'll find a complete description of when to choose each earlier in this book in Chapter 6. Your options are:

- **Autofocus mode.** Select Single-servo AF or Full-time servo AF. Again, choose Single-servo AF (AF-S) for relatively stationary subjects, or Full-time servo AF (AF-F) for moving subjects. However, where AF-C mode (when using the optical viewfinder) continues to refocus until you press the shutter release down all the way to take a picture, AF-F refocuses at all times during Live View, and stops focusing when you press the shutter release halfway.

- **AF area mode.** Choose Face-priority AF (for scenes with human faces); Wide-area AF (for scenes with objects throughout the frame); Normal-area AF (for average subjects, generally centered in the middle of the frame); or Subject-tracking AF (for moving subjects; the camera will lock focus and then refocus as your subject moves within the frame).

b. Metering/Exposure

The orange-coded Metering/Exposure Custom Settings (see Figure 9.4) let you define five different parameters that affect exposure metering in the Nikon D7000.

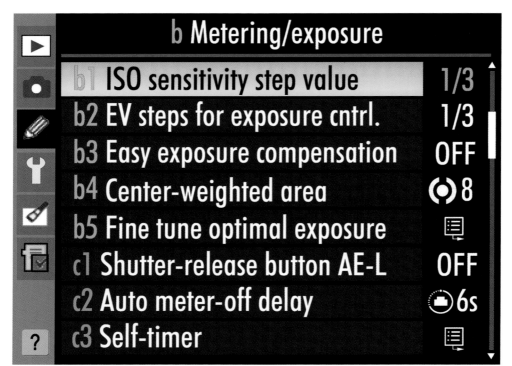

Figure 9.4
There are five metering/exposure options.

b1 ISO Sensitivity Step Value

This setting determines the size of the "jumps" it should use when making ISO adjustments—either one-third or one-half stop. At the one-third stop setting, typical ISO values would be 200, 250, 320, 400, 500, 640, 800, 1000, 1250, 1600, and so forth. Choose 1/2 stop settings, and your choices would be 200, 280, 400, 500, 560, 800, 1100, and 1600 over the same range. For really large increments, set the full-stop option, and choose 200, 400, 800, and 1600, and so forth. The larger increment can help you leap from one ISO setting to one that's much larger with one click in environments where you don't care to fine-tune sensitivity. As you've surmised, your choices include 1/3 step (the default); 1/2 step; and 1 step.

b2 EV Steps for Exposure Cntrl.

This setting tells the Nikon D7000 the size of the "jumps" it should use when making exposure adjustments—either one-third or one-half stop. The increment you specify here applies to f/stops, shutter speeds, EV changes, and autoexposure bracketing. As with ISO sensitivity step value, you can select from 1/3 step (the default); or 1/2 step.

Choose the 1/3 stop setting when you want the finest increments between shutter speeds and/or f/stops. For example, the D7000 will use shutter speeds such as 1/60th, 1/80th, 1/100th, 1/125th, and 1/160th second, and f/stops such as f/5.6, f/6.3, f/7.1, and f/8, giving you (and the autoexposure system) maximum flexibility.

With 1/2-stop increments, you will have larger and more noticeable changes between settings. The D7000 will apply shutter speeds such as 1/60th, 1/125th, 1/250th, and 1/500th second, and f/stops including f/5.6, f/6.7, f/8, f/9.5, and f/11. These coarser adjustments are useful when you want more dramatic changes between different exposures, or want to create a series of more widely spaced shots for high dynamic range (HDR) photography.

b3 Easy Exposure Compensation

This setting potentially simplifies dialing in EV (exposure value compensation) adjustments by specifying whether the exposure compensation button must be pressed while adding or extracting EV compensation. Because of the possibility of confusion or error, I tend to leave this setting turned off. Your choices are as follows:

- **Reset On (Auto reset).** This setting allows you to add or subtract exposure by rotating the sub-command dial when in Program (P) or Shutter-priority (S) exposure modes, or by rotating the main command dial when using Aperture-priority (A) mode. Rotating either dial has no effect in Manual (M) exposure mode. (If you've reversed the behavior of the command dials using CSM #f6, the "opposite" command dial must be used to make the changes.) Any adjustments you've made are canceled when the camera is shut off, or the meter-off time expires and the D7000's exposure meters go back to sleep. That's a useful mode, because most of us have made an EV adjustment and then forgotten about it, only to expose a whole series of improperly exposed photos. You can still have "sticky" EV settings when Easy Exposure Compensation is turned on: just hold down the exposure compensation button when you make your changes.

- **On.** This setting brings the Easy Exposure Compensation mode into conformance with the D7000's behavior when the exposure compensation button is pressed: in either case, any EV modifications you make will remain until you countermand them. As I have mentioned several times, forgetting to "turn off" EV changes after you've moved on to a different shooting environment is a primary cause of over- and underexposure among those of us who are forgetful or who ignore the D7000's flashing EV warnings.

- **Off.** With this default setting, you must always press the exposure compensation button while rotating the main command dial to add or subtract exposure. Use this choice when you don't want any EV changes unless you deliberately make them by pressing the button. This is your safest option in most cases.

b4 Center-Weighted Area

This setting changes the size of the center-weighted exposure spot (except when the D7000 is used with a non-CPU [generally older AI and AI-S and earlier lenses that haven't been updated with a "computer" chip]). Your choices include 6mm, 8mm, 10mm, 13mm, or full-frame average (which turns the metering mode from a center-weighted system to an old-fashioned averaging system). If you're using a non-CPU lens, the center-weighted area is fixed at 8mm, and the camera ignores whatever choice you may have entered here. Because the D7000 does not show the default 8mm area in the viewfinder, you don't have any visual indication of what area is being emphasized by the metering system. Personally, I don't think that's much of a problem, so go ahead and choose whatever center-weighted area works best for you.

b5 Fine-Tune Optimal Exposure

This setting is a powerful adjustment that allows you to dial in a specific amount of exposure compensation that will be applied, invisibly, to every photo you take using each of the three metering modes. No more can you complain, "My D7000 always underexposes by 1/3 stop!" If that is actually the case, and the phenomenon is consistent, you can use this custom menu adjustment to compensate.

Exposure compensation is usually a better idea (does your camera *really* underexpose that consistently?), but this setting does allow you to "recalibrate" your D7000 yourself. Your dialed in modifications will survive a two-button reset. However, you have no indication that fine-tuning has been made, so you'll need to remember what you've done. After all, you someday might discover that your camera is consistently *over*exposing images by 1/3 stop, not realizing that your CSM #b5 adjustment is the culprit.

In practice, it's rare that the Nikon D7000 will *consistently* provide the wrong exposure in any of the three metering modes, especially Matrix metering, which can alter exposure dramatically based on the D7000's internal database of typical scenes. This feature may be most useful for Spot metering, if you always take a reading off the same type of subject, such as a human face or 18-percent gray card. Should you find that the gray card readings, for example, always differ from what you would prefer, go ahead and fine-tune optimal exposure for Spot metering, and use that to read your gray cards. To use this feature:

1. Choose b5 Fine-tune Optimal Exposure from the Custom Settings menu.

2. In the screen that appears, choose Yes after carefully reading the warning that Nikon insists on showing you each and every time this option is activated.

3. Choose Matrix metering, Center-weighted, or Spot metering in the screen that follows by highlighting your choice and pressing the multi selector right button.

4. Press the up/down buttons to dial in the exposure compensation you want to apply. You can specify compensation in increments of 1/6 stop, half as large a change as conventional exposure compensation. This is truly *fine-tuning*.

5. Press OK when finished. You can repeat the action to fine-tune the other two exposure modes if you wish.

c. Timers/AE Lock

This category (see Figure 9.5) is a mixed bag of settings, covering both entries that adjust delay times (c2 through c4) and how the shutter release and AE-L buttons interact (c1). I think the latter setting, should have been placed in the purple f-coded Controls section. Go figure.

c1 Shutter Release Button AE-L

This is another of Nikon's easily confusing options for controlling how and when autofocus and exposure are activated and locked. The intent is to allow you to separate autofocus and autoexposure activation and locking.

Figure 9.5
The Timers/AE Lock settings.

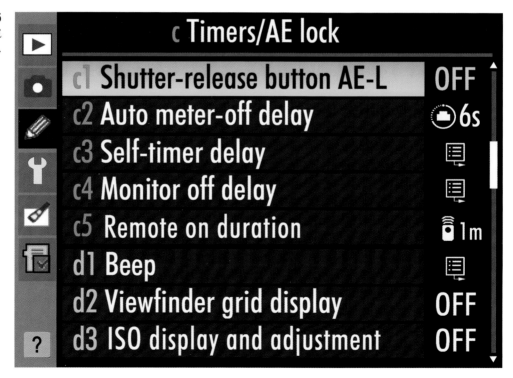

All you need to know is:

- **Off.** Exposure is locked *only* when the AE-L/AF-L button is pressed. This is the default.

- **On.** Exposure locks when either the shutter release button is depressed halfway or the AE-L/AF-L button is held down.

c2 Auto Meter-Off Delay

Use this setting to determine how long the D7000's exposure meter continues to operate after the last operation, such as autofocusing, focus point selection, and so forth, was performed. The default value is 6 seconds, but you can also select 4, 8, 16, and 30 seconds, as well as 1, 5, 10, and 30 minutes, or No limit, which keeps the meter active until the camera is switched off.

To save power, you should select an intermediate value, such as 8, 16, or 30 seconds if the default 6 seconds is not long enough. When the Nikon EH5a/EP5b AC adapter is connected to the D7000, the exposure meter will remain on indefinitely, just as if you'd specified No limit. Absent an external power source, any setting longer than 8 seconds will definitely eat up power.

Even so, sports shooters and some others prefer a longer delay, because they are able to keep their camera always "at the ready" with no delay to interfere with taking an action shot that unexpectedly presents itself. Extra battery consumption is just part of the price paid. For example, when I am shooting football, a meter-off delay of 16 seconds is plenty, because the players lining up for the snap is my signal to get ready to shoot. But for basketball or soccer, I typically set the meter-off delay for No Limit, because action is virtually continuous. I typically use the MB-D11 battery pack/grip at these events, so my D7000 has plenty of power, and I carry two sets of spare batteries. I rarely shoot much more than 1000-1200 shots at any sports event, so that's sufficient juice even with meter-off delay set for No Limit.

Of course, if the meters have shut off, and the power switch remains in the On position, you can bring the camera back to life by tapping the shutter button.

c3 Self-Timer

This setting lets you choose the length of the self-timer shutter release delay, the number of shots taken, and the interval between those shots. Your options include:

- **Self-timer delay.** The default value is 10 seconds. You can also choose 2, 5, 10, or 20 seconds. If I have the camera mounted on a tripod or other support and am too lazy to dig around for my wired or IR remote, I can set a two-second delay that is sufficient to let the camera stop vibrating after I've pressed the shutter release. I use a longer delay time if I am racing to get into the picture myself and am not sure I can make it in 10 seconds.

■ **Number of shots.** After the timer finishes counting down, the D7000 can take from 1 to 9 different shots. This is a godsend when shooting photos of groups, especially if you want to appear in the photo itself. You'll always want to shoot several pictures to ensure that everyone's eyes are open and there are smiling expressions on each face. Instead of racing back and forth between the camera to trigger the self-timer multiple times, you can select the number of shots taken after a single countdown. For small groups, I always take at least as many shots as there are people in the group—plus one. That gives everybody a chance to close their eyes. Of course, the ML-L3 IR remote is often your best choice, but this facility works well if you don't have one handy.

■ **Interval between shots.** If you've selected 2 to 9 as your number of shots to be snapped off, you can use this option to space out the different exposures. Your choices are 0.5 seconds, 1, 2, or 3 seconds. Use a short interval when you want to capture everyone saying "Cheese!" The 3-second option is helpful if you're using flash, as 3 seconds is generally long enough to allow the flash to recycle and have enough juice for the next photo.

Tip

If you want a longer delay and are *really* lazy, just turn the D7000's release mode dial to the Mup position. No menu changes required! When you press the shutter release all the way down, the mirror will raise (reducing vibration so you can take a picture immediately), but if you do nothing else, the picture will be taken anyway 30 seconds later. (To take a picture immediately after the mirror is raised, press the shutter release a second time.) Return the release mode dial to the Single frame or continuous shooting modes to cancel this temporary self-timer option.

c4 Monitor Off Delay

You can adjust the amount of time the monitor remains on when no other operations are being performed. You can select separate times for Playback, Menus, Information Display, Image Review, and Live View. All allow you to choose times from four seconds to 10 minutes, except for Live View, which offers only 5, 10, 15, 20, and 30 minute options.

Choosing a brief duration can help preserve battery power. However, the D7000 will always override the review display when the shutter button is partially or fully depressed, so you'll never miss a shot because a display image was on the monitor screen.

SAVING POWER WITH THE Nikon D7000

There are six settings and several techniques you can use to help you stretch the longevity of your D7000's battery. To get the most from each charge, consider these steps:

- **Playback menu.** Image Review: Turn off image review after each shot. You can still review your images by pressing the Playback button.

- **Auto meter-off delay.** Set to 4 seconds if you can tolerate such a brief active time.

- **Monitor off delay.** Set for the minimum, 10 seconds. That big three-inch LCD uses a lot of juice, so reducing the amount of time it is used when you don't turn it off manually (either for automatic review or for playing back your images) can boost the effectiveness of your battery.

- **Reduce LCD illumination.** Set CSM #d10 to Off, so the monochrome LCD status panel will be backlit only when you manually use the switch around the shutter release.

- **Reduce LCD brightness.** In the Setup menu, select the lowest of the seven brightness settings that work for you under most conditions. If you're willing to shade the LCD with your hand, you can often get away with lower brightness settings outdoors, which will further increase the useful life of your battery.

- **Turn off modeling flash.** Set CSM #e4 to Off.

- **Reduce internal flash use.** No flash at all or fill flash use less power than a full blast.

- **Cancel VR.** Turn off vibration reduction if your lens has that feature and you feel you don't need it.

- **Use a card reader.** When transferring pictures from your D7000 to your computer, use a card reader instead of the USB cable. Linking your camera to your computer and transferring images using the cable takes longer and uses a lot more power.

c5 Remote on Duration

You can adjust the amount of time the D7000 "looks" for an IR signal from its front and rear infrared sensors. You can select 1, 5, 10, or 15 minutes. Use a shorter active interval to save power.

d. Shooting/Display

This menu section (see Figure 9.6) offers a variety of mostly unrelated shooting and display options not found elsewhere, but which are not frequently changed, making them suitable for a Custom Settings entry. The figure shows only the first eight entries; you must scroll down to see the last five.

Figure 9.6
A mixed bag of entries is found in the Shooting/ Display submenu.

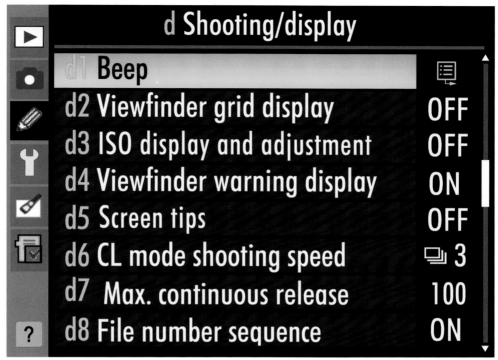

d1 Beep

The Nikon D7000's internal beeper provides a (usually) superfluous chirp to signify various functions, such as the countdown of your camera's self-timer or autofocus confirmation in AF-S mode (unless you've selected Release Priority in CSM #a2). You can (and probably should) switch it off if you want to avoid the beep because it's annoying, impolite, distracting (at a concert or museum), or undesired for any other reason. It's one of the few ways to make the D7000 a bit quieter. (I've actually had new dSLR owners ask me how to turn off the "shutter sound" the camera makes; such an option was available in the point-and-shoot camera they'd used previously.) Select d1: Beep from the menu, and select one of the following:

- **Volume.** Select Off to disable the beeper, or values of 1 (soft) through 3 (loud). A quarter-note icon appears in the monochrome LCD status panel and the shooting information display.

- **Pitch.** Select High for a high-pitched beep, or Low for a deeper tone.

d2 Viewfinder Grid Display

The D7000 can display a grid of lines overlaid on the viewfinder (see Figure 9.7), offering some help when you want to align vertical or horizontal lines. Note that the

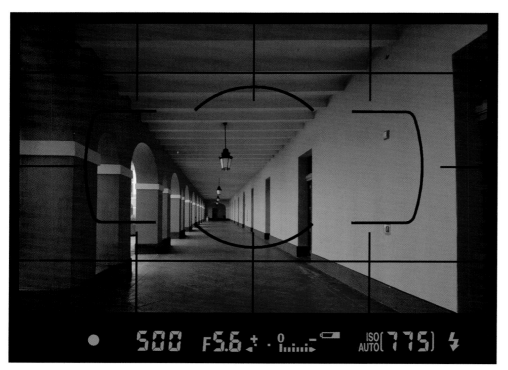

Figure 9.7
The D7000's
optional grid
display can
help with com-
posing and
aligning images
in the
viewfinder.

intersections of these lines do *not* follow the Rule of Thirds convention, and so are less useful for composition, assuming you want to follow the Rule of Thirds guideline in the first place. If you happen to subscribe to the Rule of Quarters, you're all set. Note that for critical applications, it's possible that your D7000's viewfinder isn't absolutely accurate. I sometimes have to rotate images slightly in Photoshop because the grid is not perfectly aligned. Your options for this grid display are On and Off (the default).

d3 ISO Display and Adjustment

This entry controls whether ISO or frame count are displayed in the viewfinder and top-panel monochrome LCD. You have three options.

- **Show ISO sensitivity.** Choose this option, and the viewfinder and top-panel LCD will display the current ISO sensitivity in the position where the frame count is normally shown. Use it if knowing the ISO setting is more important than having ready access to the number of frames remaining. (For example, you're using a very large card with thousands of exposures available.)

- **Show ISO/Easy ISO.** This option also replaces the frame count with the ISO display, but when active you can change the ISO quickly by rotating the sub-command dial (when using P or S exposure modes) or by rotating the main command dial (when using A mode). This feature can come in handy when you're adjusting the ISO frequently under changing light conditions, or are using ISO adjustments to allow changing exposure while keeping the aperture and shutter speeds the same. For example, say you're using Aperture-priority at ISO 200 to shoot a sports event and, under the current lighting, the D7000 is choosing 1/250th second as a shutter speed. With Easy ISO active, you can bump the ISO up to ISO 400. The camera will automatically increase the shutter speed to 1/500th second.

■ **Show Frame Count.** In this default mode, the number of exposures remaining is shown in the viewfinder and monochrome LCD.

d4 Viewfinder Warning Display

The D7000 has a low-battery, black-and-white mode warning, and a "no card loaded" advisory that can be superimposed on the screen. If you find this distracting, you can change from On (the default) to Off, and disable the warning.

d5 Screen Tips

The shooting information display can include "tool tips" that explain the function of any highlighted adjustable item in the bottom two rows. You can turn this feature from the default On to Off once you've learned which task each entry performs.

d6 CL Mode Shooting Speed

While the frames per second shooting rate at the Continuous high speed shooting mode (C$_H$) is fixed at 6 fps, you can adjust the speed for the Continuous low speed mode (C$_L$). You can select 1 to 5 fps rates. Choose a firing speed suitable for the kind of shooting environment you're in:

■ **Normal continuous shooting.** I set my D7000 to the 1 fps rate most of the time, so that I can take multiple shots quickly without needing to press the shutter release repeatedly. A one-second rate isn't so fast that I end up taking a bunch of shots that I don't want, but it is fast enough that I can shoot a series.

■ **Bracketing.** When I'm using bracketing, I generally have the D7000 set to shoot a bracketed set of three pictures: normal, over-, and underexposure. With the camera set to 3 fps, I can press the shutter once and take all three bracketed shots, with basically the same framing, within about one second.

■ **Slower action sequences.** The 6 fps rate available for sports photography often produces an embarrassing plethora of pictures that are a pain to wade through after the event is over. For some types of action, such as long distance running, golf, swimming, or routine baseball plays, a rate of 3 to 5 fps might be sufficient. You can make this more reasonable speed available by defining it here.

d7 Max. Continuous Release

Use this setting to limit the number of consecutive shots that can be taken in one burst when using continuous shooting modes. Your choices are any value between 1 and 100. Choosing a particular setting does not mean that the D7000 will actually *take* that many shots if you hold down the shutter button long enough. As your buffer fills, continuous shooting will slow down and eventually pause while the D7000 dumps pictures to the memory card.

However, there are many image quality and size settings that will allow the D7000 to shoot more or less forever when equipped with a very fast memory card. For example, at the JPEG Normal setting, you can theoretically shoot dozens of full-resolution images consecutively, and even using JPEG Fine you may be able to fire off more than 40 pictures in one burst. If you'd rather not accumulate that many images of one action and don't trust yourself to let up on the shutter release (it would take about 17 seconds to shoot 100 pictures at 6 fps), you can limit the maximum burst here.

d8 File Number Sequence

The Nikon D7000 will automatically apply a file number to each picture you take, using consecutive numbering for all your photos over a long period of time, spanning many different memory cards, starting over from scratch when you insert a new card, or when you manually reset the numbers. Numbers are applied from 0001 to 9999, at which time the D7000 "rolls over" to 0001 again.

The camera keeps track of the last number used in its internal memory and, if File Number Sequence is turned On, will apply a number that's one higher, or a number that's one higher than the largest number in the current folder on the memory card inserted in the camera. You can also start over each time a new folder has been created on the memory card, or reset the current counter back to 0001 at any time. Here's how it works:

- **On.** At this default setting, the D7000 will use the number stored in its internal memory any time a new folder is created, a new memory card inserted, or an existing memory card formatted. If the card is not blank and contains images, then the next number will be one greater than the highest number on the card *or* in internal memory (whichever is higher). Here are some examples.

    - You've taken 1,235 shots with the camera, and you insert a blank/reformatted memory card. The next number assigned will be 1,236, based on the value stored in internal memory.

    - You've taken 1,235 shots with the camera, and you insert an old memory card you previously used with the D7000, but which has a picture numbered 0728. The next picture will be numbered 1,236.

- You've taken more than 9,999 shots with the camera and the counter has rolled over to 0001 again, and your new total is 1,235 shots. You insert an old memory card with a picture from before the rollover that's numbered 8,281. The next picture will be numbered 8,282, and that value will be stored in the camera's menu as the "high" shot number (and will be applied when you next insert a blank card). This misnumbering makes it a good idea to always reformat your memory cards before taking a photo, if at all possible.

- **Off.** If you're using a blank/reformatted memory card, or a new folder is created, the next photo taken will be numbered 0001. File number sequences will be reset every time you use or format a card, or a new folder is created (which happens when an existing folder on the card contains 999 shots).

- **Reset.** The D7000 assigns a file number that's one larger than the largest file number in the current folder, unless the folder is empty, in which case numbering is reset to 0001. At this setting, new or reformatted memory cards will always have 0001 as the first file number.

HOW MANY SHOTS, REALLY?

The file numbers produced by the D7000 don't provide information about the actual number of times the camera's shutter has been tripped—called actuations. For that data, you'll need a third-party software solution, such as the free Opanda iExif (www.opanda.com) for Windows (see Figure 9.8) or the non-free ($34.95) GraphicConverter for Macintosh (www.lemkesoft.com). These utilities can be used to extract the true number of actuations from the Exif information embedded in a JPEG file.

Figure 9.8
Opanda iExif shows the exact number of pictures that have been taken with your camera.

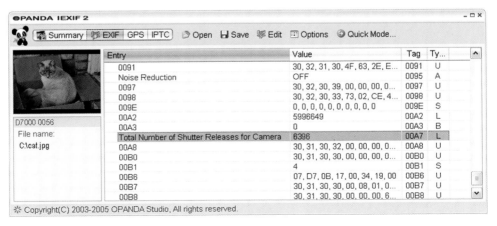

d9 Information Display

The shooting information display that appears when you press the Info button can be set to change automatically from dark lettering on a light background to light lettering on a dark background (see Figure 9.9), or you can select one or the other to be used all the time. The color LCD monitor will automatically change its brightness to provide the best contrast for the selected text display. Your choices are:

■ **Auto.** If the scene as viewed through the lens indicates a bright environment, the shooting info display will appear as black letters on a white background, producing an improved view in full daylight. If the scene appears dark, the display will have lighter letters on a dark background. Note that it's easy to "fool" the camera. Until you take the lens cap off, you'll see the dark background display regardless of your shooting environment. If you're standing in a darkened location, but point the camera at a bright scene, the D7000 will show you the "daylight" display.

■ **Manual.** Select this option and you can choose B (Dark on light) or W (Light on dark).

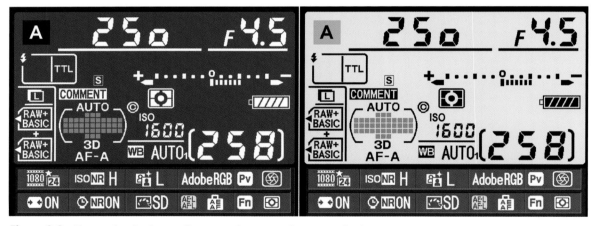

Figure 9.9 Choose the display configuration for your information display.

d10 LCD Illumination

When set to Off (the default), the monochrome LCD status panel (and the status LCDs on any attached compatible Nikon Speedlight, such as the Nikon SB-900) will illuminate for as long as the exposure meters are active, but only when the switch around the shutter release is pressed towards the maximum clockwise direction, just past the On indicator. Choose On, and the panel will be illuminated any time the exposure meters are active (and thus using more power), without the need to press the switch.

d11 Exposure Delay Mode

This is a marginally useful feature you can use to force the Nikon D7000 to snap a picture about one second after you've pressed the shutter release button all the way. It's useful when you are using shutter speeds of about 1/8th to 1/60th second hand-held and want to minimize the effects of the vibration that results when you depress the shutter button. It can also be used when the camera is mounted on a tripod, although the self-timer function, set to a two-second delay, is more useful in that scenario. When switched On, the camera will pause while you steady your steely grip on the camera, taking the picture about one second later. When turned Off, the picture is taken when the shutter release is pressed, as normal. One interesting side-effect of this mode is that it separates the normally invisible pre-flash produced by the D7000's internal flash (or any external flash that's connected) with the delay, so, if you're shooting living subjects (human or animal) they may be startled by the initial flash and close their eyes just before the main flash fires 1000 milliseconds later.

d12 Flash Warning

You can choose On to display a flash-ready indicator in the viewfinder if flash is required to produce an acceptable exposure. Select Off to disable this warning.

d13 MB-D11 Battery Type

This option is needed to communicate to the D7000 what type of AA batteries are being used in the MB-D11 battery pack/grip, because the different varieties of AA batteries provide slightly different voltages, and change voltages at different rates as they are used up. The setting you select here has no effect when you're using an EN-EL15. Your choices include:

- **LR6 (AA alkaline).** For ordinary alkaline batteries
- **HR6 (AA NiMH).** For Nickel-Metal Hydride rechargeable batteries
- **FR6 (AA lithium).** For non-rechargeable lithium batteries

Because of their limited capacity, you'll want to use conventional AA alkaline batteries only as a last resort, and then only when the weather is warmer than 68 degrees Fahrenheit, because the chemical reactions that provide power decline at lower temperatures. Alkalines retain their power longer when not used, so they may be a reasonable choice if you rarely use your MB-D11 and want to keep it ready to go. But I expect few readers will have this useful accessory sitting on a shelf gathering dust.

d14 Battery Order

When using the MB-D11 battery pack/grip, the batteries in the pack and in your D7000 are used consecutively. That is, one of them powers the camera until it is exhausted, and then the D7000 switches to the other. You can choose the order in which this switch-off takes place.

The default setting is MB-D11: Use MB-D11 Batteries First. You can also specify D7000: Use Camera Battery First. If you were using AA alkaline batteries in the MB-D11 as an emergency reserve, you'd probably want to use the D7000's internal battery first, so the alkalines wouldn't be prematurely exhausted and could live to shoot as backup another day. If you're using an EN-EL15 in the MB-D11, and shooting a lot, you might want to use the MB-D11 battery first, and use the camera's battery as a backup, because the MB-D11 battery can be changed more quickly, and without removing the grip from the D7000.

e. Bracketing/Flash

There are lots of useful settings in this submenu (see Figure 9.10) that deal with bracketing and electronic flash (hence the cleverly concocted name). I'll provide a thorough description of using bracketing in Chapter 4, and a complete rundown of flash options in Chapter 12. Here, I'll offer an introduction to the settings at your disposal.

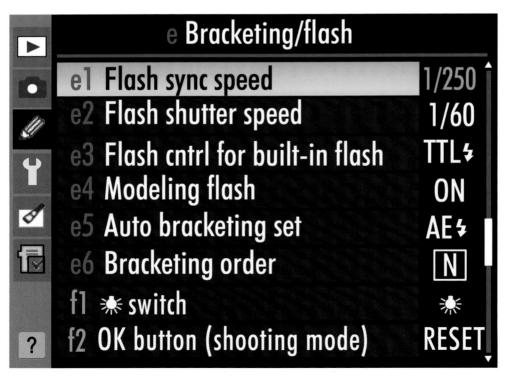

Figure 9.10
Bracketing and flash options are available in this menu.

e1 Flash Sync Speed

As you may already know (or will learn in Chapter 12), the focal plane shutter in the Nikon D7000 must be fully open when the flash fires; otherwise, you'll image one edge or the other of the vertically traveling shutter curtain in your photo. Ordinarily, the fastest shutter speed during which the shutter is completely open for an instant is 1/250th second. However, there are exceptions when you can use faster shutter speeds with certain flash units (such as the Nikon SB-900, SB-700, SB-800, SB-600, and SB-R200) for automatic FP (focal plane) synchronization. There are also situations in which you might want to set flash sync speed to *less* than 1/250th second, say, because you *want* ambient light to produce secondary ghost images in your frame. (I'll address all these sync issues in Chapter 12.) You can choose the following settings:

- **1/320 s (Auto FP).** This setting can allow use of flash with any shutter speed from 1/320th second to 1/8,000th second, with certain external flash units, *but not with the D7000's built-in flash.* If you're using the Nikon SB-900, or SB-700, the earlier SB-800, the SB-600, or SB-R200 external flash unit, shutter speeds from 1/320th to 1/8,000th second can be used; synchronization is produced by firing the unit continuously over a longer time period in short repeating bursts, so the effective power of the flash is reduced (meaning that the *distance range* of the flash is curtailed). You'll need to shoot subjects that are closer to the camera. When using Program or Aperture-priority mode (which both automatically select a shutter speed), high-speed sync will kick in whenever the actual shutter speed is faster than 1/320th second. Other flash units, including the D7000's *built-in* flash allow the D7000 to sync with flash at speeds of up to 1/320th second.

- **1/250 s (Auto FP).** This setting allows using the named external flash units with high-speed synchronization at 1/250th second or faster, and activates auto FP sync when the camera selects a shutter speed of 1/250th second or faster in Program and Aperture-priority modes. Other flash units, including the D7000's built-in flash, will be used at speeds no faster than 1/250th second.

- **1/250 s-1/60 s.** You can specify a shutter speed from 1/250th second to 1/60th second to be used as the synchronization speed for internal and external flash units.

e2 Flash Shutter Speed

This setting determines the *slowest* shutter speed that is available for electronic flash synchronization when you're not using a "slow sync" mode (described in Chapter 12). As you may know, when you're using flash, the flash itself provides virtually all of the illumination that makes the main exposure, and the shutter speed determines how much, if any, of the ambient light contributes to that second, non-flash exposure. Indeed, if the camera or subject is moving, you can end up with two distinct exposures in the same frame: the sharply defined flash exposure, and a second, blurry "ghost" picture created by the ambient light.

If you *don't* want that second exposure, you should use the highest shutter speed that will synchronize with your flash. This setting prevents Program or Aperture-priority modes (which both select the shutter speed for you) from inadvertently selecting a "too slow" shutter speed. You can select a value from 30 s to 1/60 s, and the D7000 will avoid using speeds slower than the one you specify with electronic flash (unless you've selected slow sync, slow rear-curtain sync, or red-eye reduction with slow sync, as described in Chapter 12). The "slow sync" modes do permit the ambient light to contribute to the exposure (say, to allow the background to register in night shots, or to use the ghost image as a special effect). For brighter backgrounds, you'll need to put the camera on a tripod or other support to avoid the blurry ghosts that can occur from camera shake, even if the subject is stationary.

If you are able to hold the D7000 steady, a value of 1/30 s is a good compromise; if you have shaky hands, use 1/60 s or higher. Those with extraordinarily solid grips can try the 1/15 s setting. Remember that this setting only determines the slowest shutter speed that will be used, not the default shutter speed.

e3 Flash Cntrl for Built-in Flash

The Nikon D7000's built-in flash has four modes, which I'll describe in a lot more detail in Chapter 12. Your four options are as follows:

- **TTL.** When the built-in flash is triggered, the D7000 first fires a pre-flash and measures the light reflected back and through the lens to calculate the proper exposure when the full flash is emitted a fraction of a second later.

- **Manual.** You can set the level of the built-in flash from full power to 1/128 power.

- **Repeating flash.** The flash fires multiple bursts, producing a stroboscopic lighting effect. As I'll describe in Chapter 12, when you choose repeating flash you'll be asked to select Output (flash power level), Times (the number of times the flash is fired at the output level you specify), and Frequency (how often the flash fires per second). Note that these factors are interdependent. For example, if you tell the flash to fire at 1/8 output power, you can select from 2 to 5 flashes, at a rate of 1 to 50 flashes per second. That's because the flash has only enough power for a maximum of 5 flashes at the 1/8 output setting. At 1/128 power, there's enough juice for 2 to 35 individual flashes, at a rate of no more than 50 flashes per second.

- **Commander mode.** If you never use external flash, you can safely ignore this setting. If you do, you'll want to set up the D7000 for your most frequently used options, to avoid having to fiddle with the camera if you decide to pull your SB-900 out of your bag for some impromptu multi-flash shooting. In Commander mode, the built-in flash emits pre-flashes that can be used to wirelessly control one or more remote external flash units.

Tip

If the Nikon SB-400 flash unit is attached and turned on, this menu choice is not available, because the SB-400 unit, unlike the D7000's built-in flash and other external flash units, cannot function in Commander mode. You'll be able to set flash compensation and flash mode for the built-in flash as well as individual "groups" of flashes (Groups A and B) and the triggering channels. As you'll see, using electronic flash with the Nikon D7000 is worth a book of its own, but I'll do my best to explain the vagaries in Chapter 12.

e4 Modeling Flash

The Nikon D7000, and certain compatible external flash units (the SB-900, SB-800, SB-700, SB-600, and SB-R200) have the capability of simulating a modeling lamp, which gives you the limited capability of previewing how your flash illumination is going to look in the finished photo. The modeling flash is not a perfect substitute for a real incandescent or fluorescent modeling lamp, but it does help you see how your subject is illuminated, and spot any potential problems with shadows.

When this feature is activated, pressing the depth-of-field button on the D7000 briefly triggers the modeling flash for your preview. Selecting Off disables the feature. You'll generally want to leave it On, except when you anticipate using the depth-of-field preview button for depth-of-field purposes (imagine that) and do *not* want the modeling flash to fire when the flash unit is charged and ready. Some external flash units, such as the SB-900, have their own modeling flash buttons. Although the SB-600 does not have this button, it works fine with the D7000's modeling flash feature.

e5 Auto Bracketing Set

The Nikon D7000 can automatically take several pictures using slightly different settings within a range that you specify, and apply the changes to automatic exposure, electronic flash, or white balance. This setting allows you to specify whether bracketing is used for both automatic exposure *and* flash (AE & flash), automatic exposure only (AE), flash bracketing only (Flash only), or white balance color bracketing alone (WB bracketing). No autoexposure or flash bracketing will be performed when white balance bracketing is activated. Because you can specify white balance manually when importing a RAW file, WB bracketing is not available when Quality has been set to NEF (RAW) or NEF (RAW)+JPEG. The results you get with flash bracketing can vary quite a bit, depending on the amount of ambient illumination and flash mode you've chosen, but exposure bracketing is fairly consistent. I tend to leave this option set to AE most of the time. White balance bracketing is useful when you're not quite sure of the color balance of your illumination.

e6 Bracketing Order

Use this setting to define the sequence in which bracketing is carried out. Your choices are the default: MTR>Under>Over (metered exposure, followed by the version receiving less exposure, and finishing with the picture receiving the most exposure) and Under>MTR>Over, which orders the exposures from least exposed to most exposed (for both ambient and flash exposures). The same order is applied to white balance bracketing, too, but the values are Normal>More Yellow>More Blue and More Yellow>Normal>More Blue. (Nikon actually calls "yellow" by the term "amber," but I've found "yellow" easier to understand.) You'll find lots more about bracketing in Chapter 4.

f. Controls

You can modify the way various control buttons and dials perform by using the options in this submenu, shown in Figure 9.11.

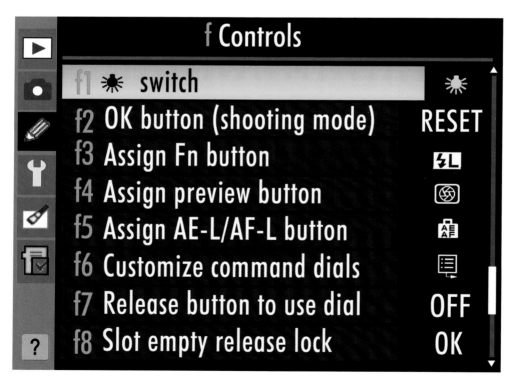

Figure 9.11
Modify the behavior of the D7000's controls with these menu options.

f1 Illuminator Switch

When you rotate the power switch, located concentrically with the shutter release, all the way to the clockwise position, the monochrome LCD control panel is backlit for approximately six seconds. Choose the LCD Backlight option, the default, and that's exactly what happens. The Switch and Information Display also turns on the shooting information display on the color LCD.

f2 OK Button (Shooting Mode)

You can define a function for the multi selector center button.

- **RESET Select center focus point.** This default setting lets you quickly select the center focus point in the viewfinder simply by pressing the multi selector center button.

- **Highlight active focus point.** This setting is useful when the active focus point is not illuminated in the viewfinder, and you want to determine what it is. Just press the multi selector center button, and presto, there it is.

- **Not used.** Nothing happens when the multi selector center button is pressed. If you find yourself sloppily pressing the center button in the heat of the moment while shooting, use this setting to deactivate it and avoid unwanted actions.

f3 Assign Fn. Button

You can also define the function of the Fn button. Your choices are:

- **Preview.** Depth-of-field preview. Perhaps you'd like to use the DOF preview button for something else, and substitute the Fn button for DOF preview.

- **FV Lock.** Press the Fn button to lock the value of the built-in or external flash, and press again to unlock it. This is the default value for the button.

- **AE/AF Lock.** Lock both focus and exposure while the Fn button is pressed. Use this setting or one of the next three when you want to have a specific mode of operation normally available from the AE-L/AF-L button, but would prefer to trigger the behavior with the Fn button pressed instead.

- **AE Lock only.** Lock only the exposure while the Fn button is pressed.

- **AE Lock (Hold).** Exposure is locked when the Fn button is pressed, and remains locked until the button is pressed again, or the exposure meter-off delay expires.

- **AF Lock only.** Focus is locked in while the Fn button is held down.

- **Flash off.** The built-in flash (if elevated) and any external flash attached and powered up will not fire while the Fn button is held down. Handy if you want to temporarily disable the flash, say, to take a picture or two by available light, and then return to normal flash operation.

- **Bracketing burst.** If the Fn button is pressed while exposure or flash bracketing have been activated in Single frame mode, all the shots will be taken, one after another, each time the shutter release is pressed. If Continuous high speed or Continuous low speed shooting modes (C_H or C_L) are active (or if white balance bracketing is active), the D7000 will repeat the bracketing bursts for as long as the shutter release button is pressed down.

- **Active D-Lighting.** Press the Fn button and rotate the main command dial to choose Active D-Lighting.

- **+NEF (RAW).** If your D7000 is currently set to shoot JPEG only, use this setting so that when you press the Fn button, the next shot will be recorded as a RAW+JPEG set. I use this option when shooting sports or other fast-moving events, then decide to shoot an image, say, along the sidelines, that could benefit from RAW manipulation later.

- **Matrix metering.** Switch from the current metering mode to Matrix metering while the Fn button is held down. You can use this to switch rapidly, say, from Spot metering to Matrix metering in a single session.

- **Center-weighted metering.** Switch from the current metering mode to Center-weighted metering while the Fn button is held down.

- **Spot metering.** Switch from the current metering mode to Spot metering while the Fn button is held down. This is my favorite setting, because I like to switch from Matrix to Spot metering from time to time.

- **Framing grid.** Hold down the Fn button and rotate the main command dial to turn the framing grid on or off.

- **Viewfinder virtual horizon.** Press the Fn button to view or hide the Virtual Horizon indicators in the viewfinder. The display shows the degree of tilt of the camera, with the bars to the left and right of center disappearing as the D7000 is leveled. (See Figure 9.12.)

- **Access top item in My Menu.** Another new option, this one summons the first entry in your My Menu roster. Effectively, you can select *any* menu item that you access frequently, place it at the top of My Menu (as described in Chapter 10), and jump to that item by pressing the Fn button.

Figure 9.12
Virtual horizon indicators in the viewfinder show the degree of tilt of the camera.

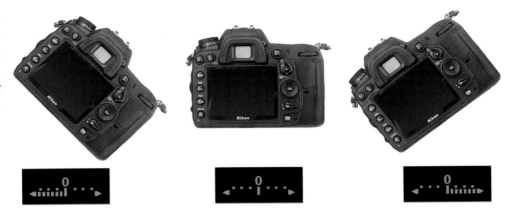

- **1 step spd/aperture.** If you sometimes prefer coarser exposure settings of 1 whole step (instead of the 1/3 or 1/2 step increments that are normally set), use this option. When holding down the Fn button and rotating a command dial, shutter speed and aperture changes are made in whole step increments instead.

- **Choose non-CPU lens number.** If you swap out older non-CPU manual lenses frequently, this option provides a quicker way of telling the D7000 which lens number (1 to 9) to use. I often mount an old manual focus 85mm f/1.8 lens or 55mm f/3.5 Micro Nikkor on my D7000, and can use this facility to switch back and forth between the lens settings I've manually entered for these lenses. (Chapter 10 will show you how to do that in the Setup menu.)

- **Playback.** This option redefines the Fn button to provide the same function as the Playback button. You'll find this useful when a long, heavy lens is mounted on your camera and it's difficult to press the Playback button with the left hand.

- **Start movie recording.** Use this choice to be able to start movie recording by pressing the Fn button.

f4 Assign Preview Button

The depth-of-field button can also be defined as you wish, with the same options and limitations as for the Fn button, but the default action for the DOF button is Preview.

f5 Assign AE-L/AF-L Button

As if the Nikon D7000 didn't have enough buttons that are user-definable, you can change the behavior of the AE-L/AF-L button, too! The default value for the AE-L/AF-L button is AE/AF Lock.

To recap your options:

- **AE/AF Lock.** Lock both focus and exposure while the AE-L/AF-L button is pressed.

- **AE Lock only.** Lock only the exposure while the AE-L/AF-L button is pressed.

- **AF Lock only.** Focus is locked in while the AE-L/AF-L button is held down.

- **AE Lock (Hold).** Exposure is locked when the AE-L/AF-L button is pressed, and remains locked until the button is pressed again, or the exposure meter-off delay expires.

- **AF-ON.** The AE-L/AF-L button is used to initiate autofocus.

- **FV Lock.** Press the AE-L/AF-L button to lock the value of the built-in or external flash, and press again to unlock it.

f6 Customize Command Dials

You can use the options in this menu entry to change the behavior of the command dials. Use the available tweaks to change the behavior of the dials to better suit your preferences, or if you're coming to the Nikon world from another vendor's product that uses a different operational scheme. Keep in mind that redefining basic controls in this way can prove confusing if someone other than yourself uses your camera, or if you find yourself working with other Nikon cameras that have retained the normal command dial behavior. The reason that the dials are set for their default directions is to match the direction of rotation of the aperture ring/sub-command dial (when changing the aperture). Turning any of the three to the left decreases exposure, while rotating to the right increases exposure. Your options include:

- **Reverse rotation.** Rotating the main command dial (on both the camera and MB-D11 battery pack) counterclockwise causes shutter speeds to become shorter in Manual and Shutter-priority modes; rotating the sub-command dial counter-clockwise selects larger f/stops. If you want to reverse the directional orientation of the dials (so you'll need to rotate the main command dial clockwise to specify shorter shutter speeds, etc.), set this option to Yes. Set to No to return to the original D7000 scheme of things.

- **Change main/sub.** Select On to exchange the functions of the main and sub-command dials. When activated, the main dial will set the aperture in Manual and Aperture-priority modes, and the sub-command dial will adjust the shutter speed in Manual and Shutter-priority modes. All other normal functions are swapped, as well. Select Off to return to the Nikon D7000's default arrangement.

- **Aperture setting.** Ordinarily, autofocus lenses having an aperture ring are locked at their smallest aperture when mounted on the Nikon D7000 (and other Nikon models) and f/stops are set using the sub-command dial (unless you've used the

Change main/sub option above). The default setting of Sub-Command Dial retains this behavior. If you'd rather unlock the aperture ring on the lens and use that instead, choose Aperture ring. Type G lenses, which lack an aperture ring, will still be adjusted using the sub-command dial, regardless of how this setting is made. Non-CPU lenses, which lack an electronic connection to the camera, are always set using the aperture ring.

- **Menus and playback.** You can change the orientation of the command dials when navigating menus and playback options, too. By default, the main command dial is used to select an image during full-frame playback; move the cursor left or right during thumbnail viewing, and move the menu highlighting up or down. The sub-command dial is used to display additional photo information in full-frame play-back, to move the cursor up and down, and to move back and forth between menus and submenus. (Note that you can also use the multi selector directional buttons for these functions.) When set to On, the functions assigned to the dials are reversed. Choose On (Image Review Excluded) to reverse the functions of the dials *except during image review.*

f7 Release Button to Use Dial

Normally, any button used in conjunction with a command dial must be held down while the command dial or sub-command dial is rotated. Choose Yes for this option if you want to be able to press the button and release it, and then rotate the command dial. You can continue to make adjustments until the button is pressed again, or you press the metering mode, exposure compensation, flash, ISO, Qual, or WB buttons, or the shutter release button is pressed halfway. Exposure meter time-out also turns off Setting mode, unless the D7000 is connected to an AC adapter. Chose No to return to the D7000's default behavior, which requires that the button be held down while the adjustment is made.

f8 Slot Empty Release Lock

This entry gives you the ability to snap off "pictures" without a memory card installed—or to lock the camera shutter release if that is the case. It is sometimes called Play mode, because you can experiment with your camera's features or even hand your D7000 to a friend to let him fool around, without any danger of pictures actually being taken.

Back in our film days, we'd sometimes finish a roll, rewind the film back into its cassette surreptitiously, and then hand the camera to a child to take a few pictures—without actually wasting any film. It's hard to waste digital film, but "shoot without card" mode is still appreciated by some, especially camera vendors who want to be able to demo a camera at a store or trade show, but don't want to have to equip each and every demonstrator model with a memory card. Choose Enable Release to activate "play" mode or Release Locked to disable it.

The pictures you actually "take" are displayed on the LCD with the legend "Demo" superimposed on the screen, and they are, of course, not saved. Note that if you are using the optional Camera Control Pro 2 software to record photos from a USB-tethered D7000 directly to a computer, no memory card is required to unlock the shutter even if Release Locked has been selected.

f9 Reverse Indicators

Refugees from the Canon world or other dSLR product lines are sometimes put off that Nikon cameras place the plus exposure values on the left side of the analog exposure display in the control panel, viewfinder, and shooting information display, with the negative values on the right, to match the rotation of the aperture ring (if used). This default setting (+0–) can be swapped for the opposite orientation (–0+) to change the display to the other orientation. My take is that if you've fled to Nikonland, you might as well get used to it. I suppose this setting is useful for a dedicated Canon shooter who sometimes uses a Nikon dSLR, and who never needs to change exposure using an aperture ring.

f10 Assign MB-D11 AE-L/AF-L Button

If you are using the MB-D11 grip, you can define the function of the AE-L/AF-L button, just as you can its counterpart on the camera body. Your choices are:

- **AE/AF Lock.** Lock both focus and exposure while the AE-L/AF-L button is pressed.

- **AE Lock only.** Lock only the exposure while the AE-L/AF-L button is pressed.

- **AF Lock only.** Focus is locked in while the AE-L/AF-L button is held down.

- **AE Lock (Hold).** Exposure is locked when the AE-L/AF-L button is pressed, and remains locked until the button is pressed again, or the exposure meter-off delay expires.

- **AF-ON.** The AE-L/AF-L button is used to initiate autofocus.

- **FV Lock.** Press the AE-L/AF-L button to lock the value of the built-in or external flash, and press again to unlock it.

- **Same as Fn. Button.** The button on the grip performs the same function you've assigned to the camera body's Fn button.

10

Setup: The Setup Menu, Retouch Menu, and My Menu

We're not done covering the Nikon D7000's Setup options yet. There are three more menus to deal with. These include the Setup menu (which deals with adjustments that are outside the actual shooting experience, such as formatting a memory card, adjusting the time, or checking your battery); the Retouch menu (which enables you to fine-tune the appearance of images by trimming, adding filter effects, or removing red-eye); and the My Menu system, which can help you set up a customized menu that contains only the entries you want.

Setup Menu Options

There is a long list of 24 entries in the orange-coded Setup menu (see Figure 10.1), in which you can make additional adjustments on how your camera *behaves* before or during your shooting session, as differentiated from the Shooting menu, which adjusts how the pictures are actually taken.

Your choices include:

- Format memory card
- Save user settings
- Reset user settings
- LCD brightness
- Clean image sensor
- Lock mirror up for cleaning
- Video mode
- HDMI
- Flicker reduction
- Time zone and date
- Language
- Image comment

- Auto image rotation
- Image Dust Off ref photo
- Battery info
- Wireless transmitter
- Image authentication
- Copyright information
- Save/load settings
- GPS
- Virtual horizon
- Non-CPU lens data
- AF fine tune
- Firmware version

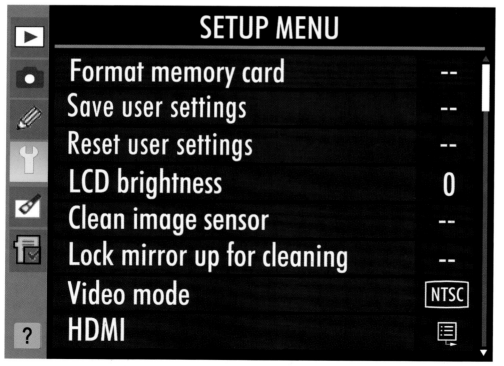

Figure 10.1
The Setup menu allows you to adjust how the D7000 behaves.

Format Memory Card

I recommend using this menu entry to reformat your memory card after each shoot. While you can move files from the memory card to your computer, leaving behind a blank card, or delete files using the Playback menu's Delete feature, both of those options can leave behind stray files (such as those that have been marked as Protected). Format removes those files completely and beyond retrieval (unless you use a special utility program as described in Chapter 14) and establishes a spanking new fresh file system on the card, including a spanking new DCIM (Digital Camera Images) folder, which will contain subfolders for each model camera that the card happens to be used in. (That's why you can remove a card from your D7000, use it in another model camera, and find that the images from each type of camera reside in folders of their own within the main DCIM folder.) Reformatting resets all the file allocation table (FAT) pointers (which tell the camera and your computer's operating system where all the images reside) efficiently pointing where they are supposed to on a blank card.

If you're an efficiency nut, you can reformat a memory card without a visit to the Setup menu by holding down the metering and Trash buttons (both marked with red Format labels) for about two seconds. If you'd rather format the other card, rotate the main command dial to select that slot. Then press the pair of buttons again, and the D7000 will format your card. To cancel the format, press any other button.

Or, select this menu entry, choose which memory card to format (Slot 1 or Slot 2), and select Yes from the screen that appears. Press OK to begin the format process. Wait until the For indicator has finished flashing on the monochrome LCD status panel.

Save User Settings

Use this entry to register your camera's current settings in either of two special memory banks, marked with U1 and U2 on the mode dial, where they can be retrieved and re-established simply by rotating the dial to the bank you want to use. For example, you might want to have one user setting for outdoor sports photography, with the D7000 set to Shutter-priority, a shutter speed of 1/1000th second, AF-C autofocus mode, and 3D-tracking AF-area mode. To save your settings, just follow these steps:

1. **Choose a semi-automatic/manual exposure mode.** Select from Program, Aperture-priority, Shutter-priority, or Manual modes.

2. **Adjust settings.** You need to set the camera to the parameters you want to store in the U1 and U2 banks. You can select a flexible Program (P) mode setting, specify a particular shutter speed (with the camera set to S or M modes), preferred aperture (if the camera is set to A or M modes), plus exposure and flash compensation adjustments. You can also select a flash mode, focus point, metering mode, AF and

AF-area modes to be applied when using the optical viewfinder, as well as bracketing parameters, and choices in the Shooting and Custom Settings menus. All these can be registered and retrieved. However, you can't register a particular storage folder or file naming scheme, nor Picture Controls, multiple exposure settings, or interval timer shooting. Those parameters are common to all your camera mode dial settings (U1, U2, or otherwise).

3. **Choose Save User Settings from the Setup menu.** Press the right directional button.

4. **Select U1 or U2 from the menu.** Press the right directional button to be taken to a confirmation screen.

5. **Save settings.** Highlight Save Settings (rather than Cancel) and press OK to register your current settings to U1 or U2. The stored settings can be retrieved by rotating the mode dial to U1 or U2.

Reset User Settings

Select this, and you can set either U1 or U2 (individually, or both if you repeat the process) to the default camera settings. The exposure mode registered to a reset user slot will be P, and the Shooting and Custom Settings menus will be the defaults (see Table 8.1 and Tables 9.1 to 9.6 in Chapters 8 and 9, respectively).

LCD Brightness

Choose this menu option and a grayscale strip appears on the LCD, as shown in Figure 10.2. Use the multi selector up/down keys to adjust the brightness to a comfortable viewing level. Under the lighting conditions that exist when you make this adjustment, you should be able to see all 10 swatches from black to white. If the two end swatches blend together, the brightness has been set too low. If the two whitest swatches on the right end of the strip blend together, the brightness is too high. Brighter settings use more battery power, but can allow you to view an image on the LCD outdoors in bright sunlight. When you have the brightness you want, press OK to lock it in and return to the menu.

Clean Image Sensor

This entry gives you some control over the Nikon D7000's automatic sensor cleaning feature, which removes dust through a vibration cycle that shakes the sensor until dust, presumably, falls off and is captured by a sticky surface at the bottom of the sensor area. If you happen to take a picture and notice an artifact in an area that contains little detail (such as the sky or a blank wall), you can access this menu choice, place the camera with its base downward, and choose Clean Now. A message Cleaning Sensor now appears, and the dust you noticed has probably been shaken off.

Figure 10.2
Adjust the LCD brightness so that all the grayscale strips are visible.

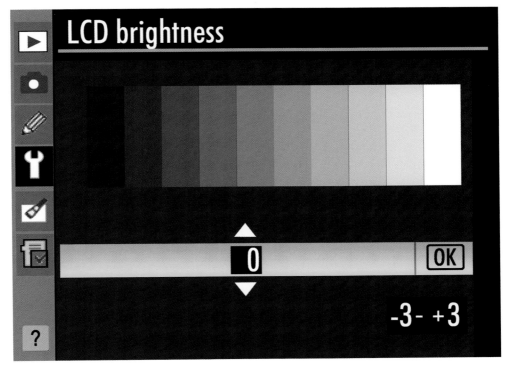

You can also tell the D7000 when you'd like it to perform automatic cleaning without specific instructions from you. Select from:

- **ON.** Clean at startup. This allows you to start off a particular shooting session with a clean sensor.

- **OFF.** Clean at shutdown. This removes any dust that may have accumulated since the camera has been turned on, say, from dust infiltration while changing lenses. Note that this choice does not turn off automatic cleaning; it simply moves the operation to the camera power-down sequence.

- **ON/OFF.** Clean at both startup and shutdown. Use this setting if you're paranoid about dust and don't mind the extra battery power consumed each time the camera is turned on or off. If you only turn off the D7000 when you're finished shooting, the power penalty is not large, but if you're the sort who turns off the camera every time you pause in shooting, the extra power consumed by the dust removal may exceed any savings you get from leaving the camera off.

- **Cleaning Off.** No automatic dust removal will be performed. Use this to preserve battery power, or if you prefer to use automatic dust removal only when you explicitly want to apply it.

Lock Mirror Up for Cleaning

You can also clean the sensor manually. Use this menu entry to raise the mirror and open the shutter so you'll have access to the sensor for cleaning with a blower, brush, or swab, as described in Chapter 14. You don't want power to fail while you're poking around inside the camera, so this option is available only when sufficient battery power (at least 60 percent) is available. Using a fully charged battery or connecting the D7000 to an EH-5/EH5a AC adapter is an even better idea.

Video Mode

This setting controls the output of the Nikon D7000 to a conventional video system through the video cable when you're displaying images on a monitor or connected to a VCR through the external device's yellow video input jack. You can select either NTSC, used in the United States, Canada, Mexico, many Central, South American, and Caribbean countries, much of Asia, and other countries; or PAL, which is used in the UK, much of Europe, Africa, India, China, and parts of the Middle East.

HDMI

The Nikon D7000 has a High-Definition Multimedia Interface (HDMI) video connection, so you can play back your camera's images on HDTV or HD monitors using a type A cable, which Nikon does not provide to you, but which is readily available from third parties. Before you link up you'll want to choose the HDMI resolution to be used, from 480p (640 × 480 progressive scan); 576p (720 × 576 progressive scan); 720p (1280 × 720 progressive scan); or 1080i (1920 × 1080 interlaced scan).

You can also choose to turn Device Control on or off. When On is chosen and the camera is connected to a television that supports the HDMI-CEC protocol, when both are turned on you'll see PLAY and SLIDE SHOW messages on the television. You can then use the television's compatible remote control instead of the multi selector and OK buttons to review images and play slide shows. Choose Off, and this capability is disabled.

Flicker Reduction

This option, the first on the second page of the Setup menu (see Figure 10.3), reduces flicker and banding, which can occur when shooting in Live View mode and Movie mode under fluorescent and mercury vapor illumination, because the cycling of these light sources interacts with the frame rate of the camera's video system. In the United States, you'd choose the 60Hz frequency; in locations where 50Hz current is the norm, select that option instead.

Figure 10.3
Flicker reduction is the first choice on the second page of the Setup menu.

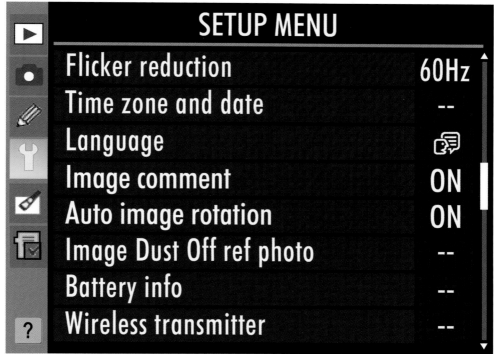

Time Zone and Date

Use this menu entry to adjust the D7000's internal clock. Your options include:

■ **Time zone.** A small map will pop up on the setting screen and you can choose your local time zone. I sometimes forget to change the time zone when I travel (especially when going to Europe), so my pictures are all time-stamped incorrectly. I like to use the time stamp to recall exactly when a photo was taken, so keeping this setting correct is important.

■ **Date and time.** Use this setting to enter the exact year, month, day, hour, minute, and second, using a 24-hour clock.

■ **Date format.** Choose from Y/M/D (year/month/day), M/D/Y (month/day/year), or D/M/Y (day/month/year) formats.

■ **Daylight saving time.** Use this to turn daylight saving time On or Off. Because the date on which DST goes into effect each year has been changed from time to time, if you turn this feature on you may need to monitor your camera to make sure DST has been implemented correctly.

Language

Choose from 22 languages for menu display, choosing from Czech, Danish, German, English, Spanish, French, Indonesian, Italian, Dutch, Norwegian, Polish, Portuguese, Russian, Finnish, Swedish, Turkish, Arabic, Traditional Chinese, Simplified Chinese, Japanese, Korean, or Thai.

Image Comment

The Image Comment is your opportunity to add a copyright notice, personal information about yourself (including contact info), or even a description of where the image was taken (e.g., Browns Super Bowl 2012), although text entry with the Nikon D7000 is a bit too clumsy for doing a lot of individual annotation of your photos. (But you still might want to change the comment each time, say, you change cities during your travels.) The embedded comments can be read by many software programs, including Nikon View NX or Capture NX2.

The standard text entry screen described in Chapter 8 can be used to enter your comment, with up to 36 characters available. For the copyright symbol, embed a lowercase "c" within opening and closing parentheses: (c). You can input the comment, turn attachment of the comment On or Off using the Attach Comment entry, and select Done when you're finished working with comments. If you find typing with a cursor too tedious, you can enter your comment in Nikon Capture NX2 and upload it to the camera through a USB cable.

Auto Image Rotation

Turning this setting On tells the Nikon D7000 to include camera orientation information in the image file. The orientation can be read by many software applications, including Adobe Photoshop, Nikon View NX, and Capture NX2, as well as the Rotate Tall setting in the Playback menu. Turn this feature Off, and none of the software applications or Playback's Rotate Tall will be able to determine the correct orientation for the image. Nikon notes that only the first image's orientation is used when shooting continuous bursts; subsequent photos will be assigned the same orientation, even if you rotate the camera during the sequence (which is something I have been known to do myself when shooting sports like basketball).

Image Dust Off Ref Photo

This menu choice lets you "take a picture" of any dust or other particles that may be adhering to your sensor. The D7000 will then append information about the location of this dust to your photos, so that the Image Dust Off option in Capture NX 2 can be used to mask the dust in the NEF image.

To use this feature, select Image Dust Off Ref Photo, choose either Start or Clean Sensor and then Start, and then press OK. If directed to do so, the camera will first perform a self-cleaning operation by applying ultrasonic vibration to the low-pass filter that resides on top of the sensor. Then, a screen will appear asking you to take a photo of a bright featureless white object 10 cm from the lens. Nikon recommends using a lens with a focal length of at least 50mm. Point the D7000 at a solid white card and press the shutter release. An image with the extension NDF will be created, and can be used by Nikon Capture NX 2 as a reference photo if the "dust off" picture is placed in the same folder as an image to be processed for dust removal.

Battery Info

This screen is purely informational; there are no settings to be made. When invoked, you can see the following information:

- **Bat. Meter.** The current battery level, shown as a percentage from 100 to 0 percent.

- **Pic. Meter.** This shows the number of actuations with the current battery since it was last recharged. This number can be larger than the number of photos taken, because other functions, such as white balance presetting, can cause the shutter to be tripped. This display is not shown when the MB-D11 battery pack is attached and loaded with AA batteries.

- **Battery age.** Eventually, a battery will no longer accept a charge as well as it did when it is new, and must be replaced. This indicator shows when a battery is considered new (0); has begun to degrade slightly (1,2,3); or has reached the end of its charging life and is ready for replacement (4). Batteries charged at temperatures lower than 41 degrees F may display an impaired charging life temporarily, but return to their true "health" when recharged above 68 degrees F. This display is not shown when the MB-D11 battery pack is attached and loaded with AA batteries.

Wireless Transmitter

This menu entry is used to modify settings for connecting to a wireless network using the optional WT-4 wireless transmitter. Consult the manual furnished with your transmitter for instructions on configuring the device and your computer's WiFi network. This menu entry is grayed out, and available only when the WT-4 is connected.

Copyright Information

This choice, which appears on the third page of the Setup menu when you scroll down (see Figure 10.4) is an expansion of the Image Comment capability, allowing you to specify the name of the "artist" (photographer), and enter copyright information. Use

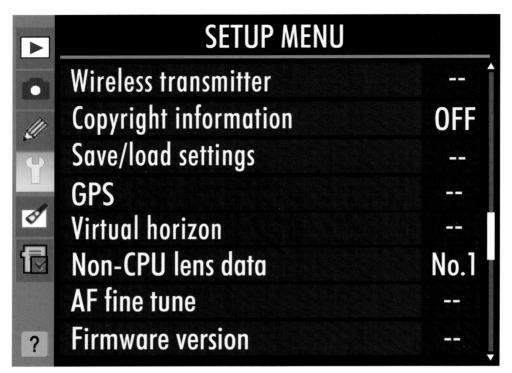

Figure 10.4
Copyright
Information is
on the third
screen of the
Setup menu.

the standard Nikon text entry screen described earlier. Highlight the Attach Copyright Information option and press the right multi selector button to mark/unmark it to control whether your copyright data is embedded in each photo as taken.

Save/Load Settings

You can store many camera settings to your memory card in a file named NCSETUP5, and then reload them later using this menu item. This is a good way to archive your favorite camera settings for the Playback menu, Shooting menu, Custom Settings menus, Setup menu, and all My Menu items. You can restore your settings if you've messed them up, or save multiple sets of settings to multiple memory cards. You can save only one group of settings at a time to a particular card; the default name NCSETUP5 cannot be changed. Well, it *can* be changed in your computer, but if you do, the D7000 will not be able to find it on the memory card. If you want to save multiple settings, simply use multiple memory cards. This might be a good use for all those 256MB SD cards you have left over from your point-and-shoot days.

Note that storing/restoration is an all-or-nothing proposition. When you select Save Settings, all your current settings are stored on the memory card; choose Load Settings, and the camera's current settings are replaced with the values stored on the memory card.

The following settings are saved:

- **Playback menu.** Display mode, Image Review, After Delete, Rotate tall.

- **Shooting menu.** File naming, Role played by card in Slot 2, Image quality, Image size, JPEG compression, NEF (RAW) recording, White balance, Set Picture Control, Auto distortion control, Color space, Active D-Lighting, Long exp. NR, High ISO NR, ISO sensitivity settings, Movie settings, Remote control mode.

- **Custom Settings menu.** All settings are stored.

- **Setup menu.** Clean image sensor, Video mode, HDMI, Flicker reduction, Time zone and date, Language, Image comment, Auto image rotation, Copyright information, GPS, Non-CPU lens data.

- **My Menu/Recent Settings.** All My Menu entries, All recent settings, active tab.

GPS

This menu entry has options for using the Nikon GP-1 Global Positioning System (GPS) device, shown mounted on my D7000 in Figure 10.5. It has three options, none of which turn GPS features on or off, despite the misleading "Enable" and "Disable" nomenclature (what you're enabling and disabling is the automatic exposure meter turn-off):

- **Auto meter-off.** You can choose Enable or Disable. Enabling reduces battery drain by allowing the D7000 to turn off exposure meters while using the GP-1 after the time specified in CSM #c2 (Auto meter-off delay, discussed in Chapter 9) has elapsed. When the meters turn off, the GP-1 becomes inactive and must reacquire at least three satellite signals before it can begin recording GPS data once more. When you choose Disable, the exposure meters to remain on while using the GP-1, so that GPS data can be recorded at any time, despite increased battery drain.

Figure 10.5
The Nikon GP-1 GPS device can be clipped to your camera strap or mounted on the accessory shoe on top of the camera.

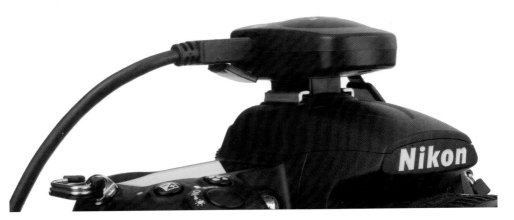

- **Position.** This is an information display, rather than a selectable option. It appears when the GP-1 is connected and receiving satellite positioning data. It shows the latitude, longitude, altitude, and Coordinated Universal Time (UTC) values.

- **Use GPS to set camera clock.** Select Yes or No. When enabled, your D7000's internal camera clock will be set using UTC values whenever the GP-1 is attached to the camera. If you use the device frequently, this will ensure that your camera's clock is always set accurately, and won't require a manual update periodically.

Virtual Horizon

Some people like this feature, which provides a virtual bubble level display on the LCD that acts like the horizon indicator in an airplane, ostensibly to help you keep your image level as you shoot. I'm less than enamored, finding it to be an interesting toy that really doesn't do the job sufficiently.

When activated, a circular indicator like the one shown in Figure 10.6 appears on the LCD. Of course, you can't frame a picture through the viewfinder very easily while monitoring this display, and it's difficult to keep the camera on a level plane, so you'll find that the Virtual Horizon works best when the D7000 is mounted on a tripod.

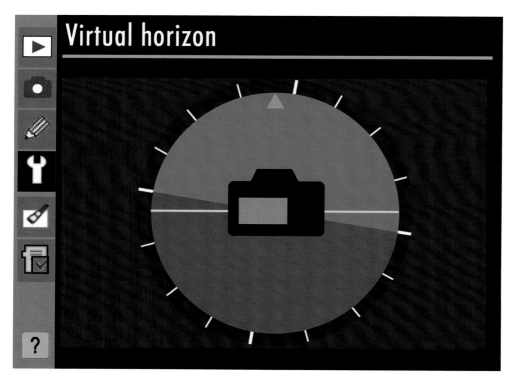

Figure 10.6
The Virtual Horizon serves as a kind of bubble level for your camera.

That's the problem. All my tripods and tripod heads already *have* bubble levels built in. So, when I'm using the D7000 on a tripod, I really don't need the Virtual Horizon. In addition, the feature only shows when you've rotated the camera along the axis of the lens. If you tilt it forward or back (pointing the lens a bit towards the sky or ground), that angling won't be detected. The bubble levels on my tripods and tripod heads can do that, with no problems. I know folks who like and use the virtual horizon, but I find it just a cute way to use the sensor built into your camera, which sends vertical/horizontal orientation information to the various rotation features.

Non-CPU Lens Data

You can specify lens focal length data and maximum aperture for up to nine older manual focus, non-CPU chipped lenses. When both values are entered, the D7000 can use older lenses (including AI manual focus lenses) that are not equipped with a CPU chip for color matrix metering to calculate exposure in Aperture-priority and Manual exposure modes. The data also enables automatic power zoom when using the Nikon SB-900, SB-700, and discontinued SB-800/SB-600 Speedlights, as well as improved flash exposures and balanced iTTL fill-flash. In addition, the current aperture can be listed in the monochrome LCD status panel and camera viewfinder, as well as embedded in the photo playback display.

This is a great feature for those of us who have a large collection of manual focus lenses that work just fine on modern Nikon digital cameras. I happen to use a manual focus 16mm f/3.5 Nikkor fisheye, a 55mm f/3.5 Micro-Nikkor, and an 85mm f/1.8 Nikkor several times a week, with other older lenses seeing occasional use.

The Nikon D7000 allows defining up to nine different lenses, and I can choose any of them with a quick trip to this menu entry (or to the equivalent menu item in My Menu, described later in this chapter).

To enter this information, follow these steps using the screen shown in Figure 10.7:

1. Choose Non-CPU lens data from the Setup menu.

2. Highlight Lens Number and press the multi selector left/right buttons to choose a number between 1 and 9.

3. Scroll down to Focal Length (mm) and use the multi selector left/right buttons to choose a focal length between 6mm and 4000mm.

4. Scroll down to Maximum Aperture and use the multi selector left/right buttons to choose a maximum f/stop between f/1.2 and f/22.

5. Choose Done. You can now select the lens number using any of several controls you can define for the Fn button, or depth-of-field preview button as described in Chapter 9 under CSM #f3, or CSM #f4.

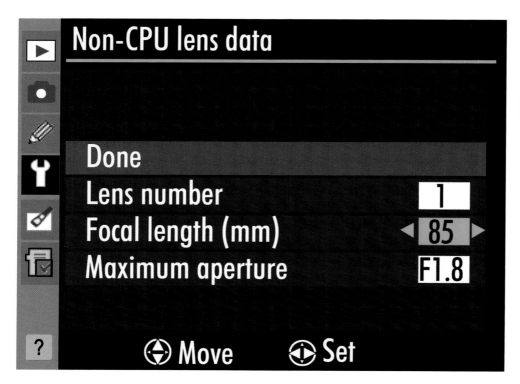

Figure 10.7
You can enter focal length and maximum aperture of up to nine manual focus lenses.

AF Fine Tune

Troubled by lenses that don't focus exactly where they should, producing back-focus or front-focus problems? No need to send your lens and/or camera into Nikon for servicing. The Nikon D7000 allows you to fine-tune focus for up to 12 different lenses. You'll probably never need to use this feature, but if you do, it's priceless. To fine-tune your lenses, first perform some tests to see just how much fine-tuning is required. The only problem I've run into is that with some lenses, particularly short-focal length lenses, using large negative values (−10 to −20) to move the focal point closer to the camera sometimes results in being unable to focus to infinity. If you run into that, you may be better off sending the lens to Nikon so they can recalibrate the focus for you.

This menu option has four choices, shown in Figure 10.8:

- **AF Fine tune (On/Off).** Enable/disable application of your AF Fine tuning changes.

- **Saved value.** View or enter an adjustment for the lens currently mounted on your camera.

Figure 10.8
The autofocus
of lenses can be
adjusted here.

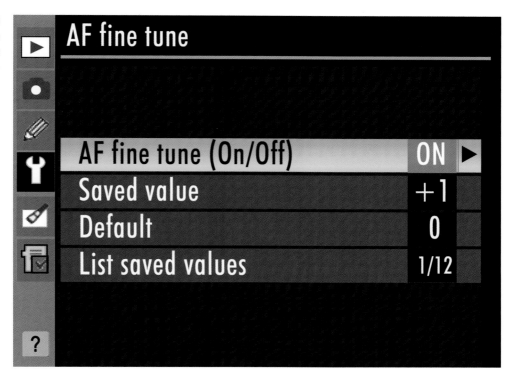

- **Default.** Set the default value to be applied to lenses that haven't been recalibrated. You'd use this if your D7000 has a certain amount of front- or back-focus problems with all lenses. Use with caution, as it affects every CPU lens that you use.

- **List saved values.** View and delete tuning values you've saved for up to 12 different lenses.

Because the adjustments made with the AF Fine tune setting are potentially so dangerous to your focusing health, I'm not even going to provide an overview in this chapter. (Knowing just enough to hurt yourself can be a real possibility.) Instead, you'll find a complete discussion of using this feature at the end of Chapter 11, which deals with lens issues.

Eye-Fi Upload

This option (which doesn't show up in Figure 10.4) is displayed in the menu only when a compatible Eye-Fi memory card is being used in the D7000. The Eye-Fi card looks like an ordinary SDHC memory card, but has built-in WiFi capabilities, so it can be used to transmit your photos as they are taken directly to a computer over a WiFi network. When an Eye-Fi card (see Figure 10.9) is inserted, and you've enabled the card by choosing Enable in this menu entry, one of four informational icons will appear in the shooting information screen, shown, left to right in Figure 10.10.

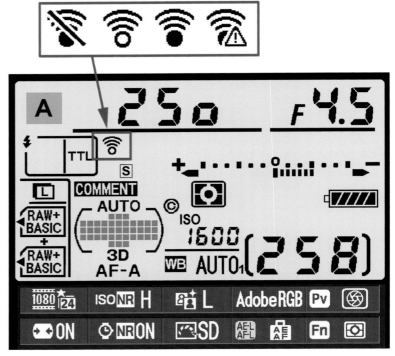

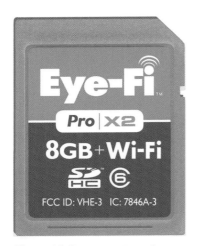

Figure 10.9 An Eye-Fi card can be inserted in either slot.

Figure 10.10 The icons show the Eye-Fi card's status. Left to right: Eye-Fi upload disabled; Eye-Fi upload enabled, but no images available for upload; Waiting to begin upload (if static)/Uploading (if animated); Error.

Firmware Version

You can see the current firmware release in use in the menu listing. You can learn how to update firmware in Chapter 14.

Retouch Menu Options

- D-Lighting
- Red-eye correction
- Trim
- Monochrome
- Filter effects

- Color balance
- Small picture
- Image overlay
- NEF (RAW) Processing
- Quick Retouch

The Retouch menu (see Figure 10.11) is most useful when you want to create a modified copy of an image on the spot, for immediate printing or e-mailing without first importing into your computer for more extensive editing. You can also use it to create

Figure 10.11
The Retouch menu allows simple in-camera editing.

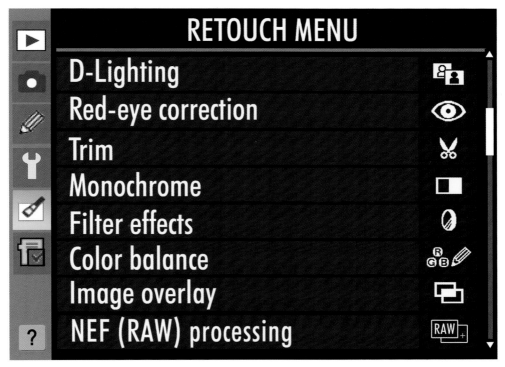

a JPEG version of an image in the camera when you are shooting RAW-only photos. While you can retouch images that have already been processed by the Retouch menu, each retouch option can be applied only once, except for the Image Overlay and Edit Movie tools. You may notice some quality loss when applying more than one retouch option. To create a retouched copy of an image:

1. While browsing among images in Playback mode, press OK when an image you want to retouch is displayed on the screen. The Retouch menu will pop up, and you can select a retouching option.

2. From the Retouch menu, select the option you want and press the multi selector right button. The Nikon D7000's standard image selection screen appears. Scroll among the images as usual with the left/right multi selector buttons, press the Zoom In button to examine a highlighted image more closely, and press OK to choose that image.

3. Work with the options available from that particular Retouch menu feature and press OK to create the modified copy, or Playback to cancel your changes.

4. A retouched JPEG image will be the same size and quality as the original, except for copies created from NEF and TIFF images (which are always saved as JPEG Fine images).

D-Lighting

This option brightens the shadows of pictures that have already been taken. Once you've selected your photo for modification, you'll be shown side-by-side images with the unaltered version on the left, and your adjusted version on the right. Press the multi selector's up/down buttons to choose from High, Normal, or Low corrections. Press the Zoom In button to magnify the image. When you're happy with the corrected image on the right, compared to the original on the left, press OK to save the copy to your memory card.

Red-Eye Correction

This Retouch menu tool can be used to remove the residual red-eye look that remains after applying the Nikon D7000's other remedies, such as the red-eye reduction lamp. (You can use the red-eye tools found in most image editors, as well.)

Your Nikon D7000 has a fairly effective red-eye reduction flash mode. Unfortunately, your camera is unable, on its own, to totally *eliminate* the red-eye effects that occur when an electronic flash (or, rarely, illumination from other sources) bounces off the retinas of the eye and into the camera lens. Animals seem to suffer from yellow or green glowing pupils, instead; the effect is equally undesirable. The effect is worst under low-light conditions (exactly when you might be using a flash) as the pupils expand to allow more light to reach the retinas. The best you can hope for is to *reduce* or minimize the red-eye effect.

The best way to truly eliminate red-eye is to raise the flash up off the camera so its illumination approaches the eye from an angle that won't reflect directly back to the retina and into the lens. The extra height of the built-in flash may not be sufficient, however. That alone is a good reason for using an external flash. If you're working with your D7000's built-in flash, your only recourse may be to switch on the red-eye reduction flash mode. That causes a lamp on the front of the camera to illuminate with a half-press of the shutter release button, which may result in your subjects' pupils contracting, decreasing the amount of the red-eye effect. (You may have to ask your subject to look at the lamp to gain maximum effect.)

If your image still displays red-eye effects, you can use the Retouch menu to make a copy with red-eye reduced further. First, select a picture that was taken with flash (non-flash pictures won't be available for selection). After you've selected the picture to process, press OK. The image will be displayed on the LCD. You can magnify the image with the Zoom In button, scroll around the zoomed image with the multi selector buttons, and zoom out with the Zoom Out button. While zoomed, you can cancel the zoom by pressing the OK button.

When you are finished examining the image, press OK again. The D7000 will look for red-eye, and, if detected, create a copy that has been processed to reduce the effect.

Figure 10.12
Wider pupils (left) can lead to red-eye effects; the Nikon D7000's red-eye reduction lamp can cause pupils to contract (right).

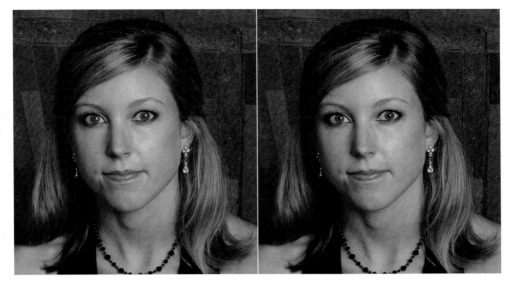

If no red-eye is found, a copy is not created. Figure 10.12 shows an original image (left) and its processed copy (right).

Trim

This option creates copies in specific sizes based on the final size you select, chosen from among 3:2, 4:3, and 5:4 aspect ratios (proportions). You can use this feature to create smaller versions of a picture for e-mailing without the need to first transfer the image to your own computer. If you're traveling, create your smaller copy here, insert the memory card in a card reader at an Internet café, your library's public computers, or some other computer, and e-mail the reduced-size version. Just follow these steps:

1. **Select your photo.** Choose Trim from the Retouch menu. You'll be shown the standard Nikon D7000 image selection screen. Scroll among the photos using the multi selector left/right buttons, and press OK when the image you want to trim is highlighted. While selecting, you can temporarily enlarge the highlighted image by pressing the Zoom In button.

2. **Choose your aspect ratio.** Rotate the main command dial to change from 3:2, 4:3, 5:4, 1:1, and 16:9 aspect ratios. These proportions happen to correspond to the proportions of common print sizes, including the two most popular sizes: 4 × 6 inches (3:2) and 8 × 10 inches (5:4).

3. **Crop in on your photo.** Press the Zoom In button to crop in on your picture. The pixel dimensions of the cropped image at the selected proportions will be displayed in the upper-left corner (see Figure 10.13) as you zoom. The current framed size is outlined in yellow.

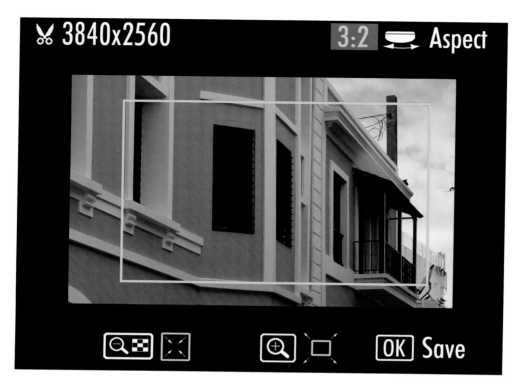

Figure 10.13
The Trim feature of the Retouch menu allows in-camera cropping.

Table 10.1 Trim Sizes

Aspect Ratio	Sizes Available
3:2	4480 × 2984, 3840 × 2580, 3200 × 2128, 2560 × 1704, 1920 × 1280, 1280 × 856, 960 × 640, 640 × 424
4:3	3840 × 2880, 3200 × 2400, 2560 × 1920, 1920 × 1440, 1280 × 960, 960 × 720, 640 × 480
5:4	3600 × 2880, 2992 × 2400, 2400 × 1920, 1808 × 1440, 1200 × 960, 986 × 720, 608 × 480
1:1	2880 × 2880, 2400 × 2400, 1920 × 1920, 1440 × 1440, 960 × 960, 720 × 720, 480 × 480
16:9	4480 × 2520, 3840 × 2160, 3200 × 1800, 2560 × 1440, 1920 × 1080, 1280 × 720, 960 × 536, 640 × 480

4. **Move cropped area within the image.** Use the multi selector left/right and up/down buttons to relocate the yellow cropping border within the frame.

5. **Save the cropped image.** Press OK to save a copy of the image using the current crop and size, or press the Playback button to exit without creating a copy. Copies created from JPEG Fine, Normal, or Standard have the same Image Quality setting as the original; copies made from RAW files or any RAW+JPEG setting will use JPEG Fine compression.

Monochrome

This Retouch choice allows you to produce a copy of the selected photo as a black-and-white image, sepia-toned image, or cyanotype (blue-and-white). You can fine-tune the color saturation of the previewed Sepia or Cyanotype version by pressing the multi selector up button to increase color richness, and the down button to decrease saturation. When satisfied, press OK to create the monochrome duplicate. Cancel by pressing the Playback button.

Filter Effects

Add tones to your images using this Retouch option. You have seven choices: Skylight, Warm, Red/Green/Blue intensifiers, Cross Screen, and Soft. Preview the effects in the color LCD before pressing OK to create the modified copy.

Color Balance

This Retouch effect allows you to create a copy with modified color balance. When you press the OK button while viewing a selected image, a screen like the one shown in Figure 10.14 appears with the photo shown in thumbnail size at the upper-left corner, and red/green/blue histograms at the right. You can bias the image along the magenta/green axis or blue/yellow (amber) axis based on your perception of the thumbnail or, as you gain experience, from your estimation of the distribution of tones as shown by the histograms.

Press the multi selector up button to increase the amount of green, the down button to increase the amount of magenta, the right button to increase the bias towards yellow/amber, and the left button to increase the amount of blue. As you make these modifications, the changes will be reflected in the histograms.

Image Overlay

This feature allows you to combine two RAW photos (only NEF files can be used) in a composite image that Nikon claims is better than a "double exposure" created in an image-editing application, because the overlays are made using RAW data.

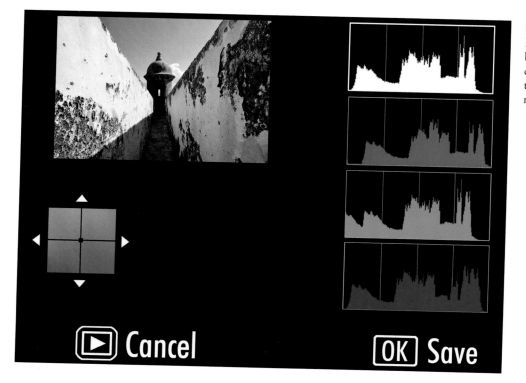

Figure 10.14
Fine-tune color
balance in the
camera using
this Retouch
menu screen.

To produce this composite image, follow these steps:

1. Choose Image Overlay. The screen shown in Figure 10.15 will be displayed, with the Image 1 box highlighted. If you want to choose an image from a card in another slot in the camera, in the playback mode, press and hold the BKT button and then press the multi selector up button to choose the other slot.

2. Press OK and the Nikon D7000's image selection screen appears. Choose the first image for the overlay and press OK.

3. Press the multi selector right button to highlight the Image 2 box, and press OK to produce the image selection screen. Choose the second image for the overlay.

4. By highlighting either the Image 1 or Image 2 boxes and pressing the multi selector up/down buttons, you can adjust the "gain," or how much of the final image will be "exposed" from the selected picture. You can choose from X0.5 (half-exposure) to X2.0 (twice the exposure) for each image. The default value is 1.0 for each, so that each image will contribute equally to the final exposure.

5. Use the multi selector right button to highlight the Preview box and view the combined picture. Press the Zoom In button to enlarge the view.

Figure 10.15
Overlay two
RAW images
to produce
a "double
exposure."

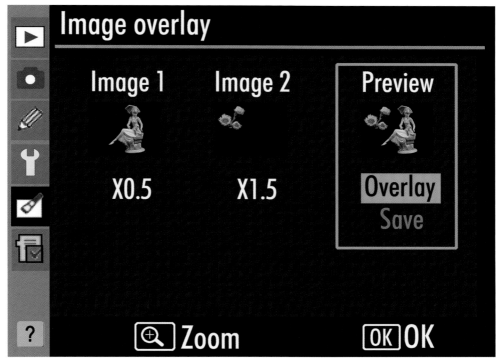

6. When you're ready to store your composite copy, press the multi selector down button when the Preview box is highlighted to select Save, and press OK. The combined image is stored on the memory card.

NEF (RAW) Processing

Use this tool to create a JPEG version of any image saved in either straight RAW (with no JPEG version) or RAW+Basic (with a Basic JPEG version). You can select from among several parameters to "process" your new JPEG copy right in the camera.

1. Choose a RAW image. Select NEF (RAW) processing from the Retouch menu. You'll be shown the standard Nikon D7000 image selection screen. Use the left/right buttons to navigate among the RAW images displayed. Press OK to select the highlighted image.

2. In the NEF (RAW) processing screen, shown in Figure 10.16, you can use the multi selector up/down keys to select from eight different attributes of the RAW image information to apply to your JPEG copy. Choose Image Quality (Fine, Normal, or Basic), Image Size (Large, Medium, or Small), White Balance, Exposure Compensation, Picture Control, High ISO Noise Reduction, Color Space, and D-Lighting parameters.

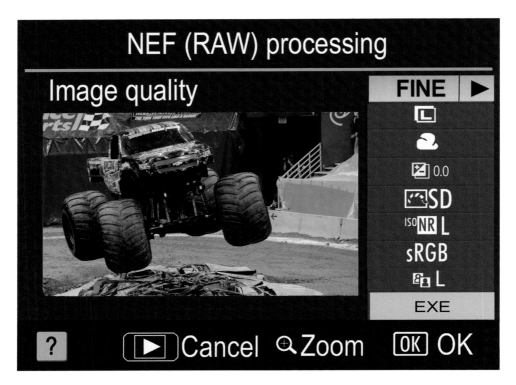

Figure 10.16
Adjust eight
parameters and
then save your
JPEG copy
from a RAW
original file.

Tip

The White Balance parameter cannot be selected for images created with the
Image Overlay tool, and the Preset manual white balance setting can be fine-
tuned only with images that were originally shot using the Preset white balance
setting. Exposure compensation cannot be adjusted for images taken using Active
D-Lighting, and both white balance and optimize image settings cannot be
applied to pictures taken using any of the Scene modes.

3. Press the Zoom In button to magnify the image temporarily while the button is
   held down.

4. Press the Playback button if you change your mind, to exit from the processing
   screen.

5. When all parameters are set, highlight EXE (for Execute) and press OK. The D7000
   will create a JPEG file with the settings you've specified, and show an Image Saved
   message on the LCD when finished.

Resize

This option, the first on the second page of the Retouch menu (see Figure 10.17), creates smaller copies of the selected images. It can be applied while viewing a single image in full-frame mode (just press the OK button while viewing a photo), or accessed from the Retouch menu (especially useful if you'd like to select and resize multiple images).

1. **Select images.** If accessing from the Retouch menu, you can choose to select multiple images, or jump directly to the following two steps.

2. **Choose destination.** If two memory cards are inserted, you can choose either Slot 1 or Slot 2 as the destination.

3. **Choose Size.** Next, select the size for the finished copy, from 2.5M (1920×1280 pixels), 1.1M (1280×856 pixels), 0.6M (960×640 pixels), 0.3M (640×424 pixels), or 0.1M (320×216 pixels).

4. **Confirm.** Press OK to create your copy.

Figure 10.17
Resize is the first entry on the second page of the Retouch menu.

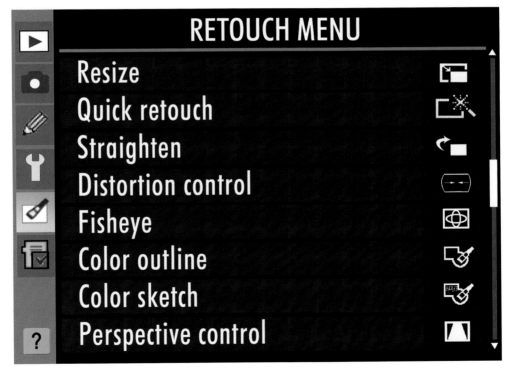

Quick Retouch

This option brightens the shadows of pictures that have already been taken. Once you've selected your photo for processing, use the multi-selector up/down keys in the screen that pops up (see Figure 10.18). The amount of correction that you select (High, Normal, or Low) will be applied to the version of the image shown at right. The left-hand version of the image shows the uncorrected version. While working on your image, you can press the Zoom In image to temporarily magnify the original photo.

Quick Retouch brightens shadows, enhances contrast, and adds color richness (saturation) to the image. Press OK to create a copy on your memory card with the retouching applied.

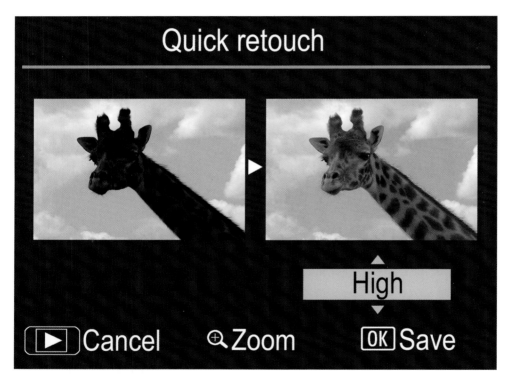

Figure 10.18
Quick Retouch applies D-Lighting, enhanced contrast, and added saturation to an image.

Straighten

Use this to create a corrected copy of a crooked image, rotated by up to five degrees, in increments of one-quarter of a degree. Use the right directional button to rotate clockwise, and the left directional button to rotate counterclockwise. Press OK to make a corrected copy, or the Playback button to exit without saving a copy.

Distortion Control

This option produces a copy with reduced barrel distortion (a bowing out effect) or pincushion distortion (an inward-bending effect), both most noticeable at the edges of a photo. You can select Auto to let the D3100 make this correction, or use Manual to make the fix yourself visually. Use the right directional button to reduce barrel distortion and the left directional button to reduce pincushion distortion. In both cases, some of the edges of the photo will be cropped out of your image. Press OK to make a corrected copy, or the Playback button to exit without saving a copy. Note that Auto cannot be used with images exposed using the Auto Distortion Control feature described earlier in this chapter. Auto works only with type G and type D lenses (see Chapter 11 for a description of what these lenses are), and does not work well with certain lenses, such as fisheye lenses and perspective control lenses.

Fisheye

This feature emulates the extreme curving effect of a fisheye lens. Use the right directional button to increase the effect, and the left directional button to decrease it. Press OK to make a corrected copy, or the Playback button to exit without saving a copy. Figure 10.19 shows an example image.

Figure 10.19
You can apply a
fisheye effect to
an image.

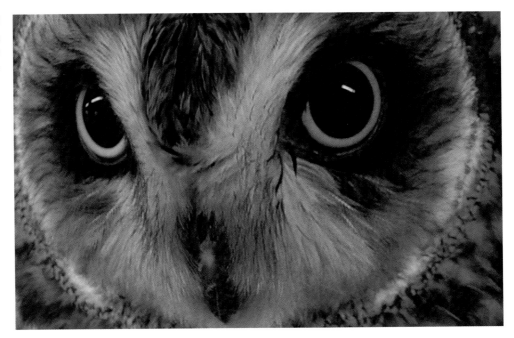

Color Outline

This option creates a copy of your image in outline form (see Figure 10.20), which Nikon says you can use for "painting." You might like the effect on its own. It's a little like the Find Edges command in Photoshop and Photoshop Elements, but you can perform this magic in your camera!

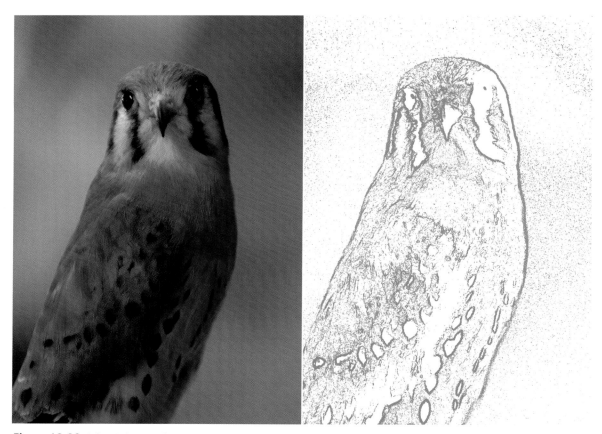

Figure 10.20 The Color Outline retouching feature creates an outline image (right), but it's not in color (like the original, left).

Perspective Control

This option lets you adjust the perspective of an image, reducing the falling back effect produced when the camera is tilted to take in the top of a tall subject, such as a building. Use the multi selector buttons to "tilt" the image in various directions and visually correct the distortion as in Figure 10.21.

Figure 10.21

Perspective Control lets you fix "falling back" distortion when photographing tall subjects.

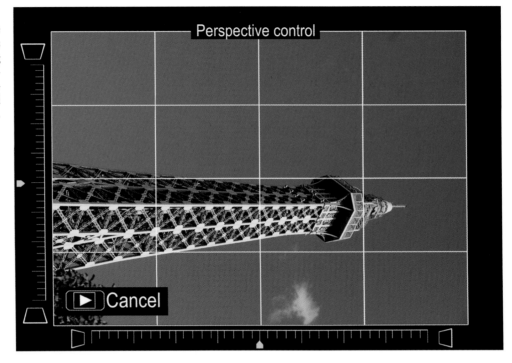

Miniature Effect

This is a clever effect, and it's hampered by a misleading name and the fact that its properties are hard to visualize (which is not a great attribute for a visual effect). This tool doesn't create a "miniature" picture, as you might expect. What it does is mimic tilt/shift lens effects that angle the lens off the axis of the sensor plane to drastically change the plane of focus, producing the sort of look you get when viewing some photographs of a diorama, or miniature scene. Confused yet?

Perhaps the best way to understand this capability is to actually modify a picture using it. Just follow these steps:

1. **Take your best shot.** Capture an image of a distant landscape or other scene, preferably from a slightly elevated viewpoint.

2. **Access Miniature Effect.** When viewing the image during playback, press the multi selector center button to access the Retouch menu, and select Miniature Effect. A screen like the one shown in Figure 10.22 appears.

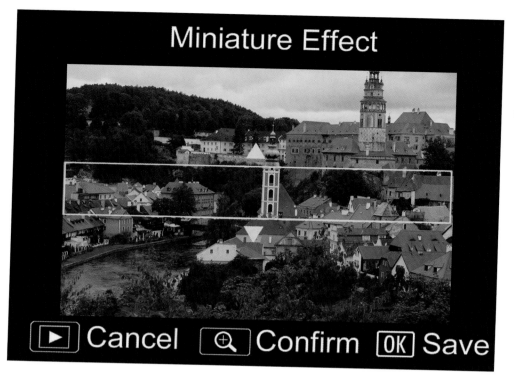

Figure 10.22
Choose the area for sharp focus by moving the yellow box within the frame.

3. **Adjust selected area.** A wide yellow box (or a tall yellow box if the image is rotated to vertical perspective on playback) highlights a small section of the image. (No, we're not going to create a panorama from that slice; this Nikon super-tricky feature has fooled you yet again.) Use the up/down buttons (or left/right buttons if the image is displayed vertically) to move the yellow box, which represents the area of your image that will be rendered in (fairly) sharp focus. The rest of the image will be blurred.

4. **Preview area to be in sharp focus.** Press the Zoom In button to preview the area that will be rendered in sharp focus. Nikon labels this control Confirm, but that's just to mislead you. It's actually just a preview that lets you "confirm" that this is the area you want to emphasize.

5. **Apply the effect.** Press the OK button to apply the effect (or the Playback button to cancel). Your finished image will be rendered in a weird altered-focus way, as shown in Figure 10.23.

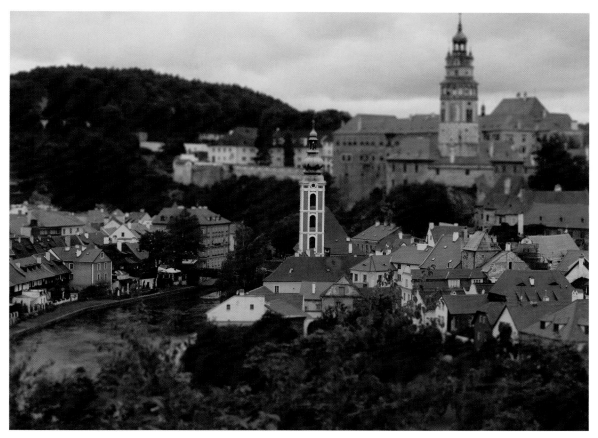

Figure 10.23 The same photo with the diorama/miniature effect applied.

Side-by-Side Comparison

Use this option to compare a retouched photo side-by-side with the original from which it was derived. Don't look for Side-by-Side Comparison in the Retouch menu. It doesn't appear there. Instead, this option is shown at the bottom of the pop-up menu that appears when you are viewing an image (or copy) full screen and press the OK button.

To use Side-by-Side Comparison:

1. Press the Playback button and review images in full-frame mode until you encounter a source image or retouched copy you want to compare. The retouched copy will have the retouching icon displayed in the upper-left corner. Press OK.

2. The original and retouched image will appear next to each other, with the re-touching options you've used shown as a label above the images, as you can see in Figure 10.24.

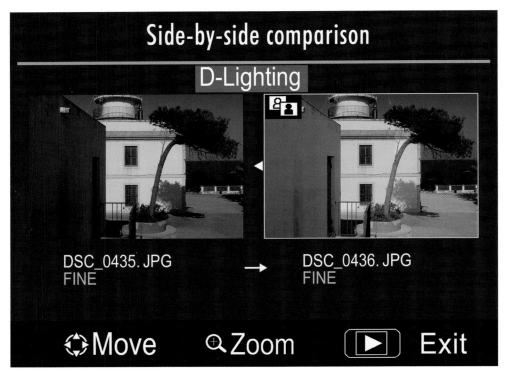

Figure 10.24
You can easily compare an original image and the retouched version side-by-side.

3. Highlight the original or the copy with the multi selector left/right buttons, and press the Zoom In button to magnify the image to examine it more closely.

4. If you have created more than one copy of an original image, select the retouched version shown, and press the multi selector up/down buttons to view the other retouched copies. The up/down buttons will also let you view the other image used to create an Image Overlay copy.

5. When done comparing, press the Playback button to exit.

Edit Movie

You can edit movies as you view them, pausing (using the down directional button) and clipping off portions from the beginning and/or end of the movie to create an edited version. Movie editing can be done from this menu entry, or accessed by pausing and pressing the AE-L/AF-L button to display a retouching menu.

I'll describe editing movies using this capability in detail in Chapter 6.

Using My Menu

The last menu in the D7000's main menu screen has two versions: Recent Settings and My Menu. The default mode is Recent Settings, which simply shows an ever-changing roster of the 20 menu items you used most recently. You'll probably find it more useful to activate the My Menu option instead, which contains only those menu items that you deposit there extracted from the Playback, Shooting, Custom Settings, Setup, and Retouch menus, based on your own decisions on which you use most. Remember that the D7000 always returns to the last menu and menu entry accessed when you press the MENU button. So you can set up My Menu (see Figure 10.25) to include just the items accessed most frequently, and (as long as you haven't used another menu), jump to those items instantly by pressing the MENU button.

Switching back and forth is easy. The My Menu and Recent Settings menus each has a menu choice called Choose Tab. Highlight that entry and press the right multi selector button to view a screen that allows you to activate either the My Menu or Recent Settings menu. Press OK to confirm. If you find your needs change so often that My Menu is of little use, you might find the Recent Settings tab a better choice, because it displays the actual menu items you've been using recently.

Figure 10.25
You can include your favorite menu items in the fast-access My Menu.

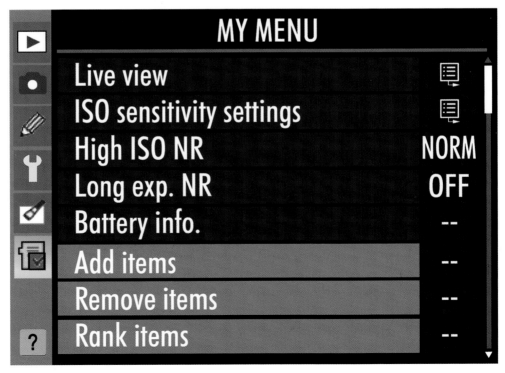

I tend to include frequently used functions that aren't available using direct access buttons in My Menu. For example, I include High ISO NR and Long Exp. NR, and Battery Info there, because I may want to turn noise reduction on or off, or check the status of my battery during shooting. I *don't* include ISO, Qual, or WB changes in My Menu, even though they are available in the menu system, because I can quickly change those values by pressing their dedicated buttons and rotating the main and sub-command dials.

You can add or subtract entries on My Menu at any time, and re-order (or rank) the entries so the ones you access most often are shown at the top of the list. Here's all you need to know to work with My Menu. To add entries to My Menu:

1. Select My Menu and choose Add Items.

2. A list of the available menus will appear (Playback, Shooting, Custom Settings, Setup, and Retouch menus). Highlight one and press the multi selector's right button.

3. Within the selected menu, choose the menu item you want to add and press OK.

4. The label Choose Position appears at the top of the My Menu screen. Use the up/down buttons to select a rank among the entries, and press OK to confirm and add the new item.

5. Repeat steps 1-4 if you want to add more entries to My Menu.

To reorder the menu listings:

1. Within the My Menu screen, choose Rank Items.

2. Use the up/down buttons to select the item to be moved, and press OK.

3. Use the up/down buttons to relocate the selected item and press OK.

4. Repeat steps 2-3 to move additional entries.

To remove entries from the list you can simply press the Trash button while an item is highlighted in the My Menu screen. To remove multiple items, follow these steps:

1. Within the My Menu screen, choose Remove Items.

2. A list with checkboxes next to the menu items appears. Scroll down to an item you want to remove and press the multi selector right button to mark its box. If you change your mind, highlight the item and press the right button again to unmark the box.

3. When finished, highlight Done and press the OK button.

4. Press OK to confirm the deletion.

11

Working with Lenses

If Nikon has one advantage over many of the other vendors of digital SLRs (other than making great, affordable cameras), it's the mind-bending assortment of high-quality lenses available to enhance the capabilities of cameras like the Nikon D7000. You can use thousands of current and older lenses introduced by Nikon and third-party vendors since 1959 (although lenses made before 1977 may need an inexpensive modification). These can give you a wider view, bring distant subjects closer, let you focus closer, shoot under lower light conditions, or provide a more detailed, sharper image for critical work. Other than the sensor itself, the lens you choose for your dSLR is the most important component in determining image quality and perspective of your images.

This chapter explains how to select the best lenses for the kinds of photography you want to do.

Sensor Sensibilities

From time to time you've heard the term *crop factor*, and you've probably also heard the term *lens multiplier factor*. Both are misleading and inaccurate terms used to describe the same phenomenon: the fact that cameras like the D7000 (and most other affordable digital SLRs) provide a field of view that's smaller and narrower than that produced by certain other (usually much more expensive) cameras, when fitted with exactly the same lens.

Figure 11.1 quite clearly shows the phenomenon at work. The outer rectangle, marked 1X, shows the field of view you might expect with a 28mm lens mounted on one of Nikon's "full-frame" (non-cropped) cameras, like the Nikon D700, D3s, or D3x. The area marked 1.5X shows the field of view you'd get with that 28mm lens installed on a

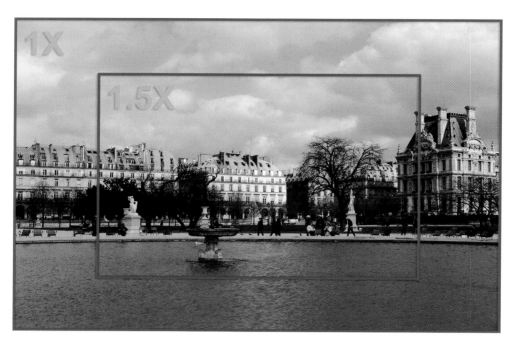

Figure 11.1
Nikon offers
digital SLRs
with full-frame
(1X) crops, as
well as 1.5X.

D7000. It's easy to see from the illustration that the 1X rendition provides a wider, more expansive view, while the inner field of view is, in comparison, *cropped.*

The cropping effect is produced because the sensors of DX cameras like the Nikon D7000 are smaller than the sensors of the D700, D3, or D3x. These "full-frame" cameras (which Nikon calls *FX format*) have a sensor that's the size of the standard 35mm film frame, 24mm × 36mm. Your D300's sensor does *not* measure 24mm × 36mm; instead, it specs out at 23.6 × 15.6 mm, or about 66.7 percent of the area of a full-frame sensor, as shown by the red boxes in the figure. You can calculate the relative field of view by dividing the focal length of the lens by .667. Thus, a 100mm lens mounted on a D7000 has the same field of view as a 150mm lens on the Nikon D700. We humans tend to perform multiplication operations in our heads more easily than division, so such field of view comparisons are usually calculated using the reciprocal of .667—1.5—so we can multiply instead. (100 / .667=150; 100 × 1.5=150)

This translation is generally useful only if you're accustomed to using full-frame cameras (usually of the film variety) and want to know how a familiar lens will perform on a digital camera. I strongly prefer *crop factor* over *lens multiplier*, because nothing is being multiplied; a 100mm lens doesn't "become" a 150mm lens—the depth-of-field and lens aperture remain the same. (I'll explain more about these later in this chapter.) Only the field of view is cropped. But *crop factor* isn't much better, as it implies that the 24 × 36mm frame is "full" and anything else is "less." I get e-mails all the time from photographers who point out that they own full-frame cameras with 36mm × 48mm sensors (like the Mamiya 645ZD or Hasselblad H3D-39 medium format digitals). By their reckoning, the "half-size" sensors found in cameras like the Nikon D700 and D3/D3x are "cropped."

If you're accustomed to using full-frame film cameras, you might find it helpful to use the crop factor "multiplier" to translate a lens's real focal length into the full-frame equivalent, even though, as I said, nothing is actually being multiplied. Throughout most of this book, I've been using actual focal lengths and not equivalents, except when referring to specific wide-angle or telephoto focal length ranges and their fields of view.

Crop or Not?

There's a lot of debate over the "advantages" and "disadvantages" of using a camera with a "cropped" sensor, versus one with a "full-frame" sensor. The arguments go like these:

■ **"Free" 1.5X teleconverter.** The Nikon D7000 (and other cameras with the 1.5X crop factor) magically transforms any telephoto lens you have into a longer lens, which can be useful for sports, wildlife photography, and other endeavors that benefit from more reach. Yet, your f/stop remains the same (that is, a 300mm f/4 becomes a very fast 450mm f/4 lens). Some discount this advantage, pointing out that the exact same field of view can be had by taking a full-frame image, and trimming it to the 1.5X equivalent. While that is strictly true, it doesn't take into account a factor called *pixel density*. A 12-megapixel DX camera like the Nikon D5000 has the same absolute resolution as a full-frame D3s, but the D5000 packs all those pixels together much more tightly, into that 23.6 × 15.8mm area. So, a 300mm f/4 lens delivers the same field of view as a 450mm optic at the D5000's full 12MP resolution. When you crop the D3s image to get the same FOV, you're using only 5 megapixels worth of resolution. So, while both images will be framed the same, the D5000 version, with its higher pixel density, will be sharper. This comparison becomes even more dramatic when you make the comparison with a camera having a much higher resolution, such as the D7000. The D7000 packs 16.2 megapixels into a DX-sized frame, while the D3s still has 5MP—less than a third the resolution—in the same DX frame when using crop mode.

■ **Dense pixels=more noise.** The other side of the pixel density coin is that the denser packing of pixels in the D7000 sensor means that each pixel must be smaller, and will have less light-gathering capabilities. Larger pixels capture light more efficiently, reducing the need to amplify the signal when boosting ISO sensitivity, and, therefore, producing less noise. In an absolute sense, this is true, and cameras like the D3s *do* have sensational high-ISO performance. However, the D7000's sensor is improved over earlier cameras, so you'll find it performs very well at higher ISOs. You needn't hesitate to use ISO 1600 (or even higher) with the Nikon D7000: just don't expect the same low-noise results at ISO 6400 as D3s owners get from their cameras.

■ **Lack of wide-angle perspective.** Of course, the 1.5X "crop" factor applies to wide-angle lenses, too, so your 20mm ultrawide lens becomes a hum-drum 30mm near-wide-angle, and a 35mm focal length is transformed into what photographers call a "normal" lens. Zoom lenses, like the 18-105mm lens that is often purchased with the D7000 in a kit, have less wide-angle perspective at their minimum focal length. The 18-105mm optic, for example, is the equivalent of a 27mm moderate wide angle when zoomed to its widest setting. Nikon has "fixed" this problem by providing several different extra-wide zooms specifically for the DX format, including the (relatively) affordable 10-24mm f/3.5-4.5 DX Nikkor shown in Figure 11.2. You'll never really lack for wide-angle lenses, but some of us will need to buy wider optics to regain the expansive view we're looking for.

■ **Mixed body mix-up.** The relatively small number of Nikon D7000 owners who also have a Nikon full-frame camera can't ignore the focal-length mix-up factor. If you own both FX and DX-format cameras (some D7000 owners use them as a backup to an FX model, for example), it's vexing to have to adjust to the different fields of view that the cameras provide. If you remove a given lens from one camera and put it on the other, the effective focal length/field of view changes. That 17-35mm f/2.8 zoom works as an ultra-wide to wide angle on an FX camera, but functions more as a moderate wide-angle to normal lens on a D7000. To get the "look" on both cameras, you'd need to use a 10-24mm zoom on the D7000, and the 17-35mm zoom on the D700. It's possible to become accustomed to this FOV shake-up and, indeed, some photographers put it to work by mounting their longest telephoto lens on the D7000 and their wide-angle lenses on their full-frame camera. But, even if you've never owned both an FX and DX camera, you should be aware of the possible confusion.

Your First Lens

Some Nikon dSLRs are almost always purchased with a lens. The entry- and mid-level Nikon dSLRs, including the D7000, are often bought by those new to digital photography, frequently by first-time SLR or dSLR owners who find the AF-S DX Nikkor 18-105mm f/3.5-5.6G ED VR or AF-S DX Zoom-Nikkor 18-55mm f/3.5-5.6G ED II, both with vibration reduction, irresistible bargains. Other more advanced Nikon models are often purchased without a lens by veteran Nikon photographers who already have a complement of optics to use with their cameras.

I bought my D7000 as a body-only (which was a somewhat rare configuration at the time of introduction), because I already had a (large) collection of lenses. But you might have purchased your D7000 with a lens, because it's an excellent first Nikon camera for photographers experienced with another camera line, or for ambitious beginners. That makes an economical "kit" lens very attractive. When the D7000 was first introduced,

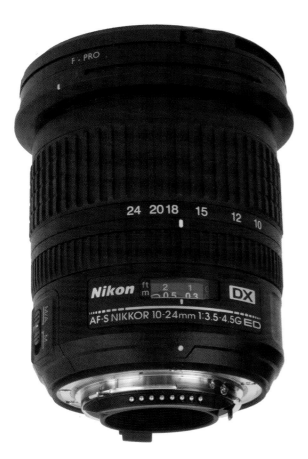

Figure 11.2 This 10-24mm zoom gives the Nikon D7000 true ultra-wide capabilities.

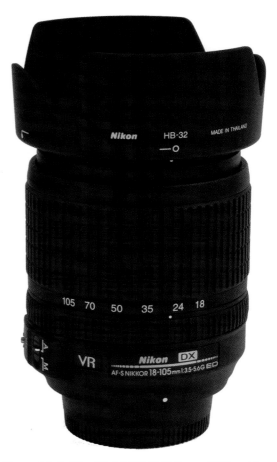

Figure 11.3 The AF-S DX VR II Zoom-Nikkor 18-105mm f/3.5-5.6G IF-ED is one of the most popular basic lenses for the Nikon D7000.

Nikon offered it as a kit with the 18-200mm f/3.5-5.6G IF-ED VR II zoom. (See Figure 11.3.) However, the body was also readily available for many purchasers who, like me, fall into one of the following categories: Those who are upgrading from the Nikon D300, from a Nikon film camera, or who are buying the D7000 as a second camera body to complement their more advanced DX model, or even as an adjunct to their full-frame camera. These owners, too, generally have lenses they can use with their new D7000.

So, depending on which category you fall into, you'll need to make a decision about what kit lens to buy, or decide what other kind of lenses you need to fill out your complement of Nikon optics. This section will cover "first lens" concerns, while later in the chapter we'll look at "add-on lens" considerations.

When deciding on a first lens, there are several factors you'll want to consider:

- **Cost.** You might have stretched your budget a bit to purchase your Nikon D7000, so you might want to keep the cost of your first lens fairly low. Fortunately, there are excellent lenses available that will add from $100 to $300 to the price of your camera if purchased at the same time.

- **Zoom range.** If you have only one lens, you'll want a fairly long zoom range to provide as much flexibility as possible. Fortunately, the two most popular basic lenses for the D7000 have 3X to 5X zoom ranges, extending from moderate wide-angle/normal out to medium telephoto. Either are fine for everyday shooting, portraits, and some types of sports.

- **Adequate maximum aperture.** You'll want an f/stop of at least f/3.5 to f/4 for shooting under fairly low light conditions. The thing to watch for is the maximum aperture when the lens is zoomed to its telephoto end. You may end up with no better than an f/5.6 maximum aperture. That's not great, but you can often live with it, particularly with a lens having vibration reduction (VR) capabilities, because you can often shoot at lower shutter speeds to compensate for the limited maximum aperture.

- **Image quality.** Your starter lens should have good image quality, because that's one of the primary factors that will be used to judge your photos. Even at a low price, several of the different lenses that can be packaged with the D7000 kit include extra-low dispersion glass and aspherical elements that minimize distortion and chromatic aberration; they are sharp enough for most applications. If you read the user evaluations in the online photography forums, you know that owners of the kit lenses have been very pleased with their image quality.

- **Size matters.** A good walking-around lens is compact in size and light in weight.

- **Fast/close focusing.** Your first lens should have a speedy autofocus system (which is where the Silent Wave motor found in all but the older or bargain basement third-party lenses is an advantage). Close focusing (to 12 inches or closer) will let you use your basic lens for some types of macro photography.

You can find comparisons of the lenses discussed in the next section, as well as third-party lenses from Sigma, Tokina, Tamron, and other vendors, in online groups and websites. I'll provide my recommendations, but more information is always helpful.

Buy Now, Expand Later

The D7000 is commonly available with several good, basic lenses that can serve you well as a "walk-around" lens (one you keep on the camera most of the time, especially when you're out and about without your camera bag). The number of options available to you is actually quite amazing, even if your budget is limited to about $100-$350 for your first lens. Here's a list of Nikon's best-bet "first" lenses. Don't worry about sorting out the alphabet soup right now; I provide a complete list of Nikon lens "codes" later in the chapter.

- **AF-S DX Nikkor 18-105mm f/3.5-5.6G ED VR.** This lens, introduced at the same time as the D90, is an excellent choice as a "walking around" lens for the D7000. It's more compact than the 18-200mm VR II (described later), and has a more limited zoom range. Its focal length range is quite sufficient for most general photography, and at around $300 with the camera (or slightly more when purchased separately), it's a real bargain. (See Figure 11.3.)

- **AF-S DX Nikkor 18-55mm f/3.5-5.6G VR.** If you owned an earlier entry-level Nikon dSLR, you may have a lens in this focal length left over. The vibration reduction ("anti-shake") feature of this lens partially offsets the relatively slow maximum aperture of the lens at the telephoto position. It can be mated with Nikon's AF-S DX VR Zoom-Nikkor 55-200mm f/4-5.6G IF-ED to give you a two-lens VR pair that will handle everything from 18mm to 200mm, at a relatively low price.

- **AF-S DX Nikkor 16-85mm f/3.5-5.6G ED VR.** The 16-85mm VR lens is the zoom that would make a lot of sense as a kit lens for the D7000. If you really want to use just a single lens with your camera, and don't need much in the way of telephoto focal lengths, this one provides an excellent combination of zoom range, image quality, and features. Unlike the 18-200mm kit lens, this one has a zoom range that extends from a true wide angle (equivalent to a 24mm lens on a full-frame camera) to useful medium telephoto (about 128mm equivalent), and so can be used for everything from architecture to portraiture to sports. If you think vibration reduction is useful only with longer telephoto lenses, you may be surprised at how much it helps you hand-hold your D7000 even at the widest focal lengths. The only disadvantage to this lens is its relatively slow speed (f/5.6) when you crank it out to the telephoto end. (See Figure 11.4.)

- **AF-S DX Zoom-Nikkor 18-70mm f/3.5-4.5G IF-ED.** If you don't plan on getting a longer zoom-range basic lens and can't afford the 16-85 zoom, I highly recommend this aging, but impressive lens, if you can find one in stock or available used at relatively low prices. Originally introduced as the kit lens for the venerable Nikon D70, the 18-70mm zoom quickly gained a reputation as a very sharp lens at a bargain price. It doesn't provide a view that's as long or as wide as the 16-85, but it's a half-stop faster at its maximum zoom position. You may have to hunt around to find one of these, but they are available for $250-$300 and well worth it. I own one to this day, and use it regularly, although it spends most of its time installed on my D70, which has been converted to infrared-only photography. (See Figure 11.5.)

■ **AF-S DX Zoom-Nikkor 18-135mm f/3.5-5.6G IF-ED.** This lens has been sold
as a kit lens for intermediate amateur-level Nikons, and some retailers with stock
on hand are packaging it with the D7000 body as well. While decent, it's really best
suited for the crowd who buys one do-everything lens and then never purchase
another. Available for less than $300, you won't tie up a lot of money in this lens.
There's no VR, so, for most, the 18-105mm VR lens is a better choice.

■ **AF-S DX VR II Zoom-Nikkor 18-200mm f/3.5-5.6G IF-ED.** I owned the original version of this lens for about three months, and decided it really didn't meet
my needs. That version was introduced as an ideal "kit" lens for the Nikon D200
a few years back, and, at the time had almost everything you might want. The new
VR II version is much better, with improved sharpness at the telephoto end, and

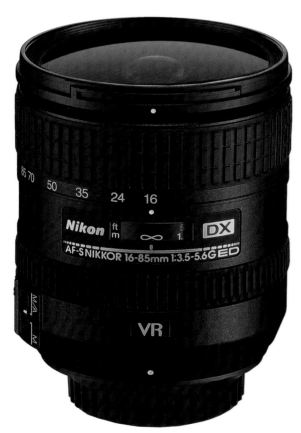

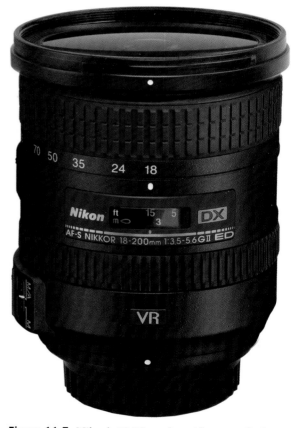

Figure 11.4 Nikon's 16-85mm VR lens provides an
excellent range from wide angle to short telephoto.

Figure 11.5 Nikon's 18-70mm lens, if you can find
one, is very sharp and very affordable.

elimination of "zoom creep," which caused the original to zoom out when tilted down. The new lens retains the stunning 11X zoom range and covers everything from the equivalent of 27mm to 300mm when the 1.5X crop factor is figured in, and its VR capabilities plus light weight let you use it without a tripod most of the time.

■ **AF-S VR Zoom-Nikkor 24-120mm f/3.5-5.6G IF-ED.** I felt I had to mention this lens because I see a large number of them available used at low prices. There are two versions, an older non-VR lens, and this model, which added vibration reduction, internal focusing, and some extra low dispersion (ED) elements to improve image quality. Unfortunately, while image quality is very good at the maximum 120mm, the lens softens quite a bit at shorter focal lengths and at larger apertures, making it less suitable as an all-around tool.

■ **AF-S NIKKOR 24-120mm f/4G ED VR.** This newer lens is the one to get if you want this useful focal length range. It's much sharper than the older models, and has a constant f/4 maximum aperture at all focal lengths. It's also a lot more expensive, at $1,100-plus.

What Lenses Can You Use?

The previous section helped you sort out what basic lens you need to buy with your Nikon D7000. Now, you're probably wondering what lenses can be added to your growing collection (trust me, it will grow). You need to know which lenses are suitable and, most importantly, which lenses are fully compatible with your Nikon D7000.

With the Nikon D7000, the compatibility issue is a simple one: It can use any modern-era Nikon lens with the AF-S or AF designation, with full availability of all autofocus, auto aperture, autoexposure, and image-stabilization features (if present). You can also use any Nikon AI, AI-S, or AI-P lens, which are manual focus lenses produced starting in 1977 and effectively through the present day, because Nikon continues to offer a limited number of manual focus lenses for those who need them. With the D7000, you can even use Aperture-priority metering with older manual focus lenses.

Nikon lenses produced prior to 1977 must have a minor conversion done to be used safely, because cameras other than certain Nikon entry-level models (such as the D3100) have a pin on the lens mount that can be damaged by an older, unmodified lens. John White at www.aiconversions.com will do the work for about $35 to allow these older lenses to be safely used on any Nikon digital camera.

As far as third-party (non-Nikon) lenses go, your D7000 will accept virtually all modern lenses produced by Tokina, Tamron, Sigma, and other vendors. They will autofocus just fine on a Nikon D7000, but if you also own a D40/D40x/D60, they will autofocus only with those lenses that contain an internal focusing motor. Vendors have different designators to indicate these lenses, such as HSM (for hyper-sonic motor). You'll have to check with the manufacturer of non-Nikon lenses to see if they are compatible with the D7000, particularly since some vendors have been gradually introducing revamped versions of their existing lenses with the addition of an internal motor.

Today, in addition to its traditional full-frame lenses, Nikon offers lenses with the DX designation, which is intended for use only on DX-format cameras. While the lens mounting system is the same, DX lenses have a coverage area that fills only the smaller frame, allowing the design of more compact, less-expensive lenses especially for non-full-frame cameras.

Ingredients of Nikon's Alphanumeric Soup

Nikon has always been fond of appending cryptic letters and descriptors onto the names of its lenses. Some of the first Nikon lenses I purchased had names like 35mm f/2 Auto Nikkor-O, 85mm f/1.8 Auto Nikkor-H, 105mm Auto Nikkor-P, and 200mm f/4 Auto Nikkor-Q. At the time, I didn't know what the funny letters represented, but I did know that the "Auto" portion of the name meant that, when you pressed the shutter release button, the lens would actually *stop down automatically* to the aperture you'd selected for the exposure. Don't laugh. Many lenses required rotating a ring manually after focusing and before taking the picture in order to close the lens down to the so-called *pre-set* aperture.

I actually still own all those lenses, because they work just fine on my Nikon digital camera bodies, including my beloved D7000. And I now know that the funny letters stood for the number of elements in the lens, which was apparently a more important attribute for a photographer to know than it is today. P stood for *penta* (five elements); H represented *hexa* (six elements); S stood for *septa* (seven elements); and so on through *octa*, *nona*, and *deca* (eight, nine, and ten). I'd finally found a use for my high-school Latin, even though Nikon substituted penta for *quinta*, because Q was already taken by *quadra* (four elements).

In the years since, Nikon lens nomenclature has become considerably more complex. Even the basic name of the company's lenses can be a source of confusion. Back when Paul Simon wrote his hit *Kodachrome* the popular terminology was always a "Nikon camera." And a "Nikkor lens." Today, even though Kodachrome itself is no longer with us, *Nikkor* is officially part of the name of each lens produced by Nikon, with the exception of the company's "budget" line of 30 years ago, which were called *Nikon Lens Series E* to differentiate them from all the other "top of the line" lenses. But it's become more common to informally refer to a Nikon lens without fear of being corrected.

Here's an alphabetical list of lens terms you're likely to encounter, either as part of the lens name, or in reference to the lens's capabilities. Not all of these are used as parts of a lens's name, but you may come across some of these terms in discussions of particular Nikon optics:

- **AF, AF-D, AF-I, AF-S.** In all cases, AF stands for *autofocus* when appended to the name of a Nikon lens. An extra letter is added to provide additional information. A plain-old AF lens is an autofocus lens that uses a slot-drive motor in the camera body to provide autofocus functions (and so cannot be used in AF mode on the Nikon D40, D40x, D60, D3000, or D5000 which lack the camera body motor). The D means that it's a D-type lens (described later in this listing); the I indicates that focus is through a motor inside the lens; and the S means that a super-special (Silent Wave) motor in the lens provides focusing. (Don't confuse a Nikon AF-S lens with the AF-S [Single-servo autofocus mode].) Nikon is currently upgrading its older AF lenses with AF-S versions, but it's not safe to assume that all newer Nikkors are AF-S, or even offer autofocus. For example, the PC-E Nikkor 24mm f/3.5D ED perspective control lens must be focused manually, and Nikon offers a surprising collection of other manual focus lenses to meet specialized needs.

- **AI, AI-S.** All Nikkor lenses produced after 1977 have either automatic aperture indexing (AI) or automatic indexing-shutter (AI-S) features that eliminate the previous requirement to manually align the aperture ring on the camera when mounting a lens. When AI/AI-S was introduced, Nikon included the designation in the lens name and offered a service to convert most older lenses to the new configuration. Within a few years, all Nikkors had this automatic aperture indexing feature (except for G-type lenses, which have no aperture ring at all), including Nikon's budget-priced Series E lenses, so the designation was dropped at the time the first autofocus (AF) lenses were introduced. The most important difference between AI and AI-S lenses is that the aperture action of the AI-S versions is *linear*, theoretically allowing for more efficient shutter priority and programmed exposure metering on cameras of the time. Current models make no distinction between AI and AI-S lenses. These lenses can be used for Aperture-priority and Manual mode metering on the Nikon D7000 and other Nikon "pro" bodies.

- **AI-P.** A lens with an AI-P designation is an AI lens that has the CPU chip included, which allows the transfer of basic lens information to the camera. It was possible to add an appropriate chip to most AI and AI-S lenses, upgrading them to AI-P status, but there are few companies offering this service anymore. "Chipped" AI/AI-S/AI-P lenses are manual focus optics that can be used with the full range of metering options, the same as with autofocus lenses.

- **CRC (Close Range Correction).** The so-called "floating element" system allowed lens elements to shift position to reduce curvature of field and spherical aberrations at close-focusing distances. It is available with certain lenses, including the AF Micro-Nikkor 60mm f/2.8D, which was replaced by the AF-S Micro-Nikkor 60mm f/2.8G ED.

- **E.** The E designation was used for Nikon's budget-priced E Series optics, five prime and three zoom manual focus lenses built using aluminum or plastic parts rather than brass, the preferred material in those days, so they were less rugged. All are effectively AI-S lenses. They do have good image quality, which makes them a bargain for those who treat their lenses gently and don't need the latest autofocus features. They were available in 28mm f/2.8, 35mm f/2.5, 50mm f/1.8, 100mm f/2.8, and 135mm f/2.8 focal lengths, plus 36-72mm f/3.5, 75mm-150mm f/3.5, and 70-210mm f/4 zooms. (All these would be considered fairly "fast" today.)

- **D.** Appended to the maximum f/stop of the lens (as in f/2.8D), a D Series lens is able to send focus distance data to the camera, which uses the information for flash exposure calculation and 3D Color Matrix II matrix metering.

- **DC.** The DC stands for defocus control, which allows managing the out-of-focus parts of an image to produce better-looking portraits and close-ups.

- **DX.** The DX lenses are designed for use with digital cameras using the APS-C–sized sensor having the 1.5X crop factor. Their image circle isn't large enough to fill up a full 35mm frame at all focal lengths, but they can be used on Nikon's full-frame D3/D3x and D700 models using the automatic/manual DX crop mode. Theoretically, these lenses can be built smaller and lighter than their full-frame counterparts, but there are some hefty DX lenses available, including the AF-S DX Zoom-Nikkor 17-55mm f/2.8G IF-ED.

- **ED (or LD/UD).** The ED (extra low dispersion) designation indicates that some lens elements are made of a special hard and scratch-resistant glass that minimizes the divergence of the different colors of light as they pass through, thus reducing chromatic aberration (color "fringing") and other image defects. A gold band around the front of the lens indicates an optic with ED elements. You sometimes find LD (low dispersion) or UD (ultra-low dispersion) designations.

- **FX.** When Nikon introduced the Nikon D3 full-frame camera, it coined the term "FX," representing the 23.9 × 36mm sensor format as a counterpart to "DX," which was used for its 15.8 × 23.6mm APS-C-sized sensors. Although FX hasn't been officially applied to any Nikon lenses so far, expect to see the designation used more often to differentiate between lenses that are compatible with any Nikon digital SLR (FX) and those that operate only on DX-format cameras, or in DX mode when used on an FX camera like the D3.

- **G.** G-type lenses have no aperture ring, and you can use them at other than the maximum aperture only with electronic cameras like the D7000 that set the aperture automatically or by using the command dial while the exposure compensation/aperture button is depressed. This includes all Nikon digital dSLRs.

- **IF.** Nikon's *internal focusing* lenses change focus by shifting only small internal lens groups with no change required in the lens's physical length, unlike conventional double helicoid focusing systems that move all lens groups toward the front or rear during focusing. IF lenses are more compact and lighter in weight, provide better balance, focus more closely, and can be focused more quickly.

- **IX.** These lenses were produced for Nikon's long-discontinued Pronea 6i and S APS film cameras. While the Pronea could use many standard Nikon lenses, IX lenses cannot be mounted on any Nikon digital SLR.

- **Micro.** Nikon uses the term *micro* to designate its close-up lenses. Most other vendors use *macro* instead.

- **NAI.** This is not an official Nikon term, but it is widely used to indicate that a manual focus lens is *Not-AI*, which means that it was manufactured before 1977, and therefore cannot be used safely on modern digital Nikon SLRs without modification.

- **NOCT (Nocturnal).** Used primarily to refer to the prized Nikkor AI-S Noct 58mm f/1.2, a "fast" (wide aperture) prime lens, with aspherical elements, capable of taking photographs in very low light.

- **PC (Perspective Control).** A PC lens is capable of shifting the lens from side to side (and up/down) to provide a more realistic perspective when photographing architecture and other subjects that otherwise require tilting the camera so that the sensor plane is not parallel to the subject. Older Nikkor PC lenses offered shifting only, but more modern models, such as the PC-E Nikkor 24mm f/3.5D ED lens introduced early in 2008 allow both shifting and tilting.

- **UV.** This term is applied to special (and expensive) lenses designed to pass ultraviolet light.

- **UW.** Lenses with this designation are designed for underwater photography with Nikonos camera bodies, and cannot be used with Nikon digital SLRs.

- **VR.** Nikon has an expanding line of vibration reduction (VR) lenses, including several very affordable models, which shift lens elements internally to counteract camera shake. The VR feature allows using a shutter speed up to four stops slower than would be possible without vibration reduction.

What Lenses Can Do for You

I'm something of a lens nut. Because my work requires me to evaluate lots of different lenses and provide recommendations for specific lenses that may have overlapping focal lengths and features, I'm able to justify owning many more optics than the average person wants or needs. It probably wouldn't make sense for you to own 10-24mm,

14-24mm, 17-35mm, 24-70mm, 18-70mm, and 28-200mm zooms as I do. Indeed, a much saner approach to expanding your lens collection is to consider what each of your options can do for you and then choose the type of lens and specific model that will really boost your creative opportunities.

So, in the sections that follow, I'm going to provide a general guide to the sort of capabilities you can gain for your D7000 by adding a lens to your repertoire. Then, at the end of the chapter, I'll provide a more detailed discussion of some specific lenses and how they might fit into your camera bag toolkit.

- **Wider perspective.** Your 18-55mm f/3.5-5.6 or 16-85mm f/4-5.6 lens has served you well for moderate wide-angle shots. Now you find your back is up against a wall and you *can't* take a step backwards to take in more subject matter. Perhaps you're standing on the rim of the Grand Canyon, and you want to take in as much of the breathtaking view as you can. You might find yourself just behind the baseline at a high school basketball game and want an interesting shot with a little perspective distortion tossed in the mix. There's a lens out there that will provide you with what you need, such as the 12-24mm and 10-24mm Nikon zooms I'll describe later in this chapter.

- **Bring objects closer.** A long lens brings distant subjects closer to you, offers better control over depth-of-field, and avoids the perspective distortion that wide-angle lenses provide. They compress the apparent distance between objects in your frame. Don't forget that the Nikon D7000's crop factor narrows the field of view of all these lenses, so your 70-300mm lens looks more like a 105mm-450mm zoom through the viewfinder. The image shown in Figure 11.6 was taken using a wide 16mm lens, while the images in Figures 11.7 and 11.8 were taken from the same position as Figure 11.6, but with focal lengths of 70mm and 200mm, respectively.

- **Bring your camera closer.** Macro lenses allow you to focus to within an inch or two of your subject. Nikon's best close-up lenses are all fixed focal length optics in the 60mm to 200mm range. But you'll find good macro zooms available from Sigma and others. They don't tend to focus quite as close, but they provide a bit of flexibility when you want to vary your subject distance (say, to avoid spooking a skittish creature).

- **Look sharp.** Many lenses are prized for their sharpness and overall image quality. While your run-of-the-mill lens is likely to be plenty sharp for most applications, the very best optics are even better over their entire field of view (which means no fuzzy corners), are sharper at a wider range of focal lengths (in the case of zooms), and have better correction for various types of distortion.

Figure 11.6
An ultra-wide-angle lens provided this view of Sedona's Cathedral Rock.

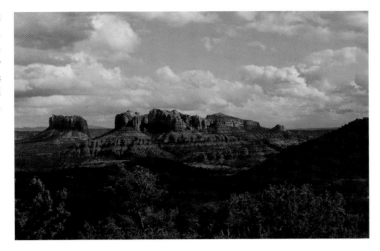

Figure 11.7
This photo, taken from roughly the same distance shows the view using a short telephoto lens.

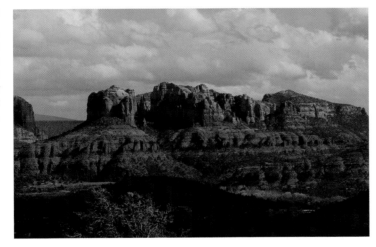

Figure 11.8
A long telephoto lens captured this close-up view of Cathedral Rock from approximately the same shooting position.

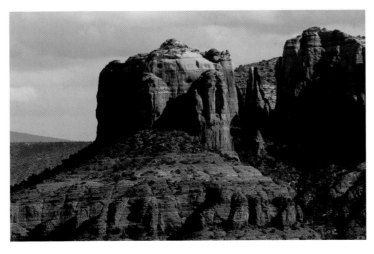

- **More speed.** Your Nikon 70-300mm f/4.5-5.6 telephoto zoom lens might have the perfect focal length and sharpness for sports photography, but the maximum aperture won't cut it for night baseball or football games, or, even, any sports shooting in daylight if the weather is cloudy or you need to use some ungodly fast shutter speed, such as 1/4,000th second. You might be happier to gain a full f/stop with an AF-S Nikkor 300mm f/4D IF-ED for a little more than $1,000, or even the pricier Nikon AF-S VR II Zoom-Nikkor 70-200mm f/2.8G VR II mated to a 1.4x teleconverter (giving you a 98-280mm f/4 lens). If money is no object, you can spring for Nikon's superfast 400mm f/2.8 and 600mm f/4 (both with vibration reduction and priced in the $6,500-and-up stratosphere). Or, maybe you just need the speed and can benefit from an f/1.8 or f/1.4 prime lens. They're all available in Nikon mounts (there's even an 85mm f/1.4 and 50mm f/1.4 for the real speed demons). With any of these lenses you can continue photographing under the dimmest of lighting conditions without the need for a tripod or flash, or boosting the ISO to noise-producing levels.

- **Special features.** Accessory lenses give you special features, such as tilt/shift capabilities to correct for perspective distortion in architectural shots. You'll also find macro lenses, including the new AF-S Micro-Nikkor 60mm f/2.8G ED, fisheye lenses like the AF DX Fisheye-Nikkor 10.5mm f/2.8G ED, and all VR (vibration reduction) lenses also count as special-feature optics.

Zoom or Prime?

Zoom lenses have changed the way serious photographers take pictures. One of the reasons that I own 12 SLR film bodies dating back to the pre-zoom days is that in ancient times it was common to mount a different fixed focal length prime lens on various cameras and take pictures with two or three cameras around your neck (or tucked in a camera case) so you'd be ready to take a long shot or an intimate close-up or wide-angle view on a moment's notice, without the need to switch lenses. It made sense (at the time) to have a half-dozen or so bodies (two to use, one in the shop, one in transit, and a couple backups). Zoom lenses of the time had a limited zoom range, were heavy, and not very sharp (especially when you tried to wield one of those monsters hand-held).

That's all changed today. Lenses like the razor-sharp AF-S VR II Zoom-Nikkor 70-200mm f/2.8G IF-ED boast longer zoom ranges, in a package that's about 8.5-inches long, and while not petite at 3.2 pounds, quite usable hand-held (especially with VR switched on). Although such a lens might seem expensive at $2,200-plus, it's actually much less costly than the six or so lenses it replaces. I'll explain more about this particular lens later in the chapter.

When selecting between zoom and prime lenses, there are several considerations to ponder. Here's a checklist of the most important factors. I already mentioned image quality and maximum aperture earlier, but those aspects take on additional meaning when comparing zooms and primes.

- **Logistics.** As prime lenses offer just a single focal length, you'll need more of them to encompass the full range offered by a single zoom. More lenses mean additional slots in your camera bag, and extra weight to carry. Just within Nikon's line alone you can choose from a good selection of general purpose prime lenses in 28mm, 35mm, 50mm, 85mm, 100mm, 135mm, and 200mm focal lengths, all of which are overlapped by the 28-200mm zoom I mentioned earlier. Even so, you might be willing to carry an extra prime lens or two in order to gain the speed or image quality. The relatively new Nikkor 35mm f/1.8 DX lens offers a fast "normal" focal length for those owning APS-C cameras at an economical price.

- **Image quality.** Prime lenses usually produce better image quality at their focal length than even the most sophisticated zoom lenses at the same magnification. Zoom lenses, with their shifting elements and f/stops that can vary from zoom position to zoom position, are in general more complex to design than fixed focal length lenses. That's not to say that the very best prime lenses can't be complicated as well. However, the exotic designs, aspheric elements, and low-dispersion glass can be applied to improving the quality of the lens, rather than wasting a lot of it on compensating for problems caused by the zoom process itself.

- **Maximum aperture.** Because of the same design constraints, zoom lenses usually have smaller maximum apertures than prime lenses, and the most affordable zooms have a lens opening that grows effectively smaller as you zoom in. The difference in lens speed verges on the ridiculous at some focal lengths. For example, an 18mm-55mm basic zoom gives you a 55mm f/5.6 lens when zoomed all the way out, while prime lenses in that focal length commonly have f/1.8 or faster maximum apertures. Indeed, the fastest f/2, f/1.8, f/1.4, and f/1.2 lenses are all primes, and if you require speed, a fixed focal length lens is what you should rely on. Figure 11.9 shows an image taken with a Nikon 85mm f/1.4 lens in low-light conditions.

- **Speed.** Using prime lenses takes time and slows you down. It takes a few seconds to remove your current lens and mount a new one, and the more often you need to do that, the more time is wasted. If you choose not to swap lenses, when using a fixed focal length lens you'll still have to move closer or farther away from your subject to get the field of view you want. A zoom lens allows you to change magnifications and focal lengths with the twist of a ring and generally saves a great deal of time.

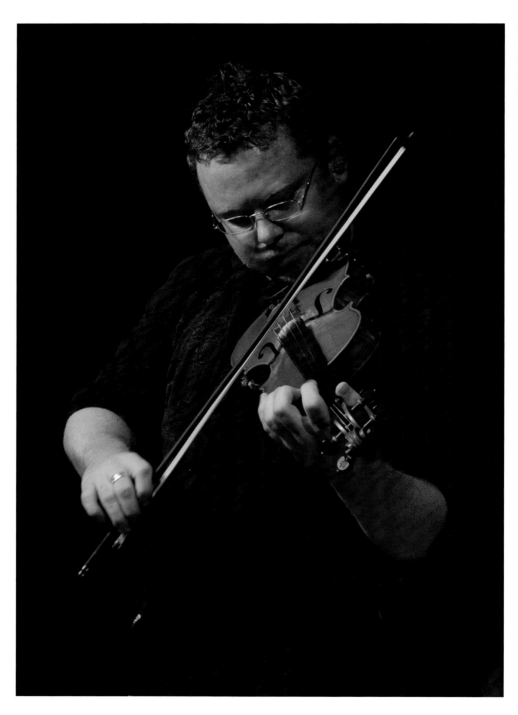

Figure 11.9
An 85mm f/1.4 lens was perfect for this hand-held photo.

Categories of Lenses

Lenses can be categorized by their intended purpose—general photography, macro photography, and so forth—or by their focal length. The range of available focal lengths is usually divided into three main groups: wide-angle, normal, and telephoto. Prime lenses fall neatly into one of these classifications. Zooms can overlap designations, with a significant number falling into the catch-all wide-to-telephoto zoom range. This section provides more information about focal length ranges, and how they are used.

When the 1.5X crop factor (mentioned at the beginning of this chapter) is figured in, any lens with an equivalent focal length of 10mm to 16mm is said to be an *ultrawide-angle lens*; from about 16mm to 30mm is said to be a *wide-angle lens*. *Normal lenses* have a focal length roughly equivalent to the diagonal of the film or sensor, in millimeters, and so fall into the range of about 30mm to 40mm on a D7000. *Short telephoto lenses* start at about 40mm to 70mm, with anything from 70mm to 250mm qualifying as a conventional *telephoto*. For the Nikon D7000, anything from about 300mm-400mm or longer can be considered a *super-telephoto*.

Using Wide-Angle and Wide-Zoom Lenses

To use wide-angle prime lenses and wide zooms, you need to understand how they affect your photography. Here's a quick summary of the things you need to know.

- **More depth-of-field.** Practically speaking, wide-angle lenses offer more depth-of-field at a particular subject distance and aperture. (But see the sidebar below for an important note.) You'll find that helpful when you want to maximize sharpness of a large zone, but not very useful when you'd rather isolate your subject using selective focus (telephoto lenses are better for that).

- **Stepping back.** Wide-angle lenses have the effect of making it seem that you are standing farther from your subject than you really are. They're helpful when you don't want to back up, or can't because there are impediments in your way.

- **Wider field of view.** While making your subject seem farther away, as implied above, a wide-angle lens also provides a larger field of view, including more of the subject in your photos. Table 11.1 shows the diagonal field of view offered by an assortment of lenses, taking into account the crop factor introduced by the Nikon D7000's smaller-than-full-frame sensor.

- **More foreground.** As background objects retreat, more of the foreground is brought into view by a wide-angle lens. That gives you extra emphasis on the area that's closest to the camera. Photograph your home with a normal lens/normal zoom setting, and the front yard probably looks fairly conventional in your photo (that's why they're called "normal" lenses). Switch to a wider lens and you'll discover that your lawn now makes up much more of the photo. So, wide-angle lenses are great when you want to emphasize that lake in the foreground, but problematic when your intended subject is located farther in the distance.

- **Super-sized subjects.** The tendency of a wide-angle lens to emphasize objects in the foreground, while de-emphasizing objects in the background can lead to a kind of size distortion that may be more objectionable for some types of subjects than others. Shoot a bed of flowers up close with a wide angle, and you might like the distorted effect of the larger blossoms nearer the lens. Take a photo of a family member with the same lens from the same distance, and you're likely to get some complaints about that gigantic nose in the foreground.

- **Perspective distortion.** When you tilt the camera so the plane of the sensor is no longer perpendicular to the vertical plane of your subject, some parts of the subject are now closer to the sensor than they were before, while other parts are farther away. So, buildings, flagpoles, or NBA players appear to be falling backwards, as you can see in Figure 11.10. While this kind of apparent distortion (it's not caused by a defect in the lens) can happen with any lens, it's most apparent when a wide angle is used.

- **Steady cam.** You'll find that you can hand-hold a wide-angle lens at slower shutter speeds, without need for vibration reduction, than you can with a telephoto lens. The reduced magnification of the wide-lens or wide-zoom setting doesn't emphasize camera shake like a telephoto lens does.

Table 11.1 Field of View at Various Focal Lengths

Diagonal Field of View	Focal Length at 1X Crop	Focal Length Needed to Produce Same Field of View at 1.5X Crop
107 degrees	16mm	10.5mm
94 degrees	20mm	13mm
84 degrees	24mm	16mm
75 degrees	28mm	19mm
63 degrees	35mm	23mm
47 degrees	50mm	33mm
28 degrees	85mm	56mm
18 degrees	135mm	90mm
12 degrees	200mm	133mm
8.2 degrees	300mm	200mm

■ **Interesting angles.** Many of the factors already listed combine to produce more interesting angles when shooting with wide-angle lenses. Raising or lowering a telephoto lens a few feet probably will have little effect on the appearance of the distant subjects you're shooting. The same change in elevation can produce a dramatic effect for the much-closer subjects typically captured with a wide-angle lens or wide-zoom setting.

Figure 11.10
Tilting the camera back produces this "falling back" look in architectural photos.

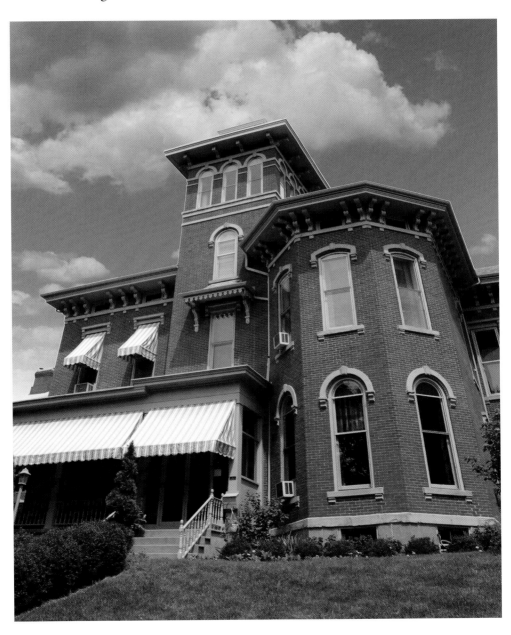

Table 11.1 turns the conventional "equivalent" listing on its head. Usually, you'll see a table that tells you that, say, a 100mm lens when used on a camera like the Nikon D7000, will have an equivalent field of view of a 150mm lens on a full-frame camera. That's actually not a difficult calculation, and might not be as useful as you think. If you're concerned about focal length equivalents, you probably have some experience using full-frame cameras.

So, what you really want to know is, if I want the same field-of-view that I got with my old 20mm lens on my film camera, what focal length lens do I need to use *now?* The fact that your 20mm lens is now the equivalent of a 30mm lens on the D7000 isn't as important as the question, *"Do I own a lens that will provide the same field of view that I used to get with my trusty 20mm lens?"* That's what the table shows you. In the center column, you find a list of common focal lengths for prime lenses originally designed for full-frame cameras. You can scan down the column to see that, if you want the same field of view that you got with your 35mm lens, you'll need to use a 23mm focal length or zoom position when you're shooting with the D7000. Or, if you preferred 85mm as a focal length for portraits, that you'll need a 56mm focal length when the 1.5X crop factor is figured in. The left column shows the angle of the field of view of each lens's focal length, because many old-timers sometimes think in those terms.

The crop factor strikes again! You can see from this table that wide-angle lenses provide a broader field of view, and that, because of the D7000's 1.5X crop factor, lenses must have a shorter focal length to provide the same field of view. If you like working with a 28mm lens with your full-frame camera, you'll need a 19mm lens for your Nikon D7000 to get the same field of view. (Some focal lengths have been rounded slightly for simplification.)

DOF IN DEPTH

The DOF advantage of wide-angle lenses is diminished when you enlarge your picture; believe it or not, a wide-angle image enlarged and cropped to provide the same subject size as a telephoto shot would have the *same* depth-of-field. Try it: take a wide-angle photo of a friend from a fair distance, and then zoom in to duplicate the picture in a telephoto image. Then, enlarge the wide shot so your friend is the same size in both. The wide photo will have the same depth-of-field (and will have much less detail, too).

Avoiding Potential Wide-Angle Problems

Wide-angle lenses have a few quirks that you'll want to keep in mind when shooting so you can avoid falling into some common traps. Here's a checklist of tips for avoiding common problems:

- **Symptom: converging lines.** Unless you want to use wildly diverging lines as a creative effect, it's a good idea to keep horizontal and vertical lines in landscapes, architecture, and other subjects carefully aligned with the sides, top, and bottom of the frame. That will help you avoid undesired perspective distortion. Sometimes it helps to shoot from a slightly elevated position so you don't have to tilt the camera up or down.

- **Symptom: color fringes around objects.** Lenses are often plagued with fringes of color around backlit objects, produced by *chromatic aberration*, which comes in two forms: *longitudinal/axial*, in which all the colors of light don't focus in the same plane; and *lateral/transverse*, in which the colors are shifted to one side. Axial chromatic aberration can be reduced by stopping down the lens, but transverse CA cannot. Both can be reduced by using lenses with low diffraction index glass (or ED elements, in Nikon nomenclature) and by incorporating elements that cancel the chromatic aberration of other glass in the lens. For example, a strong positive lens made of low dispersion crown glass (made of a soda-lime-silica composite) may be mated with a weaker negative lens made of high-dispersion flint glass, which contains lead.

- **Symptom: lines that bow outward.** Some wide-angle lenses cause straight lines to bow outwards, with the strongest effect at the edges. In fisheye (or *curvilinear*) lenses, this defect is a feature, as you can see in Figure 11.11. When distortion is not desired, you'll need to use a lens that has corrected barrel distortion. Manufacturers like Nikon do their best to minimize or eliminate it (producing a *rectilinear* lens), often using *aspherical* lens elements (which are not cross-sections of a sphere). You can also minimize barrel distortion simply by framing your photo with some extra space all around, so the edges where the defect is most obvious can be cropped out of the picture. Some image editors, such as Photoshop and Photoshop Elements have a lens distortion correction feature.

- **Symptom: dark corners and shadows in flash photos.** The Nikon D7000's built-in electronic flash is designed to provide even coverage for lenses as wide as 17mm. If you use a wider lens, you can expect darkening, or *vignetting*, in the corners of the frame. At wider focal lengths, the lens hood of some lenses (my 18mm-70mm lens is a prime offender) can cast a semi-circular shadow in the lower portion of the frame when using the built-in flash. Sometimes removing the lens hood or zooming in a bit can eliminate the shadow. Mounting an external flash unit, such as the mighty Nikon SB-800 can solve both problems, as it has zoomable coverage up to as wide as the field of view of a 14mm lens when used with the included adapter. Its higher vantage point eliminates the problem of lens hood shadow, too.

- **Symptom: light and dark areas when using polarizing filter.** If you know that polarizers work best when the camera is pointed 90 degrees away from the sun and have the least effect when the camera is oriented 180 degrees from the sun, you know only half the story. With lenses having a focal length of 10mm to 18mm (the equivalent of 15mm-27mm lens on a full-frame camera), the angle of view is extensive enough to cause problems. Think about it: when a 10mm lens is pointed at the proper 90-degree angle from the sun, objects at the edges of the frame will be oriented at 135 to 41 degrees, with only the center at exactly 90 degrees. Either edge will have much less of a polarized effect. The solution is to avoid using a polarizing filter with lenses having an actual focal length of less than 18mm (or 27mm equivalent).

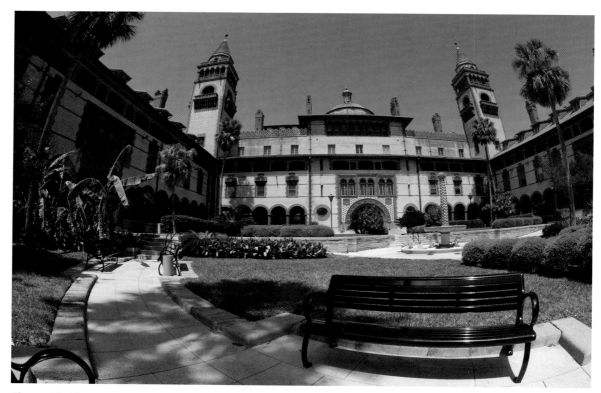

Figure 11.11 Many wide-angle lenses cause lines to bow outwards towards the edges of the image; with a fisheye lens, this tendency is considered an interesting feature.

Using Telephoto and Tele-Zoom Lenses

Telephoto lenses also can have a dramatic effect on your photography, and Nikon is especially strong in the long-lens arena, with lots of choices in many focal lengths and zoom ranges. You should be able to find an affordable telephoto or tele-zoom to enhance your photography in several different ways. Here are the most important things you need to know. In the next section, I'll concentrate on telephoto considerations that can be problematic—and how to avoid those problems.

- **Selective focus.** Long lenses have reduced depth-of-field within the frame, allowing you to use selective focus to isolate your subject. You can open the lens up wide to create shallow depth-of-field, or close it down a bit to allow more to be in focus. The flip side of the coin is that when you *want* to make a range of objects sharp, you'll need to use a smaller f/stop to get the depth-of-field you need. Like fire, the depth-of-field of a telephoto lens can be friend or foe. Figure 11.12 shows a photo of a statue, photographed using a telephoto lens and wider f/stop to de-emphasize the distracting background.

- **Getting closer.** Telephoto lenses bring you closer to wildlife, sports action, and candid subjects. No one wants to get a reputation as a surreptitious or "sneaky" photographer (except for paparazzi), but when applied to candids in an open and honest way, a long lens can help you capture memorable moments while retaining enough distance to stay out of the way of events as they transpire.

- **Reduced foreground/increased compression.** Telephoto lenses have the opposite effect of wide angles: they reduce the importance of things in the foreground by squeezing everything together. This compression even makes distant objects appear to be closer to subjects in the foreground and middle ranges. You can use this effect as a creative tool to squeeze subjects together.

- **Accentuates camera shakiness.** Telephoto focal lengths hit you with a double-whammy in terms of camera/photographer shake. The lenses themselves are bulkier, more difficult to hold steady, and may even produce a barely perceptible see-saw rocking effect when you support them with one hand halfway down the lens barrel. Telephotos also magnify any camera shake. It's no wonder that vibration reduction is popular in longer lenses.

- **Interesting angles require creativity.** Telephoto lenses require more imagination in selecting interesting angles, because the "angle" you do get on your subjects is so narrow. Moving from side to side or a bit higher or lower can make a dramatic difference in a wide-angle shot, but raising or lowering a telephoto lens a few feet probably will have little effect on the appearance of the distant subjects you're shooting.

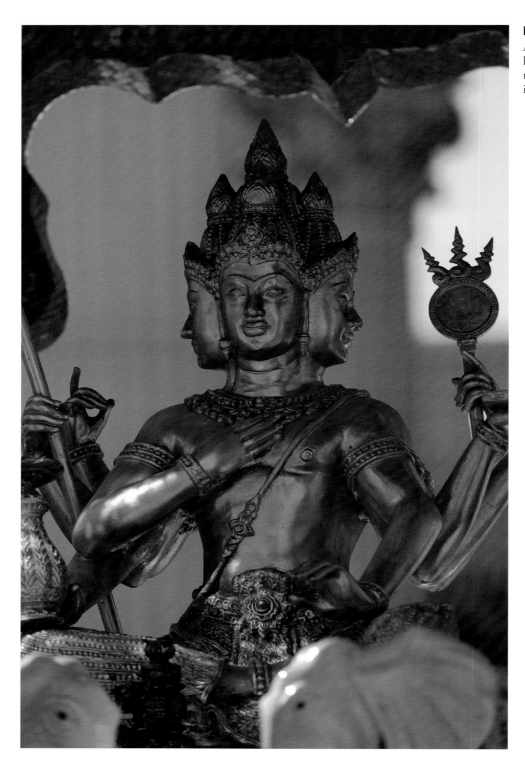

Figure 11.12
A wide f/stop helped isolate the statue from its background.

Avoiding Telephoto Lens Problems

Many of the "problems" that telephoto lenses pose are really just challenges and not that difficult to overcome. Here is a list of the seven most common picture maladies and suggested solutions.

- **Symptom: flat faces in portraits.** Head-and-shoulders portraits of humans tend to be more flattering when a focal length of 50mm to 85mm is used. Longer focal lengths compress the distance between features like noses and ears, making the face look wider and flat. A wide-angle might make noses look huge and ears tiny when you fill the frame with a face. So stick with 50mm to 85mm focal lengths, going longer only when you're forced to shoot from a greater distance, and wider only when shooting three-quarters/full-length portraits, or group shots.

- **Symptom: blur due to camera shake.** Use a higher shutter speed (boosting ISO if necessary), consider an image-stabilized lens, or mount your camera on a tripod, monopod, or brace it with some other support. Of those three solutions, only the first will reduce blur caused by *subject* motion; a VR lens or tripod won't help you freeze a racecar in mid-lap.

- **Symptom: color fringes.** Chromatic aberration is the most pernicious optical problem found in telephoto lenses. There are others, including spherical aberration, astigmatism, coma, curvature of field, and similarly scary-sounding phenomena. The best solution for any of these is to use a better lens that offers the proper degree of correction, or stop down the lens to minimize the problem. But that's not always possible. Your second-best choice may be to correct the fringing in your favorite RAW conversion tool or image editor. Photoshop CS5's Lens Correction filter (found in the Distort menu) offers sliders that minimize both red/cyan and blue/yellow fringing.

- **Symptom: lines that curve inwards.** Pincushion distortion is found in many telephoto lenses. You might find after a bit of testing that it is worse at certain focal lengths with your particular zoom lens. Like chromatic aberration, it can be partially corrected using tools like the correction tools built into Photoshop and Photoshop Elements. You can see an exaggerated example in Figure 11.13; pincushion distortion isn't always this obvious.

- **Symptom: low contrast from haze or fog.** When you're photographing distant objects, a long lens shoots through a lot more atmosphere, which generally is muddied up with extra haze and fog. That dirt or moisture in the atmosphere can reduce contrast and mute colors. Some feel that a skylight or UV filter can help, but this practice is mostly a holdover from the film days. Digital sensors are not sensitive enough to UV light for a UV filter to have much effect. So you should be prepared to boost contrast and color saturation in your Picture Controls menu or image editor if necessary.

■ **Symptom: low contrast from flare.** Lenses are furnished with lens hoods for a good reason: to reduce flare from bright light sources at the periphery of the picture area, or completely outside it. Because telephoto lenses often create images that are lower in contrast in the first place, you'll want to be especially careful to use a lens hood to prevent further effects on your image (or shade the front of the lens with your hand).

■ **Symptom: dark flash photos.** Edge-to-edge flash coverage isn't a problem with telephoto lenses as it is with wide angles. The shooting distance is. A long lens might make a subject that's 50 feet away look as if it's right next to you, but your camera's flash isn't fooled. You'll need extra power for distant flash shots, and probably more power than your D7000's built-in flash provides. The Nikon SB-900 Speedlight, for example, can automatically zoom its coverage down to that of a 105mm medium telephoto lens, providing a theoretical full-power shooting aperture of about f/11 at 30 feet and ISO 400. (Try *that* with the built-in flash!)

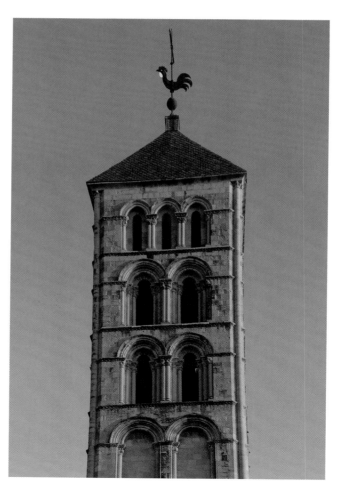

Figure 11.13
Pincushion distortion in telephoto lenses causes lines to bow inwards from the edges.

Telephotos and Bokeh

Bokeh describes the aesthetic qualities of the out-of-focus parts of an image and whether out-of-focus points of light—circles of confusion—are rendered as distracting fuzzy discs or smoothly fade into the background. *Boke* is a Japanese word for "blur," and the h was added to keep English speakers from rendering it monosyllabically to rhyme with *broke*. Although bokeh is visible in blurry portions of any image, it's of particular concern with telephoto lenses, which, thanks to the magic of reduced depth-of-field, produce more obviously out-of-focus areas.

Bokeh can vary from lens to lens, or even within a given lens depending on the f/stop in use. Bokeh becomes objectionable when the circles of confusion are evenly illuminated, making them stand out as distinct discs, or, worse, when these circles are darker in the center, producing an ugly "doughnut" effect. A lens defect called spherical aberration may produce out-of-focus discs that are brighter on the edges and darker in the center, because the lens doesn't focus light passing through the edges of the lens exactly as it does light going through the center. (Mirror or *catadioptric* lenses also produce this effect.)

Other kinds of spherical aberration generate circles of confusion that are brightest in the center and fade out at the edges, producing a smooth blending effect, as you can see at right in Figure 11.14. Ironically, when no spherical aberration is present at all, the

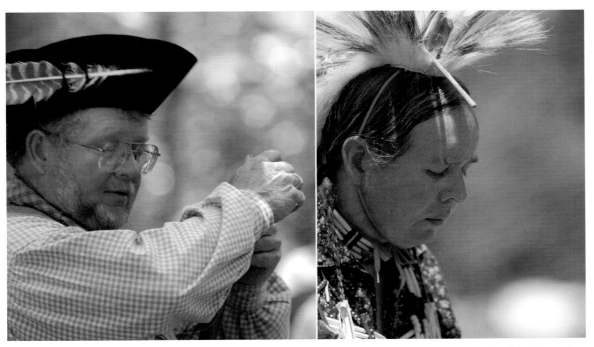

Figure 11.14 Bokeh is less pleasing when the discs are prominent (left), and less obtrusive when they blend into the background (right).

discs are a uniform shade, which, while better than the doughnut effect, is not as pleasing as the bright center/dark edge rendition. The shape of the disc also comes into play, with round smooth circles considered the best, and nonagonal or some other polygon (determined by the shape of the lens diaphragm) considered less desirable.

If you plan to use selective focus a lot, you should investigate the bokeh characteristics of a particular lens before you buy. Nikon user groups and forums will usually be full of comments and questions about bokeh of particular lenses, so the research is fairly easy.

Add-ons and Special Features

Once you've purchased your telephoto lens, you'll want to think about some appropriate accessories for it. There are some handy add-ons available that can be valuable. Here are a couple of them to think about.

Lens Hoods

Lens hoods are an important accessory for all lenses, but they're especially valuable with telephotos. As I mentioned earlier, lens hoods do a good job of preserving image contrast by keeping bright light sources outside the field of view from striking the lens and, potentially, bouncing around inside that long tube to generate flare that, when coupled with atmospheric haze, can rob your image of detail and snap. In addition, lens hoods serve as valuable protection for that large, vulnerable, front lens element. It's easy to forget that you've got that long tube sticking out in front of your camera and accidentally whack the front of your lens into something. It's cheaper to replace a lens hood than it is to have a lens repaired, so you might find that a good hood is valuable protection for your prized optics.

When choosing a lens hood, it's important to have the right hood for the lens, usually the one offered for that lens by Nikon or the third-party manufacturer. You want a hood that blocks precisely the right amount of light: neither too much light nor too little. A hood with a front diameter that is too small can show up in your pictures as vignetting. A hood that has a front diameter that's too large isn't stopping all the light it should. Generic lens hoods may not do the job.

When your telephoto is a zoom lens, it's even more important to get the right hood, because you need one that does what it is supposed to at both the wide-angle and telephoto ends of the zoom range. Lens hoods may be cylindrical, rectangular (shaped like the image frame), or petal shaped (that is, cylindrical, but with cut-out areas at the corners which correspond to the actual image area). Lens hoods should be mounted in the correct orientation (a bayonet mount for the hood usually takes care of this).

Telephoto Converters

Teleconverters (often called telephoto extenders outside the Nikon world) multiply the actual focal length of your lens, giving you a longer telephoto for much less than the price of a lens with that actual focal length. These converters fit between the lens and your camera and contain optical elements that magnify the image produced by the lens. Available in 1.4X, 1.7X, and 2.0X configurations from Nikon, a teleconverter transforms, say, a 200mm lens into a 280mm, 340mm, or 400mm optic, respectively. Given the D7000's crop factor, your 200mm lens now has the same field of view as a 420mm, 510, or 600mm lens on a full-frame camera. At around $300-$400 each, converters are quite a bargain, aren't they?

The only drawback is that Nikon's TC II and TC III teleconverters can be used only with a limited number of Nikkor AF-S lenses. The compatible models include the 200mm f/2G ED-IF AF-S VR Nikkor, 300mm f/2.8G ED-IF AF-S VR Nikkor, 400mm f/2.8D ED-IF AF-S II Nikkor, 80-200mm f/2.8D ED-IF AF-S,70-200mm f/2.8G ED-IF AF-S VR Zoom-Nikkor, 200-400mm f/4G ED-IF AF-S VR Zoom-Nikkor, 300mm f/4D ED-IF AF-S Nikkor, 500mm f/4D ED-IF AF-S II Nikkor, and 600mm f/4D ED-IF AF-S II Nikkor. These tend to be pricey (or ultra-pricey lenses). Teleconverters from Sigma, Kenko, Tamron, and others cost less, and may be compatible with a broader range of lenses. (They work especially well with lenses from the same vendor that produces the teleconverter.)

There are other downsides. While extenders retain the closest focusing distance of your original lens, autofocus is maintained only if the lens's original maximum aperture is f/4 or larger (for the 1.4X extender) or f/2.8 or larger (for the 2X extender). The components reduce the effective aperture of any lens they are used with, by one f/stop with the 1.4X converter, 1.5 f/stops with the 1.7X converter, and 2 f/stops with the 2X extender. So, your 200mm f/2.8 lens becomes a 280mm f/4 or 400mm f/5.6 lens. Although Nikon converters are precision optical devices, they do cost you a little sharpness, but that improves when you reduce the aperture by a stop or two. Each of the converters is compatible only with a particular set of lenses greater, so you'll want to check Nikon's compatibility chart to see if the component can be used with the lens you want to attach to it.

If your lenses are compatible and you're shooting under bright lighting conditions, the Nikon extenders make handy accessories. I recommend the 1.4X version because it robs you of very little sharpness and only one f/stop. The 1.7X version works well, too, but I've found the 2X older TC II teleconverter to exact too much of a sharpness and speed penalty to be of much use. (See Figure 11.15.) The newer TC III model is a better bet.

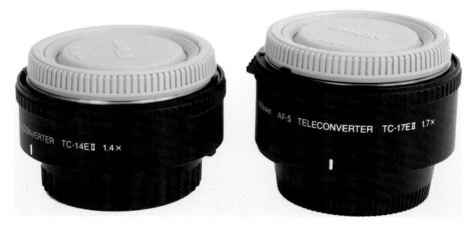

Figure 11.15
Telephoto converters increase the effective focal length of your lenses.

Macro Focusing

Some telephotos and telephoto zooms available for the Nikon D7000 have particularly close focusing capabilities, making them *macro* lenses. Of course, the object is not necessarily to get close (get too close and you'll find it difficult to light your subject). What you're really looking for in a macro lens is to magnify the apparent size of the subject in the final image. Camera-to-subject distance is most important when you want to back up farther from your subject (say, to avoid spooking skittish insects or small animals). In that case, you'll want a macro lens with a longer focal length to allow that distance while retaining the desired magnification.

Nikon makes five lenses that are officially designated as macro lenses. They include:

- **AF-S Micro-Nikkor 60mm f/2.8G ED.** This new type G lens supposedly replaces the type D lens listed next, adding an internal Silent Wave autofocus motor that should operate faster, and which is also compatible with cameras lacking a body motor, such as the Nikon D40/D40x and D60. It also has ED lens elements for improved image quality. However, because it lacks an aperture ring, you can control the f/stop only when the lens is mounted directly on the camera or used with automatic extension tubes. Should you want to reverse a macro lens (which can improve image quality) or mount it on a bellows, you're better off with a lens having an aperture ring.

- **AF Micro-Nikkor 60mm f/2.8D.** This older lens's aperture ring gives it a little more versatility but, realistically, only fanatical close-up shooters actually use the Nikon BR-2a lens reversing ring (which can improve image quality) or mount the lens on a bellows. I happen to belong in that camp, so I am hanging onto mine.

- **AF-S VR Micro-Nikkor 105mm f/2.8G IF-ED.** This G-series lens did replace a similar D-type, non-AF-S version that also lacked VR. I own the older lens, too, and am keeping it for the same reasons described above—but also because I find

VR a rather specialized tool for macro work. Some 99 percent of the time, I shoot close-ups with my D7000 mounted on a tripod or, at the very least, on a monopod, so camera vibration is not much of a concern. Indeed, *subject* movement is a more serious problem, especially when shooting plant life outdoors on days plagued with even slight breezes. Because my outdoor subjects are likely to move while I am composing my photo, I find both VR and autofocus not very useful. I end up focusing manually most of the time, too. This lens provides a little extra camera-to-subject distance, so you'll find it very useful, but consider the older non-G, non-VR version, too, if you're in the market.

- **AF Micro-Nikkor 200mm f/4D IF-ED.** With a price tag of about $1,300, you'd probably want this lens only if you planned a great deal of close-up shooting at greater distances. It focuses down to 1.6 feet, but provides enough magnification to allow interesting close-ups of subjects that are farther away. A specialized tool for specialized shooting.

- **PC Micro-Nikkor 85mm f/2.8D.** Priced about the same as the 200mm Micro-Nikkor, this is a manual focus lens that offers both tilt and shift capabilities, so you can adjust the perspective of the subject as you shoot. The tilt feature lets you "tilt" the plane of focus, providing the illusion of greater depth-of-field (the actual DOF is just distributed differently), while the shift capabilities make it possible to shoot down on a subject from an angle and still maintain its correct proportions. If you need one of these, you already know it; if you're still wondering how you'd use one, you probably have no need for these specialized capabilities.

You'll also find macro lenses, macro zooms, and other close-focusing lenses available from Sigma, Tamron, and Tokina. If you want to focus closer with a macro lens, or any other lens, you can add an accessory called an *extension tube*, like the one shown in Figure 11.16, or a *bellows extension.* These add-ons move the lens farther from the focal plane, allowing it to focus more closely. Nikon and other vendors also sell add-on close-up lenses, which look like filters, and allow lenses to focus more closely.

Figure 11.16
Extension tubes enable any lens to focus more closely to the subject.

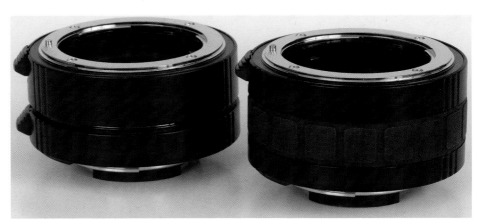

Vibration Reduction

Nikon has a burgeoning line of about a dozen and a half lenses with built-in vibration reduction (VR) capabilities. I expect another half dozen or so new VR lenses to be introduced rather early in the life of this book.

The VR feature uses lens elements that are shifted internally in response to vertical or horizontal motion of the lens, which compensates for any camera shake in those directions. Vibration reduction is particularly effective when used with telephoto lenses, which magnify the effects of camera and photographer motion. However, VR can be useful for lenses of shorter focal lengths, such as Nikon's 16-85mm and 18-55mm VR lenses. Other Nikon VR lenses provide stabilization with zooms that are as wide as 24mm.

Vibration reduction offers two to three shutter speed increments' worth of shake reduction. (Nikon claims a four-stop gain, which I feel may be optimistic.) This extra margin can be invaluable when you're shooting under dim lighting conditions or hand-holding a lens for, say, wildlife photography. Perhaps that shot of a foraging deer would require a shutter speed of 1/2,000th second at f/5.6 with your AF-S VR Zoom-Nikkor 200-400mm f/4G IF-ED lens. Relax. You can shoot at 1/250th second at f/11 and get a photo that is just as sharp, as long as the deer doesn't decide to bound off. Or, perhaps you're shooting indoors and would prefer to shoot at 1/15th second at f/4. Your 16mm-85mm VR lens can grab the shot for you at its wide-angle position. However, consider these facts:

- **VR doesn't freeze subject motion.** Vibration reduction won't freeze moving subjects in their tracks, because it is effective only at compensating for *camera* motion. It's best used in reduced illumination, to steady the up-down swaying of telephoto lenses, and to improve close-up photography. If your subject is in motion, you'll still need a shutter speed that's fast enough to stop the action.

- **VR adds to shutter lag.** The process of adjusting the lens elements, like autofocus, takes time, so vibration reduction may contribute to a slight increase in shutter lag. If you're shooting sports, that delay may be annoying, but I still use my VR lenses for sports all the time!

- **Use when appropriate.** You may find that your results are worse when using VR while panning, although newer Nikon VR lenses work fine when the camera is deliberately moved from side to side during exposure. Older lenses can confuse the panning motion with camera wobble and provide too much compensation. If you're not sure how your particular lens performs, you might want to switch off VR when panning or when your camera is mounted on a tripod.

- **Do you need VR at all?** Remember that an inexpensive monopod might be able to provide the same additional steadiness as a VR lens, at a much lower cost. If you're out in the field shooting wild animals or flowers and think a tripod isn't practical, try a monopod first.

VIBRATION REDUCTION: IN THE CAMERA OR IN THE LENS?

Sony's acquisition of Konica Minolta's dSLR assets and the introduction of an improved in-camera image-stabilization system has revised an old debate about whether VR belongs in the camera or in the lens. Perhaps it's my Nikon bias showing, but I am quite happy not to have vibration reduction available in the body itself. Here are some reasons:

- Should in-camera VR fail, you have to send the whole camera in for repair, and camera repairs are generally more expensive than lens repairs. I like being able to simply switch to another lens if I have a VR problem.

- VR in the camera doesn't steady your view in the viewfinder, whereas a VR lens shows you a steadied image as you shoot.

- You're stuck with the VR system built into your camera. If an improved system is incorporated into a lens and the improvements are important to you, just trade in your old lens for the new one.

The original AF-S VR Zoom-Nikkor 70-200mm f/2.8G IF-ED, which I discuss next in terms of its role in the Nikon lens menagerie's ideal "Magic Three" (discussed below) is typical of the VR lenses Nikon offers. It has the basic controls shown in Figure 11.17, to adjust focus range (full, or limited to infinity down to 2.5 meters); VR On/Off; and Normal VR/Active VR (the latter an aggressive mode used in extreme situations, such as a moving car). Not visible (it's over the horizon, so to speak) is the M/A-M focus mode switch, which allows changing from autofocus (with manual override) to manual focus. There's also a focus lock button near the front of the lens (see Figure 11.18). I often use the rotating tripod mount collar as a grip for the lens when shooting hand-held, and, as you can see in Figure 11.19, I've replaced the factory tripod mounting foot with Kirk's Arca-Swiss-compatible quick release mount foot.

Figure 11.17
On the Nikon 70-200mm VR zoom you'll find (top to bottom): the focus limit switch, VR on/off switch, and Normal/ Active VR adjustment.

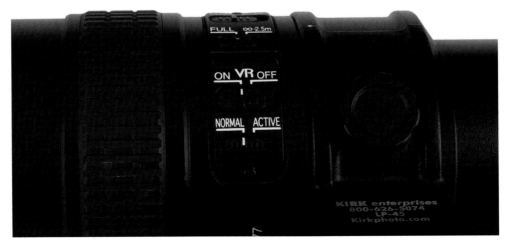

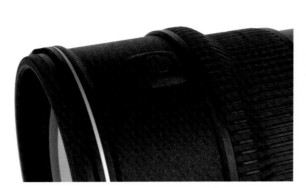

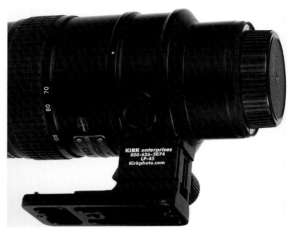

Figure 11.18 The lens also includes an autofocus lock button that can be activated while holding the lens.

Figure 11.19 The rotating collar allows mounting the lens/camera to a tripod in vertical or horizontal orientations—or anything in-between.

Your Second (and Third…) Lens

There are really only two advantages to using just a single lens. One of them is creative. Keeping one set of optics mounted on your D7000 all the time forces you to be especially imaginative in your approach to your subjects. I once visited Europe with only a single camera body and a 35mm f/2 lens. The experience was actually quite exciting, because I had to use a variety of techniques to allow that one lens to serve for landscapes, available light photos, action, close-ups, portraits, and other kinds of images.

Of course, it's more likely that your "single" lens is actually a zoom, which is, in truth, many lenses in one, taking you from, say, 16mm to 85mm (or some other range) with a rapid twist of the zoom ring. You'll still find some creative challenges when you stick to a single zoom lens's focal lengths.

The second advantage of the unilens camera is only a marginal technical benefit since the introduction of the Nikon D7000. If you don't exchange lenses, the chances of dust and dirt getting inside your D7000 and settling on the sensor is reduced (but *not* eliminated entirely). Although I've known some photographers who minimized the number of lens changes they made for this very reason, reducing the number of lenses you work with is not a productive or rewarding approach for most of us. Recent Nikon cameras, like the D7000, have an automatic sensor cleaning feature that has made this "advantage" much less significant than it was in the past.

It's more likely that you'll succumb to the malady known as *Lens Lust*, which is defined as an incurable disease marked by a significant yen for newer, better, longer, faster, sharper, anything-er optics for your camera. (And, it must be noted, this disease can *cost* you significant yen—or dollars, or whatever currency you use.) In its worst manifestations, sufferers find themselves with lenses that have overlapping zoom ranges or capabilities, because one or the other offers a slight margin in performance or suitability for specific tasks. When you find yourself already lusting after a new lens before you've really had a chance to put your latest purchase to the test, you'll know the disease has reached the terminal phase.

In this final part of the chapter, I'm going to discuss some specific Nikon lenses that I have experience with, and provide some recommendations. That's not to say that I use only Nikon lenses; I absolutely love my 10-17mm Tokina fisheye zoom lens, and couldn't afford a zoom that reaches all the way out to 500mm if I hadn't been able to pick up my 170-500mm Sigma zoom lens second-hand for an excellent price. But there are so many lens options available that it makes more sense to confine my comments to the true-blue Nikkors that I've had experience with.

The Magic Three

If you cruise the forums, you'll find the same three lenses mentioned over and over, often referred to as "The Trinity," "The Magic Three," or some other affectionate nickname. They are the three lenses you'll find in the kit of just about every serious Nikon photographer (including me). They're fast, expensive, heavier than you might expect, and provide such exquisite image quality that once you equip yourself with the Trinity, you'll never be happy with anything else.

Until, perhaps, now. Nikon has muddied the waters recently by introducing some new lenses that have displaced the original magic trio. Moreover, D7000 owners just might be happier with a triad-plus-one that I'm going to describe.

The Original Magic Three

For a significant number of years, the most commonly cited "ideal" lenses for "serious" Nikon digital SLRs (meaning the D200, D300, and D2xs) were the 17-35mm f/2.8, 28-70mm f/2.8, and 70-200 f/2.8 VR. The trio share a number of attributes. All three are non-DX lenses that (theoretically) work equally well on film cameras, the full-frame Nikon D3/D3x and D700, as well as DX cameras like the D7000, making for a sound investment in optics that could be used on any Nikon SLR, past or future.

All three incorporate internal Silent Wave motors and focus incredibly fast. They all have f/2.8 maximum apertures that are *constant*; they don't change as the lens is zoomed in or out. All three are internal focusing (IF) models that don't change length as they focus, and include extra-low dispersion (ED) elements. And, all three are expensive, at $1,400-$1,600. But, as I discovered when I added this set, once you have them, you don't need any other lenses unless you're doing field sports like football or soccer, extreme wide-angle, or close-up photography. I generally take these three lenses with me every-where, adding another lens or two as required for specialized needs.

- **AF-S Zoom-Nikkor 17-35mm f/2.8D IF-ED.** When I am shooting landscapes, doing street photography, or some types of indoor sports, this lens goes on my D7000 and never comes off. It was my main lens on my last trip to Europe; I was traveling light and took this one, a 10-17mm Tokina fisheye zoom, and my 28-200mm Nikkor G lens (in place of my humongous 70-200 VR lens), and didn't need anything else. It's one of the two or three sharpest lenses I own, and focuses down to about 1 foot, so I can use it for close-ups of flowers and other macro sub-jects. With the DX 1.5X crop factor, it serves as a highly versatile medium wide-angle to normal lens.

- **AF-S Zoom-Nikkor 28-70mm f/2.8D IF-ED.** Nicknamed "The Beast" because of its size and weight, this lens, too, is wonderfully sharp, and well-suited for any-thing from sports to portraiture that falls within its focal length lens. I know many photographers who aren't heavily into landscapes who use this lens as their main lens. With its impressive lens hood mounted, The Beast is useful for terrifying small children, too.

- **AF-S VR Zoom-Nikkor 70-200mm f/2.8G IF-ED.** This legendary lens is perfect for some indoor and many outdoor sports, on a monopod, or hand-held, and can be used for portraiture, street photography, wildlife (especially with the 1.4X tele-converter), and even distant scenics. I use it for concerts, too, alternating between this lens and my 85mm f/1.4. It takes me in close to the performer, and can be used wide-open or at f/4 with good image quality. The only time I leave it behind is when I need to travel light (although it's not really that huge). This is the only lens of the magic trio that lacks an aperture ring, but you probably won't be using it with a bel-lows extension, anyway.

FULL-FRAME FOLLY?

The only "problem" with the original 70-200mm lens is that it produces noticeable vignetting and reduced sharpness in the corners at many focal lengths when used on a full-frame camera like the Nikon D3s/D3x, or D700. D7000 owners won't see any of these characteristics at all, because of the crop factor, and the vignetting and slight soft-ness disappear on full-frame cameras when used with a 1.4X teleconverter. To be honest, I've had wonderful results with this lens even with my full-frame cameras. I don't shoot landscapes or brick walls with 70 to 200mm focal lengths, and for the portrait and fash-ion work I do, the corners aren't important. If you plan to use your D7000 and a full-frame Nikon camera, you should keep this "shortcoming" of the original 70-200mm zoom in mind.

To the Original Magic Trio, I often recommend adding one (or both) of these lenses:

- **AF Nikkor 85mm f/1.4D IF.** The nickname of this lens is "The Cream Machine" because of its remarkably smooth bokeh, which provides absolutely gorgeous out-of-focus backgrounds, especially when the lens is used with a wide aperture. It's incredibly sharp, and can definitely be used at f/1.4. The 85mm f/1.4 is the perfect portrait lens, and can be used wide-open without qualms. If you need this sort of lens, it's almost a bargain at its $1,000 price, and worth the extra $600 over its 85mm f/1.8 counterpart. Both Nikon 85mm lenses are D-series AF, rather than G-type AF-S lenses, and are becoming long in the tooth, so you might want to look for one now before they are entirely supplanted by the much more expensive new AF-S 85mm f/1.4G version, which has a $1,700 price tag.

- **AF-S DX Zoom-Nikkor 10-24mm f/3.5-4.5G IF-ED.** If you need a slightly wider view than that provided by the Trio's 17-35mm f/2.8, this lens makes a good supplement. It could never replace my 17-35 fave in terms of sharpness and freedom from aberrations, but, since I already own one, I'm keeping it for those times when I want to capture something requiring the field of view of a 10-16mm (or slightly longer) lens. The overlap between this lens and the 17-35mm doesn't bother me; it just means I don't have to swap lenses quite as often. Each will do a little of what the other one is best at. One disadvantage of this lens is that it won't cover the full-frame of an FX-format camera like the Nikon D3s, so you can't use it effectively if you upgrade in the future.

The New Magic Three

There are new sheriffs in town: a whole new Magic 3. Two were introduced with the original D3 and D300: an AF-S Nikkor 14-24mm f/2.8G ED, and an AF-S Nikkor 24-70mm f/2.8G ED lens. Both are G-type lenses (they lack an aperture ring), have AF-S focusing, and have constant f/2.8 apertures. In 2009, Nikon announced a replacement for the 70-200mm VR lens, rounding out the Magic Trio with an all new lineup. Like the original big three, these are all full-frame lenses that work with any DX or FX-format Nikon camera.

The chief advantage of the new lineup (if you can call it that) is that there is no overlap. You can go from 14-24mm to 24-70mm to 70-200mm with no gaps in coverage. I don't find that an overwhelming advantage, because there are lots of situations in which the 17-35mm range of my existing lens is exactly what I need; if I used the "new" trio exclusively, I'd find myself swapping lenses whenever I needed more than a 24mm focal length.

So, I now own both the new 14-24mm f/2.8 zoom *and* the old 17-35mm f/2.8 lens—and I use them both about equally. The 14-24mm gives me a bit more wide-angle perspective than the 17-35mm lens, and it is fabulously sharp. I use the 17-35mm lens when I think I'll need the longer focal length, when I want to shoot semi-macro pictures of, say, flowers, and when I am traveling light. For example, when shooting in Europe I take along the 17-35mm lens (which is *much* smaller than the 14-24, and can be used with polarizing filters, to boot), and my 28-200mm zoom.

Carefully consider the focal lengths you need before deciding which "magic" triad is best for you. The new lineup looks like this:

- **AF-S Nikkor 14-24mm f/2.8G ED.** I never cease to be amazed by this lens, and its image quality is incredible, with very low barrel distortion (outward bowing at the edges) and very little of the chromatic aberrations common to lenses this wide. Because it has full-frame coverage, it's immune to obsolescence. It focuses down to 10.8 inches, allowing for some interesting close-up/wide-angle effects. The downside? The outward curving front element precludes the use of most filters, although I haven't tried this lens with add-on Cokin-style filter holders yet. (The one from Lee is very, very expensive.) Lack of filter compatibility isn't a fatal flaw for D7000 users, as the use of polarizers would be problematic in any case. The polarizing effect would be highly variable because of this lens's extremely wide field of view.

- **AF-S Nikkor 24-70mm f/2.8G ED.** This lens seems to provide even better image quality than the legendary Beast, especially when used wide open or in flare-inducing environments. (You can credit the new internal Nano Crystal Coat treatment for that improvement.) My recommendation is that if you already own The Beast, or can get one used for a good price ($1,000 or less), you don't sacrifice much going with the older 28-70mm lens, and may find the overlap with the 14-24mm lens useful. But if you have the cash and opportunity to purchase this newer lens, you won't be making a mistake. Some were surprised when it was introduced without the VR feature, but Nikon has kept the size of this useful lens down, while maintaining a reasonable price for a "pro" level lens.

- **AF-S VR II Zoom-Nikkor 70-200mm f/2.8G IF-ED.** Not a lot to be added about the latest version of this lens, which is a worthy representative of the telephoto zoom range in this "ideal" trio of lenses. It does have better performance in the corners on full-frame cameras, but its other attributes remain the same. The one exception is the magnification at long focal lengths and very close focusing distances. Due to a quirk in optical design (common to many zoom lenses of this type, not just this particular Nikon lens), the magnification or image size is much less when you're shooting subjects at focal lengths from about 150-200mm at distances of a couple yards. You might end up with an image that is the same size, in the frame, as one taken with a 135mm fixed focal length lens. That's quite a reduction in magnification, but it won't affect most people. I *do* happen to shoot with my 70-200mm lens at close distances and zoomed all the way to 200mm, so I've retained my old VR I version and have no plans to upgrade to this newer lens.

Fine-Tuning the Focus of Your Lenses

In Chapter 10, I introduced you to the D7000's AF Fine tune capability. In this section, I'll show you how to calibrate your lenses using this feature.

Why is the focus "off" for some lenses in the first place? There are lots of factors, including the age of the lens (an older lens may focus slightly differently), temperature effects on certain types of glass, humidity, and tolerances built into a lens's design that all add up to a slight misadjustment, even though the components themselves are, strictly speaking, within specs. A very slight variation in your lens's mount can cause focus to vary slightly. With any luck (if you can call it that) a lens that doesn't focus exactly right will at least be consistent. If a lens always focuses a bit behind the subject, the symptom is *back focus*. If it focuses in front of the subject, it's called *front focus*.

As I noted, you're almost always better off sending such a lens in to Nikon to have them make it right. But that's not always possible. Perhaps you need your lens recalibrated right now, or you purchased a gray market lens that Nikon isn't willing to fix. If you want to do it yourself, the first thing to do is determine whether or not your lens has a back focus or front focus problem.

For a quick-and-dirty diagnosis (*not* a calibration; you'll use a different target for that), lay down a piece of graph paper on a flat surface, and place an object on the line at the middle, which will represent the point of focus (we hope). Then, shoot the target at an angle using your lens's widest aperture and the autofocus mode you want to test. Mount the camera on a tripod so you can get accurate, repeatable results.

If your camera/lens combination doesn't suffer from front or back focus, the point of sharpest focus will be the center line of the chart, as you can see in Figure 11.20. If you do have a problem, one of the other lines will be sharply focused instead. Should you discover that your lens consistently front or back focuses, it needs to be recalibrated. Unfortunately, it's only possible to calibrate a lens for a single focusing distance. So, if you use a particular lens (such as a macro lens) for close-focusing, calibrate for that. If you use a lens primarily for middle distances, calibrate for that. Close-to-middle distances are most likely to cause focus problems, anyway, because as you get closer to infinity, small changes in focus are less likely to have an effect.

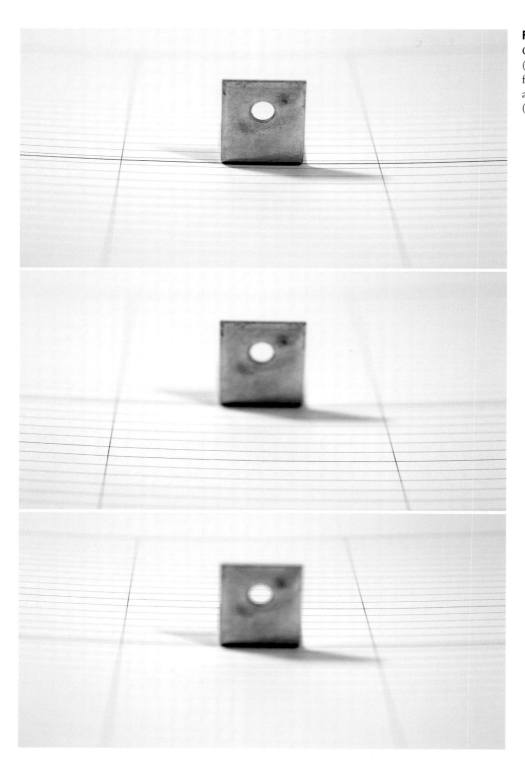

Figure 11.20
Correct focus (top), front focus (middle), and back focus (bottom).

Lens Tune-up

The key tool you can use to fine-tune your lens is the AF Fine tune entry in the Setup menu, shown in Figure 11.21. You'll find the process easier to understand if you first run through this quick overview of the menu options:

- **AF fine tune (On/Off).** This option enables/disables AF fine-tuning for all the lenses you've defined using the menu entry. If you discover you don't care for the calibrations you make in certain situations (say, it works better for the lens you have mounted at middle distances, but is less successful at correcting close-up focus errors) you can deactivate the feature as you require. You should set this to On when you're doing the actual fine-tuning.

- **Saved value.** This setting lets you tune the autofocus calibration for the current CPU-chipped lens (virtually all Nikon-brand autofocus lenses) mounted on the D7000. When you first fine-tune a lens, the saved value will be 0 (zero). You can press the multi selector up/down buttons to choose a value between +20 and –20. Positive numbers move the focal point farther from the camera, and would be used if your lens consistently suffers from front focus problems. Negative numbers move the focal point closer to the camera, and would be used if your lens is plagued with consistent back focus. The value is relative, and doesn't correlate to any particular distance or percentage.

Figure 11.21
The AF Fine tune menu.

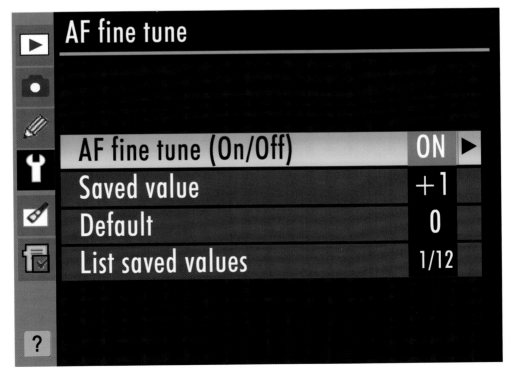

■ **Default.** This entry often confuses. It is a value that is applied to *every* lens mounted on the camera that doesn't already have a customized saved value associated with it. That is, if your D7000 has consistent front or back focus problems with *all* lenses, you can enter a value here, and the camera will apply the correction to each CPU lens you use. This default setting can be overridden by saved values you've stored for particular lenses. So, you can change the default focal plane for all lenses, and still further fine-tune specific lenses that need more autofocus correction. My recommendation is that if your camera and lenses are so out of whack that you need global correction and individual fine-tuning, you *really* ought to consider shipping the whole kit off to Nikon for proper calibration.

■ **List saved values.** This screen shows you the saved fine-tuning values for all lenses. If the currently mounted lens has a stored value, it will be marked with a solid black box icon. You can delete lenses from this list by highlighting them and pressing the Trash button. You can also change the number (a two-digit number from 00-99) used to identify a particular lens.

Evaluate Current Focus

The first step is to capture a baseline image that represents how the lens you want to fine-tune autofocuses at a particular distance. You'll often see advice for photographing a test chart with millimeter markings from an angle, and the suggestion that you auto-focus on a particular point on the chart. Supposedly, the markings that actually *are* in focus will help you recalibrate your lens. The problem with this approach is that the information you get from photographing a test chart at an angle doesn't actually tell you what to do to make a precise correction. So, your lens back focuses three millimeters behind the target area on the chart. So what? Does that mean you change the Saved Value by –3 clicks? Or –15 clicks? Angled targets are a "shortcut" that don't save you time.

Instead, you'll want to photograph a target that represents what you're actually trying to achieve: a plane of focus locked in by your lens that represents the actual plane of focus of your subject. For that, you'll need a flat target, mounted precisely perpendicular to the sensor plane of the camera. Then, you can take a photo, see if the plane of focus is correct, and if not, dial in a bit of fine-tuning in the AF Fine tuning menu, and shoot again. Lather, rinse, and repeat until the target is sharply focused.

You can use the focus target shown in Figure 11.22, or you can use a chart of your own, as long as it has contrasty areas that will be easily seen by the autofocus system, and without very small details that are likely to confuse the AF. Download your own copy of my chart from www.nikonguides.com/FocusChart.pdf. Then print out a copy on the

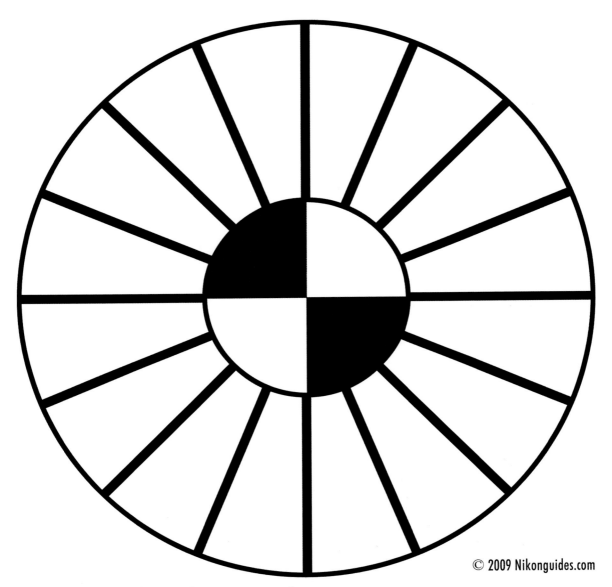

© 2009 Nikonguides.com

Figure 11.22 Use this focus test chart, or create one of your own.

largest paper your printer can handle. (I don't recommend just displaying the file on your monitor and focusing on that; it's unlikely you'll have the monitor screen lined up perfectly perpendicular to the camera sensor.) Then, follow these steps:

1. **Position the camera.** Place your Nikon D7000 on a sturdy tripod with a remote release attached, positioned at roughly eye-level at a distance from a wall that represents the distance you want to test for. Keep in mind that autofocus problems can be different at varying distances and lens focal lengths, and that you can enter only *one* correction value for a particular lens. So, choose a distance (close-up or mid range) and zoom setting with your shooting habits in mind.

2. **Set the autofocus mode.** Choose the autofocus mode (AF-C or AF-S) you want to test.

3. **Level the camera (in an ideal world).** If the wall happens to be perfectly perpendicular, you can use a bubble level, plumb bob, or other device of your choice to ensure that the camera is level to match. Many tripods and tripod heads have bubble levels built in. Avoid using the center column, if you can. When the camera is properly oriented, lock the legs and tripod head tightly.

4. **Level the camera (in the real world).** If your wall is not perfectly perpendicular, use this old trick. Tape a mirror to the wall, and then adjust the camera on the tripod so that when you look through the viewfinder at the mirror, you see directly into the reflection of the lens. Then, lock the tripod and remove the mirror.

5. **Mount the test chart.** Tape the test chart on the wall so it is centered in your camera's viewfinder.

6. **Photograph the test chart using AF.** Allow the camera to autofocus, and take a test photo, using the remote release to avoid shaking or moving the camera.

7. **Make an adjustment and rephotograph.** Make a fine-tuning adjustment and photograph the target again. Follow the instructions in the next section. I've separated the fine-tuning adjustments from these steps because some people may want to just tweak the focus at a later time without going through all these evaluation steps. Repeat steps 1-8 in the section that follows this one to make evaluation images at a range of corrections, say, −5 through +5.

8. **Evaluate the image.** If you have the camera connected to your computer with a USB cable and Camera Control Pro or other linkup software such as Nikon Transfer, or through a WiFi connection, so much the better. You can view the image after it's transferred to your computer. Otherwise, *carefully* open the camera card door and slip the memory card out and copy the images to your computer.

9. **Evaluate focus.** Which image is sharpest? That's the setting you need to use for this lens. If your initial range doesn't provide the correction you need, repeat the steps between −20 and +20 until you find the best fine-tuning.

Changing the Fine-Tuning Setting

Adjust the fine-tuning for the lens you have mounted on the camera by following these steps:

1. If you haven't been running the test described previously, mount the CPU-equipped lens you want to fine-tune on the Nikon D7000. The camera will automatically recognize the lens you are using during the "calibration" process and display its name on the screen.

2. If you haven't already done so, choose AF Fine tune (On/Off) and turn it ON.

3. Select Saved Value.

4. Press the multi selector up/down buttons to tell the D7000 to adjust the autofocus from +20 (move the focal point away from the camera to fix front-focus problems) to –20 values (move the focal point toward the camera to fix back focus). (See Figure 11.23.)

5. Press OK when the value you want is entered. You may have to run the test described above several times and use some trial and error to determine the correct adjustment.

Figure 11.23
Change a Saved Value for a particular lens.

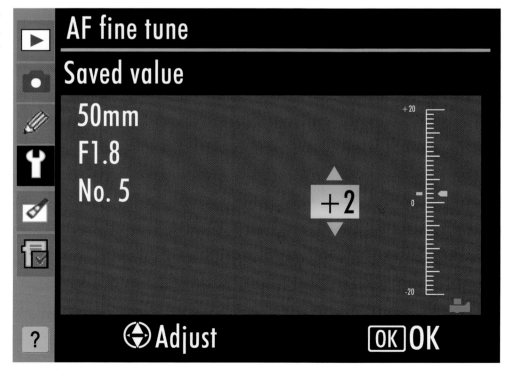

6. Choose List Saved Values to see the lenses you've fine-tuned. (See Figure 11.24.)

7. Assign a lens identifier from 00 to 99 to the lens you've just calibrated. This identifier can be used to differentiate a particular lens from other lenses of the same type, if you own, say, some duplicate lenses. That's not as far-fetched as you might think. Some organizations, such as newspapers, allow their photographers to use favorite lenses exclusively, but may need to share other optics among several photographers. If you don't know which of the pooled AF-S Nikkor 600mm f/4G ED VR lenses you'll be using on any particular day, you can calibrate your camera separately for each of them. (See Figure 11.25.)

8. Press MENU to exit.

Set Default Value

If you want to set a default value for lenses that aren't in your Saved Values list (say, because your camera always back or front focuses slightly), choose the Default setting from the AF Fine Tune menu, and adjust as shown in Figure 11.26.

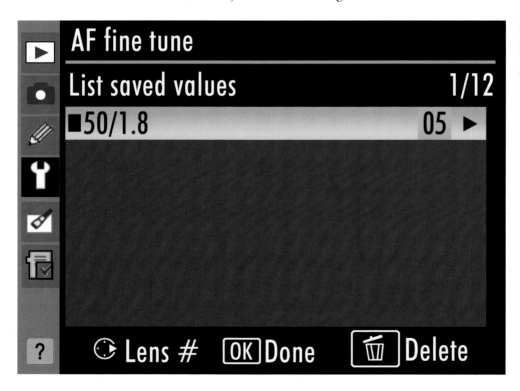

Figure 11.24
List the Saved Values you've stored.

Figure 11.25
Assign a lens number, if necessary, to differentiate a particular lens from other lenses of the same type you may use.

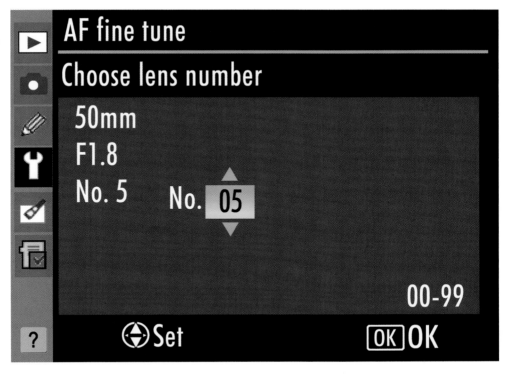

Figure 11.26
Choose a default value to be applied to all lenses not already fine-tuned.

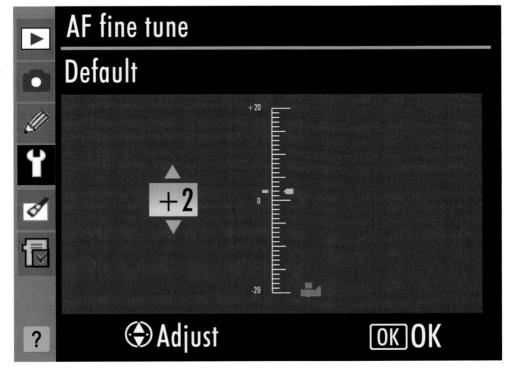

12

Making Light Work for You

Successful photographers and artists have an intimate understanding of the importance of light in shaping an image. Rembrandt was a master of using light to create moods and reveal the character of his subjects. Artist Thomas Kinkade's official tagline is "Painter of Light." The late Dean Collins, co-founder of Finelight Studios, revolutionized how a whole generation of photographers learned and used lighting. Photo guru Ed Pierce conducts seminars called "Captivated by the Light," that reveal his secrets for portrait lighting. It's impossible to underestimate how the use of light adds to—and how misuse can detract from—your photographs.

All forms of visual art use light to shape the finished product. Sculptors don't have control over the light used to illuminate their finished work, so they must create shapes using planes and curved surfaces so that the form envisioned by the artist comes to life from a variety of viewing and lighting angles. Painters, in contrast, have absolute control over both shape and light in their work, as well as the viewing angle, so they can use both the contours of their two-dimensional subjects and the qualities of the "light" they use to illuminate those subjects to evoke the image they want to produce.

Photography is a third form of art. The photographer may have little or no control over the subject (other than posing human subjects) but can often adjust both viewing angle *and* the nature of the light source to create a particular compelling image. The direction and intensity of the light sources create the shapes and textures that we see. The distribution and proportions determine the contrast and tonal values: whether the image is stark or high key, or muted and low in contrast. The colors of the light (because even "white" light has a color balance that the sensor can detect), and how much of those colors the subject reflects or absorbs, paint the hues visible in the image.

As a Nikon D7000 photographer, you must learn to be a painter and sculptor of light if you want to move from *taking* a picture to *making* a photograph. This chapter provides an introduction to using the two main types of illumination: *continuous* lighting (such as daylight, incandescent, or fluorescent sources) and the brief, but brilliant snippets of light we call *electronic flash*.

Continuous Illumination versus Electronic Flash

Continuous lighting is exactly what you might think: uninterrupted illumination that is available all the time during a shooting session. Daylight, moonlight, and the artificial lighting encountered both indoors and outdoors count as continuous light sources (although all of them can be "interrupted" by passing clouds, solar eclipses, a blown fuse, or simply by switching a lamp off). Indoor continuous illumination includes both the lights that are there already (such as incandescent lamps or overhead fluorescent lights indoors) and fixtures you supply yourself, including photoflood lamps or reflectors used to bounce existing light onto your subject.

Electronic flash is notable because it can be much more intense than continuous lighting, lasts only a brief moment, and can be much more portable than supplementary incandescent sources. It's a light source you can carry with you and use anywhere.

Indeed, your Nikon D7000 has a flip-up electronic flash unit built in, as shown in Figure 12.1. But you can also use an external flash, either mounted on the D7000's

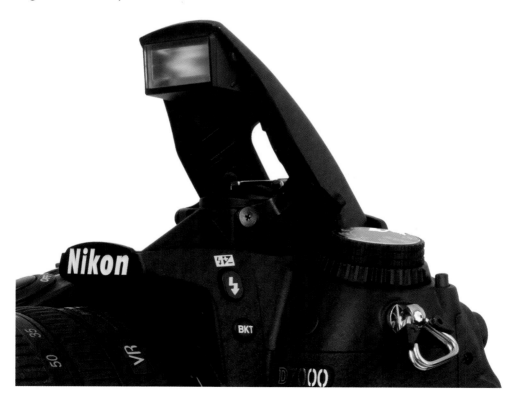

Figure 12.1
One form of light that's always available is the flip-up flash on your Nikon D7000.

accessory shoe or used off-camera and linked with a cable or triggered by the D7000's wireless Commander mode. Studio flash units are electronic flash, too, and aren't limited to "professional" shooters, as there are economical "monolight" (one-piece flash/power supply) units available in the $200 price range. Anyone can buy a couple to store in a closet and use to set up a home studio, or use as supplementary lighting when traveling away from home.

Figure 12.2
You always know how the lighting will look when using continuous illumination.

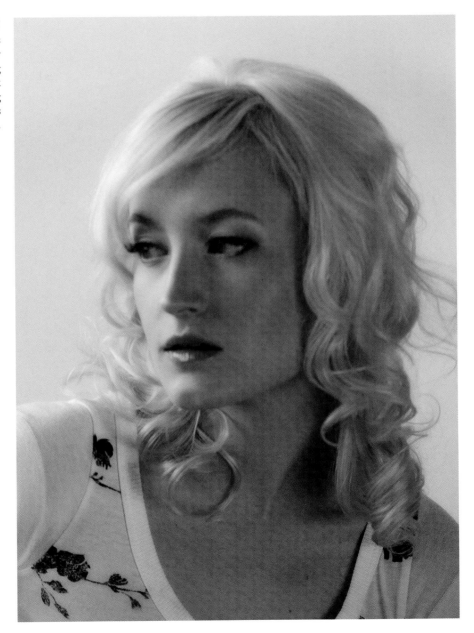

There are advantages and disadvantages to each type of illumination. Here's a quick checklist of pros and cons:

- **Lighting preview—Pro: continuous lighting.** With continuous lighting, you always know exactly what kind of lighting effect you're going to get and, if multiple lights are used, how they will interact with each other (see Figure 12.2).

- **Lighting preview—Con: electronic flash.** With flash, the general effect you're going to see may be a mystery until you've built some experience, and you may need to review a shot on the LCD, make some adjustments, and then reshoot to get the look you want. (In this sense, a digital camera's review capabilities replace the Polaroid test shots pro photographers relied on in decades past.)

- **Exposure calculation—Pro: continuous lighting.** Your D7000 has no problem calculating exposure for continuous lighting, because it remains constant and can be measured through a sensor that interprets the light reaching the viewfinder. The amount of light available just before the exposure will, in almost all cases, be the same amount of light present when the shutter is released. The D7000's Spot metering mode can be used to measure and compare the proportions of light in the highlights and shadows, so you can make an adjustment (such as using more or less fill light) if necessary. You can even use a hand-held light meter to measure the light yourself.

- **Exposure calculation—Con: electronic flash.** Electronic flash illumination doesn't exist until the flash fires, and so can't be measured by the D7000's exposure sensor when the mirror is flipped up during the exposure. Instead, the light must be measured by metering the intensity of a pre-flash triggered an instant before the main flash, as it is reflected back to the camera and through the lens. An alternative is to use a sensor built into the external flash itself and measure reflected light that has not traveled through the lens. If you have a do-it-yourself bent, there are hand-held flash meters, too, including models that measure both flash and continuous light.

- **Evenness of illumination—Pro/con: continuous lighting.** Of continuous light sources, daylight, in particular, provides illumination that tends to fill an image completely, lighting up the foreground, background, and your subject almost equally. Shadows do come into play, of course, so you might need to use reflectors or fill-in light sources to even out the illumination further, but barring objects that block large sections of your image from daylight, the light is spread fairly evenly. Indoors, however, continuous lighting is commonly less evenly distributed. The average living room, for example, has hot spots and dark corners. But on the plus side, you can *see* this uneven illumination and compensate with additional lamps.

- **Evenness of illumination—Con: electronic flash.** Electronic flash units, like continuous light sources such as lamps that don't have the advantage of being located 93 million miles from the subject, suffer from the effects of their proximity. The *inverse square law*, first applied to both gravity and light by Sir Isaac Newton, dictates that as a light source's distance increases from the subject, the amount of light reaching the subject falls off proportionately to the square of the distance. In plain English, that means that a flash or lamp that's eight feet away from a subject provides only one-quarter as much illumination as a source that's four feet away (rather than half as much). (See Figure 12.3.) This translates into relatively shallow "depth-of-light."

- **Action stopping—Con: continuous lighting.** Action stopping with continuous light sources is completely dependent on the shutter speed you've dialed in on the camera. And the speeds available are dependent on the amount of light available and your ISO sensitivity setting. Outdoors in daylight, there will probably be enough sunlight to let you shoot at 1/2,000th second and f/6.3 with a non-grainy sensitivity setting of ISO 400. That's a fairly useful combination of settings if you're not using a super-telephoto with a small maximum aperture. But inside, the reduced illumination quickly has you pushing your D7000 to its limits. For example, if you're shooting indoor sports, there probably won't be enough available light to allow you to use a 1/2,000th second shutter speed (although I routinely shoot indoor basketball with my D7000 at ISO 1600 and 1/500th second at f/4). In many indoor sports situations, you may find yourself limited to 1/500th second or slower.

Figure 12.3

A light source that is twice as far away provides only one-quarter as much illumination.

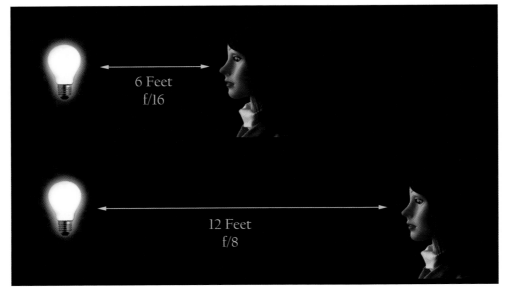

6 Feet
f/16

12 Feet
f/8

■ **Action stopping—Pro: electronic flash.** When it comes to the ability to freeze moving objects in their tracks, the advantage goes to electronic flash. The brief duration of electronic flash serves as a very high "shutter speed" when the flash is the main or only source of illumination for the photo. Your D7000's shutter speed may be set for 1/250th second during a flash exposure, but if the flash illumination predominates, the *effective* exposure time will be the 1/1,000th to 1/50,000th second or less duration of the flash, as you can see in Figure 12.4, in a shot by Cleveland photographer Kris Bosworth, because the flash unit reduces the amount of light released by cutting short the duration of the flash. The only fly in the ointment is that, if the ambient light is strong enough, it may produce a secondary, "ghost" exposure, as I'll explain later in this chapter.

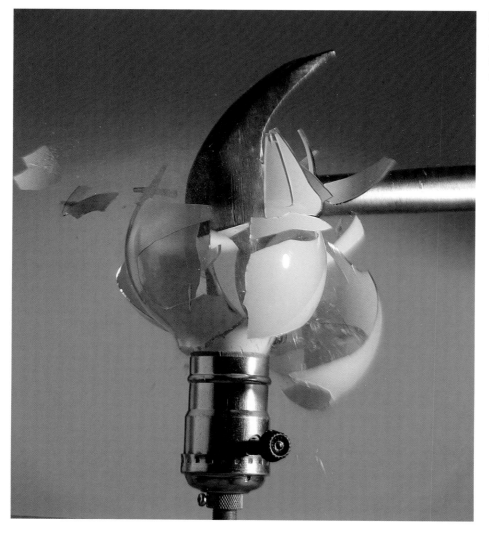

Figure 12.4
Electronic flash can freeze almost any action.

- **Cost—Pro: continuous lighting.** Incandescent or fluorescent lamps are generally much less expensive than electronic flash units, which can easily cost several hundred dollars. I've used everything from desktop high-intensity lamps to reflector flood lights for continuous illumination at very little cost. There are lamps made especially for photographic purposes, too. Maintenance is economical, too: many incandescent or fluorescents use bulbs that cost only a few dollars.

- **Cost—Con: electronic flash.** Electronic flash units aren't particularly cheap. The lowest-cost dedicated flash designed specifically for the Nikon dSLRs is about $110. Such units are limited in features, however, and intended for those with entry-level cameras. Plan on spending some money to get the features that a sophisticated electronic flash offers.

- **Flexibility—Con: continuous lighting.** Because incandescent and fluorescent lamps are not as bright as electronic flash, the slower shutter speeds required (see Action stopping, above) mean that you may have to use a tripod more often, especially when shooting portraits. The incandescent variety of continuous lighting gets hot, especially in the studio, and the side effects range from discomfort (for your human models) to disintegration (if you happen to be shooting perishable foods like ice cream). The heat also makes it more difficult to add filtration to incandescent sources.

- **Flexibility—Pro: electronic flash.** Electronic flash's action-freezing power allows you to work without a tripod in the studio (and elsewhere), adding flexibility and speed when choosing angles and positions. Flash units can be easily filtered, and, because the filtration is placed over the light source rather than the lens, you don't need to use high-quality filter material. For example, Roscoe or Lee lighting gels, which may be too flimsy to use in front of the lens, can be mounted or taped in front of your flash with ease.

Continuous Lighting Basics

While continuous lighting and its effects are generally much easier to visualize and use than electronic flash, there are some factors you need to take into account, particularly the color temperature of the light. (Color temperature concerns aren't exclusive to continuous light sources, of course, but the variations tend to be more extreme and less predictable than those of electronic flash, which output relatively consistent daylight-like illumination.)

Color temperature, in practical terms, is how "bluish" or how "reddish" the light appears to be to the digital camera's sensor. Indoor illumination is quite warm, comparatively, and appears reddish to the sensor. Daylight, in contrast, seems much bluer to the sensor. Our eyes (our brains, actually) are quite adaptable to these variations, so white objects don't appear to have an orange tinge when viewed indoors, nor do they seem excessively blue outdoors in full daylight. Yet, these color temperature variations are real and the sensor is not fooled. To capture the most accurate colors, we need to take the color temperature into account in setting the color balance (or *white balance*) of the D7000—either automatically using the camera's smarts or manually using our own knowledge and experience.

The only time you need to think in terms of actual color temperature is when you're making adjustments using the Choose Color Temp. setting in the White Balance entry within the Shooting menu (which, as described in Chapter 8, allows you to dial in exact color temperatures, if known). So, those occasions are the only times you're likely to be confused by a seeming contradiction in how color temperatures are named: warmer (more reddish) color temperatures (measured in degrees Kelvin) are the *lower* numbers, while cooler (bluer) color temperatures are *higher* numbers. It might not make sense to say that 3,400K is warmer than 6,000K, but that's the way it is. If it helps, think of a glowing red ember contrasted with a white-hot welder's torch, rather than fire and ice.

The confusion comes from physics. Scientists calculate color temperature from the light emitted by a mythical object called a black body radiator, which absorbs all the radiant energy that strikes it, and reflects none at all. Such a black body not only *absorbs* light perfectly, but it *emits* it perfectly when heated (and since nothing in the universe is perfect, that makes it mythical).

At a particular physical temperature, this imaginary object always emits light of the same wavelength or color. That makes it possible to define color temperature in terms of actual temperature in degrees on the Kelvin scale that scientists use. Incandescent light, for example, typically has a color temperature of 3,200K to 3,400K. Daylight might range from 5,500K to 6,000K. Each type of illumination we use for photography has its own color temperature range—with some cautions. The next sections will summarize everything you need to know about the qualities of these light sources.

Daylight

Daylight is produced by the sun, and so is moonlight (which is just reflected sunlight). Daylight is present, of course, even when you can't see the sun. When sunlight is direct, it can be bright and harsh. If daylight is diffused by clouds, softened by bouncing off objects such as walls or your photo reflectors, or filtered by shade, it can be much dimmer and less contrasty.

Daylight's color temperature can vary quite widely. It is highest in temperature (most blue) at noon when the sun is directly overhead, because the light is traveling through a minimum amount of the filtering layer we call the atmosphere. The color temperature at high noon may be 6,000K. At other times of day, the sun is lower in the sky and the particles in the air provide a filtering effect that warms the illumination to about

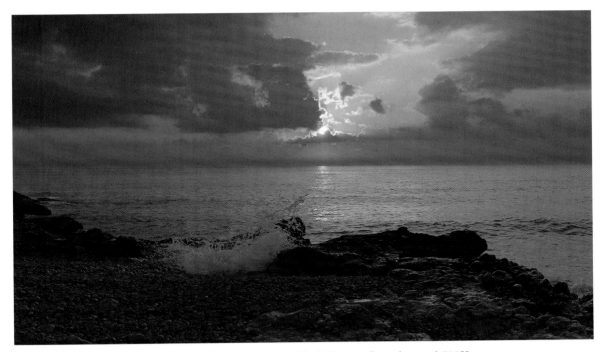

Figure 12.5 At dawn and dusk, the color temperature of daylight may dip as low as 4,500K.

5,500K for most of the day. Starting an hour before dusk and for an hour after sunrise, the warm appearance of the sunlight is even visible to our eyes when the color temperature may dip to 5,000-4,500K, as shown in Figure 12.5.

Because you'll be taking so many photos in daylight, you'll want to learn how to use or compensate for the brightness and contrast of sunlight, as well as how to deal with its color temperature. I'll provide some hints later in this chapter.

Incandescent/Tungsten Light

The term incandescent or tungsten illumination is usually applied to the direct descendents of Thomas Edison's original electric lamp. Such lights consist of a glass bulb that contains a vacuum, or is filled with a halogen gas, and contains a tungsten filament that is heated by an electrical current, producing photons and heat. Tungsten-halogen lamps are a variation on the basic light bulb, using a more rugged (and longer-lasting) filament that can be heated to a higher temperature, housed in a thicker glass or quartz envelope, and filled with iodine or bromine ("halogen") gases. The higher temperature allows tungsten-halogen (or quartz-halogen/quartz-iodine, depending on their construction) lamps to burn "hotter" and whiter. Although popular for automobile headlamps today, they've also been used for photographic illumination.

Although incandescent illumination isn't a perfect black body radiator, it's close enough that the color temperature of such lamps can be precisely calculated and used for photography without concerns about color variation (at least, until the very end of the lamp's life).

Of course, old-style tungsten lamps are on the way out, to be replaced either by compact fluorescent lights (CFL) or newer, more energy efficient (and expensive) tungsten lights. Despite government regulations, tungsten lamps can't be phased out completely, because CFLs don't work in all fixtures and for all applications, such as dimmers (even if you purchase special "dimmable" CFLs), electronic timer or "dusk-to-dawn" light controllers, some illuminated wall switches, or with motion sensors. Only certain types of CFLs (cold cathode models) operate outside in cold weather; they emit IR signals that can confuse the remote control of your TV, air-conditioner, etc, and the typical CFL has a Color Rendering Index of 80, compared to the virtually perfect 100 rating of incandescent lights.

The other qualities of this type of lighting, such as contrast, are dependent on the distance of the lamp from the subject, type of reflectors used, and other factors that I'll explain later in this chapter.

Fluorescent Light/Other Light Sources

Fluorescent light has some advantages in terms of illumination, but some disadvantages from a photographic standpoint. This type of lamp generates light through an electrochemical reaction that emits most of its energy as visible light, rather than heat, which is why the bulbs don't get as hot. The type of light produced varies depending on the phosphor coatings and type of gas in the tube. So, the illumination fluorescent bulbs produce can vary widely in its characteristics.

That's not great news for photographers. Different types of lamps have different "color temperatures" that can't be precisely measured in degrees Kelvin, because the light isn't produced by heating. Worse, fluorescent lamps have a discontinuous spectrum of light that can have some colors missing entirely. A particular type of tube can lack certain shades of red or other colors (see Figure 12.6), which is why fluorescent lamps and other alternative technologies such as sodium-vapor illumination can produce ghastly looking human skin tones. Their spectra can lack the reddish tones we associate with healthy skin and emphasize the blues and greens popular in horror movies.

Also gaining in popularity are LED light sources, particularly for movies, in the form of compact units that clip onto the camera and provide a continuous beam of light to fill in shadows indoors or out, and/or to provide the main illumination when shooting video inside.

Figure 12.6
The uncorrected fluorescent lighting in the gym added a distinct greenish cast to this image when exposed with a daylight white balance setting.

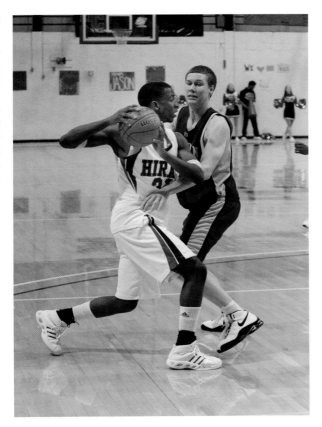

Adjusting White Balance

I showed you how to adjust white balance in Chapter 8, using the D7000's built-in presets, white balance shift capabilities, setting exact color temperatures, and white balance bracketing (there's more on bracketing in Chapter 4, too).

In most cases, however, the Nikon D7000 will do a good job of calculating white balance for you, so Auto can be used as your choice most of the time. Use the preset values or set a custom white balance that matches the current shooting conditions when you need to. The only really problematic light sources are likely to be fluorescents. Vendors, such as GE and Sylvania, may actually provide a figure known as the *color rendering index* (or CRI), which is a measure of how accurately a particular light source represents standard colors, using a scale of 0 (some sodium-vapor lamps) to 100 (daylight and most incandescent lamps). Daylight fluorescents and deluxe cool white fluorescents might have a CRI of about 79 to 95, which is perfectly acceptable for most photographic applications. Warm white fluorescents might have a CRI of 55. White deluxe mercury vapor lights are less suitable with a CRI of 45, while low-pressure sodium lamps can vary from CRI 0-18.

Remember that if you shoot RAW, you can specify the white balance of your image when you import it into Photoshop, Photoshop Elements, or another image editor using Nikon Capture NX2, Adobe Camera Raw, or your preferred RAW converter. While color-balancing filters that fit on the front of the lens exist, they are primarily useful for film cameras, because film's color balance can't be tweaked as extensively as that of a sensor.

Electronic Flash Basics

Until you delve into the situation deeply enough, it might appear that serious photographers have a love/hate relationship with electronic flash. You'll often hear that flash photography is less natural looking, and that the built-in flash in most cameras should never be used as the primary source of illumination because it provides a harsh, garish look. Indeed, the most advanced "pro" cameras like the Nikon D2xs and D3 don't have a built-in flash at all. Available ("continuous") lighting is praised, and built-in flash photography seems to be roundly denounced.

In truth, however, the bias is against *bad* flash photography. Indeed, flash has become the studio light source of choice for pro photographers, because it's more intense (and its intensity can be varied to order by the photographer), freezes action, frees you from using a tripod (unless you want to use one to lock down a composition), and has a snappy, consistent light quality that matches daylight. (While color balance changes as the flash duration shortens, some Nikon flash units can communicate to the camera the exact white balance provided for that shot.) And even pros will cede that the built-in flash of the Nikon D7000 has some important uses as an adjunct to existing light, particularly to fill in dark shadows.

But electronic flash isn't as inherently easy to use as continuous lighting. As I noted earlier, electronic flash units are more expensive, don't show you exactly what the lighting effect will be (unless you use a second source or mode called a *modeling light* for a preview), and the exposure of electronic flash units is more difficult to calculate accurately.

For the pop-up flash built into the Nikon D7000, the full burst of light lasts about 1/1,000th second and provides enough illumination to shoot a subject 10 feet away at f/5.6 using the ISO 200 setting. As you can see, the built-in flash is somewhat limited in range; you'll realize why external flash units are often a good idea later in this chapter.

An electronic flash (whether built in or connected to the Nikon D7000 through a cable or the hot shoe or fired wirelessly) is triggered at the instant of exposure, during a period when the sensor is fully exposed by the shutter. As I mentioned earlier in this book, the D7000 has a vertically traveling shutter that consists of two curtains. The first curtain opens and moves to the opposite side of the frame, at which point the shutter is completely open. The flash can be triggered at this point (so-called *front-curtain sync*), making the flash exposure. Then, after a delay that can vary from 30 seconds to 1/250th second (with the Nikon D7000; other cameras may sync at a faster or slower speed), a second curtain begins moving across the sensor plane, covering up the sensor again. If the flash is triggered just before the second curtain starts to close, then *second-curtain sync* is used. (I'll describe these in more detail later in this chapter.) In both cases, though, a shutter speed of 1/250th second is ordinarily the maximum that can be used to take a photo. If you use a faster shutter speed, you'll expose only the part of the sensor exposed by the gap between the shutter curtains when the flash fires.

Determining Exposure

Calculating the proper exposure for an electronic flash photograph is a bit more complicated than determining the settings for continuous light. The right exposure isn't simply a function of how far away your subject is (which the D7000 can figure out based on the autofocus distance that's locked in just prior to taking the picture). Various objects reflect more or less light at the same distance so, obviously, the camera needs to measure the amount of light reflected back and through the lens. Yet, as the flash itself isn't available for measuring until it's triggered, the D7000 has nothing to measure.

The solution is to fire the flash twice. The initial shot is a *monitor pre-flash* that can be analyzed, then followed virtually instantaneously by a main flash (to the eye the bursts appear to be a single flash) that's given exactly the calculated intensity needed to provide a correct exposure. As a result, the primary flash may be longer in duration for distant objects and shorter in duration for closer subjects, depending on the required intensity for exposure. This through-the-lens evaluative flash exposure system is called i-TTL (intelligent Through The Lens), and it operates whenever the pop-up internal flash is used, or you have attached a Nikon dedicated flash unit to the D7000.

Guide Numbers

Guide numbers, usually abbreviated GN, are a way of specifying the power of an electronic flash in a way that can be used to determine the right f/stop to use at a particular shooting distance and ISO setting. In fact, before automatic flash units became prevalent, the GN was actually used to do just that. A GN is usually given as a pair of numbers for both feet and meters that represent the range at ISO 100. For example, the Nikon D7000's built-in flash has a GN in i-TTL mode of 12/39 (meters/feet) at ISO 100. To calculate the right exposure at that ISO setting, you'd divide the guide number by the distance to arrive at the appropriate f/stop.

Using the D7000's built-in flash as an example, at ISO 100 with its GN of 39, if you wanted to shoot a subject at a distance of 10 feet, you'd use f/3.9 (39 divided by 10), rounded to f/4. At 5 feet, an f/stop rounded to f/8 would be used. Some quick mental calculations with the GN will give you any particular electronic flash's range. You can easily see that the built-in flash would begin to peter out at about 20 feet, where you'd need an aperture of f/2 (with a fast prime lens) at ISO 100. Of course, in the real world you'd probably bump the sensitivity up to a setting of ISO 800 so you could use a more practical f/5.6 at that distance.

Today, guide numbers are most useful for comparing the power of various flash units, rather than actually calculating what exposure to use. You don't need to be a math genius to see that an electronic flash with a GN in feet of, say, 157 (like the SB-900) would be *a lot* more powerful than your built-in flash. At ISO 100, you could use f/8 instead of f/2 at 20 feet, an improvement of about 4 stops.

How Electronic Flash Works

The bursts of light we call electronic flash are produced by a flash of photons generated by an electrical charge that is accumulated in a component called a *capacitor* and then directed through a glass tube containing xenon gas, which absorbs the energy and emits the brief flash. For the pop-up flash built into the D7000, the full burst of light lasts about 1/1,000th of a second and provides enough illumination to shoot a subject 10 feet away at f/4 using the ISO 100 setting. In a more typical situation, as noted earlier, you'd use ISO 200, f/5.6 to f/8 and photograph something 8 to 10 feet away. As you can see, the built-in flash is somewhat limited in range; you'll see why external flash units are often a good idea later in this chapter.

An electronic flash (whether built in, attached to the accessory shoe, or connected to the D7000 through a cable plugged into a hot shoe adapter in the accessory shoe) is triggered at the instant of exposure, during a period when the sensor is fully exposed by the shutter. As I mentioned earlier in this book, the D7000 has a vertically traveling shutter that consists of two curtains. The first curtain opens and moves to the opposite side of the frame, at which point the shutter is completely open. The flash can be triggered at this point (so-called *first-curtain sync*), making the flash exposure. Then, after a delay that can vary from 30 seconds to 1/250th second (with the D7000; other cameras may sync at a faster or slower speed), a second curtain begins moving across the sensor plane, covering up the sensor again. If the flash is triggered just before the second curtain starts to close, then *second-curtain sync* is used. In both cases, though, a shutter speed of 1/250th second is the maximum that can be used to take a photo, unless you're using the high-speed 1/320th second sync.

Figure 12.7 illustrates how this works, with a fanciful illustration of a generic shutter (your D7000's shutter does *not* look like this, and some vertically traveling shutters move bottom to top rather than the top-to-bottom motion shown). Both curtains are tightly closed at upper left. At upper right, the first curtain begins to move downwards, starting to expose a narrow slit that reveals the sensor behind the shutter. At lower left, the first curtain moves downwards farther until, as you can see at lower right in the figure, the sensor is fully exposed.

Figure 12.7
A focal plane shutter has two curtains, the lower, or first curtain, and an upper, second curtain.

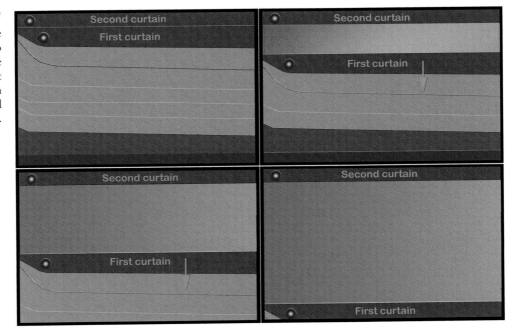

When first-curtain sync is used, the flash is triggered at the instant that the sensor is completely exposed. The shutter then remains open for an additional length of time (from 30 seconds to 1/250th second), and the second curtain begins to move downward, covering the sensor once more. When second-curtain sync is activated, the flash is triggered *after* the main exposure is over, just before the second curtain begins to move downward.

A Typical Electronic Flash Sequence

Here's what happens when you take a photo using electronic flash, either the unit built into the Nikon D7000 or an external flash like the Nikon SB-900, all within a few milliseconds of time:

1. **Sync mode.** After you've selected a shooting mode, choose the flash sync option available in that mode by holding down the Flash button and rotating the main command dial until the icon representing the choice you want is displayed in the top-panel monochrome LCD. (See Figure 12.8.)

2. **Metering method.** Choose the metering method you want, from Matrix, Center-weighted, or Spot metering.

3. **Activate flash.** Press the flash pop-up button to flip up the built-in flash, if necessary, or mount (or connect with a cable) an external flash and turn it on. A ready light appears in the viewfinder and on the back of an external flash when the unit is ready to take a picture.

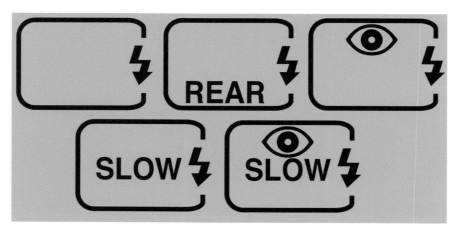

Figure 12.8
Icons for flash sync modes include front sync (top left), rear sync (top middle), red-eye reduction (top right), slow sync (lower left), and slow sync with red-eye reduction (lower right).

4. **Check exposure.** Select a shutter speed when using Manual, Program, or Shutter-priority modes; select an aperture when using Aperture-priority and Manual exposure modes.

5. **Preview lighting.** If you want to preview the lighting effect, press the depth-of-field button to produce a modeling flash burst (unless you've redefined this control in the Custom Settings menu as described in Chapter 9).

6. **Lock flash setting (if desired).** Optionally, if the main subject is located significantly off-center, you can frame so the subject is centered, lock the flash at the exposure needed to illuminate that subject, and then reframe using the composition you want. Lock the flash level using the Flash Value Lock button (which is, by default, the Fn button, but can also be assigned to the Fn, Preview, or AE-L/AF-L buttons in CSM #f3, CSM #f4, or CSM #f5). Press the FV lock button, and the flash will emit a pre-flash to determine the correct flash level, and then the D7000 will lock the flash at that level until you press the FV lock button again to release it. FV lock icons appear in the monochrome LCD status panel and the viewfinder.

7. **Take photo.** Press the shutter release down all the way.

8. **D7000 receives distance data.** A D- or G-series lens now supplies focus distance to the D7000.

9. **Pre-flash emitted.** The internal flash, if used, or external flash sends out one or two pre-flash bursts. One burst can be used to control additional wireless flash units in Commander mode, while one burst is used to determine exposure.

10. **Exposure calculated.** The pre-flash bounces back and is measured by the 2,016-pixel RGB sensor in the viewfinder. It measures brightness and contrast of the image to calculate exposure. If you're using Matrix metering, the D7000 evaluates the scene to determine whether the subject may be backlit (for fill flash), a subject that requires extra ambient light exposure to balance the scene with the flash exposure,

or classifies the scene in some other way. The camera to subject information as well as the degree of sharp focus of the subject matter is used to locate the subject within the frame. If you've selected Spot metering, only standard i-TTL (without balanced fill flash) is used.

11. **Mirror up.** The mirror flips up. At this point exposure and focus are locked in.

Tip

If you want to confirm that the pre-flash fires before the mirror flips up, set the D7000 to Mup (Mirror Up) mode using the release mode dial. (This separates the firing of the pre-flash from the flash used to make the exposure.) Press the shutter release as you look through the viewfinder. You'll see the pre-flash fire, and *then* the mirror will flip up, obscuring your view. Press the shutter release a second time to take the actual picture. Only *then* will the main flash fire.

---

12. **Flash fired.** At the correct triggering moment (depending on whether front or rear sync is used), the camera sends a signal to one or more flashes to start flash discharge. The flash is quenched as soon as the correct exposure has been achieved.

13. **Shutter closes.** The shutter closes and the mirror flips down. You're ready to take another picture. Remember to press the FV lock button again to release the flash exposure if your next shot will use a different composition.

14. **Exposure confirmed.** Ordinarily, the full charge in the flash may not be required. If the flash indicator in the viewfinder blinks for about three seconds after the exposure, that means that the entire flash charge was required, and it *could* mean that the full charge wasn't enough for a proper exposure. Be sure to review your image on the LCD to make sure it's not underexposed, and, if it is, make adjustments (such as increasing the ISO setting of the D7000) to remedy the situation.

Choosing a Flash Sync Mode

The Nikon D7000 has five flash sync modes, selected by holding down the Flash button while rotating the main command dial. (See Figure 12.8 for the icons.) Those modes (which I've listed in logical order, so the explanation will make more sense, rather than the order in which they appear during the selection cycle) are as follows:

■ **Front-curtain sync.** This setting should be your default setting. In this mode the flash fires as soon as the front curtain opens completely. The shutter then remains open for the duration of the exposure, until the rear curtain closes. If the subject is moving and ambient light levels are high enough, the movement will cause a secondary "ghost" exposure that appears in front of the flash exposure.

- **Rear-curtain sync.** With this setting, which can be used with Shutter-priority, Aperture-priority, Program, or Manual exposure modes, the front curtain opens completely and remains open for the duration of the exposure. Then, the flash is fired and the rear curtain closes. If the subject is moving and ambient light levels are high enough, the movement will cause a secondary "ghost" exposure that appears behind the flash exposure (trailing it). You'll find more on "ghost" exposures next. In Program and Aperture-priority modes, the D7000 will combine rear-curtain sync with slow shutter speeds (just like slow sync, discussed below) to balance ambient light with flash illumination. (It's best to use a tripod to avoid blur at these slow shutter speeds.)

- **Red-eye reduction.** In this mode, there is a one-second lag after pressing the shutter release before the picture is actually taken, during which the D7000's red-eye reduction lamp lights, causing the subject's pupils to contract (assuming they are looking at the camera), and thus reducing potential red-eye effects. Don't use with moving subjects or when you can't abide the delay.

- **Slow sync.** This setting allows the D7000 in Program and Aperture-priority modes to use shutter speeds as slow as 30 seconds with the flash to help balance a background illuminated with ambient light with your main subject, which will be lit by the electronic flash. You'll want to use a tripod at slower shutter speeds, of course. As shown in Figure 12.9, it's common that the ambient light will be incandescent illumination that's much warmer than the electronic flash's "daylight" balance, so, if you want the two sources to match, you may want to use a warming filter on the flash. That can be done with a gel if you're using an external flash like the SB-900, or by taping an appropriate warm filter over the D7000's built-in flash. (That's not a convenient approach, and many find the warm/cool mismatch unobjectionable and don't bother with filtration.)

- **Red-eye reduction with slow sync.** This mode combines slow sync with the D7000's red-eye reduction behavior when using Program or Aperture-priority modes.

In Shutter-priority and Manual exposure modes, you can select the following three flash synchronization settings:

- **Front-curtain sync/fill flash.** This setting should be your default setting. This mode is also available in Program and Aperture-priority mode, as described above, and, with high ambient light levels, can produce ghost images, discussed below.

- **Red-eye reduction.** This mode, with its one-second lag and red-eye lamp flash, is described above.

■ **Rear-curtain sync.** As noted previously, in this sync mode, the front curtain opens completely and remains open for the duration of the exposure. Then, the flash is fired and the rear curtain closes. If the subject is moving and ambient light levels are high enough, the movement will cause that "ghost" exposure that appears to be trailing the flash exposure.

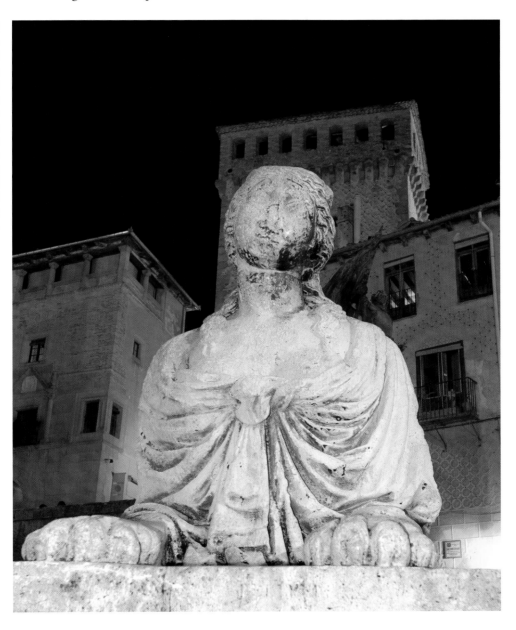

Figure 12.9
I deliberately used flash and slow sync to separate this Roman sphinx sculpture (limned in bluish light from the flash) from the background illuminated by warmer incandescents.

Ghost Images

The difference might not seem like much, but whether you use first-curtain sync (the default setting) or rear-curtain sync (an optional setting) can make a significant difference to your photograph *if the ambient light in your scene also contributes to the image.* At faster shutter speeds, particularly 1/250th second, there isn't much time for the ambient light to register, unless it is very bright. It's likely that the electronic flash will provide almost all the illumination, so first-curtain sync or second-curtain sync isn't very important.

However, at slower shutter speeds, or with very bright ambient light levels, there is a significant difference, particularly if your subject is moving, or the camera isn't steady. In any of those situations, the ambient light will register as a second image accompanying the flash exposure, and if there is movement (camera or subject), that additional image will not be in the same place as the flash exposure. It will show as a ghost image and, if the movement is significant enough, as a blurred ghost image trailing in front of or behind your subject in the direction of the movement.

As I mentioned earlier, when you're using first-curtain sync, the flash goes off the instant the shutter opens, producing an image of the subject on the sensor. Then, the shutter remains open for an additional period (which can be from 30 seconds to 1/250th second). If your subject is moving, say, towards the right side of the frame, the ghost image produced by the ambient light will produce a blur on the right side of the original subject image, making it look as if your sharp (flash-produced) image is chasing the ghost. (See Figure 12.10, top.) For those of us who grew up with

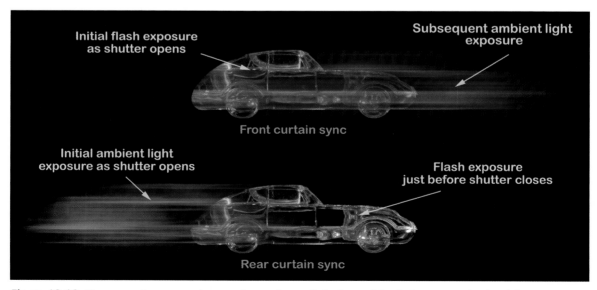

Figure 12.10 Front-curtain sync produces an image that trails in front of the flash exposure (top), while rear-curtain sync creates a more "natural looking" trail behind the flash image (bottom).

lightning-fast superheroes who always left a ghost trail *behind them*, that looks unnatural (see Figure 12.10, bottom).

So, Nikon provides rear (second) curtain sync to remedy the situation. In that mode, the shutter opens, as before. The shutter remains open for its designated duration, and the ghost image forms. If your subject moves from the left side of the frame to the right side, the ghost will move from left to right, too. *Then*, about 1.5 milliseconds before the second shutter curtain closes, the flash is triggered, producing a nice, sharp flash image *ahead* of the ghost image. Voilà! We have monsieur *le Flash* outrunning his own trailing image.

EVERY WHICH WAY, INCLUDING UP

Note that, although I describe the ghost effect in terms of subject matter that is moving left to right in a horizontally oriented composition, it can occur in any orientation, and with the subject moving in *any* direction. (Try photographing a falling rock, if you can, and you'll see the same effect.) Nor are the ghost images affected by the fact that modern shutters travel vertically rather than horizontally. Secondary images are caused between the time the first curtain fully opens, and the second curtain begins to close. The direction of travel of the shutter curtains, or the direction of your subject, does not matter.

Avoiding Sync Speed Problems

Using a shutter speed faster than 1/250th second can cause problems. Triggering the electronic flash only when the shutter is completely open makes a lot of sense if you think about what's going on. To obtain shutter speeds faster than 1/250th second, the D7000 exposes only part of the sensor at one time, by starting the second curtain on its journey before the first curtain has completely opened, as shown in Figure 12.11. That effectively provides a briefer exposure as a slit of the shutter passes over the surface of the sensor. If the flash were to fire during the time when the first and second curtains partially obscured the sensor, only the slit that was actually open would be exposed.

You'd end up with only a narrow band, representing the portion of the sensor that was exposed when the picture is taken. For shutter speeds *faster* than 1/250th second, the second curtain begins moving *before* the first curtain reaches the bottom of the frame. As a result, a moving slit, the distance between the first and second curtains, exposes one portion of the sensor at a time as it moves from the top to the bottom. Figure 12.11 shows three views of our typical (but imaginary) focal plane shutter. At left is pictured the closed shutter; in the middle version you can see the first curtain has moved down about 1/4 of the distance to the top; and in the right-hand version, the second curtain has started to "chase" the first curtain across the frame towards the bottom.

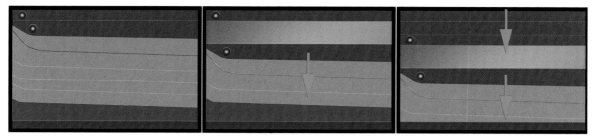

Figure 12.11 A closed shutter (left); partially open shutter as the first curtain begins to move downwards (middle); only part of the sensor is exposed as the slit moves (right).

If the flash is triggered while this slit is moving, only the exposed portion of the sensor will receive any illumination. You end up with a photo like the one shown in Figure 12.12. Note that a band across the bottom of the image is black. That's a shadow of the second shutter curtain, which had started to move when the flash was triggered. Sharp-eyed readers will wonder why the black band is at the *bottom* of the frame rather than at the top, where the second curtain begins its journey. The answer is simple: your lens flips the image upside down and forms it on the sensor in a reversed position. You never notice that, because the camera is smart enough to show you the pixels that make up your photo in their proper orientation during picture review. But this image flip is why, if your sensor gets dirty and you detect a spot of dust in the upper half of a test photo, if cleaning manually, you need to look for the speck in the *bottom* half of the sensor.

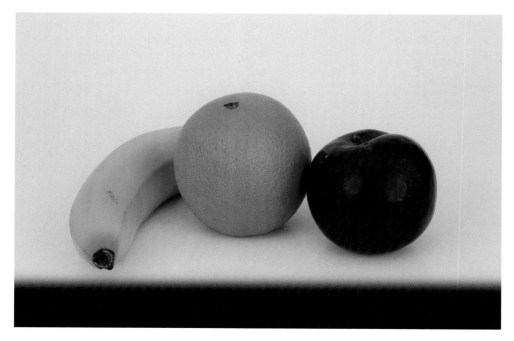

Figure 12.12 If a shutter speed faster than 1/250th second is used, you can end up photographing only a portion of the image.

I generally end up with sync speed problems only when shooting in the studio, using studio flash units rather than my D7000's built-in flash or a Nikon dedicated Speedlight. That's because if you're using either type of "smart" flash, the camera knows that a strobe is attached, and remedies any unintentional goof in shutter speed settings. If you happen to set the D7000's shutter to a faster speed in S or M mode, the camera will automatically adjust the shutter speed down to 1/250th second as soon as you flip up the flash (or prevent you from choosing a faster speed if the flash is already up). In A, P, or any of the Scene modes, where the D7000 selects the shutter speed, it will never choose a shutter speed higher than 1/250th second when using flash. In P mode, shutter speed is automatically set between 1/60th to 1/250th second when using flash.

But when using a non-dedicated flash, such as a studio unit plugged into an optional accessory hot shoe adapter, the camera has no way of knowing that a flash is connected, so shutter speeds faster than 1/250th second can be set inadvertently. To avoid that problem with studio flash, I strongly recommend setting your camera to Manual exposure, and using the x250 shutter speed, which is located *past* the Bulb speed when rotating the main command dial all the way to the left. You won't have to worry as much about accidentally changing the shutter speed to an unusable setting; there is no speed *beyond* x250th second, and if you nudge the main command dial to the right, you'll get a Bulb exposure, which will immediately become evident.

Note that the D7000 can use a feature called *high-speed sync,* described next, that allows shutter speeds faster than 1/250th second with certain external dedicated Nikon flash units. When using high-speed sync, the flash fires a continuous serious of bursts at reduced power for the entire duration of the exposure, so that the illumination is able to expose the sensor as the slit moves. HS sync is set using the controls that adjust the compatible external flash.

High-Speed (FP) Sync

While the D7000 prevents you from using a shutter speed faster than 1/250th second when working with the built-in flash, if you use certain external dedicated Nikon flash units, you have an additional option: high-speed (FP) sync. You don't need to make any special settings on the flash; the D7000 takes care of the details for you, as I'll describe in this section.

As I said earlier, triggering the electronic flash only when the shutter is completely open makes a lot of sense if you think about what's going on. To obtain shutter speeds faster than 1/250th second, the D7000 exposes only part of the sensor at one time, by starting the second curtain on its journey before the first curtain has completely opened. That effectively provides a briefer exposure as a slit of the shutter passes over the surface of the sensor. If the flash were to fire during the time when the first and second curtains partially obscured the sensor, only the area defined by the slit that was actually open would be exposed.

However, the D7000 and certain Nikon flashes provide a partial solution, called *high-speed sync* or *FP sync* (focal plane sync). Those flash units can fire a series of flashes consecutively in rapid succession, producing the illusion of a longer continuous flash, although at reduced intensity. These multiple flashes have a duration long enough to allow exposing the area of the sensor revealed by the traveling slit as it makes its full pass. However, the reduced intensity means that your flash's range is greatly reduced.

This technique is most useful outdoors when you need fill-in flash, but find that 1/250th second is way too slow for the f/stop you want to use. For example, at ISO 200, an outdoors exposure is likely to be 1/250th second at, say, f/14, which is perfectly fine for an ambient/balanced fill-flash exposure if you don't mind the extreme depth-of-field offered by the small f/stop. But, what if you'd rather shoot at 1/1,600th second at f/5.6? High-speed sync will let you do that, and you probably won't mind the reduced flash power, because you're looking for fill flash, anyway. This sync mode offers more flexibility than, say, dropping down to ISO 100.

High-speed sync is also useful when you want to use a larger f/stop to limit the amount of depth-of-field. Select a shutter speed higher than 1/250th second, and the faster-sync speed automatically reduces the effective light of the flash, without other intervention from you.

To use Auto FP sync with units like the Nikon SB-900, SB-700, SB-800 (now discontinued), SB-600, and SB-R200 units, there is no setting to make on the flash itself. You need to use CSM #e1 to specify either 1/320 s (Auto FP) or 1/250 s (Auto FP). When either of those settings is activated, when using P or A exposure modes, the shutter speed will be set to 1/320th or 1/250th second (respectively) when a compatible external flash is attached. Higher shutter speeds than 1/320th or 1/250th second can then be used with full synchronization, at reduced flash output.

Working with Nikon Flash Units

If you want to work with dedicated Nikon flash units, at this time you have six choices, the D7000's built-in flash, the Nikon SB-900, SB-700, SB-800, SB-600, SB-400 on-camera flash units, and the SB-R200 wireless remote flash. (The discontinued SB-800 can still be found on the used market, while the SB-600 is slated for replacement soon.) These share certain features, which I'll discuss while pointing out differences among them. Nikon may introduce additional flash units during the life of this book, but the current batch and the Nikon Creative Lighting System ushered in with them were significant steps forward, so I don't expect any major changes in the near future. First, a quick introduction to the separate flash units currently available:

Nikon D7000 Built-in Flash

The built-in flash has a guide number of 12/39 (meters/feet) at ISO 100 and must be activated by manually flipping it up (It will also pop up automatically when using certain Scene modes any time it's needed). This flash is powerful enough to provide primary direct flash illumination when required, but can't be angled up for diffuse bounce flash off the ceiling. It's useful for balanced fill flash (more on that later) and for use in Commander mode, which allows the built-in flash to trigger one or more off-camera flash units in up to four separate groups wirelessly. You can use CSM #e3 to dial down the intensity of the built-in flash to 1/128 power so that, in Commander mode, it will activate off-camera flash units but not contribute much (if at all) to the exposure. The built-in flash can also be set to fire only as a pre-flash that will trigger external units, without setting off its main burst. The built-in flash has useful modeling light and repeating flash modes, which will be described later in this chapter.

Because the built-in flash draws its power from the D7000's battery, extensive use will reduce the power available to take pictures. For that reason alone, use of an external flash unit can be a good idea when you plan to take a lot of flash pictures.

Nikon SB-900

The Nikon SB-900 (see Figure 12.13) is currently the flagship of the Nikon flash line up, and has a guide number of 34/111.5 (meters/feet) when the "zooming" flash head (which can be set to adjust the coverage angle of the lens) is set to the 35mm position. It has all the features of the D7000's flash unit, including Commander mode, repeating flash, modeling light, and selectable power output, along with some extra capabilities.

For example, you can angle the flash and rotate it to provide bounce flash. It includes additional, non-through-the-lens exposure modes, thanks to its built-in light sensor, and can "zoom" and diffuse its coverage angle to illuminate the field of view of lenses from 8mm (with the wide-angle/diffusion dome attached) to 120mm on a D7000. The SB-900 also has its own powerful focus assist lamp to aid autofocus in dim lighting, and has reduced red-eye effects simply because the unit, when attached to the D7000, is mounted in a higher position that tends to eliminate reflections from the eye back to the camera lens.

Nikon SB-700

This lower-cost unit has a guide number of 28/92 (meters/feet) at ISO 100 when set to the 35mm zoom position. It has many of the SB-900's features, including zoomable flash coverage equal to the field of view of a 16-56mm lens on the D7000 (24-120mm settings with a full-frame camera), and 14mm with a built-in diffuser panel. It has a built-in modeling flash feature, but lacks repeating flash, accessory filters, and an

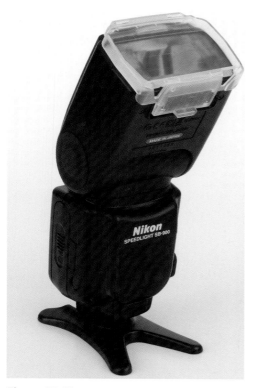

Figure 12.13 The Nikon SB-900 is currently the flagship of the Nikon electronic flash line up.

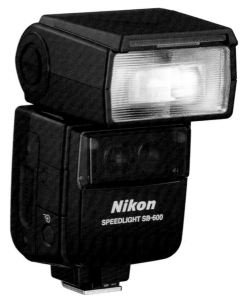

Figure 12.14 The Nikon SB-600 is a popular medium-priced electronic flash with most of the features of the SB-900, except for Commander mode to control remote units.

included flash diffuser dome, which can be purchased separately. Other differences include a wireless Commander mode, and automatic detection of DX format when mounted on the D7000.

Nikon SB-600

This lower-cost unit (see Figure 12.14) has a guide number of 30/98 (meters/feet) at ISO 100 when set to the 35mm zoom position. It has many of the SB-900's features, including zoomable flash coverage equal to the field of view of a 16-56mm lens on the D7000 (24-85mm settings with a full-frame camera), and 14mm with a built-in diffuser panel. Like the SB-700, it has a built-in modeling flash feature, and does not have repeating flash, accessory filters, or the optional flash diffuser. Other differences include:

■ **Multiple flash exposure modes.** The SB-600 does not offer AA or A automatic, non-TTL exposure modes, but does support i-TTL, D-TTL (for the Nikon D1 series and D100), TTL Auto Flash for many Nikon film cameras, and Manual flash modes. (Output can be varied only from 1/1 to 1/64 power.)

■ **Flash groups.** The SB-600 cannot function in Commander mode to control other Nikon flash units, but it can serve as a slave unit triggered by a commander as part of a flash group.

■ **Bounce capability.** The flash head tilts upwards up to 90 degrees, plus 180 degrees to the left or 90 degrees to the right.

The SB-600 is long overdue for replacement. There's nothing in the works as I write this, so you'd be smart to do some Googling before buying this unit.

Nikon SB-400

The entry-level SB-400 (see Figure 12.15) is a good choice for most Nikon D7000 applications. It's built specifically for entry-level Nikon cameras like the D40 or D7000, and has a limited, easy-to-use feature set. It has a limited ISO 100 guide number of 21/68 at the 18mm zoom-head position. It tilts up for bounce flash to 90 degrees, with click detents at the 0, 60, 75, and 90 degree marks. Unless you feel the need for an emergency flash or fill flash unit that's only slightly more powerful than the D7000's built-in flash, for the most flexibility, you might want to consider the SB-600.

Nikon SB-R200

This is a specialized wireless-only flash (see Figure 12.16) that's especially useful for close-up photography, and is often purchased in pairs for use with the Nikon R1 and R1C1 Wireless Close-Up Speedlight systems. Its output power is low at 10/33 (meters/feet)

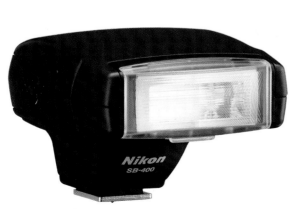

Figure 12.15 The Nikon SB-400 is an entry-level flash best suited for Nikon's entry-level dSLRs.

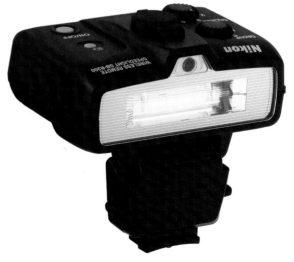

Figure 12.16 The Nikon SB-R200 is a wireless macro-only flash supplied with the Nikon R1 and R1C1 Wireless Close-Up Speedlight systems.

for ISO 100 as you might expect for a unit used to photograph subjects that are often inches from the camera. It has a fixed coverage angle of 78 degrees horizontal and 60 degrees vertical, but the flash head tilts down to 60 degrees and up to 45 degrees (with detents every 15 degrees in both directions). In this case, "up" and "down" has a different meaning, because the SB-R200 can be mounted on the SX-1 Attachment Ring mounted around the lens, so the pair of flash units are on the sides and tilted toward or away from the optical axis. It supports i-TTL, D-TTL, TTL (for film cameras), and Manual modes.

Flash Techniques

Entire books have been written on using Nikon electronic flash units, and the Nikon Creative Lighting System (CLS). Even in a 500-plus page book like this one, I don't have room to show you how to use every feature of every flash unit. Instead, I'm going to use this next section to discuss what specific capabilities are included in the Nikon D7000's built-in flash, as well as some of the key features of the Nikon dedicated external flash units.

After reading this, you'll know more about what you can do, and will explore the controls and settings that will let you move beyond this overview. If you'd like an amazing practical guide to flash photography in general, I recommend Joe McNally's *Hot Shoe Diaries*. You can find basic information on flash photography and lighting techniques in my book *David Busch's Quick Snap Guide to Lighting*. Like Joe's book, it is non-Nikon-specific, but shows you tricks of studio lighting, and other techniques that you can easily apply to your D7000 camera and its flash units.

Using Zoom Heads

External flash zoom heads can adjust themselves automatically to match lens focal lengths in use reported by the D7000 to the flash unit, or you can adjust the zoom head position manually if you want to use a setting that doesn't correspond to the automatic setting the flash will use. With older flash units, like the SB-600, automatic zoom adjustment wastes some of your flash's power, because the flash unit assumes that the focal length reported comes from a full-frame camera. Because of the 1.5X crop factor, the flash coverage when the flash is set to a particular focal length will be wider than is required by the D7000's cropped image.

You can manually adjust the zoom position yourself, using positions built into the flash unit that more closely correspond to your D7000's field of view when using a flash that does not, like the SB-900, automatically take into account the difference between FX (full-frame) and DX (APS-C) coverage. Table 12.1 shows the actual focal length of a lens (or focal length position of a zoom lens) in the left column, with the closest zoom head position on the flash unit in the right column.

Table 12.1 Zoom Head Equivalents for DX Mode

Lens Focal Length	Zoom Head Position
14mm	20mm
18mm	24mm
20mm	28mm
24mm	35mm
28mm	50mm
35mm	50mm
50mm	50mm
70mm	85mm
85mm	105mm

To set the zoom position manually, follow one of these steps:

■ **SB-900.** Press the Zoom button (located southwest of the selector dial/OK button pad) once, release it, and then rotate the selector dial until the zoom setting you want appears on the LCD. An "M" appears on the LCD above the Zoom indicator to show that the zoom setting has been made manually. An FX or DX indicator appears to the left, just above the Zoom indicator to show that the SB-900 is set for FX or DX coverage. You can also change the zoom setting by pressing the Zoom button repeatedly, in which case the focal length setting will jump from one increment to the next, wrapping around at 200mm back to the 12mm setting. Figure 12.17 shows the controls on the back of the SB-900.

■ **SB-700.** Press the Zoom button to the left of the selector dial to highlight Zoom on the flash's LCD screen. Then, rotate the control dial to the zoom position you want. Press the center OK button on the selector dial to confirm your setting. (You can also cycle through the available zoom settings by pressing the Zoom button repeatedly.) An M appears above the Zoom indicator on the LCD to show you've set the zoom value manually. To switch back to power zoom, press the Zoom button until the power zoom icon appears (it's the word "zoom" with a back-looping arrow). Then press the Sel (Select) button to confirm.

■ **SB-600.** Press the Zoom button and adjust zoom position manually. M appears above Zoom in the LCD. To cancel manual zoom, press the Zoom button until it matches the focal length set on the lens.

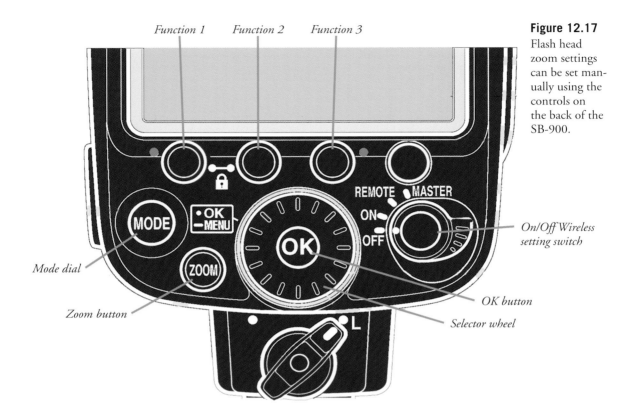

Function 1 *Function 2* *Function 3*

Figure 12.17
Flash head
zoom settings
can be set man-
ually using the
controls on
the back of the
SB-900.

On/Off Wireless setting switch

Mode dial

OK button

Zoom button

Selector wheel

Flash Modes

The external flash units have various flash modes included, which are available or not available with different camera models, categorized into nine different groups. A table showing most of the groups is included in the manuals for the external flash units, but the table is irrelevant for D7000 users (unless you happen to own an older digital or film SLR, as well). For digital cameras, there are two main groups: digital cameras *not* compatible with the Nikon Creative Lighting System (Nikon D1-series cameras, and the Nikon D100), and digital cameras that *are* compatible with CLS (including the D7000). Groups I through VII, which support various combinations of features, consist of various film SLRs. You can ignore those options, unless you're using your external flash with an older film camera.

To change flash mode with the SB-900, press the Mode button on the back left edge, then release it and rotate the selector dial until the mode you want appears on the LCD. The TTL automatic flash modes available for the SB-900 are described next. (The SB-700 has a sliding mode selector switch to the left of the speedlight's LCD with positions for TTL, Manual, and GN settings. Those are the only modes available with that flash when you're using it as a Master. However, when the SB-700 is used as a remote flash triggered by a Master Commander flash, it can operate in Repeating mode.)

- **iTTL Automatic Balanced Fill Flash.** In both Matrix and Center-weighted camera exposure modes, the camera and flash balance the exposure so that the main subject and background are well-exposed. A TTL BL indicator appears on the LCD. However, if you switch to Spot metering, the flash switches to standard iTTL, described next.

- **Standard iTTL.** In this mode, the exposure is set for the main subject, and the background exposure is not taken into account. A TTL indicator appears on the LCD. In either iTTL Automatic Balanced Fill Flash or Standard iTTL modes, if the full power of the flash is used, the ready light indicator on the flash and in the camera viewfinder will blink for three seconds. This is your cue that perhaps even the full power of the flash might not have been enough for proper exposure. If that's the case, an EV indicator will display the amount of underexposure (–0.3 to –3.0 EV) on the LCD while the ready light indicator flashes.

- **AA: Auto Aperture flash.** An A indicator next to an icon representing a lens opening/aperture is shown on the LCD when this mode is selected. The SB-900 uses a built-in light sensor to measure the amount of flash illumination reflected back from the subject, and adjusts the output to produce an appropriate exposure based on the ISO, aperture, focal length, and flash compensation values set on the D7000. This setting on the flash can be used with the D7000 in Program or Aperture-priority modes.

- **A: Non-TTL auto flash.** To work with this mode, you must set the SB-900 for its use using the flash's (not the camera's) Custom Settings menu. Press the OK button in the center of the flash unit's selector dial for about one second, and when the Custom Settings menu appears, rotate the selector dial to choose A. Press OK again, and you can choose from among four variations, Auto Aperture Flash (described above) with or without monitor pre-flash, or Non-TTL auto flash, with or without monitor pre-flash. (Note that the SB-900 manual calls these options "modeling illumination" instead.) In this mode, the SB-900's sensor measures the flash illumination reflected back from the subject, and adjusts the output to provide an appropriate exposure, without the feedback about the aperture setting of the camera that's used with AA mode. This setting on the flash can be used when the D7000 is set to Aperture-priority or Manual modes. You can use this setting to manually "bracket" exposures, as adjusting the aperture value of the lens will produce more or less exposure; the flash has no idea what aperture you've changed to.

- **GN: Distance priority manual.** You enter a distance value, and the SB-900 adjusts light output based on distance, ISO, and aperture to produce the right exposure in either Aperture-priority or Manual exposure modes. Press the Mode button on the flash and rotate the selector dial until the GN indicator appears (the GN option appears only when the flash is pointed directly ahead, or is in the downward bounce position). Then press the OK button to confirm your choice. After that, you can specify a shooting distance by pressing Function Button 2, and then rotating the selector dial until the distance you want is indicated on the LCD. Press the OK button to confirm. The SB-900 will indicate a recommended aperture, which you then set on the lens mounted on the D7000 in Manual exposure mode.

- **M: Manual flash.** The flash fires at a fixed output level. Press the Mode button and rotate the selector dial until M appears on the SB-900's LCD panel. Press the OK button to confirm your choice. Press the Function Button 1 and rotate the selector dial to dial in the power output level you want. Calculate the correct f/stop to use, either by taking a few test photos, with a flash meter, or by the seat of your pants. Then, set the D7000 to Aperture-priority or Manual exposure and choose the f/stop you've decided on. (You can also use manual flash with the D7000's built-in unit by choosing a flash level in CSM #e3, as described in Chapter 9, and calculating the appropriate aperture.) (Good luck. I use test shots to calculate the f/stop, myself.)

- **RPT: Repeating flash.** The flash fires repeatedly to produce a multiple flash strobing effect. To use this mode, set the D7000's exposure mode to Manual. Then set up the number of repeating flashes per frame, frequency, and flash output level, as described in Chapter 9. When using the D7000's built-in flash, use CSM #e3; with the SB-900, press the Mode button and rotate the selector dial to display RPT. Set the flash output level with Function Button 1 and the selector dial, and choose the number of flashes with the Function Button 2 and the selector dial. Finally, press Function Button 3 and rotate the selector dial to choose the frequency. If you don't have a flash meter, the best way to decide what aperture to use on the camera in repeating mode is to take a few test shots.

BURN OUT

When using repeating flash with the built-in flash or the SB-900 or SB-700, or *any* large number of consecutive flashes in any mode (more than about 15 shots at full power), allow the flash to cool off (Nikon recommends a 10-minute time out) to avoid overheating the flash. The SB-900 and SB-700 will signal you with a warning chime that rings when it's time for a cooling-off period. The flash will actually disable itself, if necessary, to prevent damage.

Working with Wireless Commander Mode

The D7000's built-in flash can be set to Commander mode (as described in Chapter 9) and used to control other compatible flash units. The Nikon SB-900 and SB-700 can also be a flash "Commander" to communicate with and trigger other flash units. Nikon offers a unit called the SU-800, which is a commander unit that has no built-in visible flash, and which controls other units using infrared signals.

The SU-800 has several advantages. It's useful for cameras like the D3s and D3x, which have no built-in flash to function in Commander mode, and could also be used with the D7000 to function as a commander that doesn't have any effect on the exposure. However, you can achieve much the same effect by dialing down the D7000's built-in flash to 1/128 power, or by setting the built-in flash to - - (flash cancelled) in Commander mode to turn off the built-in flash during exposure. The real advantage the SU-800 has over the D7000's built-in flash is its "reach." Because it uses IR illumination rather than visible light to communicate with remote flashes, the infrared burst can be much stronger, doubling its effective control range to 66 feet.

To use the D7000 to control other flash units in Advanced Wireless Lighting mode, if you want the built-in flash as the commander, you need to set it to that mode using CSM #e3, as described next. Once you have set either the D7000's built-in flash or the SB-900 as the Master/Commander, you can specify a shooting mode, either Manual with a power output setting you determine from 1/1 to 1/128, or for TTL automatic exposure. When using TTL, you can dial in from –1.0 to +3.0 flash exposure compensation for the master flash. You can also specify a channel (1, 2, 3, or 4) that all flashes will use to communicate among themselves. (If other Nikon photographers are present, choosing a different channel prevents your flash from triggering their remotes, and vice versa.)

Each remote flash unit can also be set to one of three groups (A, B, or C), so you can set the exposure compensation and exposure mode of each group separately. For example, one or more flashes in one group can be reduced in output compared to the flashes in the other group, to produce a particular lighting ratio of effect. You'll find instructions for setting exposure mode, channel, and compensation next (for the built-in flash).

Setting Commander Mode for the D7000's Built-in Flash

Setting Commander mode for the built-in flash unit may seem complicated, but it's fairly easy once you've gone through it a few times. Here are the instructions you need.

1. Navigate to CSM #e3, and choose Commander Mode (see Figure 12.18).

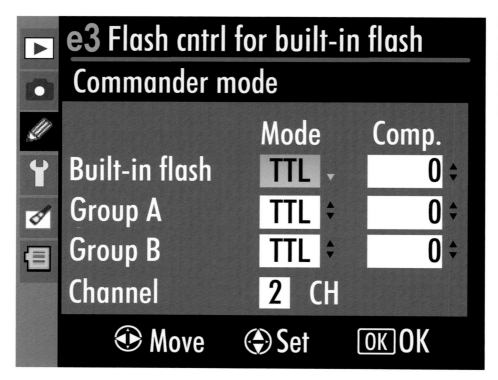

Figure 12.18
Commander mode for the built-in flash can be set in the Custom Settings menu.

2. Use the multi selector left/right buttons to highlight Mode in the Built-in Flash row, then press the up/down buttons to choose TTL, M, or - - (flash disabled). Then use the multi selector right button to highlight the Comp. parameter in the third column. If you chose TTL, you can select exposure compensation from –1 to +3.0; choose M, and you can set flash output from 1/1 to 1/128; choose - - and the pre-flashes will still be used to control any remote units in use, but the built-in flash will not fire to contribute to the exposure.

3. Use the multi selector right button to move down to Group A to select TTL, Manual, AA, or - - exposure (to deactivate that group), then highlight the Comp. column to set the exposure compensation/output power as above. Repeat for any additional groups you want to set up.

4. Use the multi selector right button to highlight the Channel setting, and use the up/down buttons to select the channel that all the flash units will communicate over.

5. Press OK when finished.

Setting Commander and Remote Modes for the SB-900

Setting modes for the SB-900 has been greatly simplified, compared to the previous SB-900. Just rotate the On/Off/Wireless mode switch to the Remote or Master positions. In Remote mode, the SB-900 will be triggered by the Commander flash unit in its group. In Master mode, the SB-900 will serve as the trigger for the other flash units in a group.

You'll want to tell the SB-900 which Channel to use, and which Group it belongs to so that it responds to/controls the other units in its group. You'll need to do this separately for each of the SB-900 units you are working with, if you're using more than one. Here are the (confusing) steps to follow (I recommend doing several dry runs to see how setting up multiple flashes works before trying it "live."):

1. On the master flash, press Function Button 1 to highlight M (Master).

2. Press the Mode button, then spin the selector dial to choose the flash mode you want to use for that flash unit, from among TTL, A (Auto Aperture), M (Manual), or - -. Then, press OK.

> **Tip**
>
> At the - - setting, the master flash is disabled; it will trigger the other units, but its flash won't contribute to the exposure—except if you're shooting very close to the subject using a high ISO setting. If an external flash is the master, try tilting or rotating the flash head away from your subject to minimize this spill-over effect.

3. Press Function Button 2, and rotate the selector dial to choose the flash compensation level. The amount of EV correction appears at the right side, opposite the master flash's mode indicator.

4. Press Function Button 1 to move on to the Group Selection option. Press OK to choose Group A, or rotate the selector dial to choose Group B or C, then press OK to confirm the group you've chosen.

5. If you're using additional SB-900 flash units with this master flash, set their flash modes and exposure compensation individually by repeating Steps 2, 3, and 4 with the master flash.

6. If you'll be using even more SB-900 flash units, set up those groups as you did for Group A, but specify the group name you'll be using for the additional units (either B or C).

7. Once the modes for all the flash units have been set on the master flash, press Function Button 2 and rotate the selector dial to set a channel number that the master flash will use to control its groups.

8. Now take each of the remote flash units and set the correct group and channel number you want to use. Just press Function Button 1 on each remote flash, and rotate the selector dial to specify the group name. Press OK. Then press Function Button 2 and rotate the selector dial to choose the channel number, and then press the OK button. You're all set! If a Nikon-compatible flash is used as a remote, both the rear and front ready lights will blink when the unit is charged, at full power, and communicating properly with the Master flash.

Connecting External Flash

You have five basic choices for linking an external flash unit to your Nikon D7000. They are as follows:

■ **Mount on the accessory shoe.** Sliding a compatible flash unit into the Nikon D7000's accessory shoe provides a direct connection. With a Nikon dedicated flash, all functions of the flash are supported.

■ **Connect to the accessory shoe with a cable.** The Nikon SC-28 and SC-29 TTL coiled remote cords have an accessory shoe on one end of a nine-foot cable to accept a flash, and a foot that slides into the camera accessory shoe on the other end, providing a link that is the same as when the flash is mounted directly on the camera. The SC-29 version also includes a focus assist lamp, like that on the camera, SB-900, and SB-700.

■ **Multi-flash cables.** The Nikon SC-27/SC-26 TTL Multi-Flash Sync Cords can be used to connect TTL flash units to each other or through the AS-10 TTL Multi-Flash Adapter or SC-28 TTL Remote Cord for multi-flash operation. However, this three-pin connector does not support i-TTL or D-TTL operation. You may wish to use it with older Nikon flash units.

■ **Connect to a PC/X connector.** Some external flash units, including studio units, can connect to the Nikon D7000 through an adapter that clips in the accessory shoe and provides a PC/X connector. These adapters can be especially useful if they are combined with a voltage limiter so you needn't fear frying your camera with an older flash unit that has a triggering voltage that's too high. I sometimes use a wireless flash trigger that plugs into a PC connector, and sets off flash units through radio waves.

■ **Wireless link.** As described earlier in this chapter, a Nikon electronic flash can be triggered by another Master flash in Commander mode or by the RU-800 infrared unit.

- **Third-party wireless solutions.** I'm especially impressed with the RadioPopper JrX line of wireless flash triggers, particularly since they can be used to control the output levels of Nikon flash units attached to them, and also the output of the Alien Bees flash units I use in my studio. Pocket Wizards are another wireless trigger product line that can be adapted for use with Nikon flash.

Using Flash Exposure Compensation

You can manually add or subtract exposure to the flash exposure calculated by the D7000. Just press the Flash button on the camera (just below the flash pop-up button) and rotate the sub-command dial until the amount of exposure compensation you want appears on the monochrome LCD and in the viewfinder. You can make adjustments from −3EV to +1EV in 1/3 EV increments. As with ordinary exposure compensation, the adjustment you make remains in effect until you zero it out by pressing the Flash button and rotating the sub-command dial until 0 appears on the monochrome control panel and in the viewfinder.

To view the current flash exposure compensation setting, press the Flash button. When compensation is being used, an icon will be displayed in the viewfinder and on the monochrome LCD.

More Advanced Lighting Techniques

As you advance in your Nikon D7000 photography, you'll want to learn more sophisticated lighting techniques, using more than just straight-on flash, or using just a single flash unit. Entire books have been written on lighting techniques, and I've written multiple chapters on them in books of my own. I'm going to provide a quick introduction to some of the techniques you should be considering.

Diffusing and Softening the Light

Direct light can be harsh and glaring, especially if you're using the flash built into your camera, or an auxiliary flash mounted in the hot shoe and pointed directly at your subject. The first thing you should do is stop using direct light (unless you're looking for a stark, contrasty appearance as a creative effect). There are a number of simple things you can do with both continuous and flash illumination.

- **Use window light.** Light coming in a window can be soft and flattering, and a good choice for human subjects. Move your subject close enough to the window that its light provides the primary source of illumination. You might want to turn off other lights in the room, particularly to avoid mixing daylight and incandescent light. (See Figure 12.19.)

- **Use fill light.** Your D7000's built-in flash makes a perfect fill-in light for the shadows, brightening inky depths with a kicker of illumination. (See Figure 12.20.)

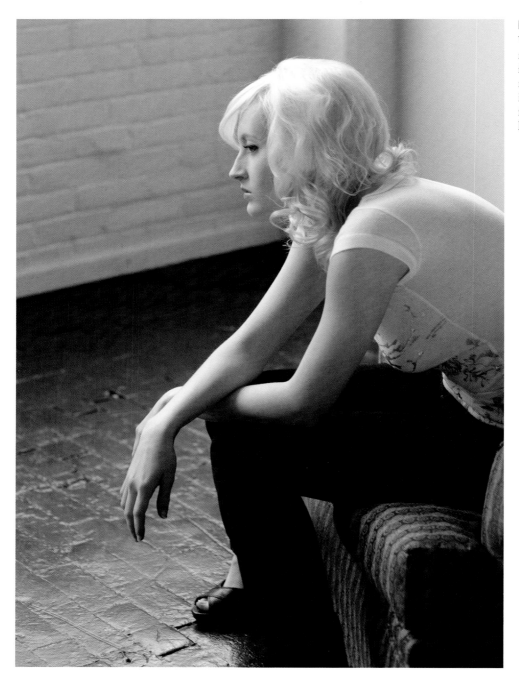

Figure 12.19
Window light makes the perfect diffuse illumination for informal soft-focus portraits like this one.

Figure 12.20
Fill flash
brightened up
the shadows in
this photo.

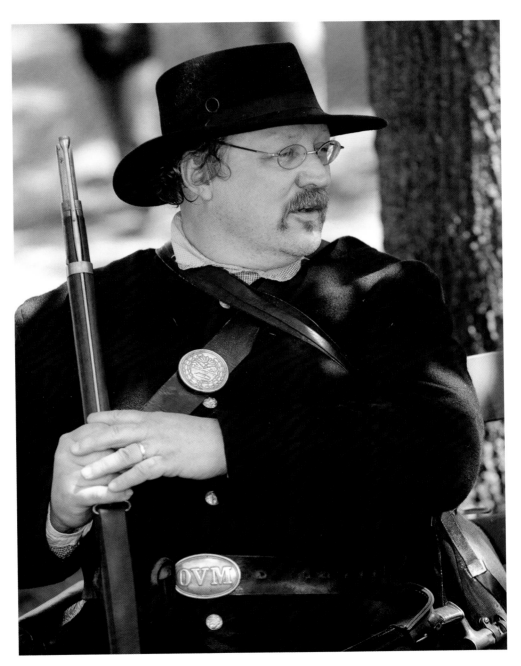

- **Bounce the light.** External electronic flash units mounted on the D7000 usually have a swivel that allows them to be pointed up at a ceiling for a bounce light effect. You can also bounce the light off a wall. You'll want the ceiling or wall to be white or have a neutral color to avoid a color cast.

- **Use reflectors.** Another way to bounce the light is to use reflectors or umbrellas that you can position yourself to provide a greater degree of control over the quantity and direction of the bounced light. Good reflectors can be pieces of foamboard, Mylar, or a reflective disk held in place by a clamp and stand. Although some expensive umbrellas and reflectors are available, spending a lot isn't necessary. A simple piece of white foamboard does the job beautifully. Umbrellas have the advantage of being compact and foldable, while providing a soft, even kind of light. They're relatively cheap, too, with a good 40-inch umbrella available for as little as $20. I purchased some collapsible round aluminized reflectors used to block an automobile's windshield from the rays of the sun—at a remarkable two for $7.98.

- **Use diffusers.** Nikon supplies a Sto-Fen-style diffuser dome with the SB-900 and SB-700 flash. You can purchase a similar diffuser for the SB-600 from Nikon, Sto-Fen, and some other vendors that offer clip-on diffusers. The two examples shown in Figures 10.21 and 10.22 fit over your electronic flash head and provide a soft, flattering light. These add-ons are more portable than umbrellas and other reflectors, yet provide a nice diffuse lighting effect.

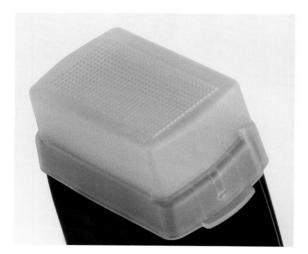

Figure 12.21 This diffuser dome is provided by Nikon with the SB-900, and softens the light of an external flash unit.

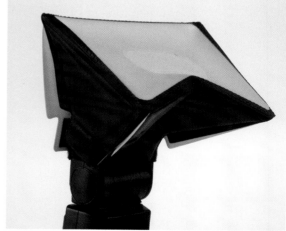

Figure 12.22 Soft boxes use Velcro strips to attach them to just about any shoe-mount flash unit.

Using Multiple Light Sources

Once you gain control over the qualities and effects you get with a single light source, you'll want to graduate to using multiple light sources. Using several lights allows you to shape and mold the illumination of your subjects to provide a variety of effects, from backlighting to side lighting to more formal portrait lighting. You can start simply with several incandescent light sources, bounced off umbrellas or reflectors that you construct. Or you can use more flexible multiple electronic flash setups.

Effective lighting is the one element that differentiates great photography from candid or snapshot shooting. Lighting can make a mundane subject look a little more glamorous. Make subjects appear to be soft when you want a soft look, or bright and sparkly when you want a vivid look, or strong and dramatic if that's what you desire. As you might guess, having control over your lighting means that you probably can't use the lights that are already in the room. You'll need separate, discrete lighting fixtures that can be moved, aimed, brightened, and dimmed on command.

Selecting your lighting gear will depend on the type of photography you do, and the budget you have to support it. It's entirely possible for a beginning D7000 photographer to create a basic, inexpensive lighting system capable of delivering high-quality results for a few hundred dollars, just as you can spend megabucks ($1,000 and up) for a sophisticated lighting system.

Basic Flash Setups

If you want to use multiple electronic flash units, the Nikon Speedlights described earlier will serve admirably. The higher-end models can be used with Nikon's wireless i-TTL features, which allows you to set up to three separate groups of flash units (several flashes can be included in each group) and trigger them using a master flash and the camera. Just set up one master unit, and arrange the compatible slave units around your subject. You can set the relative power of each unit separately, thereby controlling how much of the scene's illumination comes from the main flash, and how much from the auxiliary flash units, which can be used as fill flash, background lights, or, if you're careful, to illuminate the hair of portrait subjects.

Studio Flash

If you're serious about using multiple flash units, a studio flash setup might be more practical. The traditional studio flash is a multi-part unit, consisting of a flash head that mounts on your light stand, and is tethered to an AC (or sometimes battery) power supply. A single power supply can feed two or more flash heads at a time, with separate control over the output of each head.

When they are operating off AC power, studio flash don't have to be frugal with the juice, and are often powerful enough to illuminate very large subjects or to supply lots and lots of light to smaller subjects. The output of such units is measured in watt seconds (ws), so you could purchase a 200ws, 400ws, or 800ws unit, and a power pack to match.

Their advantages include greater power output, much faster recycling, built-in modeling lamps, multiple power levels, and ruggedness that can stand up to transport, because many photographers pack up these kits and tote them around as location lighting rigs.

A more practical choice these days are *monolights* (see Figure 12.23), which are "all-in-one" studio lights that sell for about $200-$400. They have the flash tube, modeling light, and power supply built into a single unit that can be mounted on a light stand. Monolights are available in AC-only and battery-pack versions, although an external battery eliminates some of the advantages of having a flash with everything in one unit. They are very portable, because all you need is a case for the monolight itself, plus the stands and other accessories you want to carry along. Because these units are so popular with photographers who are not full-time professionals, the lower-cost monolights are often designed more for lighter duty than professional studio flash. That doesn't mean they aren't rugged; you'll just need to handle them with a little more care, and, perhaps, not expect them to be used eight hours a day for weeks on end. In most other respects, however, monolights are the equal of traditional studio flash units in terms of fast recycling, built-in modeling lamps, adjustable power, and so forth.

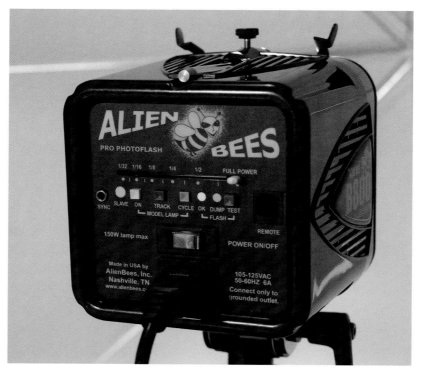

Figure 12.23
All-in-one "monolights" contain flash, power supply, and a modeling light in one compact package (umbrella not included).

Connecting Multiple Non-Dedicated Units to Your Nikon D7000

Non-dedicated electronic flash units can't use the automated i-TTL features of your Nikon D7000; you'll need to calculate exposure manually, through test shots evaluated on your camera's LCD, or by using an electronic flash meter. Moreover, you don't have to connect them to the accessory shoe on top of the camera. Instead, you can use a PC/X connector.

You should be aware that older electronic flash units sometimes use a triggering voltage that is too much for your D7000 to handle. You can actually damage the camera's electronics if the voltage is too high. You won't need to worry about this if you purchase brand new units from Alien Bees, Adorama, or other vendors. But if you must connect an external flash with an unknown triggering voltage, I recommend using a Wein Safe Sync (see Figure 12.24), which isolates the flash's voltage from the camera triggering circuit.

Another safe way to connect external cameras is through a radio-control device, such as the RadioPopper or PocketWizard triggers I mentioned earlier. They clip on the hot shoe and transmit a signal to a matching receiver that's connected to your flash unit. The receiver may have a hot shoe, PC connector, and "monoplug" connector (it looks like a headphone plug) that links to a matching port on compatible flash units.

Finally, some flash units have an optical slave trigger built in, or can be fitted with one, so that they fire automatically when another flash, including your camera's built-in unit, fires. Make sure the slave feature has a "digital" mode, which is designed to fire the flash when the main flash burst is detected, not the initial monitor pre-burst.

Figure 12.24
A voltage isolator can prevent frying your D7000's flash circuits if you use an older electronic flash.

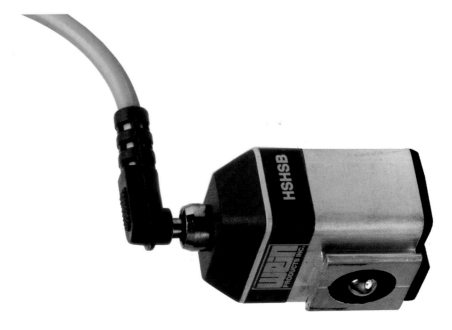

Other Lighting Accessories

Once you start working with light, you'll find there are plenty of useful accessories that can help you. Here are some of the most popular that you might want to consider.

Soft Boxes

Soft boxes are large square or rectangular devices that may resemble a square umbrella with a front cover, and produce a similar lighting effect. They can extend from a few feet square to massive boxes that stand five or six feet tall—virtually a wall of light. With a flash unit or two inside a soft box, you have a very large, semi-directional light source that's very diffuse and very flattering for portraiture and other people photography.

Soft boxes are also handy for photographing shiny objects. They not only provide a soft light, but if the box itself happens to reflect in the subject (say you're photographing a chromium toaster), the box will provide an interesting highlight that's indistinct and not distracting.

You can buy soft boxes or make your own. Some lengths of friction-fit plastic pipe and a lot of muslin cut and sewed just so may be all that you need. (See Figure 12.25.)

Light Stands

Both electronic flash and incandescent lamps can benefit from light stands. These are lightweight, tripod-like devices (but without a swiveling or tilting head) that can be set on the floor, tabletops, or other elevated surfaces and positioned as needed. Light stands should be strong enough to support an external lighting unit, up to and including a relatively heavy flash with soft box or umbrella reflectors. You want the supports to be capable of raising the lights high enough to be effective. Look for light stands capable of extending six to seven feet high. The nine-foot units usually have larger, steadier bases, and extend high enough that you can use them as background supports. You'll be using these stands for a lifetime, so invest in good ones. I bought my light stands when I was in college, and I have been using them for decades.

Backgrounds

Backgrounds can be backdrops of cloth, sheets of muslin you've painted yourself using a sponge dipped in paint, rolls of seamless paper, or any other suitable surface your mind can dream up. Backgrounds provide a complementary and non-distracting area behind subjects (especially portraits) and can be lit separately to provide contrast and separation that outlines the subject, or which helps set a mood.

I like to use plain-colored backgrounds for portraits, and white or gray seamless backgrounds for product photography. You can usually construct these yourself from cheap materials and tape them up on the wall behind your subject, or mount them on a pole stretched between a pair of light stands.

Snoots and Barn Doors

These fit over the flash unit and direct the light at your subject. Snoots are excellent for converting a flash unit into a hair light, while barn doors give you enough control over the illumination by opening and closing their flaps that you can use another flash as a background light, with the capability of feathering the light exactly where you want it on the background. (See Figure 12.26.)

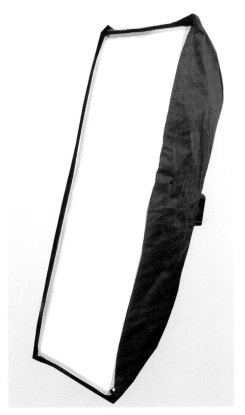

Figure 12.25 Soft boxes provide a diffuse light source.

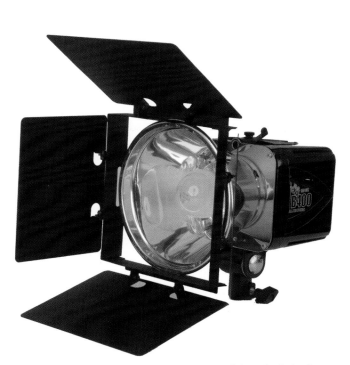

Figure 12.26 Barn doors allow you to modulate the light from a flash or lamp, and they are especially useful for hair lights and background lights.

Part IV

Enhancing Your Experience

What do you do after the shutter clicks and your image has been captured in electrons for posterity? This final part of the book will help you get more from your Nikon D7000 as you download and edit the pictures you've taken, and take the steps necessary to keep your camera humming like the finely (non-oiled) machine that it really is.

Chapter 13 details some of your options for downloading and editing your photographs. I'll provide quick introductions to the software bundled with your camera, and describe some of the other applications available to convert RAW files and fine-tune images. The chapter is not a software how-to—this book is virtually 100 percent devoted to photographic shooting techniques. (I want to help you *avoid* having to patch up your pictures in Photoshop where possible, by capturing them correctly in the camera.)

Chapter 14 tells you everything you need to know about upgrading your camera's firmware, protecting your LCD and memory card data, and, when necessary, cleaning your sensor manually.

13

Useful Software for the Nikon D7000

Unless you only take pictures, and then immediately print them directly to a PictBridge-compatible printer, somewhere along the line you're going to need to make use of the broad array of software available for the Nikon D7000. The picture-fixing options in the Retouch menu let you make only modest modifications to your carefully crafted photos. If your needs involve more than fixing red-eye, cropping and trimming, and maybe adjusting tonal values with D-Lighting, you're definitely going to want to use a utility or editor of some sort to perfect your images. After you've captured some great images and have them safely stored on your Nikon D7000's memory card, you'll need to transfer them from your camera and memory card to your computer, where they can be organized, fine-tuned in an image editor, and prepared for web display, printing, or some other final destination.

Fortunately, there are lots of software utilities and applications to help you do all these things. This chapter will introduce you to a few of them. Please note that this is *not* a "how-to-do-it" software chapter. This book has already expanded to more than twice the size of my previous camera guides, and I'm going to use every available page to offer advice on how to get the most from your D7000. There's no space to explain how to use all the features of Nikon Capture NX2, nor how to tweak RAW file settings in Adobe Camera Raw. Entire books have been written about both products. This chapter is intended solely to help you get your bearings among the large number of utilities and applications available, to help you better understand what each does, and how you might want to use them. At the very end of the chapter, however, I'm going to make an exception and provide some simple instructions for using Adobe Camera Raw, to help those who have been using Nikon's software exclusively get a feel for what you can do with the Adobe product.

The basic functions found in most of the programs discussed in this chapter include image transfer and management, camera control, and image editing. You'll find that many of the programs overlap several of these capabilities, so it's not always possible to categorize the discussions that follow by function. In fact, I'm going to start off by describing a few of the offerings available from Nikon.

Nikon's Applications and Utilities

If nothing else, Nikon has made sorting through the software for its digital cameras an interesting pursuit. Through the years, we've had various incarnations of programs with names like PictureProject, Nikon View, and Nikon Capture. Some have been compatible with both the Nikon dSLR and amateur Coolpix product lines. Many of them have been furnished on disc with the cameras. Others, most notoriously Nikon Capture, have been an extra-cost option, which particularly infuriated those of us who had paid several thousand dollars for a Nikon dSLR, and found that we'd need to pay more to get the software needed for the camera.

Recently, Nikon has begun splitting their software offerings into separate programs that are sort of standalone products, but which integrate with the others. For example, if you bought Nikon Capture NX2 you found that the program didn't really capture anything, as the previous Nikon Capture 4 did. If you wanted to operate the camera remotely, you needed to buy the off-shoot program, Nikon Camera Control Pro, which cost even *more* money.

The next few sections provide some descriptions of the Nikon software you'll want to use with your D7000.

Nikon View NX 2

This latest incarnation of Nikon's basic file viewer is better than ever, making it easy to browse through images, convert RAW files to JPEG or TIFF, and make corrections to white balance and exposure, either on individual files or on batches of files. It now includes Nikon Transfer and a movie editing tool, and works in tandem with Nikon Capture NX2, as you can open files inspected in View NX in one of the other programs—or within a third-party application you "register."

First and foremost, Nikon View NX is a great file viewer. There are three modes for looking at images: a thumbnail grid mode for checking out small previews of your images; an image viewer mode (see Figure 13.1) that shows a group of thumbnails along with an enlarged version of a selected image; and full screen mode, which allows you to examine an image in maximum detail.

Figure 13.1
Nikon View
NX is a great
basic file view-
ing utility.

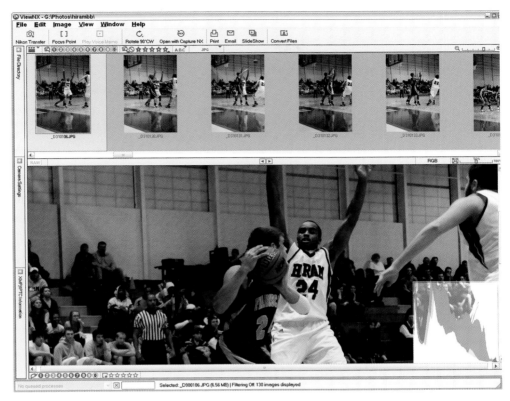

If you like to shoot RAW+JPEG, you can review image pairs as if they were a single image (rather than view the RAW and JPEG versions separately), and work with whichever version you need. The active focus area can be displayed in the image (see Figure 13.1 again), and there are histogram, highlight, and shadow displays to help you evaluate an image.

Should you want to organize your images, there are 10 labels available to classify images by criteria such as images printed, images copied, or images sent as e-mail, and you can mark your best shots for easier retrieval with a rating system of one to five stars. ViewNX also allows you to edit embedded XMP/IPTC information in fields such as Creator, Origin, Image Title, and suitable keywords. The utility can be downloaded from the support/download pages of the Nikon website at www.nikonusa.com.

Nikon Transfer

It seems like everyone offers some sort of image transfer system that automatically recognizes when a memory card is inserted in a reader, or a digital camera like the Nikon D7000 is attached to a computer using a USB cable. The most popular operating systems, from Mac OS X to Windows XP, Vista, and Windows 7 have their own built-in transfer programs, and Adobe Photoshop Elements includes one in its suite of utilities.

Nikon Transfer, now included with Nikon View NX 2, is particularly well-suited for D7000 owners, because it integrates easily with other Nikon software products, including View NX and Nikon Capture NX2. You can download photos to your computer, and then continue to work on them in the Nikon application (or third-party utility) of your choice.

When a memory card is inserted into a card reader, or when the D7000 is connected to your computer through a USB cable, Nikon Transfer recognizes the device, searches it for thumbnails, and provides a display like the one shown in Figure 13.2. You can preview the images and mark the ones you want to transfer with checks to create a Transfer Queue.

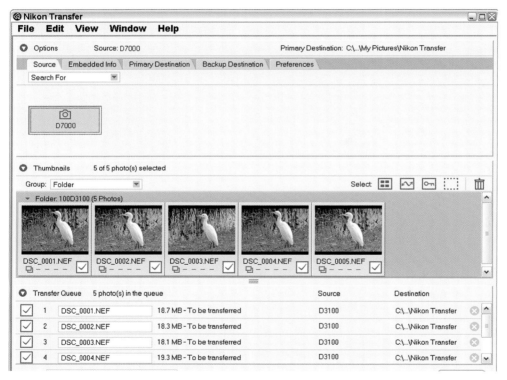

Figure 13.2
After Nikon Transfer displays thumbnails of the images on your memory card or camera, mark the ones you want to transfer.

Then, click on the Primary Destination tab (see Figure 13.3) and choose a location for the photos that will be transferred. Nikon Transfer can create a new folder for each transfer based on a naming convention you set up (click the Edit button next to the box at top center in the figure), or copy to a folder named after the current folder in the D7000's memory card. You can keep the current filename as the files are transferred, or assign a new name with a prefix you designate, such as Spain07_ . The program will add a number from 001 to 999 to the filename prefix you specify.

Figure 13.3
Copy files to a destination you specify using an optional file-name template you can define.

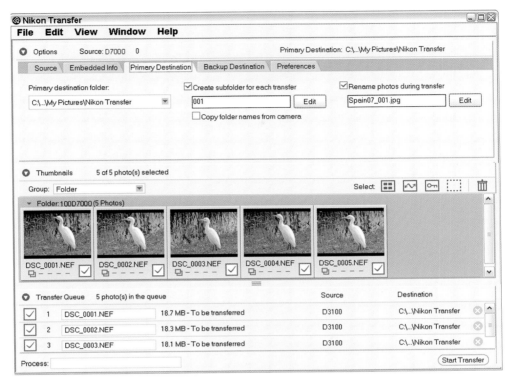

One neat feature is the ability to name a Backup Destination location, so that all transferred pictures can also be copied to a second folder, which can be located on a different hard disk drive or other media. You can embed information such as copyright data, star ratings, and labels in the images as they are transferred. When the file transfer is complete, Nikon Transfer can launch an application of your choice, set with a few clicks in the Preferences tab (see Figure 13.4).

Nikon Capture NX2

Capture NX2 is a pretty hefty chunk of software for the typical entry-level Nikon owner, but you, as a D7000 buyer, should be up to it. However, this program is challenging to master (and is somewhat expensive at about $150), but if you're ambitious and willing to plant your pitons for a steep climb up the learning curve, the program is indeed a powerful image-editing utility. It's designed specifically to process Nikon's NEF-format RAW files (although this edition has added the ability to manipulate JPEG and TIFF images as well). It includes an image browser (with labeling, sorting, and editing) that can be used to make many adjustments directly through the thumbnails. It also has advanced color management tools, impressive noise reduction capabilities, and batch processing features that allow you to apply sets of changes to collections of images.

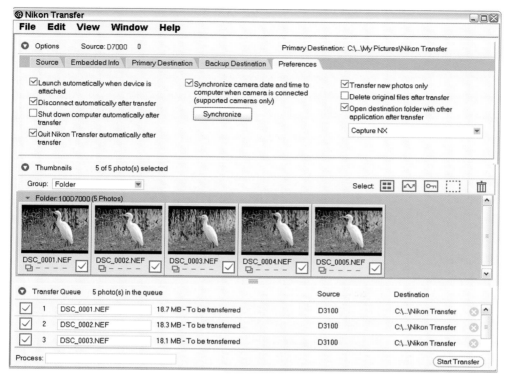

Figure 13.4
You can tell Nikon Transfer what to do after images are transferred in the Preferences tab.

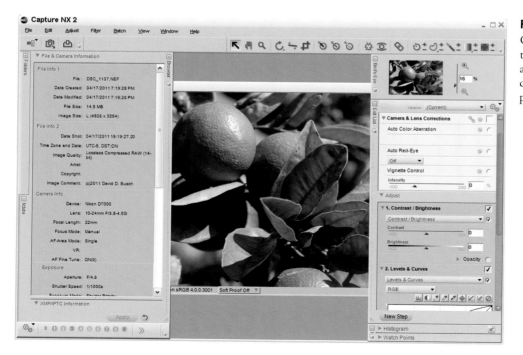

Figure 13.5
Capture NX2's tools are arranged in dockable palettes.

All the tools are arranged in dockable/expandable/collapsible palettes (see Figure 13.5) that tell you everything you need to know about an image, and provide the capabilities to push every pixel in interesting ways.

Photographers tend to love Capture NX or hate it, particularly in the NX 2 version that was current when I wrote this book, and it's easy to separate the fans from the furious. Those who are enamored of the program have invested a great deal of time in learning its quirky paradigm and now appreciate just how powerful Capture NX is. The detractors are usually those who are comfortable with another program, such as Photoshop or even Capture 4, this program's predecessor, and are upset that even the simplest functions can be confoundingly difficult for a new user to figure out. Capture NX's murky Help system isn't a lot of help; there's room for a huge book (or two) to explain how to use this program.

For example, instead of masks, Capture NX2 uses Nik Software's U Point technology, which applies Control Points to select and isolate parts of an image for manipulation. There are Color Control Points, with up to nine different sliders for each selected area. (See Figure 13.6.) There are also Black and White Control points for setting dynamic range, Neutral Control Points for correcting color casts, and a Red-Eye Reduction Control Point that removes crimson glows from pupils.

The workflow revolves around an Edit List, which contains a list of enhancements, including Camera Adjustments, RAW Adjustments, Light & Color Adjustments, Detail Adjustments, and Lens Adjustments, which can each be controlled separately. You can add steps of your own, cancel adjustments individually, and store steps in the Edit List as Settings that can be applied to individual images or batches.

Figure 13.6
Control Points are used to make common adjustments.

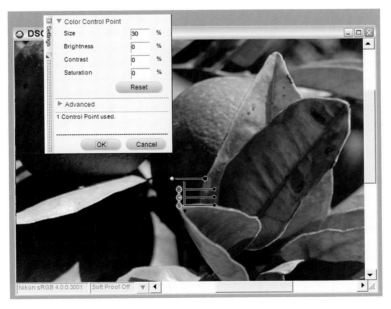

There are also Color Aberration Controls, D-Lighting, Image Dust Off, Vignette Control, Fisheye-to-Rectilinear Image Transformation ("de-fishing"), and a Distortion Control to reduce pincushion and barrel distortion.

Nikon Camera Control Pro 2

Nikon's Camera Control Pro 2 is a versatile utility that allows you to communicate directly with your camera from your computer through a USB cable. Once the two are linked, you can perform a variety of functions:

- **Shoot remotely.** Just about any shooting function you can adjust on the camera can be performed remotely, as you can see from the cluster of tabbed dialog boxes. Set exposure mode, adjust the aperture, add or subtract exposure compensation, choose a focus area, change ISO sensitivity or white balance—all are at your command through the software. You can even change Quality and Size settings, turn on auto bracketing, and change image optimization settings. You can optionally disable the controls on the camera, to prevent having settings you made at the computer changed accidentally.

- **Download directly to your computer.** When doing time-lapse photography using a tethered camera, you can use Camera Control Pro to transfer the images you take directly to the computer.

- **Upload comments.** Frustrated by the Nikon D7000's text entry screen? Edit your Image Comment and upload it directly to the camera from your computer keyboard.

- **Create and save custom curves.** You can load a sample image and create a special tone compensation custom curve for that image using tools similar to those found in Photoshop.

- **View and change Custom Settings.** This is one of my favorite features. While changing the Custom Settings for any of the Custom Settings options using the D7000's menus isn't difficult (particularly after you've absorbed the information in Chapter 9), Camera Control Pro makes playing with these options a joy.

Other Software

Other useful software for your Nikon D7000 falls into several categories. You might want to fine-tune your images, retouch them, change color balance, composite several images together, and perform other tasks we know as image editing, with a program like Adobe Photoshop, Photoshop Elements, or Corel Photo Paint.

You might want to play with the settings in RAW files, too, as you import them into an image editor. There are specialized tools expressly for tweaking RAW files, ranging from Adobe Camera Raw to PhaseOne's Capture One Pro (C1 Pro). A third type of manipulation is the specialized task of noise reduction, which can be performed within Photoshop, Adobe Camera Raw, or tools like Bibble Professional. There are also specialized tools just for noise reduction, such as Noise Ninja (also included with Bibble) and Neat Image. Some programs, like the incomparable DxO Optics Pro perform magical transformations that you can't achieve any other way.

Each of these utilities and applications deserves a chapter of its own, so I'm simply going to enumerate some of the most popular applications and utilities and tell you a little about what they do.

DxO Optics Pro

DxO Labs (www.DxO.com) offers an incredibly useful program called Optics Pro ($170-$300) that is unique in the range of functions it provides. Ostensibly an image quality enhancement utility that "cures" some of the ills that plague even the best lenses, the latest release also features a new RAW conversion engine that uses a new demosaicing algorithm to translate your NEF files into images with more detail, less noise, and fewer artifacts. These features meld well with the program's original mission: fixing the optical "geometry" of images, using settings custom-tailored for each individual lens. (I'm not kidding: when you "assemble" the program, you specify each and every camera body you want to use with Optics Pro, and designate exactly which lenses are included in your repertoire.)

Once an image has been imported into Optics Pro, it can be manipulated within one of four main sections: Light, Color, Geometry, and Details. It's especially useful for correcting optical flaws, color, exposure, and dynamic range, while adjusting perspective, distortion, and tilting. If you own a fisheye lens, Optics Pro will "de-fish" your images to produce a passable rectilinear photo from your curved image. A new Dust/Blemish Removal tool operates something like a manual version of the D7000's Dust Off Reference Photo. The user creates a dust/blemish template, and the program removes dust from the marked area in multiple images. Figure 13.7 shows you DxO Optics Pro's clean user interface.

Phase One Capture One Pro (C1 Pro)

If there is a Cadillac of RAW converters for Nikon and Canon digital SLR cameras, C1 Pro has to be it. This premium-priced program from Phase One (www.phaseone.com) does everything, does it well, and does it quickly. If you can't justify the price tag of this professional-level software (as much as $399 for the top-of-the-line edition), there are "lite" versions for serious amateurs and cash-challenged professionals for as little as $130.

Aimed at photographers with high-volume needs (that would include school and portrait photographers, as well as busy commercial photographers), C1 Pro is available for both Windows and Mac OS X, and supports a broad range of digital cameras. Phase

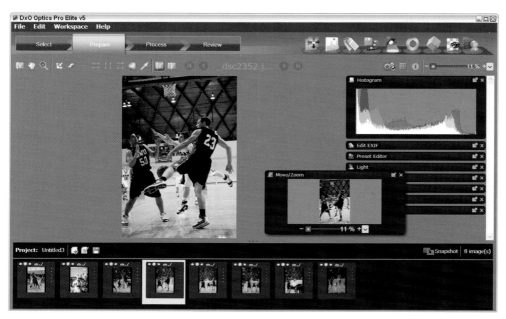

Figure 13.7
DxO Optics
Pro fixes lens
flaws, and
functions as a
high-tech RAW
converter and
noise reduction
utility, too.

One is a leading supplier of megabucks digital camera backs for medium and larger format cameras, so they really understand the needs of photographers.

The latest features include individual noise reduction controls for each image, automatic levels adjustment, a "quick develop" option that allows speedy conversion from RAW to TIFF or JPEG formats, dual-image side-by-side views for comparison purposes, and helpful grids and guides that can be superimposed over an image. Photographers concerned about copyright protection will appreciate the ability to add watermarks to the output images.

Bibble Pro

One of my personal favorites among third-party RAW converters is Bibble Pro. It supports one of the broadest ranges of RAW file formats available (which can be handy if you find yourself with the need to convert a file from a friend or colleague's non-Nikon camera), including NEF files from Nikon cameras dating as far back as the Nikon D1, D1x/h, D2H, and D100. The utility supports lots of different platforms, too. It's available for Windows, Mac OS X, and, believe it or not, Linux.

Bibble (www.bibblelabs.com) works fast, which is important when you have to convert many images in a short time (event photographers will know what I am talking about!). Bibble's batch-processing capabilities also let you convert large numbers of files using settings you specify without further intervention. Its customizable interface lets you organize and edit images quickly and then output them in a variety of formats, including 16-bit TIFF and PNG. You can even create a web gallery from within Bibble. I often find myself disliking the generic filenames applied to digital images by cameras, so I really like Bibble's ability to rename batches of files using new names that you specify.

Bibble is fully color managed, which means it can support all the popular color spaces (Adobe sRGB and so forth) and use custom profiles generated by third-party color-management software. There are two editions of Bibble, a Pro version and a Lite version. The Pro version is reasonably priced at $199, but you can save $100 with the Lite edition, which lacks the top-line's options for tethered shooting, embedding IPTC-compatible captions in images, and can also be used as a Photoshop plug-in (if you prefer not to work with the application in its standalone mode). Bibble Pro now incorporates Noise Ninja technology, so you can get double-duty from this valuable application.

BreezeBrowser Pro

A versatile program you want to consider is BreezeBrowser Pro, from Breeze Systems (www.breezesys.com), which performs several useful functions in addition to RAW file conversion and image browsing. It can produce contact sheets and proof images, generate nifty web pages with only a little input on your part, and, importantly in this GPS-crazy age, link geo-tagged images with Google Earth and online maps. Now that the Nikon D7000 provides the compact Nikon GP-1 geo-tagging unit, which clips onto the camera's accessory shoe, software like BreezeBrowser provides an actual real-world application for this kind of data.

A real bargain at $69.95, BreezeBrowser Pro offers all the basic conversion, sharpening, resizing, and adjustments for your RAW images. You can create captioned web pages from within the program, and, if you want to sell your pictures, it will protect them with watermarking and provide a system for online ordering of images/prints. Batch rename features let you change the filename applied in the camera to something more useful, and edit the date/time stamps of your files. The Windows-only program is shown in Figure 13.8.

BreezeSystems NKRemote

You may find BreezeSystems' NKRemote an attractive $175 alternative. It links to your camera through the USB cable, and offers direct control of virtually every camera control through a well-designed user interface. It has a couple quirks—for example, you can discern the original Canon-oriented underpinnings of the program by the use of the label Tv (Time Value) for Shutter-priority. But the features are solid.

The program works with a variety of Nikon cameras; check out the website at www.breezesys.com for a complete list. So, if you add another model to your kit, you won't have to buy new software. NKRemote allows focusing automatically and manually from your PC (you can choose the focus point by checking one of boxes in the AF interface), thanks to its support for the Live View feature. You'll enjoy setting up your

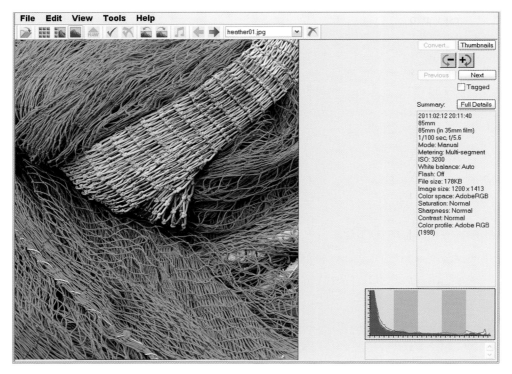

Figure 13.8
BreezeBrowser Pro offers geotagging and support for web image sales among its innovative features.

D7000 on a long USB tether, and relaxing while you wait for that elusive plaid-bellied sapgrabber to perch within view of your lens.

You can shoot time-lapse photos to capture flowers blooming, construction sites constructing, or dawns breaking. It's easy to adjust Picture Controls from your PC, too. One of my favorite features is the Photo Booth capability, which you can set up to operate like one of those three-shots-for-a-dollar photo booths at the County Fair. In this mode, the software automatically takes a series of photos in sequence, and then immediately prints them out. If you're a professional (or aspiring pro), you can set up your photo booth at an event; otherwise, the feature is great fun to use at home.

Photoshop/Photoshop Elements

Photoshop is the high-end choice for image editing, and Photoshop Elements is a great alternative for those who need some of the features of Photoshop, but can do without the most sophisticated capabilities, including editing CMYK files. Both editors use the latest version of Adobe's Camera Raw plug-in, which makes it easy to adjust things like image resolution, white balance, exposure, shadows, brightness, sharpness, luminance, and noise reduction. One plus with the Adobe products is that they are available in identical versions for both Windows and Macs.

The latest version of Photoshop includes a built-in RAW plug-in that is compatible with the proprietary formats of a growing number of digital cameras, both new and old, and which can perform a limited number of manipulations on JPEG and TIFF files, too. This plug-in also works with Photoshop Elements, but with fewer features. Here's how easy it is to manipulate a RAW file using the Adobe converter:

1. Transfer the RAW images from your camera to your computer's hard drive.

2. In Photoshop, choose Open from the File menu, or use Organizer or Bridge (depending on the version you have installed).

3. Select a RAW image file. The Adobe Camera Raw plug-in will pop up, showing a preview of the image, like the one shown in Figure 13.9.

4. If you like, use one of the tools found in the toolbar at the top left of the dialog box. From left to right, they are:

   ■ **Zoom.** Operates just like the Zoom tool in Photoshop.

   ■ **Hand.** Use like the Hand tool in Photoshop.

   ■ **White Balance.** Click an area in the image that should be neutral gray or white to set the white balance quickly.

   ■ **Color Sampler.** Use to determine the RGB values of areas you click with this eyedropper.

   ■ **Crop.** Pre-crops the image so that only the portion you specify is imported into Photoshop. This option saves time when you want to work on a section of a large image, and you don't need the entire file.

   ■ **Straighten.** Drag in the preview image to define what should be a horizontal or vertical line, and ACR will realign the image to straighten it.

   ■ **Retouch.** Used to heal or clone areas you define.

   ■ **Red-Eye Removal.** Quickly zap red pupils in your human subjects.

   ■ **ACR Preferences.** Produces a dialog box of Adobe Camera Raw preferences.

   ■ **Rotate Counterclockwise.** Rotates counterclockwise in 90-degree increments with a click.

   ■ **Rotate Clockwise.** Rotates clockwise in 90-degree increments with a click.

5. Using the Basic tab, you can have ACR show you red and blue highlights in the preview that indicate shadow areas that are clipped (too dark to show detail) and light areas that are blown out (too bright). Click the triangles in the upper-left corner of the histogram display (shadow clipping) and upper-right corner (highlight clipping) to toggle these indicators on or off.

6. Also in the Basic tab you can choose white balance, either from the drop-down list or by setting a color temperature and green/magenta color bias (tint) using the sliders.

7. Other sliders are available to control exposure, recovery, fill light, blacks, brightness, contrast, vibrance, and saturation. A checkbox can be marked to convert the image to grayscale.

8. Make other adjustments (described in more detail below).

9. ACR makes automatic adjustments for you. You can click Default and make the changes for yourself, or click the Auto link (located just above the Exposure slider) to reapply the automatic adjustments after you've made your own modifications.

10. If you've marked more than one image to be opened, the additional images appear in a "filmstrip" at the left side of the screen. You can click on each thumbnail in the filmstrip in turn and apply different settings to each.

11. Click Open Image/Open Image(s) into Photoshop using the settings you've made.

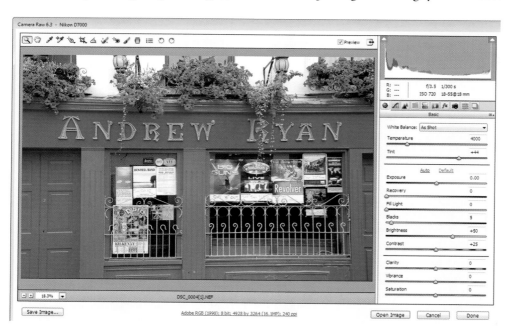

Figure 13.9
The basic ACR dialog box looks like this when processing a single image.

The Basic tab is displayed by default when the ACR dialog box opens, and it includes most of the sliders and controls you'll need to fine-tune your image as you import it into Photoshop. These include:

- **White Balance.** Leave it As Shot or change to a value such as Daylight, Cloudy, Shade, Tungsten, Fluorescent, or Flash. If you like, you can set a custom white balance using the Temperature and Tint sliders.

- **Exposure.** This slider adjusts the overall brightness and darkness of the image.

- **Recovery.** Restores detail in the red, green, and blue color channels.

- **Fill Light.** Reconstructs detail in shadows.

- **Blacks.** Increases the number of tones represented as black in the final image, emphasizing tones in the shadow areas of the image.

- **Brightness.** This slider adjusts the brightness and darkness of an image.

- **Contrast.** Manipulates the contrast of the midtones of your image.

- **Convert to Grayscale.** Mark this box to convert the image to black-and-white.

- **Vibrance.** Prevents over-saturation when enriching the colors of an image.

- **Saturation.** Manipulates the richness of all colors equally, from zero saturation (gray/black, no color) at the −100 setting to double the usual saturation at the +100 setting.

Additional controls are available on the Tone Curve, Detail, HSL/Grayscale, Split Toning, Lens Corrections, Camera Calibration, and Presets tabs, shown in Figure 13.10. The Tone Curve tab can change the tonal values of your image. The Detail tab lets you adjust sharpness, luminance smoothing, and apply color noise reduction. The HSL/Grayscale tab offers controls for adjusting hue, saturation, and lightness and converting an image to black-and-white. Split Toning helps you colorize an image with sepia or cyanotype (blue) shades. The Lens Corrections tab has sliders to adjust for chromatic aberrations and vignetting. The Camera Calibration tab provides a way for calibrating the color corrections made in the Camera Raw plug-in. The Presets tab (not shown) is used to load settings you've stored for reuse.

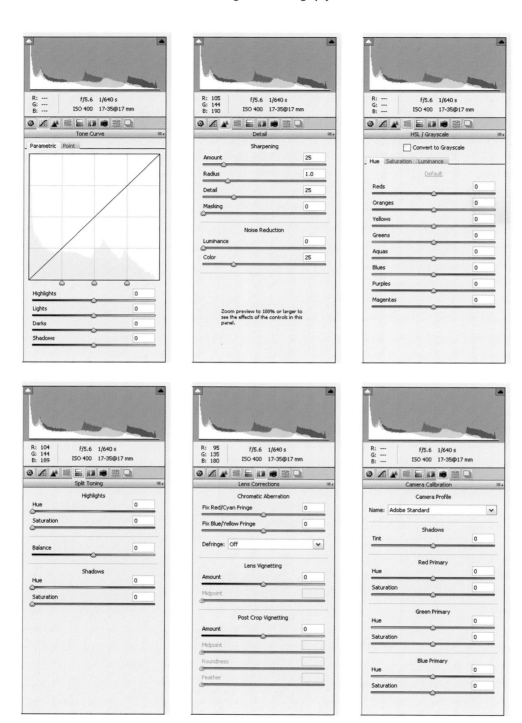

Figure 13.10 More controls are available within the additional tabbed dialog boxes in Adobe Camera Raw.

Nikon D7000: Troubleshooting and Prevention

One of the nice things about modern electronic cameras like the Nikon D7000 is that they have fewer mechanical moving parts to fail, so they are less likely to "wear out." No film transport mechanism, no wind lever or motor drive, no complicated mechanical linkages from camera to lens to physically stop down the lens aperture. Instead, tiny, reliable motors are built into each lens (and you lose the use of only that lens should something fail), and one of the few major moving parts in the camera itself is a lightweight mirror (its small size is one of the advantages of the D7000's 1.5X crop factor) that flips up and down with each shot.

Of course, the camera also has a moving shutter that can fail, but the shutter is built rugged enough that you can expect it to last 150,000 shutter cycles or more. Unless you're shooting sports in continuous mode day in and day out, the shutter on your D7000 is likely to last as long as you expect to use the camera.

The only other things on the camera that move are switches, dials, buttons, the flip-up electronic flash, and the door that slides open to allow you to remove and insert the Secure Digital card. Unless you're extraordinarily clumsy or unlucky and manage to bend the internal pins in the Secure Digital card slot, or give your built-in flash a good whack while it is in use, there's not a lot that can go wrong mechanically with your Nikon D7000.

On the other hand, one of the chief drawbacks of modern electronic cameras is that they are modern *electronic* cameras. Your D7000 is fully dependent on two different batteries. Without them, the camera can't be used. There are numerous other electrical and electronic connections in the camera (many connected to those mechanical switches and dials), and components like the color LCD and top-panel status LCD that can potentially fail or suffer damage. The camera also relies on its "operating system," or *firmware*, which can be plagued by bugs that cause unexpected behavior. Luckily, electronic components are generally more reliable and trouble-free, especially when compared to their mechanical counterparts from the pre-electronic film camera days. (Film cameras of the last 10 to 20 years have had almost as many electronic features as digital cameras, but, believe it or not, there were whole generations of film cameras that had *no* electronics or batteries.)

Digital cameras have problems unique to their breed, too; the most troublesome being the need to clean the sensor of dust and grime periodically. This chapter will show you how to diagnose problems, fix some common ills, and, importantly, learn how to avoid them in the future.

Battery Powered

I've grown to live with the need for batteries even though I shot for years using all-mechanical Nikon cameras that had no batteries (or even a built-in light meter!). The need for electrical power is the price we pay for modern conveniences like autofocus, autoexposure, LCD image display, backlit menus, and, of course, digital images.

One of the batteries you rely on is the EN-EL15 battery installed in the grip. It's rechargeable, can last for as long as 1,000 shots, and is user-replaceable if you have a spare. The second power cell in your camera is a so-called *clock battery,* which is also rechargeable, but is tucked away within the innards of the camera and can't be replaced by the user. The clock battery retains the settings of the camera when it's powered down, and, even, when the main battery is removed for charging. If you remove the EN-EL15 for long periods, the clock battery may discharge, but it will be quickly rejuvenated when you replace the main battery. (It's recharged by juice supplied by the EN-EL15.) Although you can't replace this battery yourself, you can expect it to last for the useful life of the camera.

So, your main concern will be to provide a continuous, reliable source of power for your D7000. As I noted in Chapter 1, you should always have a spare battery or two so you won't need to stop shooting when your internal battery dies. I recommend buying Nikon-brand batteries: saving $20 or so for an after-market battery may save you a few dollars, but can cost you much more than that if the battery malfunctions and damages your camera.

KEEPING TRACK OF YOUR BATTERIES AND MEMORY CARDS

Here's a trick I use to keep track of which batteries are fresh/discharged, and which memory cards are blank/exposed. I cut up some small slips of paper and fold them in half, forming a tiny "booklet." Then I write EXPOSED in red on the "inside" pages of the booklet and UNEXPOSED in green on the outside pages. Folded one way, the slips read EXPOSED; folded the other way, the slips read UNEXPOSED. I slip them inside the plastic battery cover, which you should *always* use when the batteries are not in the camera (to avoid shorting out the contacts), folded so the appropriate "state" of the batteries is visible. The same slips are used in the translucent plastic cases I use for my memory cards. (See Figure 14.1.) For my purposes, EXPOSED means the same as DISCHARGED, and UNEXPOSED is the equivalent of CHARGED. The color coding is an additional clue as to which batteries/memory cards are good to go, or not ready for use.

Figure 14.1
Mark your batteries—or memory cards—so you'll know which are ready for use.

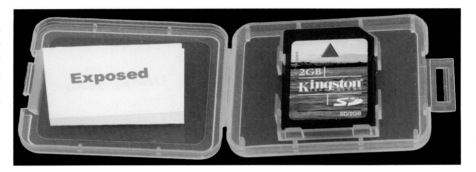

A good use for those extra batteries is in the Nikon MB-D11 Multi-Power Battery Pack (about $250), which holds an EN-EL15 battery, effectively doubling your total shooting time. The MB-D11 can also be used with the included AA Battery Holder, allowing you to use six AA batteries in a pinch (included) so users can use AA batteries as a power backup.

The MB-D11 power pack is sometimes called a *vertical grip*, because it includes a supplemental AE-L/AF-L button, vertically oriented shutter release button with lock, and front and rear command dials. The control combo makes it more convenient to shoot vertically oriented photos with the camera rotated 90 degrees.

There are several techniques you can use to stretch the longevity of your D7000's battery. To get the most from each charge, consider these steps:

■ **Playback menu: Image Review.** Turn off automatic image review after each shot using this menu option. You can still review your images by pressing the Playback button. Or, leave image review on, but set the display for the minimum 4 seconds as described next.

- **Monitor Off Delay.** In CSM #c4, set for the minimum, 4 seconds, for playback, menus, shooting info display, and image review. That three-inch LCD uses a lot of juice, so reducing the amount of time it is active when you don't turn it off manually can boost the effectiveness of your battery.

- **Auto meter off-delay.** Set to 4 seconds in CSM #c2 if you can tolerate such a brief active time.

- **Reduce LCD brightness.** In the Setup menu's LCD Brightness option, select the lowest of the seven brightness settings that work for you under most conditions. If you're willing to shade the LCD with your hand, you can often get away with lower brightness settings outdoors, which will further increase the useful life of your battery.

- **Turn off the shooting information display.** Turn it on or off manually as needed by pressing the Info button.

- **Reduce internal flash use.** No flash at all or fill flash use less power than a full blast.

- **Cancel VR.** Turn off vibration reduction if your lens (such as the 18-200mm VR II lens) has that feature and you feel you don't need it.

- **Use a card reader.** When transferring pictures from your D7000 to your computer, use a card reader instead of the USB cable. Linking your camera to your computer and transferring images using the cable takes longer and uses a lot more power.

Upgrading Your Firmware

The camera relies on its "operating system," or *firmware*, which should be updated in a reasonable fashion as new releases become available. The firmware in your Nikon D7000 handles everything from menu display (including fonts, colors, and the actual entries themselves), what languages are available, and even support for specific devices and features. Upgrading the firmware to a new version makes it possible to add or fine-tune features while fixing some of the bugs that sneak in.

Firmware upgrades are used most frequently to fix bugs in the software, and much less frequently to add or enhance features. The exact changes made to the firmware are generally spelled out in the firmware release announcement. You can examine the remedies provided and decide if a given firmware patch is important to you. If not, you can usually safely wait a while before going through the bother of upgrading your firmware—at least long enough for the early adopters (such as those who haunt the Digital Photography Review forums at www.dpreview.com) to report whether the bug fixes have introduced new bugs of their own. Each new firmware release incorporates the changes from previous releases, so if you skip a minor upgrade you should have no problems.

WHEN TO UPGRADE YOUR FIRMWARE

I *always* recommend waiting at least two weeks after a firmware upgrade is announced before changing the software in your camera. This is often in direct contradiction to the online Nikon "gurus" who breathlessly announce each new firmware release on their web pages, usually with links to where you can download the latest software. *Don't do it!* Yet. Nikon has, in the past, introduced firmware upgrades that were buggy and added problems of their own. If you own a camera affected by a new round of firmware upgrades, I urge you to wait and let a few million over-eager fellow users "beta test" this upgrade for you. Within a few weeks, any problems (although I don't expect there will be any) will surface and you'll know whether the update is safe. Your camera is working fine right now, so why take the chance?

How It Works

If you're computer savvy, you might wonder how your Nikon D7000 is able to over-write its own operating system—that is, how can the existing firmware be used to load the new version on top of itself? It's a little like lifting yourself by reaching down and pulling up on your bootstraps.

Not ironically, that's almost exactly what happens: At your command (when you start the upgrade process), the D7000 shifts into a special mode in which it is no longer operating from its firmware but, rather, from a small piece of software called a *bootstrap loader*, a separate, protected software program that functions only at startup or when upgrading firmware. The loader's function is to look for firmware to launch or, when directed, to copy new firmware from a memory card to the internal memory space where the old firmware is located. Once the new firmware has replaced the old, you can "reboot" the camera using the new operating system.

Why Three Firmware Modules?

Your Nikon D7000's firmware is divided into three parts; most earlier Nikon models had the firmware in just two sections. Why chop the firmware up in the first place? And what's that third module for, anyway?

Previous Nikon cameras had an A and B firmware listing, located in the Firmware Version entry in the Setup menu. There's a good reason why the firmware was previously divided in twain. Each of the two modules was "in charge" of particular parts of the camera's operating system. So, when a bug was found, or a new feature added, it was possible, in many cases, to offer only an upgrade for either Firmware A or Firmware B, depending on which module was affected. Although mistakes in upgrading firmware are rare, you cut the opportunities for user errors in half when only one of the modules needs to be replaced.

But there's a more important reason for having at least two firmware modules. If your camera had just one, and you had the misfortune to munge that firmware during an ill-fated upgrade, it's very likely your camera would be magically transformed into a digital doorstop. Part of the firmware is needed simply to install (or re-install firmware) in the first place. With all Nikon cameras, Firmware A and Firmware B each has the capability of locating and installing replacement firmware. So, if A is ruined, you can use the routines in B to re-install a new copy of A. And vice versa. We can all agree that this is a wise move on Nikon's part.

So, what's Firmware L, currently found only in a few Nikon cameras, like the D7000, used for? Some have speculated that the L firmware was a Language database, so that support for the camera could be expanded to include other languages without the need to mess with the A and B entries. I suspected that the L represented a lens database, perhaps to allow the EXPEED processor to compensate for vignetting or aberrations.

The L firmware is so mysterious that the first few Nikon representatives I asked didn't know exactly what it was for, either, but I managed to track down a techie who filled me in, while providing some additional insight into the workings of all three firmware modules. He confirmed that the Nikon D90 was the first Nikon camera to include this third firmware module, and that it was, indeed, a lens database that could be updated from time to time with information about new lenses as they were introduced. The function, he said, was to allow more sophisticated distortion control and other features, such as distance integration information provided by Nikon D and G lenses.

> ## WARNING
>
> Use a fully charged EN-EL15 charged battery or a Nikon EH-5/EH-5a AC adapter to ensure that you'll have enough power to operate the camera for the entire upgrade. Moreover, you should not turn off the camera while your old firmware is being overwritten. Don't open the memory card door or do anything else that might disrupt operation of the D7000 while the firmware is being installed.

Getting Ready

Before you get started, I have to emphasize that at the time this book was written, only one firmware release has been made available, Version 1.01, which fixed some problems with movie shooting. So, the procedure I am going to describe is the recommended process used for that update. But when it comes time to do an actual firmware upgrade for your D7000, you should double-check the instructions below against the recommended procedure that Nikon implements at that time. It should be very close to the steps I outline, but there may be some small differences.

The first thing to do is determine whether you need the current firmware update. First, confirm the version number of your Nikon D7000's current firmware:

1. Turn on the D7000.
2. Press the MENU button and select Firmware Version from the Setup menu. The camera's firmware version will be displayed. (See Figure 14.2.)
3. Write down the Version number for Parts A, B, and L.
4. Turn off the D7000.

Figure 14.2
View your current firmware versions before upgrading.

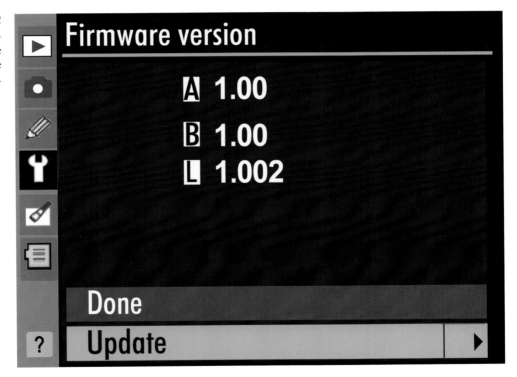

Next, go to the Nikon support site, locate, and download the firmware update. In the USA, the place to go is http://support.nikonusa.com/, which will offer a list of choices, including one that says Current Firmware Downloads available for Nikon Products. Click that link, then click the DSLR link on the page displayed next. Scroll down to the D7000 row in the table, and review the version number for the current update.

If the version is later than the one you noted in your camera, click the firmware link in either the Windows or Macintosh columns (depending on your computer) to download the file. It will have a name like D7000-V101W.exe (Windows) or F-D7000-V101M.dmg (Macintosh). Extract the file to a folder on your computer using the unzipping or unstuffing software of your choice.

The D7000's firmware comes in two parts, A and B, which can be updated individually (plus the third, L file, which is updated less often). The actual update files will be named something like:

D7000_0101.bin

For the most recent update, both A and B modules were included in a single file. In the past, Nikon has also used separate files for the A and B modules. Because it was mandatory to update *both* A and B firmware for the 1.01 upgrade, Nikon avoided potential user error by combining the firmware modules into one installation pack. The final preparation you need to make is to decide whether you'd like to upgrade your firmware using a memory card reader, or by transferring the software to the D7000 using the UC-E4 USB cable. In either case, you'll need to format a memory card in the D7000. Then, perform one of the sets of steps in the sections that follow.

Updating from a Card Reader

To update from a card reader, use a reader connected to your computer with a USB cable. Then, follow these steps:

1. Insert a formatted memory card into the card reader. If you have been using Nikon transfer or the "autoplay" features of your operating system to transfer images from your memory card to the computer, the automated transfer dialog box may appear. Close it.

2. The memory card will appear on your Macintosh desktop, or in the Computer/My Computer folders under Windows 7/Windows Vista/Windows XP.

3. Drag one of the firmware files to the memory card. You can install "A" or "B" first (if two files are provided), or, only the L file if that is the only one included. It doesn't matter. If your particular upgrade consists of only one of the two files, drag that to the memory card. Remember to copy the firmware to the *root* (top) directory of the memory card. The D7000 will be unable to find it if you place it in a folder.

Updating with a USB Connection

You can also copy the firmware to the D7000's memory card using a USB connection. Just follow these steps:

1. With the camera turned off, insert the formatted memory card. Then, turn the camera back on.

2. Press the MENU button and navigate to the Setup menu.

3. Turn the D7000 off and connect it to your computer using the UC-E4 USB cable.

4. Turn the camera back on. If you have been using Nikon transfer or the "autoplay" features of your operating system to transfer images from your memory card to the computer, the automated transfer dialog box may appear. Close it.

5. The camera will appear on the Macintosh desktop, or in the Computer/My Computer folders under Windows 7/Windows Vista/Windows XP.

6. Drag one of the firmware files to the memory card. It doesn't matter whether you install "A" or "B", if two are available. If your particular upgrade consists of only one .bin file, drag that to the memory card. Remember to copy the firmware to the *root* (top) directory of the memory card. The D7000 will be unable to find it if you place it in a folder.

7. Disconnect the camera from the computer.

Starting the Update

To perform the actual update, follow these steps:

1. With the memory card containing the firmware update software in the camera, turn the camera on.

2. Press the MENU button and select Firmware Version in the Setup menu.

3. Select Update and press the multi selector button to the right.

4. When the firmware update screen appears, highlight Yes and press OK to begin the update.

5. The actual process may take a few minutes (from two to five). Be sure not to turn off the camera or perform any other operations while it is underway. (See Figure 14.3.)

6. When the update is completed, the warning message will no longer be displayed on the screen. You can turn off the camera when the message disappears. (See Figure 14.4.)

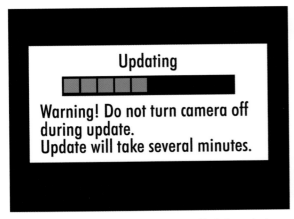

Figure 14.3 Don't turn the camera off while updating is underway.

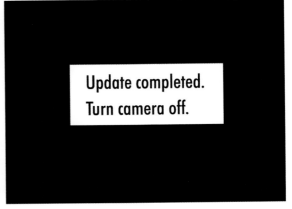

Figure 14.4 Turn the camera off when update is finished.

7. Remove the memory card.

8. Turn the D7000 back on to load the updated firmware.

9. Press the MENU button and select Firmware Version in the Setup menu to view the current firmware number. If it matches the update, you've successfully upgraded that portion of the firmware.

10. Reformat the memory card.

11. If there is a second part to your firmware upgrade ("A" or "B"), then repeat all the steps for the additional firmware software.

12. Reformat the memory card to return it to a "clean" condition.

Protect Your LCD

The massive three-inch color LCD on the back of your Nikon D7000 almost seems like a target for banging, scratching, and other abuse. The camera is furnished with the plastic Nikon BM-8 LCD protector, which I dislike strongly, as it tends to scratch easily and tends to fog up when you breathe on it while peering through the viewfinder. The LCD itself is quite rugged, and a few errant knocks are unlikely to shatter the protective cover over the LCD, and scratches won't easily mar its tempered glass surface. However, if you want to be on the safe side, there are a number of protective products you can purchase to keep your LCD safe—and, in some cases, make it a little easier to view. Here's a quick overview of your options.

- **Plastic overlays.** The simplest solution (although not always the cheapest) is to apply a plastic overlay sheet or "skin" cut to fit your LCD. These adhere either by static electricity or through a light adhesive coating that's even less clingy than stick-it notes. You can cut down overlays made for PDAs (although these can be pricey at up to $19.95 for a set of several sheets), or purchase overlays sold specifically for digital cameras. Vendors such as Hoodman (www.hoodmanusa.com) offer overlays of this type. These products will do a good job of shielding your D7000's LCD screen from scratches and minor impacts, but will not offer much protection from a good whack.

- **Acrylic shields.** These scratch-resistant acrylic panels, laser cut to fit your camera perfectly, are my choice as the best protection solution, and what I use on my own D7000. At about $6 each, they also happen to be the least expensive option as well. I get mine from a company called 'da Products (www.daproducts.com). They attach using strips of sticky adhesive that hold the panel flush and tight, but which allow the acrylic to be pried off and the adhesive removed easily if you want to remove or replace the shield. They don't attenuate your view of the LCD and are non-reflective enough for use under a variety of lighting conditions. I also like the glass covers from GGS, available from a variety of sources, and shown in Figure 14.5.

Figure 14.5
A tough glass shield can protect your LCD from scratches.

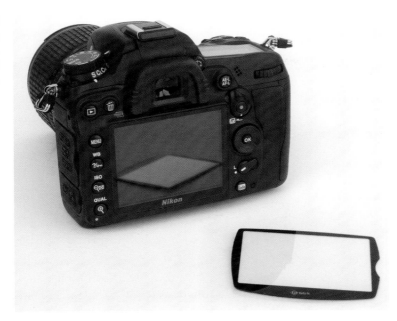

- **Flip-up hoods.** These protectors slip on using the flanges around your D7000's eyepiece, and provide a cover that completely shields the LCD, but unfolds to provide a three-sided hood that allows viewing the LCD while minimizing the extraneous light falling on it and reducing contrast. They're sold for about $40 by Delkin (www.delkin.com) and Hoodman. If you want to completely protect your LCD from hard knocks and need to view the screen outdoors in bright sunlight, there is nothing better. However, I have a couple problems with these devices. First, with the cover closed, you can't peek down after taking a shot to see what your image looks like during picture review. You must open the cap each time you want to look at the LCD. Moreover, with the hood unfolded, it's difficult to look through the viewfinder: Don't count on being able to use the viewfinder *and* the LCD at the same time with one of these hoods in place.

- **Magnifiers.** If you look hard enough, you should be able to find an LCD magnifier that fits over the monitor panel and provides a 2X magnification. These often strap on clumsily, and serve better as a way to get an enlarged view of the LCD than as protection. Hoodman and other suppliers offer these specialized devices.

Troubleshooting Memory Cards

Sometimes good memory cards go bad. Sometimes good photographers can treat their memory cards badly. It's possible that a memory card that works fine in one camera won't be recognized when inserted into another. In the worst case, you can have a card full of important photos and find that the card seems to be corrupted and you can't access any of them. Don't panic! If these scenarios sound horrific to you, there are lots of things you can do to prevent them from happening, and a variety of remedies available if they do occur. You'll want to take some time—before disaster strikes—to consider your options.

All Your Eggs in One Basket?

The debate about whether it's better to use one large memory card or several smaller ones has been going on since even before there were memory cards. I can remember when computer users wondered whether it was smarter to install a pair of 200MB (not *gigabyte*) hard drives in their computer, or if they should go for one of those new-fangled 500MB models. By the same token, a few years ago the user groups were full of proponents who insisted that you ought to use 128MB memory cards rather than the huge 512MB versions. Today, most of the arguments involve 8GB cards versus 16GB cards, and I expect that as prices for larger capacity cards continue to drop, they'll find their way into the debate as well.

Why all the fuss? Are 8GB memory cards more likely to fail than 4GB cards? Are you risking all your photos if you trust your images to a larger card? Isn't it better to use several smaller cards, so that if one fails you lose only half as many photos? Or, isn't it wiser to put all your photos onto one larger card, because the more cards you use, the better your odds of misplacing or damaging one and losing at least some pictures?

In the end, the "eggs in one basket" argument boils down to statistics, and how you happen to use your D7000. The rationales can go both ways. If you have multiple smaller cards, you do increase your chances of something happening to one of them, so, arguably, you might be boosting the odds of losing some pictures. If all your images are important, the fact that you've lost 100 rather than 200 pictures isn't very comforting.

After all, the myth assumes that a damaged card will always be full before it becomes corrupted. Fortunately, memory cards don't magically wait until they are full before they fail. In a typical shooting session, it doesn't matter whether you've shot 3.5GB worth of pictures on a 4GB card or 3.5GB worth of pictures on an 8GB card. If either card fails, you've lost the same number of images. Your risk increases *only* when you start shooting additional photos on the larger card. In the real world, most of us who use larger memory cards don't fill them up very often. We just like having the extra capacity there when we need it.

The myth also says that by using several smaller cards, you're spreading the risk around so that only some pictures will be lost in case of a failure. What is more important to you, your photographs or the members of your family? When going on vacation, do you insist on splitting your kin up and driving several smaller cars?

If you shoot photojournalist-type pictures, you probably change memory cards when they're less than completely full in order to avoid the need to do so at a crucial moment.

(When I shoot sports, my cards rarely reach 80 to 90 percent of capacity before I change them.) Using multiple smaller cards means you have to change them that more often, which can be a real pain when you're taking a lot of photos. As an example, if you use 1GB memory cards with a Nikon D7000 and shoot RAW+JPEG FINE, you may get only a few dozen pictures on the card. That's not even twice the capacity of a 36-exposure roll of film (remember those?). In my book, I prefer keeping all my eggs in one basket, and then making very sure that nothing happens to that basket.

Preventive Measures

Here are some options for preventing loss of valuable images:

- **Interleaving.** One option is to *interleave* your shots. Say you don't shoot weddings, but you do go on vacation from time to time. Take 50 or so pictures on one card, or whatever number of images might fill about 25 percent of its capacity. Then, replace it with a different card and shoot about 25 percent of that card's available space. Repeat these steps with diligence (you'd have to be determined to go through this inconvenience), and, if you use four or more memory cards you'll find your pictures from each location scattered among the different memory cards. If you lose or damage one, you'll still have *some* pictures from all the various stops on your trip on the other cards. That's more work than I like to do (I usually tote around a portable hard disk and copy the files to the drive as I go), but it's an option.

- **In-camera backup.** Fortunately, if you own a Nikon D7000, you don't need to restrict yourself to a single basket. Load your camera with two Secure Digital cards, then go to the Shooting menu and set Role Played by Card in Slot 2 to Backup, so that each shot you take is copied to both cards simultaneously. This will slow down your maximum shooting speed significantly (don't try this backup method when shooting sports), but for ordinary photography, this provides the peace of mind of knowing you're making a spare copy of each image right on the spot.

EXTREME BACKUP

I probably took the dual-card technique to the extreme recently while on a trip. I had my D7000 stocked with a pair of 32GB cards, and was shooting in RAW+JPEG mode. I happened to be shooting three-exposure brackets, which I was going to process as HDR (high dynamic range) photos. With the camera set to copy to both cards at the same time, and using Continuous high, every time I pressed the shutter release, the D7000 took a three-shot set in both RAW+JPEG Fine (six pictures) and copied them to both cards (12 files in all). That was 218MB of images per shot! I managed the dubious feat of filling up 64GB of memory cards while pressing the shutter release fewer than 300 times.

■ **Transmit your images.** Another option is to transmit your images, as they are shot, over a network to your laptop, assuming a network and a laptop are available. You can use Nikon's Wireless Transmitter WT-4a, and beam the images over to a computer as you shoot them using the gadget's Image Transfer mode. A company called Eye-Fi (www.eye.fi) markets a clever Secure Digital card with wireless capabilities built-in (covered more in Chapter 10). They currently offer four models, including the basic Eye-Fi Home (about $50), which can be used to transmit your photos from the D7000 to a computer on your home network (or any other network you set up somewhere, say, at a family reunion). Eye-Fi Share and Eye-Fi Share Video (about $60 and $80, respectively), which are basically exactly the same (Share Video is 4GB instead of 2GB in capacity), include software to allow you to upload your images from your camera through your computer network directly to websites such as Flickr, Facebook, Shutterfly, Nikon's own My Picturetown, and digital printing services that include Walmart Digital Photo Center. The most sophisticated option is Eye-Fi Explore, which I use, a 4GB SDHC card that adds geographic location labels to your photo (so you'll know where you took it), and frees you from your own computer network by allowing uploads from more than 10,000 WiFi hotspots around the USA. Very cool, and the ultimate in picture backup.

■ **External backup.** You can purchase external hard disk gadgets called Personal Storage Devices (see Figure 14.6), which can copy files from your memory cards automatically. More expensive models have color LCD screens so you can review your images. I tend to prefer using a netbook, like the one shown in Figure 14.7. I can store images on the netbook's internal hard disk, and make an extra backup copy to an external drive as well. Plus, I can access the Internet from WiFi hotspots, all using a very compact device. Lately, I've been backing up many images on my iPad, which has 64GB of storage—enough for short trips.

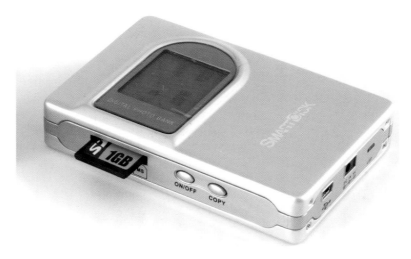

Figure 14.6
Small battery-operated personal storage devices can back up your images.

Figure 14.7
A small net-book, with or without an external hard drive, is another backup option.

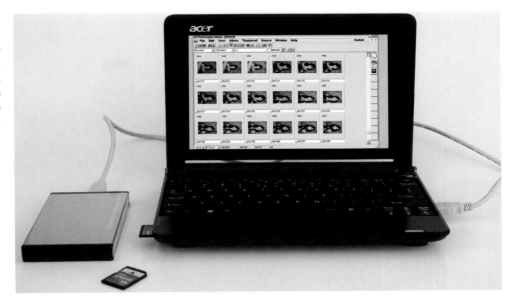

What Can Go Wrong?

There are lots of things that can go wrong with your memory card, but the ones that aren't caused by human stupidity are statistically very rare. Yes, a memory card's internal bit bin or controller can suddenly fail due to a manufacturing error or some inexplicable event caused by old age. However, if your card works for the first week or two that you own it, it should work forever. There's really not a lot that can wear out.

The typical memory card is rated for a Mean Time Between Failures of 1,000,000 hours of use. That's constant use 24/7 for more than 100 years! According to the manufacturers, they are good for 10,000 insertions in your camera, and should be able to retain their data (and that's without an external power source) for something on the order of 11 years. Of course, with the millions of cards in use, there are bound to be a few lemons here or there.

Given the reliability of solid-state memory compared to magnetic memory, though, it's more likely that your problems will stem from something that you do. Secure Digital cards are small and easy to misplace if you're not careful. For that reason, it's a good idea to keep them in their original cases or a "card safe" offered by Gepe (www.gepe.com), Pelican (www.pelican.com), and others. Always placing your memory card in a case can provide protection from the second-most common mishap that befalls memory cards: the common household laundry. If you slip a card in a pocket, rather than a case or your camera bag often enough, sooner or later it's going to end up in the washing machine and probably the clothes dryer, too. There are plenty of reports of relieved digital camera owners who've laundered their memory cards and found they still worked fine, but it's not uncommon for such mistreatment to do some damage.

Memory cards can also be stomped on, accidentally bent, dropped into the ocean, chewed by pets, and otherwise rendered unusable in myriad ways. It's also possible to force a Secure Digital card into your D7000's Secure Digital card slot incorrectly if you're diligent enough, doing little damage to the card itself, but bending the connector pins in the camera, eliminating its ability to read or write to any memory card.

Or, if the card is formatted in your computer with a memory card reader, your D7000 may fail to recognize it. Occasionally, I've found that a memory card used in one camera would fail if used in a different camera (until I reformatted it in Windows, and then again in the camera). Every once in awhile, a card goes completely bad and—seemingly—can't be salvaged.

Another way to lose images is to do commonplace things with your card at an inopportune time. If you remove the card from the D7000 while the camera is writing images to the card, you'll lose any photos in the buffer and may damage the file structure of the card, making it difficult or impossible to retrieve the other pictures you've taken. The same thing can happen if you remove the memory card from your computer's card reader while the computer is writing to the card (say, to erase files you've already moved to your computer). You can avoid this by *not* using your computer to erase files on a memory card but, instead, always reformatting the card in your D7000 before you use it again.

What Can You Do?

Pay attention: If you're having problems, the *first* thing you should do is *stop* using that memory card. Don't take any more pictures. Don't do anything with the card until you've figured out what's wrong. Your second line of defense (your first line is to be sufficiently careful with your cards that you avoid problems in the first place) is to *do no harm* that hasn't already been done. Read the rest of this section and then, if necessary, decide on a course of action (such as using a data recovery service or software described later) before you risk damaging the data on your card further.

Now that you've calmed down, the first thing to check is whether you've actually inserted a card in the camera. If you've set the camera so that shooting without a card has been turned on, it's entirely possible (although not particularly plausible) that you've been snapping away with no memory card to store the pictures to, which can lead to massive disappointment later on. Of course, the –E- warning appears on the LCD when the camera is powered up, and the Demo message is superimposed on the review image after every shot (assuming you've enabled the D7000 to take photos when a card is not inserted), but maybe you're inattentive, aren't using picture review, or have purchased one of those LCD fold-up hoods mentioned earlier in this chapter. You can avoid all this by setting the No Memory Card? (CSM #f10) feature to Release Locked, and leaving it there.

THE ULTIMATE IRONY

I recently purchased an 8GB Kingston memory card that was furnished with some nifty OnTrack data recovery software. The first thing I did was format the card to make sure it was okay. Then I hunted around for the free software, only to discover it was preloaded onto the memory card. I was supposed to copy the software to my computer before using the memory card for the first time.

Fortunately, I had the OnTrack software that would reverse my dumb move, so I could retrieve the software. No, wait. I *didn't* have the software I needed to recover the software I erased. I'd reformatted it to oblivion. Chalk this one up as either the ultimate irony or Stupid Photographer Trick #523.

Things get more exciting when the card itself is put in jeopardy. If you lose a card, there's not a lot you can do other than take a picture of a similar card and print up some Have You Seen This Lost Flash Memory? flyers to post on utility poles all around town.

If all you care about is reusing the card, and have resigned yourself to losing the pictures, try reformatting the card in your camera. You may find that reformatting removes the corrupted data and restores your card to health. Sometimes I've had success reformatting a card in my computer using a memory card reader (this is normally a no-no because your operating system doesn't understand the needs of your D7000), and *then* reformatting again in the camera.

If your memory card is not behaving properly, and you *do* want to recover your images, things get a little more complicated. If your pictures are very valuable, either to you or to others (for example, a wedding), you can always turn to professional data recovery firms. Be prepared to pay hundreds of dollars to get your pictures back, but these pros often do an amazing job. You wouldn't want them working on your memory card on behalf of the police if you'd tried to erase some incriminating pictures. There are many firms of this type, and I've never used them myself, so I can't offer a recommendation. Use a Google search to turn up a ton of them.

DIMINISHING RETURNS

Usually, once you've recovered any images on a memory card, reformatted it, and returned it to service, it will function reliably for the rest of its useful life. However, if you find a particular card going bad more than once, you'll almost certainly want to stop using it forever. See if you can get it replaced by the manufacturer if you can, but, in the case of Secure Digital card failures, the third time is never the charm.

A more reasonable approach is to try special data recovery software you can install on your computer and use to attempt to resurrect your "lost" images yourself. They may not actually be gone completely. Perhaps your card's "table of contents" is jumbled, or only a few pictures are damaged in such a way that your camera and computer can't read some or any of the pictures on the card. Some of the available software was written specifically to reconstruct lost pictures, while other utilities are more general purpose applications that can be used with any media, including floppy disks and hard disk drives. They have names like OnTrack, Photo Rescue 2, Digital Image Recovery, MediaRecover, Image Recall, and the aptly named Recover My Photos. You'll find a comprehensive list and links, as well as some picture recovery tips at www.ultimateslr.com/memory-card-recovery.php. I like the RescuePRO software that SanDisk supplies (see Figure 14.8), especially since it came on a mini-CD that I was totally unable to erase by mistake.

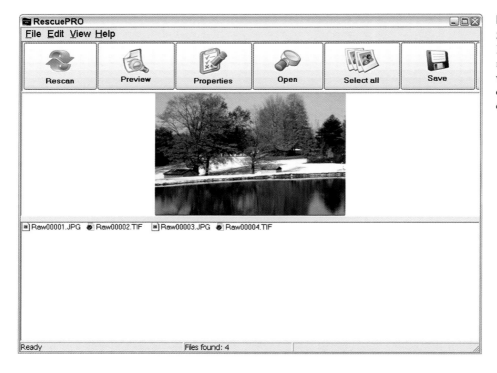

Figure 14.8
SanDisk supplies RescuePRO recovery software with some of its memory cards.

Clean Your Sensor

Yes, the Nikon D7000 has a two-pronged sensor dust prevention scheme: an innovative air control system that keeps dust away from the sensor in the first place, and a sensor-shaking cleaning mechanism. But no dust-busting technology is 100-percent effective.

Indeed, there's no avoiding dust. No matter how careful you are, some of it is going to settle on your camera and on the mounts of your lenses, eventually making its way inside your camera to settle in the mirror chamber. As you take photos, the mirror flipping up and down causes the dust to become airborne and eventually make its way past the shutter curtain to come to rest on the anti-aliasing filter atop your sensor. There, dust and particles can show up in every single picture you take at a small enough aperture to bring the foreign matter into sharp focus. No matter how careful you are and how cleanly you work, eventually you will get some of this dust on your camera's sensor. Some say that CMOS sensors, like the one found in the Nikon D7000, "attract" less dust than CCD sensors found in cameras from other vendors. But even the cleanest-working photographers using the Nikon D7000 are far from immune.

Fortunately, one of the Nikon D7000's most useful features is the automatic sensor cleaning system that reduces or eliminates the need to clean your camera's sensor manually. The sensor vibrates ultrasonically each time the D7000 is powered either on or off (or both, at your option), shaking loose any dust.

Although the automatic sensor cleaning feature operates when you power the camera up or turn it off (depending on the behavior you specify in the Setup menu), you can activate it manually at any time. Choose Clean Image Sensor from the Setup menu, and select Clean Now. If you'd rather specify when automatic cleaning occurs, choose On (clean at power up), Off (clean when the camera is switched off), On/Off (clean at both power up and power down), or Cleaning Off (no automatic sensor cleaning will take place).

If some dust does collect on your sensor, you can often map it out of your images (making it invisible) using software techniques with the Image Dust Off Ref Photo feature in the Setup menu. Operation of this feature is described in Chapter 10.

Of course, even with the Nikon D7000's automatic sensor cleaning/dust resistance features, you may still be required to manually clean your sensor from time to time. This section explains the phenomenon and provides some tips on minimizing dust and eliminating it when it begins to affect your shots.

Dust the FAQs, Ma'am

Here are some of the most frequently asked questions about sensor dust issues.

Q. I see tiny specks in my viewfinder. Do I have dust on my sensor?

A. If you see sharp, well-defined specks, they are clinging to the underside of your focus screen and not on your sensor. They have absolutely no effect on your photographs, and are merely annoying or distracting.

Q. I can see dust on my mirror. How can I remove it?

A. Like focus-screen dust, any artifacts that have settled on your mirror won't affect your photos. You can often remove dust on the mirror or focus screen with a bulb air blower, which will loosen it and whisk it away. Stubborn dust on the focus screen can sometimes be gently flicked away with a soft brush designed for cleaning lenses. I don't recommend brushing the mirror or touching it in any way. The mirror is a special front-surface-silvered optical device (unlike conventional mirrors, which are silvered on the back side of a piece of glass or plastic) and can be easily scratched. If you can't blow mirror dust off, it's best to just forget about it. You can't see it in the viewfinder, anyway.

Q. I see a bright spot in the same place in all of my photos. Is that sensor dust?

A. You've probably got either a "hot" pixel or one that is permanently "stuck" due to a defect in the sensor. A hot pixel is one that shows up as a bright spot only during long exposures as the sensor warms. A pixel stuck in the "on" position always appears in the image. Both show up as bright red, green, or blue pixels, usually surrounded by a small cluster of other improperly illuminated pixels, caused by the camera's interpolating the hot or stuck pixel into its surroundings, as shown in Figure 14.9. A stuck pixel can also be permanently dark. Either kind is likely to show up when they contrast with plain, evenly colored areas of your image.

Figure 14.9
A stuck pixel is surrounded by improperly interpolated pixels created by the D7000's demosaicing algorithm.

Finding one or two hot or stuck pixels in your sensor is unfortunately fairly common. They can be "removed" by telling the D7000 to ignore them through a simple process called *pixel mapping*. If the bad pixels become bothersome, Nikon can remap your sensor's pixels with a quick trip to a service center.

Bad pixels can also show up on your camera's color LCD panel, but, unless they are abundant, the wisest course is to just ignore them.

Q. I see an irregular out-of-focus blob in the same place in my photos. Is that sensor dust?

A. Yes. Sensor contaminants can take the form of tiny spots, larger blobs, or even curvy lines if they are caused by minuscule fibers that have settled on the sensor. They'll appear out of focus because they aren't actually on the sensor surface but, rather, a fraction of a millimeter above it on the filter that covers the sensor. The smaller the f/stop used, the more in-focus the dust becomes. At large apertures, it may not be visible at all.

Q. I never see any dust on my sensor. What's all the fuss about?

A. Those who never have dust problems with their Nikon D7000 fall into one of four categories: those for whom the camera's automatic dust removal features are working well; those who seldom change their lenses and have clean working habits that minimize the amount of dust that invades their cameras in the first place; those who simply don't notice the dust (often because they don't shoot many macro photos or other pictures using the small f/stops that makes dust evident in their images); and those who are very, very lucky.

Identifying and Dealing with Dust

Sensor dust is less of a problem than it might be because it shows up only under certain circumstances. Indeed, you might have dust on your sensor right now and not be aware of it. The dust doesn't actually settle on the sensor itself, but, rather, on a protective filter a very tiny distance above the sensor, subjecting it to the phenomenon of *depth-of-focus*. Depth-of-focus is the distance the focal plane can be moved and still render an object in sharp focus. At f/2.8 to f/5.6 or even smaller, sensor dust, particularly if small, is likely to be outside the range of depth-of-focus and blur into an unnoticeable dot.

However, if you're shooting at f/16 to f/22 or smaller, those dust motes suddenly pop into focus. Forget about trying to spot them by peering directly at your sensor with the shutter open and the lens removed. The period at the end of this sentence, about .33mm in diameter, could block a group of pixels measuring 40 × 40 pixels (160 pixels in all!). Dust spots that are even smaller than that can easily show up in your images if you're shooting large, empty areas that are light colored. Dust motes are most likely to show up in the sky, as in Figure 14.10, or in white backgrounds of your seamless product shots and are less likely to be a problem in images that contain lots of dark areas and detail.

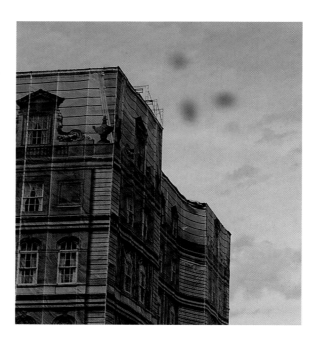

Figure 14.10
Only the dust spots in the sky are apparent in this shot.

To see if you have dust on your sensor, take a few test shots of a plain, blank surface (such as a piece of paper or a cloudless sky) at small f/stops, such as f/22, and a few wide open. Open Photoshop or another image editor, copy several shots into a single document in separate layers, then flip back and forth between layers to see if any spots you see are present in all layers. You may have to boost contrast and sharpness to make the dust easier to spot.

Avoiding Dust

Of course, the easiest way to protect your sensor from dust is to prevent it from settling on the sensor in the first place. Here are my stock tips for eliminating the problem before it begins.

- **Clean environment.** Avoid working in dusty areas if you can do so. Hah! Serious photographers will take this one with a grain of salt, because it usually makes sense to go where the pictures are. Only a few of us are so paranoid about sensor dust (considering that it is so easily removed) that we'll avoid moderately grimy locations just to protect something that is, when you get down to it, just a tool. If you find a great picture opportunity at a raging fire, during a sandstorm, or while surrounded by dust clouds, you might hesitate to take the picture, but, with a little caution (don't remove your lens in these situations, and clean the camera afterwards!) you can still shoot. However, it still makes sense to store your camera in a clean environment. One place cameras and lenses pick up a lot of dust is inside a camera bag. Clean your bag from time to time, and you can avoid problems.

- **Clean lenses.** There are a few paranoid types that avoid swapping lenses in order to minimize the chance of dust getting inside their cameras. It makes more sense just to use a blower or brush to dust off the rear lens mount of the replacement lens first, so you won't be introducing dust into your camera simply by attaching a new, dusty lens. Do this before you remove the current lens from your camera, and then avoid stirring up dust before making the exchange.

- **Work fast.** Minimize the time your camera is lens-less and exposed to dust. That means having your replacement lens ready and dusted off, and a place to set down the old lens as soon as it is removed, so you can quickly attach the new lens.

- **Let gravity help you.** Face the camera downward when the lens is detached so any dust in the mirror box will tend to fall away from the sensor. Turn your back to any breezes, indoor forced air vents, fans, or other sources of dust to minimize infiltration.

- **Protect the lens you just removed.** Once you've attached the new lens, quickly put the end cap on the one you just removed to reduce the dust that might fall on it.

- **Clean out the vestibule.** From time to time, remove the lens while in a relatively dust-free environment and use a blower bulb like the one shown in Figure 14.11 (*not* compressed air or a vacuum hose) to clean out the mirror box area. A blower bulb is generally safer than a can of compressed air, or a strong positive/negative airflow, which can tend to drive dust further into nooks and crannies.

- **Be prepared.** If you're embarking on an important shooting session, it's a good idea to clean your sensor *now*, rather than come home with hundreds or thousands of images with dust spots caused by flecks that were sitting on your sensor before you even started.

Figure 14.11
Use a robust air bulb for cleaning your sensor.

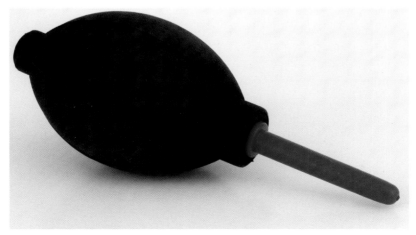

- **Clone out existing spots in your image editor.** Photoshop and other editors have a clone tool or healing brush you can use to copy pixels from surrounding areas over the dust spot or dead pixel. This process can be tedious, especially if you have lots of dust spots and/or lots of images to be corrected. The advantage is that this sort of manual fix-it probably will do the least damage to the rest of your photo. Only the damaged pixels will be affected.

- **Use filtration in your image editor.** A semi-smart filter like Photoshop's Dust & Scratches filter can remove dust and other artifacts by selectively blurring areas that the plug-in decides represent dust spots. This method can work well if you have many dust spots, because you won't need to patch them manually. However, any automated method like this has the possibility of blurring areas of your image that you didn't intend to soften.

Sensor Cleaning

Those new to the concept of sensor dust actually hesitate before deciding to clean their camera themselves. Isn't it a better idea to pack up your D7000 and send it to a Nikon service center so their crack technical staff can do the job for you? Or, at the very least, shouldn't you let the friendly folks at your local camera store do it?

Of course, if you choose to let someone else clean your sensor, they will be using methods that are more or less identical to the techniques you would use yourself. None of these techniques are difficult, and the only difference between their cleaning and your cleaning is that they might have done it dozens or hundreds of times. If you're careful, you can do just as good a job.

Of course vendors like Nikon won't tell you this, but it's not because they don't trust you. It's not that difficult for a real goofball to mess up a camera by hurrying or taking a shortcut. Perhaps the person uses the "Bulb" method of holding the shutter open and a finger slips, allowing the shutter curtain to close on top of a sensor cleaning brush. Or, someone tries to clean the sensor using masking tape, and ends up with goo all over its surface. If Nikon recommended *any* method that's mildly risky, someone would do it wrong, and then the company would face lawsuits from those who'd contend they did it exactly in the way the vendor suggested, so the ruined camera is not their fault.

You can see that vendors like Nikon tend to be conservative in their recommendations, and, in doing so, make it seem as if sensor cleaning is more daunting and dangerous than it really is. Some vendors recommend only dust-off cleaning, through the use of reasonably gentle blasts of air, while condemning more serious scrubbing with swabs and cleaning fluids. However, these cleaning kits for the exact types of cleaning they recommended against are for sale in Japan only, where, apparently, your average photographer is more dexterous than those of us in the rest of the world. These kits are similar to those used by official repair staff to clean your sensor if you decide to send your camera in for a dust-up.

As I noted, sensors can be affected by dust particles that are much smaller than you might be able to spot visually on the surface of your lens. The filters that cover sensors tend to be fairly hard compared to optical glass. Cleaning the 23.6mm × 15.8mm sensor in your Nikon D7000 within the tight confines of the mirror box can call for a steady hand and careful touch. If your sensor's filter becomes scratched through inept cleaning, you can't simply remove it yourself and replace it with a new one.

There are four basic kinds of cleaning processes that can be used to remove dusty and sticky stuff that settles on your dSLR's sensor. All of these must be performed with the shutter locked open. I'll describe these methods and provide instructions for locking the shutter later in this section.

- **Air cleaning.** This process involves squirting blasts of air inside your camera with the shutter locked open. This works well for dust that's not clinging stubbornly to your sensor.

- **Brushing.** A soft, very fine brush is passed across the surface of the sensor's filter, dislodging mildly persistent dust particles and sweeping them off the imager.

- **Liquid cleaning.** A soft swab dipped in a cleaning solution such as ethanol is used to wipe the sensor filter, removing more obstinate particles.

- **Tape cleaning.** There are some who get good results by applying a special form of tape to the surface of their sensor. When the tape is peeled off, all the dust goes with it. Supposedly. I'd be remiss if I didn't point out right now that this form of cleaning is somewhat controversial; the other three methods are much more widely accepted.

Placing the Mirror/Shutter in the Locked and Fully Upright Position for Landing

Make sure you're using a fully charged battery or an AC adapter. Fortunately, the Nikon D7000 is smart enough that it won't let you try to clean the sensor manually unless the battery has a sufficient charge.

1. Remove the lens from the camera and then turn on the camera.

2. You'll find the Lock Mirror Up for Cleaning menu choice in the Setup menu. Select it.

3. Choose Start. The mirror will flip up and the shutter will open.

4. Use one of the methods described below to remove dust and grime from your sensor. Be careful not to accidentally switch the power off or open the Secure Digital card or battery compartment doors as you work. If that happens, the shutter may be damaged if it closes onto your cleaning tool.

5. When you're finished, turn off the power, replace your lens, and switch your camera back on.

Air Cleaning

Your first attempts at cleaning your sensor should always involve gentle blasts of air. Many times, you'll be able to dislodge dust spots, which will fall off the sensor and, with luck, out of the mirror box. Attempt one of the other methods only when you've already tried air cleaning and it didn't remove all the dust.

Here are some tips for doing air cleaning:

- **Use a clean, powerful air bulb.** Your best bet is bulb cleaners designed for the job, like the Giottos Rocket. Smaller bulbs, like those air bulbs with a brush attached sometimes sold for lens cleaning or weak nasal aspirators may not provide sufficient air or a strong enough blast to do much good.

- **Hold the camera upside down.** Then look up into the mirror box as you squirt your air blasts, increasing the odds that gravity will help pull the expelled dust downward, away from the sensor. You may have to use some imagination in positioning yourself. (See Figure 14.12, which illustrates how I clean my Nikon D7000.)

- **Never use air canisters.** The propellant inside these cans can permanently coat your sensor if you tilt the can while spraying. It's not worth taking a chance.

- **Avoid air compressors.** Super-strong blasts of air are likely to force dust under the sensor filter.

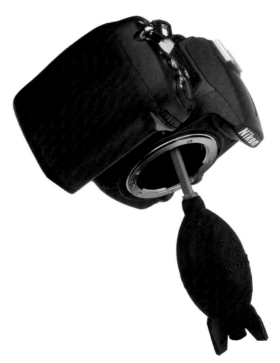

Figure 14.12
Hold the camera upside down and blow the dust off the sensor.

Brush Cleaning

If your dust is a little more stubborn and can't be dislodged by air alone, you may want to try a brush, charged with static electricity, which can pick off dust spots by electrical attraction. One good, but expensive, option is the Sensor Brush sold at www.visible-dust.com. A cheaper version can be purchased at www.copperhillimages.com. You need a 16mm version, like the one in Figure 14.13. It can be stroked across the short dimension of your D7000's sensor.

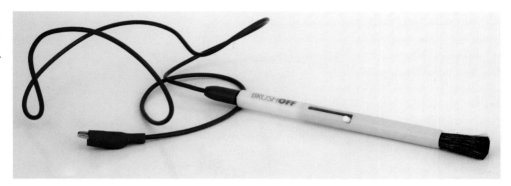

Figure 14.13
A proper brush is required for dusting off your sensor.

Ordinary artist's brushes are much too coarse and stiff and have fibers that are tangled or can come loose and settle on your sensor. A good sensor brush's fibers are resilient and described as "thinner than a human hair." Moreover, the brush has a wooden handle that reduces the risk of static sparks.

Brush cleaning is done with a dry brush by gently swiping the surface of the sensor filter with the tip. The dust particles are attracted to the brush particles and cling to them. You should clean the brush with compressed air before and after each use, and store it in an appropriate air-tight container between applications to keep it clean and dust-free. Although these special brushes are expensive, one should last you a long time.

Liquid Cleaning

Unfortunately, you'll often encounter really stubborn dust spots that can't be removed with a blast of air or flick of a brush. These spots may be combined with some grease or a liquid that causes them to stick to the sensor filter's surface. In such cases, liquid cleaning with a swab may be necessary. During my first clumsy attempts to clean my own sensor, I accidentally got my blower bulb tip too close to the sensor, and some sort of deposit from the tip of the bulb ended up on the sensor. I panicked until I discovered that liquid cleaning did a good job of removing whatever it was that took up residence on my sensor.

You want a sturdy swab that won't bend or break so you can apply gentle pressure to the swab as you wipe the sensor surface. Use the swab with methanol (as pure as you can get it, particularly medical grade; other ingredients can leave a residue), or the Eclipse solution also sold by Photographic Solutions. Eclipse is actually quite a bit purer than even medical-grade methanol. A couple drops of solution should be enough, unless you have a spot that's extremely difficult to remove. In that case, you may need to use extra solution on the swab to help "soak" the dirt off.

You can make your own swabs out of pieces of plastic (some use fast food restaurant knives, with the tip cut at an angle to the proper size) covered with a soft cloth or Pec-Pad, as shown in Figure 14.14. However, if you've got the bucks to spend, you can't go wrong with good-quality commercial sensor cleaning swabs, such as those sold by Photographic Solutions, Inc. (www.photosol.com/swabproduct.htm).

Once you overcome your nervousness at touching your D7000's sensor, the process is easy. You'll wipe continuously with the swab in one direction, then flip it over and wipe in the other direction. You need to completely wipe the entire surface; otherwise, you may end up depositing the dust you collect at the far end of your stroke. Wipe; don't rub.

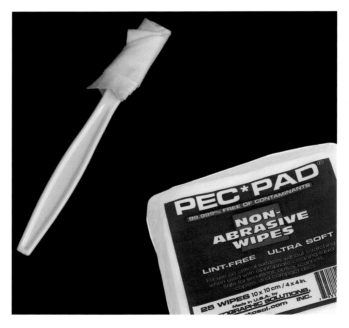

Figure 14.14
Carefully wrap a Pec-Pad around a plastic knife that you've truncated.

Tape Cleaning

There are people who absolutely swear by the tape method of sensor cleaning. The concept seems totally wacky, and I have never tried it personally, so I can't say with certainty that it either does or does not work. In the interest of completeness, I'm including it here. I can't give you a recommendation, so if you have problems, please don't blame me. The Nikon D7000 is still too new to have generated any reports of users accidentally damaging the anti-dust coating on the sensor filter using this method.

Tape cleaning works by applying a layer of Scotch Brand Magic Tape to the sensor. This is a minimally sticky tape that some of the tape cleaning proponents claim contains no adhesive. I did check this out with 3M, and can say that Magic Tape certainly *does* contain an adhesive. The question is whether the adhesive comes off when you peel back the tape, taking any dust spots on your sensor with it. The folks who love this method claim there is no residue. There have been reports from those who don't like the method that residue is left behind. This is all anecdotal evidence, so you're pretty much on your own in making the decision whether to try out the tape cleaning method.

Magnifier Assisted Cleaning

Using a magnifier to view your sensor as you clean it is a good idea. I rely on two types. I have four Carson MiniBrite PO-25 magnifiers (see Figure 14.15), and keep one in each camera bag. So, no matter where I am shooting, I have one of these $8.95 gadgets with me. You can read more about this great tool at my blog (http://dslrguides.com/blog/?p=274). When I'm not traveling, I use a SensorKlear loupe. It's a magnifier with a built-in LED illuminator. There's an opening on one side that allows you to insert a SensorKlear cleaning wand, a pen-like stylus with a surface treated to capture dust particles. (See Figure 14.16.) Both the SensorKlear loupe and the SensorKlear wand are available from www.lenspen.com.

Figure 14.15
The Carson MiniBrite is a good value sensor magnifier.

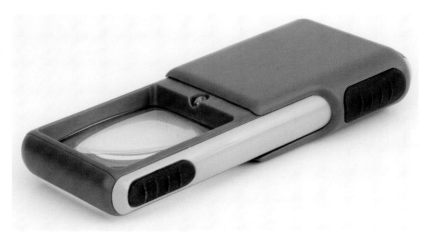

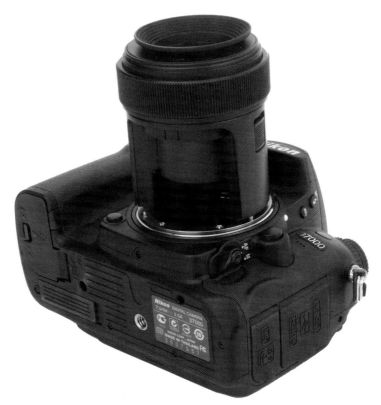

Figure 14.16
The SensorKlear
Loupe and
wand allow
quickly remov-
ing multiple
dust particles.

When I'm using the MiniBrite, I locate the dust on the sensor with the magnifier, remembering that the position of the dust will be *reversed* from what I might have seen on an image on the camera's LCD (because the camera lens flips the image when making the exposure). Then, I use the SensorKlear wand or the blower brush to remove the artifact.

The SensorKlear loupe actually allows you to keep your eye on the prize as you do the cleaning. You can peer through the viewer, rotate the opening to the side opposite the position of the dust, then insert the hinged wand to tap the dust while you're watching. This method allows removing a bunch of dust particles quickly, so it's my preferred procedure when I have the loupe with me.

Glossary

It's always handy to have a single resource where you can look up various terms you'll encounter while working with your digital camera. Here is the latest update of a glossary I've compiled over the years, with some new additions specifically for the Nikon D7000.

AE-L/AF-L A button on the D7000 that allows locking exposure and/or focus point prior to taking a photo.

ambient lighting Diffuse, non-directional lighting that doesn't appear to come from a specific source but, rather, bounces off walls, ceilings, and other objects in the scene when a picture is taken.

analog/digital converter The EXPEED module in the camera that electronically converts the analog information captured by the D7000's sensor into digital bits that can be stored as an image.

angle of view The area of a scene that a lens can capture, determined by the focal length of the lens. Lenses with a shorter focal length have a wider angle of view than lenses with a longer focal length.

anti-alias A process that smoothes the look of rough edges in images (called *jaggies* or *staircasing*) by adding partially transparent pixels along the boundaries of diagonal lines that are merged into a smoother line by our eyes. *See also* jaggies.

aperture The size of the opening in the iris or diaphragm of a lens, relative to the lens's focal length. Also called an *f/stop*. For example, with a lens having a focal length of 100mm, an f/stop with a diameter of 12.5mm would produce an aperture value of f/8.

Aperture-priority A camera setting that allows you to specify the lens opening or f/stop that you want to use, with the camera selecting the required shutter speed automatically based on its light-meter reading. *See also* Shutter-priority.

artifact A type of noise in an image, or an unintentional image component produced in error by a digital camera during processing, usually caused by the JPEG compression process in digital cameras, or, in some cases, by dust settling on the sensor.

aspect ratio The proportions of an image as printed, displayed on a monitor, or captured by a digital camera. The D7000's movie feature, for example, includes options for HDTV's 16:9 aspect ratio.

Autofocus A camera setting that allows the Nikon D7000 to choose the correct focus distance for you, based on the contrast of an image (the image will be at maximum contrast when in sharp focus). The camera can be set for *Single-servo Autofocus (AF-S)*, in which the lens is not focused until the shutter release is partially depressed, *Continuous-servo Autofocus (AF-C)*, in which the lens refocuses constantly as you frame and reframe the image, and *Automatic-autofocus (AF-A)*, in which the D7000 focuses using AF-S mode, but switches to AF-C mode if the subject starts to move. The D7000 can also be set for *Manual* focus. In Live View mode, your two choices are AF-S and AF-F.

backlighting A lighting effect produced when the main light source is located behind the subject. Backlighting can be used to create a silhouette effect, or to illuminate translucent objects. *See also* front lighting and side lighting.

barrel distortion A lens defect that causes straight lines at the top or side edges of an image to bow outward into a barrel shape. *See also* pincushion distortion.

blooming An image distortion caused when a photosite in an image sensor has absorbed all the photons it can handle so that additional photons reaching that pixel overflow to affect surrounding pixels, producing unwanted brightness and overexposure around the edges of objects.

blur To soften an image or part of an image by throwing it out of focus, or by allowing it to become soft due to subject or camera motion. Blur can also be applied creatively in an image-editing program.

bokeh A term derived from the Japanese word for blur, which describes the aesthetic qualities of the out-of-focus parts of an image. Some lenses produce "good" bokeh and others offer "bad" bokeh. Some lenses produce uniformly illuminated out-of-focus discs. Others produce a disc that has a bright edge and a dark center, producing a "doughnut" effect, which is the worst from a bokeh standpoint. Lenses that generate a bright center that fades to a darker edge are favored, because their bokeh allows the circle of confusion to blend more smoothly with the surroundings. The bokeh characteristics of a lens are most important when you're using selective focus (say, when shooting a portrait) to deemphasize the background, or when shallow depth-of-field is a given because you're working with a macro lens, with a long telephoto, or with a wide-open aperture. *See also* circle of confusion.

bounce lighting Light bounced off a reflector, including ceiling and walls, to provide a soft, natural-looking light.

buffer The digital camera's internal memory where an image is stored immediately after it is taken until it can be written to the camera's non-volatile (semi-permanent) memory card.

burst mode The digital camera's equivalent of the film camera's motor drive, used to take multiple shots within a short period of time, each stored in a memory buffer temporarily before writing them to the media.

calibration A process used to correct for the differences in the output of a printer or monitor when compared to the original image. Once you've calibrated your scanner, monitor, and/or your image editor, the images you see on the screen more closely represent what you'll get from your printer, even though calibration is never perfect.

Camera Raw A plug-in included with Photoshop and Photoshop Elements that can manipulate the unprocessed images captured by digital cameras, such as the Nikon D7000's NEF files. The latest versions of this module can also work with JPEG and TIFF images.

camera shake Movement of the camera, aggravated by slower shutter speeds, which produces a blurred image.

Center-weighted meter A light-measuring device that emphasizes the area in the middle of the frame when calculating the correct exposure for an image. *See also* Matrix metering and Spot meter.

channel In an electronic flash, a channel is a protocol used to communicate between a master flash unit and the remote units slaved to that main flash. The ability to change channels allows several master flash units to operate in the same environment without interfering with each other.

chromatic aberration An image defect, often seen as green or purple fringing around the edges of an object, caused by a lens failing to focus all colors of a light source at the same point. *See also* fringing.

circle of confusion A term applied to the fuzzy discs produced when a point of light is out of focus. The circle of confusion is not a fixed size. The viewing distance and amount of enlargement of the image determine whether we see a particular spot on the image as a point or as a disc. *See also* bokeh.

close-up lens A lens add-on that allows you to take pictures at a distance that is less than the closest-focusing distance of the lens alone.

color correction Changing the relative amounts of color in an image to produce a desired effect, typically a more accurate representation of those colors. Color correction can fix faulty color balance in the original image, or compensate for the deficiencies of the inks used to reproduce the image.

compression Reducing the size of a file by encoding using fewer bits of information to represent the original. Some compression schemes, such as JPEG, operate by discarding some image information, while others have options that preserve all the detail in the original, discarding only redundant data.

Continuous-servo autofocus An automatic focusing setting (AF-C) in which the camera constantly refocuses the image as you frame the picture. This setting is often the best choice for moving subjects. *See also* Single-servo autofocus.

contrast The range between the lightest and darkest tones in an image. A high-contrast image is one in which the shades fall at the extremes of the range between white and black. In a low-contrast image, the tones are closer together.

Creative Lighting System (CLS) Nikon's electronic flash system used to coordinate exposure, camera information, and timing between a camera's built-in flash (if present) and external flash units, which can be linked through direct electrical connections or wirelessly. Some external flash units can act as a "master" to command other external units.

dedicated flash An electronic flash unit, such as the Nikon SB-700 Speedlight, designed to work with the automatic exposure features of a specific camera.

depth-of-field A distance range in a photograph in which all included portions of an image are at least acceptably sharp.

diaphragm An adjustable component, similar to the iris in the human eye, which can open and close to provide specific-sized lens openings, or f/stops, and thus control the amount of light reaching the sensor or film.

diffuse lighting Soft, low-contrast lighting.

digital processing chip A solid-state device found in digital cameras that's in charge of applying the image algorithms to the raw picture data prior to storage on the memory card.

diopter A value used to represent the magnification power of a lens, calculated as the reciprocal of a lens's focal length (in meters). Diopters are most often used to represent the optical correction used in a viewfinder to adjust for limitations of the photographer's eyesight, and to describe the magnification of a close-up lens attachment.

equivalent focal length A digital camera's focal length translated into the corresponding values for a 35mm film camera. This value can be calculated for lenses used with the Nikon D7000 by multiplying by 1.5.

exchangeable image file format (Exif) Developed to standardize the exchange of image data between hardware devices and software. A variation on JPEG, Exif is used by most digital cameras, and includes information such as the date and time a photo was taken, the camera settings, resolution, amount of compression, and other data.

Exif *See* exchangeable image file format (Exif).

exposure The amount of light allowed to reach the film or sensor, determined by the intensity of the light, the amount admitted by the iris of the lens, the length of time determined by the shutter speed, and the sensitivity of the sensor or film to light.

exposure compensation Exposure compensation, which uses exposure value (EV) settings, is a way of adding or decreasing exposure without the need to reference f/stops or shutter speeds. For example, if you tell your camera to add +1EV, it will provide twice as much exposure, either by using a larger f/stop, slower shutter speed, or both. The D7000 offers both conventional exposure compensation and flash exposure compensation.

fill lighting In photography, lighting used to illuminate shadows. Reflectors or additional incandescent lighting or electronic flash can be used to brighten shadows. One common technique outdoors is to use the camera's flash as a fill in sunlit situations.

filter In photography, a device that fits over the lens, changing the light in some way. In image editing, a feature that changes the pixels in an image to produce blurring, sharpening, and other special effects. Photoshop includes several interesting filter effects, including Lens Blur and Photo Filters.

flash sync The timing mechanism that ensures that an internal or external electronic flash fires at the correct time during the exposure cycle. A digital SLR's flash sync speed is the highest shutter speed that can be used with flash, ordinarily 1/250th of a second with the Nikon D7000. *See also* front-curtain sync and rear-curtain sync.

focal length The distance between the film and the optical center of the lens when the lens is focused on infinity, usually measured in millimeters.

focal plane A line, perpendicular to the optical axis, which passes through the focal point forming a plane of sharp focus when the lens is set at infinity. A focal plane indicator is etched into the Nikon D7000 on the top panel.

focus tracking The ability of the automatic focus feature of a camera to change focus as the distance between the subject and the camera changes. One type of focus tracking is *predictive,* in which the mechanism anticipates the motion of the object being focused on, and adjusts the focus to suit.

format To erase a memory card and prepare it to accept files.

fringing A chromatic aberration that produces fringes of color around the edges of subjects, caused by a lens's inability to focus the various wavelengths of light onto the same spot. Purple fringing is especially troublesome with backlit images.

front-curtain sync (first-curtain sync)   The default kind of electronic flash synchronization technique, originally associated with focal plane shutters, which consists of a
traveling set of curtains, including a *front curtain*, which opens to reveal the film or sensor, and a *rear curtain*, which follows at a distance determined by shutter speed to conceal the film or sensor at the conclusion of the exposure. For a flash picture to be taken,
the entire sensor must be exposed at one time to the brief flash exposure, so the image
is exposed after the front curtain has reached the other side of the focal plane, but before
the rear curtain begins to move. Front-curtain sync causes the flash to fire at the beginning of this period when the shutter is completely open, in the instant that the first curtain of the focal plane shutter finishes its movement across the film or sensor plane.
With slow shutter speeds, this feature can create a blur effect from the ambient light,
showing as patterns that follow a moving subject with the subject shown sharply frozen
at the beginning of the blur trail. *See also* rear-curtain sync.

front lighting   Illumination that comes from the direction of the camera. *See also* backlighting and side lighting.

f/stop   The relative size of the lens aperture, which helps determine both exposure and
depth-of-field. The larger the f/stop number, the smaller the f/stop itself.

graduated filter   A lens attachment with variable density or color from one edge to
another. A graduated neutral-density filter, for example, can be oriented so the neutral-
density portion is concentrated at the top of the lens's view with the less dense or clear
portion at the bottom, thus reducing the amount of light from a very bright sky while
not interfering with the exposure of the landscape in the foreground. Graduated filters
can also be split into several color sections to provide a color gradient between portions
of the image.

gray card   A piece of cardboard or other material with a standardized 18-percent
reflectance. Gray cards can be used as a reference for determining correct exposure or
for setting white balance.

group   A way of bundling more than one wireless flash unit into a single cluster that
all share the same flash output setting, as controlled by the master flash unit.

high contrast   A wide range of density in a print, negative, or other image.

highlights   The brightest parts of an image containing detail.

histogram   A kind of chart showing the relationship of tones in an image using a series
of 256 vertical bars, one for each brightness level. A histogram chart, such as the one
the Nikon D7000 can display during picture review, typically looks like a curve with
one or more slopes and peaks, depending on how many highlight, midtone, and shadow
tones are present in the image.

hot shoe A mount on top of a camera used to hold an electronic flash, while providing an electrical connection between the flash and the camera. Also called an accessory shoe.

hyperfocal distance A point of focus where everything from half that distance to infinity appears to be acceptably sharp. For example, if your lens has a hyperfocal distance of four feet, everything from two feet to infinity would be sharp. The hyperfocal distance varies by the lens and the aperture in use. If you know you'll be making a grab shot without warning, sometimes it is useful to turn off your camera's automatic focus, and set the lens to infinity, or, better yet, the hyperfocal distance. Then, you can snap off a quick picture without having to wait for the lag that occurs with most digital cameras as their autofocus locks in.

image rotation A feature that senses whether a picture was taken in horizontal or vertical orientation. That information is embedded in the picture file so that the camera and compatible software applications can automatically display the image in the correct orientation.

image stabilization A technology that compensates for camera shake, usually by adjusting the position of the camera sensor or (with the implementation used by Nikon) by re-arranging the position of certain lens elements in response to movements of the camera.

incident light Light falling on a surface.

International Organization for Standardization (ISO) A governing body that provides standards used to represent film speed, or the equivalent sensitivity of a digital camera's sensor. Digital camera sensitivity is expressed in ISO settings.

interpolation A technique digital cameras, scanners, and image editors use to create new pixels required whenever you resize or change the resolution of an image based on the values of surrounding pixels. Devices such as scanners and digital cameras can also use interpolation to create pixels in addition to those actually captured, thereby increasing the apparent resolution or color information in an image.

ISO *See* International Organization for Standardization (ISO).

i-TTL Nikon's intelligent Through-The-Lens flash metering system, which uses pre-flashes to calculate exposure and to communicate between flash units, using the camera's 2,016-segment RGB sensor viewfinder exposure meter.

jaggies Staircasing effect of lines that are not perfectly horizontal or vertical, caused by pixels that are too large to represent the line accurately. *See also* anti-alias.

JPEG A file "lossy" format (short for Joint Photographic Experts Group) that supports 24-bit color and reduces file sizes by selectively discarding image data. Digital cameras generally use JPEG compression to pack more images onto memory cards. You can select how much compression is used (and, therefore, how much information is thrown away) by selecting from among the Standard, Fine, Super Fine, or other quality settings offered by your camera. *See also* RAW.

Kelvin (K) A unit of measure based on the absolute temperature scale in which absolute zero is zero; it's used to describe the color of continuous-spectrum light sources and applied when setting white balance. For example, daylight has a color temperature of about 5,500K, and a tungsten lamp has a temperature of about 3,400K.

lag time The interval between when the shutter is pressed and when the picture is actually taken. During that span, the camera may be automatically focusing and calculating exposure. With digital SLRs like the Nikon D7000, lag time is generally very short; with non-dSLRs, the elapsed time easily can be one second or more under certain conditions.

latitude The degree by which exposure can be varied and still produce an acceptable photo.

lens flare A feature of conventional photography that is both a bane and a creative outlet. It is an effect produced by the reflection of light internally among elements of an optical lens. Bright light sources within or just outside the field of view cause lens flare. Flare can be reduced by the use of coatings on the lens elements or with the use of lens hoods. Photographers sometimes use the effect as a creative technique, and Photoshop includes a filter that lets you add lens flare at your whim.

lighting ratio The proportional relationship between the amount of light falling on the subject from the main light and other lights, expressed in a ratio, such as 3:1.

lossless compression An image-compression scheme, such as TIFF, that preserves all image detail. When the image is decompressed, it is identical to the original version.

lossy compression An image-compression scheme, such as JPEG, that creates smaller files by discarding image information, which can affect image quality.

macro lens A lens that provides continuous focusing from infinity to extreme close-ups, often to a reproduction ratio of 1:2 (half life-size) or 1:1 (life-size).

Matrix metering A system of exposure calculation that looks at many different segments of an image to determine the brightest and darkest portions, and base f/stop and shutter speed on settings derived from a database of images. *See also* Center-weighted meter and Spot meter.

maximum burst The number of frames that can be exposed at the current settings until the buffer fills.

midtones Parts of an image with tones of an intermediate value, usually in the 25 to 75 percent brightness range. Many image-editing features allow you to manipulate midtones independently from the highlights and shadows.

mirror lock-up The ability of the D7000 to retract its mirror out of the light path to allow access to the sensor for cleaning, or to reduce the effect of vibration when using the Mup setting.

neutral color A color in which red, green, and blue are present in equal amounts, producing a gray.

neutral-density filter A gray camera filter reducing the amount of light entering the camera without affecting the colors.

noise In an image, pixels with randomly distributed color values. Noise in digital photographs tends to be the product of low-light conditions and long exposures, particularly when you've set your camera to a higher ISO rating than normal.

noise reduction A technology used to cut down on the amount of random information in a digital picture, usually caused by long exposures or increased ISO sensitivity ratings.

normal lens A lens that makes the image in a photograph appear in a perspective that is like that of the original scene, typically with a field of view of roughly 45 degrees.

overexposure A condition in which too much light reaches the film or sensor, producing a dense negative or a very bright/light print, slide, or digital image.

pincushion distortion A type of lens distortion in which lines at the top and side edges of an image are bent inward, producing an effect that looks like a pincushion. *See also* barrel distortion.

Playback menu The D7000's list of settings and options that deal with reviewing and printing images that you've shot. *See also* Retouch menu, Setup menu, and Shooting menu.

polarizing filter A filter that forces light, which normally vibrates in all directions, to vibrate only in a single plane, reducing or removing the specular reflections from the surface of objects and darkening blue skies.

RAW An image file format, such as the NEF format in the Nikon D7000, which includes all the unprocessed information captured by the camera after conversion to digital form. RAW files are very large compared to JPEG files and must be processed by a special program such as Nikon Capture NX2 or Adobe's Camera Raw filter after being downloaded from the camera.

rear-curtain sync (second-curtain sync) An optional kind of electronic flash synchronization technique, originally associated with focal plane shutters, which consists of a traveling set of curtains, including a *front (first) curtain* (which opens to reveal the film or sensor) and a *rear (second) curtain* (which follows at a distance determined by shutter speed to conceal the film or sensor at the conclusion of the exposure). For a flash picture to be taken, the entire sensor must be exposed at one time to the brief flash exposure, so the image is exposed after the front curtain has reached the other side of the focal plane, but before the rear curtain begins to move. Rear-curtain sync causes the flash to fire at the end of the exposure, an instant before the second or rear curtain of the focal plane shutter begins to move. With slow shutter speeds, this feature can create a blur effect from the ambient light, showing as patterns that follow a moving subject with the subject shown sharply frozen at the end of the blur trail. If you were shooting a photo of The Flash, the superhero would appear sharp, with a ghostly trail behind him. *See also* front-curtain sync (first-curtain sync).

red-eye An effect from flash photography that appears to make a person's eyes glow red, or an animal's yellow or green. It's caused by light bouncing from the retina of the eye and is most pronounced in dim illumination (when the irises are wide open) and when the electronic flash is close to the lens and, therefore, prone to reflect directly back. The D7000's red-eye lamp can reduce the effect during picture taking by causing the subjects' irises to contract just prior to the exposure. Image editors can fix red-eye after the fact through cloning other pixels over the offending red or orange ones.

Retouch menu The D7000's list of special effects and editing changes you can make to images you've already taken. Choices in this menu allow you to trim/crop photos, and add effects such as fisheye looks. *See also* Playback menu, Setup menu, and Shooting menu.

RGB color A color model that represents the three colors—red, green, and blue—used by devices such as scanners or monitors to reproduce color. Photoshop works in RGB mode by default, and even displays CMYK images by converting them to RGB.

saturation The purity of color; the amount by which a pure color is diluted with white or gray.

selective focus Choosing a lens opening that produces a shallow depth-of-field. Usually this is used to isolate a subject in portraits, close-ups, and other types of images, by causing most other elements in the scene to be blurred.

self-timer A mechanism that delays the opening of the shutter for some seconds after the release has been operated.

sensitivity A measure of the degree of response of a film or sensor to light, measured using the ISO setting.

Setup menu The D7000's list of settings and options that deal with overall changes to the camera's operation, such as Date/time, LCD brightness, sensor cleaning, self-timer delay, and so forth. *See also* Playback menu, Retouch menu, and Shooting menu.

shadow The darkest part of an image, represented on a digital image by pixels with low numeric values.

sharpening Increasing the apparent sharpness of an image by boosting the contrast between adjacent pixels that form an edge.

Shooting menu The D7000's list of settings and options that deal with how the camera behaves as you take pictures, such as image size and quality, white balance, autofocus settings, ISO sensitivity, or movie shooting options. *See also* Playback menu, Retouch menu, and Setup menu.

shutter In a conventional film camera, the shutter is a mechanism consisting of blades, a curtain, a plate, or some other movable cover that controls the time during which light reaches the film. Digital cameras can use both a mechanical shutter and an electronic shutter for higher effective speeds.

Shutter-priority An exposure mode in which you set the shutter speed and the camera determines the appropriate f/stop. *See also* Aperture-priority.

side lighting Applying illumination from the left or right sides of the camera. *See also* backlighting and front lighting.

Single-servo autofocus An automatic focusing setting (AF-S) in which the camera focuses once when the shutter release is pressed down halfway. *See also* Continuous-servo autofocus.

slave unit An accessory flash unit that supplements the main flash, usually triggered electronically when the slave senses the light output by the main unit, or through infrared or radio waves.

slow sync An electronic flash synchronizing method that uses a slow shutter speed so that ambient light is recorded by the camera in addition to the electronic flash illumination. This allows the background to receive more exposure for a more realistic effect.

specular highlight Bright spots in an image caused by reflection of light sources.

Spot meter An exposure system that concentrates on a small area in the image. *See also* Center-weighted meter and Matrix metering.

time exposure A picture taken by leaving the shutter open for a long period, usually more than one second. The camera is generally locked down with a tripod to prevent blur during the long exposure. The D7000 can automatically shoot time exposures up to 30 seconds, as well as much longer exposures with the camera set to Bulb and the shutter opened/closed manually.

Through-The-Lens (TTL) A system of providing viewing and exposure calculation through the actual lens taking the picture.

tungsten light Light from ordinary room lamps and ceiling fixtures, as opposed to fluorescent illumination.

underexposure A condition in which too little light reaches the film or sensor, producing a thin negative, a dark slide, a muddy-looking print, or a dark digital image.

unsharp masking The process for increasing the contrast between adjacent pixels in an image, increasing sharpness, especially around edges.

vignetting Dark corners of an image, often produced by using a lens hood that is too small for the field of view, a lens that does not completely fill the image frame, or generated artificially using image-editing techniques.

white balance The adjustment of a digital camera to the color temperature of the light source. Interior illumination is relatively red; outdoor light is relatively blue. Digital cameras like the Nikon D7000 set correct white balance automatically or let you do it through menus. Image editors can often do some color correction of images that were exposed using the wrong white balance setting, especially when working with RAW files that contain the information originally captured by the camera before white balance was applied.

zoom head The capability of an external electronic flash to change the area of its coverage to more closely match the focal length setting of a prime or zoom lens.

Index

D

D-lighting. *See also* Active D-Lighting
  Retouch menu options, 328
D series lenses, 356
'da Products, acrylic shields from, 10, 468
Dali, Salvador, 184
dark flash photos with telephoto lenses, 372
dark frame subtraction, 120
darkness with long exposures, 186, 189
data in Playback menu's display options, 220
Datacolor's Spyder products, 261
dates and times. *See also* clock; interval photography
  Calendar view, working in, 64–65
  deleting images by date, 216–217
  file information screen data, 70
  overview data screen information, 74
  Setup menu options, 317
David Busch's Quick Snap Guide to Lighting, 422
dawn, color temperature at, 403
daylight, color temperature of, 402–403
Daylight Savings Time, 16
  Setup menu options, 317
DC lenses, 356
DCIM (Digital Camera Images) folder, 313
default settings, 41–46
  Custom Settings menu options, resetting, 277–280
  front-curtain sync as, 411
  lenses, focus values for, 388, 392–393
  recommended default changes, 45–46
  Reset Shooting menu options, 229–230
  two-button reset, 42–44
degrees Kelvin, 244–245
  and continuous light, 402
  of fluorescent light, 404

delayed exposures, 191–193. *See also* interval photography; self-timer
Delayed Remote, 28
deleting
  After Delete options, Playback menu, 223
  Calendar view, deleting images in, 65
  My Menu entries, 344
  Picture Controls, 257
  Playback menu options, 216–217
  on reviewing images, 61
  thumbnail images, 64
Delkin flip-up hoods for LCD, 468
depth-of-field. *See* DOF (depth-of-field); DOF (depth-of-field) button
depth-of-focus and dust, 479–480
depth-of-light, 399
Design Rule for Camera File System (DCF) specifications, 218, 231
diaphragm lever, 84–85
diffusers, 434
diffusing light, 431–434
digital image process (DIP) chip, 237
Digital Image Recovery, 476
Digital Photography Review forums, 462
dimming compact fluorescent lights (CFLs), 404
diopter correction
  adjusting, 20
  Diopter adjustment wheel, 56–57
Direct Sunlight WB (white balance), 245
Display mode entry, Playback menu, 69
distortion. *See also* auto distortion control; barrel distortion; pincushion distortion
  converging lines with wide-angle lenses, 367
  falling back effect with wide-angle lenses, 363, 365
  Retouch menu's distortion control option, 337
  with wide-angle lenses, 364–365

Z

WE'VE GOT YOUR SHOT COVERED

New Releases

**A Shot in the Dark:
A Creative DIY Guide to
Digital Video Lighting on
(Almost) No Budget**
1-4354-5863-X • $44.99

**Fashion Flair for
Portrait and Wedding
Photography**
1-4354-5884-2 • $34.99

**Fearless Photographer:
Portraits**
1-4354-5824-9 • $34.99

**Picture Yourself Making
Creative Movies with Corel
VideoStudio Pro X4**
1-4354-5726-9 • $29.99

**Complete Digital
Photography,
Sixth Edition**
1-4354-5920-2 • $44.99

**David Busch's Master
Digital SLR Photograp
Third Edition**
1-4354-5832-X • $39.9

**The Linked Photographers'
Guide to Online Marketing
and Social Media**
1-4354-5508-8 • $29.99

**Picture Yourself
Learning Corel PaintShop
Photo Pro X3**
1-4354-5674-2 • $29.99

**Fearless Photographer:
Weddings**
1-4354-5724-2 • $34.99

**Photographs from
the Edge of Reality**
1-4354-5782-X • $39.99

**Killer Photos
with Your iPhone**
1-4354-5689-0 • $24.99

**Photo Restoration a
Retouching Using Co
PaintShop Photo Pro
Second Edition**
1-4354-5680-7 • $39.9

New from #1 Bestselling Author David Busch!

To learn more about the author and our complete collection of David Busch products please visit www.courseptr.com/davidbusch.
David Busch, Your Complete Solution

**David Busch's Canon
PowerShot G12 Guide
to Digital Photography**
1-4354-5950-4 • $29.99

**David Busch's Sony α SLT-
A55/A33 Guide to Digital
Photography**
1-4354-5944-X • $29.99

**David Busch's Nikon
D3100 Guide to Digital
SLR Photography**
1-4354-5940-7 • $29.99

**David Busch's
Compact Field Guide
for the Nikon D3100**
1-4354-5994-6 • $13.99

**David Busch's Canon EOS
60D Guide to Digital SLR
Photography**
1-4354-5938-5 • $29.99

**David Busch's
Compact Field Guid
for the Canon EOS 6**
1-4354-5996-2 • $13.9

**David Busch's
Compact Field Guide
for the Canon EOS 7D**
1-4354-5878-8 • $13.99

**David Busch's Nikon
D7000 Guide to Digital
SLR Photography**
1-4354-5942-3 • $29.99

**David Busch's
Compact Field Guide
for the Nikon D7000**
1-4354-5998-9 • $13.99

**David Busch's Canon EOS
Rebel T3i/600D Guide to
Digital SLR Photography**
1-4354-6028-6 • $29.99

**David Busch's Compact
Field Guide for the Canon
EOS Rebel T3i/600D**
1-4354-6032-4 • $13.99

**David Busch's Sony
DSLR-A580/A560 Gu
to Digital Photograp**

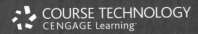

**COURSE TECHNOLOGY
CENGAGE Learning**
Professional • Technical • Reference

Our comprehensive list of digital photography books can be fou
online at **www.courseptr.com**, by phone at **1.800.354.9706**, a
at Amazon, Barnes & Noble, and other fine retailers nationwi

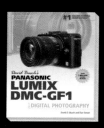

David Busch
YOUR COMPLETE SOLUTION

Course Technology PTR has your complete digital photography solution. Created with the expertise of bestselling author and photographer David Busch, we now offer books, iPhone applications, and field guides on the latest digital and digital SLR cameras from Canon, Nikon, Sony, Olympus, and Panasonic. These three formats allow you to have a comprehensive book to keep at home, an iPhone app to take with you when you're on-the-go, and a pocket-sized compact guide you can store in your camera bag. Now all the camera information you need is at your fingertips in whatever format you prefer.

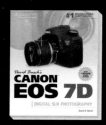 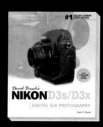 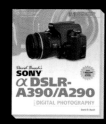 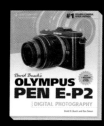 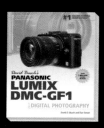

David Busch's CANON EOS 7D DIGITAL SLR PHOTOGRAPHY

David Busch's NIKON D3s/D3x DIGITAL SLR PHOTOGRAPHY

David Busch's SONY α DSLR-A390/A290 DIGITAL PHOTOGRAPHY

David Busch's OLYMPUS PEN E-P2 DIGITAL PHOTOGRAPHY

David Busch's PANASONIC LUMIX DMC-GF1 DIGITAL PHOTOGRAPHY

Camera Guides

David Busch is the #1 bestselling camera guide author. A professional photographer with more than 20 years of experience and over a million books in print, David provides expert authority to these guides, covering digital and digital SLR cameras from Canon, Nikon, Sony, Olympus, and Panasonic. Featuring beautiful full-color images, David Busch camera guides show you how, when, and, most importantly, why to use all the cool features and functions of your camera to take stunning photographs.

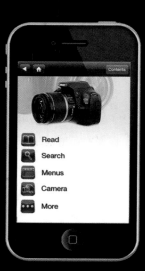

iPhone Apps NEW!

Now take the expert advice of bestselling camera guide author David Busch with you wherever you take your iPhone! You'll find the same rich information as our camera guides as well as new interactive and multimedia elements in an easy-to-access, searchable, portable format for your on-the-go needs. Visit the iTunes store for more information and to purchase.

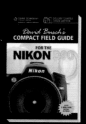

David Busch's COMPACT FIELD GUIDE FOR THE NIKON D90

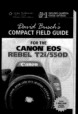

David Busch's COMPACT FIELD GUIDE FOR THE CANON EOS REBEL T2i/550D

Compact Field Guides NEW!

Are you tired of squinting at the tiny color-coded tables and difficult-to-read text you find on the typical laminated reference card or cheat sheet that you keep with you when you're in the field or on location? *David Busch's Compact Field Guides* are your solution! These new, lay-flat, spiral bound, reference guides condense all the must-have information you need while shooting into a portable book you'll want to permanently tuck into your camera bag. You'll find every settings option for your camera listed, along with advice on why you should use—or not use—each adjustment. Useful tables provide recommended settings for a wide variety of shooting situations, including landscapes, portraits, sports, close-ups, and travel. With this guide on hand you have all the information you need at your fingertips so you can confidently use your camera on-the-go.